The Adams Papers

C. JAMES TAYLOR, EDITOR IN CHIEF

SERIES II

Adams Family Correspondence

Adams Family Correspondence

MARGARET A. HOGAN, C. JAMES TAYLOR,
KAREN N. BARZILAY, HOBSON WOODWARD,
MARY T. CLAFFEY, ROBERT F. KARACHUK,
SARA B. SIKES, GREGG L. LINT

EDITORS

Volume 9 • *January 1790 – December 1793*

THE BELKNAP PRESS
OF HARVARD UNIVERSITY PRESS
CAMBRIDGE, MASSACHUSETTS
AND LONDON, ENGLAND

2009

Funds for editing *The Adams Papers* were originally furnished by Time, Inc., on behalf of *Life*, to the Massachusetts Historical Society, under whose supervision the editorial work is being done. Further funds were provided by a grant from the Ford Foundation to the National Archives Trust Fund Board in support of this and four other major documentary publications. In common with these and many other enterprises like them, *The Adams Papers* has continued to benefit from the guidance and cooperation of the National Historical Publications and Records Commission, chaired by the Archivist of the United States, which from 1975 to the present has provided this enterprise with major financial support. Important additional funds were supplied from 1980 to 1993 by The Andrew W. Mellon Foundation, The J. Howard Pew Freedom Trust, and The Charles E. Culpeper Foundation through the Founding Fathers Papers, Inc. Since 1993, *The Adams Papers* has received major support from the National Endowment for the Humanities, and matching support from The Packard Humanities Institute, through the Founding Fathers Papers, Inc., and from The Charles Francis Adams Charitable Trust, The Florence J. Gould Foundation, The Lyn and Norman Lear Fund, and anonymous donors. Any views, findings, conclusions, or recommendations expressed in this publication do not necessarily reflect those of the National Endowment for the Humanities.

∞ This volume meets all ANSI/NISO Z39.48–1992 standards for permanence.

Library of Congress Cataloging in Publication Data (Revised for vols. 5–9)

Adams family correspondence.
    (The Adams papers: Series II, Adams family correspondence)
    Vols. 3–4 edited by L. H. Butterfield and Marc Friedlaender.
    Vols. 5–6 edited by Richard Alan Ryerson et al.
    Vols. 7–9 edited by Margaret A. Hogan et al.
    Includes bibliographical references and index.
    Contents: v. 1. December 1761 – May 1776–v. 2. June 1776 – March 1778–[etc.]–v. 9. January 1790 – December 1793.
    I. Butterfield, L. H. (Lyman Henry), 1909–1982. II. Friedlaender, Marc, 1905–1992. III. Ryerson, Richard Alan, 1942– . IV. Hogan, Margaret A. V. Series: Adams papers: Series II, Adams family correspondence.
E322.1.A27   929'.2   63–14964

ISBN 0–674–00400–0 (v. 1–2)
ISBN 0–674–00405–1 (v. 3–4)
ISBN 0–674–00406–X (v. 5–6)
ISBN 0–674–01574–6 (v. 7)

ISBN–13 978–0–674–02278–2 (v. 8)
ISBN–10 0–674–02278–5 (v. 8)
ISBN–13 978–0–674–03275–0 (v. 9)
ISBN–10 0–674–03275–5 (v. 9)

Out of the highest admiration
this volume
of the *Adams Family Correspondence*
is dedicated to

HILLER B. ZOBEL

in recognition of his fifty years as
an editor, advisor, and friend
of the Adams Papers.

This edition of *The Adams Papers*

is sponsored by the MASSACHUSETTS HISTORICAL SOCIETY

to which the ADAMS MANUSCRIPT TRUST

by a deed of gift dated 4 April 1956

gave ultimate custody of the personal and public papers

written, accumulated, and preserved over a span of three centuries

by the Adams family of Massachusetts

The Adams Papers

The acorn and oakleaf device on the preceding page is redrawn from a seal cut for John Quincy Adams after 1830. The motto is from Cæcilius Statius as quoted by Cicero in the First Tusculan Disputation: *Serit arbores quæ alteri seculo prosint* ("He plants trees for the benefit of later generations").

Contents

Descriptive List of Illustrations

On 6 April 1790, George Washington "Sat for Mr. Savage, at the request of the Vice-President, to have my Portrait drawn for him." The artist, Edward Savage (1761–1817), executed a companion portrait of Martha Washington around the same time. He depicted the president in a navy and buff military uniform with gold epaulets and ruffled jabot, and the first lady in an elaborate fluted hat and intricately laced shawl.

Although the circumstances of Savage's formal training are unknown, the technical detail of his compositions reflects the influence of John Singleton Copley. A similar portrait of George Washington painted by Savage and donated to Harvard University in 1790 is considered one of the best likenesses of the president. Savage later combined the portrait sketches for his well-received painting and engraving "The Washington Family."

Eleven days after the president sat for Savage, both images were completed and delivered to the Adamses. A receipt signed by Savage and endorsed by Abigail records the date: "Received New York the 17th of April 1790 of the Vice President of the U.S. forty six Dollars and 2/3ds for a portrait of the President of the U.S. & His Lady– Signed Edward Savage." On display in the Adams family home in Quincy ever since, the paintings hang in the dining room of the Old House as part of the Adams National Historical Park's collection (Washington, *Diaries*, 6:57; Edmund Quincy, *Life of Josiah Quincy of Massachusetts*, Boston, 1867, p. 51; vol. 8:xvi–xvii, 381; Washington, *Papers, Presidential Series*, 4:286–289; Grove *Dicy. of Art*; Wilhelmina S. Harris, *Furnishings Report of the Old House, The Adams National Historic Site, Quincy, Massachusetts*, 10 vols., Quincy, 1966–1974, 2:242–244).

Courtesy of the Adams National Historical Park.

Writing to John Quincy Adams on 11 July 1790 (below), Abigail noted, "you will see by the publick papers that we are destined to Philadelphia, a Grievous affair to me I assure you, but so it is ordained–" The Residence Act, which established the permanent seat of government on the Potomac with a temporary residence in Philadelphia for ten years, was signed by George Washington five days later. After a seven-year debate, two lingering problems of the Revolution–the location of the capital and the financing of the war debt–were resolved.

Disagreement on these issues, which fell largely along sectional lines, reached a peak in the spring of 1790. Northerners and southerners alike wanted the permanent capital located close to home. In Congress, representatives and senators lobbied on behalf of their own cities and districts, many acting with blatant economic self-interest. With respect to the war debt, most northerners supported Alexander Hamilton's long-term funding plan—in particular, federal assumption of state obligations—as a means not only to strengthen the federal union but also to free their own states from crushing financial burdens. Southerners, however, widely feared assumption as an unconstitutional violation of states' rights. Leaders in Congress and the Washington administration worked out a compromise whereby northerners gave sufficient support to pass the Residence Act on 16 July, and southerners did the same for the Funding Act, which the president signed into law on 9 August.

Not surprisingly, the New York press criticized the decision to move the capital. The stinging "View of Con–ss on the Road to Philadelphia" was one of many opposition political cartoons sold on the streets of New York in early July. Captioned "What think ye of Con–ss now," the print, by an anonymous engraver, shows Robert Morris leading Congress by the nose to the temporary seat in Philadelphia. Morris, who had extensive property interests on the Delaware River, had attempted to steer the permanent seat to Philadelphia but settled for a temporary placement there—no doubt assuming that, once situated, Congress would be difficult to move. As George Washington, Alexander Hamilton, James Madison, and others sought a compromise on the location of the capital, the temporary move to Philadelphia successfully secured the votes of Morris and his supporters (Kenneth R. Bowling, *Creating the Federal City, 1774–1800: Potomac Fever*, Washington, D.C., 1988, p. 61–78; Wilhelmus Bogart Bryan, *A History of the National Capital*, 2 vols., N.Y., 1914–1916, 1:30–31, 34–35, 42–43; Elizabeth M. Nuxoll, "The Financier as Senator: Robert Morris of Pennsylvania, 1789–1795," in Kenneth R. Bowling and Donald R. Kennon, eds., *Neither Separate nor Equal: Congress in the 1790s*, Athens, Ohio, 2000, p. 104–108; *First Fed. Cong.*, 5:713–937, 6:1767–1791).

Courtesy of the Historical Society of Pennsylvania.

4. "BUSH HILL. THE SEAT OF WM. HAMILTON ESQR. NEAR PHILADELPHIA," BY JAMES PELLER MALCOM, 1787   III

Arriving at the property of William Hamilton in November 1790, Abigail found that "Bush Hill is a very beautiful place. But the grand and sublime I left at Richmond Hill" (to AA2, 21 Nov., below). Located two miles outside of Philadelphia, the mansion was constructed about 1740 by William's grandfather Andrew Hamilton, a lawyer and architect. The house, which had stood unoccupied for many years, was still undergoing repairs and renovations when the family leased it. Abigail wrote later to her sister, "When I got to this place, I found this house just calculated to make the whole family sick; cold, damp, and wet with new paint." Despite its inconveniences, Abigail came to appreciate the home and reflected fondly on it as the family prepared to depart in the spring of 1791: "I shall have some regrets at leaving this place, just as the season begins to open all its beauties upon me" (to Elizabeth Smith Shaw, 20 March 1791, below; vol. 8:xv–xvi, 352).

Bush Hill remained empty until the 1793 yellow fever outbreak when it was turned into a hospital. The once noble mansion became known as "a great human slaughter house, where numerous victims were immolated at the altar of riot and intemperance." In an effort to improve the situation, citizens formed a committee to oversee the facility and the care of the infirm. In subsequent years, the Hamilton family converted the building to a tavern and resort. The mansion was demolished in 1875 to make way for new residences (J. H. Powell, *Bring Out Your Dead: The Great Plague of Yellow Fever in Philadelphia in 1793*, Phila., 1949, p. 61, 143–144, 275; JA, *D&A*, 3:184; Thompson Westcott, *The Historic Mansions and Buildings of Philadelphia*, Phila., 1877, p. 417, 421–423; Mathew Carey, *A Short Account of the Malignant Fever Lately Prevalent in Philadelphia*, 4th rev. edn., Phila., 1794, p. 32, Evans, No. 35586).

James Peller Malcom (1767–1815) produced this illustration for the December 1787 issue of the London *Universal Magazine*. Born in Philadelphia, Malcom (or Malcolm) trained at the Royal Academy in London and worked in England as a writer and engraver of noted technical skill (*Universal Magazine*, 81:361 [Dec. 1787]; *DAB*).

Courtesy of the Massachusetts Historical Society.

5. COTTON TUFTS TO ABIGAIL ADAMS, APPLETON'S LOAN CERTIFICATE, 21 AUGUST 1792   197

On 17 January 1790, Abigail Adams wrote to her uncle Cotton Tufts: "The little matter you have belonging to me I wish you to dispose of as you would of your own property to the best advantage by changing or selling according to your judgment" (below). The "little matter" was government bonds, in which Abigail had quietly invested since 1777. That year, she purchased her first federal bond, which paid her a 24 percent annual return for almost five years. Over the next fifteen years, Abigail continued to invest small portions of the family savings in the risky but profitable bond market. Abigail was keenly aware of the legal limits on female property ownership and enlisted her uncle and sons to complete transactions. In an effort to keep her activities private, she repeatedly requested that Cotton Tufts invest "in your own Name, giving me some memorandum that you hold in your Hands such an interest belonging to me" (2 Aug. 1790, below).

Abigail and John, while complementary in many respects, were sharply divided over how to invest their modest income. John, who disdained "stock-jobbing" and speculation, preferred land. Abigail, who rarely criticized her husband to others, lamented to her sister Mary Cranch that she "never desired so much Land unless we could have lived upon it. the Money paid for useless land I would have purchased publick Securities . . . but in these Ideas I have always been so unfortunate as to differ from my partner who thinks he never saved any thing but what he vested in Land" (10 Oct. 1790, below). After more than a decade of managing the farm and accounts on her own while John was in Philadelphia and Europe, Abigail was extremely reluctant to forfeit her control, particularly since she found greater success in the market than in managing tenants and their meager crops.

On 4 August 1790, Congress passed the Funding Act providing for the assumption of state debt by the federal government. Under this legislation, the government converted 90 percent of each Massachusetts bond holder's securities into federal bonds, with the balance covered by the state. By the time Abigail converted her Massachusetts bonds into federal securities on 21 August 1792, their market value had appreciated considerably. Cotton Tufts signed the receipt as "Trustee to Mrs. Abig.ͨ Adams" (Woody Holton, "Abigail Adams, Bond Speculator," *WMQ*, 3d series, 64:821–838 [Oct. 2007]).

Courtesy of the Adams Papers.

6. "TOM PAINE'S NIGHTLY PEST," BY JAMES GILLRAY, 1792   285

Thomas Paine responded to criticism of his *Rights of Man* with a second volume in 1792. Using the American government as a model, *Rights of Man, Part II*, employed economic reasoning to argue for the financial efficacy of a democratic republic over a monarchy. Experiencing the reaction in England firsthand, Abigail Adams Smith wrote to her father that *Part II* "has been stiled in the House of Commons an Infamous Libell upon the Constitution" (7 May 1792, below). Paine was indeed charged with sedition and answered a court summons on 8 June 1792, but his trial was postponed to 18 December.

In "Tom Paine's Nightly Pest," noted satirist James Gillray (1757–1815) alludes to Paine's upcoming trial. Three faceless judges haunt Paine as he sleeps and proclaim the charges against him: "Libels / Scurrilities / Falshoods / Perjuries / Rebellions / Treasons." The scales of justice hang in the balance. Despite the "Guardian Angels" of Charles James Fox and Joseph Priestley gracing Paine's headboard, the verdict is pronounced that those who "mix in treason" are "sure to die like dogs!" An imp hurriedly escaping out a window draped with fleur-de-lis patterned curtains symbolizes Paine's flight from Britain to France just prior to his trial.

Tried in absentia, Paine was defended by Thomas Erskine, attorney general to the Prince of Wales, who offered a four-hour argument for the freedom of the press. But the prosecution, as John informed Abigail, "was pleased to quote large Passages from Publicola, with Some handsome Compliments: so that Publicola is become a Law Authority" (27 Feb. 1793, below). A reputedly stacked jury promptly ruled in favor of the prosecution, and Paine was ordered to be hanged if captured. He spent the rest of his life in France and the United States (Craig Nelson, *Thomas Paine: En-*

lightenment, Revolution, and the Birth of Modern Nations, N.Y., 2006, p. 216, 219, 245–246; *DNB*; Richard Godfrey, *James Gillray: The Art of Caricature*, London, 2001, p. 101–102).
Courtesy of the British Museum.

7. "JOURNÉE DU 10 AOÛST 1792 AU CHÂTEAU DES THUILLERIE," BY
MADAME JOURDAN, CA. 1792   307

Abigail Adams Smith sailed with her husband and two sons to London in the spring of 1792 and for the next ten months kept the Adams family apprised of the revolution in France. Declaring that "the accounts from Paris are shocking to every humane mind, and too dreadful to relate," Nabby enclosed newspapers to tell the story and warned her mother not to assume that the English press "exaggerate in their accounts; . . . I fear they do not, for I saw, on Sunday last, a lady who was in Paris on the 10th of August, and she heard and saw scenes as shocking as are related by any of them; they seem to have refined upon the cruelties of the savages" (13 Sept. 1792, below).

After two years of intermittent violence and plodding progress toward building a republic, the revolutionary spirit in France reached a boiling point in the summer of 1792, culminating in the siege of the Tuileries Palace and the launch of the Terror. On 10 August, spurred by leaders from the Jacobin Club, National Guard soldiers, joined by *fédérés*—armed volunteers from the provinces—and Parisian citizens, marched over the bridges crossing the Seine to attack the palace. Within hours, "the justice of the people displayed itself in all its horror." Upon the capitulation of the guard, the mob murdered several hundred people, including the palace domestic service and groups of men loyal to the crown. Soldiers attempting to escape were hunted down in the streets of Paris and killed. Following the arrest of the royal family, "the mob in their fury seemed determined to destroy every vestige of Royalty." Just a week later, a guillotine was set up in front of the palace, foreshadowing the larger massacres to come with the Reign of Terror (Philadelphia *National Gazette*, 10 Nov.; New York *Daily Advertiser*, 1 Oct.).

The siege was quickly immortalized in artwork as a symbol of the defeat of the monarchy. Madame Jourdan's engraving, after G. Texier's painting, shows the victorious National Guard executing some Swiss soldiers while driving others to fling themselves from the second-story windows. Commoners carrying pikes, at right, include two women ready for battle.

The Adamses shared their horror at the reports of riots and mob violence. Thomas Boylston lamented to his father that "the dreadful scenes . . . has excited terrors even in the breasts of the warmest enthusiasts for Revolution" (30 Oct. 1792, below). Abigail, who counted friends among some of the early leaders of the Revolution, remarked to John, "when I read citizen President, & citizens Equality, I cannot help feeling a mixture of Pitty and contempt for the Hypocrisy I know they are practising and for the Tyranny they are Executing" (2 Jan. 1793, below; Bosher, *French Rev.*, p. xix, 168–179; Schama, *Citizens*, p. 611–619).

Courtesy of the Bibliothèque nationale de France.

8. "HIGH STREET, FROM NINTH STREET. PHILADELPHIA," BY WILLIAM
RUSSELL BIRCH AND THOMAS BIRCH, 1799   327

When John Adams returned to Philadelphia by himself in 1792, rather than live in a boardinghouse he decided to stay at the home of Abigail's cousins Samuel Alleyne and Mary Smith Gray Otis. While John was well accommodated at their residence, he missed Abigail and told her that he was "So little pleased with living alone at any Lodgings, that this shall be the last time" (to AA, 7 Dec., below). Nevertheless, he stayed with the Otises again the following winter. Abigail would not join him in Philadelphia until 1797 when they moved into the president's mansion (JA, *D&A*, 3:229; JA to AA, 1 Dec. 1793, below).

The Otises' home was located at 198 High Street, across the street from the president's house and just a few blocks from Congress. High Street was commonly known as Market Street because of the prevalence of open-air markets, and in this engraving, the cupola of the market shed between Third and Fourth Streets is just visible in the distance. Artist William Russell Birch (1755–1834) captures the Otises' neighborhood with "the street-scenes all accurate as they now stand," including a detachment of the First City Troop, a mounted military unit organized to defend the city.

"High Street" is part of a series of 27 views that represent Philadelphia at the turn of the nineteenth century—an ode to urban life and a celebration of city commerce. Already an established miniature artist, William, with his son Thomas (1779–1851), also a painter, arrived in America from England in 1794 and began a series of sketches reflecting "the eminence of an opulent city." Funded via a subscription campaign, the prints were a substantial investment at $28 for an unbound set and $44.50 for a bound and hand-colored edition (*Philadelphia Directory*, 1793, Evans, No. 25585; Agnes Addison Gilchrist, "Market Houses in High Street," *Amer. Philos. Soc.*, *Trans.*, 43:304, 310 [1953]; *DAB*; William R. Birch and Thomas Birch, *The City of Philadelphia, in the state of Pennsylvania North America*, Phila., 1800, repr. edn., Phila., 1982).

Courtesy of the Print and Picture Collection, The Free Library of Philadelphia.

9, 10. LOUIS XVI, BY JOSEPH DUCREUX, 1793, AND "LA REINE MARIE-ANTOINETTE EN HABIT DE VEUVE À LA PRISON DE LA CONCIERGERIE," BY ALEXANDRE KUCHARSKI, 1793   392, 393

In April 1793, when early reports in the American press indicated that Louis XVI and Marie Antoinette had been executed, Thomas Boylston Adams wrote to his father, "Since the Execution of the King & Queen nothing can be thought too mad or extravagant for the National Convention to commit, and the conjecture is not unfair that the Royal Family is e're this extinct" (7 April 1793, below). Although the king was dead, it would still be several months until Marie Antoinette's execution. Like many Americans, the Adamses opposed the fate of the French royal family. Charles Adams wrote to John in May that "most Americans are friends to the Revolution of France however they may view with horror the enormities which have been committed" (10 May 1793, below). Abigail's sister Elizabeth Smith Shaw mourned the king in a letter to Mary Smith Cranch: "I am sure you could not read the fate of his unhappy Family without tender regret— It was his misfortune, & seems to be his only crime that he was born, & a King at this particular period of time" (21 April 1793, below).

After their arrest on 10 August 1792, the royal family was removed to the medieval Temple Prison for several months. At first, the family was housed on two floors and allowed a staff of fourteen. The king and queen were provided with books, the children with toys, and they even enjoyed walks in the gardens. But on 3 December, the National Convention brought charges against Louis XVI for "conspiracy against the liberty of the nation." In mid-January 1793, he was found guilty and sentenced to death. The portraitist Joseph Ducreux (1735–1802) visited the king in prison several days before his execution by guillotine on 21 January. Avoiding the flattering angles and smooth lines favored by court painters, Ducreux captured him in a charcoal drawing as "Citizen Capet," wearing a simple coat.

Marie Antoinette remained in the Temple until 2 August when she was taken to the notorious Conciergerie. In early summer, the Committee of Public Safety had undergone a turnover in leadership, and the new regime was determined to see the "Widow Capet" to the guillotine. Labelled by her accusers the "scourge and blood sucker of the French," Marie Antoinette was tried in October in the midst of the Terror. She faced charges ranging from causing a famine in Paris and destroying the "energy" of the constitution to being the "authoress of all those reverses of fortune" of the republic's armies. During this time one of the queen's favorite painters, Alexandre Kucharski (1741–1819), stole into the Conciergerie to visit her. Kucharski later painted her from memory, showing a woman with a sunken face wearing a widow's black headdress. Like the portrait of Louis XVI, this painting captures the stark resignation of its subject as Marie Antoinette awaited her execution on 16 October (Bosher, *French Rev.*, p. xix–xxi, 168–183; Charles Downer Hazen, *Modern European History*, N.Y., 1917, p. 122–124; David P. Jordan, *The King's Trial: Louis XVI vs. The French Revolution*, Berkeley, Calif., 1979, p. 83; Schama, *Citizens*, p. 653–663, 795–796; *The Trial of Louis XVI Late King of France, and Marie Antoinette, His Queen*, Lansingburgh, N.Y., 1794, Evans, No. 47100; Caroline Weber, *Queen of Fashion: What Marie Antoinette Wore to the Revolution*, N.Y., 2006, p. 271–272).

Courtesy of Musée Carnavalet / Roger-Viollet, and Réunion des Musées Nationaux / Art Resource, New York.

Introduction

Volume 9 of the *Adams Family Correspondence* covers an eventful four years in the life of the Adams family and in the history of the United States. Spanning the period from 1790 through 1793, these letters chronicle the early years of the federal government under the Constitution, including such milestones as the funding of the national debt and the assumption of state debts, the choice of a permanent site for the government, the creation of a national bank, the reestablishment of an army, and the election of 1792. In the background, the French Revolution influenced ongoing debates about the nature of democracy and inflamed tensions among political factions, which would soon develop into full-fledged political parties.

For the family itself, these years concluded the transition of the second generation of Adamses from children to adults. The youngest, Thomas Boylston, completed his schooling at Harvard, and all three brothers finished their legal training and embarked on careers as lawyers. The eldest son, John Quincy, began his political career, appropriately enough in Boston and Braintree, where he lobbied successfully for the incorporation of the town of Quincy, and began to publish his writings under a variety of pseudonyms. Daughter Abigail Adams Smith continued to raise her first two sons and gave birth to another, Thomas Hollis Smith, who lived less than a year. John and Abigail meanwhile settled uncomfortably into their roles as vice president and second lady of the nation. John found his work onerous and unsatisfying, while Abigail, troubled with ill health, eventually retreated to Braintree to escape the social whirlwind in successive capital cities.

Unlike previous volumes in the *Family Correspondence* series, which predominantly feature either letters between Abigail and John or those among Abigail and her sisters, this volume moves the younger generation front and center, with a particular emphasis on the correspondence of the three Adams sons, John Quincy, Charles, and Thomas Boylston, among themselves and with their parents and sister, Abigail (Nabby) Adams Smith. In general, this is a period of relative scarcity of letters for the Adams family—from over four years, a mere 360 are extant, of which 289 are published here. As usual, Abigail Adams remains the most prominent author, having written 87 letters (30 percent) in the book. John Adams accounts for another 64 (22 percent), and the three sons for 78 (27 percent) more. The latter half of the volume is a virtual round-robin among the three sons and their parents, with occasional additions by Nabby, Elizabeth Smith Shaw, and a handful of others. With fewer letters among Abigail and her sisters, the focus of the correspondence is less on domestic matters and more on national and international events, though Abigail's efforts to manage her various homes remain a topic of concern.

1. AFFAIRS OF STATE

The year 1789 marked John Adams' return to the American political scene. For the previous decade, he and his family had been on the periphery of the U.S. government—deeply involved in its diplomatic affairs, no doubt, but physically removed from its actual operations. At a distance, they worried about what Congress was doing (or, equally often, not doing) and considered how best to reform the government to better serve the nation's needs. They missed the debates over the Constitution while in Europe, though that did not stop them from commenting on the results or speculating on revisions. John, in particular, had reservations but indicated that he was "clear for accepting the present Plan as it is and trying the Experiment."[1]

Now, in the early 1790s, John and Abigail found themselves at the center again, discovering all that had changed in America in the years following the Revolution and realizing that it was not always to their liking. John's role as vice president—what he called "the most insignificant Office that ever the Invention of Man contrived or his Imagination conceived"—limited him to presiding over the Senate and casting the occasional tie-breaking vote. Nonetheless, he filled the position faithfully. Abigail reported to her sister Mary Cranch that John "has not mist one hour from attendance at Congress. he goes from Home at ten and seldom gets back till four, and

[1] JA to Cotton Tufts, 23 Jan. 1788, vol. 8:220.

5 hours constant sitting in a day for six months together, (for He can not leave his Chair) is pretty tight service." Worse yet, he had to read bills and listen to debates without interjecting or offering his own views on the matters at hand—frustrating service indeed for an opinionated man like John.[2]

Meanwhile, Abigail shared hostessing duties with the other leading ladies of the government: Martha Washington, of course, but also Sarah Jay, Lucy Flucker Knox, and even Lady Elizabeth Temple, wife of British consul general Sir John Temple. Hosting dinners and entertaining visitors were integral parts of Abigail's role in the capital, and they took up much of her time and energy. At one point, she reported to her son John Quincy, "we have regularly dined from 16 to 18 and sometimes 20 person every wednesday in the week Since I removed into Town, and on Mondays I see company. the rest of the week is or might be altogether taken up in Par[ties] abroad." Only her poor health gave her an excuse to step back from the endless series of social obligations.[3]

The Adamses had a warm relationship with George and Martha Washington, which made the intense social and political environment more palatable. Abigail "lived in habits of intimacy and Friendship" with Martha, taking excursions with her outside New York City and enjoying their mutual interest in grandchildren. They dined at one another's homes when in the same town and corresponded when apart. Martha invited Abigail's niece Louisa Smith to join her grandchildren for dancing lessons. George made certain that Abigail had the place of honor at Martha's levees, "always at the right hand of Mrs W." And Abigail as usual extolled George Washington, finding him "polite with dignity, affable without familiarity, distant without Haughtyness, Grave without Austerity, Modest, Wise, & Good."[4]

Abigail was shrewd enough, however, to recognize that if Washington "was not really one of the best intentiond Men in the world he might be a very dangerous one." His stature was critical to the stability of the new government, but this situation gave him a worrisome amount of power. When he became gravely ill in the late spring of 1790, Abigail agonized that "the union of the states, and concequently the permanancy of the Government depend under

[2] JA to AA, 19 Dec. 1793, and AA to Mary Smith Cranch, 4 July 1790, both below.
[3] AA to Mary Smith Cranch, 24 Jan. [1790], and to JQA, 5 Feb. 1792, both below.
[4] AA to Mary Smith Cranch, 29 Aug. 1790; to AA2, 8 Jan. 1791; Martha Washington to AA, 25 Jan.; and AA to Cranch, 5 Jan. 1790, all below.

Providence upon his Life. at this early day when neither our Finances are arranged nor our Government Sufficiently cemeted to promise duration, His death would I fear have had most disasterous Consequences." Her fears were not only for the nation. If Washington died, John would succeed him—a situation Abigail dreaded. "Most assuredly," she wrote to her sister, "I do not wish for the highest Post. I never before realizd what I might be calld to, and the apprehension of it only for a few days greatly distresst me."[5]

All of the Adamses were engrossed by the political affairs of the United States and closely followed state and national events. Abigail attended sessions of Congress herself and learned much about behind-the-scenes maneuvers through socializing with legislators and administration officials. Family members batted back and forth their opinions on such issues as the representation debate, Alexander Hamilton's funding plan, the war with Native Americans in the Ohio Country, and the impact of financial speculation, though they generally found themselves on common ground. They kept abreast of news of their home state as well, watching with interest local elections and the doings of the Massachusetts General Court. With Charles in New York and John Quincy in Boston, the family had eyes and ears in three of the country's major cities, and Thomas Boylston was expected to report events from Philadelphia whenever John and Abigail were not in residence.[6]

The Adamses also read the newspapers avidly. Ever more important in shaping the political debates of the period, the press of the early republic made no claims to objectivity but rather gave voice to different political factions. Like others, the Adams family deplored the vitriolic (sometimes even libelous) tone of many newspapers but had no difficulty endorsing papers that supported their own views. The Adamses were equally happy to take aim at any newspapers that did not adhere to their political agenda. Abigail condemned Benjamin Edes' *Boston Gazette* as a "fountain of Sedition"; John Quincy, decrying the inaccurate representations of popular opinion generated by "the paltry malevolence of a few contemptible scribblers in our News papers," singled out Philip Freneau's *National Gazette* as "virulent and abusive." The Adamses canceled their subscriptions to Boston papers that they considered too Antifederalist, such as the

[5] AA to Mary Smith Cranch, 5 Jan. and 30 May 1790, both below. See also Martha Washington to AA, 12 May, below.

[6] See, for instance, AA to Mary Smith Cranch, 20 Feb. 1790; to Cotton Tufts, 6 Sept.; JQA to TBA, 3 Dec. 1791; TBA to William Cranch, 23 Jan. 1792; and CA to AA, 22 April, all below.

Independent Chronicle and the *Herald of Freedom*. Nonetheless, they kept tabs on what was being written and routinely recommended to one another items of interest.[7]

The increasing factionalism that both fed on and nourished newspaper polemics transformed the political landscape. Differences in ideology came to be identified with organized parties, which in turn promoted an us-versus-them mentality that hardened those differences. The Adamses were not immune to these divisions and held their own views as strongly as any partisan. But they did lament how such fights cheapened the political process. Abigail agonized that "the more I see of Mankind, and of their views and designs, (the more Sick I am of publick Life) and the less worthy do they appear to me, and the less deserving of the Sacrifices which Honest men make to serve them." Regional differences only magnified these disagreements. Following the congressional debates over Hamilton's funding system, Abigail noted to her sister Mary, "I firmly believe if I live Ten years longer, I shall see a devision of the Southern & Northern states, unless more candour & less intrigue, of which I have no hopes, should prevail." Charles, likewise, found "too much local partiality in the administration of our Government."[8]

One of the earliest manifestations of political parties was in the presidential and congressional elections of 1792. John, of course, did not "run" for reelection; he allowed his name to be put forward. Even in this evolving political landscape, candidates did not actively campaign but rather allowed surrogates to promote their interests through the press and through personal connections. John professed indifference to the outcome, telling Nabby that he was "more anxious to get out of public life than to continue in," but fooled no one in his desire to continue as vice president. Members of the Federalist and Democratic-Republican parties lobbied for their candidates—John Adams and George Clinton, respectively—but managed to maintain a certain level of civility. John reported, "We, indeed, have our parties and our sophistry, and our rivalries, but they proceed not to violence. The elections are going on in New-England with a spirit of sobriety and moderation, which will do us honour;

---

[7] AA to Cotton Tufts, 17 Jan. 1790; JQA to AA, 17 Oct.; JQA to TBA, 2 Sept. 1792; and Cotton Tufts to JA, 6 Jan. 1791, all below. For a thorough discussion of newspaper culture during this period, see Jeffrey L. Pasley, *"The Tyranny of Printers": Newspaper Politics in the Early American Republic*, Charlottesville, Va., 2001.

[8] AA to Cotton Tufts, 7 March 1790; to Mary Smith Cranch, 20 April 1792; and CA to AA, 22 April, all below.

and, I have not heard of any thing more intemperate than might be expected, in the southward or middle states."[9]

John's sanguine attitude, however, proved premature and understated the divisiveness of the election. Thomas Boylston in the fall of 1792 begged John to come to Philadelphia as soon as possible. " 'Tis said to be your *happy fate*," he wrote, "to be the most obnoxious character in the United States, to a certain party, (whose hatred & opposition is the glory of every honest man) who for a long time have considered you as the first barrier to be removed in order to the success of their designs." John too found "Stories of Marches and Countermarches Intrigues and Manœuvres" when he arrived in New York City en route to Philadelphia. Because the Democratic-Republicans knew that they had no chance of unseating Washington, they had instead made John Adams their primary target.[10]

The results of the election remained uncertain throughout the fall. John counted votes, warning Abigail that "I am told that an unanimous Vote will be for me in Vermont New Hampshire, Connecticut and Rhode Island. This is generally expected, but I know full well the Uncertainty of Such Things, and am prepared to meet an Unanimous Vote against me." He had low expectations for taking any of the southern states. In the end he won decisively, receiving 77 electoral votes to Clinton's 50. On 5 December, the day the votes were cast, John wrote to Abigail, "This Day decides whether I shall be a Farmer or a Statesman after next March." The country had decided that he should remain a statesman a few years longer.[11]

2. THE HOME FRONT

Abigail's ultimate response to the political bickering and the social bustle surrounding the federal government was to remove herself from the scene. She had dutifully followed John first to New York, then to Philadelphia when it became the capital in the fall of 1790. In the spring of 1792, she and John went home for the summer to Quincy—now split off from Braintree as a separate town—as they had done the previous year. That fall, when John returned to Philadelphia, Abigail remained in Massachusetts. Poor health spurred the initial decision: Abigail, suffering from rheumatism and the re-

[9] JA to AA2, 29 Oct. 1792, but see also TBA to AA, 17 Oct., both below.
[10] TBA to JA, 30 Oct. 1792, and JA to AA, 2 Dec., both below.
[11] JA to AA, 24 Nov. and 5 Dec. 1792, both below. For the final electoral vote tally, see JQA to JA, 8 Dec., and note 1, below.

sidual effects of malaria, was too ill to travel. Philadelphia's unhealthy climate—including a major yellow fever epidemic in 1793—also encouraged her to stay away. Abigail ultimately decided to make the arrangement permanent for the remainder of John's vice presidency. She and John contented themselves with summers together, which afforded them more time in the same place than they had had for much of their marriage. Abigail's choice to remain in Quincy stemmed from various factors. It moved her closer to her sisters and extended family. It spared her the limelight of Philadelphia society, where she had to be on her guard socially and politically. It allowed her to enjoy the quieter pleasures of life in Quincy. And it freed her to run her own household and manage the family's properties directly rather than through agents and surrogates (most notably, Cotton Tufts, Mary Cranch, and John Quincy Adams).

In all the places she lived, Abigail faced the usual difficulties in managing her household, including high prices, obstreperous servants, and continual maintenance problems. When Abigail and John arrived at Bush Hill, the house they initially rented on the outskirts of Philadelphia, they found "the workmen there with their brushes in hand. This was cold comfort in a house, where I suppose no fire had been kindled for several years. . . . What confusion! Boxes, barrels, chairs, tables, trunks, &c.; every thing to be arranged, and few hands to accomplish it." Another house, rented the second year in Philadelphia, had "Rooms so small and not able to lay two together, [which] renders it very troublesome to see so much company as we must be obliged to." Even worse, Abigail struggled to find adequate servants: "I brought all my servants from N york, cook excepted and, thought I could not be worse of than I had been. I have had in the course of 18 months Seven, and I firmly believe in the whole Number, not a virtuous woman amongst them all; the most of them drunkards." One was "so indecent, that footman Coachman & all were driven out of the House." She sent a stream of pleas to Mary Cranch in Braintree to find her better help, preferring good, reliable people from Massachusetts to what she considered the lazy and immoral servants in New York, "all Foreigners & chiefly vagabonds."[12]

Running the household included making financial decisions, both day-to-day and long-term. Abigail as always was deeply engaged in

---

[12] AA to AA2, 21 Nov. 1790; to Mary Smith Cranch, 30 Oct. 1791; to Cranch, 9 Jan.; and to Cranch, 28 April 1790, all below. See also AA's letters to Mary Cranch of 5 Jan. and 21 April 1790, both below.

investing the Adamses' money. Unlike John, she had no interest in land and preferred securities, which she believed would be "less troublesome to take charge of then Land and much more productive, but in these Ideas I have always been so unfortunate as to differ from my partner who thinks he never saved any thing but what he vested in Land." John's love of land obliged Abigail and her main agent in Braintree, Cotton Tufts, to spend much of their time searching out adequate tenants to farm these properties and care for the houses. Few tenants lived up to their exacting standards, and Abigail and John had difficulty profiting from their landholdings. Abigail was more successful with her own investments in bonds and loan certificates, making handsome profits for the family through shrewd purchases and timely sales, with the assistance of a federal economic policy (supported by her husband) that funded war bonds at par, regardless of the price at which a speculator had acquired them. Tufts handled most of the transactions for Abigail because she, as a woman, could not make them directly. Conscious of her image in the political world, Abigail also attempted to keep these dealings anonymous.[13]

Despite Abigail's success with investing, the Adamses' day-to-day finances remained precarious. John's salary for the vice presidency, $5,000 per year, was not sufficient to maintain two residences, one in the capital and one at home in Massachusetts, and the situation only grew worse, first with the government's move to Philadelphia and later with rapid inflation striking the American economy and undercutting his salary's value. In 1790 and 1791, Abigail missed Braintree and wished to return there more frequently, but "reasons, not of state, but of purse" prevented it. She complained that Congress refused to increase John's salary and forced him "to remove twice at his own expence in the course of two years—and to a city where the expence of living is a third dearer than at N york." The need to support their children further taxed John and Abigail's resources. Nonetheless, they never reached the point of true want and, despite their complaints, found means enough to live in style and to give to those less fortunate.[14]

[13] AA to Mary Smith Cranch, 10 Oct. 1790, and to Cotton Tufts, 18 April, both below. For most of the discussion on the Adamses' finances, see AA's correspondence with Cotton Tufts throughout the volume. For AA's investing, see Woody Holton, "Abigail Adams, Bond Speculator," *WMQ*, 3d series, 64:821–838 (Oct. 2007).

[14] AA to JQA, 20 Aug. 1790, and to Cotton Tufts, 11 March 1791, both below.

Abigail, when absent from Quincy, remained deeply concerned with the goings-on and well-being of her neighbors and friends in the area. She welcomed news of marriages, births, and deaths in town as well as word of who had moved in and who had moved out. She made a point of ensuring that the indigent Mary Palmer, who stayed at the Old House during the winter of 1790, received "a couple of loads of wood" to help with the heating. After Palmer's death, Abigail insisted that Palmer's two daughters, Polly and Elizabeth, remain in the house rent free until they made alternative arrangements. She gave small gifts to various poor widows and tried to quietly assist her sister Mary Cranch when she struggled owing to her husband Richard's ill health. These acts of generosity helped Abigail to keep close to the Braintree community, even when she was away, and allowed her to fulfill her sense of obligation to give back for the many blessings that she had received in her life.[15]

3. YOUNG LAWYERS AND GROWING FAMILIES

During these initial years of the early republic, the three Adams sons all attempted to establish themselves in the legal profession. John Quincy was the first to complete his apprenticeship, with Theophilus Parsons in Newburyport, Massachusetts, and receive admission to the bar. He moved in the summer of 1790 to Boston where he set up office in the Adams family's Court Street house while boarding with his mother's cousins Dr. Thomas and Abigail Welsh. There John Quincy continued to study and slowly began to take cases. Arguing his first lawsuit in October 1790, he felt that he "was too much agitated to be possessed of proper presence of mind" and lost to the respected Harrison Gray Otis. Nevertheless, his practice grew, as did his political standing. On his father's advice, he began to attend the Boston town meeting, where he was eventually invited to sit on a committee advocating reform of the police. He also played an active role in support of the incorporation of a new town—Quincy—out of certain districts in Braintree. His writings under various pseudonyms put him at the center of debates regarding Thomas Paine's *Rights of Man* and the French Revolution.[16]

---

[15] AA to Cotton Tufts, 17 Jan. 1790; to Mary Smith Cranch, 20 Feb.; to Cranch, 15 March; and to Cotton Tufts, 18 Dec. 1791, all below.

[16] JA to JQA, 9 Feb. 1790; JQA to JA, 19 March; JQA to AA, 17 Oct.; and JQA to TBA, 1 Feb. 1792, all below. For JQA's writings as Publicola, see TBA to AA, 27 May, note 5, below.

Charles too had a budding legal career, apprenticing with John Laurance in New York City and later working with Robert Troup. Having previously caused the family some concern due to questionable acquaintances and occasional inappropriate behavior while at Harvard, he was now settling down well. Even John, who was rarely generous with his praise, noted that "Charles is uncommonly assiduous in his office, and very attentive to his studies. He is acquiring [a] Reputation for the Ease and Elegance of his manners as well as for the solidity of his Pursuits." Charles passed his examinations in the summer 1792 and set up his own office in Hanover Square, right in the heart of the city. By December he had argued and won his first case and seemed well on the way to a successful career.[17]

Thomas Boylston, who graduated from Harvard in the summer of 1790, quickly joined his parents in New York and in the fall of the same year moved with them to Philadelphia. It was not always clear that he would pursue the law like his father and older brothers (his mother and John Quincy thought he might be better suited to business), but he decided in the end to go that route, though Abigail speculated it was "rather from necessity than inclination." He went to work in the office of Jared Ingersoll and, after initial delays due to ill health, made good progress. He also became John and Abigail's agent in Philadelphia during the periods when they were staying in Braintree, making arrangements for their housing and organizing the paperwork necessary for John to receive his salary. By late 1793, Thomas Boylston too had passed the bar, in Pennsylvania, and declared himself ready "to undertake the cause of the oppressed, & attempt to render justice to him that is wronged."[18]

John was proud of his sons but could not restrain himself from offering advice—in large quantities, usually unsolicited—on appropriate readings, study techniques, managing a law office, and other "tricks of the trade" for his young lawyers. He counseled them "to make yourself Master of the Roman Learning" and to make "Love of study an increasing Passion." Still, he was sympathetic to the difficulty of building a practice and recommended patience. To John Quincy he noted, "You must expect an Interval of Leisure, and Ennui." He later reiterated, "Some odd incident, altogether unforeseen and unexpected, will very probably bring you into some popular

---

[17] JA to JQA, [*ante* 8] Sept. 1790; CA to AA, 15 Aug. 1792; to JA, 20 Aug.; and JA to AA, 2 Dec., all below.

[18] AA to JQA, 12 Sept. 1790, and TBA to AA, 9 Dec. 1793, both below.

Cause, and Spread your Character with a thousand Trumpetts at a time. Such a Thing may not happen however in several years. meantime Patience Courage." John knew from personal experience that a young lawyer starting out in Boston would struggle to compete against more experienced attorneys and that John Quincy would need to allow his business to build slowly.[19]

The brothers likewise provided encouragement to one another, particularly to John Quincy, who found the transition especially stressful. Prone to worry and depression, he agonized over his prospects and his failure to find immediate success, even as he acknowledged that he could "have but little expectations at present from business." When Charles received John Quincy's report on his first case, Charles noted that "the person who is unintimidated upon such occasions has not the common feelings of human nature." He found it no surprise that John Quincy should be bested by a more experienced lawyer or that he might need to practice his public-speaking skills. But Charles believed John Quincy's greatest obstacle was his own attitude: "I cannot conclude," Charles wrote, "without wishing you could persuade yourself to take the world a little more fair and easy I am confident you raise hills in your imagination more difficult to ascend than you will in reality find them. May you have great fortitude and a more peaceful mind is the wish of your brother." Charles knew that he would have to walk the same "anxious path. . . . A prospect is before me not less clouded than yours." But he seemed better able to face the stress of the situation—or, if he suffered from such anxiety, was unwilling to commit those thoughts to paper.[20]

Of course, life was not only work for the three sons. All had active social lives, attending assemblies and dances, weddings, ordinations, and even a balloon launch. Thomas Boylston developed a rapport with a circle of Quakers in Philadelphia, while Charles, in New York, came to know Nabby's in-laws, the Smiths, and the company of young men surrounding Baron von Steuben. The brothers made visits, as time allowed, to one another as well as to their parents in Braintree and Philadelphia.

Naturally, some of this socializing led to romance. During his time in Newburyport, John Quincy had become involved with Mary Frazier, a young woman from the area. Unprepared to make a com-

[19] JA to JQA, 4 Oct. 1790; to CA, 5 June 1793; to JQA, 19 Feb. 1790; and to JQA, 13 Dec., all below.
[20] JQA to AA, 14 Aug. 1790; CA to JQA, 21 Oct., and 7 Nov., all below.

mitment to her, John Quincy nonetheless felt "a total impossibility to help myself" from the strength of his feelings for her. Consequently, he determined, "I am more than ever convinced of the absolute necessity for me, to leave this town very soon" to escape the situation. Charles met his future wife, Sarah Smith, while socializing with his sister Nabby's in-laws in New York. Sarah, one of William Stephens Smith's younger sisters, had evidently caught his eye by early 1792. The relationship progressed sufficiently to excite the concern of Nabby, who tried to remove Sarah from the scene by bringing her with the Smiths to England. Sarah's mother objected "because she would not go free and unbiassed in her mind," and little more was said on the subject for the time being.[21]

Not surprisingly, the Adams parents had thoughts on such relationships. Abigail especially counseled her sons to avoid early marriage.[22] Nabby too suggested that John Quincy ought to wait: "I could wish to see you a few years further advanced in Life before you engage in a Connection which if you form at present must impede your progress and advancement." John Quincy tried to reassure both mother and sister that he had no intention of moving hastily toward gaining a wife he felt unable to support without his parents' assistance: "You may rest assured, my dear Madam, that I am as resolutely determined never to connect a woman to desperate Fortunes, as I am never to be indebted to a woman for wealth." While his interest in Mary Frazier continued for several years—he did not absolutely break off the relationship until he was on the verge of leaving for Europe in 1794—John Quincy held to his resolve not to act upon his feelings and remained unattached. Likewise, Charles and Sarah Smith waited until 1795 before they finally married.[23]

Meanwhile, daughter Nabby was attending to her growing family and her husband's career, which faced its own challenges. William Stephens Smith had hoped to receive a diplomatic appointment be-

---

[21] JQA to William Cranch, 7 April 1790, and note 5; and AA2 to AA, 27 March 1792, both below.

[22] Interestingly, AA believed that she herself had married too young. She wrote to TBA some years later, in response to his thoughts on his growing relationship with Ann Harrod, "I once heard you say, you would not give a copper to be married after 30. but I must add, few gentlemen are fit to be married untill that age; nor do I think a Lady less qualified to make a good wife with the judgement and experience of even that age. sure I am too many enter that state prematurely, with experience upon my side. I say of myself that I did, much too young for the proper fulfillment of duties which soon devolved upon me" (20 March 1803, private owner).

[23] AA2 to JQA, 18 April 1790, and JQA to AA, 29 Aug., both below.

fore he and Nabby left Great Britain in the spring of 1788. When that opportunity failed to materialize, they returned to his home in New York to build their family and pursue other options. In the fall of 1789, Smith was made marshal for the district of New York, not an especially remunerative job. The Adams family as a whole took this situation amiss, believing that Smith was being penalized for his connection to the Adamses. Abigail considered him "poorly provided for in the distribution of offices," and Smith himself described his situation as "Mortifying."[24]

In an effort to improve his financial circumstances, Smith embarked on a "sudden and unexpected" trip to England in December 1790, in part to collect some debts owed to his father's estate and also to assist in a speculative venture organized by Richard Platt. This left Nabby alone in New York with her children, including young Thomas Hollis Smith, born the previous August. She felt the separation keenly, especially with her parents now removed to Philadelphia. She lamented to a cousin, "the absence of my Husband— leaves a blank in my mind which may be alleviated in some degree by the Kind attentions of my friends; but which nothing can fill up." She also worried about her children's development, fearing that she lacked the "firmness and authority" necessary to train them properly and declaring their education "a task which I feel myself incompetant to the proper performance of." Smith returned in June 1791, having been offered a more lucrative public position, supervisor of revenue for the New York district.[25]

In March 1792, however, the whole Smith family traveled to England to allow Smith to try to make a greater fortune through "advantageous private contracts." He had resigned his position as supervisor of revenue, believing he could do better outside the public sphere and frustrated by what he considered inadequate regard for his earlier sacrifices for the country. He proved successful in this latest venture and was able to bring his family home again by early 1793 with ready means. Smith relished the freedom this newfound wealth provided him: "I feel myself in a great measure independent

[24] Vol. 8:228, 274–275; JQA to AA2, 20 Nov. 1790; AA to Mary Smith Cranch, 12 Dec.; and AA2 to AA, 30 Dec., all below.

[25] AA to Mary Smith Cranch, 12 Dec. 1790; AA2 to Elizabeth Cranch Norton, 7 Feb. 1791; AA2 to Cranch, 8 Feb.; and JA to WSS, 14 March, all below. TBA seconded AA2's concerns about her ability to properly raise her children. Writing to William Cranch, TBA commented that if the Smith sons "could be under the government of your good mother for one week before you come, you would be pleased with their vivacity; but under present management I fear you will perceive very soon where the defect lies" (4 Sept., below).

of the smiles or frowns of Courtiers, which I am grevied to find our Capital abounds, with." He was pleased to no longer be reliant on public offices to maintain his status or provide for his family.[26]

Despite this success, the Adamses had reservations about Smith. John complained that he had returned from England "almost a Revolutionist" and that Nabby's "Adventurer of an Husband is so proud of his Wealth that he would not let her go I suppose without a Coach and four." He felt compelled to warn Smith against boastfulness. But John also found Smith "clever and agreable: . . . I wish . . . that my Boys had a little more of his Activity." Despite the Adamses' initial pleasure at their daughter's match, they had begun to exhibit a pattern of concern that in time would only increase.[27]

The Smiths, however, provided one unmistakable joy for the family: grandchildren. Abigail and John reveled in their roles as grandparents. For the Adamses, one of the most difficult aspects of the government's relocation from New York to Philadelphia was that it separated Abigail from Nabby and her children. Abigail, while still in New York, could barely tolerate their short absences to visit Nabby's in-laws on Long Island: "the House really felt so lonely after [ma]ster william went, that I sent for him back yesterday." Moving a hundred miles away was infinitely more difficult. For a time, the Smith's middle child, John Adams Smith, stayed with the Adamses in Philadelphia, and both grandparents had a wonderful time doting on him. Abigail informed Nabby that "Every day, after dinner, he sets his grandpapa to draw him about in a chair, which is generally done for half an hour, to the derangement of my carpet and the amusement of his grandpapa." Abigail revealed her feelings for her grandchildren when she wrote to her sister Mary Cranch, who had recently become a grandmother for the first time. Abigail asked, "Can you really believe that you are a Grandmamma? does not the little fellow feel as if he was really your own. if he does not now, by that time you have lived a year with him, or near you, I question if you will be able to feel a difference." As her own children grew up, grew more independent, and moved on, Abigail looked to her grandchildren to fill her desire to nurture a new generation.[28]

---

[26] AA to JQA, 5 Feb. 1792, and WSS to JA, 5 Oct., both below.

[27] JA to AA, 27 Feb. and 2 March 1793, both below.

[28] AA to Mary Smith Cranch, 3 April 1790, and to AA2, 21 Feb. 1791, both below. See also AA to Abigail Bromfield Rogers, [5 *Sept. 1790*], below.

4. ANOTHER REVOLUTION

The most important international event of this period was the French Revolution, beginning with the storming of the Bastille in 1789 and growing in intensity throughout these years. More than a backdrop to American politics, it served as yet another divide between Federalists and Democrats. The Adamses raised objections to the French Revolution far earlier than most American observers, who tended to view events in France sympathetically, as a counterpart to or even continuation of the American Revolution. Prior to the Terror, the French seemed to stand for the same ideals of republicanism and opposition to tyrannical monarchy as the American colonists had. But John Quincy argued that "the national Assembly in tearing the lace from the garb of government, will tear the coat itself into a thousand rags.— That nation may for ought I know finally be free; but I am firmly persuaded it will not be untill they have undergone another revolution. . . . rights like these, blown to the winds, by the single breath of a triumphant democracy are inauspicious omens for the erection of an equitable government of Laws.—"[29]

Daughter Nabby, living in England with her husband and children in the summer and fall of 1792, had the closest vantage point on events in France. In London, the Smiths were privy to extensive newspaper coverage and also met refugees on a regular basis, including some people whom the Adamses had known when they lived in Auteuil in the mid-1780s. Nabby reported to her mother that "The accounts from Paris are shocking to every humane mind, and too dreadful to relate. . . . I think the King and Queen will fall a sacrifice to the fury of the *mobites*, and is it not even better they should, than that the people should be annihilated by a general massacre?" Coyly she continued, "I wonder what Mr. Jefferson says to all these things?" William Stephens Smith himself visited Paris and was even offered a commission in the French Army, which desperately sought experienced officers to help the French in their war with the other European powers. Nabby refused to allow her husband to go off on this adventure, however, declaring, "it is too uncertain a cause to volunteer in."[30]

As the violence escalated in France, opposition grew in America. When news of the overthrow of the monarchy and the attack on the

[29] JQA to JA, 19 Oct. 1790, below.
[30] AA2 to AA, 13 Sept. 1792, below.

Tuileries reached Philadelphia in the fall of 1792, Thomas Boylston found that "The dreadful scenes now acting in France, and the universal anarchy which appears to prevail, has excited terrors even in the breasts of the warmest enthusiasts for Revolution." Similarly, Abigail's sister Elizabeth Shaw inquired whether people had "put on any *external* marks of mourning for the unfortunate Lewis to whom America is so much indebted." But some Americans remained committed to the French cause. Charles reported that "The success of The French against the combined armies has excited a blind joy" in New York. In Boston, attendees at a "Civic Feast," held in January 1793, ate a large ox and drank toasts to liberty and fraternity to celebrate the success of the French Revolution. Abigail wrote to Nabby, "you will see by our Newspapers how citizen Mad our people are, and what a jubelee they have exhibited for the success of the French Arms over the Prussians & Austerians. when they establish a good Government upon a solid Basis then will I join them in rejoicing."[31]

The appearance in the United States of "Citizen" Edmond Genet to represent France as its minister plenipotentiary highlighted the importance—and challenges—of Franco-American relations. The United States wanted to honor its long-standing friendship with France but also feared being drawn into a raging European war. The unstable nature of France's government created additional complications. Charles reported that many in New York debated how to respond to Genet's arrival: "Some say that we cannot but receive him out of a principle of gratitude to France who was so early in acknowledging our Independence! but should we carry this so far as to draw all the Nations of Europe into a war with us? Can we receive a minister who comes from we know not who?" The difficulty was exacerbated by Genet's own behavior, in particular his strident promotion of French interests in violation of the United States' neutrality. Washington eventually felt compelled to issue a proclamation of neutrality and, when that failed to quell Genet's mischievous activities, to demand his recall.[32]

Genet's removal did little to settle debate over how the United States should respond to the volatile circumstances in France. John believed that Washington needed to take stronger measures lest

---

[31] TBA to JA, 30 Oct. 1792; Elizabeth Smith Shaw to Mary Smith Cranch, 21 April 1793; CA to JA, 5 Jan.; and AA to AA2, 10 Feb., all below.
[32] CA to JA, 19 Feb. 1793, below. See also CA to JA, 25 Aug.; TBA to AA, 3 Nov.; and JA to AA, 5 Dec., all below.

French-inspired Democratic-Republicans topple the American government: "If the President has made any Mistake at all, it is by too much Partiality for the French Republicans and in not preserving a Neutrality between the Parties in France as well as among the Belligerent Powers. . . . A Party Spirit will convert White into black and Right into Wrong." But with the French Revolution, as with so many other aspects of American affairs, events were largely out of John's control. The Adamses could do little but observe as the situation unfolded, discuss it among themselves, and hope that others with more power would steer the right course.[33]

5. NOTES ON EDITORIAL METHOD

In 2007, the Adams Papers editorial project undertook a full review of its editorial practices and developed a new policy consistent with current standards for documentary editing. For a full statement of that policy, see *Adams Family Correspondence*, 8:xxxv–xliii. Readers may still wish to consult the descriptions of editorial policy established at the beginning of the project, as contained in the *Diary and Autobiography of John Adams*, 1:lii–lxii, and the *Adams Family Correspondence*, 1:xli–xlviii. These statements document the original conception of the Adams Papers project, though parts of them have now been superseded.

6. RELATED DIGITAL RESOURCES

The Massachusetts Historical Society continues to support the work of making Adams family materials available to scholars and the public online. Three digital resources in particular complement the *Adams Family Correspondence* volumes: The Adams Family Papers: An Electronic Archive, The Diaries of John Quincy Adams: A Digital Collection, and Founding Families: Digital Editions of the Papers of the Winthrops and the Adamses. All of these are available through the Historical Society's website at www.masshist.org.

The Adams Family Papers Electronic Archive contains images and text files of all of the correspondence between John and Abigail Adams owned by the Massachusetts Historical Society as well as John Adams' diaries and autobiography. The files are fully searchable and can also be browsed by date.

[33] JA to AA, 19 Dec. 1793, below.

The Diaries of John Quincy Adams Digital Collection provides images of John Quincy Adams' entire 51-volume diary, which he composed over nearly 70 years. The images can be searched by date or browsed by diary volume.

The Founding Families Digital Editions, a project cosponsored by the National Endowment for the Humanities, Harvard University Press, and the Massachusetts Historical Society, provides searchable text files of the 38 Adams Papers volumes published prior to 2007 (excluding the *Portraits* volumes) as well as the 7 volumes of the Winthrop Family Papers. The Adams Papers volumes are supplemented by a cumulative index prepared by the Adams Papers editors. This digital edition is designed not to replace the letterpress edition but rather to complement it by providing greater access to a wealth of Adams material.

Readers may wish to supplement the letters included in volume 9 of the *Adams Family Correspondence* with material from the same time period included in John Adams' *Diary and Autobiography*, 3:223–225; in John Quincy Adams' Diary available online (as described above); and in the letters of John Adams and John Quincy Adams published, respectively, in *The Works of John Adams*, edited by Charles Francis Adams, 8:496–515, 9:563–574, and *Writings of John Quincy Adams*, edited by Worthington Chauncey Ford, 1:44–176. Future volumes of the *Papers of John Adams* will expand on John's public life during these important years of the early republic.

The value of the *Family Correspondence* series lies only in part with the insight that the letters of the Adamses provide into the public affairs of their times. This volume, like the others that have preceded it, does indeed discuss the growth of the American nation, but it also reveals an intimate portrait of one of the country's first families. The Adamses may have been at the forefront of major events, but the challenges that they faced—rearing children, building careers, managing households, sustaining relationships across long distances—were in many ways quite ordinary. And it is their eloquently written record, balancing the mundane and the extraordinary, that makes the *Family Correspondence* such compelling reading.

Margaret A. Hogan
November 2008

Acknowledgments

Every volume of the Adams Papers benefits greatly from the assistance of many people beyond the editors.

We particularly appreciate the efforts of several members of the Adams Papers staff past and present, including former transcriber Nathaniel Adams; James Connolly and Amanda Mathews, our current transcribers; Judith S. Graham, former editorial assistant and current editor of the Louisa Catherine Adams diaries; and Sara Martin, assistant editor. All of them provided invaluable help with the preparation of materials for this and future volumes of the *Adams Family Correspondence* and assisted with the production of this book. They pitched in with grace and good humor on a wide array of tasks large and small, always with care and great skill.

Our copyeditor Ann-Marie Imbornoni reviewed the entire manuscript with her usual precision and consideration, saving us from any number of embarrassing errors.

Many people contributed to the research behind this book. We particularly wish to thank Edward B. Doctoroff, Head of the Library Privileges and Billing Division at Harvard's Widener Library; and the reference staffs at Harvard University's Houghton, Lamont, and Widener libraries, the Rare Books and Manuscripts Department at the Boston Public Library, and the New England Historic Genealogical Society.

As with previous volumes, Kevin and Kenneth Krugh of Technologies 'N Typography in Merrimac, Massachusetts, ably typeset the volume. At Harvard University Press, we thank John F. Walsh, Associate Director for Design and Production; Abigail Mumford, Production Supervisor; and Kathleen McDermott, Senior Editor in History and the Social Sciences, for their continuing assistance with the publication, marketing, and sales of this book and all Adams Papers titles.

The Massachusetts Historical Society continues to provide this project with the use of its unrivaled collections and the support of its knowledgeable staff. In particular, we thank Dennis A. Fiori, President; Peter Drummey, Stephen T. Riley Librarian; Conrad E. Wright, Worthington C. Ford Editor; Brenda M. Lawson, Director of Collections Services; Mary E. Fabiszewski, Senior Cataloger; Nancy Heywood, Digital Projects Coordinator; and all of the members of the Library–Reader Services department. Finally, we also greatly appreciate the ongoing contributions made by the Adams Papers Administrative Committee to the success of this project.

Guide to Editorial Apparatus

The first three sections (1–3) of this guide list, respectively, the arbitrary devices used for clarifying the text, the code names for prominent members of the Adams family, and the symbols that are employed throughout *The Adams Papers*, in all its series and parts, for various kinds of manuscript sources. The final three sections (4–6) list, respectively, the symbols for institutions holding original materials, the various abbreviations and conventional terms, and the short titles of books and other works that occur in volume 9 of the *Adams Family Correspondence*.

1. TEXTUAL DEVICES

The following devices will be used throughout *The Adams Papers* to clarify the presentation of the text.

[. . .]	One word missing or illegible.
[. . . .]	Two words missing or illegible.
[. . . .]¹	More than two words missing or illegible; subjoined footnote estimates amount of missing matter.
[ ]	Number or part of a number missing or illegible. Amount of blank space inside brackets approximates the number of missing or illegible digits.
[roman]	Conjectural reading for missing or illegible matter. A question mark is inserted before the closing bracket if the conjectural reading is seriously doubtful.
~~roman~~	Canceled matter.
[*italic*]	Editorial insertion.
{roman}	Text editorially decoded or deciphered.

2. ADAMS FAMILY CODE NAMES

First Generation

JA	John Adams (1735–1826)
AA	Abigail Adams (1744–1818), *m.* JA 1764

Second Generation

AA2	Abigail Adams (1765–1813), daughter of JA and AA, *m.* WSS 1786
WSS	William Stephens Smith (1755–1816), brother of SSA
JQA	John Quincy Adams (1767–1848), son of JA and AA
LCA	Louisa Catherine Johnson (1775–1852), *m.* JQA 1797
CA	Charles Adams (1770–1800), son of JA and AA
SSA	Sarah Smith (1769–1828), sister of WSS, *m.* CA 1795
TBA	Thomas Boylston Adams (1772–1832), son of JA and AA
AHA	Ann Harrod (1774?–1845), *m.* TBA 1805

Third Generation

GWA	George Washington Adams (1801–1829), son of JQA and LCA
JA2	John Adams (1803–1834), son of JQA and LCA
MCHA	Mary Catherine Hellen (1806–1870), *m.* JA2 1828
CFA	Charles Francis Adams (1807–1886), son of JQA and LCA
ABA	Abigail Brown Brooks (1808–1889), *m.* CFA 1829
ECA	Elizabeth Coombs Adams (1808–1903), daughter of TBA and AHA

Fourth Generation

LCA2	Louisa Catherine Adams (1831–1870), daughter of CFA and ABA, *m.* Charles Kuhn 1854
JQA2	John Quincy Adams (1833–1894), son of CFA and ABA
CFA2	Charles Francis Adams (1835–1915), son of CFA and ABA
HA	Henry Adams (1838–1918), son of CFA and ABA
MHA	Marian Hooper (1842–1885), *m.* HA 1872
MA	Mary Adams (1845–1928), daughter of CFA and ABA, *m.* Henry Parker Quincy 1877
BA	Brooks Adams (1848–1927), son of CFA and ABA

Fifth Generation

CFA3	Charles Francis Adams (1866–1954), son of JQA2
HA2	Henry Adams (1875–1951), son of CFA2
JA3	John Adams (1875–1964), son of CFA2

3. DESCRIPTIVE SYMBOLS

The following symbols are employed throughout *The Adams Papers* to describe or identify the various kinds of manuscript originals.

D	Diary (Used only to designate a diary written by a member of the Adams family and always in combination with the short form of the writer's name and a serial number, as follows: D/JA/23, i.e., the twenty-third fascicle or volume of John Adams' manuscript Diary.)
Dft	draft
Dupl	duplicate
FC	file copy (A copy of a letter retained by a correspondent other than an Adams, no matter the form of the retained copy; a copy of a letter retained by an Adams other than a Letterbook copy.)
IRC	intended recipient's copy (Generally the original version but received after a duplicate, triplicate, or other copy of a letter.)
Lb	Letterbook (Used only to designate an Adams Letterbook and always in combination with the short form of the writer's name and a serial number, as follows: Lb/JQA/29, i.e., the twenty-ninth volume of John Quincy Adams' Letterbooks.)
LbC	letterbook copy (Used only to designate an Adams Letterbook copy. Letterbook copies are normally unsigned, but any such copy is assumed to be in the hand of the person responsible for the text unless it is otherwise described.)

M	Miscellany (Used only to designate materials in the section of the Adams Papers known as the "Miscellanies" and always in combination with the short form of the writer's name and a serial number, as follows: M/CFA/32, i.e., the thirty-second volume of the Charles Francis Adams Miscellanies—a ledger volume mainly containing transcripts made by CFA in 1833 of selections from the family papers.)
MS, MSS	manuscript, manuscripts
RC	recipient's copy (A recipient's copy is assumed to be in the hand of the signer unless it is otherwise described.)
Tr	transcript (A copy, handwritten or typewritten, made substantially later than the original or later than other copies—such as duplicates, file copies, or Letterbook copies—that were made contemporaneously.)
Tripl	triplicate

4. LOCATION SYMBOLS

DLC	Library of Congress
Ia-HA	Iowa State Department of History and Archives
MeHi	Maine Historical Society
MB	Boston Public Library
MBBS	Bostonian Society
MBNEH	New England Historic Genealogical Society
MH-Ar	Harvard University Archives
MH-H	Houghton Library, Harvard University
MHi	Massachusetts Historical Society
MQA	Adams National Historical Park
MQHi	Quincy Historical Society
MWA	American Antiquarian Society
NhHi	New Hampshire Historical Society
NHi	New-York Historical Society
NNC	Columbia University
OCHP	Cincinnati Historical Society
PHC	Haverford College
PHi	Historical Society of Pennsylvania
PPAmP	American Philosophical Society
PPPrHi	Presbyterian Historical Society
PWacD	David Library of the American Revolution
ViMtvL	Mount Vernon Ladies' Association

5. OTHER ABBREVIATIONS AND CONVENTIONAL TERMS

Adams Papers

Manuscripts and other materials, 1639–1889, in the Adams Manuscript Trust collection given to the Massachusetts Historical Society in 1956 and enlarged by a few additions of family papers since then. Citations in the present edition are simply by date of the original document if the original is in the main chronological series of the Papers and therefore readily found in the microfilm edition of the Adams Papers (see below).

The Adams Papers

The present edition in letterpress, published by The Belknap Press of Harvard University Press. References to earlier volumes of any given unit take this form: vol. 2:146. Since there is no overall volume numbering for the edition, references from one series, or unit of a series, to another are by writer, title, volume, and page, for example, JA, *D&A*, 4:205.

Adams Papers, Adams Office Manuscripts

The portion of the Adams manuscripts given to the Massachusetts Historical Society by Thomas Boylston Adams in 1973.

APM

Formerly, Adams Papers, Microfilms. The corpus of the Adams Papers, 1639–1889, as published on microfilm by the Massachusetts Historical Society, 1954–1959, in 608 reels. Cited in the present work, when necessary, by reel number. Available in research libraries throughout the United States and in a few libraries in Canada, Europe, and New Zealand.

PCC

Papers of the Continental Congress. Originals in the National Archives: Record Group 360. Microfilm edition in 204 reels. Usually cited in the present work from the microfilms but according to the original series and volume numbering devised in the State Department in the early nineteenth century; for example, PCC, No. 93, III, i.e., the third volume of series 93.

Thwing Catalogue, MHi

Annie Haven Thwing, comp., Inhabitants and Estates of the Town of Boston, 1630–1800. Typed card catalogue, with supplementary bound typescripts, in the Massachusetts Historical Society. Published on CD-ROM with Annie Haven Thwing, *The Crooked and Narrow Streets of the Town of Boston, 1630–1822*, Massachusetts Historical Society and New England Historic Genealogical Society, 2001.

6. SHORT TITLES OF WORKS FREQUENTLY CITED

AA, *Letters*, ed. CFA, 1848
  Letters of Mrs. Adams, the Wife of John Adams. With an Introductory Memoir by Her Grandson, Charles Francis Adams, 4th edn., rev. and enl., Boston, 1848.

AA, *New Letters*
  New Letters of Abigail Adams, 1788–1801, ed. Stewart Mitchell, Boston, 1947.

AA2, *Jour. and Corr.*
  Journal and Correspondence of Miss Adams, Daughter of John Adams, . . . Edited by Her Daughter [Caroline Amelia (Smith) de Windt], New York and London, 1841–[1849]; 3 vols.
    Note: Vol. [1], unnumbered, has title and date: *Journal and Correspondence of Miss Adams*, 1841; vol. 2 has title, volume number, and date: *Correspondence of Miss Adams . . . Vol. II*, 1842; vol. [3] has title, volume number, and date: *Correspondence of Miss Adams . . . Vol. II*, 1842, i.e., same as vol. 2, but preface is signed "April 3d, 1849," and the volume contains as "Part II" a complete reprint-

ing, from same type and with same pagination, of vol. 2, above, originally issued in 1842.

AFC
> *Adams Family Correspondence*, ed. L. H. Butterfield, Marc Friedlaender, Richard Alan Ryerson, Margaret A. Hogan, and others, Cambridge, 1963– .

Amer. Antiq. Soc., *Procs.*
> American Antiquarian Society, *Proceedings*.

Amer. Philos. Soc., *Memoirs, Procs., Trans.*
> American Philosophical Society, *Memoirs, Proceedings,* and *Transactions*.

Amer. State Papers
> *American State Papers: Documents, Legislative and Executive, of the Congress of the United States,* Washington, 1832–1861; 38 vols.

Annals of Congress
> *The Debates and Proceedings in the Congress of the United States* [1789–1824], Washington, 1834–1856; 42 vols.

Ann. Register
> *The Annual Register; or, A View of the History, Politics, and Literature for the Year,* ed. Edmund Burke and others, London, 1758– .

Biog. Dir. Cong.
> *Biographical Directory of the United States Congress, 1774–1989,* Washington, 1989.

Bosher, *French Rev.*
> J. F. Bosher, *The French Revolution,* New York, 1988.

Boston Directory, [year]
> *Boston Directory,* issued annually with varying imprints.

Boston, [vol. no.] *Report*
> City of Boston, Record Commissioners, *Reports,* Boston, 1876–1909; 39 vols.

Braintree Town Records
> *Records of the Town of Braintree, 1640 to 1793,* ed. Samuel A. Bates, Randolph, Mass., 1886.

Brewer, *Reader's Handbook*
> E. Cobham Brewer, *The Reader's Handbook of Famous Names in Fiction, Allusions, References, Proverbs, Plots, Stories, and Poems,* rev. edn., London, 1902.

Cambridge Modern Hist.
> *The Cambridge Modern History,* Cambridge, Eng., 1902–1911; repr. New York, 1969; 13 vols.

Catalogue of JA's Library
> *Catalogue of the John Adams Library in the Public Library of the City of Boston,* Boston, 1917.

Catalogue of JQA's Books
> Henry Adams and Worthington Chauncey Ford, *A Catalogue of the Books of John Quincy Adams Deposited in the Boston Athenæum with Notes on Books, Adams Seals and Book-Plates,* Boston, 1938.

CFA, *Diary*
> *Diary of Charles Francis Adams,* ed. Aïda DiPace Donald, David Donald, Marc Friedlaender, L. H. Butterfield, and others, Cambridge, 1964– .

Colonial Collegians
: *Colonial Collegians: Biographies of Those Who Attended American Colleges before the War of Independence*, CD-ROM, ed. Conrad Edick Wright, Robert J. Dunkle, and others, Boston, 2005.

Col. Soc. Mass., *Pubns.*
: Colonial Society of Massachusetts, *Publications*.

DAB
: Allen Johnson, Dumas Malone, and others, eds., *Dictionary of American Biography*, New York, 1928–1936; repr. New York, 1955–1980; 10 vols. plus index and supplements.

Dexter, *Yale Graduates*
: Franklin Bowditch Dexter, *Biographical Sketches of the Graduates of Yale College with Annals of the College History*, New York and New Haven, 1885–1912; 6 vols.

DNB
: Leslie Stephen and Sidney Lee, eds., *The Dictionary of National Biography*, New York and London, 1885–1901; repr. Oxford, 1959–1960; 21 vols. plus supplements.

Doc. Hist. Ratif. Const.
: *The Documentary History of the Ratification of the Constitution*, ed. Merrill Jensen, John P. Kaminski, Gaspare J. Saladino, and others, Madison, Wis., 1976– .

Doc. Hist. Supreme Court
: *The Documentary History of the Supreme Court of the United States, 1789–1800*, ed. Maeva Marcus, James R. Perry, and others, New York, 1985–2007; 8 vols.

Evans
: Charles Evans and others, *American Bibliography: A Chronological Dictionary of All Books, Pamphlets and Periodical Publications Printed in the United States of America* [1639–1800], Chicago and Worcester, 1903–1959; 14 vols.

Ferguson, *Power of the Purse*
: E. James Ferguson, *The Power of the Purse: A History of American Public Finance, 1776–1790*, Chapel Hill, 1961.

First Fed. Cong.
: *Documentary History of the First Federal Congress of the United States of America, March 4, 1789 – March 3, 1791*, ed. Linda Grant De Pauw, Charlene Bangs Bickford, Helen E. Veit, William C. diGiacomantonio, and Kenneth R. Bowling, Baltimore, 1972– .

First Fed. Elections
: *The Documentary History of the First Federal Elections, 1788–1790*, ed. Merrill Jensen, Robert A. Becker, Gordon DenBoer, and others, Madison, Wis., 1976–1989; 4 vols.

Grandmother Tyler's Book
: *Grandmother Tyler's Book: The Recollections of Mary Palmer Tyler (Mrs. Royall Tyler), 1775–1866*, ed. Frederick Tupper and Helen Tyler Brown, New York and London, 1925.

Greenleaf, *Greenleaf Family*
: James Edward Greenleaf, comp., *Genealogy of the Greenleaf Family*, Boston, 1896.

Grove *Dicy. of Art*
: Jane Turner, ed., *The Dictionary of Art*, New York, 1996; 34 vols.

Hamilton, *Papers*
> *The Papers of Alexander Hamilton*, ed. Harold C. Syrett, Jacob E. Cooke, and others, New York, 1961–1987; 27 vols.

Haraszti, *Prophets*
> Zoltán Haraszti, *John Adams and the Prophets of Progress*, Cambridge, 1952.

Harvard *Quinquennial Cat.*
> Harvard University, *Quinquennial Catalogue of the Officers and Graduates, 1636–1930*, Cambridge, 1930.

History of Hingham
> *History of the Town of Hingham, Massachusetts*, Hingham, 1893; 3 vols. in 4.

History of Weymouth
> *History of Weymouth Massachusetts*, Weymouth, 1923; 4 vols.

Hoefer, *Nouv. biog. générale*
> Jean Chrétien Ferdinand Hoefer, ed., *Nouvelle biographie générale depuis les temps les plus reculés jusqu'à nos jours*, Paris, 1852–1866; 46 vols.

JA, *D&A*
> *Diary and Autobiography of John Adams*, ed. L. H. Butterfield and others, Cambridge, 1961; 4 vols.

JA, *Defence of the Const.*
> John Adams, *A Defence of the Constitutions of Government of the United States of America*, London, 1787–1788; repr. New York, 1971; 3 vols.

JA, *Earliest Diary*
> *The Earliest Diary of John Adams*, ed. L. H. Butterfield and others, Cambridge, 1966.

JA, *Legal Papers*
> *Legal Papers of John Adams*, ed. L. Kinvin Wroth and Hiller B. Zobel, Cambridge, 1965; 3 vols.

JA, *Letters*, ed. CFA
> *Letters of John Adams, Addressed to His Wife*, ed. Charles Francis Adams, Boston, 1841; 2 vols.

JA, *Papers*
> *Papers of John Adams*, ed. Robert J. Taylor, Gregg L. Lint, and others, Cambridge, 1977– .

JA, *Works*
> *The Works of John Adams, Second President of the United States: with a Life of the Author*, ed. Charles Francis Adams, Boston, 1850–1856; 10 vols.

JCC
> *Journals of the Continental Congress, 1774–1789*, ed. Worthington Chauncey Ford, Gaillard Hunt, John C. Fitzpatrick, Roscoe R. Hill, and others, Washington, 1904–1937; 34 vols.

Jefferson, *Papers*
> *The Papers of Thomas Jefferson*, ed. Julian P. Boyd, Charles T. Cullen, John Catanzariti, Barbara B. Oberg, and others, Princeton, 1950– .

JQA, *Diary*
> *Diary of John Quincy Adams*, ed. David Grayson Allen, Robert J. Taylor, and others, Cambridge, 1981– .

JQA, *Writings*
    Writings of John Quincy Adams, ed. Worthington Chauncey Ford, New York, 1913–1917; 7 vols.

Laurens, *Papers*
    The Papers of Henry Laurens, ed. Philip M. Hamer, George C. Rogers Jr., David R. Chesnutt, C. James Taylor, and others, Columbia, S.C., 1968–2003; 16 vols.

Malone, *Jefferson*
    Dumas Malone, *Jefferson and His Time*, Boston, 1948–1981; 6 vols.

Mass., *Acts and Laws*
    Acts and Laws of the Commonwealth of Massachusetts [1780–1805], Boston, 1890–1898; 13 vols.

MHS, *Colls., Procs.*
    Massachusetts Historical Society, *Collections* and *Proceedings*.

Monaghan, *John Jay*
    Frank Monaghan, *John Jay, Defender of Liberty*, New York and Indianapolis, 1935.

Morison, *Three Centuries of Harvard*
    Samuel Eliot Morison, *Three Centuries of Harvard, 1636–1936*, Cambridge, 1936.

NEHGR
    New England Historical and Genealogical Register.

NEHGS, *Memorial Biographies*
    Memorial Biographies of the New England Historic Genealogical Society, Boston, 1880–1908; 9 vols.

New-York Directory, [year]
    New-York Directory [title varies], issued annually with varying imprints.

Notable Amer. Women
    Edward T. James and others, eds., *Notable American Women, 1607–1950: A Biographical Dictionary*, Cambridge, 1971; 3 vols.

OED
    The Oxford English Dictionary, 2d edn., Oxford, 1989; 20 vols.

Oxford Classical Dicy.
    Simon Hornblower and Antony Spawforth, eds., *The Oxford Classical Dictionary*, 3d edn., New York, 1996.

Parliamentary Hist.
    The Parliamentary History of England, from the Earliest Period to the Year 1803, London, 1806–1820; 36 vols.

Pattee, *Old Braintree*
    William S. Pattee, *A History of Old Braintree and Quincy, with a Sketch of Randolph and Holbrook*, Quincy, 1878.

Philadelphia Directory, [year]
    Philadelphia Directory [title varies], issued annually with varying imprints.

PMHB
    Pennsylvania Magazine of History and Biography.

Repertorium
    Ludwig Bittner and others, eds., *Repertorium der diplomatischen Vertreter aller Länder seit dem Westfälischen Frieden (1648)*, Oldenburg, &c., 1936–1965; 3 vols.

Rowen, *Princes of Orange*
> Herbert H. Rowen, *The Princes of Orange: The Stadholders in the Dutch Republic*, Cambridge, Eng., 1988.

Rush, *Letters*
> *Letters of Benjamin Rush*, ed. L. H. Butterfield, Princeton, 1951; 2 vols.

Schama, *Citizens*
> Simon Schama, *Citizens: A Chronicle of the French Revolution*, New York, 1989.

Shaw-Shoemaker
> Ralph R. Shaw and Richard H. Shoemaker, *American Bibliography: A Preliminary Checklist for 1801–1819*, New York, 1958–1966; 22 vols.

Sibley's Harvard Graduates
> John Langdon Sibley, Clifford K. Shipton, Conrad Edick Wright, Edward W. Hanson, and others, *Biographical Sketches of Graduates of Harvard University, in Cambridge, Massachusetts*, Cambridge and Boston, 1873– .

Smith, *Letters of Delegates*
> *Letters of Delegates to Congress, 1774–1789*, ed. Paul H. Smith and others, Washington, 1976–2000; 26 vols.

Sprague, *Annals Amer. Pulpit*
> William B. Sprague, *Annals of the American Pulpit; or, Commemorative Notices of Distinguished American Clergymen of Various Denominations*, New York, 1857–1869; 9 vols.

Sprague, *Braintree Families*
> Waldo Chamberlain Sprague, comp., *Genealogies of the Families of Braintree, Mass., 1640–1850*, Boston, 1983; repr. CD-ROM, Boston, 2001.

Stewart, *Opposition Press*
> Donald H. Stewart, *The Opposition Press of the Federalist Period*, Albany, 1969.

U.S. Census, 1790
> *Heads of Families at the First Census of the United States Taken in the Year 1790*, Washington, 1907–1908; 12 vols.

U.S. House, *Jour.*
> *Journal of the House of Representatives of the United States*, Washington, 1789– .

U.S. Senate, *Jour.*
> *Journal of the Senate of the United States of America*, Washington, 1789– .

U.S. Statutes at Large
> *The Public Statutes at Large of the United States of America, 1789– *, Boston and Washington, 1845– .

Washington, *Diaries*
> *The Diaries of George Washington*, ed. Donald Jackson and Dorothy Twohig, Charlottesville, 1976–1979; 6 vols.

Washington, *Papers, Presidential Series*
> *The Papers of George Washington: Presidential Series*, ed. Dorothy Twohig, Mark A. Mastromarino, Jack D. Warren, Robert F. Haggard, Christine S. Patrick, John C. Pinheiro, and others, Charlottesville, 1987– .

Winsor, *Memorial History of Boston*
> Justin Winsor, ed., *The Memorial History of Boston, Including Suffolk County, 1630–1880*, Boston, 1880–1881; 4 vols.

Winter, *Amer. Finance and Dutch Investment*
    Pieter J. van Winter and James C. Riley, *American Finance and Dutch Investment,*
    1780–1805, New York, 1977; 2 vols.

WMQ
    William and Mary Quarterly.

Wyman, *Charlestown Genealogies*
    Thomas Bellows Wyman, *The Genealogies and Estates of Charlestown: In the*
    County of Middlesex and Commonwealth of Massachusetts, 1629–1818, Boston,
    1879; 2 vols.

Young, *Democratic Republicans*
    Alfred F. Young, *The Democratic Republicans of New York: The Origins, 1763–1797,*
    Chapel Hill, N.C., 1967.

VOLUME 9

Family Correspondence

January 1790 – December 1793

Adams Family Correspondence

Abigail Adams to Mary Smith Cranch

my dear sister   Jan^{ry} 5th 1790

I begin my Letter with the congratulations of the season, to you and all my other Friends & for many happy returns in Succeeding years. the New years day in this State, & particularly in this city is celebrated with every mark of pleasure and satisfaction. the shops and publick offices are Shut, there is not any market upon this day, but every person laying aside Buisness devote the day to the Social purpose of visiting & receiving visits. the churches are open & divine Service performed begining the year in a very proper manner by giving Thanks to the great Governour of the universe for past mercies, & imploring his future Benidictions there is a kind of cake in fashion upon this day call'd New years cooky. this & cherry Bounce as it is calld is the old Dutch custom of treating their Friends upon the return of every New Year.[1] the common people who are very ready to abuse Liberty, on this day are apt to take rather too freely of the good things of this Life, and finding two of my servants not alltogether qualified for Buisness, I remonstrated to them, but they excused it saying it was new year, & every body was joyous then. the V P. visited the President & then returnd home to receive His Friends. in the Evening I attended the drawing Room, it being mrs W——s publick day. it was as much crowded as a Birth Night at St James, and with company as Briliantly drest, diamonds & great hoops excepted my station is always at the right hand of Mrs W. through want of knowing what is right, I find it some times occupied, but on such an occasion the President never fails of Seeing that it is relinquishd for me, and having removed Ladies Several times, they have now learnt to rise & give it me, but this between our selves, as *all distinction* you know is unpopular. Yet this same P.

I

has so happy a faculty of appearing to accommodate & yet carrying his point, that if he was not really one of the best intentiond Men in the world he might be a very dangerous one. he is polite with dignity, affable without familiarity, distant without Haughtyness, Grave without Austerity, Modest, Wise, & Good these are traits in his Character which peculiarly fit him for the exalted station he holds—and God Grant that he may Hold it with the same applause & universal Satisfaction for many many years—as it is my firm opinion that no other man could rule over this great peopl & consolidate them into one mighty Empire but He who is Set over us.

I thank you my dear sister for several kind Letters,[2] the reason why I have not written to you has been that the post office would not permit Franks even to the V. P. and I did not think my Letters worth paying for— I wrote you a long Letter a little before mr Adams's return, but being under cover to him, I had the mortification to receive it back again. I am perfectly satisfied with what you did for son Thomas, and thank you for all your kind care of him it has saved me much trouble, but I do not think his Health good, he is very thin pale & sallow. I have given him a puke, & think he is the better for it. Charls is quite fat. he is very steady and studious. there is no fault to be found with his conduct, he has no company or companions but known & approved ones, nor does he appear to wish for any other. I some times think his application too intence, but better so, than too remis.

I was really surprizd to learn that Sister Shaw was likly to increase her Family.[3] I wish her comfortably through, but shall feel anxious for her feeble constitution as to my Neice mrs Norten I doubt not she will find her Health mended by becomeing a mother, and you will soon be as fond of your Grandchildren as ever you was of your own.[4] I hope however she will not follow her cousins example, and be like always to have one, before the other is weaned.[5] John does not go alone yet. William becomes every day more & more interesting he is a very pleasant temperd Boy, but the other will require the whole house to manage him. with Regard to the cellar I know if very cold weather should come we shall lose our red wine & Porter, but as to the key, tis a point I do not chuse to meddle with tho all the Liquors shoud suffer by it. I did not leave it where it is, nor do I hold myself answerable for the concequences of neglect. the fruit which came here was like refuse, rotton & Bruised, a specimin of what I expected but you know there are cases where silence is prudence, and I think without flattering myself I have attaind to some share of that virtue. we live in a world where having Eyes, we must not see, and Ears we must not hear

10 Jan^ry

I designd to have written much more to you and some other Friends, but publick days, dinning parties &c have occupied me so much for this fort night, that I must close my Letter now or lose the conveyance.

remember me affectionatly to all Friends. living two miles from meeting obliges me to hasten or lose the afternoon Service. adieu yours   A Adams—

RC (MWA:Abigail Adams Letters).

[1] The New York tradition of distributing *Nieuwjaar koeken* (New Year's cookies) and cherry bounce (a cherry cordial) on New Year's Day was introduced by Dutch settlers in the seventeenth century (Andrew F. Smith, ed., *The Oxford Encyclopedia of Food and Drink in America*, 2 vols., Oxford, 2004, 1:317; Alan Davidson, *The Oxford Companion to Food*, Oxford, 1999, p. 212).

[2] Cranch to AA, 1 Nov. 1789, vol. 8:433–434. Other letters beyond that date have not been found.

[3] Elizabeth Smith Shaw was almost forty years old when her third child, Abigail Adams Shaw, was born on 2 March 1790; see Elizabeth Smith Shaw to AA, 14 March, below.

[4] Elizabeth Cranch Norton gave birth to her first child, Richard Cranch Norton, on 12 March (*History of Weymouth*, 4:444).

[5] This is the first reference to AA2's third pregnancy. She gave birth to Thomas Hollis Smith on 7 Aug., her third son in as many years; see AA to Mary Smith Cranch, 8 Aug., below.

Abigail Adams to Cotton Tufts

my dear sir   [*post 8 January* 1790][1]

I have to acknowledge two kind Letters[2] from you which I should sooner have replied to, but the post office would make me pay more than I thought my Letters would be worth. the Members of both Houses have been more punctual in meeting this year than they were the last, & the third day they made a House.[3] you will see, & I doubt not be pleased with the Presidents Speach. great National objects will come before the two Houses, perhaps none of greater magnitude than the National Debt. I hope to see an adoption of all the state debts, and ways and means devised to pay them but whether there will be sufficient courage in the Legislature to take so desicive a step, must be left to time to devellope but it is one of the main pillars upon which the duration of the Government rests. the Bill you drew was immediatly Honourd, the inaccuracy was discoverd, but it did not injure the validity of it. I received all the

3

things you mention by Barnard. Butter is sold here at a shilling York currency by the Quantity, if it should be sold again at six pence with you I wish you to send me two more firkins, and Hams I would not fail to have a dozen engaged for me, or a dozen & half we cannot get such pork or Hams here as massachusetts affords. Barnard talks of comeing again this winter, but if he should not, he will be out early in the Spring. we have had an uncommon pleasent Season, mild as may, but I fear not so Healthy as Severer weather would be

in one of Your Letters you mentiond that the G——r was a little hurt that mr A did not call to take leave of him. when he first arrived he went to see him, but indisposition prevented the G——r from receiving him. after this he received a message from the G——r requesting him to dine with him when *ever the President* did. you know how that matter was conducted, and that mr Adams was with the President, when the G——r sent his excuse for not waiting upon the President, and received for answer, that if he was too much indisposed to come out, he certainly was unfitt to receive company, and therefore he must decline dinning with him, upon which mr A. to the President observed that as his invitation was conditional he presumed he was excused and accordingly dinned with the President at his Apartments. the Gr conduct was Such as to *belittle* him, to use the expression of a Great Man; in the Eyes of every person not totally blinded to his foibles. inclosed is the late speach—[4]

The accounts you mention you may charge if you please; Brislers I wish you to forward that I may know how to Settle it with him.

All Friends here desire to be affectionatly rememberd to you, particularly your / affectionate Neice   A Adams

RC (NHi:Misc. Mss. Adams, Abigail); endorsed: "rec[d] Jan[y] 18. 1790"; docketed: "Mrs Abigail Adams / Letter" and "Jan[y] 1790." Filmed at [*ante 18 Jan. 1790*].

[1] The dating is based on George Washington's speech, for which see note 4.

[2] Tufts to AA, 20 Dec. 1789, vol. 8:448–449. The other letter has not been found.

[3] It had taken over a month for both the Senate and the House of Representatives to achieve quorums at the start of the first congressional session the previous spring. This time it took only a few days, with both houses reaching quorums by 7 Jan. 1790 (*First Fed. Cong.*, 1:3–7, 213–214; 3:3–7).

[4] Not found. Washington gave his first State of the Union address before both houses of Congress on 8 January. Touching on a number of subjects, including the need to create a uniform currency and regulate naturalization, a possible war with the Indians, and the federal government's role in promoting "Agriculture, Commerce and Manufactures" as well as "Science and Literature," the president's speech particularly stressed the importance of military preparedness (*First Fed. Cong.*, 1:215–218). The speech appeared in the New York *Gazette of the United States* the following day.

Abigail Adams to Cotton Tufts

Dear Sir: New York, Jan'ry 17, 1790.

I think our dear state makes full use of the liberty of the press, but they who write for the benefit of mankind whether learned or unlearned will always find more utility in reasoning than writing; I am led to these observations by several pieces, some in Edes paper, that fountain of Sedition, and a piece in Adams paper signed "a New England man."[1] This same writer and many others will find their hands full, whenever the systems and plans of the Secretary of the Treasury come before them. Many copies are ordered to be printed. They are not yet published, but are spoken of by many members of the House, as a performance which does much honour to the abilities of the Secretary.[2] The two Houses are going on upon business and are now pretty full. The *House* condescended to go in a body to the President with their answer to his speech, tho' many of them warmly opposed it, yet as the Senate, with their president at their Head, had done it, they did not know how very well to get over it. But the Senate all rode, & how should they look on foot with a rabble after them splashing through the mud, & this objection was obviated, by a member proposing that the Hackney men should be sent, to supply those with carriages, who had not them of their own.

"Then it looks so monarchial," to go to the president, that they had best send a committee first to know when & where he would receive their answer, this was done, and the president returned for answer, that as the Senate had come to him, he could not think proper to make a distinction, besides it was the usage & custom of particular states to send answers to speeches made them by their Governours, & he would not *wish* to make innovations, and this polite answer being reported, a member moved that as the president had been so very delicate upon the subject, he would not any longer oppose the House going, so the Mountain went to Mahomet, and in style too.

Their Sergeant at Arms preceeded the carriage of the Speaker, bearing his maise before on horse back & carriages followed. Thus this mighty business was accomplished. Pray do not tell anybody from whence you get this story, I dare say it will not be entered upon the journals.[3]

The Ancient Ballad & the Hartford News Boys New Years Address should be bound up together, let those feel the rod who deserve it. Mac Fingal has not yet lost his talent at satire.[4]

I suppose Boston is not behind hand with New York in speculation. I have thought whether it would not be best to sell the indents & purchase certificates.[5] I suppose they have risen with you, they are seven & six pence here, indents I mean. The little matter you have belonging to me I wish you to dispose of as you would of your own property to the best advantage by changing or selling according to your judgment. The small pitance distributed to the widows is but a mite, my Heart is much larger than my purse and I think I should experience a great pleasure and satisfaction if I could make the Fatherless and widows heart sing for joy. I wish you to order Pratt to carry to Mrs. Palmer a couple of loads of wood, it will be necessary to have fires in all the chimneys in the course of the winter and I wish to give her two cords of wood in that way, for several reasons, and you will order it done in the manner you think best.

My best regards to Mrs. Tufts, to all other friends, will you be so good as to give Mrs. Hunt a dollar on my account.

Sir your very / Affectionate Niece   Abigail Adams

MS not found. Printed from Walter R. Benjamin, ed., *The Collector*, 26:86–87 (June 1913).

[1] Benjamin Edes' *Boston Gazette*, which enjoyed great prestige during the Revolution but suffered a gradual decline in the 1790s, was a strongly Antifederalist and then Republican publication. AA probably refers here to items in the 11 Jan. 1790 issue, including the reprinting of a portion of JA's "Dissertation on the Canon and the Feudal Law" defending freedom of the press, first published in the *Gazette* years before, with a preamble noting, "the manly, and truly democratic sentiments they contain, entitles them to the notice of every *consistent Republican*. How far they correspond with recent opinions *privately* and *publicly* advanced by certain great Characters, the candid must declare. . . . The comparison may at least amuse your readers, and perhaps, may be a lesson to the very learned, and 'Most Honorable' Author." For JA's "Dissertation," see *Papers*, 1:103–128.

Thomas Adams' thriving Boston *Independent Chronicle* was similarly partisan. The piece signed "a New-England man," from the 7 Jan. issue, contended that, taxed by the federal government, Americans would "suffer the insults and abuse which the peasants in a government of despotism, are constantly experiencing." The author asked, "Is the aggrandizing of a few . . . and fatening with exorbitant salaries, those who are near the throne of despotism, what you suffered to purchase?" (Stewart, *Opposition Press*, p. 616; Jeffrey L. Pasley, *"The Tyranny of Printers": Newspaper Politics in the Early American Republic*, Charlottesville, Va., 2001, p. 107–108).

[2] Alexander Hamilton presented his "Report of the Secretary of the Treasury on the Public Credit" to the House of Representatives on 14 January. The House ordered that 300 copies of the document be printed and resolved to open debate on the subject in two weeks' time (*First Fed. Cong.*, 3:263; 5:743). For the text of the report, see *First Fed. Cong.*, 5:743–777.

[3] According to the journal of the House of Representatives, the members of the House waited on George Washington at his home on 14 Jan. to deliver their reply to his State

of the Union speech. The Senate also visited the president that morning (*First Fed. Cong.*, 1:222; 3:262). The following day, the *New York Daily Gazette* reported, "Yesterday the Members of the Senate and House of Representatives of the United States went in their carriages, preceded by the Serjeant at Arms on horseback, and presented their Addresses to the President, in answer to his Address to both Houses."

[4] "The Ancient Ballad" probably refers to the poem titled "Fragments of Ancient Ballads," dated 1 Jan., which appeared in the *Massachusetts Centinel*, 6 January. An indictment of Gov. John Hancock's behavior during Washington's visit to Massachusetts in the fall of 1789, a portion read: "They rais'd a grand Triumphal Arch / With trophies on the top, / And all agreed in *form* to march / And meet him, when he'd stop. / But then this City govern'd was, / By such a little man. / That he determin'd, ah! alas! / To intercept their plan." The other piece was likely "The News-Boy's Address to His Customers," which appeared in the *Connecticut Courant*, 7 Jan. 1790. Touching on a number of political subjects, it also alluded to Hancock: "Now states, 'tis clearly proved at Boston, / Their sovereignty should make the most on, / Each State, in governor's opinion, / At home should rank before the Union; / And should our President but doubt, / We'll try the reasoning force of gout." This poem was probably drafted by one of the Connecticut Wits—perhaps, as AA suggests, by John Trumbull, the author of *McFingal*.

[5] For AA's activities as a bond speculator, see Descriptive List of Illustrations, No. 5, above.

Abigail Adams to Mary Smith Cranch

my dear sister   Richmond Hill Jan^ry 24 1789 [*1790*]

I embrace this opportunity By my Brother to write you a few lines tho it is only to tell you what you would have learnt from him, Namely that we are all well. he is come in persuit of Betsy Crosby. how well the child might have been provided for if the dr had lived, I cannot pretend to say, but two thirds of her property is already consumed, every minutia being charged to her as the account will shew, however this is no concern of mine.[1] I am not without hopes my dear [Sis]ter of comeing to Braintree and spending several months [wit]h you during the next recess of congress.[2] how long they [wil]l set this Session I cannot pretend to say, but rather think they will rise early in the Spring.[3] I think it would be a pleasure to me to have a small Family, and be able when I returnd to visit my Friends a little more than I have done. I never rode so little as I have done Since I resided here there are no pleasent rides no, variety of Scenes round Newyork, unless you cross ferrys over to long Island or to the Jerseys. I have however enjoyd a greater share of Health than I have for some years past & been less afflicted with the Complaint which used to allarm as well as distress me

How is my Neice mrs Norten? give my Love to her & tell her I hope to find her with a fine Girl in her Arms when I return to Braintree. tell Lucy she is quite as usefull as if she was married. I want to see her much as well as the rest of my dear Fiends, to many of them

I owe Letters, but I really hate to touch a pen. I am ashamed to Say how laizy I am grown in that respect

I could give an account of visiting and receiving visits, but in that there is so little variety that one Letter only might contain the whole History. for Instance on Monday Evenings Mrs Adams Receives company, that is her Rooms are lighted, & put in order Servants &c Gentlemen and Ladies, as many as inclination curiosity or Fashion tempts come out to make their Bow & curtzy take coffe & Tea chat an half hour, or longer, and then return to Town again on twesday the same Ceremony is performd at Lady Temples on wednesday at mrs Knoxs on Thursdays at mrs Jays and on Fryday at mrs Washingtons, So that if any person has so little to employ themselves in as to want an amusement, five Evenings in a week, they may find it at one or other of these places. to Mrs Washingtons I usually go as often as once a fortnight, and to the others occasionally.

So I learn that my Young Friend Nancy is seariously thinking of becomeing the Madam of a Parish be sure to tell her, that I like it much as it will be so fine a half way House to call at when I go & come From N york to Braintree, but laying Selfish considerations aside I hope she is like to be setled to the mind of herself & Family.[4]

my best Regards to mrs Quincy and all other Friends.

Brother says You wrote to me by mrs Cushing. she is not yet arrived—[5] adieu yours most tenderly   A Adams

RC (MWA:Abigail Adams Letters); addressed by CA: "Mrs Mary Cranch / Braintree." Some loss of text where the seal was removed.

[1] Elizabeth Anne Crosby's father, the minister Joseph Crosby Jr., had died in May 1783 with few assets. His brother, Dr. Ebenezer Crosby, professor at Columbia College, acted as Betsy's guardian until his death in July 1788, at which time six-year-old Betsy went to live with Peter Boylston Adams, who had been married to Joseph and Ebenezer's late sister Mary. Betsy would eventually marry their son, Boylston Adams, in 1802. Although Betsy was named in Ebenezer Crosby's will, she did not receive her inheritance until 1807 when his youngest son turned 21 (vol. 5:187–188; *Sibley's Harvard Graduates*, 18:53–54, 19:forthcoming).

[2] Although AA was unable to return to Massachusetts during the summer of 1790, she did visit Braintree in the summer of 1791 and lived there permanently from 1792 to 1797. Throughout JA's presidency, she returned to Quincy every summer.

[3] The session of Congress, which lasted longer than AA anticipated, adjourned on 12 Aug. 1790 (*First Fed. Cong.*, 3:568).

[4] For Nancy Quincy's marriage to Rev. Asa Packard, see vol. 8:448.

[5] Hannah Phillips Cushing (1754–1834), originally of Middletown, Conn., was the wife of U.S. Supreme Court justice William Cushing (*DAB*, entry on William Cushing).

Abigail Adams to Hannah Quincy Lincoln Storer

my dear Friend   Jan'ry 29 1790 Richmond Hill

By my son who Sets out in the morning on his return to Boston, I write to thank you for your kind Letter of december, and for the present which accompanied it.[1] the Butter was very fine, and much Superiour to any that I have been able to procure here. if I did not hear others complain of that article, I should be led to doubt my own judgment, and to suppose that I had brought my Yankee fancies with me. I know there are certain tastes, and Habits which we contract in early Life, which grow up with us, and lead us to think that they have no equal. a free intercourse with the world, and observation upon the Habits and customs of other states, Nations, & Kingdoms, tends in a great measure to wear of these local attachments, to enlarge our Ideas, and Liberalize our Sentiments, and teach us that the Bontifull Hand of Providence has Strewed comforts and Blessings within the reach of all his creatures, and that it is civilisation cultivation and improvement which enhances their value to us.

You ask my opinion of Nancys match? that she shoud marry a Clergyman I do not think strange, her most worthy Grandmamma did so,[2] they are certainly a most respectable *order* of Men with us, Men of Learning of Religion, and in general of Liberality. from my own personal knowledge and acquaintance with a large Number of those Gentleman, I do not believe that in either of the 12 other states can be selected an equal Number of So respectable for their ingenuity and abilities, their Gentlemanly deportment and manners as our State furnishes. Yet very few of those Gentlemen think themselves qualified to open the Bible and give you a discourse of half an hour or more, without having previously studied their discourse, & committed it to writing. if the Clergymen here study, it is too deeply for me. I cannot comprehend or believe all their doctrines. they are worthy Good Men, but deciples of good old Calvin, and will Scarcly allow Man to be a free Agent. having said no more than what I think really true with respect to the Clergy I have only to add, that I hope my Friend Nancy will find herself very happy with the Gentleman She has chosen a Clergyman is more like to be a domestick man, than either of the other Learned Professions. Nancy is domestick and will make a very pretty Madam of a Parish.

Pray my good Lady get some of your acquaintance to move in the Legislature to have a Bedlam Erected; there is a member belonging to it, who gives such proof of Insanity that he certainly ought not to go at large. his imagination paints Giants, and he appears in all the Horrors of a man fit for war treason and Rebelion what astonishes me is, that he has Supporters.[3]

I think it probable that congress will rise early in the spring, if so I promise myself the pleasure of visiting my Friends, to whom I must request you to present my Regards, particularly to Mary I wish this had been the winter instead of the last, that She had visited Newyork. I saw George to day, & would have had him dined with me, but he was engaged. my Love to the little Family. present me respectfully to your Worthy Partner & to your Mamma.[4] tell Mrs Guile there is a Lady in Newyork to whom I felt a partiality on my first seeing her, merely because she reminded me of her, and upon a further acquaintance I esteemed her upon her own account, tho the similarity always gives her an additional Weight.

I can scarcly describe to you my feelings the other Day upon receiving a Letter from my dear old Friend Hannah Green, the Friend of my earliest Years, the companion of my juvenile days. I read it, & laid it down to indulge a crowd of reflections which Instantly rushd into my mind. O thou star! was one of them, how has thy Beams been clowded and thy Glory obscured![5] yet hast thou shone through all the visisitudes of fortune. I have not written to her, but I do not mean to omit it. when I look Back my dear Friend upon those whose circumstances were formerly affluent and whose expectation were promising; and see them placed in a situation so much inferiour in point of wealth, at the same time, behold them submitting with a patient cheerfullness to the reverse of fortune, I admire that greatness of mind, and that resignation to the dispensations of Providence which shines so conspicuously in their Characters.[6] To know how to be exalted and how to be abased; is a great attainment in the Christian Character—but my pen runs on strangly.

I will return your Box by Barnard. it was my intention before, but I was too late it is so dark that I can only see to add that I am both in darkness, and Light your sincere and / affectionate Friend

A Adams

RC (Adams Papers).

[1] Storer to AA, 12 Dec. 1789, vol. 8:448.

[2] Nancy Quincy's maternal grandmother, Ann Fiske, had married Rev. Joseph Marsh, former pastor of the First Church of Braintree, in 1709 (D. W. Marsh, ed., *Genealogy of the Marsh Family*, Amherst, Mass., 1886, p. 10).

[3] John Gardiner (1737–1793), who had been elected representative from Pownalborough in 1789, introduced a motion on 13 Jan.

1790 proposing that the legislature consider "the state of the law and the Professors thereof" and subsequently put forth a bill outlining a number of reforms to law and legal practice in the state. Although many were dismissive of Gardiner, who was by all accounts an eccentric and a troublemaker, several of his ideas, such as the decriminalization of debt, eventually made their way into Massachusetts law (T. A. Milford, *The Gardiners of Massachusetts: Provincial Ambition and the British-American Career*, Durham, N.H., 2005, p. 1, 2, 115, 117–121, 253; Boston *Herald of Freedom*, 15 Jan.). See also AA to Mary Smith Cranch, 20 Feb., below.

[4] Presumably Ann Marsh Quincy, the third wife of Hannah's father. For Mary and George Storer, see vol. 6:118.

[5] Possibly a reference to Milton's *Paradise Lost*, Book I, lines 589–596: "Thir dread commander: he above the rest / In shape and gesture proudly eminent / Stood like a Towr; his form had yet not lost / All her Original brightness, nor appear'd / Less then Arch Angel ruind, and th' excess / Of Glory obscur'd: As when the Sun new ris'n / Looks through the Horizontal misty Air / Shorn of his Beams."

[6] In her letter of 17 Nov. 1789 (Adams Papers), Hannah Green confided in AA about her family's misfortunes since the Revolution: "'Tis true we never were at the *height* of Affluence yet we had all the *comforts* of life—but the War which has made such devastation in our land, has almost been our ruin—we have been drove from our home & stript of our property." AA apparently replied to her old friend sometime before 7 Nov. 1790, when Green wrote AA another letter thanking her for her "kind remembrance." Green added, "I assure you my heart was much affected, when I saw your writing & receiv'd your present, it [bro]ught to mind many happy days that are [pa]st & gone" (Adams Papers). Hannah and her husband, Joshua Green, a Boston merchant, fled their home during the British occupation of the city at the onset of the Revolution. They returned to find their house in shambles, reporting property losses of over £3,500 (Samuel Abbott Green, *An Account of Percival and Ellen Green and of Some of Their Descendants*, Groton, Mass., 1876, p. 19–20, 62).

Abigail Adams Smith to Lucy Cranch

Richmond Hill Jany 31ˢᵗ 1790

I cannot omit so good an opportunity as now Presents to acknowledge the receipt of your kind letter of Nov. my Dear Lucy—,[1] my Brother has made us a very agreeable visit and I hope when he returns he will give a favourable account of his friends;—and of New York. he has been danceing amongst the Ladies and has been much approved. but what will you think of their ideas of Beauty, when I tell you that he has also borne away the Palm upon this subject— against the fairer Part of the family—, we are very reluctant at parting with him— but as it is necessary we must Submit—

what a Beautifull Winter we have. the weather here has been very fine. for two months past with very few exceptions we have not had more than one inch of snow at a fall, which has not Continued for any time—and it is almost as mild as April—, but we cannot enjoy the present pleasure without some apprehension least the future should prove unfavourable— the farmers tremble for their Crops, least the spring should prove unfriendly to them, thus it is the past and the future oftentimes prevent us from enjoying the Present Blessings with a proper gratitude— it often surprises me to hear Persons of good judgent—regreting the Scences which they have passed— looking back to the pleasures they injoyed in situations in which I recollect to have known them imployed in anticipating the pleasures of those stations in which they are at present placed— there is a certain unsattisfying principle in our dispositions which deprives us of much Sattisfaction,— those who are Conscious of it and indeavour to Correct it have some chance to overcome it and to enjoy the greatest of all blessings a Contented mind—

Mrs Norton wrote me that you were to spend most of the Winter with her.[2] perhaps this may find you employed in the gratefull office of Confering, pleasure upon others—which I am sure must be the Case in whatever situation it meets you—

our friend N—— Q.—I hear is soon to become Mrs Packard how do her friends approve of her settling at such a distance from them and how can she reconcile her mind to quit her Native Town to which She is so much attached;— I expect in the Common Course of Human events that Parson W–b–d–will soon drop off, and that some smart young Parson will be put into his Place who will present himself to my friend Lucy—and I hope he will prove worthy of her acceptance this will be very agreeable to all Parties;— you must Compleat the trio—[3] be so good when you see Miss Quincy to present my regards to her— present me respectfully to Your Pappa & Mamma— and to all friends who may inquire after your / friend

A Smith—

RC (MHi:Christopher P. Cranch Papers); addressed: "Miss Lucy Cranch / Braintree / Massachusetts"; internal address: "Miss Lucy Cranch."; notation: "favourd by / Mr Thomas Adams."

[1] Not found.
[2] Not found.
[3] That is, with Lucy Cranch's distant cousin Nancy Quincy and Lucy's sister, Elizabeth, both of whom married ministers.

Abigail Adams Smith to Elizabeth Cranch Norton

My Dear Cousin—   Richmond Hill Jany 31st 1790—

your letter of December 14th I had the pleasure to receive the last week.[1] and by my Brother Thomas who leaves us tomorrow I have an opportunity to Convince you that I am determined to fullfill my late promises of future attention to my Cousin—, Thomas has made us a sociable visit, and we are very Sorry to part with him even now,— the necessity of his attending his Studies must reconcile us to it. I beleive he has been gratified with his visit although he does not appear to have received such a favourable prepossession for New York as to determine to return hither when he has finished his Studies at Colledge

we expect that Congress will adjourn in the spring—and Mamma intends if they do, to spend her summer at Braintree which will I am sure be a great addition to your Happiness, as well as all her other friends— it too frequently so happens that such events as deprives some of us of our greatest pleasure Contributes in an equal degree to the Happiness of others, Perhaps it is designed for some wise purposes— I am sure that I have no disposition to doubt upon this Head we are informed that your friend Nancy Quincy is soon to say Love Honour and *obey* you are I presume acquainted with the Gentleman, does her choice receive the sanction of your approbation!— She expressed a partiallity for the profession when I last saw her;— I know *she* is very deserving, and I hope she has found a Person of equal Merrit, and who will prove deserving of her;—

there is a great pleasure in renewing an acquaintance with an old friend after we have been seperated from each other by any intervening Circumstances, for any length of time. there is at present a great Collection of persons from all quarters in this City—and I sometimes meet with those whith whom I was formerly acquainted. Mrs Roggers whom we knew in London—Spends the winter here. she is an amiable Benevolent Woman, and we enjoy much pleasure from her society.— the manner of visiting here is not so well calculated to promote intimacies and sociability as in Boston, but when you are obliged to keep up an extensive visitting acquaintance—it may be done with less inconvenience here most of the Ladies whose Husbands are in Publick offices have their particular day on which they are at home to receive Company. at all other times they are at liberty to refuse themselvs if they choose, and they are *obliged* to keep up such an extensive acquaintance as would take up their whole time otherwise you may return a dozen of thease visits in an evening— it is not expected (if you find the family at home) that you will set more than a quarter of an Hour, and if you do not a Card answers every purpose— in this way you will readily suppose that one cannot form intimate acquaintances—but you are at liberty to make choice of such a Number as please you the most and with them you may Live less ceremoniously—, I have met with some very amiable and agreeable Women, in whose acquaintance I find much pleasure, and gratification— when we meet at any of thease Evening Parties we make a little circle amongst ourselvs—and can enjoy our own observations upon the Characters arround us—

there is a Lady here from Virginia who reminds me of our friend Mrs Russell—by a simularity of manners—which has prepossessed me much in her favour.

be so good as to Present my Compliments to Mr Norton, in which M^r. Smith joins me and be assured that I am very sincerely your friend   A Smith—

RC (MHi:Christopher P. Cranch Papers); addressed: "Mrs Elizabeth Norton. / Weymouth— / Massachusetts"; endorsed: "M^rs. A Smith to M^rs. / Norton 1790."; notation: "favoured by / Mr T. Adams."

[1] Not found.

John Adams to John Quincy Adams

My dear son   New York Feb. 9. 1790

I hope your Anxiety, about your Prospects of future Life, will not be indulged too far. If, after your Term with Mr Parsons expires your Judgment, Inclination and Advice of your Friends lead you to Boston, you shall have my full Consent and Approbation.

If you could contrive to get a Small Family into my House with whom you could reputably board: and could reserve the best Room and Chamber, for your office and Lodging Room, I should not be displeased with the Arrangement. an office you must have. enquire into this matter, and let me know upon what Terms you can board, and have an office.— Upon this Plan, you might make an Excursion sometimes to Braintree, and pursue your studies there, especially in the Heat of summer when the Air of Boston is unwholesome.

inclosed is a Copy of Mr Fitsimmons's Motions Yesterday on the national Debt.[1]

May the Blessing of God attend you my dear son. so wishes and prays your / Affectionate Father   John Adams

RC (Adams Papers); internal address: "Mr J. Q. Adams."

[1] Enclosure not found. Thomas Fitzsimmons (1741–1811), congressman from Pennsylvania, introduced on 8 Feb. a set of eight resolutions summarizing the central points of Alexander Hamilton's report on the public credit. Following a similar motion by William Loughton Smith, Fitzsimmons successfully argued that debating the report in the form of resolutions was the most expedient way to discuss its content (*DAB*; New York *Daily Advertiser*, 9 Feb.).

Cotton Tufts to Abigail Adams

Dear Mad^m   Boston Feby 10. 1789 [1790]

Our Genl Court is now in the Fourth Week of its Session; very little Business of Importance as yet finished[1] The Leisure Season of the Year invites many of our good Folks to spin out the Session to a Length more favourable to their Purses than to the Interest of their Constituents.[2] Much has been said of the Necessity of making Provision for restoring the public Credit, However no Tax or any other effectual Measure is as yet agreed upon— whether any Thing will be done to purpose before the Court rises is uncertain as many of the Members are of opinion that it will be best to wait the Decision of Congress on the Report of the Secretary of the Treasury—[3]

The Cold has been severe for several Days— the Thermometer stood at. o. this Morning— Sudden Deaths have ben frequent for a Week past— M^rs. Palmer was seized with a Paralisis on Friday Evening last & died the Night following—[4]

Your Son Mr Thos. arrived in Boston last Saturday & is well— By a Letter from Mr Shaw I find M^rs. Shaw is well.

Mr Joy has offered the Land bought of S. Quincy at the Price He gave for it with the Interest from the Time of Purchase— his Mem^m. is enclosed for Your Consideration—[5]

Be pleased to present my Affectionate Regards to M^r. Adams & Your Children—

I am with sincere Affection / Yours   Cotton Tufts

RC (Adams Papers); addressed: "M^rs. Abigail Adams"; endorsed: "dr Tufts / Febry 10 1789." Filmed at 10 Feb. 1789.

[1] The Mass. General Court met from 13 Jan. to 9 March, after which it adjourned until 26 May (Mass., *Acts and Laws*, 1788–1789, p. 611, 725; 1790–1791, p. 91).

[2] Members of the General Court were paid per diem, with senators earning six shillings and six pence per day and members of the House of Representatives six shillings per day. Legislators were also compensated for their travel time, receiving one day's pay for every ten miles they traveled to attend the session (Mass., *Acts and Laws*, 1788–1789, p. 679).

[3] On 3 March, the General Court passed a revised "Act to Raise a Public Revenue by Excise, and to Regulate the Collection Thereof," which included a list of items to

be taxed and a detailed explanation of how the law would be enforced (*Boston Gazette*, 8 Feb.; Mass., *Acts and Laws*, 1788–1789, p. 462–476).

[4] Mary Cranch Palmer, Richard Cranch's sister, died on 6 Feb. at seventy years of age; see also AA to Mary Smith Cranch, 20 Feb., and Mary Smith Cranch to AA, 28 Feb., both below.

[5] The enclosure was possibly a document entitled "Extract from Mr Quincey's Deed" (Adams Papers, Adams Office Manuscripts, Box 2, folder 16), which describes two parcels of land in Braintree previously owned by Samuel Quincy Jr. but purchased by John and Abigail Joy in March 1788. JA would purchase both parcels from the Joys for £250

in June 1791. The first piece was thirty acres bordering the Adamses' land to the north, and the second was twenty acres of woodland adjacent to the Adamses' land to the west (John and Abigail Joy to JA, 18 June 1791, Adams Papers, Adams Office Manuscripts, Box 2, folder 16). See also AA's reply to Tufts on 7 March, below.

John Adams to John Quincy Adams

My dear son   New York Feb. 19. 1790

There is a sett of Scotch Writers that I think deserve your Attention in a very high Degree. There are Speculations in Morals Politicks and Law that are more luminous, than any other I have read. The Elements of Criticism and other of Lord Kaims's Writings—Historical Law Tracts—sir James Steuart—Adam Smith &c both his Theory of Moral Sentiments and his Wealth of Nations—[1] There are several others whose Names and Titles I dont at present recollect.

Your Project of going to Boston, I think of, every day.— You may divide your time between Braintree and Boston to great Advantage, or reside constantly at Boston if your Business should require it. But my Son, You must expect an Interval of Leisure, and Ennui.

Whether those who ought to be my Friends will be yours or not, I cant say.— Whether they are mine or not is at least problematical in some Instances— Yet I think you will find Friends in Boston.

Write me as often as you can. I hope the contracted ignorant Prejudice against your Profession will not be pushed so far as to render you uncomfortable.—

Preserve my Son, at every Risque;—at every Loss;—even to extreme Poverty and obscurity; Your Honour and Integrity Your Generosity and Benevolence, your enlarged Views and liberal Philanthropy. Candour and Honour, are of more importance in your Profession even than Eloquence Learning or Genius. You will be miserable without them whatever might be your Success. The Family is well— Yours affectionatly   John Adams

RC (Adams Papers); internal address: "J. Q. Adams." Tr (Adams Papers).

[1] Several of these works, including Adam Smith's *An Inquiry into the Nature and Causes of the Wealth of Nations*, London, 1778; and Henry Home, Lord Kames' *Elements of Criticism*, Edinburgh, 1788, and *Historical Law Tracts*, Edinburgh, 1761, are in JA's library at MB (*Catalogue of JA's Library*). JA also recommended the writings of Sir James Stewart, which include *Dirleton's Doubts and Questions in the Law of Scotland*, Edinburgh, 1715. JQA apparently took his father's advice; his personal library at the Stone Library, MQA, includes a 1791 edition of *Wealth of Nations*, a 1792 edition of *Theory of Moral Sentiments*, and a 1788 edition of *Elements of Criticism*.

Abigail Adams to Mary Smith Cranch

My dear sister   Richmond Hill Febry 20 1790

I yesterday received a Letter from dr Tufts and an other from Thomas informing me of the death of Mrs Palmer.[1] the good old Lady is gone to rest, happily for her I doubt not, but what will become of her daughters Heaven only knows, Polly in particular. I feel very unhappy for them, and you I am sure must be still more so. I suppose you was too heavily loaded with care, and affliction to write me by the last post. they may continue in the House untill we want it, if it would any way serve them, but I presume there cannot be any thing for their support after their Mothers discease. I am sure you cannot help looking back for 20 years and exclaming what a change! but such are the visisitudes of Life, and the Transitory fleeting state of all sublinary things; of all pride that which persons discover from Riches is the weakest. if we look over our acquaintance, how many do we find who were a few years ago in affluence, now reduced to real want but there is no Family amongst them all whose schemes have proved so visionary, and so abortive as the unhappy one we are now commisirating. better is a little with contentment than great Treasure; and trouble therewith. it would be some consolation to the Sisters if they had a Brother in whom they could take comfort. if ever convents are usefull, would be for persons thus circumstanced.[2]

I did not write to you by Thomas as I thought he could give you every information you wish'd for respecting us. he writes that he got home well, but appears in Some anxiety about the Measles. I would not wish him to avoid them, but only to be watchfull when he takes them and to be particularly attentive to himself during the period. this care I know you will have of him, if he should get them, and if he does not take them, he will always have an anxiety upon his mind increasing too as he advances in Life, every time he is liable to be exposed to them.

From all the Debates in Congress upon the subject of a discrimination, I presume the vote will be that there shall be none, but that some one or other of the plans proposed by the Secretary of the Treasury will be adopted it is thought that tomorrow will be the desisive day with respect to the question, as the vote will be calld for.[3] on this occasion I am going for the first Time to the House with mrs dalton[4] mrs Jay & Mrs Cushing to hear the debate. if you read the papers you will find Some very judicious debates.[5] mr Smith of S C who married a daughter of mr Izard, is one of the first from that state, & I might add from the Southern states.[6] mr Ames from our state & mr Sedwick and mr Gerry are all right upon this Question & make a conspicuous figure in the debates.[7] I hope some method will be adopted Speedily for the relief of those who have so long been the sufferers by the instability of Government. the next question I presume that will occupy Congress will be the Assumption of the state debts and here I apprehend warm work, and much opposition, but I firmly believe it will terminate for the General Good.

What a disgrace upon the Legislature of our state that they should permit Such a Madman as Gardner to occupy their time, to vilify Characters to propogate grose falshoods to the world under their Sanction. I should feel more trust for them if I did not foresee that good would come out of it in time. if the Bar possess that Honour which I presume they Have, they will combine to defeat Gardner and his Abetters and establish such Rules & Regulations as will tend to restore their profession to the same Reputation which they held before the Revolution. you and I feel peculiarly interested in this matter as we have children rising into Life educated to the Law, without a competant knowledge of which no Man is fit for a Legislator or a statesman. let us look into our National Legislature, Scarcly a man there makes any figure in debate, who has not been Bred to the Law

pray give my Love to my worthy Brother Cranch & tell him that I sympathize with him in his affliction Remember me affectionatly to my Neices & Nephew and believe / that your happiness is very near the Heart / of your ever affectionat   A Adams

RC (MWA:Abigail Adams Letters); addressed by CA: "Mrs Mary Cranch / Braintree."

[1] The letter from TBA has not been found.

[2] Gen. Joseph Palmer suffered a financial reversal after the Revolution that culminated in the loss of the family's Germantown estate. Palmer invested his few remaining assets building saltworks on the Boston Neck but died in 1788 before they were fully operational, leaving the family destitute. Mary Cranch Palmer and her two daughters had moved into the Old House in the Adamses' absence the previous fall (*Grandmother Tyler's Book*, p. 83–95; vol. 8:385).

[3] Part of the ongoing debate in the House of Representatives regarding Alexander Hamilton's report on the public credit, James Madison's discrimination amendment would have made a distinction, when debt certificates were repaid, between the original holders of government securities and the people who subsequently purchased them at a depreciated cost, dividing compensation between the two. The proposal was soundly rejected on 22 Feb. 1790 (*First Fed. Cong.*, 12:283, 473).

[4] Ruth Hooper Dalton (1739–1826), daughter of Robert and Ruth Hooper of Marblehead, was the wife of Massachusetts

senator Tristram Dalton (*Vital Records of Marblehead*, Salem, 1903, p. 275; *Salem Gazette*, 17 Jan. 1826; *Sibley's Harvard Graduates*, 13:569).

[5] Coverage of debates in the House of Representatives on Madison's motion appeared in the *New York Daily Gazette*, 16–20 Feb., and New York *Gazette of the United States*, 17, 20 Feb. (*First Fed. Cong.*, 12:322–345, 355–369).

[6] William Loughton Smith (ca. 1758–1812), married to Charlotte Izard (d. 1792), was a South Carolina lawyer and staunch Federalist who served in the U.S. House of Representatives from 1789 until 1797, when he became minister to Portugal (*DAB*).

[7] Congressmen Fisher Ames, Elbridge Gerry, and Theodore Sedgwick all spoke at length in opposition to Madison's plan. Sedgwick argued, "What merit would the government possess, if it stripped one class of citizens who had acquired by the known and established rules of law, property, of that property, under the specious pretence of doing justice to another class of citizens" (*First Fed. Cong.*, 12:335–345, 451–459).

Abigail Adams to Mary Smith Cranch

my dear sister   Newyork Feb'ry 28 1790

on the 17 of this Month cousin William wrote his uncle,[1] that he had carried his cousin Tom Home to Braintree with the Symptoms of the Measles upon him; you will easily Suppose that I waited for the next post with great anxiety but how was I dissapointed last Evening when mr Adams returnd from Town, and the Roads being very bad the post had not arrived. I could not content myself without sending into Town again before I went to Bed, but the Servant returnd with two Newspapers only. I am the more anxious because I know that Thomas was not well during the whole time that [he] was with us. I gave him a puke, after which he appeard [bet]ter. he appeard to me to have lost his appetite his flesh and his coulour, & I am fearfull he was in a poor state to take the measles. I know that he will have every care & attention under your Roof that he could have, if I was with him and this is a great relief to my mind; but to hear that he was sick, and to be ten days in suspence, & how much longer I know not; has made me very unhappy. if you have occasion for wine as no doubt you will, pray send for the Key and get it; and let Pratt bring you wood.— The trouble you must necessarily be in upon the death of Mrs Palmer, and the distrest Situation of the Family, anxiety which I know you feel for Mrs Norten, and now the Sickness of Thomas I fear will prove too much for your Health. I wrote to you by the last post and to Thomas, but tis a long time since I had a Letter from you.[2] I think the House had better be shut up than permitt any Body that I can think of, to go into it especially as I think it probable we shall spend a large part of the year there. I wish however that the dr might be consul[ted] with regard to the Safety of the House; pray write to me and relieve my mind as soon as possible.

I have never heard how Brother got home with his charge. is Polly married? I did not mention it to him while he was here, but mr A did. I knew it to be so much against his inclination that I thought it best to be silent.[3] our Family are all well. mrs Cushing and mrs Rogers Spent the day with me yesterday. the judg and his Lady appear very happy, and well pleasd with their situation & reception at Newyork. I am very well pleasd to find that Gardner is returning to his former insignifica[nce] Strange that he should be attended to, or have any weight with sensible Men—

my Love to cousin Lucy whom with the rest of my Friends I long to see. Believe me dear sister most / affectionatly yours

A Adams

RC (MWA:Abigail Adams Letters); addressed by CA: "Mrs Mary Cranch / Braintree." Some loss of text where the seal was removed.

[1] Not found.
[2] The letter to TBA has not been found.
[3] For Mary (Polly) Adams' marriage, see Cranch to AA, 28 Feb., and note 4, below.

Mary Smith Cranch to Abigail Adams

My dear Sister   Braintree February 28th 1790.

I know you Will rejoice to hear that cousin Tom has got comfortable through the Measles. He caught them at Cambridge the day he arriv'd from new york— He came here the Monday after & told me he thought he had them but return'd the next day—promising to return as soon as he felt the Symtoms The Monday following his cousin William brought him home in a close carriage but he did not break out till Wednesday. he was pretty sick but not very bad till they came out. He had Several faint turns before & sometimes felt as if he did not weigh a pound after they broke out— The rash came first but the measles soon follow'd thick enough, his cough was troublesome & his Fever pretty high but upon the whole I think he has had them light to what people in general have or to what you & I had. There are many People Who have them now extreamly bad & many have died with them— I have two in my Family still to have them Cornelius & Ben.[1] Cornelius complains a little to day— I expect it will be out in a few days— cousin did not lay upon the bed an hour for them— He Sleep in the easy chair half his time— the greatest difficulty attending his disorder was there turning upon his Bowels— I was oblig'd to give him two or three portions of Rhubarb before I could carry it of– this circumstance has weakend him—but I do not design he shall return to college till he is quite well— He has been below Stairs these two days, but the weather has been so wet that he has not been out He has had a dull time in his confinment— Neither of his cousins were at home & his eyes were so affected that he could not read & unluckyly I had caught such a cold that I could only wisper great part of the time—

You may have heard of the sudden Death of Sister Palmer. She was seeiz'd with a Palsy—from being to all appearances well— she said "Betsy I am frighted my hand feels so numb." She endeavour'd to say more but could not speak & did not appear to have the full use of her reason. I got there in about an hour after she was taken she then knew us all & seem'd senseble that she was going, by the mottion of her hand, she could only say yes & no–& that with difficulty one side was wholly dead. She was taken at sun set. She gap'd often & had all the appearence of a person very sleepy. She was carried up stairs in a chair & put to Bed after being Bleed & went to sleep as quietly as any body but it was never to awake again— She fell into a Lethargy & ceas'd to breathe about sundown the next day she had not a pain nor did she move a Limb or a feature of her Face after she went to sleep— The Loss is great indeed to her Daughters—but all the horrows of Death were taken away by such an easy dismisson & to so good a woman what a favour— Mr Cranch was much affected you may be sure— He is now the last of the Family & may heaven long preserve him— we had the corps brought to our House & the Funiral went out from it. She was plac'd in mr Alleynes Tomb.[2]

Cousin Polly & Betsy behave with christian resignation but are greatly distress'd at the situation they find themselves in. Cousin Betsy can support herself in some way or other but her Sister cannot They are yet in your house & I suppos'd you had rather they should be athough they should not be able to pay you any thing than have it stand alone they take good care of it— Jo Cranch has been there these six weeks–& is only waiting to get into some business to be married. mr Cranch wrote a Letter to General Knox desiring him to give him some establishment in his profession as a Gunsmith if he could. He sent it by Mr Adams.[3] I wish my dear Sister you would be so kind as to mention the thing where you think it will do the best The General knows him to be a capable honest man If he can get into any business he will take both my Cousins with him. you cannot Serve us more than by being able to froward him in this way—, They have no where else to look but to us— I am very willing to do all I can for them, but to maintain them wholly is more than we can do & would be very painful to them There stores cannot hold out long & then they must come here—

Mrs Norton holds out yet & is very well for her. What you tell me of Mrs Smith I expected to hear My Love to her & her little ones— your Son John is in Boston attending the Court. I hear he is well but have not seen him. Mrs Hall has had a dreadfull eye but it is better Miss Polly Adams was married in her Fathers absence & looks quite stately— They are going to Boston to live he is an excellent Bootmaker & has the character of a very steady well behav'd man— but somehow or other it was not agreable to her Father— did he not tell you of it?[4] cousin Tom did not know it till he return'd—

Mr Cranch is much worried with a salt [. . .] humour in his arms I sometimes think tis ring worms but let it be what it will— it causes him a great many little Blind Boils I have try'd many things but cannot cure it Cousin Tom Says you have a Tar ointment[5] which you have used for Mr Adams[6]

RC (Adams Papers).

[1] Probably Cornelius Hunt, brought from the West Indies by Boston merchant Cornelius Durant to be raised by the Cranches; see vol. 8:395-396. For Benjamin Guild Jr., see vol. 8:285, 286.

[2] Mary Cranch Palmer possibly was buried in a tomb at the Christ Church burial ground originally intended for Thomas Alleyne, who died out of state in 1787 (vol. 8:165, 166).

[3] Not found. For the marriage of cousins Joseph Cranch and Elizabeth Palmer, see vol. 8:148, note 6.

[4] Mary (Polly) Adams, eldest daughter of Peter Boylston Adams, married Elisha Turner (1762–1806) of Braintree on 17 Jan. 1790. Their unnamed infant died in the spring during an influenza epidemic (*Braintree Town Records*, p. 870; Sprague, *Braintree Families*; Mary Smith Cranch to AA, 16 May and 4 July, both below).

[5] Tar ointment was used to treat both diseases of the skin and digestive problems (John Elliot, *The Medical Pocket-Book*, Boston, 1795, p. 131).

[6] The RC ends here, presumably missing one or more additional pages.

Abigail Adams to Cotton Tufts

Dear sir   Newyork March 7th 1790

I received your Letter inclosing mr joys proposals and I have omitted answering it because I wished mr Adams to determine himself. he says that he had already offerd mr joy what he gave, which he considerd quite as much as the place was worth, that it will not yeald him half the interest of the Money unless he was to live at home & be able to improve it, that mr Joys present proposal of the interest and commissions will not do, and I add that if mr Adams was to purchase it he must Sell a Bill at 8 pr ct discount to pay for it. indeed I do not know whether Bills upon Holland are not worse still I should like to have the land as it is so near us, & would accommodate us so well, but I cannot like joys conduct with respect to it. will you be so good as to write us word how Bills Sell in Boston. I am sorry to find your Legislature acting a part so derogatary to their Honour and interest, and so little agreeable to what I know your sentiment are. it must be painfull to you to see such a combination to destroy all order, & overthrow the constitution. the proposed amendments I Sincerly hope for the Honour of the State, will be successfully combatted.[1] how can these people all of whom have solemnly sworn to support the constitution, come forward with proposals which Strike a deadly blow at the vitals of it, but I trust they will be dissapointed mr M——n is not acting a much better part here, only a more artfull and coverd one. the more I see of Mankind, and of their views and designs, (the more Sick I am of publick Life) and the less worthy do they appear to me, and the less deserving of the Sacrifices which Honest men make to serve them. I think from what I can hear & see the Assumption of the State Debts much more uncertain than I conceived a week ago—but time must determine there are some person who think the stability of the General Government rests upon that one point.

my dear sir I am extreemly anxious about my son Thomas. tis near 3 weeks Since I heard he was carried to Braintree with the Symptoms of the Measles upon him, Since which I have not been able to get a single line from any Friend. the imagination is fruitfull in uncertainty, and I have sometimes been led to fear that he is very sick, and know not how to account for this long silence with respect to him. pray Sir upon the Receipt of this write me immediatly. we are all well and desire to be affectionatly Rememberd to you and yours

most affectionatly yours   A Adams

RC (private owner, 1959); addressed by JA: "The Honourable / Cotton Tufts Esqr / Weymouth / near Boston"; endorsed: "M^rs· Ab. Adams / March 7. 1790"; notation by JA: "Free / John Adams."

[1] On 25 Sept. 1789, under pressure from James Madison and Antifederalists, Congress proposed twelve amendments to the U.S. Constitution and submitted them to the states for ratification. The Mass. General Court considered these amendments in late January and early February, approving all but three. At that time, both houses of the General Court also appointed members to a joint committee "to take into consideration what further Amendments to the Federal Constitution are necessary to be proposed to Congress." The committee's report, comprising twelve additional amendments that covered a

range of topics including elections of members to Congress, regulation of land ceded to the United States, taxation, and the militia, appeared in the Boston *Independent Chronicle* and the *Boston Gazette* in early March. A week later, the *Chronicle* reported that the General Court had postponed consideration of the proposed amendments until the following session, but they were not reintroduced for debate at that time. Massachusetts also failed to formally ratify the amendments originally proposed by Congress, ten of which became the Bill of Rights on 15 Dec. 1791 (*Doc. Hist. Ratif. Const.*, 7:xxi, xxx; *Independent Chronicle*, 4 Feb., 4, 11 March 1790; *Boston Gazette*, 8 March).

Elizabeth Smith Shaw to Abigail Adams

My Dear Sister—   Haverhill March 14th. 1790

I have a Letter partly written to you which was begun sometime ago, but as a new Seene has presented itself to my view, I will lay that aside, & ask my Sister to rejoice with me in the recovery of my Children, & Family from the Meassels, & on the birth of a fine little Daughter which was born the 2d Day of March. She has little bones, & weighed nine pound— She is as plump as a partridge, quiet as a Lamb, & Mrs Seargant says, she has a mouth *like you*, but you know every one will flatter upon those occasions— We have named her *Abigail Adams*, in respect, & gratitude to a much loved Sister—& we hope *she* will not be offended that we have given her this name, *endeared* to *me* by a *thousand kindnesses*— It is true I cannot inspire her with like Sentiments, but if I could believe like Tristam Shandy, I might hope for great things— And I think if some good Angel would permit me, to look into futurity, & I could behold my Daughter like my Sister, virtuous, & good, adorning every Station she may be called to act in, with pleasure I could foster her in my Bosom, & watch over her infant Days with unspeakable delight— But whether our Children are to be Blessings, or Curses, is not for Parents to know— It is our part to discharge our duty with Circumspection, & Fidelity— Events, are at the disposal of unerring Wisdom—

Your Son Thomas was so kind as to intend making me a visit as soon as he returned, but was detained by the meassels— I long to see him— It was rather an unfortunate circumstance for me, that we had been expecting the meassels all winter, but did not take it till the last week in February, & I was obliged to leave two of them with it just upon the turn— Betsy Quincys never come out well, & I was distressed for her, as well as for myself— We could neither get her meassels out, nor keep it out well, & she had an incessant Cough, which I feared might leave her in a poor State— Not even the *Kiss* which she was honoured with, from the President of the united

States, when he was in Haverhill, could secure her from Evils— He was almost deified, & perhaps no human Being, ever deserved it more— When Mr Shaw & I, were upon our Journey to Weymouth, the President unexpectedly went through Haverhill— Betsy Quincy, & another little Miss was so desirous of seeing this great, & good Man, that she rose 2 hours before Day, & went to Mr Harrods where he lodged, for fear she should not see him in the crowd—[1] Her wish was anounced to him by his Secretary, & he was so sweetly condescending as to come down & take them both in his Lap, & kiss them, a Circumstance, I presume, they will never forget through the whole period of their Existence— I often mention it to Betsy Quincy, as an incentive to every thing that is praiseworthy—

I suppose by this time Mrs Norton must be a Mamma, I expected it, before I kept chamber myself—but I have been rather beforehand of her Ladyship, which nobody believed from our appearance—for when I wanted the assistance of my Neighbours—they hardly could be perswaded it was necessary, & thought they were Joked with— Mrs Smith I hear, is fullfilling, & complying with the first command with great alacrity— my Love to her, I wish her good speed—& hope she may prove a rich Blessing to the World— I have received two kind letters from her, but I have not strength at present to answer them—[2]

Mr & Mrs Thaxter are well, she enjoys better health than ever— There Son is really a beautiful Child— He has been here to see his little *sweetheart*, as every-body has wisely predicted & I think I never saw a finer looking Child— you must remember I have never seen *your two Grandsons*—& alas! shall I ever be so happy as to ever, even see my Neice again— I was exceedingly dissapointed last Fall at not seeing you at Braintree, & my dear Brother Adams here— I have felt this winter as if I never should see you more, not because I was in poorer health, for I really have been better, than for several years past, but sometimes I could not help having the vapours—

Betsy Smith sends her Duty, & Love, with my Children, & Mr Shaw his best regards—but says I must not write one word than that I am your truly affectionate Sister   Eliza Shaw

RC (Adams Papers); endorsed: "Mrs Shaw."

[1] George Washington stayed with Joseph and Anna Harrod of Haverhill at their inn, the "Mason's Arms." Their daughter Ann married TBA in 1805 (Boston *Independent Chronicle*, 2 March 1786; *The Essex Antiquarian*, 3:168 [1899]).

[2] Not found.

Abigail Adams to Mary Smith Cranch

my dear sister: March 15 1790 N-york

I last Evening received your Letter of 28th of Febry which relieved my mind from a great weight of anxiety. I do not think that I have been so long a period, without Letters from some, or other of my Friends Since I first came to Newyork, or elsse the anxiety I have been under for several weeks appeard to prolong the Time

I have written to you 3 weeks Successively but you do not mention having received my Letters.[1] last week I wrote to the dr, and not to you; in some of my Letters I proposed the miss Palmers tarrying in the House as long as they could. I never expected any thing more from them, than a care of the House & furniture. I requested the dr to order them Some wood which I presume he has done. I will mention to Gen'll Knox mr Cranchs request. mr Adams deliverd the Letter and talkd with the Gen'll about him at the same time. the Gen'll mentiond him as a good workman & an honest Man. I will inquire of him when I see him if any thing can be done for Him— a Thought has just struck my mind. if we should not return to Braintree this summer, is mr Cranch Farmer enough to take that place to the Halves, provided he can do no better. I have not said any thing about it, for it this moment came into my mind. you may think upon it & give me your opinion without letting it go any further. nothing would give me more pleasure than to be able to assist two worthy people. I shall wish to hear from mrs Norten as soon as She gets to Bed. I think you told me that she expected this month and Sister Shaw too. it is really a foolish Buisness to begin after so many years, a Second crop. I expect to hear next that our good friend the dr is like to increase his Family mine is like to be very prolifick if mrs Smith continues as she has set out. she has been gone a week on a visit to Long Island. Louissa grows tall, is the same diffident modest Girll she always was. I am sending her now to dancing it is rather late for her to begin, but she learns the faster I believe. She has been only six weeks, & carried down a country dance in publick last week very well.

I hope my dear Sister you will make Thomas very carefull of himself & not let him go to cambridge till he gets well of his Cough. the march winds are cold and piercing, and the Measles never mends the constitution, the Lungs being so much affected. poor mr otis I am grieved for him. he told me to day on comeing out of meeting that he did not expected to hear that his daughter was alive; for his last intelligence was that she was very near her end.[2] this is a distress that neither you or I have yet experienced, at least not an age when the loss is so very grevious, and Heavy, yet can I most feelingly sympathize with those who have. it appears to me that more young Ladies die of consumptions in Boston than in any other place. I cannot but think that there is some cause, arising from their manner of living the too sudden change of air, from cold to Heat, & heat to cold, or a want of proper attention to their cloathing I think it ought to be a subject of investigation by the medical Society— my affectionate Regards to all Friends do not let it be so long again before I hear from you. I thank you for all your kind care of my son during his sickness. you have some times talkd of obligations, but Sure I am you ought to be satisfied upon that Head, as you so much oftner have the power of confering them, than I have of returning them to you, but you know that the will is good of your ever affectionate / Sister   Abigail Adams

RC (MWA:Abigail Adams Letters); addressed by CA: "Mrs Mary Cranch / Braintree."

[1] AA to Cranch, 20 and 28 Feb., are both above. The third letter has not been found.

[2] Abigail Otis, daughter of Samuel A. Otis, secretary of the Senate, and his first wife, Elizabeth Gray Otis, died 18 March at age sixteen. Her elder sister Elizabeth had died less than two years earlier, also after a long illness (*Sibley's Harvard Graduates*, 14:472, 475; New York *Gazette of the United States*, 31 March; *Boston Gazette*, 25 Aug. 1788).

Mary Palmer to Abigail Adams

Dear Madam   Braintree March 17th 1790

The enclosed will need your utmost candour, but as I am not able to write it over again being Still in very low health & kept so long upon Sal Vol. & Lavender that the Smell & taste of both is hateful to me & the sight of a Phial disagreable, I hope you will excuse it.[1] The very kind Letter that I reciev'd from you when you was in France to which I fear you never reciev'd any reply; emboldens me to write with the freedom of a friend.[2]

We still remain in your House but are looking out for some humble Situation where we may gain an honest tho' mean livelihood for ourselves, Integrity & independance will give a relish to every enjoyment & sweeten the coarsest food. Betsy & I wish not to be seperated, we were ever dear to each other, & affliction has been far from loosening the Cord. As yet we have not pitch'd upon a place, but hope to before your return.

I wrote to D[r] Adams soon after he left us, but suppose the Letter was lost, it was only about a Book, *Princes Chronology* you will please to tell h[im] it is in the office.[3]

Your Lark is in [good he]alth & very saucy & dainty, chooses the best of every thing [won]t eat Bread without Butter or Sugar or Meat but of the very nicest, his Seeds also must be very good & the water very clean, or he will Scold at the whole family [th]o he is not grateful enough to sing us a Song for our care of [him.]

Your Pussy is also very well & as cross as ever, & as good a [rat]catcher. but the Rats have lately left the House, so she has but little to do within doors.

Pardon Madam this triffling, when the heart is too full & afraid to vent its own feelings, it is apt to say something foolish.

I hope Betsy will be able to write to M[rs] Smith, but as every thing lays upon her I fear she wont. but She as well as her Mamma may be assured of our wishes for their prosperity & affectionate respectful Love. Our Love to Louisa, we hope She will ever approve herself worthy of so excellent an Aunt

M[rs] Briesler her sister & Children are entitled to a great share of our remembrance My love to them if you please.

I am Madam [you]r Affec[t] friend & Servant   Mary Palmer.

What I meant to enclose, is rather out of Season now, I am a little better. M. Pratt has bro't 2 Loads of Wood since Mammas death the office is safe tho' not in good order as I wish it was, I flatter myself that you will not have any cause to blame your tenants for neglect of any kind. I dare not touch upon our loss. it has been Almost too great to bear. She was a living Saint, & her departure was happy & Sweetly tranquil without a Sigh or Struggle. She is now gone to enjoy that society which her constant piety & integrity seem'd to fit her for.

March 21[st.]

I broke open the Letter to inform you of what I fear'd might be in your eyes against us if not explain'd. the day D[r] Adams went away from here, Suckey Adams came for a Hearth Brush which was in the office & was as good as new & soon after for a Cloathes Brush both which she said her Uncle had given her. & both were deliver'd to her. I am afraid we were too hasty in doing it.

RC (Adams Papers); addressed: "M[rs] Abigail Adams / New-York"; endorsed: "miss Polly / Palmer." Some loss of text where the seal was removed.

John Quincy Adams to John Adams

Dear Sir   Newbury Port March 19th: 1790.

I have to acknowledge the receipt of two Letters from you, of the 9th. and of the 19th: of last month; the former of which I received, about three weeks ago, while I was at Boston, attending upon the Session of our Supreme Court; and the latter came to hand, but two days since. I hope I shall ever feel suitably grateful, for the tender solicitude, which you express with respect to my future prospects, and I trust I shall always be sufficiently sensible of the weight and importance of your advice, and directions to regulate my conduct— The principal subject of both your Letters, has been long a matter of contemplation to my own mind; I have been for some months expecting the judicial appointments; upon the presumption that some vacancies might be made, which would open a way, for making a more advantageous settlement in some part of the Commonwealth, than there could be while those Gentlemen who were best qualified for seats upon the bench were still at the Bar.— But the appointments are now made, and have not produced the smallest alteration in the prospects of a young candidate for practice. M[r:] Paine, the late attorney general, never did any other business than that of the Commonwealth; though M[r:] Sullivan, to the same office, unites the greatest quantity of civil business of any gentleman at the bar. M[r:] Cushing was not even a practitioner; so that notwithstanding the disposal of those three important offices, the state of practice remains almost wholly as it was before.[1]

It has become necessary however for me to determine speedily upon the spot of my future residence. And in reflecting upon the subject, my mind has chiefly hesitated between, this town, Boston and Braintree. It was at one period expected that M[r:] Bradbury, who lives at Newbury-Port, would supply the place upon the bench which was vacated by the removal of Judge Sewall.[2] Had this circumstance taken place, I should have been strongly inclined, to make an experiment in this place, where a residence of three years has already made me better known than I should be in any other situation; and where an agreeable circle of acquaintance, would render the station peculiarly pleasing, so far as respects the intercourse of Society. But with the small proportion of business which is done in the County of Essex, it must be a folly to expect encouragement for a youth, in a town, where besides Mr Parsons and M^{r:} Bradbury there are two other gentlemen of the profession.[3] As I could live at less expence at Braintree than in Boston, and perhaps should have less avocations from my studies, I should without hesitation go there, and reside at least for two or three years; but my Cousin Mr. Cranch, will be there, and by opening offices in the same town, we could only divide the small pittance, which either of us singly might obtain. I could not in that case board in his father's family. There is not another family in the town (at least in that part of the town) where I could board with any convenience; and to live alone in one of your houses; besides the unpleasant circumstances of a life so solitary, would I think be quite as expensive as to live in Boston; especially when it is considered that it would be necessary for me to be as much as one third part of my time in that Town to attend upon the Sessions of the several judicial Courts— Boston therefore remains alone, upon which I am by a kind of necessity, constrained to fix my choice. I cannot say I am pleased with the manners of the Town; and I trust the opportunities and temptations to dissipation, which I shall probably find there, have no influence upon my determination, unless to increase the reluctance, with which I make it— I have consulted with D^{r:} Tufts, with Judge Dana, and with D^{r:} Welch upon the subject; and they all agree in the opinion, that I can do no better, than to fix upon Boston, and as you have in one of your last Letters express'd your approbation of the measure, there remains little doubt in my mind, but that I shall put it into execution. The Prospect it is true is not encouraging; but if a resolute determination to make my own way, in conjunction with the small talents which have been allotted to me, are sufficient to procure me even a moderate degree of success; I hope I shall not be much longer a burden to the kindest and most generous of parents.

With respect to the article of board, it would not I imagine be easy to find a family, who would resign the front room and chamber as there is but one of each in the house; and unless some advantage could be derived from the circumstance of living and keeping an office in the same house, I think it would be preferable to do otherwise. If a tenant can be found, who will upon consideration of a suitable abatement of the rent, resign the front room in your house; D^r: Tufts has promised to secure it to me for an office. And D^r: Welch, has made me an offer to board me, and let me have a chamber in a house to which he expects to remove, before I shall have occasion to go into Boston. I did not agree with him upon any settled terms; but I presume he will not demand more than three dollars by the week. In this town I have always given 2 1/2.

Should my present expectations and intentions be confirmed, I shall probably get settled in Boston sometime in August; and I shall request your permission to remove thither your law Library, which is now at Braintree. the advantage of having such a collection of books around me, will give me perhaps some opportunities, which few of the young gentlemen of the profession have possessed; and they will at least enable me to employ to some purpose a great portion of time which must otherwise lay heavy upon my hands.

I believe I have said quite enough upon a subject of so little consequence as myself.— I wish my information in the political line, were such as would enable me to supply you with any interesting communications. The public mind here seems chiefly agitated by the late discussions relation to *discrimination*, and to the *assumption* of the debts. The decision upon the former of these subjects, meets with the approbation of almost all the persons with whom I have had opportunities of conversing; but I am very apprehensive, that unless the consent of the States in their respective legislatures is requested by Congress, to the assuption, that measure will be extremely unpopular; even in this Commonwealth, burthened as it is with one of the heaviest debts in the union. And if that consent should be required, I am informed by those, who are more connected with political affairs, that even our general Court, will never grant it; though in their late Session they have not made provision for the payment of a quarter part of the interest upon their debt. New-Hampshire whose debt is comparatively trifling will be still more opposed to this measure.[4] This opposition is not confined to the party who were termed antifederalists. Some of the most strenuous advocates for the constitution, are alarmed at the prospects of a consolidation of the States and of the disolution of the particular governments. And they dread to see an article so weighty and important as the State debts taken from one scale, and added to the other.

The internal politics of the State, are in a state of tranquility, very unusual at this Season. The opposers of the Governor discouraged I presume, by the ill success which they have always experienced, seem determined to leave him in quiet possession— He has been confined as usual, all winter with the gout, and his judicial appointments, have been the only public circumstances which have for some time past been the subject of animadversion. The appointment of M^r: Paine was rather popular. That of M^r: Cushing was far otherwise. The friends of the Governor only insist upon the disinterested magnanimity, of nominating a man who it is said has been invariably opposed to his measures: while his enemies, are so far from acknowledging his disinterestedness, that they censure him very highly, for nominating to one of the most important offices in the State, a man totally unqualified to sustain it, merely to be freed from his troublesome opposition as a councillor. The late chief Justice, revered as his character universally is, does not altogether escape censure for recommending so earnestly his cousin, to an employment, to which he is almost universally said to be very inadequate—

Your dutiful Son,   J. Q. Adams.

RC (Adams Papers); endorsed: "J Q Adams. March / 19. Ans^d Ap. / 1790."

[1] Gov. John Hancock appointed Nathan Cushing and Robert Treat Paine as judges to the Mass. Supreme Judicial Court in early 1790; Paine's former position as Massachusetts attorney general was then filled by James Sullivan. Cushing (1742–1812), of Scituate, had been Judge of Admiralty for the Southern District and a member of the Council (*Massachusetts Centinel*, 3 March; *DAB*; *Sibley's Harvard Graduates*, 15:376–378).

[2] David Sewall (1735–1825) served as judge to the Mass. Supreme Judicial Court until 1789, when he was appointed judge of the U.S. District Court for Maine (*Sibley's Harvard Graduates*, 13:638, 642, 644).

[3] Dudley Atkins Tyng (1760–1829), Harvard 1781, also practiced law in Newburyport at this time (*Memorials of the Essex Bar Association*, Salem, 1900, p. 247). The other attorney has not been identified.

[4] When Congress voted on the Funding Act in July 1790, all members representing Massachusetts supported the bill. The congressmen from New Hampshire were divided: Sen. John Langdon and Rep. Abiel Foster voted in the affirmative while Sen. Paine Wingate and Reps. Nicholas Gilman and Samuel Livermore rejected the bill (*First Fed. Cong.*, 1:438; 3:533–534).

Rebecca Leppington to Abigail Adams

Boston March 20th 1790—

Encouraged Madam, by your condescention in answering a letter I not long since took the liberty to write you,[1] And relying on your candour to pardon my forwardness, I again take up the pen tho' not without fear that you will deem me an intruder on your time & patience; In your answer to the letter I have reference to, you gave me all the information I cou'd desire, & I felt myself honor'd that you noticed me as one who formerly thought herself happy in being ranked among the number of your humble friends. Without any further preface Madam, give me leave to forward another letter accompanied by one from the Gentleman with whom I have lived for Several years, to the Vice-President, soliciting his recommendation (as many others have done) for some place of trust whereby he might be usfull to the Publick & himself; I beleive few Gentlemen wou'd more faithfully discharge any obligations, You will think me partial, I acknowledge that in the four years acquaintance that I have had, I have reason to esteem him, as well for his private Character, as his universal Benevolence; And I beleive there are not many who solicit for a place under Goverment, if fidelity & honesty are requisits, who have a better claim, His own letter to the Vice-President will suggest the motives by which he is actuated, it is therefore unnessary, & might be thought impertinent in me to repeat them; You doubtless will be at a loss to account for *my* addressing *you* on this subject I am full in the beleif that many Ladies have been as instrumental in promoting both Publick & private good as the Gentlemen— And as I know from the personal acquaintance that I have with yᵒ· Madam, you are a well-wisher to all the deserving; I thought it wou'd not be amiss to ask your interest in a matter that through a multiplicity of business might be overlook'd— Your penetration, before you have read thus far, will discover that *I* feel particularly interested, Some future day perhaps may prove your conjectures are not groundless— You well know my fondness for little folks & once upon some occasion said, that had you a young family to bring up you shou'd like that I shou'd have the care of them while in that State, this I esteemed a much greater compliment than I deserved, the same Compliments however have been paid me by the person who has had an opportuinity of making observations and let it Suffice for me to say that the little family I now have the c[harge] of, are too dear to me easily to part from[2] But le[st I] trespass on your patience, I will close my [. . .] and after all proper respect for a Lady in your exalted Station subscribe myself / Madam / your very humble Servant   Rebecca Leppington

my sister desires her respectfull Compˡᵗˢ· & equally regrets that she has never had an opportuinty of seeing Mʳˢ Adams since her return from abroad.[3] My love to Louisa, the young Ladies wou'd esteem it a favor to receive a line from her—

RC (Adams Papers); addressed: "Mrs Abigail Adams / Lady of the Vice President / New-york"; endorsed: "Mrs Leppington / 20 March 1790." Some loss of text where the seal was removed.

¹ The letter from Leppington to AA has not been found but presumably inquired into Martha Washington's need for a female attendant and expressed Leppington's hope to be considered for the post. In her reply of 20 Sept. 1789 (Adams Papers), AA explained that Washington had several granddaughters as well as a niece who could fill the role of attendant as required. AA added that if Washington was "to express a wish for a young Lady as a companion, She would have more Soliciters for the place, than the President could possibly have had, for any office in his Gift."

² John Hurd (b. 1727), Harvard 1747, was a former New Hampshire land speculator and Boston insurance broker who would marry Leppington, longtime caregiver for his children, later that spring. In his letter to JA of 17 March 1790 (Adams Papers), Hurd expressed his desire for a position in the federal government, noting his many years of

public service and the financial and personal sacrifices he had made during the Revolution. Although JA thought highly of Hurd, he explained in his reply that he was unable to influence executive appointments. Hurd ultimately failed to receive a federal position, serving in local offices until his death in 1809 (*Sibley's Harvard Graduates*, 12:164–171; Rebecca Leppington Hurd to AA, 29 June 1790, Adams Papers; JA to Hurd, 5 April, LbC, APM Reel 115).

Hurd had five children from two previous marriages—two with his first wife, Elizabeth Foster (d. 1779) of Boston, and three with his second wife, Mary Russell Foster (d. 1786). Leppington cared for these latter three: twins Katharine and Elizabeth (b. 1784), and John Russell (b. 1785) (*Sibley's Harvard Graduates*, 12:164, 170–171; *Boston Gazette*, 16 Jan. 1786).

³ For Betsey Leppington, see vol. 3:319.

Abigail Adams to Mary Smith Cranch

my dear sister   N york March 21 1790

I was in hopes of hearing from you by last Nights post, as I am solicitious to learn how mrs Norten does. I had Letters from Thomas¹ and find that he is returnd to Cambridge very well he says, and he gives me the agreeable News of his Aunt shaws having got well to Bed with a daughter added to her Family. I have been anxious for her; as her Health is so slender, and I know how to feel for you too the anxiety of a Parent.

Mr Adams has spoken to Gen^ll Knox upon the subject of your Letter, and has received a [pro]mise from him, that he will do Something for mr Cranch within a [. . .]ghtnight; I wish it may put him upon such a footing as to enable him to marry. Betsy will make him an excellent wife. I wish their prospects were better. present my Regards to her and tell her that I shall always be happy to promote her interest, and wish it was more in my power—

pray what is the dismall story we hear of Mrs danfords jumping out of a 3 story window? has she been long delirious?² what was the matter with mrs Jones. she lookt as like to live last fall when she was here as any person of her age.³ How is Lucy Jones, I heard last fall a very allarming account of her Health. our Good Aunt I hope makes the dr very happy. is mrs Tufts like to increase her Family, I mean Young mrs Tufts![4] I hope nothing of the kind will take place with the other. I think it would be like to distroy the Harmony between the two Families I want to know all about the good folks in whose happiness I feel interested. I am sorry for what you write me respecting the one lately married, but I expected it. do you remember the Story of the Parissian Girl who insisted upon being hang'd because her Father and her Grand Father were hang'd.[5] it is a sad misfortune when example can be plead to satisfy scruples—but there never was any delicacy of Sentiment about her.[6] I am sorry for her Grandmother who I know it must Hurt.

Mrs Smith & children are gone on a visit to Jamaica. the House seems deserted. I expect their return soon, but not their continuence with me, as they are going to live in the city, and the cols Mother and Family are comeing into Town to live soon. my Family has been so large for this year past, that we shall not make both ends meet, as they Say the expences of Removing a Family Furniture &c was a heavy burden, and the Wages of servants is very high here, especially for such misirables as one is obliged to put up with—but I hate to complain. no one is without their difficulties, whether in High, or low Life, & every person knows best where their own shoe pinches— my Love to Mrs Norten tell her to keep up a good Heart but be sure you do not let Lucy be with her. I know her make so well that she could not stand the trial.

I have had a Nervious Headack for this week past, which has quite unfitted me for any thing, and obliges me to make my Letter shorter than I designd

Remember me kindly to all inquiring Friends and be assured of the affectionate Regards of / your sister   A Adams

Mrs Brisler Lucy & children are well

RC (MWA:Abigail Adams Letters); addressed by CA: "Mrs Mary Cranch / Braintree." Some loss of text where the seal was removed.

[1] Not found.

[2] Martha Hall Gray Danforth (b. 1760), wife of Boston physician Dr. Samuel Danforth, survived the fall but died later that year. A Salem minister recorded in his diary that Mrs. Danforth, "after delivery a few days, went into an upper chamber & covering her head with a Petticoat, leaped from the window to the Ground. She had made

several attempts to distroy life before" (Boston, *24th Report*, p. 299; *The Diary of William Bentley*, 4 vols., Gloucester, Mass., 1962, 1:153; Boston *Independent Chronicle*, 15 July).

[3] Abigail Grant Jones (b. 1765), wife of Boston merchant John Coffin Jones, died on 8 March (James N. Arnold, *Vital Record of Rhode Island, 1636–1850*, 21 vols., Providence,

1893, 4:98; *Sibley's Harvard Graduates*, 17:49, 52).

[4] Mercy Brooks Tufts was indeed pregnant, but the child would be stillborn; see Mary Smith Cranch to AA, 4 July, below.

[5] JA told the same story in his *Defence of the Const.* to illustrate that "a disposition to mischief, malice, and revenge" may descend in a family: "A young woman was lately convicted at Paris of a trifling theft, barely within the law, which decreed a capital punishment. There were circumstances, too, which greatly alleviated her fault; some things in her behaviour that seemed innocent and modest: every spectator, as well as the judges, was affected at the scene, and she was advised to petition for a pardon, as there was no doubt it would be granted. 'No,' says she, 'my grandfather, father, and brother, were all hanged for stealing; it runs in the blood of our family to steal, and be hanged; if I am pardoned now, I shall steal again in a few months more inexcuseably: and therefore I will be hanged now'" (1:115).

[6] See Mary Smith Cranch to AA, 28 Feb., and note 4, above. Peter Boylston Adams and Mary Crosby married 20 Aug. 1768; their first daughter, Mary, was born less than seven months later on 4 March 1769 (*Braintree Town Records*, p. 835, 875).

John Adams to John Quincy Adams

My dear son   New York April 1. 1790

I have this morning received your agreable Letter of the 19. Ult. and am pleased with your prudent deliberation and judicious decision, upon the Place of your future residence.

The Promotion of M[r] Sullivan, will lead him out of Town upon the Circuits and give room to others to take his Place upon occasions. You are not however to expect a run of Business at first.

Your Project of boarding with D[r] Welch is very agreable to me— and that of taking the best Room in my house for your office is equally so. The good Will of a Shop is a Point of Importance in Trade, and may have some Use in the Practice of Law.— This Circumstance may not however be of so much Weight as another vizt that that Room is the best in Boston, on account of its Situation. I would advise you to take it, at all Events.

My Law Library You may take into your office as soon as you open it, and keep it till I shall call for it.— You will find it agreable to go to Braintree and Spend a Week or a Month especially in summer. You may board at My Brothers, very agreably.— This I should recommend now and then for Variety, on account of your health; leaving it to your discretion after all.

I shall endeavour to enable D[r] Tufts at all Events to pay M[r] Parsons his Honorarium for your Education as soon as the Term expires. The D[r] may draw upon me for that when he will.[1]

Your Information on political Subjects is very Satisfactory, as it is given with that Freedom and Independence of Spirit, which I wish you always to preserve. our Family are all well. Your Brother Charles pursues his Studies with an ardour that gives me great hopes. He

reads as much as you did, and that is as much as I desire. Your / affectionate   John Adams

RC (Adams Papers); internal address: "Mr John Quincy Adams."

¹ On 2 Aug., upon the completion of JQA's clerkship in the law office of Theophilus Parsons, the Adamses paid the judge a fee of £100 (receipt printed in Goodspeed's Book Shop, Catalog No. 111, 1915, item 18).

Mary Smith Cranch to Abigail Adams

My dear Sister   Weymouth April 1^d 1790

I last Week receiv'd your Letter date 15th. of March in which you
mention writing me three weeks successivly. I have receiv'd but one
Letter before this since your Brother Adams brought me one I cannot think what is the reason I have not had them I have had that in
which you mention the miss Palmers staying in your house. They
offer you their most grateful acknowledgments for this favour, but
more particularly for giving them the rent the year past

I have talk'd with mr Jo Cranch & Cousin Betsy about taking the
Farm if you should not come your self. I know he has been use'd to
a Farm in england & he work'd with his uncle at Germantown. I
veryly believe he would do better for you than many others. he
would be careful to save & consciencius to deliver you half the produce, I shall make no comparesions mrs Palmer mourn'd to me the
Loss of mr A's young Trees by the creaturs eating the Bark last
summer mr C says he thinks every one of them are dead— I told
them It was a thing you had mention'd to me as just come into your
mind that you had not consulted mr A upon it— They have been
talking of taking a House & shop in Roxburry Street if they could do
no better—but they seem please'd with this proposal &, if it should
be agreable to mr A & you they wish to know the conditions as soon
as possible they wish doctor Tufts might have power to Lease because they wish for his advice & approbation as it will be impossible
for mr A to give it so readily & so often as they may have occation to
ask it— mr C says there is a great deal of work which ought to be
now doing. Farming Tools they have but very few of so that if they
take it they must use yours but I believe they will be carefully of
them. She will hire a good dairy maid & will exert her self to the
utmost— but my dear Sister all this dissapoints my fond hopes of
having you spend your Summer with us. Why have you made this
alteration in your Plan— I cannot give up the Idea of a visit, if but a

37

short one, & besides you have so many new relations to see that I should think your curiosity would be a little ingag'd. Do you not want to know how I behave as a Grandmother. I desir'd Lucy to inform you of Betsys & Sister Shaws Safety as soon as possible after the event, for I was hurried away immediately. Sister got to Bed but about a week before mrs Norton both of them were quick & not bad Sister wrote a long Letter to mrs N in a week & another to me in a fortnight She was well but very weak mrs N is now much better than I ever expected to see her in such a situation but she has suffer'd much from many cramps She has a Sharpness in her Blood Which has shewn it self in various shapes. She has a very bad sore mouth & Tongue & has been threaten'd with broken Breasts but they are all better

The children are fine Healthy creatures Sister says hers is so & I think I never saw one more so than my little Richard Cranch for that is his name Sister has call'd hers for you—

I do not wonder you was anxious about your son & I am sorry my Letter did not reach you sooner. He return'd before I was willing he should but his cough had left him & he promis'd me he would be very careful. he has sent me word several times that he was very well

I am griev'd for mr Otis. Nabby was a fine girl. I have made the same observation as you have done about the greater proportion of young Ladies who die of consumtions in Boston & Salem than in any other Towns Salem is as remarkable but cannot account for it

mrs Cotton Tufts is like to increase her Family again but not so the Docr. as yet I believe

you & I are like to have a lasting dispute about obligations for you will always over rate & over pay every little Service I can do you or your dear children but I can say with you that I hope you [will beli]eve the will is good of your affectionate Sister

Mary Cranch

When does mrs Smith expect to get to bed. I hope She will let you have a Grandaughter tho this time I long to see the little Boys present my Love to mr Adams & all my Cousins

mrs Norton sends her Duty & knows she says that her Aunt will rejoice with her. She makes an exellent nurse for her baby but such good nurses will be Weak & then— mrs Halls eyes are better than for several years back She was obligd to put a Blister onto one of them & it has done her great service mr Jo Cranch is greatly oblig'd to mr A & you for your exertions in his favour with Genl. Knox & hopes Something may be done to give him an extableshment

RC (Adams Papers); docketed: "Mrs M Cranch / to Mrs A Adams / April 1790." Some loss of text due to a torn manuscript.

Abigail Adams to Mary Smith Cranch

my dear sister   April 3d 1790 N york

I congratulate you and my dear Neice upon the late happy event in your Family. can you really believe that you are a Grandmamma? does not the little fellow feel as if he was really your own. if he does not now, by that time you have lived a year with him, or near you, I question if you will be able to feel a difference. have you been so much occupied by these New cares as not to be able to write me a line upon the Subject. it was from a Letter of cousin [Wi]lliams to Charles that I learnt the agreeable news, at which [I] most sincerely rejoice.[1] I doubt not as my amiable Neice has fullfild all the Relative duties in which she has been calld to act with honour to herself and satisfaction to her Friends, she will not fail to discharge the New one which has fallen to her share with equal ability. I wish my dear sister I could go with you to visit her, as we used to do, and that I could personally tell her how much her safety and happiness is dear to me. I should receive more real satisfaction in one hour, than in months of the uninteresting visits which my situation obliges me both to receive and pay. my old Friend Mrs Rogers has past the winter in N York and we have lived in our former intimacy. I shall regreet her leaving it. Mrs Smith and her Family the chief of them have been for three weeks at Jamica upon a visit. the House really felt so lonely after [ma]ster william went, that I sent for him back yesterday. John and he are both very fine children, but as yet my attachment to william is much the strongest. his temper is sweet and his disposition docile.

This place begins to reassume all its Beauty. I wish you could come and see it. For situation and prospect I know no equal. we have been gardning for more than a week. I always forgot to inquire of my Neices if the flower seeds succeeded last year.[2] I fear my prospect of visiting Braintree will be cut of, by the short recess of congress. the buisness before them is so important, and takes so much time to discus it, that they talk now of only adjourning through the

Hot Months,[3] and the breaking up a Family for a few months, the expence attending the journey with those domesticks which we must bring on, will out run the Sum allotted by our generous Country, so that I see no prospect of visiting my Friends. I must therefore content my self with hearing from them as often as I can.

I wrote you a fortnight since that Gen[ll] Knox had given his word to mr A that he would do something for mr J Cranch. I presume he will not forget him. I shall dine there on tweaday next, and as the Gen[ll] is always very civil polite and social with me, I will drop a word to him if opportunity offers. mr Jefferson is here, and adds much to the social circle[4]

I wish to have some seed Beans of scarlet and of the white kind, the pod of which is so tender. I forget the Name, but believe you will know. they grow in, joints and are very fruitfull. adieu. tis time to go to meeting, o that it was to hear good dr Price, or mr clark or Thacher, or any body whose sentiments were more conformable to mine.[5] ever yours   A Adams

RC (MWA:Abigail Adams Letters); addressed by CA: "M[rs] Mary ~~Dalton~~ / M[rs] Mary Cranch. / Braintree." Some loss of text where the seal was removed and due to a torn manuscript.

[1] Not found.

[2] At Elizabeth Cranch's request, AA returned from abroad in 1788 with flower seeds from her garden in London. In 1785, AA had sent a similar package of seeds to her niece from France, some of which thrived in Braintree (vol. 6:84; vol. 8:170).

[3] Congress debated and passed several pieces of major legislation, including the Funding Act and Residence Act, before adjourning on 12 Aug. 1790 (*First Fed. Cong.*, 5:713–937, 6:1767–1791; *Biog. Dir. Cong.*).

[4] Thomas Jefferson arrived in New York to assume his duties as secretary of state on 21 March (Jefferson, *Papers*, 16:2).

[5] For AA's previous complaints about the ministers in New York City, see AA to Mary Smith Cranch, 4 Oct. 1789, vol. 8:413–414.

John Quincy Adams to William Cranch

Newbury-Port April 7th: 1790.[1]

As you were somewhat in my debt in the article of Letters, when I left Boston, I expected ere this to have received something from you; and I was not a little disappointed when Bridge came from Boston to find he had nothing but your compliments, or some such thing to deliver me from you. I am willing however to make allowances for the multiplicity of your avocations, and not having the same excuse myself, I have seated myself to write you a Letter though I must confess I have not yet thought of a subject. I suppose however I shall still harp upon that inexhaustible subject, of all my Letters to you; I mean my single self; and I wish you would imitate my egotism, a little more than you have done; for the employments the studies the adventures, the passions, and even the amusements of a friend are always interesting in the relation; at least I always find them so; and I am willing to suppose it is from the expectation of gratifying a similar disposition in my friends, rather than from an irresistible fondness of talking about myself, that I fill so great a proportion of my letters with my own affairs.

It is just four weeks since I returned to this Town. Since which, the distribution of my time has been similar to what it was for several months, before I went to Boston. The days have pretty regularly been pass'd at our office, where a man may be lazy or indolent with as much facility, as at any other place. I have read but very little Law. Part of a volume of Burrow is all I have perused, in that line;[2] while I have been much more studious with novels, and poetry. The most weighty performance which I have attended to; has been Voltaire's Age of Lewis 14.[3] and I recollect with pleasure the time which I spent in that employment. It was not lost time. I have now begun upon Hume's Essays,[4] but Mr. Parsons has now return'd, and while he is here, we can read but very little of any thing. He goes next week to Concord; and will after that, be gone almost all the remainder of my noviciate. I hope to employ the period of his absence to some advantage— It is a subject of uncomfortable feelings to me, to find so much of my time denying me the pleasures of recollection, but I am strongly inclined to consider the evil as inevitable.

But from your observation upon the state of my mind while I was in Boston, you may perhaps feel a greater degree of curiosity, for information relating to my amusements. You were sufficiently witness to the struggle which has arisen between my *sentiments* and my *opinions*. I could not, consistent with that friendship which I trust will ever subsist between us, attempt to conceal from you feelings, which I wish not to be known to the world in general; and which I submit to, merely from a total impossibility to help myself.— Those feelings have since my return been acquiring additional strength from day to day; and I am more than ever convinced of the absolute necessity for me, to leave this town very soon.[5] Flight, and speedy flight too is the only resource that is now left me

> "My wishes, lull'd with soft inglorious dreams
> Forget the patriots' and the sages, themes"[6]

We have had three assemblies since I returned: and they have afforded me as much pleasure, as I could have expected. These assemblies are dangerous places. they are not only dangerous to females. We have in our situation quite as much real evil to apprehend from those moments "When music softens and when dancing fires."—[7] I mean not to say they are immediately dangerous to our honour and reputation, but the disposition they give to the mind, may often be fatal to the peace of a person whose welfare consists in preserving a perfect indifference. We are to have one more, on the 22d: of this month; when I very much wish to see you here; though I have almost resigned the hope.—[8] The Assemblies are however not the only occasions, when I am exposed to the perils of Sentiment. I have passed a number of evenings in companies similar to those, which I have mentioned to you; and every single instance has tended to increase my alarm. I should even at this day leave the town with great reluctance. Three months hence I fear I shall find still greater difficulty to break away.— Yet I hope you will always find the conduct of your friend to correspond with the ideas which he professed to you in some of his Letters last Summer.[9] He may suffer more in obtaining the victory, than he could at that time have imagined, but the conquest will only be the more meritorious. The following lines of your poetical friend Akenside occur to me very frequently

> "I feel diviner fires my breast inflame,
> To active Science an ingenuous fame.
> Resume the paths my earliest choice began,
> And lose with pride the Lover in the man."[10]

Putnam repeats these lines, from a little Elegy of that writer (which I pointed to him as being peculiarly applicable to his present Situation,) with more energy than I can. He is struggling with a Passion deeply rooted, and confirmed by habits of almost three years standing. His contest is infinitely more difficult in that respect than mine can be; but in the imperfections, the weaknesses and caprice of the Object of his attachment, he finds a source of support to his resolution, of which mine is altogether deprived. The two Ladies though very intimate friends, are widely different in character. And this difference is daily increasing; for they are both now at an age, when perhaps improvement is more rapid than at any other period of human life, and while the one is acquiring graces and virtues in addition to incomparable beauty, the other is increasing her power and influence, only by the refinements which experience offers to her for her System of coquetry.— Is it not a hardship that the best of the two characters should be by much the most dangerous.— Putnam sees the contrast as clearly as any one, and feels a degree of shame at having been so strongly attached to a person of so much levity and inconsistency of conduct. He is weaning himself as fast as he can, and I have so much friendship for him to wish he may completely succeed.[11] He has yet but partially obtained his end, for

> "though Reason flies the hated door,
> Yet Love, the coward Love still lags behind."[12]

Bridge, since his return affects the Philosopher, or is really so.— He did not attend our assembly, and has been as yet but very little into company; he has hitherto excused himself from the infirm state of his Health. But whether this be his real motive or not, I think him right in "laying the axe at the root of the evil."—[13] We remain excepting in these particulars as we have been for several months past, and I know of nothing further to which your curiosity would give an interest:— Pray let me hear from you as soon as possible, and believe me still your unalterable friend. J. Q. Adams.

RC (DLC:William Cranch Papers); addressed: "Mʳ William Cranch. / Boston."; endorsed: "J.Q.A. April 7. 1790."

[1] JQA placed a cross-hatch at the top of the page and wrote sideways in the margin: "Observe that in future, all my letters marked thus # are either to be burnt or kept in such a manner as will expose them to the sight of no body but yourself."

[2] Sir James Burrow, comp., *Reports of Cases Argued and Determined in the Court of King's Bench during the Time of Lord Mansfield's Presiding*, 5 vols., London, 1756–1772, and *Reports of Cases Adjudged in the Court of King's Bench since the Death of Lord Raymond*, 5 vols., London, 1766–1780 (*DNB*).

[3] Voltaire, *The Age of Lewis XIV*, 2 vols., London, 1752.

[4] David Hume, *Essays and Treatises on Several Subjects*, 4 vols., London, 1753–1754.

[5] JQA was romantically entangled with Mary Frazier (1774–1804), daughter of Moses and Elizabeth Frazier of Newburyport. In a letter written on 28 Sept., responding to a letter by JQA that has not been found, James Bridge expressed his surprise at learning the intensity of his friend's "connection with Miss F.—," quoting back to JQA his declaration, "*You* may know (though it is known to very few) that all my hopes of future happiness in this life, centre in the possession of that girl" (Adams Papers).

Before departing for Europe in 1794, JQA apparently burned a number of letters written during late 1790 that discussed his relationship with Frazier. In a letter of 29 Aug. 1794 to an unidentified correspondent, probably Thomas Woodbridge Hooper, JQA reflected on his affair, expressing gratitude that he had escaped a "web in which my own heedless passion had precipitated me" but also confessing a lingering fondness for Mary: "Far be it from me however, to utter an intimation unfavourable to the Lady, who was then the beloved of my heart. With respect to her, my *opinions* have never shared in the revolution of my *Sentiments*. Her wrong to me (which indeed never originated with herself) I freely forgave at the moment when I resigned her affections. . . . I hear her name mentioned without an emotion; I see her, without a throb of the heart; I speak to her without a faltering of the voice . . . but I remember that I *have loved* her with an affection surpassing that of Women, and there are few circumstances in the compass of human Events, that would afford me more sincere pleasure, than I should receive upon being Informed that she has become the happy wife of another Man" (Tr, MQHi).

JQA's romantic relationship with Frazier

came to an end several months after he moved to Boston to open his law practice. Nearly half a century later, JQA recalled the romance in his Diary, noting: "Dearly!—how dearly did the sacrifice of her cost me, voluntary as it was—for the separation was occasioned by my declining to contract an unqualified engagement, forbidden by my father, and by the advice of her cousin to her, to insist upon a positive engagement or a separation— Four years of exquisite wretchedness followed this separation nor was the wound in my bosom healed, till the Atlantic Ocean flowed between us." Frazier married Daniel Sargent in 1802 and died two years later of consumption (D/JQA/12, 2 Nov. 1790, APM Reel 15; *Vital Records of Newburyport Massachusetts to the End of the Year 1849*, 2 vols., Salem, Mass., 1911, 1:148; Boston *Independent Chronicle*, 2 Aug. 1804; D/JQA/33, 18 Nov. 1838, APM Reel 36; Boston, *30th Report*, p. 201).

⁶ Mark Akenside, "Love, An Elegy," lines 5–6.

⁷ Alexander Pope, *The Rape of the Lock*, Canto I, line 76.

⁸ Returning to Newburyport on 10 March 1790, JQA attended an assembly the following evening where he "danced till one." He also attended assemblies on 25 March, 6 April, and 22 April. He wrote of the last that it was "Day, before we came away." Dancing assemblies, such as the one to which JQA subscribed, were popular social events in the late eighteenth and early nineteenth centuries. At these gatherings, which were often regulated by strict rules governing everything from procedure to dress, young adults paired up to perform country dances, cotillions, and minuets (D/JQA/15, APM Reel 18; Ann Wagner, *Adversaries of Dance: From the Puritans to the Present*, Urbana, Ill., 1997, p. 82, 125–126).

⁹ Not found, but JQA recorded in his Diary that he wrote to Cranch on 7 June and 23 Aug. 1789 (D/JQA/14, APM Reel 17).

¹⁰ Mark Akenside, "Love, An Elegy," lines 131–134.

¹¹ For Samuel Putnam, JQA's Harvard classmate, see JQA, *Diary*, 2:229. Putnam's love interest was almost certainly Harriot Bradbury (1771–1798), daughter of his mentor Theophilus Bradbury, who married Thomas Woodbridge Hooper in 1792. Putnam opened a law practice in Salem in July 1790 and married Sarah Gooll (1772–1864), daughter of Lois Pickering and John Gooll of that town, on 28 Oct. 1795 (JQA, *Diary*, 2:384, 404; *Vital Records of Newburyport Massachusetts to the End of the Year 1849*, 2 vols., Salem, Mass., 1911, 2:50, 669; *Vital Records of Salem Massachusetts to the End of the Year 1849*, 6 vols., Salem, Mass., 1924, 5:289; Elizabeth Cabot Putnam and Harriet Silvester Tapley, "Hon. Samuel Putnam, LL.D, A.A.S.," Danvers Historical Society, *Historical Collections*, 10:4, 13, 31 [1922]).

¹² James Hammond, "Elegy II," lines 31–32.

¹³ "And now also the axe is laid unto the root of the trees: therefore every tree which bringeth not forth good fruit is hewn down, and cast into the fire" (Matthew, 3:10).

Abigail Adams to Cotton Tufts

Dear sir   Newyork April 18 1790

Your kind favour of the 5ᵗʰ Instant came safe to Hand.¹ I know our interest at Braintree can be of very little Service to us, seperated as we are from it, and lying so much in Buildings. I do not know what benefit was last year derived from the great Garden but unless Bass could carry manure upon it, it would soon become good for very little. if any method could be devised by which the Rent could be paid, I should have no objection to their continuing there for the last year. I was to have it in work whenever I or my Friends calld upon him, some of it has been paid in that way. I have been informd that one of the Fosters was engaged to mrs vesey for the payment of her House Rent, perhaps they might be induced to now.[2] as to Clark I should suppose there was garden enough both for Pheby & him in the peice fenced of, but if there is not, Bass & he may perhaps compound.[3] the House in Boston I do not think will let at all after the lower Room is taken of. if it should prove so, it will certainly be much more prudent to give 15£ pounds for an office than take that which yealds 36£. as to our return to Braintree during the Recess of congress—it depends upon the Length of time that they now Sit, and the period for which they adjourn. it is necessary to make nice calculations. the expence of a movement of that kind may be attended with more trouble than advantage. if the adjournment should be from june untill the Next April it might answer for us, but should they rise & make a fall Sessions, it would not answer. we must content ourselves to Tarry where we are without visiting our Friends I fear. From the progress made in Buisness it is impossible to Guess when congress will rise. The Buisness before them is a Harculian Labour the Members of different states think so widely from each other, that it is difficult to accommodate their interests to each other. what one Member esteems the pillar, the Bulwork of the constitution, an other considers as the Ruin of his State. the late vote respecting the assumption has made much ill Blood, and as the Members are not yet cool enough to persue the subject, they have taken up other Buisness for a few days— from the conversation which I have heard, I believe it will again be brought on, or Congress will rise without doing any thing more upon the subject it is impossible Sir, You must be very sensible in such an assembly those only should speak who speak to the purpose. it is frequently the case that those who have least matter, ingrose most of the Time. they must be heard and frequently answerd, or they would complain of unfair dealing for Instance, how much Time has that Mad Man Gardner expended this very year in your Legislature, to very bad purposes. Men of Sense and industery complain here as loudly as their constituents, but untill Men of Superiour abilities compose publick assemblies, Buisness will be procrastinated. the National Debt is a subject of such vast weight and importance as requires the wisest Heads, and honestest Hearts to adjust with any degree of satisfaction. mr Gerry has acquired great honour and Reputation upon this Subject, and restored his former credit.[4]

I wish sir you could find it convenient to make us a visit. it would give great pleasure to your affectionate Friends / and particularly to your Neice   Abigail Adams

Ps I should be glad of the Hams when Barnard comes— I do not find any like them here

I have received two Letters from mrs Cranch.[5] I shall write her by the next post. we have had a severe snow storm to day attended with a very high wind. it has turnd to rain but storms severely yet. my duty to your good Lady. be so good as to buy me a ticket in some of the Lotteries, I care not which.[6]

RC (NHi:Misc. Mss. Adams, Abigail).

[1] Not found.

[2] For the house and marshland formerly owned by Martha Veasey (1728–1785), which was purchased by JA from William and Sarah Veasey in Feb. 1788, see vol. 7:143-144 (Sprague, *Braintree Families*).

[3] Possibly Rev. William Clark, Harvard 1759, who served as an Anglican missionary to Christ Church in Quincy (*Sibley's Harvard Graduates*, 14:400; Cotton Tufts to JA, 25 May 1797, Adams Papers).

[4] For AA's earlier criticism of Elbridge Gerry, formerly an ardent Antifederalist, see vol. 8:389, 406. Now an enthusiastic supporter of Alexander Hamilton's plan, Gerry had recently delivered a long speech in support of the assumption of state debts that was published in the *New York Daily Gazette*, 7 April 1790 (*DAB*; *First Fed. Cong.*, 13:948-

956).

[5] See AA to Mary Smith Cranch, 21 April, note 1, below.

[6] Several lotteries were open at the time, including lotteries to finance the construction of a free school in Williamstown and to raise money for the town of Charlestown. On 2 March, the Mass. General Court also passed legislation calling for a semi-annual lottery to raise £10,000 for the state. An advertisement appeared in the Boston *Independent Chronicle*: "As the object of this Lottery is to *ease the taxes of the people*, and to *promote public credit*, the Managers flatter themselves, that principles of patriotism, as well as a spirit of adventure, will conduce to a speedy sale of the Tickets" (*Independent Chronicle*, 11, 18 March, 9 April). See also Tufts to AA, 23 Feb. 1791, below.

Abigail Adams Smith to John Quincy Adams

Richmond April 18th 1790—

I had the pleasure to receive a letter from my Dear Brother many weeks since,[1] I must acknowledge that I have been very deficient in attention by thus long neglecting to acknowledge its receipt, and I cannot find any sufficient appology to you, except a certain Indolence which at times takes possession of me and unfits me for writing—and which I presume others are not more exempt from them my self, I dare say you can as easily imagine its existance and affects as I could describe them,

the Communications which I made in my last respecting your Fathers oppinion of your going to Boston were taken from his General Conversation but was not official information but as I am informed that several Letters have passed between you since that time upon the Subject, I presume and hope that you are possessed of his sentiments upon it, and that they do accord in all respects with your wishes,– I do not think that you have any right at this period to Complain of any want of Success in your pursuits, do not anticipate such an Evil, for I cannot admit the idea that it can ever be realized, your situation will become every day more agreeable and sattisfactory as you become engaged in Business that will employ your time; engage your attention; render you independant; and enable you to promote the Happiness of others; busy minds are never Sattisfied unless their time and attention, is fully engaged, upon subjects which they esteem worthy of them

you must excuse me if I do not give any beleif to your Confession of the existance of an attachment to which "reason and Prudence would oppose their influence" I have other oppinions of your judgement and discretion than to suppose you have given your mind up uninfluenced by reason and Prudence,– I could not even advise you to permit yourself to become speedily engaged in an attachment upon which must devolve your future happiness, prosperity, and Success,– if it is not too late to advise,–I would rather offer mine, in favour of your first settling in business and takeing time to form a more extensive acquaintance with the World,– I am Sensible that your knowledge of Mankind is more enlarged and Extensive than perhaps any young Man of your age Possesses. that your knowledge of Books is Superior, and that your acquaintance with Human Nature has been derived from observation as well as from reading, that you have traversed those paths of Science and Learning which others much more advanced in years have yet to pursue—but you may yet be deficient in Practical knowledge, and as *one* who feels much interested in your Prosperity and Wellfare, I could wish to see you a few years further advanced in Life before you engage in a Connection which if you form at present must impede your progress and advancement

but if your mind is already engaged—I shall not hesitate to beleive that the object is in every respect worthy of your Partiallity, and if so time for Consideration will not abate the degree; or Chancell the weight of the engagement upon your mind,–

but I am sure that I have said enough upon a Subject which I had no pre-intention of mentioning when I took up my Pen, I hope you will not think I have been too explicit, or permit thease my Sentiments if they should not accord with your oppinions to interfere with the future Confidence of your letters, I shall ever Consider myself flattered by your Confidence and Communications upon every Subject, but I shall never excite them for unworthy purposes or to expose to others who may view things through a different medium from what they are intended

I am prepareing and expect to remove to New York the first week in May we have taken a House in Nassau Street,[2] at which, (should you make an excursion in the Course of the Summer to this place) I shall be very happy to receive you, and flatter myself it will be in my Power to Contribute more to your amusement, and Happiness, than it was at your last visit; M[r] Smith desires me to present his regards to you upon the Subject of Politicks I must refer you to Mamma and your Brother I do not pretend to understand them nor to attend to them, it seems to be a General observation that Congress set day after day and do nothing,—

My Chrildren are well and Will[m] desires to be remembered to you I am with Sincere affection your Sister   A S—[3]

RC (Adams Papers); endorsed: "My Sister. 18. April 1790."; "My Sister April 18. 1790."; and "answered May 1[st:] 1790."

[1] Not found.

[2] The Smiths moved to 13 Nassau Street, parallel to Broadway and perpendicular to Wall Street, in the heart of New York City (*New-York Directory*, 1790, Evans, No. 22724).

[3] Unable to fit her full signature at the bottom of the page, AA2 repeated her signature, "sister A Smith—," in the margin.

Abigail Adams to Mary Smith Cranch

my dear sister   Richmond Hill April 21 1790

I received your two kind Letters of April 1 & 5[1] I am extreemly sorry to hear that mrs Norten is afflicted in the way that you write me she is, but tell her to keep up a good Heart. I can Sympathize in her Sufferings a Bath of Hot Herbs was the most salutary means made use for me. a poultice of Camomile flowers is also very good, but I hope she is relieved before this time. painfull experience would teach me upon the very first chill, to apply a white Bread poultice because those cold fits are always succeeded by a fever and complaints of the Breast always follow.[2] I am glad to hear that my great Nephew [is su]ch a fine child.

When I wrote you last, you may remember that I told you I would speak to Gen[ll] Knox in behalf of mr Cranch. I thought I had best do it before I said any thing to mr A about the place as the arrangments which the Gen[ll] might make would prove more advantageous to him and require his attention upon the spot. I talkd with him and he engaged to send me a letter for him which is now inclosed to you.[3]

he told me that at west point he would find a dwelling House work shop &c and two years employ if he would go there immediatly that he believed there was yet Buisness to be compleated at Springfield. there are many applicants so that Mr Cranch should not be dilatory as there may be now a good opening for him.⁴ he will not fail of writing directly to Gen^ll Knox and giving him the information he requests The Miss Palmers may continue in the House untill mr Cranch can accommodate them better. I wish my dear sister that I could come to Braintree, but I do not see how it can be effected to any good purpose. pray can you tell me where I could get a Boy of a dozen years I would have him come round in Barnard if any one is to be had. Such a wretched crew as N york produces are scarcly to be found in any city in Europe. I am so much discouraged by every Body here that I dare not attempt to take one. I wish you would inquire of Ruthe Ludden whether she would be willing to come in Barnard & let me know. Mr Smiths Petter had a likely Boy that he askd me to take before I came here. if he is not put out, and he will Send him to me by captain Barnard I will take him—⁵ Let me hear from you soon Mrs Smith is going to House keeping in N york the 1 of May, the day when every Body Removes as they tell me here— I shall feel lost— the children amuse & divert me much but they will be here half there time. William is down on his knees searching the pictures in Milton, whilst I write. Gammar he says look here, the Man with a great sword going to cut them are Men all to pieces.— he is a lovely child with a temper as mild & sweet as one would wish. adieu my dear sister. I must quit to dress, as mrs washington Lady Temple mrs dalton mrs King & Several other Ladies drink Tea with me this afternoon

Yours most affectionatly   A Adams

wednesday Noon—

Mr Brisler desires me to ask if mr Cranch has got the Remainder of his money from mr Baxter and prays he would see mr Baxter & let him know that he wants it

RC (MWA:Abigail Adams Letters); addressed: "To / Mrs Mary Cranch / Braintree." Some loss of text where the seal was removed.

¹ The 1 April letter is above, but the 5 April letter has not been found.

² Poultices of boiled chamomile flowers and of heated white bread and milk were used to treat sore and broken breasts (Henry Wilkins, *The Family Adviser; or, A Plain and* *Modern Practice of Physic*, 3d edn., Phila., 1801, p. 22, Shaw-Shoemaker, No. 1658; Eliza Smith, *The Compleat Housewife; or, Accomplish'd Gentlewoman's Companion*, 5th edn., Williamsburg, Va., 1742, p. 204, Evans, No. 5061).

³ Not found.

⁴ The military arsenal located on the Connecticut River in Springfield, Mass., was used during the Revolution and later designated a national armory. Congress established two companies of artillery in 1786 to be stationed at Springfield and West Point, though the assignment was set to expire in early 1790. Joseph Cranch had worked briefly

as an armorer at Springfield in 1785 (David D. Hartzler and James B. Whisker, *The Northern Armory: The United States Armory at Springfield, Massachusetts, 1795–1859*, Bedford, Penn., 1997, p. 14; *First Fed. Cong.*, 1:118; Joseph Palmer to JA, 28 Nov. 1785, Adams Papers).

⁵ For Peter's son, Prince, see AA to Mary Smith Cranch, 13 June 1790, below.

Abigail Adams to Mary Smith Cranch

my dear Sister   Richmond Hill April 28 1790

I designd to have written to you by the Monday Post, but I was so very ill on Sunday that I could not set up. I have had the severest attack of the Rhumatism attended with a voilent fever which I have experienced for several years. I have not yet left my chamber, tho I am much releived. the weather has been uncommonly wet and cold, Snow we have had in the course of this fortnight more than through the whole winter. our House has been a mere Hospital ever since Saturday last. I have been confined in one chamber, col smith in an other with a Billious attack Charls is in an other with a fever, my House keeper confind to her chamber with Saint Antonys fire,¹ and a servant of col Smiths laid up with a voilent seazure of the Breast & Lungs, but thanks [to] a kind Providence we are all upon the Recovery. I was in hopes [to] have heard from you by last weeks post, & to have learnt how mrs Norten was, for whom I am much concernd. I am anxious for her, from more disinterested motives than Swifts Friend, tho perhaps I can more feelingly sympathize with her for, having "felt a pain just in the place where she complains"—²

my last letter to you was accompanied by one for mr J Cranch which I hope came safe to Hand. I wrote you something respecting Ruthe Ludden, but I wish now to be very particular. if her Time is out with her Aunt as I think it was in March, and she is inclined to come Barnard will return here sometime in May. her Passage by him will be six dollors which I shall pay. there is a mrs Laffen with whom mr Brisler is acquainted who went from here to Boston in Barnard and means to return again with him, so that she would not have to come alone. my terms to her will be three dollors a Months, and to give her the small pox. I wish to have an immediate answer because if she does not like to come, mr Brisler has a sister Betsy in Boston, who would be very glad to come and I shall write to her to come immediatly.[3] I do not wish to send Polly home till I get some-body in her Room, but send her Home I must, or I shall never have a quiet family. this I must say of her, that I have never found her otherways than stricktly honest and I have not had the least difficulty with her on account of Drink. in short it is next to im-posible here to get a servant from the highest to the lowest grade that does not drink male or Female I have at last found a footman who appears sober, but he was Born in Boston, has lived a very short time in the city & has very few acquaintance there. you would be surprizd if I was to tell you that tho I have been long trying to get a Boy here I cannot find one that any Body will Recommend, and I should be very glad to get one from Boston—I mean Peters son. my Housekeeper who on many accounts has been the most Respectable Female I have had in the Family, is so sick and infirm that she is obliged to leave me, partly I know because she will not live with Polly. if I could find any middle aged woman of a Reputable Charac-ter who understands Pastry &c in Boston I would send for her. I give 5. dollors a month to my Housekeeper, my kitchen and offices are all below stairs, and where there are a Number of Servants there must be one respectable Head amongst them to over see & take care that they do not run head long as well as to overlook the cook-ing & to make Tea for me upon my publick Evenings—to make my Pastry to assist in the Ironing &c this is the Buisness which falls to her share. Ruthe I want for a house maid. She will have no concern with cooking at all, as I keep a woman solely for that purpose. I wish you would be upon the inquiry for me. If I had not Brisler with me I should be tempted to give up publick Life. the chief of the Servants here who are good for any thing are Negroes who are slaves, the white ones are all Foreigners & chiefly vagabonds— I really know now more than ever how to Prize my English servants but I think when the cat is once gone I shall do much better do you remember the Fable of the Cat the Sow & the Eagle Scarcly a day passes that I do not think of it,[4] yet I have a real value for Polly. She has a great many good qualities, and alone in a small Family would answer very well, but Authority she cannot bear to have the least, it is only by keeping her Humble that she is any way to be bourn with. in many things as mr Althorp observed, she seems as necessary to me as my daily food, and but for that temper, I would not part with her. with that I could deal, but the eternal mischief between others, keeps the whole House in disorder, and gives a bad Name to the whole Family— thus having detaild my whole Family grievences to you I bid you adieu with Love to all Friends / from your ever affectionate sister

A Adams

RC (MWA:Abigail Adams Letters); addressed by WSS: "To / M^rs: Mary Cranch. / Braintree / near / Boston." Some loss of text where the seal was removed.

[1] Shingles, a painful skin disease (*OED*).

[2] "Yet, should some neighbour feel a pain / Just in the parts where I complain: / How many a message would he send? / What hearty prayers, that I should mend?" (Jonathan Swift, "Verses on the Death of Dr. Swift," lines 133–136).

[3] Margarette Elizabeth Briesler (b. 1762). She may have been the sister of John Briesler who AA considered taking with her to Europe in 1784, for which see vol. 5:303, 305 (Sprague, *Braintree Families*).

[4] In Aesop's fable, a cat, a sow, and an eagle all live in the same tree. The conniving cat convinces the eagle that the sow is working to uproot the tree, and the sow that the eagle has a taste for pigs, so that neither terrified animal will leave the tree to search for food. They both ultimately starve.

John Quincy Adams to Thomas Boylston Adams

Newbury. Port April 28th: 1790.

I received your short Epistle by M^r: Thomas at Ipswich,[1] where I was then attending the Court of Common Pleas: and at the same time he gave me very agreeable information respecting your performance at exhibition; which has been confirmed to me from several quarters. From the conversations which have repeatedly passed between us, you will readily imagine how much I was gratified, to hear that you acquitted yourself with so much honour; and to a mind so generous as yours, I am well perswaded, that the idea of having given pleasure to your friends, will greatly enhance the value of your own.[2]

Your Question respecting A and B. and A's Wife, may be very ingenious; but I confess it is rather beyond my comprehension. And as my imagination in pursuit of your meaning might chance to run foul of Scylla or of the other place, I will even leave it as I found it.

I presume that in the course of six weeks or two months; it will be necessary for me to take some measures in order to obtain my second degree.— But as I do not wish to take the trouble of a Journey to Cambridge; I must request you, to do the business for me.— As soon therefore as the usual advertisements to the candidates for the Master's degree, shall appear in the papers; you will apply to the Steward, the Butler; and the Sweeper, for receipts, which it seems are necessary, though, I have never owed them any thing since I left College: Doctor Tufts will supply you with ten dollars, five of which are to be paid to the President, and five to the Steward: and I herewith enclose three questions which you will deliver to the President, who will select from them that which appears to him most proper. These are all the requisites, to be complied with that have ever come to my knowledge— If any thing more should be required, you will give me the information; at any rate I suppose it will not be necessary for me to go to Cambridge, merely for the purpose of securing my degree.[3]

I should have been very happy to have seen you here in the course of the late vacation; and they had some expectation of seeing you at Haverhill; where I spent, the Sunday before last. I found almost all our friends there unwell. M[r:] Shaw's House was a mere Hospital. He was so sick himself that the public services were omitted; they were however upon the recovery; and I presume are before this wholly restored; though I have not heard from them since I came back.

I have a Letter from your father of the 16[th:] inst[t: 4] and one from your Sister of the 18[th:] they were then all well; at least as far as may be collected from negatives; I am not told that any of them were unwell.

Col[l:] Smith moves into New York in the beginning of May. They have taken a House in Nassau Street. Perhaps you know where it is.

Have you as yet determined upon your future profession? This Question I have more reasons than one to wish you immediately to answer. I shall decidedly go to Boston immediately after Commencement. If you conclude upon studying Law, and incline to become a fellow-student with me, I hope I shall be able to procure the consent of the Bar. At least you might study the two first years in my office; and the remaining year with a man of more abilities and experience. This plan would be much less expensive, and in my opinion Quite as advantageous to you, as any that could be proposed. I expect, (but this I wish you not to mention) to board with D[r:] Welch; and should you adopt this scheme, we might both I suppose, live there together; and at less expence than we could live separately. You will reflect upon the matter and determine according to your own judgment; but I wish you to inform me as soon as possible what your intentions are.

Meanwhile, I remain, your affectionate brother.

J. Q. Adams.

RC (Adams Papers); addressed: "Mʳ Thomas Boylstone Adams. / Senior Sophister, Harvard University. / Cambridge."; endorsed: "28ᵗʰ April 1790—"; docketed: "April, 28– 90." and "J Q Adams."

¹ Not found.

² TBA delivered the English oration at Harvard's public exhibition that spring (MH-Ar:Faculty Records, 6:67).

³ As was customary, JQA waited three years before taking the necessary steps to procure his master of arts. Earning the additional degree was a simple process in which the candidate responded to a question, or *quaestio*, decided in advance in consultation with the college president. JQA addressed the question *An, ubi leges sunt vagæ aut crebrò mutatæ, libertas existere possit?* (Whether, when the laws have been haphazardly or in many places changed, can freedom exist?), arguing in the negative. JQA recorded in his Diary going to commencement on 21 July, presumably attending TBA's bachelor of arts ceremony in the morning before his own ceremony that afternoon (Morison, *Three Centuries of Harvard*, p. 34–35; Quaestiones, 21 July 1790, MHi:Broadside

Coll., Evans, No. 22562; D/JQA/15, 21 July, APM Reel 18; Boston *Independent Chronicle*, 22 July).

⁴ In his letter of 16 April, JA complimented JQA on the "political Sagacity" displayed in a recent letter but warned, "be attentive: but cautious and discreet.—neglect not your private Studies and proper Business: for the sake of thinking or Speaking or writing upon public affairs." JA went on to discuss the dangers inherent in a national system in which sovereignty was divided between the state and federal governments: "Governors of states compare themselves with the President Senators of states with national Senators and Representatives of states with Representatives of the Union, and these Comparisons produce Passions and Heartburnings, which will endin Collisions Disputes perhaps seditions" (Adams Papers).

Abigail Adams to Mary Smith Cranch

my dear sister   [8 May 1790]

I wrote to you ten days ago and informd you that my Family were very sick. I did not then conceive it to be, what I have since found it the Influenza. I have got better, but my cough & some other complaints still hang about me. Polly Tailor is so bad with it, that if she is not soon relieved the concequences threaten to be fatal to her. Louissa is very sick confind to her chamber I keep a Bottle of Tarter Emetick and administer it as soon as they complain. mr Adams has kept clear of it yet, and he is the only one who has not been attack'd in a greater or less degree Mrs Smith has had a slight attack. the children appear to have it comeing and almost every Body throughout the whole city are labouring under it.¹ this afternoon I heard that my Friend mrs Rogers lies dangerously sick. this distresses me greatly because it is not in my power to render her any assistance. I last Evening heard from Thomas, and that your Family were well, but he does not mention mrs Norten by which I would fain hope that she is better. Mrs Smith Removed last week, and this makes it necessary for me to request a few articles from my House in Braintree. I must request the favour of my good Brother Cranch to get me a case made for my large looking glass, and to be so good as to pack it for me & send it by Barnard, with a note of the expence which I will pay to Barnard, my kitchen clock & press which stands in the kitchen, and two Glass Lanthorn which are in the chamber closset & the Stone Roller for the Garden. I should be glad to have all these things by Barnard. the Glass I do not know how to do without the Top I have here, I cannot afford to Buy, besides I have enough for the Braintree House, & should I purchase here must sell them again at a loss. this House is much better calculated for the glasses having all the Rooms Eleven foot high. I have not heard from you since I wrote you respecting Ruthe Ludden mrs Brisler has this disorder tho not Bad. I am impatient to hear from you pray let it be soon.

yours most affectionatly   A Adams

RC (MWA:Abigail Adams Letters); addressed: "To / Mrs Mary Cranch / Braintree"; endorsed by Richard Cranch: "Letter from Mrs· / A Adams / without Date."

[1] Influenza outbreaks occurred in the northeastern United States in the fall of 1789 and spring and fall of 1790, though the mortality rates were relatively low. Newspapers from Boston to Philadelphia noted the epidemic. On 12 May, William Maclay wrote of New York, "The whole Town, or nearly so, is sick and many die daily" (K. David Patterson, *Pandemic Influenza 1700–1900: A Study in Historical Epidemiology*, Totowa, N.J., 1986, p. 25–26; Washington, *Papers, Presidential Series*, 5:394).

Martha Washington to Abigail Adams

Wednesday– May 12. [1790]

Mrs· Washington presents her compliments to Mrs· Adams– She wishes to know how the Vice-President and Mrs· Adams are to day– Mrs· Washington is happy to inform that the President is a little better to day than he was yesterday[1]

RC (Adams Papers); addressed: "Mrs· Adams–"

[1] George Washington, unwell through much of the spring, became gravely ill from influenza and pneumonia in mid-May and did not fully recover until the middle of June (Washington, *Papers, Presidential Series*, 5:393–399).

I. GEORGE WASHINGTON, BY EDWARD SAVAGE, 1790

See page xi

2. MARTHA WASHINGTON, BY EDWARD SAVAGE, 1790
See page xi

Mary Smith Cranch to Abigail Adams

My dear Sister   Braintree May 16th 1790

I last evening receiv'd your Letter without a date but believe it was your last as you mention Mrs Smiths removal want of some Furniture &c. mr Cranch will attend to the Packing & Sending them directly— I hope you have receiv'd my last letter. you will find by that mrs Norton for whome you have been so kindly anxious was much better & had escap'd what we so much feard but She is as thin as a Lanthorn you can see thro her nose. There whole Family been sick Baby & all with this new distemper but are geting better, however bad we are if it does not run into a Lung Fever we think it light Lucy was sicker for two days than she ever was before & so was mr Norton The baby is sick now, dreadfull coughs they all have. In short I hardly know of a Person who has not been or is now sick tis not only so here but every where I believe there have been more People who have had the measles in this Parish than ever had them before & many of them attackd with the Influenzy at the same time. you will find by the publick Prints many of our acquaintance among the lists of the Dead mr Hilliard has left a large young Family & not any of them the best calculated to scrabble thro the world.[1] I Pity them from my Heart Madam Winthrop has also fallen a sacrifice to this dissorder[2] when I write to you last I was labouring under it. I thought it was the Rhumatism & treated it as such & I found Guaicum of great service to me it remov'd all the distress from my Breast & has been of service to my cough

It is really a most melancholy time your Brothers Family are rather better—but the infant dy'd last week it was pin'd to almost nothing— your poor mother can hardly crawl— Jo Fields wife has the measles now & has been very bad yesterday she got to Bed the child liv'd but one hour or too—[3] There are several women who are near geting to Bed & who have got to Bed now Sick with the measles

25th

Mrs Field remains dangerously Sick has been out of her right mind they say—for a fortnight but I do think the sickness has in some measure abated but tis a distress'd time yet mrs Norton & Baby are recover'd & Lucy has return'd to me once more. mrs Eunice Paine came here last week a perfect cripple not able to get out of her chair nor to walk a step without help is oblig'd to be carried in a chair & put into the chaise & is at times in great pain but still chearful— She sent to me to beg me to let her try for a few weeks what the country air & social company would do for her but I some times fear she will not rise again & indeed in her situation she can not much desire it— oh my Sister tis a dreadful thing to be so helpless & so dependant

Mrs Guil'd has been very bad with a Lung fever but is so recover'd as to be able to come up to her Mamas & is to sail for Europe next week & mr & mrs Wanewright with her— Such Betsy Mawyew will then be She is Publish'd—[4] Ben Guild is to stay with us till his parents return Cousin Polly Palmer is also to make one of our Family this summer mrs Cranch will spend it with mrs Norton— Mr Jo Cranch is gone to Springfield & will be in newyork as soon as he has done the work at Springfield. I cannot think why he did not do it this winter— Your House will be shut up next week the Doctor says tis best to be so untill some person can be found Who can be trusted with the care of it— we shall take care to put every thing we can under lock—but I do not think the House safe in such a Town as this I am concern'd for the Stores in the cellars.

I hope to hear that you are all better mrs Ware was last week put to Bed with Twins but they are both dead.[5] She had just got thro the measles— I was at Hingham last week. Uncles Family every root & Branch of it were weak haveing just had the influenzy— Mr Thaxter of Haverhill is in better health I hear— He has had several turns of the Gout which has been of service to him. Sister Shaws Family have all been Sick but are better

our remaining Nieghbours continue their story— The Familys had all remov'd to England I believe before you went away we never expected to hear of their arrival—but they did & have been soliciting miss Char^{lt.} to come to them—but just as she was going She receiv'd a Letter informing her that Mr Price the Gentleman she was going too had fallen from his Horse & fractur'd his scull in such a manner that he liv'd but two days The account of it you may have seen in the Boston newspapers with the sixty thousand pound he left to his widow & Twins which he had just had, one of which was nam'd for miss Char^{lt.}— This news was follow'd by another Letter from a young clergyman who was chaplain in the Family—informing them that the widow Surviv'd her Husband but Ten days & his mother but Ten more & that mr Brown was declar'd incurably mad That mr Prices Funeral cost Eleven hundred pounds Sterling & mrs Browns at Phyledilphia nine—[6] The dissapointment & the melancholy accation of it—was too much for miss Char^{lt} to bear. it depriv'd her of her reason for several weeks & they *appear'd* a very afflicted Family She would set whole days without speaking & then act like Clementina or some other character in a romance⁷ when carried out to ride she would fancy every large Building to be mr Price, would not believe he was dead sometimes—would not get out of the chaise when return'd from a ride—but must be forcably took out—would talk often as if he was present & twenty such crazy things—would scream & bite herself, but not very hard I believe We took no notice of it only once or twice Sent to know how she did. I really did not know how to act While I believ'd there was not a word of truth in all the story I could not go in & talk as if I did

I inquir'd of them who knew the Family while they liv'd in Boston besides Miss Char^lt. & was inform'd that mr Brick Govr. Bowdoin Judge Sulliven Harry Otis Jonathan Freeman ~~& Lucy Bowdoin~~ were acquainted with the Gentleman & that the young Ladies of every one of these Familys were intimate with their Daughter afterwards mrs Brown That mr otis had written her two Letters upon her marriage— mr Cranch was going to Boston to dine with mr Bowdoin I desir'd him to ask him about it. mrs Quincy undertook to ask mr Freeman & William miss Sullivan mr Cranch saw mr otis also. every one of these deny'd ever knowing or hearing of such a Family⁸

I then thought proper to send for miss Betsy & tell her that their characters suffer'd by their reporting such a story for truth & that nobody believ'd it—& that it was an affront to their understandings to suppose they believ'd it themselves She seem'd Surpriz'd & thought if I could see her mama She could convince me of the truth of it. I told her nothing could while these People deny'd any knowledge of them & advisd them to try themselves if they could find any one who knew them beside's her Sister

They have been to Boston severall times making a great noise but I believe have not found any one who knew them— however miss is come to her senses so it has had one good effect Was there ever such a Family—? They are good neighbours kind & charatable to the poor & tender to the sick & very sensible how is it possible they can be so impos'd upon & impos'd upon they must be or they are very wicked & very foolish

I believe we shall not hear of any more Letters but how she will brave it out to the world I cannot think— Mr Guild says he will give her a good price for the copy write if she will let it come out as a romance & I do not know any better way for her to save her credit—

What is to be done about commencment if you do not come home tis time to think of it It will soon be upon us Cousin Tom thinks we must do as we did for his Brother I wish you would write me about it. We will do every thing in our Power to give you satisfaction but I did hope you would have been here yourself I hope to hear that mrs Rogers is better my regards to her when you see her

My Love to all my dear Friends & believe me my dar Sister most affectionately yours   Mary Cranch

mr Cranch William & Lucy send Love & duty

RC (Adams Papers).

[1] Rev. Timothy Hilliard, minister of the First Church of Cambridge, died on 9 May, leaving behind his wife, Mary Foster Hilliard, and seven children under the age of eighteen (*Sibley's Harvard Graduates*, 16:60–63; *Massachusetts Centinel*, 12 May).

[2] Hannah Fayerweather Tolman Winthrop, widow of Prof. John Winthrop of Cambridge, died on 6 May (*Sibley's Harvard Graduates*, 9:247; *Boston Gazette*, 10 May).

[3] Mehitable Ludden Field (b. 1748), wife of Esther Briesler's brother, Joseph, died on 23 June (Sprague, *Braintree Families*).

[4] Elizabeth Mayhew (1759–1829) married Peter Wainwright on 5 June (vol. 3:108; Boston, *30th Report*, p. 414).

[5] Mary Clark Ware (1762–1805), wife of Rev. Henry Ware, minister of the First Church of Hingham, gave birth to twin daughters Fanny and Julia on 17 May. Julia died three days later and Fanny followed on 22 May (Sprague, *Annals Amer. Pulpit*, 8:202; Reuben Hersey, *Vital Records of Hingham, Massachusetts, ca. 1639–1844*, MBNEH:Mss 901).

[6] The *Massachusetts Centinel*, 21 April, reported the death in Clifton, England, of a William Price who fell from his horse. The notice also mentioned his father, Ezra Price, and that he left behind a widow and a substantial fortune. "Miss Char[lt.]" was Charlotte Apthorp (1773–1796), daughter of Sarah Wentworth and James Apthorp of Braintree. JQA had described Charlotte several years before as "affected and fantastical" and declared the Apthorp family "different from the rest of the world" (John Wentworth, *The Wentworth Genealogy: English and American*, 3 vols., Boston, 1878, 1:519, 526; JQA, *Diary*, 2:267).

[7] A reference to the madness of Clementina Porretta, a character in Samuel Richardson's novel *The History of Sir Charles Grandison* (1753). Clementina, separated from her beloved, became increasingly despondent and at one point carried on a conversation with an imaginary person she thought was hidden inside her closet.

[8] For Samuel Breck Sr., see AA to JQA, 12 May 1791, note 3, below. Cranch refers either to Capt. Jonathan Freeman (1728–1796) or to his son, also Jonathan Freeman (1761–1795), Harvard 1778, both of whom were Boston merchants (*Vital Records of Cambridge, Massachusetts, to the Year 1850*, 2 vols., Boston, 1915, 2:561; Frederick Freeman, *Freeman Genealogy*, Boston, 1875, p. 187). Mehitable Sullivan (1772–1847) was the daughter of James and Mehitable Odiorne Sullivan (*NEHGR*, 19:304–305 [Oct. 1865]).

Abigail Adams to Mary Smith Cranch

my dear sister   May 30 1790. N york

your kind Letter of various dates came safe to Hand. I was allarmed at not hearing from you, & feard that you were all sick. the disorder termd the Influenza has prevaild with much voilence, & in many places been very mortal, particularly upon long Island. not a Creature has escaped in our Family except its Head, and I compounded to have a double share myself rather than he should have it at all. heitherto he has escaped, not so the President. he has been in a most dangerous state, and for two or three days [I a]ssure you I was most unhappy. I dreaded his death from a cause that few persons, and only those who know me best would believe. it appears to me that the union of the states, and concequently the permanancy of the Government depend under Providence upon his Life. at this early day when neither our Finances are arranged nor our Government Sufficiently cemented to promise duration, His death would I fear have had most disasterous Concequences. I feard a thousand things which I pray, I never may be calld to experience most assuredly I do not wish for the highest Post. I never before realizd what I might be calld to, and the apprehension of it only for a few days greatly distresst me, but thanks to Providence he is again restored. Congress will set till july it is thought, and I fear adjourn to Philadelphia. I say I fear for it would be a sad buisness to have to Remove. besides I am sure there is not a spot in the united states So Beautifull as this upon which I live, for a summer residence but personal inconveniency out of the question I do not see any publick utility to be derived from it,—and I wish the Idea might Subside untill time should make it proper to fix a permanant Seat. I fear I must relinquish the Idea of visiting my Friends I want to see you all and my young Nephew whom you describe with all the fondness of a Grandmamma. mrs Norten will find her Health improved by Nursing I dare say. my Love to her and to cousin Lucy. how I long to have you come and see me.

I am affraid my dear sister I shall have to trouble you with the care of a commencment for Thomas, like that which you so kindly made for his Brother but I Shall know more about his inclinations when I hear from him I am unhappy at the account you give of mrs Turner poor Girl. She is going after her Mother at an early period of Life You did not say if the child was living, but I presume it is.

I do not know what to do with our House if the Ladies remove. I sometimes wish it was all in cash again do you know of any Body trusty enough to leave it with—

You will be so good as to have all Thomas things brought home and a Glass which still remains at mr Sewalls—[1] my best regards to mr Cranch & all other Friends

Yours most affectionaty   A Adams

RC (MWA:Abigail Adams Letters); addressed by CA: "Mrs Mary Cranch. / Braintree." Some loss of text where the seal was removed.

[1] While beginning his studies at Harvard, TBA boarded at the home of former Harvard professor Stephen Sewall, where he used CA's furniture (vol. 7:183, 341).

Abigail Adams to Cotton Tufts

dear sir   N york 30 May 1790.

I received your kind Letter of May   last week[1] I was very sorry to hear that you and your Family had not escaped the prevailing sickness. the disorder has universally prevaild here. not a single one of our Family, except mr Adams has escaped, and Polly, it was very near proving fatal too. We Have been in very great anxiety for the President. during the state of Suspence, it was thought prudent to say very little upon the Subject as a general allarm might have proved injurious to the present state of the Government.[2] he has been very unwell through all the Spring, labouring with a Billious disorder but thought, contrary to the advise of his Friends that he should exercise it away without medical assistance; he made a Tour upon Long Island of 8 or ten days which was a temporary Relief, but soon after his return he was Seazd with a voilent Plurisy Fever attended with every bad Symptom, and just at the Crisis was seazd with Hicups & rattling in the Throat, so that mrs washington left his Room thinking him dying the Physicians apprehended him in a most dangerous state. James powders had been administerd, and they produced a happy Effect by a profuse perspiration which reliefd his cough & Breathing, and he is now happily so far recoverd as to ride out daily.[3] I do not wish to feel again Such a state of anxiety as I experienced for several days I had never before entertaind any Idea of being calld to fill a Place that I have not the least ambition to attain to, the age of the two gentlemen being so near alike that the Life of one was as Probable as that of the other,[4] but such a Train of fearfull apprehensions allarm'd me upon the threatning prospect, that I Shudderd at the view. the weight of Empire, particularly circumstanced as ours is, without firmness without age and experienced without, a Revenue setled, & establishd, loaded with a debt, about which there is little prospect of an agreement, would bow down any man who is not supported by a whole Nation & carry him perhaps to an early Grave with misiry & disgrace. I saw a Hydra Head before me, envy Jealousy Ambition, and all the Banefull passions in League. do you wonder that I felt distrest at the view? yet I

63

could not refrain from thinking that even a Washington might esteem himself happy to close his days before any unhappy division or disasterous event had tarnishd the Lusture of his Reign

For the Assumption of the debts you will see in the papers a wise and judicious Speach of Father Sherman as he is call'd, and a very able & Lengthy one of mr Ames's.[5] all has been Said upon the subject that reason justice, good policy could dictate. I hope it will yet take place, but mr M— leads the Virginians like a flock of sheep. if congress should rise without assuming, I perdict that the Next year will not be so tranquil as the last, let who will hold the Reigns

With Regard to our own private affairs mr A says the Money for mr Parsons shall be ready at the Time when our sons time is up and that he approves of your proposal that John Should pay it himself to mr Parsons. as to the House, he thinks that, if a credible person or Family could be found to take the rest of the House at a Rent, equal to the present after deducting what must be given for an office, it would be advisable to let mr J— have it, but if not an office had better be procured else where, and he would request you to use your own judgment about it. if you are in want of 30 pounds before commencment you will draw for it. I am fully of your mind that the place which Pratt lives upon had better be let at a certain sum under restrictions. as to the other, it would be better for us if the whole sum had been laid out in paper securities, then one might have had a *chance* of some benifit from it. Pratt has such an Army to mantain, & tho an honest Man I believe, he must be embarressd with such a Numerous Family. I believe G Thayer a much better Farmer.[6]

As to commencment I do not know what Thomas wishes. if I could have been at Home to have taken the trouble upon myself I should have been willing that he should have made a similar entertainment to his Brothers, and am willing that it should be so now, but know not how to trouble our Friends with it. it has given both mr A & me great satisfaction to learn that he acquited himself so much to his Honour & the pleasure of his Friends at the exhibition

The Hams arrived safe and appear to be very fine. I shall pay Barnard the money for them.

Present me kindly to all inquiring Friends and believe me Sincerely Yours   A Adams

    you will be so good as to write me Soon

RC (Adams Papers); addressed by JA: "Honble Cotton Tufts / Boston"; endorsed: "M^rs· Abig^a· Adams / May 30. 1790—"

[1] Not found.

[2] Initially, George Washington's family and advisors attempted to keep news of his illness from the public to avoid causing any panic, but the situation was nonetheless widely known throughout New York and had been reported in the newspapers as early as 18 May (Washington, *Papers, Presidential Series*, 5:397).

[3] James' powders, a medicine containing oxide of antimony and phosphate of lime patented by Dr. Robert James (1705–1776) of London in 1746, was used to treat fevers and inflammatory conditions (*DNB*).

[4] Washington was only three years older than JA.

[5] The speeches by Roger Sherman and Fisher Ames in support of assumption were published in the New York *Daily Advertiser* on 27 and 29 May 1790, respectively (*First Fed. Cong.*, 13:1419–1424, 1432–1446).

[6] Matthew and Chloe Pratt of Weymouth, married on 21 Dec. 1775, had eight children at the time. The youngest, Elizabeth, had arrived on 4 April (*Vital Records of Weymouth Massachusetts to the Year 1850*, 2 vols., Boston, 1910, 2:152, 236; *Braintree Town Records*, p. 854). The Pratts had lived in JA's childhood home (the John Adams Birthplace) since 1778, originally sharing the house with Matthew's brother James and his wife. The family vacated the property by 1792 (Laurel A. Racine, *Historic Furnishings Report: The Birthplaces of Presidents John Adams and John Quincy Adams*, Quincy, Mass., 2001, p. 37–39).

John Quincy Adams to William Cranch

Newbury. Port June 5th: 1790.

Phillips delivered me at Exeter a half sheet of paper from you,[1] I trust I need not say it was very acceptable; I would only observe by the way, that I am no great friend to half-sheets. Sat verbum—[2]

We had a comfortable ordination.[3] Phillips can give you any particulars that your curiosity may wish to be informed of. He was however by an unfortunate accident detained from the dance in the Evening. The weather was rather too warm but we danced till between three & four in the morning. The company was not so numerous as I should have expected. Nothing like a crowd.— Of five dances in which I join'd, I had a Miss Newhall as my partner for four; she was in former times reputed to be a flame of mine; and help'd to make me pass my time tolerably—[4] There was however a weight hanging up on my spirits which she could not remove, nor could all the bustle and festivity of the time serve any further, than to make it somewhat less oppressive.— You have known me heretofore in such a state of mind for several days without any cause whatever; and I am persuaded that if from rational principles you cannot allow it to be a pitiable situation, your friendship will at least prevent you from considering it as a subject of derision. There is a passage in *Hamlet*, which describes in a striking manner that temper of mind, which you who are blest with a better flow of spirits cannot perhaps readily conceive. It is too long for a quotation, but if you wish to turn to it, you will find it in the sixth scene of the second Act. It begins "I have of late, but wherefore I know not, lost all my mirth &c"[5] Putnam who went with me, and who has a fund of Spirits almost inexhaustible, enjoyed the occasion to perfection: and if laughter is a full evidence of happiness his felicity was incessant. The people were very hospitable, and we made ourselves quite familiar at almost all the houses in the town. We returned home on Thursday in the afternoon, very much fatigued, and I rejoyced that the expedition was brought to a close.

My Forensic with Bridge is at the same period of advancement that it has been at from the creation of the world to the present day; and will continue, and from this moment to the end of time in statu quo. I know nothing of such a forensic, but from common report— At any rate it will not take place, for Bridge is gone to Pownalborough; is now I presume a sworn attorney in the County of Lincoln, and has no thoughts of attending Commencement. My ambition and vanity are at present so much swallow'd up by a stupid indolence, and an unmeaning listlessness, that I have not a wish to show myself at that time; but I hope the President will offer the forensic to you and some other of our classmates residing in Boston; and that you will accept it if offered.—[6] Little, as you know is gone to Virginia, and therefore the valedictory Oration must go to some one else: perhaps to Beale.[7]

I was at Haverhill about a fortnight since. They were then tolerably well, but I presume you saw M^r: Shaw at Election. He was at the Ordination with Betsey Smith and told me the family were all in good health. The young daughter is verily the child of their old age— For my part I cannot readily imagine how they can reconcile it to their consciences, to carry on that work yet. I wonder people at that time of life are not ashamed of getting children. I was so much scandalized, that I could hardly refrain from expostulating with them upon the subject.

I have not yet, I believe replied to a Letter of yours dated April 18th: it was written at Braintree,[8] and I did not know how long you would continue there; this was one reason which has prevented me from writing; another has been a deficiency of subject. My time has been spent of late to very little purpose. Park's Insurance, Buller's Nisi-Prius and Blackstone have employ'd my few studious hours for two months past;[9] and I have ventured to expose myself to imbibe opinions of infidelity by reading Hume's formidable essays; I have taken pleasure in the perusal; but I believe my religious principles will not suffer much from the catagion they contain.

The rest of my time has been but little diversified with Events. I have moved generally in one circle of company, and have had only a repetition of scenes which, however agreeable when they take place, would be very tedious in description.— We have had as a visitor for a month past, one of your fine Ladies, Miss K. Amory. I have been several times in company with her; and find her sensible and agreeable.[10]

The proximity of my departure from this place, has become an additional inducement to dissipation, and I shall henceforth scarcely look into a book. I feel very anxious to hear from Dr. Tufts upon the subject of an Office for me in Boston.— Never did I make an exchange in my situation with more unfavourable expectations.— Yet I believe it will be for the best— A firm determination to make the present a sacrifice to futurity is often the dictate of policy as well as of virtue

As to my being permitted as you say "to go about my business,"

"No more of that Hal, if thou lovest me,—
Perdition catch my soul but—"[11]

I am ever affectionately your's,   J. Q. Adams.

RC (private owner, 1957); addressed: "Mr. William Cranch. / Boston."; endorsed: "J.Q.A. / June 5th. 1790"; notation: "Mr. Phillips."

[1] Not found.

[2] A word is enough.

[3] Rev. William Frederick Rowland (1761–1843), originally of Plainfield, Conn., was ordained as minister of the First Church of Exeter, N.H., on 2 June (*NEHGR*, 1:155 [April 1847]).

[4] A member of JQA's social circle in Newburyport, Mary Newhall (b. 1769), daughter of Elizabeth Sprague and Samuel Newhall of Newburyport, married Rev. Ebenezer Coffin (1769–1816) in 1793 and relocated to Brunswick, Maine, where Coffin served as minister of the First Parish Church (JQA, *Diary*, 2:408, 433, 434; *Vital Records of Newburyport Massachusetts to the End of the Year 1849*, 2 vols., Salem, Mass., 1911, 1:275; Thompson Eldridge Ashby, *History of the First Parish Church in Brunswick, Maine*, Brunswick, 1969, p. 76–77).

[5] Shakespeare, *Hamlet*, Act II, scene ii, lines 307–324.

[6] In a letter of 21 June 1790, Harvard president Joseph Willard invited JQA to participate in the forensic disputation to be performed at the master's degree commencement on 21 July, suggesting that JQA find a partner (Adams Papers). JQA, in a reply to Willard that has not been found, declined to participate—seemingly because he could not perform with James Bridge, as he wished, and did not want to perform with Samuel Putnam. Bridge had left Newburyport on 20 May for his native Pownalborough, Maine, where he opened a law practice. On 10 July, he wrote to JQA, "It was a flattering circumstance to me, that the Government of H. C. had remembered me on this occasion, much more so that they thot me fit to contend with such an antagonist." It was Bridge's understanding that JQA now would be partnered with Samuel Putnam. He declared, "I shall set apart some portion of commencement day, to picture to my self Putnam & you performing— I am highly pleased that Putnam succeeds to my place, for his own sake as well as yours— I Judge that he will give is audience a better opinion of his capacity, than some have been accustomed to entertain—" (Bridge to JQA, 28 June, Adams Papers).

JQA's friend Thomas W. Thompson reported to JQA on 28 June that shortly after receiving JQA's refusal, President Willard called upon him "for an explanation of that part of your letter respecting the disagreements between Putnam and you. I told him in answer that you had mentioned the reason to me in confidence why you did not agree, but I supposed you would have no objection to his knowing it, tho' I presumed you would not wish to have it go from him. I then told him that you had no inclination that the performance should wind off in an anticlimax, and that Putnam had. He laughed, & acknowledged the propriety of your objection" (Adams Papers). Thompson went on to say he was commissioned by Willard to travel to Boston to ask William Cranch and John Murray Forbes if they would agree to present at the commencement ceremony, which they did. For JQA's attendance at commencement, see JQA to TBA, 28 April, note 3, above (D/JQA/12, 20 May, APM Reel 15; Quaestiones, 21 July 1790, MHi:Broadside Coll., Evans, No. 22562).

[7] Thaddeus Mason Harris, another former classmate of JQA, delivered the valedictory oration (JQA, *Diary*, 2:198-199; Boston *Columbian Centinel*, 24 July). For Benjamin Beale and Moses Little, see JQA, *Diary*, 2:166-167, 218. Little had temporarily relocated to Virginia to teach at an academy in Fredericksburg (Little to JQA, 29 July, Adams Papers).

[8] Not found.

[9] James Allan Park, *A System of the Law of Marine Insurances*, London, 1787; Francis Buller, *An Introduction to the Law Relative to Trials at Nisi Prius*, Dublin, 1768.

[10] Probably Catherine Amory (1769–1832), daughter of John Amory and Catherine Greene Amory of Boston and a cousin of JQA's Harvard classmate Jonathan Amory (*NEHGR*, 10:61–65 [Jan. 1856]).

[11] JQA combines two Shakespeare quotations. The first line is from *Henry IV, Part 1*, Act II, scene iv, lines 312-313; the second is from *Othello*, Act III, scene iii, lines 89-90.

Abigail Adams Smith to John Quincy Adams

New York june 6th 1790—

your letter my Dear Brother of May 1st I received three or four weeks past[1]—just at the moment when I was removeing, and Commenceing, again Housekeeping it takes three or four weeks to settle our minds to new Situations—and domestick Concerns employ a Considerable portion of the attention of *good* Housekeepers—even if they are favoured with good Servants— thease causes must Constitute my appology to you for omitting untill this time to answer your letter—which has confirmed my oppinion of your prudence, discretion,—and caution, upon *all* subjects of importance, when the Heart is so deeply interested it sometimes blinds the eyes of reason, and judgment,— I should indeed be very sorry that a first impression—of partiallity and attachment—and that excited by so amiable and deserving an object—should meet *eventually* with any efacement,— from Mercenary views—or be repulsed by too wise maxims of *Prudence*— from Charles account of *the* Lady who has had the Honour to have inspired you with a favourable opinion of the Sex—you may Worship without Idolitary—for he asserts that there is nothing so like perfection, in Human shape appeard since the World began (—and I presume would add the remainder) but to have done for the present with the subject of attachments and to turn our attention to one in which you and myself are some what interested—I mean the question of removeall of Congress to Philadelphia—which is to be decided in Senate in the Course of the week and which you will doubtless hear has passed the House in favour of that City—it is Supposed that the Senate will be equally divided—and that the V P— will decide the question and I can tell you it will be in favour of going to Phi— and I presume to add from a mistaken opinion respecting some certains matters things, oppinions, and influential, Characters.[2] it will be a disadvantage to Charles to be changeing his office—and particularly as he has become very steady and attentive to his Studies and is very happy in his circle of acquaintance here—but private interest we are taught to beleive should be sacrifised at the alter of Publick good— how they are in this instance Connected I do not see—for it is a Bargain as much as if such a sum was stipulated for the removeall. I mean with the magority—

june 16th—

Mr Charles Storer has arrived here within a few days and sets out tomorrow for Boston by him I shall forward this— the weather has been so warm the week past that it has not been in my Power to Coppy my Letter— you must excuse it— I hope to hear from you frequently—and be assured I am at all times your very sincere friend and Sister

A Sm[ith]

Colln Smith desires to be remembered to you—

RC (Adams Papers); addressed: "Mr John Quincy Adams / Newbury Port"; endorsed: "My sister—6. June 1790."; notation: "favourd by Mr / Charles Storer." Some loss of text where the seal was removed.

[1] Not found.
[2] The House of Representatives passed a resolution on 31 May in favor of the next congressional session's taking place in Philadelphia. On 8 June, the Senate voted on the House's resolution but defeated it by a vote of 13-11. Debate over the location of the seat of government for future sessions ended on 16 July with the passage of the Residence Act, which designated Philadelphia as the temporary capital until the federal government's permanent establishment at a site along the Potomac River in ten years' time (*First Fed. Cong.*, 6:1767-1768, 1770, 1774, 1775).

William Cranch to John Quincy Adams

Boston June 10th. 1790

Phillips has this moment handed me yours of the 5th. and I now throw by a *Qui tam*[1] in which I have been drudging this 1/2 hour, to thank you for your letter.– Whence comes this Listlessness–this depression of Spirits? What can relax the Elasticity of *your* Mind? I have often found myself in the same Situation. I felt it yesterday without being able to trace the least Cause. The Connection between the Soul & body is so inexplicable that I believe it impossible to account for the peculiar temper of mind which a man will frequently find himself in. I have sometimes puzzled myself much about the matter. I wish I had Shakespear by me that I might turn to the passage you allude to. Whatever may be the Cause, I will not make it a subject of derision; not from the motive of pure friendship alone, but because I think it a disorder or Disease to which a man may as necessarily be subjected as to the Stone or the Gout. The best remedy I believe is determined ~~Resolution~~ opposition. My depressions seldom last more than a few hours. I can generally reason them away. If neither Reason nor opposition will prevail, I take the first opportunity to run away from them. Some trivial Circumstance generally occurs in the Course of a few hours, which I convert into a source of Pleasure and I soon make out to dissipate the Gloom–

Just as I finished the last page I was interrupted in the office & since that time I have spent 2 hours with Betsy Foster, solus cum solâ.[2] I should not have mentioned this Circumstance, which is nothing very uncommon, but that it partly concerns you. She said she did not know any person she should be so afraid of, as you. I demanded the grounds upon which she had formed such an opinion. She said she was not much acquainted with you, but that she had in her pocketbook a little piece of satirical Poetry which she thought would justify her fears. She then produced a Copy of *the Vision*.[3] She was charmed with it, but she could not help being afraid of the Author. She read to me several of the Characters. Miss Jones's was *very beautiful*. She hoped Miss Frazier had profited by the Advice,–& she had been told that you now saw her Character in quite a different point of view. The latter part of Mrs Farris's,[4] she thought she could apply to herself and recieve much advantage from the hint. She did not read me that of Miss Bradbury, but said it was very illiberal & tho she did not know the lady, yet she presumed it very unjust,– Upon the whole she thought it an elegant performance; and I was not displeased to find that she discover'd so good a Judgment.

I assured her that you are one of the most ~~like~~ candid young men of my Acquaintance, and that if there is anything illiberal in the *Vision* I was certain you could not be the Author. She said she had her inforation from the lady who loaned her the Copy, but would not tell me who that lady was.

Last thursday I paid my Respects to *Mrs Otis*. It would be but a common place observation to say that the Bride & her husband made an elegant appearence. I do not think either of them improved by joining their Charms.[5] I n[ever] yet thought a Woman look'd better for FINERY [. . .]

Jack Forbes is in town. He becomes less erratic [as he ap]-proaches the Center of Life.[6] he sends you his Love.

Moses Little dined with me on Saturday. In the P.M. Foster & I accompanied him down the Bay in a boat. After we parted in Nantasket Road, he was soon out of sight.

It is a long time since I heard from our friends at New York. Our friends at Braintree & Weymouth are all well—

May cheerfulness & Peace be with you / yours affectionately

W. Cranch.

RC (Adams Papers); addressed: "Mr. John Quincy Adams / Mr Parsons's Office / Newbury Port."; endorsed: "W. Cranch 10. June 1790." and "Cranch. June 10th. 1790." Some loss of text where the seal was removed.

[1] A civil action brought by an informer in which penalty damages recovered from the defendant are to be shared by the plaintiff and the state.

[2] Probably Betsy Foster (b. 1770), daughter of Elizabeth Craigie and Bossenger Foster of Boston and sister of JQA's Harvard classmate Bossenger Foster Jr. (Boston, *24th Report*, p. 314, 320). "Solus cum sola" means to be alone with a woman (*OED*).

[3] For the text and history of JQA's "A Vision," see *Diary*, 2:154, 381.

[4] Frances Jenkins (1767–1839), daughter of Robert and Michal Jenkins of Newburyport, had married Capt. William Farris on 15 Dec. 1789 (*Vital Records of Newburyport Massachusetts to the End of the Year 1849*, 2 vols., Salem, Mass., 1911, 1:209; 2:158, 627).

[5] Sally Foster (1770–1836) married Harrison Gray Otis on 31 May 1790 (*DAB*; Boston, *30th Report*, p. 95).

[6] For John Murray Forbes, see JQA, *Diary*, 2:186, 188.

Abigail Adams to Mary Smith Cranch

my dear sister   N York June 13 1790

I received your Letter of May 16. and was very happy to find that you were all upon the recovery. we have daily mercies to be thankfull for, tho no state is exempt from trouble and vexation. the one which at present Torments me is the apprehension of a Removal from a very delightfull situation, to I know not where, and I am too short sighted, or too much blinded, to see any real advantage from a Removal unless a Permanant Seat was fixed. the fatigue and expence are objects not very pleasing in contemplation, and the Removal to a more southern state what I do not like, especially to Baltimore where I am told we cannot in any respect be half So well accomodated. if I could see that the publick good required it, I should submit with more Satisfaction, but to be every session disputing upon this subject, & sowerd as the Members are, is a very unpleasent thing. if we must move I must relinquish every Idea of visiting my Friends, and I had a latent hope that I should come for a few weeks merely on a visit, after Mrs Smith gets to Bed, which I presume will be in july. I wish to hear from my Mother & Brothers Family. I know not what to do with the House. I must request you to have an Eye to it, and if any trusty Body could be thought of to go into the kitchen part I could wish they might, but I own I do not know of any Body. all the interest we have must go to destruction, and we can barely live here upon the publick allowence. Your Romancing Neighbours may amuse themselves, but their storys will never gain credit. there is a Gentleman here, several indeed of whom I could inquire, but I am ashamed to ask, and indeed I do not recollect enough of the first part of the Story to inquire properly about it, and I have every reason to think it all fabulous. they are all together the strangest Family I ever heard of— I last week accompanied mrs Washington to the Jersies to visit the falls of Pasaick we were absent three days and had a very agreeable Tour.

I wish to have the articles I wrote for, sent by Captain Barnard. We have a fine growing season, is it so with you? I wish to hear from you with respect to commencment, what will be necessary and how can it be managed? I fear it will give you a great deal of trouble especially as you are not very well accomodated with help. as it will be impossible for us to be at Home, I have thought that it might be dispenced with, yet as Thomas has conducted himself so well I could wish that he might be gratified if it is his desire.

Be so good as to let mr smith know that Prince is very well and quite contented. we are all well & Polly is better, than she was. adieu write to me as soon as you can remember me affectionatly to all Friends.

Yours most tenderly   A Adams

RC (MWA:Abigail Adams Letters); addressed by CA: "Mrs Mary Cranch / Braitree."

John Quincy Adams to Cotton Tufts

Dear Sir.   Newbury-Port. June 18th: 1790.

I received a few days since your favour of the 10th: instt. 1 and as there will be a difficulty in procuring a tenant for the house, I should wish if possible to take some other office at least for a time. The multiplicity of your affairs almost precludes the hope that you can attend to this matter: if however you should hear of any room conveniently situated which might be hired for a temporary office, I shall rest assured of your goodness to engage it, or give me the information. I expect to be in Boston immediately after Commencement; and shall be quite impatient to get into my office; every day becomes additionally precious and important.

I am again obliged to request a sum similar to that for which I applied two months since. I hope I shall not incur the censure of extravagance. My horse adds to the expences to which I have formerly been subjected.— I am now quite destitute.

In three weeks from this I expect to be sworn in to the Court of Common Pleas at Salem. Mr: Parsons's fee will then be due and £6. for the fine for admission.—2 I wish I could see a prospect of ever counterbalancing all these outgoings.

I have no expectation of going to New-York this Summer; and indeed at present my sole object is, to get well settled in my office.

I am, my dear Sir, your very humble Servant and greatly obliged nephew   J. Q. Adams.

RC (NhHi:Presidential Autographs Coll.); addressed: "Hon: Cotton Tufts Esqr / Boston."; internal address: "Hon: Cotton Tufts Esqr:"; endorsed: "J. Q. Adams's Le[tter] / June 18. 1790."

[1] Not found.
[2] On 15 July, JQA received his certificate of admission as an attorney to the Court of Common Pleas for Essex County (Adams Papers).

Abigail Adams to Mary Smith Cranch

my dear sister   N. york july 4th 1790

A Memorable day in our calender a Church beloning to the dutch congregation is this day to be opened and an oration deliverd. this Church was the scene of misiry & horrour, the Prison where our poor Countrymen were confined, crowded & starved during the

War, & which the British afterwards destroyed. it has lately been rebuilt and this day is the first time that they have met in it.[1] they have done us the favour of setting apart a pew for us. the Clergyman is dr Lynn one of the Chapling to congress and I think a better preacher than most that I have heard to day; an oration is [to] be deliverd by dr Levingstone the other Minister belonging to this Church,[2] but as to an orater, the oratary of a Clergyman here consists in foaming loud speaking Working themselves up in such an enthusiam as to cry, but which has no other effect upon me than to raise my pitty. o when when shall I hear the Candour & liberal good sense of a Price again, animated with true piety without enthusiasm, Devotion without grimace and Religion upon a Rational System.

My Worthy Friend Mrs Rogers is returning to Boston. she has engaged to convey this to you with a Magizine which has for a Frontispeice a view of this House, but the great Beauty could not be taken upon so small a scale which is the Noble Hudson, as far distant from the House as the bottom of the Boston Mall is from the Governours House[3] if you see mrs Rogers, as it is probable you will at commencment, she will tell you how delightfull this spot is, and how I regreet the thoughts of quitting it. I shall miss her more than half N york besides. we are very well, but impatient to hear from you and Family. I wish Congress would so far compleat their buisness as not to have an other Session till the Spring. I really think I would then come home and pass the winter with you. mr Adams wants some exercise ever since the 4th of Jan'ry he has not mist one hour from attendance at Congress. he goes from Home at ten and seldom gets back till four, and 5 hours constant sitting in a day for six months together, (for He can not leave his Chair) is pretty tight service. reading long Bill, hearing debates, and not always those the most consonant to his mind and opinions putting questions, Stating them, constant attention to them that in putting questions they may not be misled, is no easy task what ever Grumblers may think, but Grumblers there always was & always will be—

adieu my dear sister Remember me affectionatly to all Friends yours   A Adams

RC (MWA:Abigail Adams Letters); addressed by CA: "Mrs Mary Cranch / Braintree"; notation by CA: "Hon by Mrs / Rogers." Some loss of text where the seal was removed.

¹ The Dutch Reformed Church known as Middle Dutch Church, located on Nassau Street between Cedar and Liberty Streets, opened in 1729. Occupied by the British during the Revolution, the sanctuary was used as a prison and its pews burned for fuel. The church was subsequently repaired and reopened for worship on 4 July 1790 (Jonathan Greenleaf, *A History of the Churches, of All Denominations, in the City of New York*, N.Y., 1846, p. 12–13).

² Rev. John Henry Livingston (1746–1825) of Poughkeepsie, N.Y., Yale 1762, studied theology in Holland from 1766 to 1770, earning a doctor of theology before being called as minister to the Dutch Reformed Church in New York City. Preaching in outlying churches during the British occupation, Livingston returned to the city in 1783 and served the church until 1810, when he became president of Queen's College, now Rutgers University. Livingston's oration focused on a verse in Exodus: "In all places where I record my name, I will come unto thee, and I will bless thee" (*DAB; New York Daily Gazette*, 6 July).

³ For this image of Richmond Hill, which appeared in the *New York Magazine*, June 1790, p. 317, see vol. 8:xv–xvi, 352.

Mary Smith Cranch to Abigail Adams

My dear Sister   Braintree July 4th 1789 [1790]

Mr Cranch has pack'd your things & sent them on Board Captain Barnard I hope they will go safe but since they were put on Board mr woodward has sent for the stone roler & says he lent it to mr Adams, that mr Borland sold it to him we sent him to the Doctor about it. If tis so I suppose it will be taken out—I told him you certainly suppos'd it purchase'd with the House or you would not have sent for it.

I cannot bear the thought of your removing so far from me, while you are at new york I live upon the hope that I shall see you in a few months, at least I go on pleasing my self so from one time to another but if you go so far without making us a visit I shall dispair of seeing you for a long time & this thought draws tears from my Eyes— A Sad train of Ideas will force themselves upon my imagination. The air of the more Southern States will not I fear be so friendly to the Health of my dear Friends as the pure air you now Breath— We are sadly seperated already I can see Sister Shaw tis true in a few hours but the expence of visiting you is not to be thought of— I wish I could be sent upon some publick Business like the Gentlemen—

I have been so full of cares that I have not been able to finish even a short Letter to you for a long time. Miss Eunice Paine has been with me for six weeks in much worse health than you ever saw her. She sent to me to get her a place to Board at, & mention'd Doctor Phipps,¹ & beg'd I would bring her out as she did not think she should be able to be mov'd if she stay'd in town another hot day— I told the person who came, to tell her I could not board her as our house would be full when my son & cousin Thomas came home but that I would send for her to stay a week with me in which time her Freinds might find some place for her I soon found she did not design to leave us if she could help it,— I sent to Doctor Phipps however to know if they would take her. they were willing to at two dollars a week—but she did not like to go, said if she could not stay with me, she had rather get some place at newtown Mrs Paine went but could not find one that would do—[2] six weeks were spent in this way till poor Lucy & I were almost made sick— we have not maid but celia & Miss Polly Palmer has been with us Ever since they Broke up house keeping Ben Guild is also with us till his Parents return from Europe besides this mrs Bond & her Daughter from Portland have been with us for three weeks—[3] What do you think I have done with them all? Miss Eunice is so helpless that she cannot rise or sit without help nor stand alone nor take one step she is to be carried from one room to the other in her chair & is in great pain The spasms seize her throat so badly sometimes that you would think she would choak She often finds great difficulty to swallow & sometimes I am affraid she will starve to death She is drawn almost double & one Leg is a quarter of a yard shorter than the other She is greatly to be pity'd. She is pind away to Skin & Bones

I was obligd to put a Bed into our east room for her while she stay'd She has at last consented to go to Doctor Phipps & has been there a week—but she has lost her Spirits & I think will not live long unless she has some relief

Mrs Hall din'd with us to day & I was surpriz'd to see how well she was & how active. her eyes are better, but mrs Turner she says is still in a very poor way I believe I told you that she had lost her Baby— Cousin Thomas is with us prepairing for commencment—he is well but thin—

Mrs Norton is a Shadow—but has her health pretty well She must not nurse her great Boy much longer—it make her too faint. Sister Shaws Family I hear are better but she has had a dreadfull sick one—poor William has been suffering for his gross feeding—

I hope to hear you have a Grandaughter soon my Love to mrs Smith poor mrs Tufts has got to Bed with another dead child & it has affected her much[4]

RC (Adams Papers). Filmed at 4 July 1789.

[1] Dr. Thomas Phipps (b. 1738), Harvard 1757, practiced medicine in Quincy from 1769 until his death in 1817 (*Sibley's Harvard Graduates*, 14:195–196).

[2] Sally Cobb Paine (1744–1816) was the wife of Robert Treat Paine (same, 12:469, 482).

[3] Hannah Cranch Bond and her three-year-old daughter of the same name (*Vital Records of Weymouth Massachusetts to the Year 1850*, 2 vols., Boston, 1910, 1:57).

[4] The RC ends here, presumably missing one or more additional pages.

Abigail Adams to John Quincy Adams

my dear son   N York July 11th 1790

I believe this is your Birth day, may you have many returns of this Period, encreasing in wisdom knowledge wealth and happiness at every Aniversary. it is a long time since I wrote to you, yet I have not been unmindfull of you I am anxious for your welfare,[1] and Solicitious for your success in Buisness. you must expect however to advance slowly at first and must call to your aid Patience and perseverence, keeping in mind the observation of that great Master of Life and manners who has said, "that there is a tide in the affairs of Men"[2] it must be some dire misfortune or calamity, if I judge not amiss, that will ever place you in the shallows, but you must expect to contend with envy Jealousy and other malignant passions, because they exist in Humane Nature.[3] as the poet observes "envy will merrit as its shade persue"[4] but a steady adherence to principals of Honour and integrity, will Baffel even those foes. ["]make not haste to be rich"[5] is a maxim of Sound policy tho contrary to the Sentiments of Mankind,[6] yet I have ever observed that wealth suddenly acquired is seldom balanced with discretion, but is as suddenly dissipated, and as happiness is by no means in proportion to Wealth, it ought to make us content even tho we do not attain to any great degree of it but to quit moralizing, col Hamilton has agreed to write to Gen[ll] Lincoln to furnish 5 Hundred dollars one hundred pounds of which you are to receive and the remainder is to be subject to dr Tufts order.[7] I would advise you to keep your Horse at Braintree. you can easily get him when you want him—

you will see by the publick papers that we are destined to Philadelphia, a Grievous affair to me I assure you, but so it is ordained—[8] when I shall see you and the rest of my Friends I know not, but if I can hear that you are doing well it will be a great satisfaction to me. Your sister and the children are here to day and send their Love to you. adieu it shall not be so long again before I write to you. Let me hear from you

Yours most affectionatly   A Adams

RC (Adams Papers). Dft (Adams Papers); filmed at [*July 1790*]. Tr (Adams Papers).

¹ In the Dft, AA originally finished this sentence with "and hope as you advance in Life that your prospects will brighten upon you."

² Shakespeare, *Julius Caesar*, Act IV, scene iii, line 218.

³ AA continues in the Dft, "and because they frequently serve as Agents against distinguishd abilities."

⁴ Pope, *An Essay on Criticism*, line 468.

⁵ "A faithful man shall abound with blessings: but he that maketh haste to be rich shall not be innocent" (Proverbs, 28:20).

⁶ From this point, the RC and Dft are significantly different. The Dft concludes as follows: "I know that you have ever been in the habit of economy, some times obliged to excercise more of it, than I could have wisht, but you know the causes and reasons. I do not wish to enumerate them. you will however be the less anxious at a continuance of an old habit, than if you was obliged to commence it at this day. thou shalt Love thy Neighbour as thyself is an injunction of holy Writ, but I know of no Law which obliges us to be unmindfull of ourselves. therefore my advise to my children is to look well to their own affairs. ~~and if they are calld into publick Life consider well if they can afford to aid their country to the sacrifice of their own~~ I hope they will never be calld to act in such perilous times as has fallen to the share of their Father. if they should I would ~~hope~~ have them keep in mind a maxim which tho it has not met with the Reward which it ought to, has ever been a source of satisfaction to himself. it is never to suffer private interest to Bias his judgment but to sacrifice ease convenience and interest for the general welfare of the country to this principal you must attribute his declared opinion for a Removal from hence to Philadelphia, for tho he Stands upon Record as voting against both N york & Philadelphia, it was oweing to his dislike to the Bill which confined them to Philadelphia for ten years & an agreement to make Potowmack the permanant Residence. as he conceived that ten years hence it might not be most proper place. it will be a greivious thing to me to be obliged to leave this delicious spot, your sister & the children your Brother & other connection, yet for the sake of Peace harmony and justice I am Submissive. I have just been reading the speach of mr Bland Lee and I am much pleased with the candour and good sense it contains. I am still in hopes that the Assumption will be obtaind but I do not think that Congress will rise till August. in your Letter to your Brother you mention the hundred pounds that you want to pay mr Parsons Your Father will write to genˡˡ Lincoln to pay it you and to draw upon col Hamilton who will answer the Bill. I would recommend to you to send your Horse to Braintree to pasture & you can easily get him when ever you have occasion."

On 6 July, Richard Bland Lee of Virginia delivered a "very handsome and pathetic speech, addressed to the passions as well as the understandings of the house" in support of the federal government's removal to the banks of the Potomac. Bemoaning "local animosities," Bland Lee emphasized the "ultimate harmony which was to be expected from fixing the permanent residence there" (*New York Daily Gazette*, 8 July).

⁷ On 15 July, JA enclosed in a letter to Cotton Tufts "a Bill on General Lincoln for five hundred dollars." JA instructed, "Out of it, you will let my Son John Quincy Adams receive one hundred Pounds lawful Money to pay Mr Parsons his Honorarium. The Remainder you will apply to repay the one hundred and twenty dollars you lately received of the General, and the rest you will reserve in your hands" (Adams Papers).

⁸ For Congress' move to Philadelphia, see Descriptive List of Illustrations, No. 3, above.

John Quincy Adams to William Cranch

Newbury-Port July 12ᵗʰ: 1790.

I have been wishing to write you, for several weeks past; I intended to have replied to your favour of the 10ᵗʰ: of last month, at

3. "VIEW OF CON—SS ON THE ROAD TO PHILADELPHIA," 1790

See page xi

an early period; but for sometime I was too lazy, and for this fort-night past I have been too busy. Just upon the point of going away, I find myself crowded with a hundred little trifling affairs, which at divers times during a residence of three years I have deferred to some leisure time; though the leisure time never came. so that I find myself really hurried.— Besides this I have been puzzled for a conveyance to Braintree where I supposed you would be; though by neglecting to write, I have actually lost one or two very good ones.

How do you find yourself in heart? I do not mean with respect to the Ladies, of whom I hope you still persist in your resolution to be greatly independent; but relative to the prospects of Life, as they begin to approach so near. This week is in my mind an important Epocha of my life. I consider in fact, that the critical period, within which my fate as it respects my connexion with Society is to be de-cided commences with my admission to the common pleas. The step which I have determined to take is in my own opinion hazard-ous. In that of many people it will perhaps appear compounded of impudence and vanity; but it has the sanction of all the friends upon whose judgment I can chiefly depend; and if I must fail, I hope and trust it shall be the fault of Fortune, and not mine.

Your Situation must for some time at least be vastly more eligible, than mine. You will not require so much business for your immedi-ate support. You will have no young rivals to rejoice at your failures or to envy your success; and you will not have the prejudice against you of assuming an higher tone than becomes you. All these disad-vantages will probably be mine. But are not difficulties the test of merit?— The test it is true may be too powerful, and I am persuaded you are not without anxiety with respect to your own prospects.

Thompson wrote me last week (I think it was) that he was charged by the president to propose to you and our friend Forbes, to write together for Commencement, but I have not heard what was the success of his application; I hope you will appear, for your own sake and for the sake of the class.—[1] The matter was conducted with me in such a manner that I had no option left me; I was obliged to refuse. You are in some manner personally concerned, and I there-fore hold myself accountable to you, for my conduct upon the occa-sion; and accordingly I shall take the first opportunity which shall present to relate the facts to you, in order to justify myself for refus-ing an honour which I will not affect to despise.

Do you still feel yourself sufficiently interested in the fate of our fair damsels to receive with pleasure information relating to them. If you do I have no such information to give you. Every thing remains nearly in the same situation as when I last saw you. But

> "When light wing'd toys
> Of feather'd Cupid, soil with wanton dulness,
> My *speculative*, and *offic'd* instruments;
> That my disports, corrupt and taint my business;
> Let housewives make a *ladle* of my *pen*.
> And all indign and base adversities
> Make head against my estimation."[2]

Rant enough—is there not? But I will drop this flimsy subject. I must mention to you one, of much more importance to me. It is that I am very much in want of fifteen or eighteen pounds. I have suffered a number of small debts in this town to remain unsatisfied, because I have always wished to have some cash at hand, till I find, they amount to eight or nine pounds. I shall have upon leaving this town about £3. to pay for arrears of board and washing; and upon taking the oath at Salem, I shall be called upon for £6. by the Clerk of the Court. To discharge all these sums, and to pay my expences to Commencem[t.] &c. I have about six dollars remaining of 20 that D[r:] Tufts supplied me with when I was last at Boston. I know not indeed what I shall do to pay my *Duty*, for which I understand the Clerk makes it a practice never to trust. I had hoped to have heard from the Doctor before this.— [I] can get a sum upon Newell's execution, and send it to Salem in a bill by Th[ursd]ay or Friday, the gratification which I shall feel at being relieved from my embarassment, will to a mind so benevolent as yours compensate for the trouble it will give you. But if this cannot be done, will you, if you can conveniently inform Doctor Tufts of my situation, and he will, I am sure if he can, send me a bill by the Post which will come to this Town next Monday the 19[th:] inst[t:] as I intend to go the next day to Cambridge. In the mean time I will make out as well as I can.

Adieu, my dear Friend, I am as usual, wholly your's.

J. Q. Adams.

RC (MHi:Cranch Family Papers); addressed: "M[r:] William Cranch. / Boston."; endorsed: "J.Q.A. July 12. 1790."; notation: "M[r:] Townsend." Some loss of text due to placement of the seal.

[1] See JQA to William Cranch, 5 June, note 6, above.

[2] Shakespeare, *Othello*, Act I, scene iii, lines 269–275. In line 273, JQA changes "skillet of my helm" to "ladle of my pen."

Abigail Adams to Mary Smith Cranch

my dear sister   july 27 1790 Richmond Hill

I received your kind Letter of july 4th the articles sent by captain Barnard all arrived in good order, and I have to acknowledg mr Cranchs kind care in attending to them.

you have got through commencment and I hope have not been made sick with the trouble and fatigue. we had a pleasent day here, not over Hot and I pleasd, myself with the hope that it was so with you. We got Thursdays paper, but had very little account of commencment.[1] I know you must have been too much fatigued, and too buisily occupied to be able to write

I do not know what to do with the House. I wish with all my Heart that Mears would go in. I did not once think of her, but I do not know any person I would so soon commit the care to.[2] mr Brisler is anxious about the wine Casks he says that there are only two Iron hoops on each and he fears the other will Rot off. if you have not the Keys, pray get them and let me request you to have the things lookd to. the Rats he says may undermine the Bottled wine which is pack'd in sand. he is very anxious about it, and I am not less so. I beg you my dear sister to accept of a dozen of the wine and present half a dozen bottles to my mother. if it is not drawn of let Thomas go, and do it, and send him for the Keys. if the casks look like to give way, I must request that it may be New hoopd or otheways taken care of. I do not know when I shall see you. I think it would be a cordial to me, and mr Adams pines for relaxation, tho if one was to Credit the Clamours of the Boston papers we should imagine that their was nothing going forward but dissipation, instead of which, there is nothing which wears the least appearence of it, unless they term the Pressidents Levee of a tuesday and mrs Washingtons drawing of a fryday such, one last two & the other perhaps three hours[3] She gives Tea Coffe Cake Lemonade & Ise creams in summer all other Ladies who have publick Evenings give Tea coffe & Lemonade, but one only who introduces cards, and She is frequently put to difficulty to make up one table at whist. pray is not this better than resorting to Taverns, or even having supper partys some amusement from the Business of the day is necesserry and can there be a more Innocent one than, that of meeting at Gentlemens Houses and conversing together, but faction and Antifederilism may turn every Innocent action to evil we are all well you see my pens are bad beyond description, and dinner calls.

Love to all Friends from / your ever affectionate / sister

A Adams

RC (MWA:Abigail Adams Letters); addressed by CA: "Mrs Mary Cranch. / Braintree"; notation by CA: "favd by / Mr Codman."

[1] The Boston *Independent Chronicle*, 22 July, the day after Harvard's commencement, merely listed the names of graduating bachelor's and master's students. Newspapers published during the following week included more details about the students' performances, including TBA's conference with Nahum Fay and Thomas Gray on painting, music, and oratory (Boston *Columbian Centinel*, 24 July; *Boston Gazette*, 26 July; *Independent Chronicle*, 29 July).

[2] Cranch replied to AA in a letter of 27 Aug. that George Mears was "building a house or he would have gladly have gone into yours" (Adams Papers). For the Mears family, see vol. 8:444.

[3] A piece in the Boston *Independent Chronicle*, 15 July, sharply criticized the extravagance and inaction of the federal government. Citing the enormous debt, the author asked, "Is this a moment, then, for an absurd and ridiculous imitation of European manners and establishments." The author went on to censure Congress for its "astonishing delays" and for "months idly wasted in impotent debate." A similar indictment published on 3 June declared, "Time is not to be spent in amusement, or dissipation, but attentively improved for the *dispatch* of the public business. . . . Ideas of *foreign pomp*, *parade* and *luxury*, are rather to be *spurned*, than *courted* and *fostered* by a young republic."

Abigail Adams to Cotton Tufts

my dear sir   August 2d 1790 N york

Commencment being finish'd some of your cares for my Family will be lesned. I esteem it amongst my blessings that my young Family have all past through Colledge with so much Reputation, and that in scenes strewd thick with dangers, they have escaped so well. I hope their future progress through Life may be equally pure. I feel myself indebted to many of my Friends for the kind care they have excericed towards my sons in the almost constant absence of their Parents, and particularly So to you Sir whose attention has been truly Parental. I hope they will ever mantain towards you a gratefull sense of your kindness.

Mr Adams proposes that Thomas should come on here as soon as may be. I hardly know what studies to advise him too. for some time he appeard inclined to merchandize, but without Stock, there is but a poor prospect, and I do not think that scholors ever make very good Merchants. Mr Adams remitted a Bill of 500 dollors to you which I presume was duly received, but immediatly after this he heard of the arrival of 2 casks of wine which we Suppose will more than swallow up the surpluss. his intention is to send on 40 or 50 dollors more by dr Jeffries who will leave this City in the course of the week. Congress are not yet up, they hope to rise in a few days. you have no doubt seen the funding & Assumption Bills they are not what was wisht by many members of each House, but the danger of finally loosing the Bill was so great, that it was consented to by both houses as an anchor that it would not do to quit, least the whole should go to shipwreck the funding the whole debt at once, at an interest of four pr cent and placing the indents upon the same footing, was what was most earnestly wishd for by many, but the states who were opposed to it, Clamourd so loudly that the best, is done that could be effected the House are now upon ways and means, designing that the first Quarters interest shall be paid on the first of April next. I will thank you sir to let me know by my son Thomas the amount of the little interest I have in your Hands and what proportion is state, & what continential, and whether you cannot fund it in your own Name, giving me some memorandum that you hold in your Hands such an interest belonging to me which may serve in case of accident.[1]

The wine which I suppose is in mr Codmans store we should be glad to have sent round by Barnard our present intention being, not to Remove this winter, but when Congress set mr Adams designs to go & tarry only during the session, which he flatters himself, will be a short one

my best Respects to your good Lady I am sorry for your daughters repeated misfortune I wish my dear sir you could make us a visit here. you would be delighted with this situation, and not in the least wonder, that I shall have a regreet at quitting it—

I am most affectionatly yours   A Adams

RC (NHi:Misc. Mss. Adams, Abigail); endorsed: "M^rs· A. Adams Aug. 18. 1790."

[1] Tufts enclosed the requested list of public securities in his letter of 28 Sept., below. In a letter of 3 Oct., AA again asked Tufts about putting the certificates in his name: "If you can Subscribe as a trustee for an other, I should like that method, to do it in your own Name would be equally agreeable to me, unless it should subject you to any difficulty" (NHi:Misc. Mss. Adams, Abigail). Tufts responded to AA on this point in his letter of 7 Jan. 1791, below.

Abigail Adams to Mary Smith Cranch

my dear sister   Newyork 8 August 1790

I have the pleasure to inform you that last Night mrs Smith got to Bed with an other fine Boy. We could have all wisht it had been a Girl, but rest satisfied with the sex as it a very fine large handsome Boy and both mother and child are well. She spent the day with me on fryday, and I urged her as I had Several times before, to accept a Room here, and lie in here, as the house in which she is is Small and Hot. she told me she would come out, and the next day intended [to ge]t her things ready for the purpose, but found herself so un [wel]l on Saturday, yesterday that she could not effect it. I have been very un well myself for a fortnight, so that she did not let me know she was ill, untill I had the agreeable intelligence of her being safe abed. I shall get her here as soon as possible I have both the children with me. I have not heard a word from you since commencment, and I expect all my intelligence from you. Congress rise on tuesday I wish and long to come to Braintree, but fear I shall not effect it. how does mrs Norten stand the Hot weather? your Grandson grows a fine Boy I dare say I should be quite charmd to see him & my dear cousin Lucy when is she to be married to that said Gentleman? pray give my Love to her and tell her she need not have been so sly about it.[1] I had a few lines from Thomas just before he set out for Haverhill[2] I expect him on here daily, and think he had best send his things Round by Barnard. I have nothing new to entertain you with unless it is my Neighbours the Creek Savages who visit us daily. they are lodgd at an Inn at a little distance from us. they are very fond of visiting us as we entertain them kindly, and they behave with much civility. yesterday they signd the Treaty, and last Night they had a great Bond fire dancing round it like so many spirits hooping, singing, yelling, and expressing their pleasure and Satisfaction in the true Savage Stile. these are the first savages I ever saw. mico maco, one of their kings dinned here yesterday and after dinner he confered a Name upon me the meaning of which I do not know, Mammea he took me by the Hand, bowd his Head and bent his knee, calling me Mammea, Mammea. they are very fine looking Men placid contanances & fine shape. mr Trumble says, they are many of them perfect Models. MacGillvery, dresses in our own fashion speaks English like a Native, & I should never suspect him to be of that Nation, as he is not very dark he is grave and solid, intelligent and much of a Gentleman, but in very bad Health.[3] they return in a few days.

adieu my dear sister Remember me affectionatly to all Friends I see miss Nancy Quincy is married, I wish her much happiness
 Yours   A Adams

RC (MWA:Abigail Adams Letters); addressed by CA: "Mrs Mary Cranch. / Braintree"; notation by CA: "pr favor / Doc^r Jeffries." Some loss of text where the seal was removed.

¹ In her letter of 4 Oct., Cranch seemed puzzled by AA's comment about her niece's imminent marriage: "What did you mean about Lucys going to be married there never was the least probability of it— She is a good Girl & I hope Will have a good husband Sometime or other but I Should not know What to do Without her at present" (Adams Papers). Lucy Cranch would not marry until 1795.

² Not found.

³ On 21 July 1790, Creek chief Alexander McGillivray and a delegation of approximately thirty other Creek leaders and warriors arrived in New York City to negotiate a permanent treaty with the U.S. government. McGillivray (b. ca. 1759), the son of a Scottish trader and a woman of French and Creek ancestry, was classically educated in Charleston and Savannah prior to the Revolution. When his father, a loyalist, abandoned the colonies for Scotland, McGillivray rejoined the Creeks and eventually became the chief spokesman for the Indian tribes of the South. In frequent negotiation with the governments of Spain, Georgia, and the United States, McGillivray remained a shrewd and powerful advocate for the Creek people until his death in 1793.

The visit took place at the invitation of George Washington and Henry Knox, who sought to assert executive control over Indian policy by designating each tribe as a sovereign nation with whom the United States must negotiate at the federal level. Of immediate concern was recent action by the Georgia legislature to sell large tracts of Creek land to private companies, raising the prospect of an expensive Indian war on the southern frontier.

The Creek leaders were received with great fanfare as they traveled to the nation's capital. Upon arriving in New York, they were greeted by the St. Tammany Society and paraded through the city past Federal Hall. One newspaper reported, "Col. McGil-livray was dressed in a suit of plain scarlet; and the other Chiefs and Warriors in their national habits. They appear to be men of the first distinction, and their behaviour indicated strong marks of their approbation of the reception which they met with in this city." The members of the delegation stopped at the homes of Washington and Gov. George Clinton before dining at the City Tavern, where they would lodge during their stay.

Following several weeks of negotiations and ceremony, an agreement that became known as the Treaty of New York was approved by the Senate on 7 Aug. 1790. According to the treaty, the United States displaced Spain as the Creeks' main ally and, in return, promised to protect a large area of Creek land from encroachment by white settlers. During a formal signing ceremony on 13 Aug., the treaty was read aloud before a large audience. According to one report, "The President then signed the treaty—after which he presented a string of beads as a token of perpetual peace; and a paper of tobacco to smoke in remembrance of it; Mr. McGillivray rose, made a short reply to the President, and received the tokens. This was succeeded by the shake of peace, every one of the Creeks passing this friendly salute with the President; a song of peace performed by the Creeks concluded this highly interesting, solemn and dignified transaction." The Creeks left New York shortly afterwards on 19 August. Within two years, the treaty had been rendered meaningless; the U.S. government was unable to halt white settlement in Creek territory, and McGillivray signed a new agreement with Spain in July 1792 (*DAB*; *New York Daily Gazette*, 22 July 1790; New York *Gazette of the United States*, 14, 21 Aug.; Joseph J. Ellis, *American Creation: Triumphs and Tragedies at the Founding of the Republic*, N.Y., 2007, p. 135, 149–154, 156–159).

Mary Smith Cranch to Abigail Adams

My dear Sister   Braintree August 9th 1790

It is so long since I have heard from you that I begin to be very uneasy I am the more so as I know it is about the time for mrs Smith to be confin'd & you did not give me the most favourable account of her health in your last letter. you I know feel all the anxeity of a tender mother for her but I hope to hear soon that She has presented you with a fine Grandaughter— my little Richard grows astonishingly he is not five months old & yet he can step very well & stand alone with only resting his hands upon a Chair & is so fat that I wonder how his mama can tend him, but She poor girl is wasted to nothing almost. She wants better living than a country Clergyman can afford— I made her get some wine & drink a glass or two of it every day She complains of such a faintness as you use'd to feel when you nurs'd

I dare say you thought much of us on commencment day. we had a fine day of it, but a very Crouded assembly. I did not go till the morning & then went to meeting, but I was made quite sick by it— I came home about ten a clock with a violent sick head-ack mrs Norton came the day before & keept house for me She wanted to go but I perswaid'd her not to

every thing was in very nice order: We dind above a hundred People besides the multitude who came in to drink, & eat cake & cheese in the morning & afternoon— our cake was excllint I wanted to send you a peice of it—but the company gave the best proof in the world of its being good—there was only a few Broken Peices came home. We had thirty one chickens, 2 Legs of Bacon four Tongues, a rump of Beef roast'd—& a round allamoded, Lettuce & green Peas. Lucy went up with her Brother the day before & had all the Tables sat in the morning— we had mr Beals as before for five days—[1] For care & fidelity he is another mr Brisler— We took Celia with us to be in the kitchen to Boil the Peas wash the Dishes &C— we got a lower Room for that purpose. Mr Cranch had laid up the Benches & tables we had before for this purpose—but I believe I have done now with the care of commencments— We dressd all the meat here but the roast Beef—mrs Foster did that for us[2]

you will see an account of the performances in the Paper—but it will not tell you that your son spoke as well both as to matter & manner as any of them He has left college my Sister with deservedly the best characture in the World

His behavior has been not only unexceptionable but exemplary says the President & professors & not a hint did I ever hear of his misconduct either in Publick or Private. His characture is form'd I trust go sweet youth & act your part in the world in such a manner as finally to obtain the approbation of the Judge of all the Earth— It must give you pleasure to have him with you—but I do not know how to part with him. Cousin JQA has been with us a few days this week he is well, has taken an office from one part of your house in Boston & is to Board with Doctor Welsh[3] I shall go to Town this week & see what State is cloaths & linnen are in & put him into good repair Mr Cranch has inlarg'd his Shop & made an office for William in one part of it—& now My dear Sister I know we can feel for each other— may success attend them both as they act with integrity & honour

There is a Gentleman & Lady from Demerarah who are come to this country for their health who wish to hire your house & furniture for a year or more mr Alleyne apply'd to me to know if you would lett it & desir'd me to ask you She is a cousin of his they have no children & but two Servants & mr Alleyns says they are steady good People— I told him I hop'd you would come & Spend the wintre here your self: I cannot give up the hope—how I shall feel to have you go further & not see your Face once more— we think it will not be best to remove your Books from the office they will be safer there than any where else— We go to the House & open & air it as often as we think it necessary I am more concern'd about the carpets than any thing else I am affraid the moths will get at them— we are going this week to make a Brushing & rubing— All the things which were brought from college are to be put up & stow'd away— we took part of a hamper of Porter which we found in your cellar for cousin Tom. one dozen was left which we return'd to the cellar again we did not take any of the wine, but bought a few Gallons

Miss Nancy Quincy was married, the week befor last Deacon Storys Family & mrs Quincy & Son & Deacon Marsh were all the company— William & Lucy din'd with them the next day—

Ned green is dead. What a dreadful thing it is to dye unlamented—[4]

our worthy uncle Quincy was at meeting to day & is well mrs Eunice is yet at Doctor Phipps's but is no better—I think she will never return to Boston again. if she continues to wast as fast as she had done there will not be much left to remove any where. her Brother & his wife came to see her last week & brought her every thing she wanted for her comfort mrs Paine & Mrs Greenleaf have been since—they appear to wish to make her last days as comfortable as they can—[5]

William & Lucy are gone to Weymouth their Sister was very sick yesterday & took a Puke I hope she is better but I feel uneasy she had been eating milk & made her stomach ack—

mrs Hall is well but mrs Turner does not get well—

My Love to mr Adams & My dear Cousins all— pray write soon I cannot bear to be so long without hearing from you— Shall you want any rose wather

mr Cranch sends Love— I am with the tenderest affection ever your Sister—   M Cranch

RC (Adams Papers).

[1] For Cranch's account of a similar commencement celebration for JQA, see vol. 8:132–133.

[2] Possibly Elizabeth Hiller Foster, wife of James Foster of Boston (Frederick Clifton Pierce, *Foster Genealogy*, Chicago, 1899, p. 214; vol. 7:256).

[3] JQA boarded at the home of Thomas and Abigail Kent Welsh, located at 39 Hanover Street in Boston, until his departure for Europe in 1794. A room in the Adamses' house in Boston, conveniently situated across from the courthouse at 23 Court Street, served as his law office (D/JQA/12, 22 July 1790, APM Reel 15; D/JQA/22, 21 June 1794, APM Reel 25).

[4] Edward Green (b. 1733) of Boston died in late July 1790 (Boston *Columbian Centinel*, 31 July). For his history of financial misconduct, see vol. 6:275.

[5] For Eunice Paine's sister Abigail Paine Greenleaf, see vol. 1:198.

John Quincy Adams to Abigail Adams

My dear Madam.   Boston August 14th: 1790.

I received on Commencement day, your obliging favour of the 11th: of last month, and should have replied to it before this time, had I not been constantly employ'd in making and executing my arrangements for my removal to this place. For kind wishes which you are pleased to express for my welfare and happiness, I can only return the sincerest assurances of gratitude; Thanks, are called the exchequer of the poor,[1] but there are favours, (and such must be those from Parents to their children) which can admit of compensation from no other fund. To improve for my own benefit the advantages which I owe to the goodness of my Parents, is all they require of me; and I can only lament, that so great a length of time must necessarily elapse before I can demonstrate by the Event that their labours have not been in vain.

I have this week opened an Office, in the front Room of your house in Court Street, from which place I now write. I have but little expectations at present from business, and I am sometimes tempted to regret, that I came to a place where the profession is so much crowded, and where my expences must be considerable. The only thing that keeps me here is that I know not of a more advantageous Situation; and if Fortune should be disposed to befriend me, she will have a larger scope here, than she could have in the woods.

My anxiety will be very great, untill I shall stand upon my own ground. At my time of life it is a grievous mortification to be dependant for a subsistence even though it be upon a Parent.

With respect to the horse, I have ventured to keep him here notwithstanding your direction upon a proposal of Doctor Welsh, and shall keep him untill I have your further commands. The Doctor has a very good Stable, and a boy who can take care of the horse. He has offered to stable the horse, and to be at one half the expence of keeping him for the occasional use of him, as he does not keep an horse at present himself. This will I think render it less expensive than it would be to keep him at Braintree; and it is very probable to me that the necessary occasions upon which I shall want an horse, would in the course of a year, amount to a greater sum in the hire of horses, than the keeping of this one, upon these terms. If however you should be of a different opinion, I will send him to Braintree immediately upon receiving your instructions so to do.

You will have heard before this that Miss Nancy Quincy is married, to Mr Packard, and thus you will perceive your *darling* project for the advancement of your Son blasted even before the bud.—[2]

Indeed Madam I hope you will not think the worse of your Son, if he assures you that he never will be indebted to his wife for his property. I once seriously thought that I should easily be enabled to make matrimony an instrument of my Avarice or my Ambition. But really it is not so, and I am fully perswaded like Sancho, that if it should rain *mitres* in this way, there would be never an one to fit my head.[3]

I know not of any news. The principal topic of conversation this week has been the arrival of the Columbia from an expedition which has carried her round the world. The adventurers after having their expectations raised to the highest pitch, were utterly disappointed; and instead of the immense profits upon which they had calculated, will scarcely have their outsets refunded to them. This failure has given universal astonishment, and is wholly attributed to the Captain, whose reputation now remains suspended between the qualifications of egregious knavery and of unpardonable stupidity.[4] M^r. Barrell, I am informed is not discouraged, but, intends to make the experiment once more, and if he should not meet with any body disposed to second him they say he will undertake it at his single risk and expence.—[5] The people of this vessel have brought home a number of curiosities similar to those which you have seen at Sir Ashton Lever's Museum.[6] They have likewise brought a native of the Sandwich Islands, who bound himself as a servant to one of the passengers. He was paraded, up and down our Streets yesterday, in the dress of his Country; and as he speaks our Language has been conversed with by many Gentlemen in this Town.—[7] One of the passengers it is said, has kept a very accurate Journal of the Voyage, and proposes to extract from it a relation for publication.[8] It will probably be curious; though among uncivilized and barbarous Nations it appears to me the observations of travellers, must generally consist chiefly in a repetition of what was noticed by the first adventurer who discovered them. The situation of a Country, and whatever relates to inanimate matter continues the same. The peculiarities of the animal Creation when once remarked, seldom afford any further field for information.— It is from Man that we must always derive our principal source of entertainment and instruction. And although the knowledge of the human heart may perhaps be promoted by inferences drawn from the manners and customs of a people newly discovered, yet the savage Inhabitants of a petty Island, cannot have many customs or opinions which may not be discoverable to the first Man who becomes acquainted with them;

I wish to be remembered affectionately to all my friends with you. I shall write to my brother Charles as soon as I have the courage; which will be when I shall be able to inform him that I have *one* Client.

I am your affectionate Son.   J. Q. Adams.

RC (Adams Papers); addressed: "M^rs: A. Adams. / Richmond-Hill."; docketed: "J Q Adams / to / his Mother / Boston August 14th / 1790."

[1] Shakespeare, *Richard II*, Act II, scene iii, line 65.

[2] JQA had long been teased about a potential marriage to Nancy Quincy, who was almost four years his senior (vol. 6:52; vol. 7:169).

[3] JQA paraphrases from Laurence Sterne's *The Life and Opinions of Tristram Shandy*, Vol. I, chap. 12, in which Yorick reveals his swollen head and says, "I might say with *Sancho Pança*, that should I recover, and 'Mitres thereupon be suffer'd to rain down from heaven as thick as hail, not one of 'em would fit it.'" Sterne, in turn, is borrowing from Migel de Cervantes, *Don Quixote*, Part I, book 1, ch. vii.

[4] On 9 Aug., the *Columbia* arrived in Boston Harbor following a three-year voyage. Departing from Boston in Sept. 1787 along with a sloop, *Washington*, the ship had traveled nearly 50,000 miles as it circled the globe, trading along the Northwest coast and unloading furs in China before returning to Massachusetts. The expedition was originally commanded by Capt. John Kendrick (b. ca. 1740) of Wareham, Mass., but he elected to remain with the *Washington* in the Northwest rather than return to New England. Widely regarded as incompetent and dishonest, Kendrick continued to use the sloop for trading voyages to China, pocketing the profits, until his death in 1794. It was Capt. Robert Gray (1755-1806) of Tiverton, R.I., original master of the *Washington*, who commanded the *Columbia* on its voyage back to Boston. The Boston *Columbian Centinel*, 11 Aug. 1790, reported that the ship, upon "coming to her moorings in the harbour fired a federal salute—which a great concourse of citizens assembled on the several wharfs,

returned with three huzzas, and a hearty welcome" (*Voyages of the "Columbia" to the Northwest Coast, 1787–1790 and 1790–1793*, ed. Frederic W. Howay, MHS, *Colls.*, 79:vi, viii, xi–xiv [1941]).

⁵ Joseph Barrell (1739–1804), a wealthy Boston merchant, was one of six men who financed the first expedition of the *Columbia*. Although the ship's maiden voyage was a financial failure, Barrell and a slightly different group of owners invested additional resources to launch a more successful second expedition, commanded by Capt. Robert Gray, in September (Thwing Catalogue, MHi; *Voyages*, p. vi, viii–x).

⁶ For Sir Ashton Lever's museum, see vol. 5:323, 324.

⁷ This man apparently returned to the Sandwich Islands in Nov. 1792 during the second voyage of the *Columbia* (*Voyages*, p. 417–418).

⁸ Two men kept journals during the first expedition of the *Columbia*. That of Joseph Ingraham, the first mate, has not survived. A log kept by Robert Haswell (b. 1768), who began the voyage as third mate and ended it as second officer, is extant but was not published until the late nineteenth century (same, p. xv–xviii).

Abigail Adams to John Quincy Adams

Dear Son   Richmond Hill 20 August 1790

I congratulate you upon your having setled yourself thus far, and am pleasd to find you so well accommodated. you have a good office, a Good Library, and an agreable Family to reside in. be patient and persevering. you will get Buisness in time, and when you feel disposed to find fault with your stars, bethink yourself how preferable your situation to that of many others, and tho a state of dependance must ever be urksome to a generous mind, when that dependance is not the effect of Idleness or dissapation, there is no kind parent [bu]t what would freely contribute to the Support and assistance of a child in proportion to their ability. I have been daily in expectation of seeing your Brother Thomas here. he must be expeditious in his movements or he will be calld to an account for *visiting* a most heinious offence you know in the view of those, who think there is more merrit in staying at Home. Your Father talks of taking a Tour to the eastward. it would be peculiarly agreeable to me to accompany him, but there are reasons, not of state, but of purse which must prevent it; and yet I think I could plan the matter so as that it would be no great object, to pass a couple of Months with our Friend's. Lady Temple & mrs Atkinson will set out tomorrow by way of RhoadIsland. they have offerd to take Letters to my Friends, but I have been rather neglegent in writing the weather has been so extreme Hot. I have the two Boys with me Billy & John, and it is employment enough to look after them. your sister has a third Son. heaven grant that she may add no more to the stock untill her prospects brighten. a Marshells office will poorly feed a Family and I see no prospect of any other at present.¹ I will give you

one peice of advise, never form connextions untill you see a prospect of supporting a Family, never take a woman from an Eligible
situation and place her below it. remember that as some one says in
a play ["]Marriage is chargeable"[2] and as you never wish to owe a
fortune to a wife, never let her owe Poverty to you. Misfortunes may
Surround even the fairest prospects. if so Humbly kiss the Rod in
silence, but rush not upon distress and anxiety with your Eyes
open— I approve your spirit. I should be ashamed to own him for a
son who could be so devoted to avarice as to marry a woman for her
fortune. Pride and insolence too often accompany wealth and very
little happiness is to be expected from sordid souls of earthy mould.[3]
I always loved Nancy Quincy from a native good humour and honesty of heart which she appeard to possess—but I never was in earnest in ralying you about it. (if you should perceive that the spelling
of this Letter is different from what you have been accustomed too,
you must Set it down for Websters New) plan.[4] I write in haste, as I
must dress for the *drawing Room* this Evening, and take my Letter
to Town—

We have had our Friends the Creeks very near us for a Month
and very constant visiters to us some of them have been— I have
been amused with them and their manners. tho they could not converse but by signs they appeard Friendly, manly, generous gratefull
and Honest. I was at Federal Hall when the Ceremony of Ratifying
the Treaty took place it was truly a curious scene, but my pen is so
very bad that however inclined I might be to describe it to you, I
cannot write with pleasure. I inclose you some papers that I believe
were mislaid before[5]

Remember me to the dr and mrs Welch and all other Friends—
you must go to mr Thatchers meeting and get a seat in the old
pew—

yours   A A

RC (Adams Papers); addressed by CA: "M[r:] John Quincy Adams. / Boston.";
endorsed: "My Mother: 20. Aug[t:] 1790." and "M[rs:] Adams. Aug[t:] 20[th:] 1790." Some
loss of text where the seal was removed.

[1] On 25 Sept. 1789, the Senate approved
George Washington's nomination of WSS as
marshal for the district of New York, a position he held until his appointment as supervisor of revenue for the same district in
March 1791 (*First Fed. Cong.*, 2:49, 130). See
also AA2 to Elizabeth Cranch Norton, 7 Feb.
1791, note 2, below.

[2] Thomas Otway, *Venice Preserv'd; or, A
Plot Discovered*, Act II, scene ii, line 42.

[3] Isaac Watts, "Few Happy Matches," line
13.

[4] Noah Webster (1758-1843) introduced a
spelling book in 1782 for American school-
children that sought to standardize English
spelling and pronunciation. Later known as
The American Spelling Book, the text proved
extremely popular and launched Webster's

career as a writer and lexicographer. Webster went on to advocate for reforms in English spelling, publishing in 1789 *Dissertations on the English Language*, a book based on his popular lectures and supplemented by an appendix titled "Essay on a Reformed Mode of Spelling." AA probably refers here to a 1790 publication, *A Collection of Essays and Fugitiv Writings*, in which Webster employed his ideas about spelling reform and, in doing so, subjected himself to widespread ridicule (*DAB*; Emily Ellsworth Fowler Ford, comp., and Emily Ellsworth Ford Skeel, ed., *Notes on the Life of Noah Webster*, 2 vols., N.Y., 1912, 1:295).

[5] Not found.

Abigail Adams to Mary Smith Cranch

my Dear sister   Sunday eve Nyork August 29 1790

I last Night received your Letter which I have long expected, dated 9th of August, and thank you for your account of commencment, as well as your care. I have written to you a number of times and wonderd much at not hearing from you. by dr Jeffries I wrote you an account of mrs Smiths getting well to Bed. She is very cleverly and has been once out to see me tho only three weeks last Night since she got to Bed, but the weather being so warm she has got the Air very soon or rather never Shut it out. She was going to dine below stairs to day, and said if she was not asshamed she would go with me to take leave of mrs washington who sets out tomorrow for Mount Vernon. I am [goin]g into Town for that purpose, and shall part with her, tho I hope, only for a short time, with much Regreet. no Lady can be more deservedly beloved & esteemed than she is, and we have lived in habits of intimacy and Friendship. in short the Removal of the principal connections I have here serves to render the place delightfull as it, is much less pleasent than it has been.

I have been almost upon the point of visiting Braintree. I even made several arrangments for that purpose in my own mind, but had it all overthrown by an arrangment for a Removal to Philadelphia this fall mr Adams talks now of going there, to look out a House, as he begins to think he shall be very misirable at Lodgings, but I will hope that I may come next summer, and be a Border with you for some months if we should let our House if the people you mention are responsible and worthy people I should have no objection to letting it to them with the furniture the best carpet & china & Glass tho not much excepted.— I know more injury may be done to furniture in one year than a House can easily sustain in several. a Hundred dollars goes but a little way in good furniture. perhaps they may run away with a fancy that as the house is unoccupied we would readily let it for trifle. the House I should rather let at a low

Rent than it should stand empty, but not the furniture 200 dollors a year or not much less I should expect to have for it including the Garden stables &c there are three Beds two very good and three carpets besides the best; at Philadelphia we must give four hundred for an empty house and that out of the City, but I shall ha[ve] opportunity to write you more fully if they should have any fancy for taking it and I would consult the dr about it.

we are anxious to get Thomas here and wonder that he does not come on pray hasten him as mr Adams is very ~~anxious~~ desirious to have him here— my dear Sister I never take the ten guineys so pray say no more about them I am under obligations to you for the care and attention to my children which nothing pecuniary can repay & it hurts me that I have it not in my power to do as I wish— I hope our young folks will get into Buisness I am glad mr Cranch will be like to get something for his hard Labour— I hope the remaining part of the debt will be provided for in less than ten years—[1] our publick affairs look very auspicious not withstanding the grumbling I have many more things to Say to you but am obliged to close to go into Town, but will write to you soon again— we are all well. you may write by the post they have not Chargd us postage yet and I presume will not as the New act if it had past excepts the President and vice Pressident, and as it is known to be the intention of congress, I suppose they will not tax us with postage under the present act. [2]

Love to all Friends / ever yours   A Adams

RC (MWA:Abigail Adams Letters); addressed: "To / Mrs Mary Cranch / Braintree"; endorsed by Richard Cranch: "Letter from M^rs / A Adams (NY) / Aug 29th. 1790." Some loss of text where the seal was removed.

[1] On 4 Aug., after more than six months of debate, the Funding Act became law. Under the legislation, which consolidated the debts of the individual states, owners of state bonds were to exchange their certificates for three types of federal securities: some paying 6 percent interest immediately, some 3 percent immediately, and some 6 percent in 1801 (*First Fed. Cong.*, 5:713–715, 722).

[2] Congress passed on 22 Sept. 1789 an act providing for the temporary establishment of the Post Office under the Constitution. Leaving virtually unchanged an ordinance passed under the Articles of Confederation in Oct. 1782, this legislation was subsequently renewed on 4 Aug. 1790 and 3 March 1791 when the House and Senate were unable to agree on a process for determining postal roads. The initial ordinance exempted members of Congress, the commander in chief, and other government officials from paying postage; a Post Office bill introduced in the House on 7 June 1790 that failed to pass proposed similar franking privileges for the president, vice president, and others. An act reorganizing the postal service under the new government eventually became law on 20 Feb. 1792; it too stipulated that all letters and packets to and from the president and vice president be carried free of charge (Dorothy Ganfield Fowler, *Unmailable: Congress and the Post Office*, Athens, Ga., 1977, p. 6, 9, 11, 13; *JCC*, 23:678; *First Fed. Cong.*, 6:1651–1654, 1684, 1690, 1712–1713, 1716–1718; *U.S. Statutes at Large*, 1:237).

John Quincy Adams to Abigail Adams

My dear Madam   Boston August 29th: 1790.

I received by M[rs]: Atkinson your favour of the 20th: inst[t]: which has added not a little to the weight of anxiety which, before hung heavy upon my mind. The Suspense in which I must continue, I know not how long with respect to my own prospects, has at present a constant operation to depress Spirits not naturally very lively; but when my solicitude for the welfare and happiness of my Sister is painfully excited by the circumstances which your Letter suggests, I must confess my state of mind is very far from being enviable— I am fully sensible, and I hope properly grateful, for the superior advantages with which I am favoured, above many other young people of my own standing in Life; yet perhaps the idea, that "to whom much is given, of him, *much shall be required*,"[1] does not at present tend to alleviate the disagreeable sensations, which in my present state of doubt, while the impression of *fear* is strong, and that of *hope* but weakly supported, prevail in my mind. I have so often promised on my part, that industry, application, fidelity and oeconomy, should at least concur to render Fortune propitious, that the repetition of those engagements, might wear an appearance of ostentation.— But upon one subject, on which, from a passage in your letter, I am led to suppose you are under some apprehensions on my account, I think I can safely assure you, they may be quieted. You may rest assured, my dear Madam, that I am as resolutely determined never to connect a woman to desperate Fortunes, as I am never to be indebted to a woman for wealth. The same Spirit I presume will operate equally to prevent either of these cases, and you shall never be requested for your consent to a connection of mine, until I am able to support that connection with honour and Independence.

I hope soon to have the pleasure of seeing my father here; and to converse freely with him upon my present prospects and expectations. Perhaps his presence here may be of some service to me.— I wrote to you requesting directions respecting the horse, which I have still here; and I am waiting for your orders. If you think it best that I should keep him upon the terms which I mentioned, I can purchase hay, at a cheaper rate at present than in the winter, or perhaps I could be supplied with it from the Farm; if you think otherwise I will immediately send him out to Braintree. As my expences must at present be yours, I cannot think of incurring any without your approbation.

I have been so much in the habit of complaining to you; perhaps even of whining that it is time to say something on the other side of the Question; I will therefore close this Letter, with assuring you, that except the want of business, which perhaps I ought not yet to expect, my situation here is perfectly agreeable; and that I think I should be very happy if I could only have an opportunity to work my way. And with this good news I will only add, that I am, and ever shall be, your affectionate Son.   J. Q. Adams

P. S. I attend public worship at M^{r:} Clarke's, where M^{r:} Smith, has been so kind as to offer me a seat in his pew. M^{r:} Clarke's discourses are so solid, so ingenious and so instructive, and those of M^{r:} Thacher are so empty, and flimsy, that I am sure you would approve of the principle upon which I have sacrificed the small point of policy which you suggest in your Letter, for the real advantages of improvement, which I may derive from M^{r:} Clarke's instruction— I would however observe that I shall be the only Lawyer, attending at M^{r:} Clarke's, which would not be the case at Mr Thacher's. [2]

RC (Adams Papers); addressed: "M^{rs:} A. Adams. / New-York."; docketed: "J.Q.A. 1790."

[1] Luke, 12:48.
[2] John Clarke, minister of the "Old Brick" First Church of Boston, was an early proponent of universalism known for his well-reasoned sermons and refined literary style. By contrast, Peter Thacher, leader of the Brattle Square Church and chaplain to the Mass. General Court, was a Calvinist who, while an effective and popular orator, was not an intellectual. The Brattle Square Church had long boasted the most genteel congregation in the city, counting among its members James Bowdoin, John Hancock, and Harrison Gray Otis. However, JQA apparently was not alone in preferring the Old Brick. Mary Smith Cranch reported shortly after Thacher's arrival in 1785 that a number of the Brattle Square Church's members had left for the First Church (*Sibley's Harvard Graduates,* 17:240, 243-246; 18:398, 400-402; vol. 6:99, 100). For Thacher, see also vol. 5:481.

Abigail Adams to Abigail Bromfield Rogers

dear Mrs Rogers   [5 *September* 1790] [1]

I Received by judge Cushing your very obliging Letter [2] and am very happy to find that your Health was so far restored by your journey as to enable you to attend upon commencment. it would have afforded me much pleasure to have been present as I was peculiarly interested in the day. it is a little Singular that I should have three sons graduated there and not be able to attend at one single performance of either of them. the good and amiable Character with which mr Thomas quits the university affords the most pleasing Sensations to his affectionate Parents. you must excuse this maternal effusion as I believe you too Sincerly my Friend not to participate in that which so tenderly concerns me. and now my dear Madam How do you immagine Newyork both looks, and feels to me, one attraction after an other has left me here almost alone. Mrs Smith and Family are still strong ties, but were they Removed, I should wish to follow those who are gone before me. I visited mrs Walker twice after you left Town, but as mrs Page occupied your Appartments and we did not visit, I was saved the dissagreeable sensation of entering them and finding them destitute of all that endeard them to me.[3] mrs Walker never spoke of you but in terms of most affectionate Friendship and her Eyes testified to the Sincerity of her professions. this day week I took a most tender and affectionate leave of mrs Washington She took me by Hand embraced me tenderly saying god Bless you my dear Madam we will meet again at Philadelphia but She has repeatedly told me that she shall never see N York again. She was extreemly affected the morning she left the city. I did not attend her upon the water as I had parted with her the Evening before. the Citizens of N york behaved with the greatest propriety. the Ladies who usually attended her drawing Room had taken leave of her in the course of the week, but the Govenour Clergy ministers of state and citizens who attended upon the President to the Barge which lay of just behind his House preserved a total Silence, not a word was heard, when the Barge push'd of each person took of his Hat bowd and retired.[4] mr & mrs Lear remain in the House with part of the domesticks untill they remove to Philadelphia which will be in october[5] with regard to myself I am so devided between a wish to remain with mrs Smith, and the doubt whether we ought to tarry here, that I am in a state of suspence which I am apt to think will terminate in a Removal but where ever I may be it will always afford me pleasure to see or hear from my dear Mrs Rogers. mrs Smith dinned with me yesterday being just a month since her confinement she has a fine Boy we cannot however help regretting the Sex

Dft (Adams Papers); notation: "1790." Filmed at [*Sept. 1790*].

[1] The letter is dated based on the Washingtons' departure from New York, for which see note 4.

[2] Not found.

[3] Mrs. Walker was probably Mary Robinson Walker (1756–1817), wife of New York

customs officer Benjamin Walker who had served with WSS on George Washington's staff during the Revolution. Margaret Lowther Page (1760–1835), daughter of William Lowther of Scotland, was the second wife of John Page, congressional representative from Virginia (Washington, *Papers, Presidential Series*, 2:430–431; Derick S. Hartshorn III, *The Hartshorn Families in America*, Baltimore, 1997, p. 515; New York *Evening Post*, 27 June 1817; *Richmond Enquirer*, 10 Nov. 1835; *DAB*, entry on John Page).

[4] The New York *Gazette of the United States*, 1 Sept., reported that the Washingtons departed the city on 30 Aug. from Mr. McComb's wharf, where government officials, clergymen, and "other respectable citizens" bid the couple a "solemn and affecting adieu." The account concluded, "At the moment of embarkation a federal salute was fired from the battery. By the particular request of the President, the gentlemen of the corporation had not given public notice of his intended departure on Monday; which prevented so general an attendance of the citizens as would have been desirous of paying him their respects on this interesting occasion."

[5] Tobias Lear married Mary Long (1770–1793), daughter of Pierse and Mary Long of Portsmouth, on 22 April. Mary gave birth to a son, Benjamin Lincoln, the following March (Ray Brighton, *The Checkered Career of Tobias Lear*, Portsmouth, N.H., 1985, p. 91, 98, 114; *New Hampshire Gazette*, 15 July 1785).

Abigail Adams to Thomas Brand Hollis

My Dear Sir,   New-York, September 6, 1790.

You ask, in one of your letters to Mr. Adams, what is become of Mrs. Adams that I do not hear from her?[1]

If my heart had not done you more justice than my pen, I would disown it. I have so long omitted writing to you, that my conscience has been a very severe accuser of me. But be assured, my dear sir, that I never fail to talk of you with pleasure, and think of you with affection. I place the hours spent at the Hyde amongst some of the most pleasurable of my days, and I esteem your friendship as one of the most valuable acquisitions that I made in your country:—a country that I should most sincerely rejoice to visit again, if I could do it without crossing the ocean. I have sometimes been suspected of partiality for the preference which I have given to England, but were I to live out of America, that country would have been my choice.

I have a situation here, which, for natural beauty, may vie with the most delicious spot I ever saw. It is a mile and half distant from the city of New-York. The house is situated upon an eminence; at an agreeable distance, flows the noble Hudson bearing upon her bosom the fruitful productions of the adjacent country. On my right hand are fields beautifully variegated with grass and grain to a great extent, like the valley of Honiton in Devonshire.[2] Upon my left, the city opens to view, intercepted here and there, by a rising ground, and an ancient oak. In front, beyond the Hudson, the Jersey shores present an exuberance of a rich well cultivated soil. The venerable oaks, and broken ground, covered with wild shrubs, which surround me, give a natural beauty to the spot which is truly enchanting. A lovely variety of birds serenade me morning and evening, rejoicing in their liberty and security, for I have as much as possible prohibited the grounds from invasion: and sometimes almost wished for game laws, when my orders have not been sufficiently regarded. The partridge, the woodcock, and the pigeon are too great temptations to the sportsmen to withstand. How greatly would it add to my happiness to welcome here my much esteemed friend. Tis true we have a large portion of the blue and gold, of which you used to remind me, when you thought me an Egyptian; but, however I might hanker after the good things of America, I have been sufficiently taught to value and esteem other countries besides my own.

You was pleased to inform us, that your adopted family flourished in your soil,[3] mine has received an addition. Mrs. Smith, Mr. Adams's daughter, and the wife of colonel W. Stephen Smith, respecting the name of the great literary benefactor of her native state, and in grateful remembrance of the friendly attention, and patriotic character of its present possessor, has named her new-born son Thomas-Hollis. She desires me to present you her affectionate remembrance. Mr. Adams is absent upon a journey, or he would have written you a letter of a later date than that which Mr. Knox is the bearer of.[4] This gentleman is a brother of our secretary of war, and is appointed consul to Dublin.[5] He is intelligent, and can answer you any question respecting our government, and politics, which you may wish to know; but if he should not see you, I know it will give you pleasure to learn that our union is complete by the accession of Rhode island; that our government acquires strength, confidence and stability daily. That peace is in our borders, and plenty in our dwellings; and we earnestly pray that the kindling flames of war, which appear to be bursting out in Europe, may by no means be extended to this rising nation.[6] We enjoy freedom in as great a latitude as is consistent with our security, and happiness. God grant that we may rightly estimate our blessings.

Pray remember me, in the most affectionate terms to Dr. Price, and to Mrs. Jebb, and be assured, my dear sir, that I am, with every sentiment of regard and esteem, / yours, &c.   Abigail Adams.

MS not found. Printed from John Disney, ed., *Memoirs of Thomas Brand-Hollis*, London, 1808, p. 39–40.

[1] In a letter to JA of 29 March, Hollis sent his affectionate regards to AA and noted that he "should be gratified with a line from her." Hollis also wrote to JA on 28 May (both Adams Papers).

[2] AA would have seen Honiton, a picturesque town situated in a valley near the Otter River, during the Adamses' month-long visit to southwestern England in 1787. Roughly fifteen miles east of Exeter, Honiton was renowned as a center of the lace-making trade (*Black's Guide to Devonshire*, Edinburgh, 1874, p. 164).

[3] Hollis, who named his American plants and trees after friends from the United States, noted in a letter to JA that "Mrs Adams herself & family are in perfect health at the Hide" (28 May 1790, Adams Papers; vol. 8:195).

[4] Probably that of 11 June (LbC, APM Reel 115).

[5] William Knox sailed for London aboard the brig *Rachel* on 11 Sept. (*Pennsylvania Mercury*, 16 Sept.). The London *Times* reported on 30 Nov. that he had arrived safely in Dublin.

[6] In July 1789, a Spanish ensign seized two English vessels in Nootka Sound, an action that jeopardized diplomatic relations between the two countries. Tensions escalated in the spring and early summer of 1790, with both sides preparing for war—a conflict that also could potentially involve France due to its Family Compact with Spain. The United States, too, committed to maintaining neutrality, faced the troubling possibility that Britain might attempt to march soldiers through Canada and American territory to reach Spanish possessions. Despite these concerns, the crisis was resolved without bloodshed. Although Great Britain and Spain reached a preliminary agreement on 24 July, the news did not reach the United States until months later. Discussion of a possible Anglo-Spanish war appeared in the American press throughout the summer; see, for example, New York *Daily Advertiser*, 3 Aug.; Boston *Columbian Centinel*, 4 Aug.; and *New York Daily Gazette*, 9, 17 August. The New York *Gazette of the United States*, 4 Sept., contained a report from London that began, "The question, 'are we to have a war?' has thrust 'how d'ye do?' out of place; and as no person can give a proper answer to this question, the quantity of *supposes*, *conjectures* and *ifs*, are really wonderful" (Washington, *Papers*, *Presidential Series*, 6:26, 492–493; Jefferson, *Papers*, 17:35-37, 92, 93).

Abigail Adams to Lucy Ludwell Paradise

Dear Madam [6 September 1790][1]

By mr Knox our old accquaintance who is appointed consul to dublin I embrace the opportunity of writing to you and acknowledging the Recept of your obliging Letters by col Trumble[2] whom we were all very happy to welcome to his Native Land and who has acquired to Himself and his Country an immortal Fame by his great Genius and talants in painting the Mayor and corporation of this city have employd him to take two full Length portraits one of the President of the united States the other of their Govenour at a hundred Guineys each. the first he has finished to the intire Satisfaction of every Spectator.[3] the Respectable Family from which mr Trumble is descended, his own most amiable Character and his intention of painting the great and important Scenes and principal Actors from the Life, in the late Revolution ought to ensure to him publick Patronage and I fatter myself he will meet with it before he returns to Europe. mr Jefferson whom you were so desirious of seeing return, is you know long e'er this time, our Secretary of State. he took leave of me last week to visit his Family in Virgina. the President and his Lady and Family sat of this day week for their seat at Mount Vernon. under the present administration our Government daily acquires strength and stability. the union is compleat by the late Adoption of the constitution by RhoadIsland. nothing hinders our being a very happy and prosperous people provided we have wisdom rightly to estimate our Blessings, and Hearts to improve them. I thought to have found you in America upon my return to this country and am sorry you could not make it convenient to you. I know very well by experience the strong attractions which England possesses, and Should prefer it to any other country that I have seen America excepted. Alass poor France how many direfull scenes has she yet to pass through before order will be Reestablishd. however great the Blessings to be derived from a Revolution in government, the Scenes of Anarchy cruelty and Blood which usually preceed it and the difficulty of uniting a Majority in favour of any System, are sufficent to make every person who has been an Eye witness to the demolition of one government Recoil at the prospect of over turning Empires and kingdoms[4] I hope my dear Madam that you receive agreeable accounts from the Countess your daughter and that she has increased the Family Happiness by further additions to the Family.[5] present me kindly to her when you write and to our Friend Mrs Church remember me affectionatly She is a Charming woman, we regreet her loss here, and wish she would return with her Family to her Native Land.[6] I do not know any gentleman who would be more agreeable to all those who have the pleasure of an acquaintance with him, than mr Freire in the Character you mention him, and I am satisfied from the knowledge I have of him his manners and Character would be particularly adapted to the Genius & disposition of Americans, and if his Court should appoint him, he would be received with all that Attention and Respect which is due to the Friendly conduct which the Queen of Portugal has manifested towards the Americans—[7]

Remember to mr Paradice for whom I have a real esteem & to dr Bancroft and any other of our old Friends and acquaintanc who may inquire after Your Humble Servant   A Adams

Dft (Adams Papers); notation: "Mrs Paradise. 1791." Filmed at [1791].

[1] The letter is dated based on the Washingtons' departure from New York; see AA to Abigail Bromfield Rogers, [5 *Sept. 1790*], note 4, above.

[2] John Trumbull delivered a letter of 7 Oct. 1789 (Adams Papers) in which Paradise

congratulated JA on his election as vice president and expressed her esteem for Thomas Jefferson, who recently had come to the aid of her family. She also wrote to AA on 3 June, but AA did not reply (vol. 8:367–368).

[3] Richard Varick (1753–1831), mayor of New York City, approached George Washington on 20 July 1790 about sitting for a portrait to be placed on display at City Hall. Trumbull, who had just completed a smaller full-length portrait of the president intended for Martha Washington, reported to Benjamin West in late August that he was nearly finished with the city council's commission. Trumbull described the painting as "near seven feet high compos'd with a Horse, & the background the evacuation of this Place by the British at the Peace." The artist completed a similar full-length portrait of George Clinton, governor of New York, the following year (Washington, *Papers, Presidential Series*, 6:102–103; Theodore Sizer, *The Works of Colonel John Trumbull, Artist of the American Revolution*, rev. edn., New Haven, Conn., 1967, p. 26, 82).

[4] In 1789, France abandoned absolute monarchy and formed a National Assembly, which adopted a constitution on 26 August. This new constitutional monarchy, overseen by the moderate National Assembly and sanctioned by Louis XVI, proceeded to pass a series of measures in late 1789 and 1790 that sought to reorganize and reform French society—but simultaneously rendered it increasingly unstable. During this time, there were occasional episodes of mob action, rioting, and violence both in Paris and in more rural areas throughout the country.

American newspapers reported regularly on the sittings of the National Assembly and other events in France. The New York *Daily Advertiser*, 28 Aug., published a report from France noting "the people incline to the most cruel executions. On Monday two men accused of theft were hung without any form of law." According to the New York *Gazette of the United States*, 14 Aug., "Paris has lately been troubled by some insurrections; happily a few only, who deserved it, became victims to them. In twenty-four hours peace was restored to this town."

[5] Lucy Paradise Barziza gave birth to a second son, Filippo Ignacio, in 1796 at Venice (Archibald Bolling Shepperson, *John Paradise and Lucy Ludwell of London and Williamsburg*, Richmond, Va., 1942, p. 456).

[6] For Angelica Schuyler Church, see vol. 6:10.

[7] For the appointment of Cipriáo Ribeiro, Chevalier de Freire, see vol. 8:368.

Abigail Adams to Cotton Tufts

dear sir   New york Sep[br] 6 1790

Mr Adams received your Letter dated August 31.[1] he sat of that morning after for Philadlphia and desired me to let you know that he would transmit to you an order from the treasury for the Sum you received of Generall Lincoln upon his return. where is Thomas we have been daily expecting him for near a Month, and mr Adams delay[d] going his journey a week expecting him here. he wrote me that he could not come on imediatly after commencment as you had not sufficient in your hands for that purpose. I accordingly sent on by dr Jeffries 35 dollors—directed to you, which I presume you received. I have written to his Brother & last week to him advising him to come by the Way of RhoadIsland, but have not heard a single word where he is, nor why he does not come if he is sick, or met with any accident we should be glad to know it. Mrs Cranch wrote me that a Gentleman and Lady from Demerara wanted to take a ready furnishd House, and inquired if we would Let ours. I could wish that a place which cost us so much Money might be made a little profitable to us. I have desired mrs Cranch that you might be consulted about it, and if any terms should be offerd that you think would compensate for the use of House garden and furniture, you will be so good as to inform us— things are not conducted there according to my mind, because we do not know how they are managed. mr Adams had thoughts of going to Braintree, but his journey to Philadelphia will prevent it as I suppose if he can get a House there, we must remove next month. he wishes you to inform him, the Sum you have of paper, and the different kind's

the wine which mr Codman has in his care we will thank you to Send round by Barnard as we can remove it with our other things. I do not expect to see my Friends untill an other year, when I hope to spend the summer with them.

How will Elections go? are they Still in a rage for Rotations in Massachusetts? or does the Clamour rise from a few wrestless spirits who have no other importance.[2] if they change mr Gerry for a mr any body else, they will lose one of the firmest men they have as independant a man, and as honest a one. in the first Session, his mind was irritated & he was hurt, his speaches were misrepresentd, and his conduct misconstrued, but through the whole of this last session no man has exerted himself more for the honour and Reputation of the Nation, nor more firmly gaurded the constitution against innovation. I most sincerely hope he will be reelected.[3]

I hope my dear sir that all your Family are well and that you enjoy good Health yourself. I am very sorry to hear that we are like to lose Governour Bowdoin, from the accounts we hear, I fear there is little hope of his recovery—[4]

All Letters addrest to the V President are frankd in the post office, so that you may write by that conveyance when you please.

will you be so good as to tell mr Codman that as the President and Secretary of State are both absent, there cannot any application be made at present in favour of his Brother, that on a former occasion when mr A Named a Gentleman to the Pressident as proper for consul, he replied that he had no other objection than that a much greater Number had been appointed from N England than from any other of the States, and that his object had been to distribute offices as equally as possible. mr A will however communicate to mr Lear the contents of the Letter.[5]

I am dear sir / your affectionate   A Adams

RC (NHi:Misc. Mss. Adams, Abigail); endorsed: "M^rs· Ab. Adams Sept 6. 1790."

¹ Not found.

² Amidst strong opposition in the local press to the incumbent congressional delegation, the Boston *Columbian Centinel* reported on 1 Sept., "Electioneering, for Congressional seats, is carried on with great spirit in several of the States. . . . Every error of the present Congress is pointed out with the finger of patriotism, and with infallible prescience it is *now* clearly seen how every difficulty *might have* been avoided; and if the blessed principle of *Rotation* is attended to, a NEW SET, profiting by the mistakes of the OLD, will guide the political ship to, UNIVERSAL approbation." Several days later, another piece in the *Centinel* bemoaned "the *open* condemnation of *all* the measures of Congress" in Massachusetts newspapers, concluding that the authors' "object is no other than Rotation—the *ousting* of the old, to make way for a new set of goodly rulers—men of *great abilities—profound euridition—and legislature knowledge*" (4 Sept.).

³ Elbridge Gerry was reelected to the House of Representatives, where he served until March 1793. Representatives Fisher Ames, Benjamin Goodhue, Theodore Sedgwick, George Leonard, and George Thacher were also returned to Congress. Only Jona-

than Grout of Worcester County and George Partridge of Plymouth County lost their bids for reelection, to be replaced by Artemas Ward and Shearjashub Bourne, respectively (*Biog. Dir. Cong.*). For Bourne, see also Mary Smith Cranch to AA, 12 Dec. 1790, note 1, below.

⁴ JQA reported to JA on 9 Aug. (Adams Papers) that James Bowdoin was "dangerously ill. He had at first a severe paralytic stroke, and was yesterday attacked with a Dysentery." Bowdoin died on 6 Nov. (*DAB*).

⁵ When Richard Harrison of Virginia declined the appointment of consul at Cadiz, John Codman Jr. wrote to JA requesting that his brother, Richard, be considered for the position (27 Aug., Adams Papers). JA replied on 10 Oct. (Adams Papers) that, though he would communicate Codman's letter to Thomas Jefferson, it was unlikely that the appointment would go to someone from Massachusetts. Jefferson included Codman in a list of candidates for the position in Feb. 1791, but the slot remained vacant until Feb. 1793 when the Senate confirmed Joseph Yznardi Jr., a Spanish merchant, to the post (Washington, *Papers, Presidential Series*, 5:473; Jefferson, *Papers*, 19:317, 22:431–432, 27:60).

John Adams to John Quincy Adams

Dear sir   New York [*ante 8*] September 1790¹

I received with great Pleasure your Letter of the 9 of August, inclosing a Receipt from Mr Parsons for one hundred Pounds lawful Money, which you paid him in the month of August, Second day, in full for your Tuition as a Clerk in his office for the term of three Years.²

I learned, with Pleasure also, that on the 9th of August you took Possession of an office in my house, where I wish you more pleasure and as much Profit as I once had.

At the Age of 23, My son, I know by Experience, that in the Profession of the Law, a Man is not to expect a run of Business, nor indeed enough to afford him a subsistence. I mean to assist you, till you can do without my Aid: I only ask of you to recollect that my Circumstances are not affluent: that you have Brothers and a sister who are equally intitled to assistance from me: and that therefore as

Strict an Œconomy as is consistent with your Comfort and with decency is necessary.

There is a Pew in an Obscure Corner of Mr Thatchers Church which belongs to me.[3] My Advice to you is to acquaint the Family in Possession of it, that you have the Care of it. indeed I would have you take Possession of it, and Sit in it— The Contribution I had rather pay than that you should not have a known Seat in some Meeting.

You are happy in a Connection with Dr Welsh. He is a Man of Sense and Information in publick as well as private affairs, and will be a worthy Friend to you. I hope he will introduce you to his Clubb:[4] and I know that it will be in his Power and inclination to promote your Reputation.

Dread not "unmerited Enmity" nor "unprovoked Ma[li]ce" "Industry" and "honour" will dissipate every Vapour of those kinds. Patience will be necessary. You must take large draughts of Patience. nothing is to be done in this World with out that.

If you meddle with political subjects, let me Advise you to never loose sight of Decorum. Assume a Dignity above all Personal Reflections: and avoid as much as possible a Party Spirit. The true Interest and honour of your Country should be your only Object. And may you be a Terror to those evil Doers, to whom Truth and Falshood are equally but sport, honour but a Phantom, and their own insignificant importance their only objects. The hands of two many such Creatures appear in some of the Boston Newspapers.[5]

I shall give you the Care of my House where you are and will send you a Power for that Purpose.[6] fifteen Pounds is too much to be deducted out of 36 for your office. I had however rather apply the whole 36 to your accommodation there than that you should go any where else.

Your communications on political subjects, will always be agreable.

Your Brother Charles is uncommonly assiduous in his office, and very attentive to his studies. He is acquiring [a] Reputation for the Ease and Elegance of his manners as well as for the solidity of his Pursuits.

I am uneasy at the Delay of your Brother Tho[mas.] I long to See you, as well as my Aged venerable, beloved Mother and all my other dear friends Around the Blue Hills.

I am with the tenderest Affection / your Father

John Adams.

RC (Adams Papers); addressed: "John Quincy Adams / Attorney at Law / Boston"; internal address: "Mr J. Q. Adams."; endorsed: "My Father. September 1790."; notation: "Free / John Adams." Filmed at Sept. 1790. Some loss of text due to placement and removal of the seal.

¹ The letter is dated based on the receipt of TBA's letter on 8 Sept. informing his parents he would soon arrive in New York; see AA to JQA, 9 Sept., below.

² In his letter of 9 Aug., JQA expressed gratitude for his father's ongoing financial support: "After all the trouble, and all the expence which you have so liberally bestowed upon my education, I am sensible, that I cannot with a very good grace acknowledge my dependence upon your further assistance, and that at the age of 23 it is incumbent upon a man to rely for his subsistence, only upon his own exertions. But my confidence in your goodness is too well grounded, not to be convinced, that you will make every necessary allowance for the peculiar circumstances in my education which have retarded my advancement, and for the unfavourable situation of the profession which I have embraced" (Adams Papers). For the enclosure, see JA to JQA, 1 April, note 1, above.

³ The Adamses attended the Brattle Square Church when they lived in Boston prior to the Revolution. Dr. Samuel Cooper, the minister at the time and a friend of JA,

baptized CA (JA, *Papers*, 2:viii–ix; *The Manifesto Church: Records of the Church in Brattle Square*, Boston, 1902, p. 186).

⁴ For the Wednesday Evening Club, of which Welsh was a founding member, see vol. 6:355.

⁵ In a letter to JQA of 5 Sept., AA similarly noted, "Pray who is the writer, if it was not vulgar I would say the Liar in Edes paper under the signature of a Republican? Boston has justly the Character of the Nest of Sedition. There are no papers throughout the United States half as virulent, but the Government stands now too strong, for these wrestless Spirits to overturn" (Adams Papers). In the *Boston Gazette*, 16 Aug., "A Republican" attacked the editor of the Boston *Columbian Centinel*, accusing him of forwarding "the views of the artful and designing Aristocraticks" by suggesting that the supporters of the Constitution, in order to win the endorsement of their opponents, promised additional amendments without ever intending to pursue their adoption.

⁶ JA signed a power of attorney giving JQA control over the Court Street house on 1 June 1791 (Adams Papers).

Abigail Adams to John Quincy Adams

my dear son   Newyork Sep^br 9th 1790

yesterday mr Howard arrived here and brought me Letters from your Brother Thomas, and one from you to Charles—¹ I was rejoiced to find that he was on his way here, as the delay had been the source of a good deal of uneasiness. I am fully of your mind with regard to Thomas, and know that if he studies Law it will be a force to his inclinations. the want of capital I Suppose is one great objection to Merchandise, but I think a young man who is dilligent and attentive to Buisness may make his way very [wel]l in a country like this, or suppose your Father was to send him to Holland & place him with the Willinks.² I think as far as I can judge, that it would be the best method to promote his interest. you and I know Thomas so well, as to feel satisfied that he would be steady industerous and indefatigable in his persuits, but at the same time you know that advising to a measure against which some objections arise, in case of failure the adviser must bear the blame. I have sometimes found great address necessary to carry a point, and much prudent caution to effect my scheme, yet I am sure your Father would do every thing in his power to promote the interest of his children— that they must labour for themselves is pretty plain, how foolishly so ever the world judge—and one shilling earned by their own industery is worth a pound in the publick Service. it is not grudged you may spend it, or save it without a murmer, but the people who are continually Clamouring may rest satisfied that instead of lower salleries there will be higher, and the further the Southern Gentlemen can get from the North So in proportion will there salleries be increasd, and if they Send an intire New delegation, they will very soon be converted, or what is more likly out voted. at Philadelphia they will have higher Salleries soon, than at N york, and higher still when they go to Potomack I reason from the Nature of things, and from the probable flourishing state of the Country, the burdens of which will be greatly lessned by the funding of the debt, and the measures taken to sink it.[3]

is Sullivan the inve[nome]d Snake that lifts up his head and bites, then squirms about & sneaks into the Grass? I suppose he wants a sop you must expect to feel your share of envy.

Mr Bourn wrote to your Father in favour of mr Woodard as a proper person to employ to purchase publick securities, if any Agents were employd by the commissioners—but the act does not appear to have been attended to, which says they shall be purchased openly and at the market price. the Loan officers of the several states will do the buisness—[4]

adieu yours / affectionaly   A Adams

Thomas is not yet arrived owing I suppose to contrary winds

RC (Adams Papers). Some loss of text where the seal was removed.

[1] Probably Rev. Simeon Howard or his elder son, John Clarke Howard. The letters have not been found.

[2] For Jan and Wilhem Willink, see JA, *Papers*, 13:ix–x.

[3] When the Salaries—Legislative Act first passed the House on 10 Aug. 1789, establishing generous salaries for members of Congress, all of the representatives from southern states voted for it. By contrast, the Massachusetts and New Hampshire congressmen uniformly voted against the bill, joined by several representatives from New Jersey and New York.

Newspapers throughout the nation, but especially in New England, bitterly denounced the new level of compensation for congressmen as excessive and unnecessary. The subject of federal salaries remained a frequent topic in the opposition press for over a year, and Antifederalist writers particularly emphasized it during the election campaign in the fall of 1790. A highly critical piece by Rusticus in the Boston *Independent Chronicle*, 2 Sept., recently had argued that "extravagant compensations, will, independent of the waste of money, have a pernicious tendency upon the people. There are very few men, who have an annual income equal to the wages of Congress. And there are not twenty persons, in the three millions, which compose the United States, who have an income equal to the Vice President, and to the Judges. But their stile will be imitated if they spend their salaries, and if they do not, the farmer at the plough, the mechanic in his shop, and the fisherman on the water, will stand still to enquire, why they are toiling to hoard up wealth for the children of these men?" (*First Fed. Cong.*, 3:141–142; Stewart, *Opposition Press*, p. 71–75).

⁴"An Act Making Provision for the Reduction of the Public Debt," also known as the Sinking Fund Act, was signed into law on 12 August. It provided for the appropriation from the nation's treasury of any surplus earned from duties on imported merchandise, as well as the acquisition of two million dollars in loans, all to be invested in public securities. The president of the Senate was one of five commissioners designated to handle these purchases (*First Fed. Cong.*, 6:1890–1891). In his letter to JA of 15 Aug., Sylvanus Bourne suggested Joseph Woodward as a possible agent to act on JA's behalf, noting Woodward's integrity and "thourough acquaintance in this kind of buisness" (Adams Papers).

Abigail Adams to John Quincy Adams

my dear son   N york Sep^br 12. 1790

I received by your Brother on fryday last your kind Letter; he did not get here, oweing to contrary winds untill the tenth. he appears to think of the Law, but I fear it is rather from necessity than inclination, and because he finds that his Father is fond of having him study it, and that he does not See any opening in any other buisness. I shall be better able to judge when your Father returns from Philadelphia, upon what terms he can be received there. my advice to Charles is to remain here tho tis probable mr Lawrence will be a great deal absent for he is rechosen a member of Congress. Newyork being [se]nsible when they have good & able Men, are not so swallowd up with the Idea of Rotation as Massachusetts. That I am very anxious for your sister, and Family is most certain. I do not see any present prospect which bids fair for their support. an increasing Family is sufficient to make a Man look about him and if the same degree of prudence had been persued three years ago that is practised now, I believe a Gentleman would not have been so long unemployd as he has been. the Revenue Laws are too faithfully adhered to, and too punctually obey'd for the office of Marshall to be in any degree profitable in this State. the President has said, that it his intention to give him an appointment of more consideration, as soon as the publick Service will admit of it, but had col smith persued the advise of your Father whilst in England & since his return, he need not have lookt to any Government for employ. as he had been regularly enterd into an office and studied some time before he left the Country, your Fathers advise to him, was to enter himself at the Temple, & to attend the courts at Westmister reading Law at home, then upon his return to be sworn into court and practise in this state, which he might have done to great advantage when he first returnd from England. but what Signifies looking back—let us look forward, and with regard to yourself I do not doubt you will do very well only have patience, and I will prophesy for you, that you will be able by the close of one year to pay your own Board, and if you do that tis as much as you ought to expect, and if you do not why dont worry your face into wrinkles about it. We will help you all we can, and when you are better off than those who assist you, you shall help them again if they want it, so make yourself easy and keep free from entangelments of all kinds. Thomas says you are in Love. so far as it will serve to make you attentive to your person, for you are a little inclined to be neglegent, so far it may be of service to you, besides it may keep your Head from rambling after other objects, but it if it makes you anxious & uneasy, and when you are reading, Slides in between your subject and you then you have Cause to be allarmed, so take heed—

as to your Horse I believe you had better write to your Father yourself. I think if you can get two or 3 load of Hay from your uncle Adams, it will be as well for you to keep him in Town upon the terms you mentiond, but you will be safer to have your directions from your Father. he told me sometime ago to write to you to sell him, but as I did not suppose at the time, that the order was the result of mature deliberation, I ventured to omit it, but you had better ask his advise whether you shall sell him, or keep him as you proposed in Town as we are not like to come to Braintree to use any of the Hay this year, I suppose your uncle must have more than he will want to spend there.

Sunday Noon

Your Father is just returned and has taken Bush Hill, the seat of mr Hamilton, so that matter is decided.[1] I presume we must remove next month write to me as often as you can and let me hear from time of your success & prospects. I am my dear son affectionatly /
Yours   A Adams

PS your sister asks if you have forgotten her she wrote you long ago by charles storer. her son she calls Thomas Hollis—

RC (Adams Papers); addressed: "Mr / John Quincy Adams / Boston"; endorsed: "My Mother. 12. Sept^r: 1790." and "M^rs: Adams. Sept^r: 12. 1790." Some loss of text where the seal was removed.

[1] For William Hamilton and his house, Bush Hill, see JA, *D&A*, 3:184, and Descriptive List of Illustrations, No. 4, above.

4. "BUSH HILL. THE SEAT OF WM. HAMILTON ESQR. NEAR PHILADELPHIA,"
BY JAMES PELLER MALCOM, 1787

See page xii

John Adams to John Quincy Adams

My dear John   New York Sept[r.] 13. 1790

Since my return from Philadelphia where I have been to get Lodgings, against the meeting of Congress, your Mamma has shewn me your Letter: and I consent you Should keep the Horse for the present.— My Brother may Supply you with hay, as far as your occasion for it may go.

Can nothing be done to make my Estate at Boston and Braintree more productive? The House where you are is at a miserable Rent. It ought to be higher. I am egregiously imposed upon in that instance. but much more so at Braintree. The Farm under Pratts Care is Scandalously husbanded—and my own House Garden and Land about them might be made Something of.

I must have a new Tenant both at Braintree and Boston, if I cannot have a better Rent without it. Expences are multiplying upon me, for your Brothers as well as yourself, and something must be done to assist me in the management of my Estate or I shall run behind hand and be ruined.

Your Success will depend altogether upon your Steadiness at your office. It will not be worth your while to leave your office to go much to Country Courts, without Business to lead you there at present.— While the Older Lawyers are at Country Courts, will be your best opportunities.

Your reasons for preferring M[r] Clarks Meeting may be good, but the Congregation in Brattle Street, has long given the Tone. Do however as you judge most prudent, notwithstanding what I said about my Pew in my last Letter. I am a proprietor in the House in Brattle Street to the amount of about fifty Guineas advanced when I was young, so that I have an affection for that Spot.

I know not who are the great Lawyers, at Boston at present. M[r] Tudor, Gore, Dawes, and Some others are ingenious Men: but I presume your Litterature and Science need not be discouraged.

Constancy in Attendance at Court, whether you have Business or not, and whoever is absent, will get you Business faster than any thing next to Constancy in your office. However tedious it may be, never be absent a moment nor let any thing of practice escape you. take minutes of Cases, Notes of Practice and Argument as well as Authorities and preserve them. This kind of Patience will do more than any Thing else.— You must have another kind of Patience too: a

Patience under all the mortification Humiliation and Ennui, of Want of Business for Days Weeks, Months if not Years together. Without these Several kinds of Patience, you will not succeed at last. With it, you have nothing to fear: Success is certain.

There is, between ourselves, a Savage, whose trea[chery] I would advise you to avoid like a Pestilence, but at the same time be wanting in no respect which his office Age and Rank at the Bar and in Life, entitle him to— I mean Sullivan. A more false and faithless Character is Scarcely to be found. His pretended friendship and secret [Envious?] to me, of both of which I have sufficient Evidence, I equally despise. But do you watch him. He cannot hurt me: to you he may do mischief, if you are not on your guard. You have no reason to dread him. His Learning in all kinds is as much inferiour to yours, as his Age is superiour. This must go no further than you and me, at present. I may possibly expose that fellow, if he dont mend his manners, Sometime or other. I know his hand in all his paltry Scribbles.[1]

yours   J. A.

RC (Adams Papers); internal address: "John Quincy Adams."; endorsed: "My Father. 13. Sept^r: 1790." Some loss of text where the seal was removed.

[1] James Sullivan, the new attorney general of Massachusetts, made frequent contributions to the Boston newspapers throughout his life, publishing argumentative essays under a number of different pseudonyms. A close political ally and defender of John Hancock, Sullivan had expended considerable effort in the winter of 1788–1789 to push for the election of Hancock as vice president. JA and Sullivan also found themselves on opposing sides during the bitter controversy surrounding John Temple's return to the United States following the American Revolution, for which see JA, *Papers*, 11:449–452 (JA, *Legal Papers*, 1:cx; Thomas C. Amory, *Life of James Sullivan*, 2 vols., Boston, 1859, 1:244, 249, 396–397).

John Adams to John Quincy Adams

Dear John   New York Septr. 13. 1790

I wrote you before to day: but I forgot to say Several Things.— Have you ever attended a Town Meeting? You may there learn the Ways of Men, and penetrate Several Characters which otherwise You would not know. There are Several Objects of Enquiry, which I would point out to your consideration without making any noise or parade about them.

1. The State of Parties in Religion, Government Manners, Fashions.

2. The Leading Characters in Church and State.

3. The Machines, Arts and Channels, by which Intelligence and Reports are circulated through the Town.

4. The Makers and Spreaders of Characters.

5. The State of the various Tradesmen and Mechanicks, their Views designs and Projects

6. The State, Hopes, Views, Plans, Passions, and Sentiments of the old Tories, and their Correspondencies abroad and at home in their own State and in other States.

7. Ditto of the old Whigs of 1764 and 1774.

8. Ditto of the Neutrals.

9. Ditto of those who have Sprung up Since the Revolution.

10. The Characters of all the Clergymen, of all denominations Physicians, surgeons Apothecaries, Lawyers, and Merchants of Eminence & shopkeepers

11. The Foreigners in or out of offices, French English, Dutch &c

12. The Various Combinations of all these.

13 The State of Diversions Amusements, Spectacles. &c

14. The various Clubbs, Lists of all which you should obtain.

15. The Buffoons, the Merry Andrews, the story tellers the song Singers, the Mimicks.

These are all Wheels Springs Cogs, or Pins, Some of them dirty ones which compose the Machine and make it go.

Visit my old Friend the Lt. Govr sometimes,[1] and Pay all due respect to the higher Powers. Write me as often as possible. dont shew my Letters. Yours   J. A.

RC (Adams Papers); internal address: "John Quincy Adams." Tr (Adams Papers).

[1] Samuel Adams served as lieutenant governor of Massachusetts from 1789 to 1793 (*DAB*).

John Adams to Thomas Welsh

My dear Dr Welsh   New York Septr. 13. 1790.

I received your Letter, before my Departure for Philadelphia, but had not time to answer it.[1]

It is not probable that any Special Agents will be employed in the Business you had in contemplation. The Board consists of Men, who will Study Æconomy, in that as well as in all other Affairs committed, to their Charge; and therefore the Loan Officers or Collectors or some other known Character will have this Additional Duty annexed to him, without any other Reward, than the honour of it, as I Suppose.[2]

I have much Satisfaction in finding my Son in your Family. What the Conjunctions and Oppositions of two Such political Planets may produce I know not.— Politicks are bred in the Bones of both of you. but your good Example will teach him I hope to take Politicks by Way of Amusement, or Spectacle without ever Suffering their Interference with your Professions.[3]

I recollect the painful Years, I Suffered from 1758 when I was Sworn at Boston, to the year 1761 too perfectly not to Sympathize with John. Dont let him flatter himself with hopes of a run of Business, which is neither to be expected, nor would be beneficial. His Business is to Study, and be constant to his Office and in Court. Causes and Clients will come soon enough for his Benefit, if he does that. "My Knowledge of the Law cost me Seven Years hard Study in that Great Chair" Said John Reed, who had as great a Genius and became as eminent as any Man.[4] "Attend to the Study of the Law rather than the Gain of it" Said my Master Gridley to me; and I recollect the precept with Pleasure enough to recommend it to my Sons.[5] I can ill afford to maintain my Sons at their Studies, but I had rather do that than have them overwhelmed with a run of Business at first, which must put an End to their Studies.

If a Fathers Partiality has not deceived me very much, John is as great a Schollar as this Country has produced at his Age; and I know he has a Spirit that will not stoop to dishonourable Practice or Conduct. I am therefore perfectly at ease in my Mind about his success. Whether his Reputation Spreads this year or two or three years hence, is indifferent to me, provided his Anxiety does not injure his health. I have seen too many flashing Insects in my day, glitter and glare for a moment and then disappear, to wish that my sons may Add to the Number.[6]

The best regards of my family accompany my own to M[rs] Welsh, from, my dear sir, your Fnd & ser[t]   John Adams

RC (MHi:Adams-Welsh Corr.); addressed: "D[r] Thomas Welsh / Boston"; internal address: "D[r] Welsh."; endorsed: "Vice President / Sep[tr] 13. 1790"; notation: "Free / John Adams." LbC in CA's hand (Adams Papers); APM Reel 115.

[1] Not found.

[2] On 21 Sept. Welsh again asked for inside information that JA might have as a commissioner of the federal sinking fund, saying "it might serve me and I think injure nobody" (Adams Papers). JA responded on 10 Oct.:

"It would give me great Pleasure to comply with your request, and to be of Service to you, in any Way in my Power: but I am not at Liberty to communicate the most distant hint to any one, relative to the Subject" (MHi:Adams-Welsh Corr.). Welsh apparently asked a third time through JQA; see CA to JQA, 7 Nov., below.

[3] Although Welsh's social circle included many prominent Boston politicians, he himself never served in public office.

[4] John Read (1680–1749), Harvard 1697, was the leading attorney of his day and instrumental in shaping the practice of law in early New England (*DAB*).

[5] Jeremiah Gridley, the well-respected attorney who supported JA's admission to the Boston bar, advised JA: "Pursue the Study of the Law rather than the Gain of it. Pursue the Gain of it enough to keep out of the Briars, but give your main Attention to the

study of it" (JA, *D&A*, 1:54–55). For Gridley, see also JA, *Legal Papers*, 1:ci.

[6] In his reply of 21 Sept., Welsh concurred: "The Doctrine of Patience which you emphatically inculcate I have long since been a Convert to. From the first Insertion of the Plough of the husbandman into the Soil to the Consummation of [his] Wishes in harvest a constant Exercise of this Virtue is necessary. Your Son is fully convinced of the Necessity of it and will let it have its perfect work. He is indeed what you think him to be and will in a very reasonable time acquire Business Confidence and Reputation in his Profession" (Adams Papers).

John Quincy Adams to John Adams

Dear Sir.   Boston September 21st: 1790.

I have received within a few days three Letters with which you have favoured me, and shall pay to their contents all the attention which I can command. The scheme which you have traced out in the last of them is so extensive, that I am apprehensive it will require much time, as well as very constant enquiries, to obtain the information of the several kinds which you mention. I shall endeavour to inform myself upon those several subjects with uninterrupted assiduity; and according to your directions without making any "noise or parade about it."

My circle of acquaintance at present is too much confined to enable me to obtain very rapidly any knowledge of this kind: excepting at Mr: Smiths', I am treated with cold civility by all the gentlemen in Town to whom I have been heretofore known— I am not to expect much cordiality from any of the gentlemen at the bar in town—I did not expect it, and am therefore not disappointed at finding so little as I do.— I wish not for any notice out of the line of my profession; and that must be the consequence of my own exertions.— I will be persevering as well as patient.

There are not in the profession many gentlemen inhabiting this town, whose characters are remarkably formidable from their respectability— Mr: Sullivan does more business I suppose than any four others put together.— I shall carefully remember the cautions in one of your Letters, respecting him, whatever other qualities he may possess, he may safely be taken as a model for Industry and activity.— "I believe" said Parson Clarke to me the other day "that man has not a particle of Indolence in his Nature."— He treats me civilly; and it is all I wish; I have derived even some instruction from his private conversation as well as from his arguments at the bar; and the other day, he gave me a caution, which made a singular impression upon my mind. I was sitting next to him within the bar at Concord. He took from his finger a ring, and pointed to me the motto engraved within the rim. It was "Weigh the Consequences." *Fas est et ab hoste doceri*.[1] perhaps the benefit of the admonition may not be lost, in its influence upon my conduct towards the man himself.— I have no desire to render myself personally obnoxious too him, and I trust I shall always disdain to court his favour.

M^r: Tudor is an ingenious, amiable indolent man, who will always make a respectable figure in Society, but who has not activity or application enough ever to arrive to the foremost rank of eminence in his profession: your personal acquaintance with him has made his character better known to you than it is to me; my opinion of him has been formed from the information of persons more conversant with him, and confirmed in some measure by my own observation.

M^r: Dawes, in addition to a similar indolence of disposition, labours under the disadvantage of ill health: he is supported by a very considerable weight of paternal influence, but his exertion has been blunted, by the expectation of a large patrimonial property:—he married too young.[2] To avoid an early matrimonial connection, was one of the principles which I think I have heard you say was recommended to you by Mr Gridley. Happiness in Life, I am fully perswaded must be derived principally from domestic attachments; but a foundation must be laid before the superstructure can be erected. I hope I am in no danger from this quarter.

M^r: Gore is one of those men whom Cardinal Richelieu would have employed in public affairs. He is a very fortunate man. In his profession he has been remarkably successful; from a combination of circumstances, which a man of inferior abilities to those he possesses might perhaps have improved as well.— His family connections have likewise been extremely serviceable to him, and it is said that he has made an independent Fortune, by speculation in the public funds. I have heard it asserted that he is the richest lawyer in the Commonwealth.

Mr Amory has also been successfully engaged in speculating upon public securities, as well as Mr Wetmore, and M^r: Otis. This employment does not appear to be very intimately connected with the profession. But these gentlemen I am told have played at that hazardous game with monies deposited in their hands; and have been enabled by the temporary possession of property belonging to foreigners, to become masters of sums to an equal amount before they have been called upon for payment. Amory is very attentive to his business, and has recommended himself by the expedition with which he performs that which is entrusted to him. He is a student too; but I think confines his researches rather too much within the circle of mere professional information.[3]

Otis appears to me to be advancing very rapidly to eminence. There is certainly no man in this town of the profession, who unites so many of those qualities which are calculated to attract the popular attention. He has been but four years at the bar: yet excepting Sullivan, I believe there is no one here who has a greater proportion of business. But his ambition has no limits; and I strongly suspect that the honours of a public station have such allurements to his mind, that he will catch with ardor at the first opportunity to become a public man— Such an opportunity will perhaps be presented to him before long, and if he should once get entangled in the political web, it may be presumed he will like most others find it inextricable— These are the persons who share among themselves the principal business which is done in this town. M$^{r:}$ Lowell has a Son, who was just sworn into Court at the time of his appointment, and to whom he has conveniently left all his unfinished business. The young Gentleman has talents, activity and application; with a great degree of confidence in himself; a quality which is not amiable, but which perhaps is very serviceable to him, in helping him forward.— His peculiar advantages have given him, an unusual share of business, for a person so lately admitted: he is rather disposed to attribute the circumstance to his superior abilities; and expresses some contempt for persons less successful than himself because depending solely upon their own characters: the self-sufficient airs of such a youth as this, will make me doubly sensible to the want of employment which I must submit to.[4] Disappointed emulation I have lately read, is perhaps the most cruel of all mortifications—but I shall be supported with the conviction that in the End I shall do well; and perhaps Vanity ought sometimes to meet with mortification.

With respect to the Rent of your House, from which I now write, I have made some enquiries, from the result of which I am not induced to expect I shall be able to increase it. The front Room, which I occupy is the only lower room in the house, except a small kitchen; and people here are so little used to living altogether in chambers, that they consider it as a great inconvenience. However, if you think it expedient, I can advertise it to be lett, as soon as I shall have the charge of it; and perhaps that circumstance might induce the present tenant to raise his price, as the house is much more convenient for him, than for any other man in this Town.[5] I shall punctually obey whatever directions I may receive from you upon this Subject.

The farm at Braintree I know but little about: nor am I well aware of what measures would be best calculated to render it more profitable than it is. Pratt's defect I take to be altogether *incurable*: it is want of skilful management. But a Tenant possess'd of that faculty in a high degree, unless he were very honest might be an alteration for the worse rather than the better. And I believe, that Estate, and indeed all Estates which consists in farms, will never be rendered very profitable, without the *Eye*, and the *Hand* of the Master.

With my Love to all the family at Richmond-Hill and the friends in the City I remain, dear Sir your affectionate Son.

J. Q. Adams.

RC (Adams Papers); docketed: "John Adam Jun[r.] / Sept[r] 21 –90."

[1] It is allowable to learn even from an enemy (Ovid, *Metamorphoses*, Book IV, line 428).

[2] Thomas Dawes was 24 years old when he married Margaret Greenleaf in Oct. 1781 (Boston *Continental Journal*, 11 Oct. 1781).

[3] For William Amory, see JQA, *Diary*, 2:292. For William Wetmore, see JA, *Legal Papers*, 1:cxiii.

[4] For John Lowell, who had recently received a federal judicial appointment, see vol. 7:170. His son, also John Lowell (1769-

1840), Harvard 1786, was admitted to the bar in 1789 and soon afterwards enjoyed a thriving law practice. The younger Lowell married Rebecca Amory in 1793 and later served in the Mass. General Court from 1798 to 1800 (*DAB*).

[5] Likely Thomas Adams and John Nourse, printers of the Boston *Independent Chronicle*, who had rented the Adamses' Court Street property for the past several years; see vol. 7:424, 425-426.

Mary Smith Cranch to Abigail Adams

My dear Sister   Braintree [*post 22*] September [*1790*][1]

I beleive cousin Thomas has wanted his Trunk. I hear that Barnard did not sail till last week I hope your son has arriv'd safe but wonder that we have not heard from him. He promiss'd to write. The parting on our side was hard I cannot think of it without a Tear He had so indear'd himself to us all by his affectionate behaviour & amiable manners that he was to us a Son & Brother may a good providince attend him wherever he goes—

You my dear Sister I find will soon leave new-york & altho I should not be more likely to see you when there than at Philadelphia yet I cannot bear you should move a Step farther from us—but I will please myself that you will make us a visit next Summer—

The People who apply'd to us about your House had taken a house at Cambridge but think it too far from publick amusements & are going into Boston for the winter— Mr Turner who married Mr Adams Daughter apply'd to me the other day to know if the House was to Let & wish'd to take a part of it— I told him you wish'd to let the whole but could not tell whether you would let only a part. Doctor Tufts says you had better let it be empty unless you can let it to some purpose, & to some person who will not abuse it. We will make Fires in it & preserve it from harm as well as we can

I have receiv'd your Letter of August 29th & hop'd to have had another before this time— mr Cranch says he din'd with you a few week since & that you were well I allmost begrudg'd him the pleasure—[2] mr Hunt from St Croix Lodg'd in the House with mr Adams upon his Journey to Philadelphia so that I feel as if I had been constantly knowing something about you— When you go to your new Lodgings I beg you would ask Doctor Rush about that marvellous Funeral of mrs Browns who was kill'd by falling upon a spit— miss Chartt is still in deep mourning for the Family all of whome are dead except old mr Price. I very believe her Parents are convinc'd there never were such People in Boston—but why they try to keep up the Idea I know not— We do not visit nor have for these Seven months—but are very neighbourly other ways Charles is married & is now here with his wife[3]

This week mrs Quncy & mrs Packard leave Braintree do you not pity me my sister? It was the only house I could visit at with freedom except mr Alleynes in this town What a dispersion of Friends— mr Palmers Family all going & miss otis too[4] mr otis & his wife Lodg'd here as they came from Plymouth—

Tell mrs Brisler that her Brother is to be married soon to miss Leafy Baxter so she may lay asside her mourning if she has finish'd making it— She will make him an exellent wife the Family are all pleass'd with it.[5]

Poor mr Thaxter has lost his Baby & it has been almost too much for him I hear his fits have been more frequent Since— he was very fond of his child & it was a very fine one— I do not think he will live long—[6] mrs Thaxter has a Severe trial poor woman, The Baby lay sick above two months with a dissorder in its Bowels which ended in a distress'd consumtion— I hope mrs Smith & her little ones are well my Love to her. will She go with you?

If you will not let me, I will say no more & only thank you— I hope we shall not always feel so many calls as we have done for these several years nobody but I know half the Difficultes I have had to incounter I have thoughts sometimes it would be to hard for me you & I have been better wives than the world will ever know of or give us cridit for

Mr Cranch is almost sick with one of his dreadfull colds & coughs I am much concern'd about him it has staid so long by him the rest of us are well William has some business already. He is very attentive— mrs norton & her little one are better they have been poorly with colds & the Baby with Teeth

when your carpet which is like that you gave me is wore out, I will thank you for it to mend mine—

cousin John attends to his Business too closely he ought to come to Braintree often— he will be sick if he does not ride out of Town

pray write often tis the only consolation I have for your absence & a Letter is always a cordial to the spirits of / your affectionate Sister

Mary Cranch

RC (Adams Papers); addressed by William Cranch: "Mrs Abigail Adams / New York."; endorsed: "M^rs· Cranch / 1790." Filmed at Sept. [1790].

[1] The letter is dated based on Capt. Barnard's departure from Boston on 22 or 23 Sept. (New York *Gazette of the United States*, 2 Oct.).

[2] In a letter of 27 Aug., Cranch asked AA, "Should you not be surpriz'd to see Doctor Tufts & Mr Cranch. they have really had some talks of making you a visit—but I had rather you would come here. they cannot see you for me—it will not satisfy me" (Adams Papers).

[3] Lieut. Charles Ward Apthorp (1761-1804), son of Sarah Wentworth and James Apthorp of Braintree, had married Mary Prince at St. John, New Brunswick (Boston *Columbian Centinel*, 21 Aug.; John Wentworth, *The Wentworth Genealogy: English and American*, 3 vols., Boston, 1878, 1:519,

524).

[4] Probably Hannah Otis (b. 1732), sister of Samuel Alleyne Otis and Mercy Otis Warren. Previously of Braintree, she now worked in Boston as a shopkeeper (*NEHGR*, 2:292 [July 1848]; vol. 6:232; *Boston Directory*, 1789, Evans, No. 22033).

[5] Joseph Field married his second wife, Relief Baxter (1763-1849), daughter of Daniel and Prudence Baxter of Braintree, on 3 May 1791 (Sprague, *Braintree Families*).

[6] One-year-old John Adams Thaxter died on 4 Sept. 1790 (*Vital Records of Haverhill Massachusetts to the End of the Year 1849*, 2 vols., Topsfield, Mass., 1910-1911, 2:480). For the death of John Thaxter Jr., see Elizabeth Smith Shaw to AA, 24 June 1791, and note 1, below.

Elizabeth Smith Shaw to Abigail Adams

My Dear Sister—   Haverhill September 28th. 1790

I know your tender sympathetick Heart will join with me, & drop a Tear over a lovely Child—the once beautiful John Adams Thaxter—sick—faded—withered—dead— Just as his dawning reason made us wish his stay— Just as his beauteous smile & sparkling Eye promised future Joy—

> "Tis God that lifts our Comforts high,
> Or sinks them in the Grave
> *He* gives—(& blessed be his name)
> *He* takes but what *He* gave"—[1]

It is this consideration alone that can calm the tumult of the Soul, & give peace, & serenity to the weepings Eyes, & bleeding-hearts of the fond doating Parents—

> "Religion noble comfort brings,
> Disarms our Griefs, or Blunts there Stings"—[2]

You (my Sister) know how grievous such a bereavment is, & we that are Mothers know how tenderly we love those little Sucklings— they draw love from our hearts, & are closely twisted with its fibres—
I fully intended writing to you by Cousin Thomas but Mr Thaxters Child grew so sick, that my Mind did not feel calm enough for anything, & besides that, I wished to devote all my leisure hours, to the distressed Parents— The Doctor advised Mrs Thaxter to wean her Son, but unfortunately it happened to be while he was cutting his Eye Teeth— She weaned him, & Mr Shaw carried her to Cousin Thomas's Commencement— But the dear Child was seized with a lax State, while she was gone, & was never well afterwards. They had to watch over a sick cradle for a great while, long enough to exhaust better Spirits, than poor Mr Thaxter was possessed of— It was at times in great distress—& for a whole fortnight, they did not expect its life from hour to hour— Mr Thaxter is supported much better than I feared— He behaves like a Christian— his health suffers, & it is true, that "He *thinks* like a *Sage*, but he *feels* like a *Man*"—[3]
The Death of this Child (my Sister) affects me more (perhaps) than if I had not an Infant of my own— Bearing the same name, & People talking so much about them, makes me look upon my little

Aba Adams, & consider her, as *widdowed* even in her Cradle— As her Brother & Sister were so much older, I did indeed promise myself much comfort in seeing them pleasant companions for each other, at lest in the more early part of Life, & that Protection, & attention which she could not have from her Brother, she might with propriety claim from her *Cousin*— But heaven allwise—has determined otherways, & Submission—however hard, must be our part—

Your youngest Son has now compleated his Studies at the University, & distinguished himself by his amiable Conduct, & gained the approbation, & esteem of all— So we find that merit, even in these degenerate days, does not pass unnoticed, & is not without its sincere admirers—

Mr Thomas had lived with us so long, & was now going to enter into business, on the wide world, & so far distant from me, that it affected me exceedingly— A fond Mothers heart, could not have felt more peculiar emotions— Though I wished him every Blessing, I could not *bid* him farewell—

October 16th.

This Letter has laid by me for sometime, not knowing of any direct Conveyance— But Mr & Mrs Dalton has been so kind as to call upon me, & informed me of their intended Journey to the Southward the last of this month, & politely offered to convey Letters to you— So good an Opportunity I embrace with pleasure— Mrs Dalton is indeed a fine woman, & an excellent Mother—& I am glad they are going to return for yours, & my Cousins sake— The Miss Daltons[4] I suppose will inform you, that your eldest Son has been vastly attentive to the Ladies of late—& that *one happy fair*, was distinguished— aye my Sister—what will you say, should *your Hercules* be conquered? Shall we believe Report?— And it says, that a certain Lady is highly favoured— You my Sister can easily conceive of what advantage it is, for a young Lady to have a faithful Friend—One who can kindly check the temerity of Youth, & accurately describe the Lines by which a celebrated Beauty may pass through the dangerous age of Sixteen—One who can sweetly point out the path of Duty, & make the fair Field of Science, & Literature still more pleasing, by pointing out where the sweetest flowers may be culled to adorn the female Breast,—& where the richest Fruit, to refine, & please the mental Taste—

I have given up all thoughts of visiting Braintree this Fall— Though I long to see Sister Cranch, I content myself at home, as I cannot have the pleasure of seeing you there— My little one grows finely— I was mortified that she was asleep with her night-gown on when Mrs Dalton saw her— I wish you could see her now, I fear she will not be so handsom in a year or two— I question whether Mrs Smith or Cousin Charles will ever have a Child look more like them than this sweet creature does—

It looks very dismal to think you are going so far from me, & Cousin Thomas too to settle in Pensylvania— I cannot feel willing—

I congratulate you upon the birth of a third Grandson— There will be statesmen in plenty, if Mrs Smith goes on from year to year in this way— My Love to her & the dear little Ones— I know Mrs Smith, & Cousin Charles will mourn at your leaving new york—for there is nothing better than a Fathers house—

I think I bear nursing very well, my health is certainly better than it has been for several years, or I could not tend Miss so much as I do, for she is almost as fleshy as my William was, though every body says she is much prettier— My Letter has run to a most unreasonable length— Adieu— most affectionately   E Shaw

RC (Adams Papers); addressed: "Mrs Abigail Adams / New-York"; docketed: "E Peabody to / A Adams. 1790."

[1] Isaac Watts, "Hymn 5," lines 9–12. Shaw initially quoted only the second two lines; she later interlined the first two lines.

[2] Nathaniel Cotton, "Life, Vision the Last," *Visions in Verse*, London, 1751, p. 104, lines 123–124.

[3] "He thought as a sage, but he felt as a man" (James Beattie, "The Hermit," *A Collection of Poems in Four Volumes*, London, 1770, 3:47, line 8).

[4] Tristram and Ruth Dalton had three unmarried daughters at the time: Mary (b. 1771), Sarah (b. 1775), and Catherine (b. 1777). Their eldest, Ruth (b. 1767), had married Lewis Deblois of Boston the previous summer (*Vital Records of Newburyport Massachusetts to the End of the Year 1849*, 2 vols., Salem, Mass., 1911, 1:109; 2:125).

Cotton Tufts to Abigail Adams

Dear Mad[m.]   Weymouth Sep[r.] 28. 1790

Yours of the 5[th.] I rec[d.] the 15[t.] Inst.[1] By M[r.] Thomas who has reached You before this Time I wrote & enclosed M[r.] Adams Acc[ts.] and an Answer to a former Letter of Yours.[2] Had I known that it had been necessary for Your Son to have come forward at an earlier Period and his Stay here had rested on his not being furnished with the needful. I should certainly have procured it by some means or other— His modesty joind with his Desire to Visit his Friends before He left the State prevented him I suppose from pressing the Matter—

With Respect to Your House at Braintree, No Person has presented to hire it— An Applicant would probably expect the Garden, Stables &c. with the Dwelling House—not unlikely the Land on the Back of the House, Part of these are already under the Improvement of Capt. Adams— However should any Body present to hire, I will pay ready Attention to the Business.

In the Close of last Month I paid Mr Codman for the Two Casks of Wine at which Time He engaged to forward them by Barnard— about Ten Days past I call'd on Him found they were not sent— he promised to put them on board of Barnard who was then at the Wharf or in Case He was full, by an other Vessell which would sail in a Day or two from that Time— I hope you have rec^d. them before this—

You have not mentioned in any Letter, the Receipt of the Barrell of Sugar & 1 bb. Spirits from Jamaica sent by Barnad in June last— Would you have your Cheese & Butter from Pratts sent to you— What is to be done with your farming Tools Cart & mud Boat—

Gen. Lincoln mentioned to me the 16th. Ins^t. D^r. Williamsons wish to exchange some Bank Notes for the Value to be received in New York; to oblige the D^r. I consented to Gen. Lincolns endorsing my order on M^r. Adams, it was accordingly delivered to the D^r. of which I gave information by Letter, which I hope reached M^r. Adams timely enough to prevent his sending forward the order proposed—[3]

I have enclosed a List of the public Securities, you requested, if it is not descriptive enough, Youll let me know.[4]

The Assumption of but part of our State Debt, will render it I conceive exceedingly embarrassing how to provide for the Remainder so as to facilitate the Loan of the Sum agreed to be assumed, as well as to establish a Uniformity between the measure of Congress and the State—a more full Provision than what Congress has made for Payment of Principal & Interest will be contended for, and if not allowed, I am doubtful whether any effectual Measures will be adopted— indeed at present I am entirely in the Dark, How this Business is to be settled so as to make any tolerable Consistency in the adjustment of it—

Pray what will the Commissioners employed to purchase Continental Securities, allow, or how will they conduct their Business? State Securities are sold at 8^s/P^r. £ Continental @ 12^s/2^d. Indents from 6/8 to 7^s/– Will it best to sell or best to buy—

Next Week the Choice for national Representatives will come

on— much Pains hath been taken to prejudice the Minds of People against M^r· Ames— The Votes in Suffolk Dist^t· will be divided between M^r· Ames, Judge Dawes & Mr Benj^m· Austin Junr· I think it is a Doubt whether M^r· Ames will be chosen— great Interest is making in middlesex to introduce M^r· Gorham— it is thought by some, that it will prevail— [5]

The general Dislike of the Pay, Salaries & Compen[sation] granted by Congress will lead to a Change of Men in hopes of a Change of Measures— Had Congress even with the Grants complaind off made a reasonable Dispatch in their Business Complaints would probably have subsided, more especially if they had early established a funding System upon Principles clear easy & in the Apprehensions of the Majority of the People just—upon the whole but very few People in the Massachusetts appear to be pleased with the Doings of Congress in their late Session— I do not however conceive that they have any just Reason to find fault with their own Members or indeed to treat Congress with that Rudeness which some of our Scriblers have taken the Liberty to do— [6]

M^rs· Tufts begs to be remembered to You & Yours.

Accept of the best Wishes of / Your Affec^t· Friend & H Ser^t

Cotton Tufts

Octob. 6th:

On Monday last, the Towns in this Commonwealth met for the Choice of Federal Representatives— By the Returns from a Number of Towns in this District, there is no doubt of M^r· Ames's being chosen— It is not improbable the Choice in Middlesex will fall upon Mr Gerry, notwithstanding the Pains taken to introduce M^r· Gorham—

RC (Adams Papers); addressed: "M^rs· Abigail Adams"; internal address: "M^rs· Abigail Adams"; docketed: "Dr Tufts to / Mrs Adams / September 27th 1790." Some loss of text where the seal was removed.

[1] AA to Tufts, 6 Sept., above.

[2] Not found, but AA confirmed in her response, "I received by my son your kind favour together with your statement of my papers" (3 Oct., NHi:Misc. Mss. Adams, Abigail).

[3] AA reported to Tufts that "Dr Williamson calld last week and received his money delivering your order" (same). For Dr. Hugh Williamson, see JA, D&A, 3:224–225.

[4] Not found.

[5] The Boston *Columbian Centinel*, 29 Sept., contained a piece signed "A Mechanick" lamenting, "The shifts to which the partizans for turning out the Federal Representatives are reduced, are contemptible. Mr. AMES is *now* called in the papers an *Aristocrat*, an *anti-amendmentile*, and other *equally heinous appellations*." In spite of this opposition, Fisher Ames easily defeated Benjamin Austin Jr. and Thomas Dawes, serving as congressional representative for Suffolk County until 1797. In Middlesex County, Elbridge Gerry defeated Nathaniel Gorham by a smaller margin (*Columbian Centinel*, 9 Oct. 1790).

[6] A piece by Rusticus in the Boston *Independent Chronicle*, 2 Sept., excoriated the U.S. Congress, criticizing the "extravagant compensations" of its members as well as the measures the body adopted to address the national debt. The writer noted, "The world would have supposed that fifty-six men, chosen from among three millions of people, enlightned as the Americans are acknowledged to be, would not have stood in need of having been so copiously indoctrinated in the first rudiments of government, and the first principles of national economy. We all expected that this assembly would have, without pomp, or parade, set themselves down to the business before them, expressed their sentiments to gain, or give necessary information, and stood constantly open to conviction. But instead of this, we find some of them composing long speeches to amuse an idle gallery, or fill a pompous page in Fenno's paper." Soon afterwards, "An American" complained in the Boston *Columbian Centinel* of "typographical unfairness" in the *Chronicle*, comparing the prominence and "magnitude of type" of opposition pieces to the "*little, paltry* type" of a lone essay supporting the government (4 Sept.).

Abigail Adams to Mary Smith Cranch

my dear sister   Newyork october 3^d 1790

do you not pitty me my dear sister to be so soon all in a Bustle? and wary of Removing again, as much Boxing and casing, as if we were removing to Europe. our furniture may well be stiled *movables*. the expence attending the various removals would very handsomely furnish one House. I feel low spirited and Heartless. I am going amongst an other new set of company, to form new acquaintances to make and receive a hundred ceremonious visits, not one of ten from which I shall derive any pleasure or satisfaction, obliged to leave mrs smith behind, and the Children to whom I am much attached, and many other things I have upon my mind and spirits which I cannot communicate by Letter. I live however upon the Hope that I shall come and see you next summer. I hope congress will not set out the Month of April.

I have wrote to the dr respecting the Widow Owen and Rebecca Field.[1] I had rather they should be in the House than have it left empty through the winter. they must always remember that they must remove when ever we come to want the House, and that without giving us any trouble.

you wrote me about Rose water.[2] if you have an opportunity to send me a dozen Bottles I should like to have it. I forgot to write to you Sooner, but you may have it put up and addrest to col smith Newyork when Barnard comes again we expect to get our furniture on Board by the 20th of the Month. Charles is going to Board with his sister, and Thomas will go into an office in Philadelphia. I wish he could have gone into merchandize as I am sure he has more of a Turn for active Life.

How is mrs Norten & her Boy? we have got one with a Red Head I do not know what part of the family he lays claim to. I forget whether I wrote you that they had Named him Thomas Hollis.

Let mrs Field know that Lucy and mr Brislers children have the small pox.[3] it has turnd and they have it very lightly, Lucy not more than 20 pock Nabby not a dozen, Betsy is pretty full but has a good sort and is very cleverly. I had Prince inoculated at the same time. he has about a Dozen, but has not been confined at all, nor sick a little headack excepted. be so good as to send his Father word if you have an opportunity

Mrs Smith is here to day and desires to be rememberd to all her Friends. when did you hear from sister shaw. I think I used to get Letters and write oftner when I was abroad than I do now—

Let me hear from you Soon, and believe me most affectionatly yours   A Adams

Love to mr cranch & duty to mother, I hope I shall see her again good old Lady

RC (MWA:Abigail Adams Letters); addressed by CA: "Mrs Mary Cranch / Braintree"; endorsed by Richard Cranch: "Letter from M^rs / A. Adams (NY) / Octr. 3^d 1790."

[1] In her letter to Tufts, AA asked, "If there is no probality of letting our House & furniture together, would it not be best to let the widow owen & Rebecca Field go in to the kitchen part for the winter, to have a care of it?" (3 Oct., NHi:Misc. Mss. Adams, Abigail). AA possibly refers to Elizabeth Newcomb Owen (1720–1809), widow of Joseph Owen and sister of Abigail Newcomb Field (Sprague, *Braintree Families*).

[2] Mary Smith Cranch to AA, 9 Aug., above.

[3] Lucy Field, Esther Field Briesler's sister and the youngest child of Joseph and Abigail Newcomb Field of Braintree (Frederick Clifton Pierce, *Field Genealogy*, 2 vols., Chicago, 1901, 2:962).

John Adams to John Quincy Adams

My dear Son   New York October 4. 1790

I have received and read with great Pleasure, your modest Sensible, judicious and discreet Letter of the 31. of Sept^r.[1]

The Town of Boston is at present unhappily divided into political Parties, and neither Party I presume has tried Experiments enough upon you to discover to which Side you belong. You might very easily induce either Side to make much of you, by becoming a zealot for it: but my Advice to you is Nil Admirari Nil contemni. Admire neither Party—despize neither Party.[2] Treat both Sides with Civility and respect but be the Devotee of neither. Be always on the side of

Truth Justice Honour Virtue and public Spirit. Even S. may be of service to you if you keep him at a distance, and never put yourself in his Power.

The Youth you mention has considerable Advantages, but his Contempt will hurt him, not you. Let me tell you however, once for all, that however painful, the mortifications of Emulation may be, you must learn to bear them and be Superiour to them. You will see one, preferred to you for his Party, another for his Church, a third for his family connections a fourth for an unmeaning fluencey, a fifth for his figure Air, Gate. and some for their Profligacy and De-bauchery—others for their Want of Principle. Let not those Things move you out of your Course.

In your Studies, you have yet to begin a system. from all I have Seen and read, I have formed an opinion of my own, and I now give it you as my Solemn Advice, to make yourself Master of the Roman Learning. Begin with Livy.— take your Book your Dictionary, your Grammar, your Sheet of Paper and Pen and Ink. begin at the Be-ginning and read the Work through— put down in Writing every Word with its meaning as you find it in Ainsworth. You will find it the most delightful Employment you ever engaged in. When you have finished the 35[th.] Book you will say, that you have learned more Wisdom from it than from five hundred Volumes of the trash that is commonly read.— The Writings of Cicero too, you should read in turn. When I Speak of reading I dont mean holding a book in hand and dreaming over it— take your Pen.—and make yourself Master of every Sentence.— By all means make yourself Master of the latin Tongue and that immediately. Polybius and Plutarch and Sallust as sources of Wisdom as well as Roman History, must not be forgotten, nor Dyonissius Hallicarnassensis.[3] Read them all in Latin.— Nor would I by any means consent that you forget your Greek. keep it alive at least, and improve in it by degrees.

My Brother might Supply you with Wood from my Lots as well as Hay. I wish you to ask your Uncle, respectfully as becomes you, how the account Stands between him and me and what Articles he can supply you with on my Account. I will give you the whole Manage-ment of my Estate, if you will take it— Yet I will not urge it upon you— perhaps it may interrupt your Studies too much.

Above all Things keep up your Spirits and take Care of your Health.

I long to see you in your office: but the Care of a troublesome Removal to Philadelphia, will prevent me till next year.

Your Letters give me so much pleasure as well as Information that I wish you to write as often as you can to / your Affectionate

John Adams.

Your Brother Thomas is as studious as I wish him to be.

RC (Adams Papers); internal address: "J. Q Adams." Tr (Adams Papers).

[1] JQA to JA, 21 Sept., above.

[2] A loose appropriation of Horace, *Epistles*, Book I, epistle vi, line 1.

[3] The libraries of JA and JQA, at MB and the Stone Library at MQA, respectively, contain copies of *The History of Polybius, The Megalopolitan*, London, 1698. JA's library also includes editions of Plutarch's *Lives* in French and Latin; JQA later purchased an English translation of that work. Both librar-ies also include works by the Roman historian Sallust, author of *Catiline's War* and *Jugurthine War*. The libraries have different editions of *Dionysiou Halikarnaseōs*, a history of early Rome by the Greek historian Dionysius. JA's library holds a Frankfurt edition of 1586, while JQA's includes that of Leipzig, 1774 (*Catalogue of JA's Library; Catalogue of JQA's Books*).

Abigail Adams to Mary Smith Cranch

my dear sister   Nyork october 10th 1790

I wrote to you last Sunday, and on Wednesday received your kind Letter.[1] we have begun to pack up our furniture, and expect to get it on Board by the 20th perhaps we may make it later, but I hope not as the weather will every day become more & more uncomfortable. the Idea of going so much further from you is painfull to me, and would be more so if I did not hope to Spend the next summer with you. at present you have your Family with and near you, but it is my destiny to have mine Scatered, and scarcly to keep one with us. my seperation from mrs smith is painfull to me on many accounts. there is at present no prospect of their going with us, and if their prospects here were as fair as they ought to be, I should be less solicitious for them. with Regard to our House, I should have no objection to a carefull person living in the kitchin to take care of it, but as to letting it I cannot consent unless any person offers to take House and furniture all together. there is the other part of the House in which Bass lives that might be let, but then I should be loth that a shoe makers shop should be made of either of the Rooms— in short I do not know of any persons property so unproductive as ours is. I do not believe that it yealds us one pr cent pr Annum I have the vanity however to think that if dr Tufts and my Ladyship had been left to the sole management of our affairs, they would have been upon a more profitable footing in the first place I never desired so much Land unless we could have lived upon it. the

Money paid for useless land I would have purchased publick Securities with the interest of which poorly as it is funded would have been less troublesome to take charge of then Land and much more productive, but in these Ideas I have always been so unfortunate as to differ from my partner who thinks he never saved any thing but what he vested in Land. I am really however very uneasy with Pratt as a Famer. he has got a great swarm of helpless children round him, labours hard but has no skill and the place with the addition of veseys very little more than pays the taxes; I wish mr Beals could be induced to go upon it. the other place I know no more about than if it lay in the Moon. I have written to request that the saint Germain pears and the best Russet Apples may be sent to me. the communication between Boston and Philadelphia is so frequent that I should suppose their could be no difficulty in it.

I had the pleasure of assembling yesterday mr & mrs Storer mr & mrs Atkinson mr Charles George & mary storer col & mrs smith and miss Pegy Smith who all dined with me and I felt more like Home than I have ever done since I left Braintree. mr Adams mourns that he could not make a visit Northward this fall. we are well. Brislers family all got through the small pox with only a day or twos illness— present me affectionatly to all Friends I fear mr Cranch does not put on his flannel soon enough. I grow more and more in favour of the use of it and advise you to wear it next your skin make little waistcoats & put them on with the first comeing of cold weather. I[*f*] I had as much Spair Room in my stays as you have I would not be without them

poor mr Thaxter I am grieved for him—but who is without their troubles? thank God that a larger portion has not fallen to the Lot of your ever / affectionate Sister   A Adams

RC (MWA:Abigail Adams Letters); addressed by CA: "Mrs Mary Cranch / Braintree"; endorsed by Richard Cranch: "Letter from M^rs / A Adams (N York) / Oct^r: 10th. 1790."

¹ Mary Smith Cranch to AA, [*post* 22] Sept., above.

John Quincy Adams to Abigail Adams

My dear Madam.   Boston October 17th: 1790.

I am I believe more than one Letter in your debt; but I feel if possible less inclination than ever to write to my friends as I have no good news to tell them about myself, and very little about any one else. I have now the advantage of being three hundred miles distant from every member of the family; alone in the world, without a soul to share the few joys I have, or to participate in my anxieties and suspense, which are neither few nor small. Why should I sit down to write, when I can assume no other language than that of complaint, which must be as disagreeable, to my friends who read, as it is to me who write— You may readily believe that when I have any thing favourable to say, I shall be sufficiently impatient to give you the information. My taste for politics has even become disgusting to me; I can scarcely take any pleasure in the increasing prosperity of my Country: what is the public welfare to me, if the very efforts upon which it has so much depended, have deprived me of my fundamental support, and have left me exposed to the most humiliating neglect from all the world around me; and turned me over to the delusions of Hope for my Comfort.— I am exhibiting all my weakness I am exposing myself to the Contempt as well as to the Pity of my friends, by assuming thus a style of Lamentation, unbecoming a man of Spirit. Evils I shall be told must me remedied; not deplored: but my peculiar Situation is such that there is no room for my Exertion— The day will come however, I still perswade myself that the day will come, when I shall be enabled to give you more pleasing intelligence; and as I have already said I shall then write with much more satisfaction, what will give you much more pleasure to read.

You will perceive by our Papers, that four members of our present Delegation in Congress are re-elected. It is not from the paltry malevolence of a few contemptible scribblers in our News papers, that the sense of the people is to be collected. Two candidates had been opposed to M^r: Ames with the intention to divide the votes more effectually; and so much industry and influence was exerted in *their* favour, that the result in *his* favour, was beyond the most sangwine expectations of his friends, and the friends of the national honour. In Middlesex indeed the votes were more divided. M^r: Gorham is a popular man: and if the public report be not fallacious he has been indefatigable for these two years past in the pursuit of this Election. M^r: Gerry however has a respectable majority of votes.

You mention in one of your Letters that M^r: Short is commissioned to negotiate the Loan. I should wish to know, where it is expected he will obtain it: I cannot imagine that the attempt will be made in France, where the nation are so heavily labouring under the weight of their own poverty.— Holland I presume will be the seat of the negociation. And I should be glad to be informed what is the opinion of the VP. with respect to its success.— I think the value of public paper must depend considerably upon it.[1]

Our Court of Common Pleas are sitting in this Town; and I have made my first Essay in addressing a Jury. I wish I could add that I had acquitted myself to my own Satisfaction. I had very little time for preparation and [did] not know the existence of the Cause three hours before I spoke to it.[2] From [this] circumstance, and from the novelty of the Situation, added to the diffidence I have always felt, of my talent at extemporary speechifying I was too much agitated to be possessed of proper presence of mind. You may judge of the figure I made.

I address this Letter still to New-York, presuming that if it should arrive after your departure, care will be taken to have it forwarded to Philadelphia.

Ever your's   J. Q. Adams.

RC (Adams Papers); addressed: "M^rs: A. Adams. / Richmond Hill."; docketed: "J Q Adams to / His Mother / October 17th 1790." Some loss of text where the seal was removed.

[1] In a letter of 5 Sept., AA informed JQA: "Short is commissiond to Negotiate the Loan. Humphries tis supposed is to take his place. as yet nothing is made publick respecting it. the President You know has the power of appointments in the Recess of Congress" (Adams Papers). William Short, chargé d'affaires at Paris, was instructed by Alexander Hamilton on 1 Sept. to proceed immediately to the Netherlands to secure additional U.S. loans from Amsterdam bankers. Short negotiated a $1 million loan in Feb. 1791 through Amsterdam bankers Nicolaas & Jacob van Staphorst, Wilhem & Jan Willink, and Nicholas Hubbard, the first of several loans he would open in Amsterdam and Antwerp over the next three years

(Hamilton, *Papers*, 7:6–7, 9; George Green Shackelford, *Jefferson's Adoptive Son: The Life of William Short 1759–1848*, Lexington, Ky., 1993, p. 78–80, 89–90).

[2] JQA notes in his Diary that the Court of Common Pleas met on 5 and 11 Oct. 1790 but provides no details about his first case, which he lost to Harrison Gray Otis. Thomas Welsh reported to JA, "Your son has made a Begining at the Court of Common Pleas which was the first which opend after his settling in Town. His Diffidence was remarked and the tremor which arrises from a soul alive. He has the popular Predictions in his Favor" (D/JQA/12, APM Reel 15; Welsh to JA, 20 Nov., Adams Papers).

John Quincy Adams to John Adams

Dear Sir.   Boston October 19. 1790.

I have a Letter from you which has called forth the few remaining sparks of my attenion to politics—[1] Were my own mind at ease, I should at the present time enter more than ever into the spirit of speculation upon public affairs. The prospect is really glorious; but it is perhaps impossible, at least for a man whose patriotism is not tinctured with more heroism than mine, to consider the general prosperity with such peculiar pleasure, when he is not one of the individuals who derive any immediate advantage from it, as when the fabric of his patriotic ardour is supported by the firm pillars of private interest. I feel myself growing more and more selfish and contracted in my Sentiments from day to day; and I am perswaded I shall never be much of a philanthropist or even of a Patriot, untill I have more reason to be pleased with my own Situation and prospects.

However, it was politics that I professed to make the subject of my Letter when I began, and to them I will return after this digression, which I am afraid will not please you so much as the remainder of the Letter.

I have attended Town-meeting, Sir, and it was upon the occasion of the choice of Representative for the district. I was indeed not a little diverted at the scene, and derived I believe some little Instruction as well as Entertainment from it. Three fourths of the Votes in this Town were indeed for M^r: Ames, and this perhaps may enable you to form an opinion respecting the popularity of the general Government in this State. M^r: Gerry too is reelected in the district of Middlesex, notwithstanding the whole personal interest of M^r: Gorham and his friends was very strenuously exerted to operate a change. There was not even the pretence of opposing a candidate to M^r: Goodhue, [2] and M^r: Sedgwick is also rechosen by a surprizing majority of votes in his district; these are premises from which much more accurate conclusions may be drawn, than from the senseless bawlings of a miserable faction; who are reduced to the last resource of making up in unheeded clamour, their total deficiency of influence and power.— The real fact is that the new Government is very rapidly acquiring a broad and solid foundation of popularity.— It possesses in my opinion the confidence of the people in this State to a more eminent degree than any other Government upon Earth can boast of: and it appears to me to have already acquired a stability, as astonishing as the revolution it has produced in the face of our affairs.

The effects of that revolution are already felt in a very high degree in this part of the Country. Our Commerce is increasing and extending; our manufactures multiplying very rapidly, our agriculture flourishing; industry has resumed the place which it had resigned for some time to idleness and luxury; and is seldom without employ. I am informed that the mechanics of almost every description in this Town are at present more constantly busy than they have been at any period since the Revolution. The population of the Town has increased from 14000 to 18000 inhabitants since the year 1784.[3] And the property has augmented in a much greater proportion. 1200 people are employed by one manufacture which has been only three or four years established; that of wool cards. That of Sail-Cloth, equally recent gives bread to several hundreds more: Paper hangings have become even an article of exportation from hence. Near four hundred tons of hemp, I hear have been raised this Season, within the State. This is a new Article of cultivation, and even so late as the last year there were not more than 30 tons raised within the Commonwealth. It is found to be a very profitable article, and in all probability in the course of two or three years will cease to be imported altogether; and from a calculation which I have seen we might export it and easily undersell the Russians. There is a Col^l: Wood in Charlestown who has raised more than three tons upon six acres of his land, and the produce of that small field will neat him 300 dollars.[4] There is undoubtedly a connecting chain, the commune vinculum,[5] between, all the various employments of mankind, as well as between the liberal arts & Sciences. The farmer, The tradesmen, the mechanic and the merchant, are all mutually so dependant upon one another for their prosperity, that I really know not whether most to pity the ignorance or to lament the absurdity of the partial politicians, who are constantly erecting an imaginary wall of separation between them.

The health of the Governor has been better for these two months, than for several years before. There is I think a probability that he will hold the chair of State for many years to come. It will not I presume be contested him; and indeed the bitterness of parties has been tempered very much by the favourable alteration in the public affairs. The Public Peace, and public Prosperity, appear in this instance to have possessed a mutual acting and reacting power to establish and confirm each other.

I believe no experiments have been made upon me in order to discover my political Sentiments. I have not importance enough to make it worth their while.– I have the advantage of being compleatly neglected in this line, as well as in that of my profession. But "Sweet are the uses of adversity."[6]

In the stagnation of our own politics, the people who have a fondness for the subject turn their attention to those of Europe, which seems to be now as much as ever it could be un repaire d'horreurs. The war between Spain and England has been so long suspended in

the balance, that we presume one of the scales must very soon pre-
ponderate. The last information we have has a greater appearance
of hostility than any we have hitherto received.— In France it appears to me the national Assembly in tearing the lace from the garb
of government, will tear the coat itself into a thousand rags.— That
nation may for ought I know finally be free; but I am firmly persuaded it will not be untill they have undergone another revolution.
A nobility and a clergy, church and State levelled to the ground in
one year's time; rights not inconsistent with those of man, established by a prescription uncontrovertable, if any prescription can be
so; rights like these, blown to the winds, by the single breath of a
triumphant democracy are inauspicious omens for the erection of
an equitable government of Laws.— By the politeness of the french
consul, I have perused several volumes of their debates and projects
for constitutions.[7] There are some valuable papers among them; but
it appears to me that the rabble that followed the heels of Jack Cade
could not have devised greater absurdities than many of their
propositions: some of which have been adopted by the Assembly.

I am, dear Sir, your's affectionately.   J. Q. Adams.

RC (Adams Papers); docketed: "J Q Adams to / his Father / October 19th 1790."
Tr (Adams Papers).

[1] JA to JQA, 11 Oct. (Adams Papers), in
which JA provides the history of the proverb
"Weigh the Consequences" and asks JQA
about possible candidates for Massachusetts
governor, apathy among voters of rural New
England, and the unpopularity of the federal
government in Boston.

[2] Benjamin Goodhue (1748–1814) of Salem had served in the U.S. House of Representatives since 1789 (*Biog. Dir. Cong.*).

[3] On 8 Sept. 1790 the Newburyport *Essex
Journal* compared the Boston count to an
earlier total: "The Number of Persons in this
Town, taken in Conformity to the act of the
Legislature of the United States, at this
Period, exceeds 18,000. Three or four Years
since, the whole Number was about 14,000."
The 1790 U.S. federal census reported a
Boston population of 18,038 (U.S. Census,
1790, Mass., p. 10).

[4] In 1788 Giles Richards opened a wool-
card factory near Windmill Bridge that produced 63,000 pairs of wool-carding tools
each year. Four years later the factory was
said to employ a thousand people, three-
quarters of whom were children. Sailcloth

was produced at the two-story Duck Manu-
factory in Frog Lane, where workers included African Americans and women. Paper
hangings (decorative wall panels) were produced at Joseph Hovey's American Manufac-
tory at 39 Cornhill, which advertised "elegant
Pannel Papers" at prices lower than imported
hangings. Col. David Wood (1742–1808) was
a Charlestown baker and farmer (Allan Ku-
likoff, "The Progress of Inequality in Revolutionary Boston," *WMQ*, 3d ser., 28:379 [July
1971]; Jacqueline Barbara Carr, *After the
Siege: A Social History of Boston 1775–1800*,
Boston, 2005, p. 182–185; Wyman, *Charlestown Genealogies*, 2:1047).

[5] Cicero, *Defence of Archias*, line 21.

[6] Shakespeare, *As You Like It*, Act II,
scene i, line 12.

[7] Philippe André Joseph de Létombe,
French consul in Boston, probably provided
JQA with the French National Constituent
Assembly's *Projet de constitution*, n.p., 1789–
1790, and several issues of the same body's
periodical publication, *Journal des débates et
des décrets*.

Charles Adams to John Quincy Adams

My Dear Brother   New York October 21 1790

Upon my return from Law Society this evening I found my father in my room with a letter in his hand from you to me.[1] He asked me to see what you had written concerning your downfall. Upon opening the letter I soon found what he alluded to, but could find no marks of any downfall That you should have been somewhat confused upon your first exertion was by no means a matter of astonishment to any of us The person who is unintimidated upon such occasions has not the common feelings of human nature. There is a pride a respect required by the auditors which makes a little confusion rather pleasing than disagreeable. I think that an harangue of fifteen minutes is by no means despicable for a first essay. Your father was quite consoled when he heard my letter for that written to Mamma which he had previously read had led him to suppose you had failed and suffered A Vox faucibus hasit[2] in reality. And pray how did your opponent acquit himself? I dare say well, for I think he has more command of himself than you have. Johnson in his Rambler has an excellent paper upon the nature and remedies of bashfulness a paper which will aford great consolation to those who labor under any difficulty of this kind. Number 159 Saturday September 24 1751.[3] This man certainly saw more of human nature than any other. I am delighted with his sentiments upon moral subjects. Your caution concerning postage will probably not be wanted as I am determined with the advise and consent of the Counsel to spend the three winter months in Philadelphia where I shall be under my master's care and direction. Our City seems to be quite in a lethargy since the removal of Congress, I hope we shall soon awake from this torpor. Perhaps there is no place of its bigness in the world in which so few of the inhabitants care any thing about politics. They seem to be wholly swallowed up by their business and can allow no time for recreations of this kind. The party in Boston against Mr Ames appear to have blown their blast in the newspapers, and cut but a poor figure at the election even the enemies to justice are not so numerous in Boston as some supposed. I imagine your intelligence concerning so great a change in the Representation must have been premature as by the return of the votes I find most of the former members are again elected. I suppose Grouts oration upon salt secured his election as Parkers blackguard treatment of the

Senate did his in Virginia[4] It is very strange that his conduct in that respect should have been made use of by him as an argument to his electors for his second admision into the legislature. I cannot conclude without wishing you could persuade yourself to take the world a little more fair and easy I am confident you raise hills in your imagination more difficult to ascend than you will in reality find them May you have great fortitude and a more peaceful mind is the wish of your brother

Charles Adams

RC (Adams Papers).

[1] Not found.

[2] A voice that stuck in the throat.

[3] In his essay, Samuel Johnson observes: "He that enters late into a public station, though with all the abilities requisite to the discharge of his duty, will find his powers at first impeded by a timidity which he himself knows to be vicious, and must struggle long against dejection and reluctance, before he obtains the full command of his own attention and adds the gracefulness of ease to the dignity of merit."

[4] On 6 Aug. Massachusetts congressman Jonathan Grout argued unsuccessfully in the House that a proposed duty on salt should be reduced on the grounds that fishermen and farmers would be unduly affected. Grout was not reelected. CA was probably referring to Virginia congressman Josiah Parker (1751–1810) and his active role in opposing the 1789 Senate proposal to confer titles of respect upon the president and vice president, which JA strongly supported. Parker was reelected (*New York Daily Gazette*, 9 Aug. 1790; *Biog. Dir. Cong.*; *First Fed. Cong.*, 3:554–555; 10:595, 600; Charlene Bangs Bickford and Kenneth R. Bowling, *Birth of the Nation: The First Federal Congress, 1789–1791*, Washington, D.C., 1989, p. 26–28).

John Adams to John Quincy Adams

Dear Sir   New York October 23. 1790

The Note from Piemont, I would not have Sued by any means. Hopkins's Pretentions I have no Idea of. I Suppose an account with him may be found in my Ledger, But I can Say nothing upon memory. Piemont ought to make out his Account— He says I had a Bar Wig and a Bob Wig of him. If so he should make out his Account and if they amount to as much as the Note, there is an End of the Business. If not, he ought to pay the Ballance. But in all Events dont sue him. The other Notes and Accounts, if you write to the Persons and they come and settle it will be well.[1] But dont throw away good money after bad.

I congratulate you, on your first opening at the Bar in Boston. M[r] Otis's Civility, I shall not soon forget. It is not the first Time that Otis and Adams have been concerned together in that Court. I wish you may have as good a Friend as I had in one of the Name and be to him as faithful and Useful a Friend as I was. From 1758 to the day of his Death my Friendship with his Uncle was uninterrupted.[2]

Your Anxiety is too great.— You have no right to expect and no reason to hope for more Business than you have. Remember, Your Reputation is not formed but to form.— Confidence in your Talents & Fidelity, must arise by degrees and from Experience.— The Interests of Clients are too dear and important to them to be committed by hazard to the Care of a Lawyer. Your Name can as yet be no more than that of a promising Youth— They will call you after sometime a growing young Man.

Your Sensibility at your first essay at extemporary oratory your Agitation, your Confusion, if they were as lively as you describe them, are not at all Suprizing. Had you been calm and cool, unaffected and unmoved, it would have been astonishing. Mr Pratt Said to me, "I should despair of a young Man, who could be unmoved at his first Attempt."³ This will by no means hurt your Character or your Reputation. Such Modesty is amiable. Such Bashfulness is touching: it interests the People in ones favour. I hope however, that you will never wholly conquer this Modesty. The Audience have a right to be respected and venerated. A sense of Decency; the Awe of a Gentleman ought always to be upon your Mind when you Speak in publick. The Judges, the Lawyers the Jurors, the Parties and Witnesses, have all a right to be treated with respect from You, and no other manners or Language than those of a Gentleman should ever escape you towards any of them.

Your Mother has had a severe ill turn: but is better. We expect to remove in all next Week, to Philadelphia.

It is to me a severe mortification that I cannot have more of your society: But Providence has ordered my Course of Life in such a manner, as to deprive me for the most Part of the Company of my Family. Now I totally despair of ever living with them together.

I wish I had Served a Country possessed of more generous Sentiments that I might have been able to give my Children Some better assistance: but Complaints are Follies.

The Publick in every State is rejoiced at the reelection of Mr Gerry and Mr Ames: But there is some Anxiety for the Consequences of a very restless Party in Boston. There are some Figures there of unbounded Ambition and deep Insincerity. Ambition is a good quality, when it is guided by Honour and Virtue: but when it is Selfish only, it is much to be dreaded.

I am my dear Child your affectionate   John Adams

RC (Adams Papers); addressed: "Mr John Quincy Adams / Court Street / Boston"; internal address: "Mr J. Q. Adams"; endorsed: "My Father. 23. Oct^r: 1790."; notation: "Free / John Adams." Tr (Adams Papers).

[1] JQA wrote to JA on 13 Oct. to say that Cotton Tufts had given him several of JA's old notes and accounts. One of the notes was for a debt from Boston wigmaker John Piemont (Paymount) to a Captain Hopkins, which Hopkins had endorsed to JA "For value recieved." When contacted by JQA, Piemont claimed he had paid the note years earlier. Hopkins then told JQA that he had endorsed the note to JA so that JA could sue Piemont while Hopkins was at sea and asked JQA to make good on the note. Hopkins was probably Capt. Caleb Hopkins, a Boston mariner who offered freight service to and from Philadelphia on the brig *Maria* (Adams Papers; JA, *Legal Papers*, 3:94; JA, *Papers*, 4:419; Boston *Herald of Freedom*, 31 Aug.).

[2] JA would repeat in his Autobiography that he and James Otis Jr. "lived in entire Friendship" from 1758 when Otis recommended JA's admission to the Suffolk County bar until Otis' death in 1783. Despite Otis' sometimes erratic behavior, his revolutionary ideas had a great influence on JA (JA, *D&A*, 1:56, 348–349; 3:273, 291; JA, *Papers*, 1:xxv–xxvi).

[3] A reference to Benjamin Prat, noted Boston attorney at the time JA came to the bar; see JA, *Legal Papers*, 1:cvi.

Abigail Adams to Mary Smith Cranch

my dear sister   N York october 25 1790

After I had closed my Letter to you this day fortnight,[1] I retired to my chamber, and was taken with a shaking fit which held me 2 Hours and was succeeded by a fever which lasted till near morning, attended with severe pain in my Head Back &c the next morning I took an Emetick which operated very kindly and proved to me the necessity of it. on tuesday I felt better and went below stairs, but was again Seazd with an other skaking fit which was succeeded as the former by the most voilent fever I ever felt. it quite made me delirious, no rest for 5 Night & days. it setled into a Regular intermitting Fever. the dr after having repeatedly puked me, gave me James's powders, but with very little effect I began upon the Bark the 10th day which I have taken in large Quantities and it has appeard to have put an end to my fever, but I am very low and weak.[2] I rode out yesterday and found no inconveniency from it. I shall repeat my ride to day. I have great cause to be thankfull for so speady a restoration, but I have a jouney before me which appears like a mountain & three Ferries to cross. very fortunate for me the winds have kept back the vessel from returning from Philadelphia which was to have been here the 20th to have taken our furniture Mrs smith has been with me till yesterday. her Baby is inoculated for the small pox, and she expects him to brake out this week. but here endeth not all my troubles, for the day before yesterday mrs Brisler was taken Sick of a Plurisy fever she has been 3 times Bled & is

Blisterd, and lies very ill tho I hope not dangerous. I received your Letter by mr Cranch[3] he landed I believe only a few Hours. he went to mr Laurences office to Charles and deliverd the two casks sent by Brother I believe the Ladies did not come on shore as the wind was then fair for them, and they had been out ten days, & much of the weather very stormy & Boisterous. he told Charls that they had been very sick. I am sure it would have given me great pleasure to have received & entertaind them or to have supplied them with any thing in my power

I received a few days Since by mr durant your kind Letter of october 11th which I thank you for.[4] Remember me affectionatly to mrs Eunice Paine. would a few Bottles of wine or Porter be acceptable to her. if they would will you take the trouble of getting it from our cellar for her. the dr has just left me and says he thinks mrs Brisler much relieved, and that she will be better in a few days. my Head I find as week as my body you will therefore excuse my writing more at present than to assure you that I am as ever / your affectionate sister

A Adams

P S mr Brisler would be glad the money may be sent by mr Ames when he comes to Philadelphia

RC (MWA:Abigail Adams Letters); addressed by AA2: "Mrs Mary Cranch / Braintree"; endorsed by Richard Cranch: "Letter from Mrs / A Adams (N York) / Octr 25th. 1790."

[1] AA to Mary Smith Cranch, 10 Oct., above.

[2] AA was possibly under the care of Dr. Samuel Bard, who had administered James' powders to George Washington in May when the president contracted the influenza during the New York epidemic (Washington, *Papers, Presidential Series*, 5:395–396). See AA to Cotton Tufts, 30 May, and note 3, above. AA's intermittent fever and use of

quinine suggest she may have been suffering from malaria rather than influenza.

[3] Mary Smith Cranch's letter of 4 Oct., delivered by Joseph and Elizabeth Cranch on their way to West Point, included news about members of the Cranch household as well as various other Braintree residents (Adams Papers).

[4] Not found.

Abigail Adams to John Quincy Adams

my dear son   Newyork Novbr 7th 1790

perhaps a few lines from my own Hand may serve to put you more at your ease than an account of my Health from any other person. I have indeed had a very severe sickness in which both Body and mind sufferd, and the care which devolved upon me in consequence of my being in the midst of Removal I found too much for me. the least buisness put me into such a Tremour as would prevent my getting any sleep for a whole Night. tis a Month to day since I was first taken sick—as yet I have daily returns of fever tho much lessned—and I have gained strength for this week past so much that I hope to be able to begin my journey tomorrow. the vessel saild on thursday last and I have been in Town with your sister ever Since. she thinks a little hard of you that you have not written to her She has been in great trouble for her Baby which she came very near loosing with the small Pox, but which is now happily recoverd

I received a Letter from you during my Sickness which did not add to my spirits. I was unable to answer it at the Time, or I should have chid you for your impatience, and depression of Spirits tho I know it is your Sensibility which occasions it. that received by your Brother Charls last Evening has induced me to write you this Letter.[1] there is some Money in the hands of mr Cranch which he received for mr Brisler this money I will request him to pay to you and I will repay it to Brisler as soon as the amount of the Sum is forwarded to me. the Rent of the House where you are tho a small sum you should receive and I will write to the dr to call upon Pratt who must have money in his Hands as we have concluded to take neither his Butter or cheese as we shall be so far distant. your Father wrote you to get your uncle to supply you with Hay and with wood from our own place and I would have you apply to him for it. if you have any difficulties on that account or any other write to me freely about them. I wish any method could be fallen upon to make Pratts place more productive to us— when I have more strengh I will write to you upon a subject that gives me some anxiety. common Fame reports that you are attachd to a young Lady. I am sorry such a report should prevail, because whether there is or is not cause for such a Roumour, the report may do an injury to the future prospects of the Lady as your own are not such as can warrent you in entering into any engagements, and an entanglement of this kind will only tend to depress your spirits should you be any time before you get into Buisness and believe me my dear son a too early marriage will involve you in troubles that may render you & yours unhappy the remainder of Your Life. you will say that you have no Idea of connecting yourself at present. I believe you, but why gain the affections of a woman, or why give her cause to think you attachd to her. do you not know that the most cruel of situations to a young Lady is to feel herself attachd to a Gentleman when he can testify it in no other way than by his actions; I mean when his Situation will not permit him to speak

I did not design to have said so much at this time, but my anxiety for you has led me on; perhaps I ought not to have delayd being explicit so long— my strengh will not permit me to say more than that I am ever your Affe M.   A A

RC (Adams Papers).

[1] Not found.

Charles Adams to John Quincy Adams

Dear Brother   New York Nov[r] 7[th.] 1790

I received your letter of the 29th Ult[o] by the last post.[1] The reflections which it raises in my mind are by much too interesting to afford me great pleasure. The anxious path you are now pursuing must soon be trodden by me. A prospect is before me not less clouded than yours and the faint ray of my abilities will not be able so soon to dispel the gloom which obscures the day. I have not the smallest inclination to flatter neither do I beleive that I form my judgment with jaudiced eyes. Sound sense must make its way. Do you know a man of great knowledge who has not succeeded at the bar? You yourself will not allow that you are inferior in law knowledge to any of your standing: in point of other knowledge to Otis; a fluency and elegance of style in speaking excepted. What then! are all the young men of this age to dwindle into nothing? Have they all degenerated? Are they become the grasshoppers of a summer? I trust not. I hope and firmly beleive that that spirit will still continue to illumine the rising generation which urged their fathers to great and noble deeds, That they will support as great a character and leave examples to future ages at least as glorious. If any succeed then why should you not? You must be more patient nor grate your feelings with the idea of a dependence unavoidable. Did you— but you must know with what chearfulness our parents are ready to gratify their children. They will with the utmost satisfaction relinquish the luxuries of life that they may help us. Your father says you make yourself too unhappy and if you would make yourself more contented you need not fear contempt. You have made me very happy by intimating that I could do you any kindness. Whatever is in my power shall be performed with the greatest pleasure. I showed your letter to pappa and from his direction shall give you advice as far as he will allow himself to proceed. There is a caution about him which it would be happy for this Country if more of its rulers had.

His private concerns may wither in his hands but the public trust will never suffer through him. As he is one of the commissioners concerning the loan he can only inform you that he supposes money may be borrowed to advantage in Holland: upon this point he is extremely guarded he has had many applications for advice upon the subject and answers to none.[2] He thinks it will not be proper for him to interfere in the affairs of the money due to you for Russian services. Judge Dana should write to Col Hamilton who will without doubt remit the money to him. I think there will be no difficulty in this affair. I shall go to Philadelphia the first of next month if I can then be of any service you will not fail to command me. Judge Dana can have no objection to this step: if he should your own application will be sufficient. The house of Representatives the last session were strenuous for having the indents at four per Cent. The Senate voted 3 by a majority of one only There is a rule of the house of Commons and Lords that their Presidents should always vote for the highest sums. A good rule in general from which the VP in this instance would not depart. From these hints you may enter the field of probabilities. You can as easily see what chance there will be of such a motion as any one.[3] the matter is uncertain. No one can with certainty determine. I fear very much that I shall fail in my political narrations. I will endeavor to give you what information in that line which lies in my power. But in this place the inhabitants do not trouble themselves about these subjects and my sources of information will be small. From Philadelphia I may perhaps do something. I wish however that this branch might be carried on by question and answer. Your mamma has had a troublesome fever and I forebore to acquaint you with it. knowing it would not administer comfort She has recovered and tomorrow She sets out for Phila[a] I shall miss Tom much. Your law questions I shall postpone answering. nor shall I as yet raise any objections I have not particularly examined the cases but from what knowledge I have the first appears very clear on your side the other I am not quite so confident of but from the first blush think there is but little doubt you must recover. Your father says that Doctor Tufts must make the tenants pay their rents more punctually and that you may apply to him. the two farms at Braintree the house in Boston and half the rent of the farm at Medford must yeild something. which is at your disposal. I must now wish you good night if I have not been explicit enough pray inform me and I will try to be more so.

 Yours

Cha[s] Adams.

RC (Adams Papers); addressed: "Mr John Quincy Adams / Boston"; endorsed: "Charles. 7. Nov^r: 1790."

[1] Not found.

[2] JQA apparently made this request for information on behalf of his Boston host, Thomas Welsh. See JA to Welsh, 13 Sept., and note 2, above.

[3] On 28 July the Senate considered eleven House amendments to the Funding Act. JA broke tie votes on three of them, each time siding with the faction in favor of allowing more liberal terms. The Senate, however, rejected the House proposal that indents (i.e., certificates of debt to be assumed by the federal government) should be funded at 4 rather than 3 percent interest by a vote of sixteen to eight and thus did not require a tie-breaking vote from JA (*First Fed. Cong.*, 1:447–457; Ferguson, *Power of the Purse*, p. 293, 296–297).

John Quincy Adams to Abigail Adams

Boston November 20. 1790.

I received with great pleasure, my dear Mamma, your favour of the 7th: inst^t: which relieved me in some measure from my anxiety on account of your health, though it is now again alarmed at having no letters this evening by the Post. I want exceedingly to hear of your arrival at Philadelphia, and of the thorough restoration of your health.— I hope nothing will induce you to spend another summer in that part of the Country.

I conjure you my dear Mamma, not to suffer your anxiety on my account to add to any other evils with which you are afflicted. I have been a child to complain of my situation. It has nothing really distressing in it— So long as it shall be convenient for my Parents to favour me with a continuance of their support, I can continue here, and expect some favourable chance, or the gradual operation of a good character and unblemished reputation, to place me upon my own feet: and if that assistance should become inconvenient, I can I am perswaded find some situation in the Country where I shall be able to live upon my own industry: my situation here except in my prospects of business is as agreeable as I could wish.— M^rs: Welsh is very kind and attentive, the Doctor is a man of science and genius, in whose conversation I take much pleasure, and were it not for a degree of anxiety which is incorporated into my constitution, and for one or two other circumstances which cannot continue long, I should enjoy myself as well as if Fortune were more favourable.

The other circumstances which I have mentioned, are derived from a source upon which I did not intend to have given you any concern. But as common Fame, has carried to your Ears the report of my attachment to a young Lady, I wish to give you full satisfaction by assuring you that there shall never more be any cause on my part for the continuance of it. The Lady will henceforth be at the distance of 40 miles from me, and I shall have no further opportunities to indulge a weakness, which you may perhaps censure, but which if you knew the object, I am sure you would excuse.

Upon this subject as upon several others I could converse, with more freedom than I can write; and if I could meet with the perfect approbation of my Parents, I should be happy to pay them a visit of three or four weeks this winter at Philadelphia. The expence would not be much more than I should regularly incur during the same time here. The change of air, the exercice, the novelty of the place and the variety of scenes, might have a favourable effect upon my health and Spirits. The pleasure of seeing those dear friends, from whom I am almost always separated, is an inducement of great weight. And I have at present no business with which such a tour would essentially interfere.— I only mention my wish however as an idea, which has repeatedly presented itself in agreeable colours to my mind, and shall cheerfully resign it, if it should not be altogether agreeable to my father and to you: as I well know every objection you can have will arise from a consideration of my advantage. Should the proposal obtain your consent, I shall wish to go sometime in December or January, and if any business should intervene to require my presence here at that time, I can easily postpone my visit.

The money which was due to Brissler I had received before your order came, and have paid the principal part of it to Doctor Welsh for my board. I feel too grateful to attempt expressing it for the unceasing kindness and indulgence of my parents, and I faithfully assure you, that my only present real cause of complaint is that I am obliged to rely so much upon that indulgence, my only apprehension, that I shall abuse it.

I beg to be remembered affectionately to all my friends, and am your affectionate Son.   J. Q. Adams.

RC (Adams Papers); addressed: "M^rs: A. Adams. / Philadelphia."; endorsed: "J Q. A 1790."

John Quincy Adams to Abigail Adams Smith

Boston November 20. 1790.

I have indeed, my dear Sister, been guilty of a neglect, in omitting so long to write to you, which I cannot upon any principle justify to my own heart; I am sure it has been totally inconsistent with the ardent and sincere brotherly affection which that heart invariably acknowledges for you, and which no length of time, no absence, no course of circumstances, shall ever impair: I have very frequently wished to write to you. I have many times taken my pen for the purpose, but have as often dropped it from my hand, perswaded that I could write nothing which would afford any gratification to your affection, and equally perswaded that I could not by any expressions that language affords do justice to mine.— I have been unwilling, to fatigue your patience, by a dull uniformity of peevish complaints, and I have been unable to afford pleasure to your friendship and benevolence, by any accounts of my own happiness or success.

I have indeed since I wrote you last entered upon a scene of Life different from any of those to which I have hitherto been used; I am nominally independent, though in reality very far otherwise. I have a profession without employment, and the advantage of increased present expences, with the *hope* of being able at some future period, (probably somewhat distant) of supporting them myself. My Causes for complaint, have been enlarging, in proportion as I have been advancing upon the Stage of Life, and when I write, I trouble my friends with a mere narrative of fears and disappointments. In this circumstance if you cannot find an excuse, I hope you will perceive at least an alleviation of my fault in having for so long a time apparently neglected you.— But, my dear Sister, better days will come: we shall all in our time, have comforts and enjoyments to boast of, and as time and chance happen to all men, the time must come when some favourable chances will occur to us.

You enquire whence arises the unpopularity of the V.P. There is no such unpopularity here. He has undoubtedly many enemies; and as most of them are equally enemies to the principles of honor and Justice, they will not be scrupulous in using the means of injuring him or his connections. But he has likewise many friends, many admirers, and many supporters who are fully sensible of the obligations for which his country is indebted to him; and of the sacrifices he has made of his own interest to the public welfare.— Excepting the President there is not a man in the United States of so respectable popularity as that which he possesses here; what it may be in the distant States I know not.— But a connection with a man in an eminent Station, who acts upon principles of Patriotism and Integrity, is a real injury, rather than an advantage. For all his enemies will naturally use every endeavour to obstruct, and depress persons thus connected, as their success, would not only promote his personal happiness but would tend to strengthen and confirm his public influence. His friends will never be active in their favour, because they will have personal interests and private connections, which will thoroughly counteract all active benevolence from gratitude to him.— It is one of those evils to which a man must submit, when he undertakes the generous though ungrateful task, of devoting himself to the welfare of his fellow creatures. You and I, my dear Sister, shall always find, that our near affinity, to a man, who has sacrificed himself and his family to his country, will be a real impediment to our success in the world.— I should rather have been surprized had it not deprived Col^{l:} S. of an office, to which his merits had given him an indisputable title.—[1] And I believe we shall more than once have occasion to suffer by a real partiality exerted against us in order to avoid an appearance of partiality in our favour.— For my own part, I am gradually reconciling myself to my situation. Habit enables us to endure many evils, wh[ich] would appear intolerable if contemplated only at a distance— I am alone in the world; and so long as Fortune retains the aspect in which she now presents herself to me, I shall feel a soothing consolation in the idea, that my sufferings are confined to myself, and that the happiness of no other person is dependent upon mine. I am tolerably sure of a future support for myself, and I shall I am perswaded be able to regulate my expectations and even my wishes, so as to be thoroughly satisfied with that.

I have enquired for the collection of Poems, by Tomkins, but have not as yet been able to procure them. M^{r:} Dawes tells me he owns them, and that they are principally valuable for the preface at the head of the volume.[2] I shall continue occasionally to make enquiry for them, and if I can any where purchase them, send them to you as [soon] as possible

I sincerely sympathise with you upon the removal of our Parents from New-York. Separation from all the dearest connections which give a relish to the pleasures of life, and which alleviate its evils, has been almost constantly my fate from my infancy. Habit however has not rendered me insensible to the domestic attachments, which impart almost every thing that is valuable in this world, and I readily conceive how painful your sensations must be at the departure of your friends. But Charles will remain with you. His disposition was always amiable and his manner always calculated to make him friends. He has lately imbibed a thirst for science which will infallibly render him as respectable as he is agreeable. His literary improvement since he left College is very conspicuous even to his friends here in the style of his Letters. Let us take to ourselves joy, that in the midst of all our family misfortunes we can yet glory in unimpeached honour and integrity. Let us hope that the talents which in none of us are despicable, and the virtues which it will always be in our power to retain may yet carry us credibly through the world, and if the eminence of the Parent is not to be attained let us at least resolutely determine, to show ourselves really superior to the humbler stations which Providence has assigned to us.

I beg you to present my affectionate regards to Colˡ: Smith, and remind your sons that they have an uncle at a distance, who loves them, though they remember him not. I enclose a Letter for Charles from one of his friends.[3] I will soon write to him myself.

Your ever affectionate brother. J. Q. Adams.

RC (private owner, 1990); addressed: "Mʳˢ: A. Smith / New-York." Some loss of text due to wear at the fold.

[1] In May 1789 WSS wrote to George Washington seeking a federal appointment, and a month later JA followed with a second letter in which he stated that WSS preferred a domestic assignment but would consider serving as a foreign minister in Europe. On 25 Sept. Washington named WSS marshal for the district of New York, an appointment that dissatisfied the Adams family (Washington, *Papers, Presidential Series,* 2:286–288; 4:85).

[2] Thomas Tomkins, *Poems on Various Subjects; Selected to Enforce the Practice of Virtue,* London, 1780. The preface on p. v–vii is a brief analysis of the respective functions of epic poetry, the ode, tragedy, comedy, satire, the elegy, and the pastoral. The underlying goal of all, Tomkins writes, is to "teach mankind the most important precepts of religion and virtue."

[3] Not found.

Abigail Adams to Abigail Adams Smith

My Dear, Philadelphia, 21 November, 1790.

I suppose you wish to hear from me and from your little boy. He is very well, and very amusing, as usual; talks of William, and of the other papa; is as fond as ever of the "fosses," and has a great edition to his amusement and pleasures from a flock of sheep, which are daily pastured by a shepherd and his dog upon the lawn in front of our house. Bush Hill, as it is called, though by the way there remains neither bush nor shrub upon it, and very few trees, except the pine grove behind it,—yet Bush Hill is a very beautiful place. But the grand and sublime I left at Richmond Hill. The cultivation in sight and prospect are superior, but the Schuylkill is not more like the Hudson, than I to Hercules. The house is better finished within;

but, when you come to compare the conveniences for storeroom, kitchen, closets, &c., there is nothing like it in the whole house. As chance governs many actions of my life, when we arrived in the city, we proceeded to the house. By accident, the vessel with our furniture had arrived the day before, and Briesler was taking in the first load into a house all green-painted, the workmen there with their brushes in hand. This was cold comfort in a house, where I suppose no fire had been kindled for several years, except in a back kitchen; but, as I expected many things of this kind, I was not disappointed nor discomfited. As no wood nor fodder had been provided beforehand, we could only turn about, and go to the City Tavern for the night. [1]

The next morning was pleasant, and I ventured to come up and take possession; but what confusion! Boxes, barrels, chairs, tables, trunks, &c.; every thing to be arranged, and few hands to accomplish it, for Briesler was obliged to be at the vessel. The first object was to get fires; the next to get up beds; but the cold, damp rooms, the new paint, &c., proved almost too much for me. On Friday we arrived here, and late on Saturday evening we got our furniture in. On Sunday, Thomas was laid up with rheumatism; on Monday, I was obliged to give Louisa an emetic; on Tuesday, Mrs. Briesler was taken with her old pain in her stomach; and, to complete the whole, on Thursday, Polly was seized with a violent pleuritic fever. She has been twice bled, a blister upon her side, and has not been out of bed since, only as she is taken up to have her bed made. And every day, the stormy ones excepted, from eleven until three, the house is filled with ladies and gentlemen. As all this is no more nor worse than I expected, I bear it without repining, and feel thankful that I have weathered it out without a relapse, though some days I have not been able to sit up.

Mrs. Bingham has been twice to see me. I think she is more amiable and beautiful than ever. I have seen many very fine women since I have been here. Our Nancy Hamilton is the same unaffected, affable girl we formerly knew her.[2] She made many kind inquiries after you; so did Mrs. Bingham. I have not yet begun to return visits, as the ladies expect to find me at home, and I have not been in a state of health to do it; nor am yet in a very eligible state to receive their visits. I, however, endeavoured to have one room decent to receive them, which, with my own chamber, is as much as I can boast of at present being in tolerable order. The difficulty of getting workmen, Mr. Hamilton pleads as an excuse for the house not being ready. Mrs. Lear was in to see me yesterday, and assures me that I am much better off than Mrs. Washington will be when she arrives, for that their house is not likely to be completed this year. And, when all is done, it will not be Broadway.[3] If New York wanted any revenge for the removal, the citizens might be glutted if they would come here, where every article has become almost double in price, and where it is not possible for Congress, and the appendages, to be half so well accommodated for a long time. One would suppose that the people thought Mexico was before them, and that Congress were the possessors.

28 November. Sunday.

I wrote you thus far on Sunday last. Polly is on the recovery, but your brother Thomas is very ill, and almost helpless with the rheumatism. You recollect how he formerly had it. It seems as if sickness followed me wherever I go. The President got to town on Saturday; I have not yet seen him or Mrs. Washington. We have had two severe storms; the last was snow. Poor Mrs. Knox is in great tribulation about her furniture. The vessel sailed the day before the first storm, and had not been heard of on Friday last. I had a great misfortune happen to my best trunk of clothes. The vessel sprung a leak, and my trunk got wet a foot high, by which means I have several gowns spoiled; and the one you worked is the most damaged, and a black satin;—the blessed effects of tumbling about the world. Adieu. Write me soon. Love to all.   A. A.

MS not found. Printed from AA, *Letters*, ed. CFA, 1848, p. 348–350.

[1] For the City Tavern, see JA, *D&A*, 2:114–115.

[2] For Ann (Nancy) Hamilton, see same, 3:184.

[3] In New York the Washingtons lived at 39–41 Broadway, in the Alexander Macomb mansion, which a visitor described as one of the grandest buildings in the United States. In Philadelphia the family rented a home at 190 High Street owned by Robert Morris. George Washington ordered extensive renovations in early September, but they were incomplete in late November owing in part to Morris' delay in removing his possessions (Washington, *Diaries*, 6:26; Washington, *Papers, Presidential Series*, 6:399–401, 680–681).

John Adams to Charles Adams

My dear Charles   Bush Hill Dec[r.] 4. 1790

Although I am much obliged to you for your kind Letter of the Second, and the News and Observations in it; I am disappointed in not receiving you as I expected, instead of a Letter.[1] I thought it was Sufficiently explained and understood between Us, that you were to be at Philadelphia on the first monday in December. But as it now appears otherwise I desire you to loose no time in coming on; as I want you, for the Sake of your Mother your Brother and yourself: besides a little selfish interest I have in you.

We have had a mellancholly house but are all now better. Your Brother, weak as he is, has passed the worst of his disorder, as we hope.

My Love to Col & Mrs Smith, Billy & Tommy and all Friends.— Johnny is as hearty and as gay as you can imagine. His Health has been immoveable, and his almost alone.

Judge Wilsons Lectures commence on monday fortnight: and I wish you to apply to him as early as possible. He will be pleased to have you and your Brother, as Hearers. You must take minutes of what you may hear and Send them to John.[2]

Your Haerlem Oil is pronounced to be an empirical medicine.—[3] This Town is full of Accademies Professors, Letures and Students both of Law and Physick: and will afford you a good opportunity of improvement, in various kinds of Knowledge. No Advantages or Opportunities however will avail like Patience and Study.

The great medical Characters here, Jones Shippen Rush and Khun's were educated in Europe at Leyden, Paris, London or Edinburgh: but in Law Mr Ingersol alone has Studied at the Temple— exept Mr Shippen who is not yet in Practice.[4]

on a Visit to Dr Jones Yesterday I had the Pleasure to See the Portraits of Boerhaave, Muschenbroek Mead & sloane, over his mantle Piece: and remaked the Pleasure with which he related the Lectures he had heard at Leyden and Paris.[5]

The great Judges and Masters of the Law are to be the Objects of your Admiration and Imitation. There is no Character more venerable on this side of Heaven than a wise and upright Judge. The destroyers of Mankind however glorious are hateful in comparison.

But where do I wander? I only took my Pen to desire you to come immediately to your affectionate Father   John Adams

RC (MHi:Seymour Coll.); addressed: "Mr Charles Adams / at Col Laurence's / New York"; internal address: "Mr Charles Adams."; notation: "Free / John Adams."

[1] Not found.

[2] James Wilson (1742–1798), Pennsylvania statesman and Supreme Court justice from 1789 until his death, delivered a series of lectures on the law at the College of Philadelphia starting 15 Dec. 1790. Newspapers reported that the introductory lecture was attended by leading figures in national and local politics: "The President of the United States, with his lady—also the Vice-President, and both houses of Congress, the President and both houses of the Legislature of Pennsylvania, together with a great number of ladies and gentlemen, were present;

the whole composing a most brilliant and respectable audience" (*DAB*; *Pennsylvania Packet*, 25 Dec.). This first talk was subsequently published as *An Introductory Lecture to a Course of Law Lectures*, Phila., 1791, Evans, No. 24007.

[3] Haerlem Oil, also known as Dutch Drops, was a mixture of turpentine, balsam of sulphur, and petroleum used internally to treat rheumatic complaints (Robert Dunglison, *A Dictionary of Medical Science*, 4th edn., Phila., 1844, p. 503; J. Worth Estes, *Dictionary of Protopharmacology: Therapeutic Practices, 1700–1850*, Canton, Mass., 1990, p. 71, 93).

[4] John Jones (1729–1791) studied with doctors in London, Paris, Edinburgh, and Leyden before completing his M.D. in 1751 at the University of Rheims (Martin Kaufman and others, eds., *Dictionary of American Medical Biography*, 2 vols., Westport, Conn.,

1984). For Adam Kuhn, William Shippen Jr., and Jared Ingersoll, see vol. 2:112, 171, 287; for lawyer Thomas Lee Shippen, whom the Adamses knew in London in 1786 as he pursued plans to study at the Temple, see vol. 7:303, 304.

[5] Petrus van Musschenbroek (1692–1761), a Dutch scientist who lectured at several European universities on experimental philosophy and physics, was well known for his experiments with the Leyden jar. Hans Sloane (1660–1753), the famous British physician and collector, included Queen Anne and King George II among his patients (Charles Coulston Gillispie, ed., *Dictionary of Scientific Biography*, 16 vols., N.Y., 1981; *DNB*). For Dutch botanist and physician Herman Boerhaave, see vol. 4:xiii; for Richard Mead, another British doctor, see vol. 5:171.

Elizabeth Smith Shaw to Abigail Adams

My Dear Sister—   Haverhill December 6th 1790

Major Mc Farling has just called upon us, & informed us of his intention of going to Philadephia this Week—& has intimated a wish, that some outlines of his general Character might be given to the Vice President— Mr Shaw is called away on some business, & supposes, that if it is done in the female line, it may be as efficacious as if he had written himself— Major Mc-Farling had some Conversation with the President when he was upon his Tour this way, which has encouraged him, to attend upon Congress this session— As there are Benefits to be confered, his Friends here, wish his Services, & his enfeebled State, may be thought of, & rewarded— Perhaps there but few more deserving— As a private Gentleman his Character is unblemished— He is a man of real worth, probity, & integrity, & by his industry, & the *small pittance* he has received, supported a numerous Family with decency, & reputation— As a Soldier, he was brave, & undaunted, those who fought by his side at Bunker Hill, & at white plains can witness, & his right arm can testify, that he bears about no deceitful marks of Courage, & noble resolution—for a Bullet in two different engagments, entered his arm, & is lodged there, & now, as he grows into years, he feels the pain, & inconvenience of them more, & more— He says he does not wish to spend the remainder of his life in indolence, but hopes & wishes, still to be serviceable to his Country, in some way or other— Now this is my petition, & this is my request to the Vice President, for one of my People, that as I know he delights to make a worthy man happy, he would, in his great Wisdom use his influence, to provide something for this Genttleman that he can *realize*, & be an adequate support to himself & Family in the decline of Life— So that One, who has nobly fought & bled, for his Country, should have no Cause to think her ungrateful—[1]

And now my Dear Sister, let me ask you how you do, & how you like your new Situation?— I hope you go on progressively, from good, to better—& now having a much greater number of *Friends* arround you, you will lead a pleasant, & peaceful life, for their Characteristic is hospitality kindness & Benevolence—

My kindest Love & regards attend Cousin Thomas, Tell him if you please, that we go on much in the old way—few young Ladies are courted, & less are given in marriage— In Haverhill, as in many other places there are ten young Ladies, to one Gentleman—

There has lately been two very fine, agreeable Persons from the Jersies—(Mr Newbolls by name) Cousins— They had there Education in Philadelphia— They were sensible—polite, easy in their manners, plain in th[eir] dress, but really very beautiful in their persons— I dined with them at Mr Thaxter's—& they dr[ank] Tea with us the next Day— They were detained in Town by a Storm a week— They were introduced to judge Seargants Family—& were *charmed* with Haverhill.

Mr Thaxters health is much as it has been, Mrs Thaxter is not *very well*— The loss of their Son still grieves them, but I hope they will be comforted—

Mr Shaw presents his best regards, & my Children their duty to their Uncle & Aunt

Accept my Dear Sister, & Cousins, of the Love of your ever affectionate   Elizabeth Shaw—

Excuse the writing & every inaccuracy—

RC (Adams Papers). Some loss of text where the seal was removed.

[1] Moses McFarland (1738–1802), born in Londonderry, N.H., served as a captain in the Continental Army throughout the Revolutionary War. Promoted to the rank of major in the 1780s, he died in Haverhill in 1802 (C. M. Little, *History of the Clan Macfarlane*, Tottenville, N.Y., 1893, p. 108, 109, 114). See also Elizabeth Smith Shaw to AA, 14 Feb. 1791, and note 3, below.

Abigail Adams to Mary Smith Cranch

my dear sister   Philadelphia dec^br 12 1790

I have received your two kind Letters one dated in october the 30 day I think & the 14 of Nov^br as the last came by a private Hand it did not reach me till last Evening.[1] you will suppose that I might have written to you long e'er this, but as my letters would only have been a detail of grivences and troubles I was reluctant at taking my pen, and put it of from day to day. I reachd this city after 5 days journey. I was so weak as to be able to travel only 20 miles a day, but I gaind strength daily and was much better when I got here than when I set out; my Furniture arrived the day before me. I came up to the House expecting to have found every thing in readiness to put up the furniture agreable to promise but how was I dissapointed to find the painters with their Brushes and some of the most necessary matters untouch'd the House had not been inhabited for four years & being Brick you may judge of the state of it. we had fires made in every part, the furniture must come in, and we must inhabit it unfit as it was for to go with 14 or 16, for Brislers family were all with me, to Lodings was much beyond my Revenue's I expected to suffer. We got in on fryday— on the Monday following Louissa was taken sick I gave her a puke & set her up again, but on the thursday following Polly Tailor was taken sick with a voilent Plurisy fever confined to her Bed bled 3 times puked & Blisterd; and tho it is a month she has got no further down stairs than to my chamber for after the fever left her the old Ague took her in her Head and face. She is however upon the mending order, but this is not the worst of all my troubles. Thomas has been 18 days totally deprived of the use of his Limbs by the acute Rhumatism, attended with great inflamation and fever. the fever has abated after having been 3 times Bled puked and many other applications he is yet unable to help himself. he is carried from his Bed to the Settee & fed like an infant. I have not left his Chamber excepting a nights and meal times for the whole time. the disorder seazd his Breast as well as his Limbs and produced all the complaints of Gravel by affecting his kidneys. I never knew him half so sick in my Life. I will not lay either of the disorders to this place tho I believe they were hastned & renderd worse by the dampness of the House. Polly has had 2 Fevers of the same kind since she has been with me, & Thomas Rhumatism has been comeing on for some time, yet they were peculiarly unfortunate to attack them at the time of Removal. dr Rush has attended them and I have found him a kind Friend as well as Physician. I will not detail to you that in the midst of all this, the Gentlemen and Ladies solicitious to manifest their respect were visiting us every day from 12 to 3 oclock in the midst of Rooms heepd up with Boxes trunks cases &c. thanks to a kind Providence I have got through the worst I hope of my difficulties and am in tolerable Health tho much fallen away in flesh I have a source of anxiety added to my portion on my dear daughters account, col smith having saild last week for England his going was sudden and unexpected to us, but some private family Debts which were due in England to his Fathers estate was one motive, and some prospects of assisting his Family by his voyage was a still further motive.[2] I do not know what has really been the cause why he has been so poorly provided for in the distribution of offices. the P—— has always said that he was sensible to his merrit & meant to Provide for him, but has not yet seen the way open to do it; She poor Girl is calld to quite a different trial from any she has before experienced, for tho the col was once before absent, she was in her Fathers House.[3] now she writes that she feels as if unprotected, as if alone in the wide world one of his Brothers & sisters remain with her during the cols absence. I have Johnny here with me, and would gladly send for her, to pass the winter with me, but a young Baby and some other obstacles prevent. pray my dear sister write to her and comfort her. no station in Life was ever designd by providence to be free from trouble and anxiety. the portion I believe is much more equally distributed than we imagine. Guilt of conscience is the work of our own Hands and not to be classed with the inevitable evils of Humane Life.—

Dec^{br} 14

I wrote thus far on sunday. Thomas is very little better. Charles got here on saturday and is a great assistance to me. I want my dear sisters & cousins. notwithstanding I have been such a Mover. I feel in every New place more & more the want of my own near & dear connexions. I hope to see you all next spring. pray let my son J Q A know that his Brother is sick, that we should be glad to have him come here in Jan^{ry} or this Month if more convenient to him, but that I cannot write to him till the Next post— adieu I have only time to say yours / as the Post is going   A Adams

RC (MWA:Abigail Adams Letters); endorsed by Richard Cranch: "Letter from M^rs. / A Adams (Ph^a:) / Decr. 12th. 1790"; notation: "Send this back / when you write / M C."

[1] Not found.

[2] WSS traveled to Europe on behalf of New York City speculator Richard Platt with the intention of securing a private loan using U.S. securities as collateral for the purpose of speculating in the same securities. A steep rise in their value during WSS's voyage rendered the plan impractical and WSS returned without carrying it out (Hamilton, *Papers*, 8:453–454).

[3] For WSS's extended trip to the Continent in 1787, see vol. 8:xxxi.

Mary Smith Cranch to Abigail Adams

My dear Sister   Braintree December 12th 1790

I have been waiting with impatience to hear of your arrival in Philedelphia, your health was so poor that I want to know how your Journey affected you, I hope you have found an advantage from it, but the fatigues attending moving are not very pleasing to the Body or Mind. If there could be any advantage arising from it to you, there would be something to balance the trouble, but to be at such an expence for nothing, & to be the subjects of envy too is hard— It was suppos'd that General warren was chosen to represent Plymouth county—& every body seem'd to be glad as the exchange would have been so much for the better: but alass—you will hear who it is—one who from the character he sustains you will be asham'd to invite to your table. how could the People make such a choice?[1]

I want much to hear how you like your situation. I pity mrs Smith, I am always thinking of her. I must find a way to hear from her, I think to apply to mr Storer for a private conveyence

I was at your Brother adams's the other day. Mrs Hall look'd & was very well mrs Turner is not yet mov'd I thought by what he said he was to have gone into your house immediately, she told me she thought they should soon, she is surprizingly recover'd but looks much altered

What think you my sister of the spirit of matrimony which has appear'd in Hingham— Miss Gay the younger married to Parson Howard of Boston. Major Rice Publish'd to miss Sophia Blake. & mr Caleb Thaxter to miss Fanny Gay, a Grandaughter to the late Doctor Gay—& tis said that Parson Clark of Lexington will take Miss Nabby Gay, I have not heard that any of our good cousins are spoken for.— but these are incouraging circumstances for the good

Girls. I think that Coll^n. Gay ought to find a wife among them, Betsy has something very handsome left her by Madam Derby[2]

Mr Thaxter I hear is better. Sister Shaw I have not heard from for some time, but suppose they are well– Mr Nortons Family are well. She was with me a day or two last week with her sweet little Boy– who can almost run alone & is as playful as a Lamb, he is wean'd but did not mind it in the least, he has nine or ten Teeth which he is always useing, He is very healthy & very quiet now he grows very pretty, has as fine Black eyes as you ever say, & a good animated countinance—at least this is Grandmamas oppinion– I think you must pine after mrs Smiths Children, there is nothing that enlivens us so much as having these little creatures round us–

Lucy has been making mrs Packard a visit mrs Quincy & she look sattisfied & happy, & that is enough– He has a nice house well furnish'd but neither Lucys nor my oppinion is chang'd about him, Prudence is a gift from heaven—a duplicity of character will be discover'd sooner or later wherever it is—

I know you feel interested for Williams success as well as your own sons, he has I think as much business as he could expect for the time—but not enough to maintain himself. I tell them both not to be discourag'd. good characters & good abilities will make there way good in the world– Your son keep thanksgiving with us. & I found him wanting stockings, Drawers, caps & necks– Stockings mr Turner will make for him as soon as he can. We have got him two pair from mr Hardwick[3] for the present for he could not wait he suffer'd for the want of them, the other things Lucy went to Boston & got for him, & has made them up, He appear'd very well. He shew me the Letter you wrote him from new york the day before you left it–& it was the first hint I had of his attachment—[4] his cousins knew it they have told me since– I had no time to say any thing to him after I had [read the] Letter. I was sorry as I suppest'd by his shewing [it to] me he wish'd I should—but I believe you may trust to his prudence– She is young but has had a very good education I hear, He will tell you himself how the matter stand between them. Cousin Thomas is well I hope; what is he doing? Something I know, his active spirit will never be Idle My Love to him I expect much entertainment from his letters to his cousin. he has taken an exellent likeness of him. & tell him he has left as strong an imprssion upon his Heart as he has upon his imagination, I design he shall try for your Face next—[5] my Love also to Louisa. h[er] mama complains that she has not written to her or B[roth]ers & sister. Mr Adams is always included in my wishes for your Health & happiness, & no one can wish you more than does your affectionate Sister

Mary Cranch

Lucy sends Duty & Love

RC (Adams Papers); addressed by William Cranch: "Mrs A. Adams / Philadelphia."; endorsed: "Mrs Cranch 12 / december 1790." Some loss of text where the seal was removed.

[1] Shearjashub Bourne, a Barnstable lawyer who successfully defeated James Warren and two other candidates, replaced George Partridge as congressional representative from Plymouth County. Bourne had been involved in dubious mercantile dealings during the Revolution that climaxed in a long legal battle in which JA was a brief participant. Largely overcoming widespread suspicions of disloyalty to the American cause, Bourne went on to represent Barnstable in the General Court after the Revolution and, following his two terms in the U.S. Congress, became chief justice of the Suffolk Inferior Court (JA, *Legal Papers*, 1:xcvii; vol. 8:313; Boston, *Herald of Freedom*, 9 Nov. 1790; Boston *Independent Chronicle*, 9 Dec. 1790; JA, *D&A*, 4:2–3).

[2] Jerusha Gay (1735–1812), daughter of the late Rev. Ebenezer Gay of Hingham, married Rev. Simeon Howard of Boston on 29 Nov. (*History of Hingham*, 2:264–265).

Col. Nathan Rice of Hingham wed Sophia Blake, daughter of Joseph Blake of Boston, on 16 Jan. 1791 (Boston *Columbian Centinel*, 22 Jan.; MBNEH:Mss 901, Reuben Hersey, Vital Records of Hingham, Massachusetts, ca. 1639–1844, vol. 1).

The marriage between Caleb Thaxter and Fanny Gay did not take place; Thaxter (b. 1751) died unmarried in 1828, while Frances Gay (1763–1846), daughter of Ebenezer's son Martin and his first wife Mary Pinckney, married Isaac Winslow in 1805 (*History of Hingham*, 2:265; 3:233).

Rev. Jonas Clarke (b. 1730) of the First Congregational Church in Lexington, who had lost his wife Lucy Bowes in April 1789, did not remarry prior to his death in 1805 (*Sibley's Harvard Graduates*, 13:209, 210,

215). Abigail Gay (1729–1804), eldest daughter of Ebenezer, never married. Col. Jotham Gay (1733–1802), a son of Ebenezer who served in the Continental Army during the Revolution, likewise remained unwed (*History of Hingham*, 2:265).

The cousins to whom Cranch refers were Celia (1749–1829), Hannah (1751–1807), and Elizabeth Thaxter (1753–1824), none of whom ever married (same, 3:233). Elizabeth's inheritance came from Sarah Langley Hersey Derby, widow of Richard Derby, who died on 17 June 1790, leaving behind a large fortune. The Boston *Columbian Centinel*, 26 June, reported that in her will she donated money to Harvard University as well as to the Derby school in Hingham and noted "her more than equivalent compensation of the kind offices of her particular friends."

[3] Probably John Turner, for whom see vol. 2:304–305, 341. For the Hardwick family, see vol. 1:240–241. Both Frederick Hardwick and his son John Henry Hardwick were stocking weavers (Sprague, *Braintree Families*).

[4] AA to JQA, 7 Nov., above.

[5] William Cranch sent to AA profile portraits he had made of his parents, Norton Quincy, and JQA. In his accompanying letter, he explained, "the young man who took them is a very clumsy fellow at Drapery; however, it must be said in Excuse for him, that he is very young in the business having never attempted the power of light & shade, 'till about a Month ago" (11 Dec., Adams Papers). See also AA to Mary Smith Cranch, 9 Jan. 1791, and Mary Smith Cranch to AA, 25 Jan., both below. The portraits have not been located, with the possible exception of an unattributed and undated sketch of Richard Cranch; see vol. 1:xii–xiii, 81.

John Adams to John Quincy Adams

My Dear Son   Philadelphia Dec[r] 13. 1790

Your Brother Charles arrived on Saturday night from New York and has dissipated some of the Gloom of the Family. Your Mother however Seems pretty well recovered from her Indisposition: and Your Brother Thomas, tho very weak is on the Recovery, as We hope. The rest of the Family is well.

In a Letter to your mamma, you intimate an Inclination to make Us a Visit.[1] Nothing I assure you would be more agreable to me: and I wish you to come as Soon as you find it convenient.— Philadelphia is worth Seeing. It is a great City and has Science, Litterature, Wealth and Beauty, which deserve respect, if not Admiration. The Journey by the Stage will promote your health, relax your Attention, and improve your mind.

Your old Friend M[r] Bingham is in the high road of Promotion. Member of the assembly and unanimously chosen Speaker.[2] He lives in a Style of Pomp & Splendor which is almost novel in America.

A respectful, attentive and complaisant Behaviour will engage you the good Will of the World: and your extensive Knowledge will give you great Advantages, as soon as you shall have opportunities to act yourself.

It is accident commonly which furnishes the first Occasions to a young Lawyer, to Spread his Reputation. I remember, it was neither my Friends nor Patrons among the great and learned: it was Joseph Tirrel the Horse Jockey who first raised me to fame. At Plymouth Court he had a sister, who had a popular Cause depending. He advised her to engage me in it: and I had the good fortune to conduct it in such a manner that from that time forward I was engaged in all the Causes in the County.[3] Some odd incident, altogether unforeseen and unexpected, will very probably bring you into some popular Cause, and Spread your Character with a thousand Trumpetts at a time. Such a Thing may not happen however in several years. meantime Patience Courage.

yours   John Adams

RC (Adams Papers); internal address: "M[r] J. Q. Adams." Tr (Adams Papers).

[1] JQA to AA, 20 Nov., above.
[2] William Bingham was elected to the Penn. House of Representatives in 1790 and would serve as speaker in 1791 (*Biog. Dir. Cong.*).

[3] Early in his law career JA tried at least two cases involving the family of Joseph Tirrell (b. 1723). In 1760 he successfully represented Luke Lambert in a case against Tirrell and in the same year won the case of Tirrell

v. Lawrence on behalf of a member of the Tirrell family (JA, *D&A*, 1:224; Sprague, *Braintree Families*; *Vital Records of Abington, Massachusetts*, 2 vols., Boston, 1912, 1:227).

John Quincy Adams to Abigail Adams

Boston December 14th. 1790.

I have just returned from the Post-Office, where I was in hopes of finding Letters from Philadelphia, but found myself disappointed. I wrote you almost a month ago by a private hand, (M^{r:} Gray) and I hope you received my Letter in Season. I have since thought that some of the expressions in it, upon a subject which principally concerns myself might rather tend to increase your alarm than to give you satisfaction. I must therefore again request you, my dear Madam, to remove from your mind every anxiety on that account. I am perfectly free, and you may rest assured I will remain so; I believe I may add I was never in less danger of any entanglement, which can give you pain than at present.

I am tolerably contented with my situation. Could I have just enough business to support my expences, so as to relieve me from the mortification of being at my time of life, a burthen to my Parents, there would not be I believe, a happier being in the United States. I am every day more pleased with the family where I board; and every circumstance that occurs has an agreeable aspect, except that of finding myself still an idle man.— Idle, as respects business; for I can pursue my studies perhaps even to greater advantage, than I did before I came here, and though my Time is productive of no present profit, I do not perceive that I have any of it to spare.— You will see, that my Spirits at least are in more favourable tune than they have been, when some of my former Letters were written.

But at present I have to write upon another subject. As my father in one of his late Letters to me,[1] has expressed an intention to give me the charge of the house from which I now write, I have been thinking upon the methods which might be pursued to turn it to the best account. The present Tenant for two years past has given a rent of £34. which with a deduction for necessary repairs must be reduced to something less than £30. He complains even of this rent as too high, and from several enquiries which I have made, I do not think I could get a Tenant who would give more.— I think if my father would consent to sell the house, I could undertake to be answerable to him for a principal of £500, which would be the capital of the present rent, and for an annual interest of £40 instead of 30.

Indeed I should be disappointed if I did not in both cases exceed those Sums. £500 invested in the public funds, would I think at present be as secure as in a house in Boston; and would procure in all probability a more regular and more certain interest. But there are several other modes by which I think I could secure upon such a sum, an interest of 8 or 9 per cent, without hazarding the principal, any more than the house is endangered from casualties, and from gradual decay.

I am aware of my father's predilection in favour of real Estate. But as it respects this house it seems to me, the only question must be how to make the property the most profitable. He never can live again in the house himself; in the present dispersion of his family which in all probability will continue, no one unless it be myself will ever have occasion to live in it; and this is a contingency so remote that it can have no effect upon his determination at present; it appears therefore that it will never be serviceable, only as it will produce an annual rent: from certain inconveniences attending the house itself, and from its age, which is not inconsiderable, the probability is that this rent can never be much higher than at present. Now if by changing the mode of property, an addition of a quarter part may be added to the annual income, without injuring the principal, upon all the maxims of oeconomy is it not a measure highly expedient.

I am not sure that I could sell the house, if I were authorised so to do: but if upon these considerations my father should agree with me in opinion, there can at least be no danger whatever in making the experiment; and it might possibly induce the present Tenant to raise the Rent, if he suspected the house would otherwise be sold But if it should still be concluded that the safety and permanency of landed property more than compensates for the Circumstance of its being so much less productive, at least I shall have done no harm for making these observations, which were certainly dictated by the best intentions.[2]

I enclose a Letter for my brother Charles,[3] and remain with every sentiment of affection, and gratitude your Son.   J. Q. Adams.

RC (Adams Papers); addressed: "M^rs: A. Adams. / Philadelphia."; endorsed: "J Q A 1790"; docketed: "JQ–A– Dec– / 1790."

[1] JA to JQA, 4 Oct., above.
[2] The Court Street house was not sold and the property remained in the Adams family for another century; see JA, *D&A*,
2:64.
[3] Not found, but in his Diary JQA recorded that he wrote to CA on 11 and 14 Dec. (D/JQA/15, APM Reel 18).

John Adams to Abigail Adams Smith

My Dear Child: Philadelphia, December 17th, 1790.

I have not had an opportunity to write you till now, since the departure of your Colonel Smith, for England. I presume that this voyage was undertaken on mature deliberation, and wish it may prove exactly to his satisfaction, and his interest. The state of solitude, however disagreeable, should be rendered tolerable to you, when you recollect the many years of separation which fell to the lot of your parents, in infinitely more gloomy times, and with prospects more dismal and disconsolate. Your children are a trust which will employ your mind, and occasion both business and amusement. Retirement from the world, to a great degree, of which the absence of a husband gives not only an excuse, but a peculiar grace, is not at all incompatible with the solidity, prudence, diligence, and economy, as well as thoughtfulness of your character.

This world, without constant recollection and serious reflection, is but a gay bauble.

Our family are all well, except your youngest brother, who is on the mending hand. Your little John is as healthy as he is lively and entertaining. God bless him and his brothers, is the daily prayer of

John Adams.

MS not found. Printed from AA2, *Jour. and Corr.*, 2:107–108.

Thomas Brand Hollis to Abigail Adams

My Dear Madam   Chesterfeild Street Decem. 20. 1790.

A sincere desire to hear of your welfare prompted me to write that I might have the pleasure to know from yourself, that you retained the memory of a sincere friend who has an affectionate regard for your self & family & desires the welfare of your country; being above the contracted Idea of an Insulaire who is unwilling any should enjoy Liberty but the Inhabitants of his own Island.

The love of general freedom & the Universal welfare of mankind is I deem not inconsistent with the truest regard for one's own country.

I am glad to hear the hours you spent at the Hide were agreable to you as it was my wish to make them so & I am pleased to hear you have a situation beautiful & charming[1] your description of it would raise my envy if that was part of my Constitution but I enjoy other people happiness as an addition to my own. we are here obliged to be contented with natural beauties on a smaller scale.

I have made my rivulet larger & longer & uninterrupted & it has a good effect the ends being concealed with a gravel walk on the banks.

you have made me interested in the increase of your family I know not what to write in return for the uncommon & most indearing circumstance of commemorating the memory of my friend in which also you have made me an inheritor.

The walk which Mr Bridgen appropriated to his nuns & friars will receive with Jay its new visitor endeared by every circumstance imagination could invent & he will find himself surrounded with all the charities of father mother Friends & relatives.[2]

may the young man imbibe the principles of his nominal father & as he by example & books propagated the best of principles so may the young Thomas Hollis bring them into practice for the benefit of mankind.

This attention to small matters which generally lead to good is so much in the spirit of my Dear friend Mrs Adams that whereever she passes her good deeds follow her that she will never be forgot.

I shall write to Mrs Smith & endeavour to convey in weak language the strong sense I have of her regard to the principles of Virtue & Liberty by pointing out to her son for his imitation examples of intrepid worth & persevering virtue at the same time not insensible to the ingaging attention she has paid to me & to my friends character & name.

m^r Knox had left London before my return to it. This letter should have been sent long since but waited a proper conveyance as private hands are very uncertain having but lately received an account of the receipt of 3 boxes of books sent to Boston June 1789

m^rs Jebb is alive, I dare not tell her your suspicion of which she has no fear—tho I have the greatest.

France continues to go on gloriously in spite of the clergy & Aristocraticks & will become the preceptors of mankind.

our press is under difficulties & danger paper & printing taxed & very dear penalties enormous.[3] take warning & preserve it sacred for from instructions & circulation of principles you are now a great nation long may you continue so & be happy is my earnest wish and I remain with the highest gratitude and affectionate regard— wishing every good / your obliged Friend   T Brand Hollis.

RC (Adams Papers).

¹ See AA to Hollis, 6 Sept., above.

² Edward Bridgen's portraits of nuns and monks, presented as a gift to Hollis along with accompanying verses Bridgen himself composed for the occasion, were on display in a small room at the Hyde when the Adamses visited there in 1786 (vol. 7:298; JA, *D&A*, 3:200).

³ Taxes on British newspaper sales and advertising reached unprecedented levels in the late 1780s and early 1790s. The press also faced increasingly strong libel and sedition laws that threatened publishers with fines and imprisonment (Hannah Barker, *Newspapers, Politics and English Society, 1695–1855*, N.Y., 1999, p. 66–74).

Abigail Adams to John Quincy Adams

my dear son   Dec^{br} 26 1790

I have received two Letters from you, since my arrival in this city. the sickness of your Brother Thomas must be my excuse for not sooner noticing the first, which I certainly should have done immediatly if your Father had not told me that he had written to you, and particularly answerd that part which proposed a visit to us.¹ I certainly cannot have the least objection but should be most sincerely glad to see you here, and that whilst Charles is with us. it would greatly add to my happiness if your sister could compleat the Number and I could see you all four once more together. I am very unhappy to be seperated from her during the absence of col Smith, who you must have been informd saild in the dec^{br} Packet for England. his own situation, I mean that of holding an office which has as yet been an expence to him instead of a profit, an increasing Family and no profession by which he could help himself, prey'd heavily upon his spirits and induced him to take a step from which I hope he will reap a lasting advantage both to himself and Family I presume he is engaged with, and gone for, a Gentleman who knows what he is doing. he was ready to sail before either your Father or I knew that he was going, and went in five days after his agreement with the Gentleman. this you will keep to yourself the ostensible reason is that there were some debts due to his Fathers estate which he is gone to settle, and which is really the case. the publick Rumour is that Humphies is dead, and that he was sent in his place, but I believe the death of Humphries to be a mere speculation² You will see by the Report of the Trustees to the sinking fund upon what a respectable footing our credit is, the 6 pr ct funded debt having risen to par & selling in Amsterdam at a hunderd and 24 for a Hundred.³ the state debt will rise rapidly provided a peace continues. they who have cash at command may be benefited by their purchases. they can scarcly buy a miss, I mean as it now stands.

you have made me very easy upon a Subject which I wrote to you upon from N york; I trust you will be convinced that all my anxiety was for your benifit and that your happiness will ultimately be the result of resolutions which you have wisely adopted, I have no doubt mean to adhere to, so that you shall hear no more from me upon that topick. amongst the many good Rules and Maxims of my worthy Grandmother with whom I chiefly lived during the early period of my life, I recollect with pleasure, that one of them was never to bring a painfull subject twice to recollection.[4] if a poor culprit had transgresst, she repremanded with justice with dignity, but never lessned her Authority by reproaches. the concequence was that Love towards her and respect for her opinion prevented a repition of the offence—

Poor Thomas has had a severe turn of the Rhumatism, five long weeks has he been confined to his chamber four of them totally helpless— a sympathising Parent who had realized the same painfull disorder you may be Sure, was more than commonly attentive to all his complaints and never left him an hour, Nights excepted till he was relieved Charles was of great service when he came & cheerd his spirits he had just enterd mr Ingersels office and commenced his studies when he was arrested by this cruel disease which I fear will unfit him for the Season and incapacitate him to persue them even at home for some time yet. I cannot tell you much concerning this city. I have been so much confind that excepting the visits I have received I have had [sc]arcly any intercourse tho very politely invitated in the True European stile to Tea and Cards to Several Parties. I have a bad took ack & must close this repeating my request to you to visit as soon as you can, and to present me kindly to the dr and mrs welch mr & mrs smith and all other Friends yours most tenderly

A Adams—

P S. your Father will write you respecting the house

RC (Adams Papers); addressed by CA: "John Q Adams Esqr / Boston"; endorsed: "My Mother. 26. Decr. 1790." Some loss of text due to a torn manuscript.

[1] See JA to JQA, 13 Dec., above.

[2] The rumor was indeed false. See AA to AA2, 21 Feb. 1791, and note 4, below.

[3] The commissioners of the sinking fund issued their first report on 21 Dec. 1790 and said that $278,687 had been spent to purchase securities at an average rate of 54 cents on the dollar. The government purchases had the effect of driving up the value of the securities (Edward A. Ross, *Sinking Funds*, Baltimore, 1892, p. 36–40).

[4] AA refers to her maternal grandmother, Elizabeth Norton Quincy.

Abigail Adams to Abigail Adams Smith

Dear Child,   Bush Hill, 26 December, 1790.

I would tell you that I had an ague in my face, and a violent toothache, which has prevented my writing to you all day; but I am determined to brave it out this evening, and inquire how you do. Without further complaint, I have become so tender, from keeping so much in a warm chamber, that, as soon as I set my foot out, I am sure to come home with some new pain or ache.

On Friday evening last, I went with Charles to the drawing room, being the first of my appearance in public. The room became full before I left it, and the circle very brilliant. How could it be otherwise, when the dazzling Mrs. Bingham and her beautiful sisters were there; the Misses Allen, and Misses Chew; in short, a constellation of beauties?[1] I am serious when I say so, for I really think them what I describe them. Mrs Bingham has certainly given laws to the ladies here, in fashion and elegance; their manners and appearance are superior to what I have seen. I have been employed, for several days last week, in returning visits. Mrs. Powell, I join the general voice in pronouncing a very interesting woman. She is aunt to Mrs. Bingham, and is one of the ladies you would be pleased with. She looks turned of fifty, is polite and fluent as you please, motherly and friendly.[2]

I have received many invitations to tea and cards, in the European style, but have hitherto declined them, on account of my health and the sickness of your brother. I should like to be acquainted with these people, and there is no other way of coming at many of them, but by joining in their parties; but the roads to and from Bush Hill are all clay, and in open weather, up to the horses' knees; so you may suppose that much of my time must be spent at home; but this, you know, I do not regret, nor is it any mortification to me. If I could send for you, as usual, and my dear boys, it would add greatly to my pleasure and happiness. Mrs. Otis comes frequently, and passes the day with me, and yesterday I had the whole family to keep Christmas with me.[3]

The weather is winter in all respects, and such a plain of snow puts out my eyes. We have a warm side, as well as a cold one, to our house. If there is any thing we can do for you, let me know. You cannot regret your separations more than I do, for morn, noon, and night, you rest upon the mind and heart of your ever affectionate

A. Adams.

MS not found. Printed from AA, *Letters*, ed. CFA, 1848, p. 350–351.

[1] Anne Willing Bingham had four younger unmarried sisters: Elizabeth (1768–1858), Mary (1770–1852), Dorothy (1772–1847), and Abigail (1777–1841). Benjamin Chew had eight unmarried daughters at the time, two by his first wife, Mary Galloway, and six by his second, Elizabeth Oswald: Anna Maria (1749–1812), Sarah (1753–1826), Julianna (1765–1845), Henrietta (1767–1848), Sophia (1769–1841), Maria (1771–1840), Harriet (1775–1861), and Catherine (1779–1831). The "Misses Allen" were the daughters of the late James Allen of Philadelphia and his wife Elizabeth Lawrence: Anne Penn (1769–1851), Margaret Elizabeth (1772–1798), and Mary Masters (1776–1855) (Charles P. Keith, *The Provincial Councillors of Pennsylvania,* Phila., 1883, part 1, p. 93, 98, 99, 104, 107; part 2, p. 151–152, 331, 339, 351, 355, 357; *Baltimore Patriot,* 31 May 1826).

[2] Elizabeth Willing Powel (1742–1830), a sister of Thomas Willing, was the wife of Samuel Powel of Philadelphia (Washington, *Papers, Presidential Series,* 1:125).

[3] For Mary Smith Gray Otis (1757–1839), wife of Samuel Alleyne Otis, see vol. 3:307. In addition to two grown sons from Samuel Otis' first marriage, one of whom was Harrison Gray Otis, the couple had a three-year-old daughter, Harriet (William A. Otis, *A Genealogical and Historical Memoir of the Otis Family in America,* Chicago, 1924, p. 141–144).

Charles Adams to John Quincy Adams

My dear Brother   Bush Hill Philadelphia Dec[r.] 26th 1790

I fear that my receiving your letters so late may be some disadvantage to you. The information I shall now give you perhaps may reach you too late. By the last post I received your favor of the 14th instant and this morning went into town for the one dated the 11th which Harbach brought.[1] The newspapers before this time must have informed you concerning some of the business you have written to me upon. The Presidents speech is public from that you may see that a loan of three millions of florins has been completed in Holland. The two Houses of Van Staphorst and Willinck in Amsterdam had of their own accord & without any order borrowed three millions of guilders for the United States some time in the winter of 89 and ninety. But I will copy a paragraph from a letter written your father by the houses dated February 1st 1790 The houses took on themselves to open a loan of three millions at a five pr cent interest in full confidance that our motives would be considered in their true light and not doubting but our loan would be highly approved in the United States[2] The President upon consultation has thought proper to ratify that loan upon motives best know to himself. I think that there were eleven millions to be borrowed three only have as yet been borrowed as we know. It is not certainly know whether more has been borrowed for Dutch merchants here but from the complection and interests of money lenders in Holland it is not probable There is therefore a large loan to be negotiated and it may be done upon favorable terms in Holland. The 6 per Cents are now selling in Amsterdam at 124 pr Cent as I am informed from those who know. They have been sold at par here but I beleive 18 shillings is now the price generally some thousands have been sold at par upon 90 days credit. No man can lose by bying in the public stocks *now* The three pr Cents will in my opinion be soon at 10 shillings. The resolution of the Virginia assembly will have no effect.[3] The public creditors of Pensylvania have exhibited an *arogant remostrance* to the Congress and the resolution of the Senate thereupon you will see the tenor whereof is this that it would be hurtful to the Country to make any alteration in the funding system at present[4]

There is no doubt says M[r] Lawrance that the house of Representatives will make ample provision for the remaining part of the public debt and this opinion seems to be general among the well informed. I fear very much that I have not been sufficiently accurate I think you may depend upon the information given here my desire to send by this post has made he hurry more than I could have wished. You will do well to come here this winter. All well—   C—

RC (Adams Papers); endorsed: "Charles— 26. Dec[r] 1790."

[1] Neither letter has been found. The carrier of the letter was probably John Harbach (d. 1793), a Boston securities broker (John B. Hench, "Letters of John Fenno and John Ward Fenno, 1779–1800," Amer. Antiq. Soc., *Procs.*, 90:165 [April 1980]).

[2] On 8 Dec., George Washington announced to Congress that the United States had borrowed 3 million florins in Holland. CA paraphrases here lines from Wilhem and Jan Willink's letter to JA of 1 Feb. (Adams Papers). There, the Willinks said that they and Nicolaas and Jacob van Staphorst had borrowed the money without authorization "in order to maintain the Credit of the United States" when it became clear that the United States would otherwise default on payments due on foreign debt. The loan commenced on 1 Feb. and was formally accepted by Congress seven months later (Philadelphia *Federal Gazette*, 8 Dec.; Hamilton, *Papers*, 6:210–218; 14:42, 257).

[3] In November the Va. General Assembly passed a nonbinding resolution decrying the federal Funding Act as "repugnant to the Constitution of the United States" and "subversive of the interest of the people" (Providence *United States Chronicle*, 2 Dec.).

[4] A committee of Pennsylvania citizens on 21 Aug. 1789 had submitted to Congress a "Memorial of the Public Creditors of Pennsylvania" that urged Congress to repay the federal debt over a long period of time on the theory that a slowly diminishing debt would establish public credit and motivate the states to remain unified. Congress referred the report to Secretary of the Treasury Alexander Hamilton, whose more aggressive plan was adopted by Congress instead. On 23 Dec. 1790 Congress passed a resolution refusing to reconsider the issues raised in the memorial (*First Fed. Cong.*, 5:738–743; 14:510, 515; Charlene Bangs Bickford and Kenneth R. Bowling, *Birth of the Nation: The First Federal Congress, 1789–1791*, Washington, D.C., 1989, p. 62–64).

Abigail Adams Smith to Abigail Adams

my Dear Mamma   New York Decr 30th 1790

I have this moment received your Letter of the 26th and having a Leasure moment I embrace it to reply to it— it seems to renew my spirits to get a Letter from you—and they very frequently require the aid of such incidents as arrise from Communicated friendship to keep them up—for I find it very solitary— I have no inclination to go out, and except to Mrs King I have not made any visits out of the family circle,— Bellindas Connection at this time has brought all Mr Clarksons family and Connections, which are very numerous, and respectable, to visit the two families—[1] thease visits I think it my Duty to return—and to do all in my power to accommodate upon all Sides—to stand aloof—and not associate with them would not be friendly— therefore I find myself obliged to enlarge my acquaintance— they are a plain Hospitable friendly People— Mrs Charlton is Mr Clarksons aunt and having no Chrildren of her own—She has in Part addopted him as her Child and has been very friendly to the family—and much to my surprise as I did not think myself entitled to the attention as we never had visitted I received a visit from her—[2] I returnd her visit and find her a very chearfull friendly disposed Woman— her first appearance is rather stiff and reserved—but this wears aways—upon a Short acquaintance— I expect that M^r and Mrs Clarkson will spend the Winter with me— Coll^n Smith proposed it before he went away;—and they cannot go to House keeping much before May,—and their family is so large and the House so small and inconvenient that I think they will be more comfortable here— we have ever Lived together as one family altho we are in Seperate Houses—and it is my wish to accommodate them as well as I can— for they have ever treated me with the same friendship and unreserve as they behave towards each other— and I know it is Coll^n Smiths intention that whatever advantage accrues from his present Voyage to participate it with his family— his Language to me was— this opportunity presents to me; and I see a probability of reaping advantage from undertakeing it,—the seperation from my family is a Sacrifise, which nothing but their benefit would induce me to make—but I have been waiting too Long in expectation of some appointment to releive me from the Mortifying Situation in which I have been left—and I will make this exertion chearfully for I cannot

Live myself; and behold My Mother and her family—depressed by the want of those Comforts which they have been accustomed to enjoy in a Superior degree with those who now look down upon them— I join you most sincerely in wishing that we may reap advantage from it—but I Confess that my expectations are never so Sanguine as to permit me to suffer from disappointment should it not prove equal to our wishes— you mention in one of your Letters that my Father wished to send some Papers—to Col^n Smith— there are Vessells very frequently going from hence—and the Packett will sail the 6th of January— could you forward them here I could send them soon—[3]

the weather here has been for some time past extreamly Cold—& most People are not supplied with wood— indeed the Carmen say they never knew such a Scarcity of wood— I paid the Last week three pounds for a Cord of oak Wood—and Wallnut is 18 shillings a Load— if the weather should not moderate soon—and the river not open many must Suffer—

I have frequently heard of your family from Mr Deblois and Mr King—[4] they tell me that my Brother is recovering which I am very happy to hear—and that you find yourselvs rather more retired than when you were here—

Charity says in answer to your inquiries whether She is going to be Married—that She is determined not to receive the addresses of any Gentleman untill next May, She has some body we cannot find out who in her Mind, Peggy and myself Lecture her so severely when She comes to see us—for her volatility and flirtation—that She sometimes looks quite grave Sally is much better She with Peggy is gone to dance out the old year—an ancient Dutch Custom, kept up from time out of mind—[5]

when do you expect my Brother and how does he get to Philadelphia— if he should not remember that he has a Sister in New York when he Passes I shall be very much grieved, and afflicted,—for I shall be very happy to see him here— I had a very affectionate but gloomy Letter from him— it gave me the dismals for two or three days—

I have had two invitations to be escorted to Philadelphia— M^r McCormick and the Baron Stuben have both offered to take me under their Protection but I have not the smallest idea of vissitting you this Winter I should not find Courage to undertake such a journey without my better half—unless Compelled by absolute necessity;— my own fire side has more charms for me than any other place— if I can make myself comfortable there it is all I wish altho I Long to see you all and more especially my Dear Boy—

adieu yours affectionately   A Smith

my Love to Louisa—and little John— please to Burn this—[6]

RC (Adams Papers); docketed: "Mrs Smith / to / her Mother."

[1] Belinda Smith, sister of WSS, married Matthew M. Clarkson (d. 1804) on 18 December. Clarkson, the eldest son of Matthew and Elizabeth De Peyster Clarkson, belonged to a large mercantile family that operated the firm of Clarkson, Stratfield, and Levinus at 15 Smith Street in New York City (New York *Daily Advertiser*, 21 Dec.; New York *Commercial Advertiser*, 12 Dec. 1804; Waldron Phoenix Belknap Jr., *The De Peyster Genealogy*, Boston, 1956, p. 56; *New-York Directory*, 1790, Evans, No. 22724).

[2] Mary De Peyster Charlton (1735–1819), an elder sister of Elizabeth Clarkson, was the wife of New York physician Dr. John Charlton (Belknap, *De Peyster Genealogy*, p. 23–24, 56; New York *Commercial Advertiser*, 23 Dec. 1819).

[3] AA's letter has not been found, but she accepted AA2's offer when she forwarded WSS a copy of the Revenue Bill the following March (AA to WSS, 16 March 1791, below).

[4] Lewis Deblois (1760–1833), son of loyal-ist merchant Gilbert Deblois and Ann Coffin of Boston, operated a store in Boston be-|fore pursuing a mercantile business in New York City and then Philadelphia (*NEHGR*, 67:8–10, 16 [Jan. 1913]; Boston *Independent Chronicle*, 1 June 1786; *Massachusetts Gazette*, 1 Jan. 1788; *New York Daily Gazette*, 12 Aug. 1790; Philadelphia *American Daily Advertiser*, 3 April 1792). For his recent marriage to Ruth Hooper Dalton, daughter of Massachusetts politician Tristram Dalton, see Elizabeth Smith Shaw to AA, 28 Sept. 1790, and note 4, above.

[5] Offering food and drink to neighbors on New Year's Day—following a night of revelry—was a holiday tradition in Dutch colonial New York City that persisted for many generations (Charles Burr Todd, *The Story of the City of New York*, N.Y., 1890, p. 126–128; Edwin G. Burrows and Mike Wallace, *Gotham: A History of New York City to 1898*, N.Y., 1999, p. 462, 475, 532).

[6] This sentence was written sideways next to the salutation.

Cotton Tufts to John Adams

Dear S^{r.}   Weymouth Jany. 6. 1791

We begin to feel the good Effects of our national Government— By the Presidents Speech at the opening of the present Session of Congress, our public Affairs wear a promising Appearance.[1] His Speech gave a new Spring to public Credit; in the Course of Three or Four Days after it reachd us public Securities rose 10 or 15 P^r C^t— The several Departments of Government being well filld, from the firm prudent & upright Conduct of officers, Content will follow, Murmurs cease and a general Confidence in the national Goverment be established—

Agreable to your Request, I have loand your continental Securities—have taken two sets of Certificates as per Mem. enclosed—[2] Your State Notes, I have yet on Hand, thinking it best to let them lay, till our Genl Court shall have discussed the Subject of their public Debt, which, I presume, will be taken under Consideration in their appraching Session, which commences on the Third Wednesday of the present Month—[3]

I have settled with the Printers, stopd Adams & Freeman's Paper, directed Edes & Sons to send no more after the Expiration of the present Quarter, wch. will end in February, and have continued the Centinel—[4]

I am extremely sorry to hear of the Indisposition of your Family— I hope to hear in Your next of their Restoration to Health, for Yours & their Happiness You have the ardent wishes of / Your Friend & H Ser   Cotton Tufts

RC (Adams Papers); internal address: "Hon. Jno. Adams—"; docketed: "Dr Tufts to Mr Adams / January 6 1791."

[1] George Washington spoke at the opening of the third session of Congress in Philadelphia on 8 Dec. 1790. "The abundant fruits of another year have blessed our Country with plenty, and with the means of a flourishing Commerce," he said. "The progress of public Credit is witnessed by a considerable rise of American stock abroad as well as at home." The president also mentioned the opening of a new Dutch loan, a petition for Kentucky statehood, Native American hostilities on the western frontier, and the need to protect American commerce from political upheaval in Europe (*First Fed. Cong.*, 1:497–501).

[2] Not found.

[3] The Mass. General Court convened on 26 Jan. 1791 and adjourned on 12 March. In a speech opening the session, Gov. John Hancock praised Congress' Aug. 1790 assumption of state debt but expressed concern that the amount to be paid to Massachusetts lenders was capped at $4 million. Hancock proposed that the legislature fund the residue from state revenues, and on 9 Feb. 1791 the legislature agreed to do so "whenever it is asser-

tained what Sum remains to be provided for by this State." A 24 Feb. motion to consider Hancock's proposal further was defeated in the expectation that Congress might remove the limit. The federal limit remained in place and the legislature eventually funded the shortfall (Mass., *Acts and Laws*, 1790–1791, p. 155, 168–170, 214, 559–561; Boston *Columbian Centinel*, 26 Feb.; Boston *Independent Chronicle*, 17 March; Woody Holton, "Abigail Adams, Bond Speculator," *WMQ*, 3d series, 64:837–838 [Oct. 2007]).

[4] Edmund Freeman (1764–1807) was printer of the Boston *Herald of Freedom*, a newspaper that, although ostensibly nonpartisan, leaned Antifederalist. Tufts also canceled the more overtly Antifederalist *Boston Gazette* and Boston *Independent Chronicle*; see AA to Tufts, 17 Jan. 1790, and note 1, above. Tufts continued the *Massachusetts Centinel*, the only Federalist Boston newspaper (Frederick Freeman, *The History of Cape Cod: The Annals of Barnstable County*, 2 vols., Boston, 1862, 2:148; Stewart, *Opposition Press*, p. 875).

Mary Smith Cranch to Abigail Adams

My dear Sister   Braintree January 7th 1791

What a Succession of troubles have you had to incounter & not one of us to help you through them— I have been very anxious for you & was affraid by my not hearing sooner that something had happen'd— oh my poor Thomas how I pity him—his Patience & fortitude have been put to their trial— he has a great share of it I know,

& he will find tis good to be sometimes afflicted he will feel more tenderly for others & be more ready to be "Feet to the lame, & hands to the hungry, if not eyes to the Blind["]¹ than if he had never needed the like from others tell him that Miss Paine Sends her Love to him & says she feels most sympathetickly for him & for you all & wishes you that health which she never expects her self she knows she says that cousin has thought of the poor cripple at Braintree— I hope to hear he is better soon— I wonder how you have stood such fatigues—& your house too to be in such a miserable situation not fit for well People to have gone into I wonder it had not made you all sick. I wonder if it has been as cold with you as here I never saw such a December & now we have a thaw which has Set every thing a float & makes us all feel very unwell it has given me such a head ack that I can hardly see what I write—but I could not bear to have your son visit you without a line from me. I must write a little to mrs Smith too She poor woman now knows a little & but a little of the feelings of her mama in her Friends absence She is not left with such cares as you were nor is he in any danger from an Enemy I wish she was where I could see her & her dear little Boys

It seems to me your Gentleman & Ladies were wanting in judgment to visit you before you had time to put up your Furniture I hope you will find some Friends where you can visit free from the shackels of so much ceremony as your station subjects you to you have found Doctor Rush just what I always thought him; by the way—I wish you would some time or other ask him whither he ever attend'd such a Funeral as our Neighbours have reported he did: cousin Thomas can recollect the Story & the names enough to ask the question— they say mrs Brown dy'd two year ago this winter & it was her Funeral that was so splendid. The Lady here is still in mourning for her Friends

your Friends are all well & desire to be rememberd kindly to you especially those of this household. tell cousin Thomas I long to be with him cousin Charles is a good nurse I am glad he is with you— my good Louisia does every the can to assist you I know, my Love to them all— Mr Adams with my dear Sister will always have the highest esteem & the tenderest affection of their / grateful Sister

Mary Cranch

my Love to mrs otis when you see her

RC (Adams Papers); docketed: "M^rs· Cranch 1790."

¹ "I was eyes to the blind, and feet was I to the lame" (Job, 29:15).

Abigail Adams Smith to John Adams

My Dear Pappa— New York January 7th 1791

I have received your two Kind letters of Decr 8th and 17th and am much obliged for your good wishes, and advice[1] I have no desire to mix with the World or associate with any but my friends during the absence of my Husband—retirement from the World and an intercourse with, and attention, to ones family and friends are I presume Compatiable— the former it is my wish to observe the latter Contributes much to alleviate the Solitude of my situation I am as happy in the society of Colln Smiths family as I can be during his absence— they are very friendly disposed and we have ever lived in the greatest Harmony—which has ever given me pleasure—

Colln Smiths voyage was not I *hope* undertaken without due consideration and I wish it may succeed equal to his expectations, those friends to whom he Communicated the object; have approved of it—

But if he had been treated by those in Power as he was entitled to expect he would not have been compelled to have undertaken it a paragraph in this days paper mentions that he has been sent by the President on Public Service—which Shews the Worlds opinion that he ought to have been attended to, in past appointments I most ardently wish that the result of his present voyage may render him independant of their smiles or favours—[2]

my Mamma mentions that you wished to forward to Colln Smith some journals and papers— there are frequently Vessells going from Hence—but unless some Passenger would take a Pacquet the expence of Postage would be great—

I am very happy to hear that my Brother is recovering his health sincerely do I wish that it may be permanently established— the Wellfare Health and prosperity of your family my Dear Pappa—are too nearly connected with my happiness—for me not to regret any of those events which may interfere with either—in any branch of it— and to hear of their happiness—will ever Contribute largely to that of your / Dutifull and affectionate Daughter A Smith—

RC (Adams Papers). Filmed at 17 Jan. 1791.

[1] JA's letter of 8 Dec. 1790 has not been found.

[2] The New York *Daily Advertiser* reported on 7 Jan. 1791 that "We have it from good authority, that Colonel David Humphries and William S. Smith, Esq. have lately been dispatched, by the President of the United States, to Europe, in official capacities. Mr. Smith, it is supposed to the Court of London. The object of their embassies unknown." The next day the paper printed a letter from "A. B." correcting the notice:

"Whatever might have been the object in sending the former, it is well known in this city, that the business of Mr. Smith in Europe was merely of a private nature." WSS

did in fact make diplomatic contacts while in London; see WSS to JA, 5 Aug., and note 1, below.

Cotton Tufts to Abigail Adams

Dear Madam   Weymouth Jan.ʸ 7. 1791—

I am happy to find by Mʳ Adam's's Letter of Dec. 14. that You have in a great Measure recovered Your Health.[1] I sympathize with you under the Sickness of Your Son and others in Your Family. I sincerely wish for his and their Restoration to Health, & hope by this Time that they have regain'd it and that you are sit down in some Degree of Ease & Tranquillity— Your Scituation in Life must necessarily expose You to numerous Visits, Ceremonies, Entertainments, Etiquette &c &c. these must of Course subject You to great Fatigue & much Care, and I fear has & will have a material Operation on Your Health, but as they are in some Measure unavoidable, Will it not be Wisdom to simplify so far as to make them as little burdensome as possible? Why might not You & the Presidents Lady consult & agree upon a simple Mode of conducting Visits of entertaining Company &c &c? Might You not acting in Conjunction establish a Mode respecting these that would become a Law to our American Gentry? In this Way might You not get rid of much Trouble and do essential Service to our Nation?

I have not as yet loaned your public Securities waiting for your Instructions respecting the Mode of doing it, they must either be loaned in my own Name, or as Trustee to Mʳˢ A. Adams, if taken in my own Name they must (to make them your Property) be formally transferred, if taken as Trustee they will be secured to Your Use & need no Transfer If taken in my own Name & transferred to You, as well as in the other Way, Your Name will be known— perhaps You may think of some Method that may answer Your Wishes & conceal the Name

I wish without Delay to know what measures You would have pursued the coming Year respecting the Farm on which Pratt lives; as near as I can calculate from Accᵗᵗˢ rendered in, your half produces about £26. annually, out of this Rates & Repairs are to be deducted—

I engaged the Tongues & 1 bb. Beef 5 or Six Weeks past & expected to have sent them immediately but unfortunately missd of getting them on Board the Philad Vessel, they will be sent by the first opp^y— the other Two Barrells of Beef You wrote for I concluded to delay sending them till Februay as the best Beef for Barrelling will then be at market—

M^rs· Tufts joins me in Affectionate Regards to you M^r· Adams & Family

I am Your Affectionate Friend & H Ser   Cotton Tufts

P.S. We have been much blocked up with Snow during the Week past, which will prevent my seeing M^r· J. Q. Adams before he sets off for Philadelphia[2]

RC (Adams Papers); internal address: "M^rs· Abigail Adams—"

[1] Not found.
[2] JQA noted in his Diary a "Violent Snow Storm" on 1 Jan. (D/JQA/16, APM Reel 19).

Abigail Adams to Abigail Adams Smith

My Dear Mrs. Smith,   Philadelphia, 8 January, 1791.

I received, by Mr. King, your letter of December 30th. I am uneasy if I do not hear from you once a week, though you have not any thing more to tell me than that you and your little ones are well. I think you do perfectly right in refusing to go into public during the absence of Colonel Smith. The society of a few friends is that from which most pleasure and satisfaction are to be derived. Under the wing of parents, no notice would be taken of your going into public, or mixing in any amusement; but the eyes of the world are always placed upon those whose situation may possibly subject them to censure, and even the friendly attentions of one's acquaintance are liable to be misconstrued, so that a lady cannot possibly be too circumspect. I do not mention this to you through apprehension of your erring, but only as approving your determination.

I should spend a very dissipated winter, if I were to accept of one half the invitations I receive, particularly to the routes, or tea and cards. Even Saturday evening is not excepted, and I refused an invitation of that kind for this evening. I have been to one assembly. The dancing was very good; the company of the best kind. The President and Madam, the Vice-President and Madam, Ministers of State, and their Madams, &c.; but the room despicable; the etiquette,—it was difficult to say where it was to be found. Indeed, it was not New York;[1] but you must not report this from me. The managers have been very polite to me and my family. I have been to one

177

play, and here again we have been treated with much politeness. The actors came and informed us that a box was prepared for us. The Vice-President thanked them for their civility, and told them that he would attend whenever the President did. And last Wednesday we were all there. The house is equal to most of the theatres we meet with out of France. It is very neat, and prettily fitted up; the actors did their best; "The School for Scandal" was the play. I missed the divine Farren; but upon the whole it was very well performed.[2] On Tuesday next I go to a dance at Mr. Chew's, and on Friday sup at Mr. Clymer's; so you see I am likely to be amused.[3]

We have had very severe weather for several weeks; I think the coldest I have known since my return from abroad. The climate of Old England for me; people do not grow old half so fast there; two-thirds of the year here, we must freeze or melt. Public affairs go on so smoothly here, that we scarcely know that Congress are sitting; North Carolina a little delirious, and Virginia trying to give law.[4] They make some subject for conversation; but, after all, the bluster will scarcely produce a mouse.

Present me kindly to your mamma and sisters. How I long to send for you all, as in days past; my dear little boys, too. As to John, we grow every day fonder of him. He has spent an hour this afternoon in driving his grandpapa round the room with a willow stick. I hope to see you in April. Congress will adjourn in March, and it is thought will not meet again till December.[5]

Good night, my dear. Heaven's blessings alight on you and yours,

A. Adams.

MS not found. Printed from AA, *Letters*, ed. CFA, 1848, p. 352–353.

[1] The relative merits of the cultures of New York and Philadelphia had been a subject of public debate since the Residence Act was signed by George Washington on 16 July 1790. Discussion generally focused on New York as a more sophisticated city but also one subject to European influence (Margaret M. O'Dwyer, "A French Diplomat's View of Congress, 1790," *WMQ*, 3d ser., 21:441 [July 1964]; Rush, *Letters*, 1:568; New York *Weekly Museum*, 30 Oct. 1790).

[2] AA and AA2 had both likely seen Elizabeth Farren when she appeared as Lady Teazle in Richard Brinsley Sheridan's *The School for Scandal* at Drury Lane in London in 1785 and 1786 (London *Daily Universal Register*, 14 Feb. 1785, 4 May 1786; vol. 6:185;

7:145).

[3] Philadelphia merchant George Clymer (1739–1813) had served with JA in the Continental Congress (JA, *D&A*, 2:149; JA, *Papers*, 4:398; *DAB*).

[4] On 6 Jan. 1791 Congressman John Steele of North Carolina threatened secession if the proposed Duty on Distilled Spirits Act was passed, stating that because more spirits were consumed in the South, the bill would place an undue burden on his constituents. AA's comment on Virginia likely refers to the passage of a bill in the Virginia legislature approving the separation of the District of Kentucky previous to the debate of a bill in Congress on statehood. Both federal bills became law, on 3 March and 4 Feb., respec-

tively (*First Fed. Cong.*, 1:522; 3:827, 835; 14:243–246). See also TBA to JA, 30 Oct. 1792, and note 4, below.

[5] Congress adjourned on 3 March 1791 and reconvened on 24 Oct. (*Biog. Dir. Cong.*).

Abigail Adams to Mary Smith Cranch

my dear sister   Philadelphia Jan^ry 9th 1791

I received your kind Letter of December 12th with one from my Nephew inclosing 4 Portraits[1] I instantly recognized my worthy Brother Cranch and my dear sister together with our venerable uncle Quincy. the other not one of us have skill enough to find out, by which I judge it is not a likness the three first are admirably executed and I have to request that the same hand would take my Mother and send it without letting mr Adams know for whom it is designd. you inquire how I like my situation. I answer you the one I removed from, was in Burks stile, the sublime. this is the Beautifull[2] the House is better, that is the work within is superiour. the Architecture of the other House was Grand and the Avenue to it perfectly Romantick. the British Troops rob'd this place of its principal Glory by cutting down all the Trees in front of the House and leaving it wholly Naked. behind the House is a fine Grove; through which is a gravell walk; which must in summer add greatly to the delight of the place. I am told for 8 months this place is delicious. in winter the Roads are bad and we are 2 miles & a half from the city. I have received every attention and politeness from the Gentlemen and Ladies which I could either expect or wish. Living here is more expensive than in N york, Horse keeping in particular, which we sensibly feel, as we are obliged to keep four, for during the sitting of Congress they frequently go six times to the city in the course of the day. we cannot purchase any marketing but by going into the city. we have had very Severe cold weather from the begining of December till the week past; when the snow has chiefly left us I am thinking seriously of making arrangments to come to Braintree early in the spring as the Roads will permit, for it is generally believed that Congress will not sit after march if so I hope to be with you by the last of April or begining of May and as I must leave Brisler and his Family here, I would look out early for some person in his stead. can you inform me where Nathan Tirril is, and whether he was last summer engaged.[3] he is a good Hand in a Garden and on many other accounts usefull. there are some articles which I shall want in the kitchin way, but it will be time enough to think of these things some months hence

I feel the loss of mrs smith and Family and it pains me daily that I could not have her with me this winter it is in vain to say what we ought to have been able to do, I feel what I cannot do. the Cols Family are all very kind to mrs Smith and treat her like a child, but a Fathers House is still the most desirable place. I hear every week from her. I have John with me a fine Boy he is and the enlivener of the whole Family we are a scatterd family, and I see no prospect of our ever being otherways. mr durant was here last week and said he was going to Boston in order to sail from thence for st croix, the River here being frozen up. I thought the Letter you sent to the care of Thomas would go best & soonest by him, so we gave it to him. Thomas is much better tho he does not yet go out except to ride. I have had a succession of sickness in my Family when we have been well ourselves, our servants have been laid up. when I come to this place again I am determined to bring a *decent woman* who understands plain cooking with me. Such a vile low tribe, you never was tormented with & I hope never will be. I brought all my servants from N york, cook excepted and, thought I could not be worse of than I had been. I have had in the course of 18 months Seven, and I firmly believe in the whole Number, not a virtuous woman amongst them all; the most of them drunkards. I recruited with a new one last monday, who brought written recommendations with her, and who to all appearence is very capable of her buisness, but on thursday got so drunk that she was carried to Bed, and so indecent, that footman Coachman & all were driven out of the House, concequently she has turnd herself out of doors. we know little of vileness in our state when compared to those cities who have Such Numbers of Foreigners as N york and Philadelphia— I thank you my dear sister for your kind care of your Nephew. he wanted it I believe. he mourns a want of employ, but all young men must have patience, especially in his profession. ["]there is a tide in the affairs of men" our young folks must watch for it.

I would ask dr Rush about a certain affair if I had a short detail of Names circumstances and time. if cousin Lucy thinks it worth her time to give me some account of the affair, I am upon such an intimate footing with the dr since his practise in our Family that I could easily assertain all he knows about it, but the story was so complicated that I am by no means mistress of the Subject.

my Love to mrs Norten & my young Nephew. I anticipate the pleasure of meeting you all. pray heaven nothing may arrise to prevent my realizing the Satisfaction. Let me hear from you as often you can and / believe me at all times most / affectionatly yours

A Adams

RC (MWA:Abigail Adams Letters); addressed by TBA: "M^rs: Mary Cranch / Braintree"; endorsed by Richard Cranch: "Letter from M^rs / A Adams (Ph^a:) / Jany 9th. 1791."

[1] For William Cranch's letter of 11 Dec. 1790, see Mary Smith Cranch to AA, 12 Dec., and note 5, above.

[2] Edmund Burke, *A Philosophical Enquiry into the Origin of Our Ideas of the Sublime and the Beautiful*, London, 1757.

[3] Nathan Tirrell (ca. 1754–1814) was the second son of Joseph Tirrell of Braintree (Sprague, *Braintree Families*).

Abigail Adams to Abigail Adams Smith

My Dear Child,   Philadelphia, 25 January, 1791.

You must not flatter yourself with the expectation of hearing from Colonel Smith until the February packet arrives. It is as soon as you ought to think of it. You see by the papers, that a minister is in nomination from England, and Mrs. C— writes, will come out soon.[1] Mrs. P—, from whom I received a letter, writes me by the last packet, that Mr. Friere is certainly appointed from Portugal, and that he only waits for the arrival of Count ——, his successor, in England, before he sails for America. Mrs. P— likewise communicates the agreeable intelligence of Mr. P—'s having forsaken the bottle, and that the Countess B— had another child, and was vastly happy, beloved by her dear Count, &c.; all in the true style of Mrs. P—.[2] She desires to be kindly remembered to you and the Colonel.

Present me kindly to all my New York friends. That I was attached to that place is most true, and I shall always remember with pleasure the fifteen months passed there; but, if I had you and your family, I could be very well pleased here, for there is an agreeable society and friendliness kept up with all the principal families, who appear to live in great harmony, and we meet at all the parties nearly the same company. To-morrow the President dines with us, the Governor, the Ministers of State, and some Senators.[3] Of all the ladies I have seen and conversed with here, Mrs. Powell is the best informed. She is a friendly, affable, good woman, sprightly, full of conversation. There is a Mrs. Allen, who is as well bred a woman as

I have seen in any country, and has three daughters, who may be styled the three Graces.[4]

My best respects to your good mamma and family. Tell Mrs. C— I hope she makes a very obedient wife.[5] I am sure she will be a good one. I think I shall see you in April. Why do you say that you feel alone in the world? I used to think that I felt so too; but, when I lost my mother, and afterwards my father, *that* "alone" appeared to me in a much more formidable light. It was like cutting away the main pillars of a building; and, though no friend can supply the absence of a good husband, yet, whilst our parents live, we cannot feel un-protected. To them we can apply for advice and direction, sure that it will be given with affection and tenderness. We know not what we can do or bear, till called to the trial. I have passed through many painful ones, yet have enjoyed as much happiness through life as usually falls to the lot of mortals; and, when my enjoyments have been damped, curtailed, or molested, it has not been owing to vice, that great disturber of human happiness, but sometimes to folly, in myself or others, or the hand of Providence, which has seen fit to afflict me. I feel grateful for the blessings which surround me, and murmur not at those which are withheld.— But my pen runs on, and my lads, at whose table I write, wonder what mamma can find to write about.

Adieu. My love to the children. From your ever affectionate

A. Adams.

MS not found. Printed from AA, *Letters*, ed. CFA, 1848, p. 353–355.

[1] The *Pennsylvania Mercury* reported on 22 Jan. that former New York lieutenant governor and loyalist Andrew Elliot would be named the first British minister to the United States. Elliot was proposed for the post by Henry Dundas but ultimately declined to serve and retired to Scotland (Eugene Devereux, "Andrew Elliot, Lieutenant-Governor of the Province of New York," *PMHB*, 11:149–150 [July 1887]). The letter from Susanna Clarke Copley has not been found.

[2] João Caballero de Almeida Mello e Castro succeeded Ciprião Ribeiro, Chevalier de Freire, as Portuguese minister to Great Britain (*Repertorium*, 3:317). The 2 Nov. 1790 letter from Lucy Ludwell Paradise to AA also mentioned that Paradise's husband, John, "has perfectly broke himself of the love of the Bottle. he leads a regular life, and of Course, enjoys a perfect health." The letter, however, does not indicate that the Paradises' daughter, the Countess Barziza, had had a second child (Adams Papers).

[3] Thomas Mifflin served as governor of Pennsylvania from 1790 until 1799 (*DAB*).

[4] Elizabeth Lawrence Allen (1750–1800), daughter of John and Elizabeth Lawrence of Philadelphia and widow of James Allen. She was remarried in June 1791 to John Laurance, member of the U.S. House of Representatives from New York (Charles P. Keith, *The Provincial Councillors of Pennsylvania*, Phila., 1883, p. 450–451; New York *Daily Advertiser*, 3 May 1800).

[5] That is, Belinda Clarkson, sister of WSS.

Mary Smith Cranch to Abigail Adams

My dear Sister   Braintree January 25ᵗʰ 1791

I last week receiv'd your kind Letter of the 9th of this month & rejoice to here that you are all in so much beter health than when you wrote before. I feel more pleasure at the thought of seeing you here in the Spring than I dare venture to indulge I past by your House this afternoon & the thought of seeing it again inhabited by my dear Brother & Sister gave a chearfulness to its appearence which it has not had since you left it—& beleive me my sister Joy & sorrow are so nearly alli'd in thier effects that some of the few tears which remain'd unsshed at your departure forc'd themselves from my Eyes.

every thing in your house is I believe in good order Lucy goes after every Storm & with the Boy or Girl sweeps out the Snow & whatever she finds necessary— she will send you an inventory of what things [you] have in the house that you may know what you will want & what to direct to have purchaised for you some things I can lend you—

As to help I think I can do much better for you than to get mr Tyrrel— he is not a good man & has a miserable poor Family too near for your profit There is a Negro man & his wife who have made Phebes house there home when they were not out at work for these nine months. They both were hir'd by your Brother Adams last summer the man as a Farmer & his wife as a spinner. He speaks well of them & Phebe gives them a good character She wash'd for me last summer & was with me some time as a spinner they have been hir'd servants to some of the genteelest Familys in the other states The man came from Guinea when a child & was bought by a man in connetiut who had no children & was so good to him that he gave him an education like a child— he can write & cypher &c She says she understands cooking She was born at Long Island. They appear to be very honest & good temper'd I have never heard a word amiss of them from any one they have had four children but they were dead born I have talk'd with Doctor Tufts about them—& we both think you cannot do better than to take them both if you want a servant of both sex's. They will not be above their Business nor will they have such a train after them as if you were to get servants who have connections here I have told them that I would not have them ingage themselves untill I could hear from you

183

Cousin John will be with you I hope as soon as this Letter— then prehaps you may perceive who the profile was taken for which you could not find out it cannot be so good a likeness as the others or you would have discover'd it; we thought it a good likness The one you desire will be tried for we have one of you which I think is very much like you except the nose & [. . .] he had forgot

Betsy was here yesterday & tells me Richard can run alone, he is but ten months old, Sister Shaw says she has not set her little Girl upon her Feet yet. Tis such a rarity that they are as ch[. . .] of it as if they had never had one before

remember me kindly to mr Adams & all my Cousins I have written to mrs Smith by my nephew—[1]

Yours affectionately   Mary Cranch

RC (Adams Papers); addressed by William Cranch: "Mrs A. Adams / Philadelphia"; endorsed: "Mrs Cranch / 25 Jan^ry"; docketed: "1791." Some loss of text where the seal was removed.

[1] Not found, but see AA2's reply to Mary Smith Cranch, 8 Feb., below.

Martha Washington to Abigail Adams

Tuesday morning January 25 [*1791*]

Mrs Washington, presents her compliments to Mrs Adams,— if it is agreable to her, to Let miss smith come to dance with nelly & Washington, the master[1] attends mondays wednesdays and Frydays at five oclock in the evenings— Mrs Washington will be very happy to see miss smith

RC (private owner; photocopy at ViMtvL); addressed: "Mrs Adams"; docketed: "Mrs Washington / to Mrs Adams."

[1] Martha Washington's grandchildren Eleanor Parke and George Washington Custis were receiving instruction from dancing master James Robardet. "Lately from Europe, but last from New-York," Robardet offered classes in his studio or by appointment to "those Ladies or Gentlemen who wish to be instructed at their own houses" (Washington, *Papers, Presidential Series,* 10:321; Philadelphia *American Daily Advertiser,* 20 Jan.).

Abigail Adams to Cotton Tufts

my dear sir   Philadelphia Feb^ry 6 1790 [*1791*]

I received your kind Letter of Jan^ry 7th by my son. in replie to the Buisness part, I think upon reflection and to save trouble, I would wish you to Loan my Notes as Trustee to me. I as well as many other should have liked the system of Finnance much better if the Faith pledged had been literally fullfilld; by the payment of Six pr ct interest, then let the new Loan have been fill'd at 4 or 3. the National Honour would have stood much fairer with all honest Men, and tho some individuals might have accumulated great fortunes by it, I think it would have circulated & spread abroad with more satisfaction than it will Curtaild, and part deffered as it now stands, but having been accepted & agreed to by the Government it is best to abide by it.[1]

you will Learn by the publick papers that mr Madison is come forward with all his powers, in opposition to the Bank it is difficult for the world in general to discover why a wise Man or rather so Learned a Man can take up such opinions as he has, and defend them so earnestly, but there are some who can see further through' a mill stone than others to whom mr Madisons designs are not so impenetrable, but there remains not a doubt but that the Bill will pass the House by a considerable majority.[2] Congress will rise in march, and have I hope a long recess. we propose visiting Braintree as soon as the Roads will permit and if you have not shipd the Beaf and Tongues I would have them reserved for my use there, but then I shall want only one Barrell. pork I suppose I can buy. Hams I would be glad to employ mr Foster to get for me, say one dozen I never eat finer than those which he procured for me last year

upon the subject of visits which you mention, for a publick Character like the Presidents & his Ladies I do not know how they could be visited in any other way than they are, consistant with the Rank they hold. on twesday from 3 to four the President has a Levee, when strangers are introduced *Members of the House of commons & the other House* visit him Such of the inhabitants as chuse attend. this is no more than going an hour upon the exchange an hour in Boston or Else where on thursdays he usually gives a dinner and a very handsome one too, to such company as he invites previously, and they are always properly chosen; on fryday Evenings mrs washington has a drawing Room which is usually very full of the *well Born and well Bred*. Some times it is as full as her Britanick majesties Room, & with quite as Handsome Ladies, and as polite courtiers. here the company are entertaind with Coffe Tea cake Ice creams Lemonade &c they chat with each other walk about, fine Ladies shew themselves, and as candle Light is a great improver of Beauty, they appear to great advantage; this shew lasts from seven, till Nine oclock comeing & going during those hours, as it is not

Etiquette for any person to stay Long. on other days any Lady who is in habits of intimacy may visit mrs washington with the same freedom & take Tea with her as unceremoniously as my good Aunt, your Lady will with me, when I return to Braintree, as I hope. with regard to my Ladyship, your Honours Neice it is most certainly true, that she would be very happy to See an entertain ten persons where She now does one, if her good Friends would have enabled her so to do, but as they have not she gives of such as she has with a hearty good will and be sure in as smart a manner as she can afford it is not very often that she has the pleasure. as to visits many must be of the ceremonious kind, but then there is this satisfaction that one can make 20 in a forenoon— I accept no invitation nor my Family for saturday Evening & make no sunday visits. Sometimes a Friend or intimate acquaintance will dine on sundays with us, but no invitations for that day— my dear sir I Look forward to the Spring with much pleasure as I have the prospect of seeing you then and the rest of my Friends. at present my Family are all well my three sons with me, and the Chief Justice of the united states makes this House his home during the sitting of the Court.[3]

Remember me kindly to all my connections and be assured my dear sir that I am with / Sentiments of esteem and affection / Yours

A Adams

RC (Adams Papers); addressed by TBA: "Honble: Cotton Tufts / Weymouth"; endorsed: "Mrs. Abiga. Adams Lettr / Feby 6. 1791." Filmed at 6 Feb. 1790.

[1] For the Funding Act, see AA to Mary Smith Cranch, 29 Aug. 1790, note 1, above. AA would have preferred Congress to provide 6 percent interest on the full value of all her state bonds and to offer simultaneously a new bond series that paid a lower interest rate. Despite her complaint, AA made a large profit when she redeemed state notes that she had acquired at a fraction of their face value (Woody Holton, "Abigail Adams, Bond Speculator," *WMQ*, 3d series, 64:837–838 [Oct. 2007]).

[2] During House debate of the act to establish the Bank of the United States, James Madison spoke in opposition on the grounds that the Constitution did not grant Congress the power to create such an institution and that banks established by the states were sufficient. The House nevertheless approved the bill by a vote of 39 to 20 on 8 Feb. 1791, and George Washington signed it on 25 Feb. (*First Fed. Cong.*, 4:173; 14:367, 378–381).

[3] JA wrote to John Jay on 20 Dec. 1790 to offer him and Sarah Livingston Jay a "handsome and convenient Room and Chamber, and a decent Bed" during the upcoming session of the Supreme Court (NNC:John Jay Papers). Jay accepted for himself on 4 Jan. 1791 (Adams Papers) and arrived on the 30th. The court was in session on 7 and 8 Feb., and Jay departed for New York on the 14th (*Doc. Hist. Supreme Court*, 1:341–344; 2:126, 135).

Abigail Adams Smith to Elizabeth Cranch Norton

New York Febuary 7th 1791

I received your kind Letter of 16th of January by Mr Jackson[1] and feel myself particularly obliged my Dear Cousin for your attention at this time the absence of my Husband—leaves a blank in my mind which may be alleviated in some degree by the Kind attentions of my friends; but which nothing can fill up— my Chrildren are yet so small as not to afford me much society;— in their smiles;—and Lively prattle I find an amusement;— in Mr Smiths family I have kind and attentive friends disposed to Contribute all in their power to my Happiness; we Live in the most perfect Harmony reciprocal attentions strengthenths the bond of friendship His Mamma—is a very fine Woman. possessed of a strong mind and an amiable Heart, attached to her Chrildren—to a very great degree—ever sollicitous for their wellfare and Happiness— it is no small degree of Concern to us that She does not enjoy her Health— She is greatly afflicted with a Severe pain in her Arm—which She apprehends to be the rheumatism—but which I fear will prove of a more serious nature— I am apprehensive of a paralytic dissorder— his Sisters are all fine and amiable Women— Bellinda has Married this Winter a young Gentleman Whose name is Clarkson—an amiable young Man— with whom I beleive she will be very happy— they spend the Winter with me—as also Miss Peggy the Eldest Sister who [is a] charming sprightly Companion— the Eldest Brother has taken Colln Smiths place in the Office—of Marshall—and he also is of the family—so that I am not alone,—[2] I nevertheless frequently wish that I could enjoy the society of your family—and a few of my friends—for whom I feel an attachment that is not to be abated by distance or time— the removeall of my Mamma and her family from this place is to me an irreparable Loss, of an invaluable blessing—and an event which no Length of time can reconcile me to the dispersed State of my own family is a scource of anxiety and unhappiness—to me— to look for friendship—without the Circle of ones own family and Connections whose interest as well as pleasure it is to Contribute to each others Happiness—is to expect a very great improbability if not an impossibility— if we are not disposed to contribute to each others advancement in Life—we cannot reasonably expect to interest other People in our behalf— it is a most excellent Motto—United we stand, divided we fall,—

I was I assure you my friend much gratified to hear of your prosperity and Wellfare— it would afford me much pleasure to bring our Chrildren acquainted with each other— you would be surprized to see your friend surrounded by three great Boys— I can scarce realize the idea myself I assure you— as far as one can Judge at so early a period they promise to possess amiable dispositions—and the youngest Master Thomas Hollis is not I assure you the least of a favourite altho he was considered as an *usurper*— I had anticipated the pleasure of having a Daughter— he has Carrot Colourd Hair—and consequently a fair Complexion—but every person who sees him observes a great resemblance to my family— I am happy to hear that our friend Anna is happily settled— I agree with you that She is the greatest female enthusiast I ever knew—and I beleive she stands a greater Chance for Happiness—provided the fervor—of friendship can always be kept alive— the object may perhaps change & the principle be still supported— I suppose she will think that her Chrildren should she have any—are of a superior order of beings—

with you my friend I join most sincerely in wishing that the absence of my best friend may not be of a Long Continueance—and I have no expectation of its being prolonged Later than May at fartherst but if it should;—you may bid adieu to your Cousin—for I am determined to follow him— the motives which have induced him to undertake this voyage—were the most Laudable;— you may have heard that he is gone upon Public Business—but it is not true should he succed equal to his expectations in his Business—I shall not regret having made this sacrifise—

I regreted much that I did not know of Mrs Cranch and Miss Palmers being in town when they went on to West Point I should most certainly have seen them— it was not untill a Month after their departure that Mr Greanleaf called and delivered their Letters—[3] I fear that they must have thought me unfriendly and inattentive—

be so good as to present my regards to all my friends my Love to your Mamma and Sister and my respects to Mr Norton

beleive me my Dear Cousin sincerely / your friend

A Smith—

RC (MHi:Christopher P. Cranch Papers); docketed: "Letter from M^rs. A Smith to / M^rs. Norton Feby. 1791." Some loss of text due to wear at the fold.

[1] Not found.

[2] In a letter informing George Washington of his imminent departure for England, WSS proposed to leave his office "in charge with my Brother Justus B. Smith . . . who from being constantly with me in the office is fully competent to the discharge of its duties, and for which I shall consider myself responsible" (Washington, *Papers, Presidential Series*, 7:39).

[3] Not found.

Abigail Adams Smith to Mary Smith Cranch

New York Febuary 8th 1791

your kind attention my Dear Aunt demands an early acknowl-
edgement, you judge very right that it would contribute greatly to
my happiness could I be indulged with the society of my friends in
your part of the world– I often do most ardently wish for it–but fate
has ordered it otherwise–[and] I must submit– the removeall of my
Mamma and her family from this place has deprived me of a very
great portion of Happiness I am however blessed with very Kind
friends in Coll^n Smiths family to whom I am much indebted for
friendly attentions and agreeable society– I have neither inclination
or desire to mix in society–and I have no intimate friends out of my
family– I sometimes feel as if I Stood alone in the World, seperated
from all my nearest Connections and Dearest friends– this Winter
has been a tedious and solitary one–to me– my Chrildren afford me
amusement and employment but they are yet too young to afford
me much society– William is an amiable Manly Child– John is with
my Mamma– I fear that he will require more firmness and authority
than I wish to exercise over them to Govern him–but he is a fine
Lively Animated disposition– and Hollis–bids fair from the Colour
of his Hair and Complexion to be a firebrand but at present he is
the mildest temper I ever observed in a Baby–[1] the Government of
their dispositions and a proper attention to their early education–is
a task which I feel myself incompetant to the proper performance
of– the schools in this place so far as I have had an opportunity of
judgeing are not equal to those we have in Boston–early prejudices
are not easily conquered my Dear Madam–but with respect to education its advantages and General influence upon society in my
mind we yankees far surpass thease southern People but this would
be treason if permitted to go beyond your own family

I expect that you will have the sattisfaction of my Mammas society the ensueing year it is Supposed that Congress will rise in
March and will not meet again untill the Autumn She writes me
that She shall be in New York–on her Way in April–[2] it is an ill
Wind that Blows nobody any good– I will not repine at the Loss I
shall sustain so Long as those I respect and esteem are to reap the
advantage I suppose that I shall have the pleasure of my Brother
Charles Society which is some consolation to me– it would afford
me great pleasure to make a visit to Braintree and its Environs–the

next Summer—but I scarce dare flatter myself with the idea— should my friend return early in the Spring and all matters concur—I shall indeavour to [fulfill?] this desire—

the Loss of Mrs Quincys and her Daughters society must be an unpleasant circumstance to your family Braintree has been by degrees robbed of some of its brightest ornaments— Parson Wibird I presume remains to *grace* the scene remember me to my Unkle and Cousins particularly if you please and beleive me at all times your affectionate / Neice   A Smith—

Dear Madam

I have inclosed a little parcell to my Grandmamma under cover to you & will be obliged if you will present it to her as a small token of my remembrance—and let me know how she enjoys her health this Winter—   A Smith

RC (MWA:Abigail Adams Letters); addressed: "Mrs Mary Cranch. / Braintree—"; endorsed by Richard Cranch: "Letter from M^rs / A: Smith Feb: 8th / 1791." Some loss of text where the seal was removed.

¹ This is the last reference in the Adams correspondence to Thomas Hollis Smith, who would die at age eleven months on 8 July (PPPrHi:RG 413, First Presbyterian Church [New York, N.Y.] Records).
² AA to AA2, 25 Jan., above.

Elizabeth Smith Shaw to Abigail Adams

My Dear Sister—   Haverhill February 14th· 1791

By my Sister I have been informed of your Sickness, & of the distressed State of your Family, which gave me great, pain, & anxiety— more espicially for my Cousin Thomas, who when your Letter was written was still in great distress—¹ I am sure I know how to pity a sick Family—For in the course of the last year, there were four months, when we were severely exercised with Sickness, & the voice of Health was not heard for a long time in our House—

I am very glad Cousin Louisa was with you— It is very comfortable, & an happy Circumstance, to have an amiable Neice to assist one, in such difficult times— Such a kind, tender good Nurse as I have found in my Betsy Smith, (I hope) & do not doubt, but you have experienced in your Louisa— She was always very attentive to you, & we all loved her the better for it— I hope by this time you are all happily recovered, & in the full enjoyment of the inestimable

Blessing of Health— Betsy Quincy is very sorry to hear Polly Taylor has suffered— They were great favorites of each others— She hopes she has got quite well by this time—

We have had the coldest Winter which has been known for these many Years— The coldest December that was ever felt here—[2] You, I presume have experienced nothing of our severe season— A greater state of temperature cheers your Dwelling, & the rough winds pass softly, over your dear Face—a Face—that I hope to be favoured with a sight of in the ensuing Season—& I pray nothing may prevent—

I wrote to you not long since by Major McFarland, who was going to Phyladelphia to assist his Family, by endeavouring to procure to himself some pecuniary Office— But having reached Newyork was abrubtly told of the unhappy fate of a favourite Son, who was unfortunately disappointed in transacting some commercial buisiness for the Army at the Ohio—could not bear the dishonour, & as a fool dieth, so died he—by commiting a suicide— The News so affected his poor Father, that he was obliged to return immediately home, & has hardly been seen since—[3]

The Baron Stuben was so kind as to take charge of his business, & of my Letter to you, & one to Louisa from her Sister Betsy, both of which I hope you have received—[4]

I now write expecting to send this by a couple of worthy young Gentlemen, Dr Woodbury, & Mr Henry West— They are two very active, enterprizing Men of this Town— They have carried on business for sometime in Phyladephia, & are now going for the purpose of extablishing a more regular line of Trade—[5] If it is convenient I wish my Sister would notice them— They will take pleasure in bringing Letters, & I hope you will be able to write to me by them— It is a great while since I have had a Line from you—

I believe there was never a Country more blessed than ours— The People are now enjoying there hard earnings— [There] is no murmering—no complaining in our streets—no—n[ews] of Taxs—the *six Dollors* a Day is almost forgot—[6] Health through—the Land—Peace—& Plenty crown the Year—

I suppose you have heard that Major Rice was married to Miss Sophia Blake, & that the good Dr Howard had again entered the Hymeneal Band, with Miss Jerusha Gay— Ten thousand Blessings on his head— The sagacious Hinghamites will say, that he has now, only fullfilled what he ought to have done thirty years ago—only one revolution of Saturn since—[7] I find it dificult not to contrast the celebrated beauty—the *northern* Star which once shed her benign Influences on his delighted head, with the Person, whom he is now connected— It is true that she is a most amiable woman, & has an excellent Character— But it is a degree of perfection (at which I presume *he* has arrived) to love virtue, for its own sake—[8]

Mr & Mrs Thaxter, & Cousin Betsy Smith are gone upon a visit to their Friends at Hingham, Braintree &ca I think he is really better, & has not had a Fit for several months— Cousin Betsy Thaxter spent two months in the Fall, with him— All we could do, & say, we could not prevail with her, to tarry the winter— But there was such a spirit of marrying had taken place among the Vestals at Hingham, that perhaps she wished to return before Cupids Flame was extinguished, while the Torch of Hymen was burning with unusual lustre, that she might be benifited by its sweet Influences—

Mr Shaw desires his best regards may be accepted by you, & Brother Adams, & believe me to be Yours most Affectionately

Elizabeth Shaw—

RC (Adams Papers); addressed: "M^rs· Abigail Adams / Phyladelphia"; docketed: "E Shaw to Abigail / Adams 1791." Filmed at 14 Feb. 1790. Some loss of text where the seal was removed.

[1] AA to Mary Smith Cranch, 12 Dec. 1790, above.

[2] December and January had been extremely cold. "No winter since the peace has been more rigourous, or met the city less provided against the inclemency of the weather, than the present," the *Boston Gazette* reported on 17 Jan. 1791.

[3] Nathan McFarland (b. 1768), son of Maj. Moses and Eunice Clark McFarland, was responsible for delivering food supplies to the army near Pittsburgh. On 27 Nov. 1790, failing to meet his business obligations, he shot himself (C. M. Little, *History of the Clan Macfarlane*, Tottenville, N.Y., 1893, p. 117, 133).

[4] Shaw's letter is at 6 Dec., above.

[5] Dr. Edward Woodbury (1761–1793) and Henry West (1759–1846) of Haverhill (*Vital Records of Haverhill Massachusetts to the End of the Year 1849*, 2 vols., Topsfield, Mass.,

1910–1911, 2:488, 497).

[6] In the Salaries—Legislative Act of 22 Sept. 1789 Congress had famously voted to pay its members six dollars a day for attendance and an additional six dollars for every twenty miles traveled to get to the seat of government. Critics found the amount excessive and the six dollars figure was frequently cited thereafter in discussions of the faults of government (*First Fed. Cong.*, 6:1833; Boston *Herald of Freedom*, 14 May 1790; Boston *Columbian Centinel*, 1 Sept.).

[7] It takes Saturn 29 1/2 years to complete one revolution around the sun.

[8] Rev. Simeon Howard wed his first wife, the beautiful Elizabeth Clarke Mayhew, on 3 Dec. 1771. She died on 13 April 1777, shortly after the birth of their third child (*Sibley's Harvard Graduates*, 14:282, 284). See also Mary Smith Cranch to AA, 12 Dec. 1790, and note 2, above.

Abigail Adams to Abigail Adams Smith

My Dear Child,   Philadelphia, 21 February, 1791.

I received yours of February 13th, and was happy to learn that you and your little ones were well.[1] I wrote to you by the Chief Justice, and sent your silk by him.[2] He promised me to visit you, and from him you will learn how we all are. We have had, ever since this month began, a succession of bad weather, and, for this week past, the coldest weather that I have experienced this winter. The ground is now covered with snow. This, if it would last, would let me out of my cage, and enable me to go to the assembly on the birth-day of the President, which will be on Tuesday next.[3] On Thursday last I dined with the President, in company with the ministers and ladies of the court. He was more than usually social. I asked him after Humphreys, from whom I knew he had received despatches a few days before. He said that he was well, and at Lisbon. When I returned home, I told your father that I conjectured Mr. Humphreys would be nominated for Lisbon, and the next day the Senate received a message, with his nomination, as resident minister at the Court of Portugal; the President having received official information that a minister was appointed here, Mr. Friere, as I before informed you.[4] He asked very affectionately after you and the children, and at table picked the sugar-plums from a cake, and requested me to take them for master John. Some suppose, that, if your husband was here, he would have the command of the troops which are to be raised and sent against the Indians.[5] If such an idea as that is in his mind, I am happy that your friend is three thousand miles distant. I have no fancy that a man, who has already hazarded his life in defence of his country, should risk a tomahawk and scalping-knife, where, though a conqueror, no glory is to be obtained, though much may be lost. I most sincerely hope he may be successful in his private enterprise; for the way to command Fortune is to be as independent of her as possible.

The equanimity of your disposition will lead you to a patient submission to the allotments of Providence. The education of your children will occupy much of your time, and you will always keep in mind the great importance of first principles, and the necessity of instilling the precepts of morality very early into their minds. Youth is so imitative, that it catches at every thing. I have a great opinion of Dr. Watts's "Moral Songs for Children."[6] They are adapted to

193

their capacities, and they comprehend all the social and relative duties of life. They impress the young mind with the ideas of the Supreme Being, as their creator, benefactor, and preserver. They teach brotherly love, sisterly affection, and filial respect and reverence. I do not know any book so well calculated for the early period of life; and they may be made as pleasant to them, by the method of instructing, as a hundred little stories, which are taught them, containing neither a rule of life, nor sentiment worth retaining, such as little John will now run over, of "Jack and Jill," and "Little Jack Horner." As a trial of their memory, and a practice for their tongues, these may be useful, but no other way.

I am sometimes led to think that human nature is a very perverse thing, and much more given to evil than good. I never had any of my own children so much under my eye, and so little mixed with other children or with servants, as this little boy of yours. Whatever appears is self-taught, and, though a very good boy and very orderly, he frequently surprises me with a new air, a new word, or some action, that I should ascribe to others, if he mixed with them at all. He is never permitted to go into the kitchen. Every day, after dinner, he sets his grandpapa to draw him about in a chair, which is generally done for half an hour, to the derangement of my carpet and the amusement of his grandpapa.

Remember me affectionately to all inquiring friends. I hope to see you ere long.

Your ever affectionate mother, A. Adams.

MS not found. Printed from AA, *Letters*, ed. CFA, 1848, p. 355–357.

[1] Not found.

[2] Probably 25 Jan., above.

[3] The *Gazette of the United States*, 23 Feb., reported that the city of Philadelphia celebrated George Washington's birthday on 22 Feb. with a military parade and federal salute. According to the account, "The congratulatory Compliments of the Members of the Legislature of the Union— the Heads of the Departments of State—Foreign Ministers—Officers, civil and military of the State— the Reverend Clergy—and of Strangers and Citizens of distinction, were presented to the President on this auspicious occasion."

[4] Washington nominated David Humphreys as minister resident to Portugal on 18 Feb., and the Senate confirmed his appointment three days later (Washington, *Papers, Presidential Series*, 7:384–386).

[5] On 22 Jan. Secretary of War Henry Knox had announced to Congress that a force of 3,000 soldiers was needed to put down escalating attacks by Indians against settlers along the Ohio River. In March Maj. Gen. Arthur St. Clair was chosen by Washington to lead the expedition (Wiley Sword, *President Washington's Indian War: The Struggle for the Old Northwest, 1790–1795*, Norman, Okla., 1985, p. 131–133, 145).

[6] Isaac Watts' *Divine and Moral Songs for Children* had been published in numerous editions since 1715, most recently in the United States in 1788.

Cotton Tufts to Abigail Adams

Dear Mad^m.   Boston Feby. 23. 1791–

Yours of the 6th. Inst. came safe to hand and just timely enough to counter order the Shipping of your Hams & Beef–

Some time past you requested me to purchase you a Ticket, I defered it till the Time of drawing was not far distant, & giving the Preference to our semiannual Lottery have purchased for you N°. 15533–

Will there be an advantage in becoming a Sharer in the national Bank, if so How is a Share to be obtaind– I suppose the Bill for establishing the Bank is passed– Whether the Bill reported by the Secretary has passed without any Alteration I do not know, but must confess I was not pleased with it as reported– I suspect that in operation it would have become a refind System of paper money & would more or less have had the same Effects as that work of Evils a paper medium has had,–[1]

It is expected that the Excise Bill will pass: will this not require Officers different from the Import Acts to execute it. if so I could wish that my Bro Samuel might have an honourable Appointment–[2] He has been a State Collector of Excise, which office he discharged with Reputation to himself & Benefit to the Commonwealth and has been a great Sufferer in Consequence of his Advances to the public during the War, Can you give Hints so as to obtain the Interest of such is by their Influence or otherways can obtain it– M^r. Goodhue is well acquainted with his Character–

I have taken measures to secure the Hams & shall attend to some other matters mentioned in Yours as soon as I can with Convenience and am with sincere Regards / Yours affectionately

                                                        Cotton Tufts

RC (Adams Papers); internal address: "M^rs. Abigail Adams."

[1] A 14 Dec. 1790 report of Secretary of the Treasury Alexander Hamilton recommending the establishment of a national bank was referred to a Senate committee and resulted in the 3 Jan. 1791 Bank Act. That act was amended several times in the Senate, most significantly on 14 Jan. when its charter was given an expiration date of 1811. A supplementary bill originating in the House that delayed the sale of stock in the new bank until July was signed into law on 2 March (*First Fed. Cong.*, 4:171–173, 204, 211).

[2] Samuel Tufts was not among the three men appointed in March as supervisors and inspectors of revenue for the District of Massachusetts under the new Duty on Distilled Spirits Act. See AA to Cotton Tufts, 11 March, note 5, below. AA had earlier unsuccessfully lobbied JA to help Samuel Tufts secure a federal appointment; see vol. 8:370.

Samuel Magaw, James Hutchinson, Jonathan Williams, and John Vaughan to Abigail Adams

Madam   Philad. 26 Feby 1791—

Having been honored with the Vice Presidents consent to attend the Eulogium in Memory of Dr Benjamin Franklin. We in the name of the Philosophical Society, presume to hope you will do them the honor of your presence on the Same important occasion[1]

We have the honor to be / with the greatest respect / Madam / Your obedient Servants   Sam. Magaw
                                                                James Hutchinson
                                                                Jon^a Williams
                                                                Jn Vaughan
                                                                Committee[2]

RC (Adams Papers); internal address: "Mrs Adams.—"

[1] Benjamin Franklin died in Philadelphia on 17 April 1790. Nearly a year later, on 1 March 1791, JA and AA were in attendance when American Philosophical Society vice president William Smith delivered a eulogy before members of the society at Philadelphia's German Lutheran Church: "From west to east, by land and on the wide ocean, to the utmost extents of the civilized globe, the tale hath been told—That the venerable *Sage of Pennsylvania*, the *Patriot* and *Patriarch* of America, is no more" (*DAB*; William Smith, *Eulogium on Benjamin Franklin,*

L.L.D., Phila., 1792, title page, p. 1; Philadelphia *Freeman's Journal*, 9 March).

[2] This word is written alongside the list of names preceded by a large brace. Samuel Magaw (1739–1812) was rector of St. Paul's Church, Philadelphia, and vice provost of the University of Pennsylvania. James Hutchinson (1752–1793) was a physician and University of Pennsylvania professor of medicine (*Colonial Collegians*). For Jonathan Williams, see vol. 3:72; for John Vaughan, see JA, *D&A*, 3:226.

Abigail Adams to Cotton Tufts

Dear sir   Philadelphia March 11. 1791

I received your kind Letter of the 23 Feb^ry and was happy to learn that our Friends were all well. my son Set of on his return to Boston last week, in company with mr Gerry & Ames. he was desirious of going then that he might have the pleasure of good company. this tho a very agreeable circumstance on a long journey, will I believe scarcly compensate for the badness of the Roads at this season; provided they should be eaqually so, to the Eastward as they are here.[1] March is not a favourable Month for Congress to break up. this Session sir has been marked with great dispatch of Buisness, much good humour & tho varying in sentiment upon some very important

Cotton Tufts Trustee to Mr Abigail Adams.

No. 236

COMMISSIONER'S OFFICE. 21 *August* 1792

RECEIVED OF NATHANIEL APPLETON,

COMMISSIONER OF LOANS in the STATE OF MASSACHUSETTS,

the following Certificates viz.

1 Certificate   bearing Interest at *six* per Cent. per Annum from the first day of January 1792, payable quarter yearly, and redeemable by Payments not exceeding in one year the Proportion of Eight Dollars upon a hundred on account of Principal and Interest. } 1251 . 54

1 Certificate   bearing the like Interest from the first day of January 1801, and subject to be redeemed in like manner. } 625 . 77

1 Certificate   bearing Interest at *three* per Cent. per Annum, from the first day of January 1792, payable quarter yearly, and redeemable at the pleasure of the United States. } 938 . 65

One Special Certificate for the Balance not assumable. - - - - - - - - - - - - - - - 348 . 4

Dollars   3164 .

Amounting in the whole to *Three Thousand One hundred sixty four dollars* being in full of the Certificates of Debt due by the State of Massachusetts as contained in a Statement of this Date, Numbered 936 for which I have signed Duplicate Receipts.

Cotton Tufts Trustee
to Mrs Abigail Adams

5. COTTON TUFTS TO ABIGAIL ADAMS, APPLETON'S LOAN CERTIFICATE,
21 AUGUST 1792
See page xiii

subjects those subjects have been ably discussd, and much light thrown upon them, and finally carried by large majorities. the Bank is one, which Bill as past I inclose to you and the supplement it is thought here by those who are esteemed the best judges that it will not have any of those concequences which some of its opponents have imagined. as it will be the interest of those individuals who are incorporated and subscribers, to watch carefully over its interest, and to gaurd it with Argus Eyes you will see by the Bill that you may purchase a share with four hundred dollers one fourth of which must be specie the Accession of the state of vermont during this Session to the union, and the uninimnity with which they were received is a most happy and important event in our Annals and will add weight to the Northen Scale. Kentucky is also agreed to be received but her Government is not yet organizd.[2] thus sir one pillar rises after an other, and add strength I hope to the union. the people here in this state feel the Benificial effects of their own state Governments having three Branches in lieu of one assembly, and tho the old squabling spirit is not intirely extinct, it appears to be near its dissolution.[3] they have placed their Governour upon a respectable sallery of 5 thousand dollors pr Annum, the Governour of the state upon the same footing with the V.P of the united states, whom they have obliged to remove twice at his own expence in the course of two years—and to a city where the expence of living is a third dearer than at N york. I hope to spend 5 Months of the present year at Braintree and to be there by the first of May. the Roads will not permit us to try them sooner. as my Family will consist of 8 persons I must request some little provision to be made previous to our comeing, such as wood, (Hay I presume we have in our Barn) 50 Bushels of oats. these articles I think mr Adams ought to write to his Brother to look to, and if he was not his Brother I would do it, but now I have said I will not, therefore I think it not unlikly that we may be Destitute of some of them. I have engaged to write to you for those things which may be imediatly necessary upon our arrival viz a Box of candles part mould & part dipt a Barrel of soap a Barrel of super fine flower a Loaf of sugar 14 Brown 1 pd suchong Tea half dozen pd coffe ditto chocolat. Grain Rye & Indian are easily procured suppose I need not be anxious about that. Beaf and Hams you have already secured cider is an other article of which we shall want half a dozen Barrels in Articles of furniture I want mr Pratt or any one Else to make me 2 kichin tables one a common seize one of 6 foot long 4 wide a Bread peal a roling pin, kitchin

Tongues & slice I have none a spit, I must request Miers to have them ready for me. some other articles may have escaped my memory but I have no design to get a superfluous article. a couple of wash Tubs I shall find necessary to have made. the Garden I should like to have manured and dug mrs Cranch wrote me respecting a Negro Man who lived with Pheby.[4] if you think proper you will be so good as to employ him about it. I am sorry sir to be so troublesome to you, but your many kind offices, and long habit of doing good, has always made me consider you in the different characters, of Friend, Gaurdian & Parent, and as such the whole Family look to you for advice & assistance. if you have not any cash in your Hands belonging to us, I suppose I may get credited for a month or two.

Before your Letter arrived here sir the Supervisors were all appointed for the different states. I own I was surprized to see the Name of G——m instead of Jackson who I supposed would have had it.[5] mr A after your Letter came went and talkd with the secretary of the Treasury knowing that there would be inspectors of districts, but he was told that the intention was to multiply officers as little as possible and to divide the state of Massachusetts only into two, and mr Jackson was determind upon for that part of the country the President has Appointed col smith supervisor for the state of Nyork; it will be an arduous office but one for which I believe he is very well calculated, and if he can perform the whole duty of supervisor & inspector that state will not be divided, and the compensation will be something handsome this will be much more agreeable to me & to his Family than sending him abroad.[6] we have not yet heard from him, but the packet in which he saild the Prince William Henry is upon Loyds list of arrivals the 2 of Jan[ry] which gives him a passage of 28 days my best respects to your good Lady whom I hope e'er long to embrace and the rest of my Friends. be assured dear sir that I am with sincere Regard your affectionate Neice   A. Adams

RC (NHi:Misc. Mss. Adams, Abigail); endorsed: "M[rs.] Ab. Adams March 11. 1791."

[1] JQA left Philadelphia on 3 March with Massachusetts congressmen Elbridge Gerry, Fisher Ames, George Thacher, and Jonathan Grout as well as Rhode Island congressman Benjamin Bourne, arriving in New York on 5 March. As AA predicted, he reported on "Bad roads" and "Bad fare" along the way. JQA spent several days in New York City, where he visited AA2 and was delayed until 13 March because of poor wind conditions.

Sailing to Newport aboard the packet *Hancock*, along with several members of Congress, JQA finally arrived in Boston the evening of 16 March (D/JQA/16, APM Reel 19).

[2] The Kentucky Statehood Act of 4 Feb. stipulated that Virginia's District of Kentucky would become a state on 1 June 1792 upon the organization of a state government. The Vermont Act of 2 March 1791 granted Vermont the status of the fourteenth state two

days after passage (*First Fed. Cong.*, 5:1215; 6:2003–2004).

³ On 3 Sept. 1790 a new Pennsylvania constitution replaced the constitution of 1776. The new system included a tricameral government of executive, senate, and house of representatives (instead of the unicameral Penn. Assembly), and the weak office of president of Pennsylvania was enhanced to become that of governor, with powers of appointment, veto, pardon, and command of the militia (Philip S. Klein and Ari Hoogenboom, *A History of Pennsylvania*, N.Y., 1973, p. 82–83, 100).

⁴ See Mary Smith Cranch to AA, 25 Jan. 1791, above.

⁵ On 4 March George Washington appointed Nathaniel Gorham supervisor of revenue for the District of Massachusetts to oversee the collection of duties under the new Duty on Distilled Spirits Act. Jonathan Jackson was appointed to the lesser post of inspector of revenue for the district on 15 March (Washington, *Papers, Presidential Series*, 7:511–512, 568).

⁶ Also on 4 March, Washington appointed WSS supervisor of revenue for the District of New York. The appointment entitled him to an annual salary of $800 and 1/2 of 1 percent of revenues collected. No inspectors were appointed to assist him (same, 7:511–512, 569; *First Fed. Elections*, 4:79).

Abigail Adams to Mary Smith Cranch

my dear sister   Bush Hill March 12ᵗʰ 1791

I was just going to set down to write to you, when I received your Letter of   ¹ I am sensible I was much in Arrears to you, as well as to some other of my Friend's Since the Recovery of Thomas we have had Health in our dwelling, for which I have great reason to be thankfull. I have been happy with my three sons round me, but a sigh of anxiety always hung about my Heart, for mrs smith who ought to be with me during the absence of the Col. if I had remain in N york, we should not have lived seperate this winter, but my removal here, and the expence of the removal of a Family for 5 or six months, was an obstical in the way, as the col is expected back in May. if he arrives as I hope he will, he will come immediatly into an office, which will afford to him and his Family a very handsome Support. it will be a very Arduous office in the state of N york, but he is of a very active disposition, and very well calculated for the discharge of it. a prospect of a Provision for himself and Family has releived my mind from a very heavy burden. I hope nothing will arrise to detain him abroad longer than we expect, and this provision for him at Home, is much more agreeable to us all than any employment abroad, which would have carried from me my only daughter. Charles is returnd to his office in Nyork and Boards with mrs Smith. I suppose J Q A will reach Boston by the time this Letter gets to you. he seems happy in the expectation of our passing the summer at Braintree, but he appears to have lost much of his sprightlyness and vivacity. he says that the want of Buisness in his profession and the dismal prospect for the practitioners of the Law in Massachussets, is the weight which depresses him, & that He should still be obliged at his age, to be dependant upon his parents for a support. altho these feelings are proofs of a good mind, and a sensible Heart, I could wish that they did not oppress him so much. he wishes sometimes that he had been Bred a Farmer a merchant, or an, any thing by which he could earn his Bread but we all preach Patience to him. Thomas follows his studies in the city with as much assiduity as his Health will permit, but he does not look well, and I think I cannot consent to leave him in this Hot climate during the summer. a journey may establish his Health, and prevent a return of that soar disorder the next fall as his Blood retains yet much of the materials for making it. every damp day warns him of the future, & reminds him of the past

you wrote me in your Letter of Jan^ry 25th of a Negro Man and woman whom you thought would answer for me this summer. if she is cleanly and only a tolerable cook I wish you would engage her for me. I had rather have black than white help, as they will be more like to agree with those I bring. I have a very clever black Boy of 15 who has lived with me a year and is bound to me till he is 21, my coachman will not allow that he is a negro, but he will pass for one with us.[2] Prince I believe I shall leave with mr Brisler I shall bring Polly—and dismiss the rest of my servants. tis probable we may hire the Black man part of the time as a Gardner, but I design to make those I bring with me work if I can I will be obliged to you if you will go to the House, and look over the things and write me what you think I shall have absolutely need of towards keeping House. I have written to the dr to get mr Pratt to make me two kitchin tables and some other articles there were some old Bed Steads in the House but none perfect. will you ask mr Pratt if he can make me one that is movable like one which Polly says he made for mrs Apthorp with a sacking bottom and doubles up together. I do not know any Name for them to distinguish them by; I had one made in N York which I found exceedingly usefull when Thomas was sick. I have no coars ware neither milk-pan, or bowl or dish, Broom or Brush. I shall want Some tow cloth, ten or a dozen yds at my first arrival. I do not know if the dr has any Money in his Hands, to procure me these articls but if he has not, I will send you some for the purpose. as I cannot think of comeing there with a Family—and then haveing every thing to look out for afterwards, besides I shall not have Brisler to manage for me. I shall take some spoons & what little plate I may have occasion for with me. mrs Brisler left some chairs which I shall take of her. I think I have as much table & bed linnen as I shall want I wish the Roads were such that we could set out immediatly, but that cannot be. I hope however to be with you by the first of May—and I look forward to it with great pleasure I assure you. I shall send by the first vessel a Trunk with some cloaths &c—as we wish to travell with as little Bagage as possible. I dinned yesterday at the Presidents it was a take leave dinner. the President sets of this week on a Tour to those parts of his dominions which he has not yet visited Georgia & North Carolina.[3] our publick affairs never lookt more prosperious—the people feel the benificial effects of the New Government by an increasing credit both at Home and abroad and a confidence in their Rulers. some grumbling we must always expect, but we have as a people the greatest cause for Gratitude and thankfullness to the supreme Ruler of the Universe for our present happy and prosperious circumstances as a Nation.

adieu my dear sister every blessing attend you and yours is the Sincere wish of your ever affectionate / Sister   A Adams

my kind regards to mr Cranch to mr & mrs Norten to cousin William & Lucy and a kiss for my young Richard

RC (MWA:Abigail Adams Letters); endorsed by Richard Cranch: "Letter from M^{rs} / A. Adams, Bush hill, / Mar. 12. 1791."

[1] Probably a letter of 20 Feb., in which Mary Smith Cranch observed that she had not heard from AA since her letter of 9 Jan., above, and discussed her recent correspondence with AA2. Cranch expressed concern about her niece's loneliness, remarking, "She does not know it but this feeling of hers is intirely owing to that uncommon reserve which marks her character. . . . my dear Neice wishes to retain her reserve & yet injoy all the Benfits of a more communicative disposition; this She will find She never can do I shall write to her again Soon—I feel most tenderly for her" (Adams Papers).

[2] The fifteen-year-old was probably James, who would serve the Adamses as a servant for many years; see AA to JA, 4 Dec. 1792, below. The coachman was likely Robert, who would be discharged by AA in 1792; see AA to Mary Smith Cranch, 20 April 1792, below.

[3] On 21 March 1791 George Washington departed Philadelphia for a 3-month, 1,816-mile tour of Virginia, North Carolina, South Carolina, and Georgia, fulfilling a pledge to visit all parts of the United States during his presidency. A typical stop was one made at Georgetown, S.C., on 30 April, which featured a public dinner, tea party, and ball after a grand entrance: "He was rowed over the river by seven Captains of vessels, dressed in round hats trimmed with gold lace, blue coats, white jackets, &c. in an elegant painted boat. On his arriving opposite the market he was saluted by the artillery, with fifteen guns" (Washington, *Diaries*, 6:96–98; Portsmouth *New Hampshire Spy*, 1 June).

John Adams to William Stephens Smith

My Dear Sir: Philadelphia, March 14, 1791.

I shall not entertain you with public affairs, because you will learn the state of them from the public papers more in detail. I shall only say, that the National Government has succeeded beyond the expectations, even of the sanguine, and is more popular, and has given more general satisfaction than I expected ever to live to see. The addition of Vermont and Kentucky, the augmentation of our revenues, and the rapid rise of stocks and credit, have all raised the spirits of the people, and made them as happy as their nature and state will bear.

I took my pen, however, merely to mention your appointment to the office of Supervisor for the State of New-York, which will necessarily require your personal presence before the first of July. This place, I presume, is well worth your acceptance, as it will be a decent and comfortable provision for yourself and family, while it will be an honourable and useful employment. I am therefore anxious that you should have the earliest notice of it, and return without loss of time.

Your family and friends are all well in New-York, and your son with us is as healthy and happy, and as fine a child as you could wish him to be. We are agreeably situated here; and the Session of Congress has been the most assiduous, the most harmonious, and the most efficacious I ever knew.

Present my particular regards to Mr. B. Hollis and Dr. Price, and all others who think it worth their while to ask a question concerning him who is / Yours, affectionately,   John Adams.

MS not found. Printed from AA2, *Jour. and Corr.*, 2:111–112.

Abigail Adams to William Stephens Smith

Dear Sir: Bush Hill, March 16th, 1791.

Although we have reason to expect, and hope for your speedy return, yet I would not let so good an opportunity as this, by the Portland packet, pass without writing you a few lines, partly to inform you, that your son is in perfect health, and has been so through the winter; that he is full of mirth and glee, and as fine a boy as you can wish him: and partly to congratulate you upon your appointment to the office of Supervisor for the State of New-York, under the new Revenue Bill, which I am so anxious to forward to you, that I have determined to put you to the expense of it by the packet. I have sent the bill to Mrs. Smith, that she may forward one to you by some private vessel. You will see by the bill the necessity there is of your returning with all possible despatch. The Secretary of the Treasury told Mr. Adams that he would write to you, and it is probable that he will by this opportunity. He informed Mr. Adams, that it was the President's intention to unite the office of Supervisor and Inspector for the State of New-York, and not to divide the state, as he will be obliged to do, in some states where there are many ports of entry, consequently the salary will be something handsome, and well worth your acceptance, though the duties of the office will be proportionably arduous. I thought it would be of importance to you to get sight of the bill as soon as possible.

Congress closed their session on the fourth of March, and met again the fourth Monday in October. No session has been marked with so many important events, or has been conducted with so much harmony; great despatch of important business, a most surprising rise of public credit, an increasing confidence in the national government, are some of the fruits. The accession of Vermont and Kentucky are two additional pillars to the noble building; every circumstance has conspired to add dignity and glory to our rising empire; an expiring murmur from the old dominion has been lost amidst the general peace and harmony which pervades all the states: though its noxious breath reached North Carolina and contaminated a few members, the northern climate soon dispersed the southern vapour. Rhode Island is become one of the most federal states in the union, and the antis now declare, they would willingly make any submission for their past conduct. Poor France! what a state of confusion and anarchy is it rushing into? I have read Mr. Bush's letter, and though I think he paints high, yet strip it of all its ornament and colouring, it will remain an awful picture of liberty abused, authority despised, property plundered, government annihilated, religion banished, murder, rapine and desolation scourging the land. I am sorry that my worthy and venerable divine should expose himself, at this late period of his life, to so severe a censure.[1] I love and venerate his character, but think his zeal a mistaken one, and that he is a much more shining character as a divine, than politician. To Mr. Hollis, and the rest of our friends, give my regards; I have a love for that same country, and an affection for many of its valuable inhabitants.

The President of the United States, is just setting out upon a tour to his southern dominions; he means to visit Georgia and Carolina; he will be absent three months.[2] Mr. Lewis is gone home to Virginia to be married;[3] Mr. Jackson is the only aid now remaining. We propose setting out for the eastward by the last of April, and passing the summer at Braintree. I heard this day from Mrs. Smith; she was well, and your boys—she had just received your letter, dated Falmouth, informing her of your safe arrival.[4]

I am, dear sir, with sincere regard and affection, / Yours, &c.

A. Adams.

RC not found. Printed from AA2, *Jour. and Corr.*, 2:108–111. Dft (Adams Papers), dated and filmed at 15 March.

[1] A transcription error in the printed version, the Dft identifies this as "mr Burkes Letter." Edmund Burke's *Reflections on the Revolution in France*, presented as a letter to a young Frenchman named Charles Depont, appeared in Nov. 1790. A condemnation of the recent political and social upheaval in France, Burke particularly attacked the theory of natural rights used to justify the political revolution there. He also blamed AA's "venerable divine," Richard Price, linking Price's support of the Revolution to anti-monarchical violence. Thomas Paine's *Rights of Man* was a direct response to Burke's essay (*DNB*).

[2] The Dft adds the information that "mr Lear has a son."

[3] Robert Lewis, who left Philadelphia in January, married Judith Carter Browne of Virginia (Washington, *Papers, Presidential Series*, 7:217).

[4] These letters have not been found. The Dft concludes the letter with the following paragraph: "Your little Boy runs into the Room and says by the direction of Polly—please Mamma to give my duty to dear Pappa and pray him to bring Johnny Some pretty things. my Eldst son is just returnd to Boston having made us a visit of near two Months Charles is returnd to Nyork & Thomas is with us but not in good Health, the severe sickness he had through the winter he has not yet recoverd—"

Thomas Boylston Adams to Elizabeth Smith Shaw

My dear Aunt,   Philadelphia March 17th —91.

A few days since I received your kind letter of Febry: 18th: and its being handed by a Townsman of yours was a circumstance that afforded me additional pleasure.[1] Indeed I always receive more satisfaction when I meet with any of your Neighbors, than from the inhabitants of any other place; and can account for it upon this principle chiefly, that I lived in that town at a period when objects usually make the strongest impressions on the mind, and when local attachments and prejudices, if ever, are imbibed. I hear with pleasure from Dr Woodbury that business which for some years past has been rather at a low ebb, among you, has again revived, and that its usual concomitants harmony and good humor are so remarkably prevalent. That place is by nature calculated for happiness, and nothing is requsite but the disposition of its inhabitants to render it completely delightful, and agreeable. I am often taxed by my Father with want of attachment to my native town; but I tell him, if I have any prejudices or preference, to any particular spot, that Haverhill is the center. As I have entred upon the studdy of the Law in this place it is probable I shall make it my future residence, and it is in a measure incumbent on me to adopt the interests, and conform to the manners and customs of this State; but I think neither distance of time or place will ever obliterate from my memory the favorable opinion I now entertain of Haverhill and its inhabitants.

I am glad to hear that a certain young Lady has an husband, but you cannot censure me if I say, she *might* have had a better. It was allways my opinion of the Gentleman with whom she is connected, that he thought for himself at too early a period in life; and that it was Cap^tn: W——s before he could connect the syllables which compose those two words. However he is a *good natured honest simple sort of a man*, and to sum up all his perfections at once, I believe he is calculated to make a good husband; that is, he is easily managed, a very requisite qualification with the Ladies.[2]

Your kind and friendly condolance for my illness demands my warmest thanks; it was indeed *severe*, and you who have experienced its sad effects can determine how much pain that word expresses. I have in a measure recovered my health, but the remains still lurk in my joints. Virgil when describing the mixture of grief and Sorrow which Dido expresses at the departure of Aeneas, has this expressive line, "Vulnus alit venis, cæco que carpitur igni;"[3] I will not pretend to speak with certainty, but I should immagine that the pangs and tortures of Love, are much inferior to those of the Rheumatism. I have already extended my letter beyond the usual bounds of epistolary correspondence; but when I am once engaged in writing to you, I scarcely think of closing untill I am admonished by the deficiency of my paper. You are good enough to indulge me in writing to you,— my heart follows my hand in every line, and bids it record sincerity. You will therefore believe me when I subscribe myself / Your ever affectionate nephew   Thomas B Adams.

RC (Adams Papers); addressed: "M^rs: Elizabeth Shaw. / Haverhill / Massachusetts."; notation: "Boston. 1 April. 1791. Rec^d & Ford. by Y^rs. Affec^ly. / W Smith" and, by JA, "Free / John Adams."

[1] Not found.

[2] Mary McKinstry (1770–1847) married Benjamin Willis Jr. (1768–1853) in Haverhill on 9 January. Benjamin was the son of Capt. Benjamin Willis Sr. and since the age of seventeen had called himself "the young Captain." JQA explained in his Diary in 1786 that the younger Willis "goes by that title because, he has assumed the man somewhat young" (William Willis, "Genealogy of the McKinstry Family," *NEHGR*, 12:325, 13:40 [Oct. 1858, Jan. 1859]; JQA, *Diary*, 1:368–369, 394).

[3] She feeds the wound within her veins; she is eaten by a secret flame (Virgil, *Aeneid*, Book IV, line 2).

Abigail Adams to Elizabeth Smith Shaw

Bush Hill, (near Philadelphia,)
20 March, 1791.

My Dear Sister,

I received, by Dr. W——, your kind letter of February 14th. He was very punctual to his commission. He has been three times to visit us. He came out this afternoon to let me know that he should leave Philadelphia on Tuesday. By him I have to thank my dear sister for three letters, and to confess myself much in arrears. 'Tis in vain to say that I have had a sick family; that I have had a large family; that I have been engaged in company. These are poor excuses for not writing; nor will I exculpate myself by alleging that I wanted a subject. My pride would not suffer such a plea. What, then, has been the cause? "Confess freely, and say that it was mere indolence,—real laziness," as in truth I fear it has been. Yet conscience, that faithful monitor, has reprehended me very, very often. I was very sick; (so sick, that I have not yet recovered the shock I received from it,) for near two months before I left New York. When I got to this place, I found this house just calculated to make the whole family sick; cold, damp, and wet with new paint. A fine place for an invalid; but, through a kind Providence, I sustained it, though others suffered. Happily, after a very tedious two months, Thomas recovered so as to get abroad; but his health is now very infirm, and I fear an attendance upon two offices through the day, and studying through the evening at home, is not calculated to mend it. But it is a maxim here, that he who dies with studying dies in a good cause, and may go to another world much better calculated to improve his talents, than if he had died a blockhead. Well, knowledge is a fine thing, and mother Eve thought so; but she smarted so severely for hers, that most of her daughters have been afraid of it since.

We have had a very severe winter in this State, as you may judge when I tell you that we have consumed forty cords of wood in four months. It has been as cold as any winter we have at the northward. The 17th and 18th of this month I dined with all my windows open, put out the fires, and ate ice to cool me; the glasses at 80. This is the 20th. Yesterday it snowed nearly the whole day, and to-day it is a keen northwester; and I presume it will freeze hard to-night. Yet the verdure is beautiful; full as much as I shall find by the middle of May in Massachusetts, where I hope then to be. Yet I shall have some regrets at leaving this place, just as the season begins to open all its beauties upon me. I am told that this spot is very delightful as a summer residence. The house is spacious. The views from it are rather beautiful than sublime; the country round has too much of the level to be in my style. The appearance of uniformity wearies the eye, and confines the imagination. We have a fine view of the whole city from our windows; a beautiful grove behind the house, through which there is a spacious gravel walk, guarded by a number of marble statues, whose genealogy I have not yet studied, as the last week is the first time I have visited them. A variety of fine fields of wheat and grass are in front of the house, and, on the right hand, a pretty view of the Schuylkill presents itself. But now for the reverse of the picture. We are only two miles from town, yet have I been more of a prisoner this winter than I ever was in my life. The road from hence to the pavement is one mile and a half, the soil a brick clay, so that, when there has been heavy rain, or a thaw, you must wallow to the city through a bed of mortar without a bottom, the horses sinking to their knees. If it becomes cold, then the holes and the roughness are intolerable. From the inhabitants of this place I have received every mark of politeness and civility. The ladies here are well-educated, well-bred, and well-dressed. There is much more society than in New York, and I am much better pleased and satisfied than I expected to be when I was destined to remove here. Adieu.

Your sister,

A. A.

MS not found. Printed from AA, *Letters*, ed. CFA, 1848, p. 357–359.

John Quincy Adams to Thomas Boylston Adams

Boston April 2d: 1791.

I have just received your favour of the 22d: instt:[1] thanks you know are "the exchequer of the poor." upon that exchequer of mine you are entitled to bills to a large amount. I assure you I feel the obligation of your attention to my trunk, which has not yet arrived, but which will be very acceptable when it comes. But your Letter has excited my curiosity, and I find myself very much perplexed to determine who that same "acquaintance" of yours can be, who understands the doctrine of punctuality so well, and is yet so deficient in point of practice; upon the whole I imagine it must be some of your new acquaintance, perhaps one of the clerks in Mr: Ingersoll's office. I dare say you will have too much good sense to follow his evil example—yet such characters are not uncommon in the world. Video meliora, proboque,—Deteriora sequor is a complaint of no small antiquity;[2] and the students of Horace and Cicero, will have frequent opportunities to remark, that the most prevalent foibles are not confined to their own period of Life.

The Magazines will I believe never present you with any more Rebuses, Acrostics Elegies, or other poetical effusions of my production. I must bid a long and lasting farewell to the juvenile Muses. It is to the severer toils of the Historic Matron, that I must henceforth direct all the attention that I can allow to that lovely company. Happy if they do not exclude me altogether from their train, and command me to offer all my devotions to the, eyeless dame, who holds the balance and the sword.— If I should have leisure to pursue my inclination, which I expressed to you, of venturing upon some speculations in our Newspapers, I shall willingly make a confident of you. At present I find no time to indulge myself in that kind of amusement. "He that hath little business shall become wise." says M[r:] Burke's quotation.[3] It is at least, incumbent upon him who is in that predicament, to endeavour to obtain wisdom; and in that pursuit I find that I have but little time upon my hands

You do not mention a word in your Letter upon the subject of your coming to Braintree. I hope you will come by all means. The climate of Philadelphia must be ill calculated for your northern Constitution, during the Summer months. You have been totally unused to such a climate; and after your late severe illness, I think you may very safely conclude, that by a tour hitherward, you will probably save much time, and avoid many an hour of such pains, as your experienced feelings will much better conceive than I can subscribe. Upon the fairest possible presumption, that of your preserving your health at Philadelphia, I am per[sua]ded you would not advance more in your studies, than by four or five months of peaceable application at Braintree. I assure you, I feel some anxiety [up]on the subject.— At all events I hope you will determine for the best.

Your Classmate Welles, it is greatly apprehended is lost at Sea. He sailed in December for some Island in the West Indies. There are arrivals from the port to which he was bound, which sailed from thence 88 days after his departure from this place; and the vessel in which he went has never been heard of. The only remaining hope of his friends is that he may have been taken from the wreck by some vessel bound to Europe. The chance is small, and the dependence frail.[4]

I was at Braintree on Thursday. All well.

Adieu. J. Q. Adams.

RC (Adams Papers); addressed: "M^r: Thomas B. Adams. / Bush Hill."; endorsed: "JQ Adams April 2^d / 1791." Some loss of text where the seal was removed.

[1] Not found.

[2] I see the right way and approve it, but follow the wrong (Ovid, *Metamorphoses,* Book VII, lines 20–21).

[3] Sirach (Ecclesiasticus), 38:24, quoted in Edmund Burke, *Reflections on the Revolu-*

tion in France, London, 1791, p. 39.

[4] Samuel Welles (1771–1790), Harvard 1790, apparently was lost at sea (MH-Ar: Faculty Records, 5:235; *Harvard Quinquennial Cat.,* p. 203).

Abigail Adams to John Quincy Adams

my dear son Bush Hill April 18 1791

owing to an accident your Letter of April 1^t did not reach us till the 14th I have got the power compleated and inclose it to the dr.[1] I hope your trunk & the Porter which accompanied it came safe to Hand. I put in an article or two upon the top of the Trunk which if any opportunity offers you may send to Braintree. the Porter was directed to the care of mr Smith but I did not as I ought advise him of it. Thomas said he had written to you about it. this day fortnight we set out on our journey and expect to be with you by the middle of May. I spoke to your Father upon the Subject of an Annual allowence and he agrees that you shall draw upon dr Tufts for 25 pounds a Quarter, your first Quarter to commence on the first of july. with that I think you may make it do it is agreed that your Brother accompany us. our Coachee came home to day. we should set out next week but your Sister removes then, and desires we would stay a little longer to give her time to get fix'd.[2] we are all in tolerable Health our Trees in full Bloom, the Roads pretty good

adieu yours &c A Adams

RC (Adams Papers).

[1] On 1 April, JQA noted in his Diary that Massachusetts had made a first payment of interest on state bonds. That same day, he wrote to AA, evidently indicating that JA needed to complete a power of attorney so that someone could receive his interest for him. JA, in a power of attorney dated 18 April, authorized Cotton Tufts to do so

(D/JQA/16, APM Reel 19; MBBS:Colburn Coll.). JQA's letter of 1 April has not been found.

[2] AA2 and her family moved from 13 Nassau Street to Dye (now Dey) Street in New York City (*New-York Directory,* 1790, Evans, No. 22724; *New-York Directory,* 1791, Evans, No. 23337).

Abigail Adams to Mary Smith Cranch

Dear sister   Bush Hill April 18 1791

This day fortnight the 2 of May we propose to set out on our journey to Braintree. it will be the middle of May I presume before we arrive there if we meet with no accident, So that I will thank you to attend a little to my Garden have Some sallid sewn and what ever else you think proper I wrote to you not long since requesting you to let me know what you thought I might want. you will not forget some Night Hawks.[1] be so good as to get me a dozen yds of diaper for towels I have not one there, and whatever else you think I stand in immediate want of— I cannot bear to go to a place unprovided, when a little forethought and care would save me much trouble, and I shall not have Brisler with me to provide for me. I have requested the dr to furnish you with the needfull. vendues are so frequent in Boston that I may be provided with some things perhaps. I shall want a Tea kettle dish kittle Chaffing dish a set of Brushes Brooms pails flat Irons Tubs, skillits pots &c I scarcly know what myself— I have not heard from you since I wrote to you respecting the Negro woman. I should like to have the House opend cleand and aird and to have her there when I get there, but I will write to you again and will let you know on what day tis probable I shall arrive. Remember me affectionatly to all Friends. I anticipate much satisfaction & pleasure with you this summer. I am with Sincere regard & / affection yours Sincerely   A Adams

RC (MWA:Abigail Adams Letters); addressed by TBA: "M^rs: Mary Cranch / Braintree"; endorsed by Richard Cranch: "Letter from M^rs. / A: Adams, Brush Hill, / Ap^l. 18. 1791."

[1] Chamber pots (Frederic G. Cassidy and Joan Houston Hall, eds., *Dictionary of American Regional English*, 4 vols. to date, Cambridge, 1985–2002).

John Quincy Adams to Thomas Boylston Adams

Boston April 20th: 1791.

I received by the last Post your short favour, inclosing a much longer one to Quincy which I have *punctually* delivered:[1] I know not whether this will reach you before your departure from Philadelphia; if it does not it can do no harm: and if it does, as you have concluded upon coming this way with the family it may be of some service to me.— You recollect doubtless that while I was in Philadelphia, I took some pains to make a complete collection of books and papers relative to the national government. I left one or two little minutes with you to which I requested your attention. A gentleman of your punctuality has certainly not suffered the circumstance to escape your recollection: however a little stimulus to your remembrance perhaps will not be amiss, and if you find any spare room in your trunks when you come on, I must request you to bring with you a set of the laws & journals of both Houses of the last Session, which I presume are published before this.—² Perhaps you may remember that my set of the U.S. Gazette was not complete. Mr: Fenno directed me to apply to Mr: Sigourney in this town for the numbers which I wanted, and told me, that I could probably get supplied from him. I have done so accordingly but Mr: Sigourney had sent all the papers in his possession to Mr: Fenno a few days before.³ I must therefore trouble you to send to him and request him to furnish you with as many of the following numbers as he can of the first Volume. N: 33. 36, 38, 39, 40, 41, 46, 73, 80, 85, 86, 87, 88, 89, 90, 91, 92, 98, 101, 102, 103, 104. and you will either bring them with you, or leave them to be sent by the first convenient opportunity. I shall want also of the second Volume the Numbers 88, 89, 90 which were published while I was on my passage from Philadelphia hither. I was supplied with a complete set of the second Volume to the 87th: number before I came away, and since I got home I have regularly received the numbers as they came; that little chasm, you will easily be able to assist me in filling up, and I hope you have too great a stock of patience to be wearied by my importunities.

I have little more to say. There have been great rebellions among the sons of Harvard, excited by the new regulations subjecting them to examinations. I have not at present time to give you a full account of the whole transactions; the result of the whole is that Jones, a junior is *expelled*, Trapier rusticated, Sullivan, Sophimore, suspended for nine months, and Ely, I know not of what class, to undergo a punishment not yet made public.⁴ I was at exhibition yesterday; Ellery delivered a very pretty English Oration.⁵ company pretty much as usual.

Adieu, in haste.

J. Q. Adams.

RC (Adams Papers); addressed: "Mr: Thomas B. Adams / Philadelphia."; endorsed: "Mr JQ Adams / April 20th: 1791."

¹ Letters not found.
² *Acts Passed at the Third Session of the* *Congress of the United States of America, Begun and Held at the City of Philadelphia*

on Monday the Sixth of December, in the Year M,DCC,XC, Phila., [1791], Evans, No. 23845; *Journal of the Third Session of the Senate of the United States of America, Begun and Held at the City of Philadelphia, December 6th, 1790*, Phila., 1791, Evans, No. 23901; *Journal of the House of Representatives of the United States. Anno M,DCC,XC*, Phila., 1791, Evans, No. 23899.

³John Fenno (1751–1798), an entrepreneur from Boston, established the *Gazette of the United States* in New York in April 1789 and continued it in Philadelphia after the federal capital was moved there in the autumn of 1790. Fenno envisioned the *Gazette* as a national newspaper, a publication that, circulating throughout the country, would foster American unity by promoting and defending the new government under the Constitution. Elisha Sigourney (1753–1811), a merchant in Boston, managed subscriptions to the *Gazette* there (*DAB*; Jeffrey L. Pasley, *"The Tyranny of Printers": Newspaper Politics in the Early American Republic*, Charlottesville, Va., 2001, p. 51–54; Henry H. W. Sigourney, *Genealogy of the Sigourney Family*, Boston, 1857, p. 11; Boston *Columbian Centinel*, 23 Nov. 1791).

⁴The laws of Harvard College, revised in 1790, introduced an annual public examination of each class and required all students to attend. Upset by the change in the terms of their enrollment, the senior and junior classes petitioned for exemption from the new regulation, but the overseers denied their request. On 12 April 1791, the day on which the examinations were to begin, Benjamin Foissin Trapier (b. 1774), William Sullivan (1774–1839), and Justin Ely (1772–1850) tried to stop them by putting tartar emetic in the water used to make coffee, tea, and cocoa at breakfast in the commons. With almost every student, instructor, and college officer affected, the examinations had to be postponed, though only for a day or two. The three malefactors were soon caught and obliged to leave Harvard until they passed examinations for reinstatement. While Trapier apparently never returned, Sullivan and Ely did, both graduating in 1792. In a separate incident, Henry William Jones (b. 1773) hurled a stone through a window into the room where the freshman class was being examined, an offense for which he was expelled (B. H. Hall, *A Collection of College Words and Customs*, N.Y., 1859, p. 180–182; MH-Ar:Faculty Records, 5:324–325; 6:40–41, 50, 104–109, 125, 136, 152–154; *Harvard Quinquennial Cat.*, p. 204).

⁵Abraham Redwood Ellery (1773–1820), Harvard 1791, delivered the English oration at Harvard's public exhibition on 19 April (MH-Ar:Faculty Records, 5:308–309; 6:101–103; *Harvard Quinquennial Cat.*, p. 203; D/JQA/16, 19 April, APM Reel 19).

Abigail Adams to John Quincy Adams

my dear son   Fairfield wednesday May 12ᵗʰ 1791

we have reachd this place this day, but whether I shall be able to travel tomorrow is uncertain, for I am so unfortunate as to be attackd with the intermitting fever last night was so very ill that I had not the least expectation of being able to proceed on my journey, but to day I am better. I was taken last fryday in N york with it, and prevented sitting out as we intended on monday I am now in use of the Bark and hope to prevent a return of it tomorrow, but should it attack me again I shall be obliged to lye by my sick day, and so infeebles me that I cannot travell far the day which is termd well. I left your sister and Family well. I wrote to you from N york, but as I thought your Brother had given you information of some trunks on Board Hopkins I mentiond only those by Cheeseman.¹ I inclose you Hopkins rect² if they have arrived send word to Braintree that they may be got up before I get there. I wish myself at Braintree, for travelling sick is a very dissagreeable buisness. I think if I can hold out we shall be at Braintree on wednesday next. I am too feeble to write much, so must leave it to you to give this information to your Aunt. we met mr & mrs Breck & company at kings Bridge[3]

adieu your affectionate Mother A Adams

RC (Adams Papers); addressed by TBA: "John Quincy Adams Esq[r] / Boston"; endorsed: "My Mother. 12. May 1791."; notation by JA: "Free / John Adams."

[1] Letter not found. Writing to Mary Smith Cranch from New York on 6 May (MWA: Abigail Adams Letters), AA indicated that at her departure from Bush Hill "I left to be put on Board captain Cheeseman in the Brigg Ceares one Trunk of mine and one of Pollys one Band Box and a small portmantua Trunk." The brig *Ceres*, Capt. Samuel Chesman, was scheduled to sail from Philadelphia on 5 May; she entered Boston eight days later. The brig *Maria*, Capt. Caleb Hopkins, had cleared Philadelphia on 27 April and arrived at Boston on 5 May (*Pennsylvania Mercury*, 5 May; Boston *Columbian Centinel*, 14 May; Survey of Federal Archives, Division of Professional and Service Projects, Works Progress Administration, comps., *Ship Registers and Enrollments*

of Boston and Charlestown, 1789–1795, Boston, 1942, p. 30; Philadelphia *Federal Gazette*, 27 April; Boston *Herald of Freedom*, 6 May).

[2] Not found.

[3] Boston merchant Samuel Breck Sr. (1747–1809) and his wife Hannah Andrews Breck (1747–1831) were headed to Philadelphia on a short pleasure trip. The Brecks would move there in 1792, soon after Boston introduced a system of taxation that they and other wealthy inhabitants deemed arbitrary and unjust (vol. 6:325; H. E. Scudder, ed., *Recollections of Samuel Breck with Passages from His Note-Books (1771–1862)*, Phila., 1877, p. 176–177, 186–187; Samuel Breck, *Genealogy of the Breck Family Descended from Edward of Dorchester and His Brothers in America*, Omaha, 1889, p. 40).

Martha Washington to Abigail Adams

Dear Madam Philadelphia May the 30[th.] 1791

I had the pleasure to hear of you several times while you was on your journey by persons who met you—particulary by M[r] & M[rs] Breck and M[r] & M[rs] Codman of Boston who are now in this city—[1] I was truly sorry to learn from them that you were much indisposed— I sincerely hope you will obtain a re establishment of your health by breathing the air of your country which is esteemed so salubrious— you will I conceive at any rate escape the very warm weather which we are now beginning to feel hear— It is not in my power to amuse you with a detail of what is going forward in our fashonable world hear— you know I am not much in it at any time—and at this season there is less cause for moving about than in the winter— the heat has been very oppressive for several days past—more so than common at this time of the year— those familys which usually spend the summer in the country have retired there already— I do not expect to go to Virginia till the latter part of July— I can not think of going without my dear little folks, and their vacation do not commence till that time

I had the pleasure to hear from the President the day before yesterday—from savanah and was happy to find that he has enjoyed good health— he is now on his return and will probably be at mount vernon by the middle of June and in this City by the last of the month—[2] you see my dear madam that the promise which I made of writing to you is not one of those un meaning promises which are sometimes made without ever having an intention to perform them— you will be so good as present my complements to the Vice President, and the young Gentlemen—and accept of my best wishes for the health and happy ness of your self and family in which M^r & Mrs Lear begs leve to join

I am madam with very great / regard and esteem your / affectionat Friend & / Hble servant   M Washington

the Children join me in beging to be remember to miss smith—

RC (Adams Papers).

[1] Boston merchant John Codman Jr. married Catherine Amory (1769–1832) on 14 Feb., almost two years after the death of his first wife, Margaret Russell Codman (1757–1789) (vol. 7:111; Cora C. Wolcott, *The Codmans of Charlestown and Boston*, Brookline, Mass., 1930, p. 13, 14; Boston, *30th Report*, p. 239, 303; "Memoir of the Family of Amory," *NEHGR*, 10:65 [Jan. 1856]; Roger D. Joslyn, ed., *Vital Records of Charlestown Massachusetts to the Year 1850*, 2 vols., Boston, 1984–1995, 1:394; *Massachusetts Centinel*, 14 March 1789).

[2] George Washington left Savannah, the most distant stop on his southern tour, on 15 May 1791 and arrived at Mount Vernon on 12 June. He set off again fifteen days later, reaching Philadelphia on 6 July. Washington did not expect to be back in the capital much earlier because he was scheduled to meet with the commissioners for the federal district in Georgetown, Md., on 27 June, and he foresaw that his business with them might take several days (Washington, *Diaries*, 6:96–98, 139–140, 163–164, 169; Washington, *Papers, Presidential Series*, 8:160, 264–265).

John Adams to William Stephens Smith

Dear Sir   Braintree June 19. 1791.

Give me leave to congratulate you and my daughter, as well as your venerable Mother, and her and your amiable families on your arrival in America.[1] The situation of that respectable office to which you have been promoted, and the unhappy sickness of the good Lady your Mother, made us all uncommonly anxious for your arrival, I hope you found your own family in health and your mother recovering. My dear Mrs Adams, and some others of the family, brought home the Ague, and have suffered severely, but are better. I have a great desire to see you, and converse of our friends in England, and on the state of affairs there and in France; but I presume your office and public concerns will engross all your attention for some months. I depend much on the pleasure of seeing you in October, in my way to Philadelphia.

The death of our worthy Friend Dr Price has affected me very nearly; I hope the rough usage of Mr Burke did not injure his health.[2] How is Mr Brand Hollis, and all our acquaintances? You see our American politicks go on the old way. All the winds & waves directed to the port of Elections as usual; 'tho' the reputation, credit and prosperity of the country are certainly risen and rising. Never since I was born, was America so happy as at this time, and if the French delirium should not again turn our brains, we shall continue so. The people I think have suffered and smarted under the intoxication to such a degree, that they will not suddenly run into the same error; if they do, they will resemble my Coachman, and must take an Oath I think as he does, not to taste of the Cup for some time. We hope to see our Daughter, with M^r McCormick and Charles in July, and if your affairs will permit, we shall be extreemly happy to see you, with them. My love to my daughter and my dear boys, and regards to all your family.

I am my dear Sir / Yours affectionately

FC in TBA's hand (Adams Papers); internal address: "Coll: Smith."; notation: "Copy / Coll. Smith" and "1791."

[1] WSS arrived at New York aboard the British packet on 5 June (New York *Daily Advertiser*, 7 June).

[2] Dr. Richard Price, the dissenting minister and liberal philosopher whom the Adamses had come to know and admire during their years in England, died on 19 April (vol. 6:197; *DNB*).

Elizabeth Smith Shaw to Abigail Adams

My Dear Sister—   Haverhill June 24th. 1791

As I am exceedingly grieved when I hear of the Indisposition of any of my Friends, so am I greatly rejoiced, when I hear of their Recovery—& am much gratified at hearing of yours my Sister— When Mr Shaw went to Boston we did not know of your arrival at Braintree—& since that, the Circumstances of the Parish, & Family would not admit of our leaving Home— I hope soon to have the pleasure of seeing my Brother, & my Sisters at Haverhill, I hope our Brother & Sister Cranch will accompany you— I long to see you all—

The Bitter, with the sweet we often experience in the course of our lives,—at some periods we find the portion much greater than at others— At present a gloom is spread over every other Enjoyment, by the severe illness of our worthy Friend Mr Thaxter— He was voilently seized with a pleurisy three weeks ago,— It never come to a proper Crisis, but we fear has thrown him into a Consumtive state, which must very speedily close the Scene— [1]

I suppose you have heard of Mr Shaws Fathers Death His Head was silvered o'er with age, & he was fully ripe for the Harvest—a Harvest of immortal Joys, confered on those Servants, who have been faithful in the Vineyard of their Lord— [2]

We have just heard that Sister Eunice is very sick with a Consumtion, if living— She was one of the best of Daughters, & of Sisters The whole care of the Family was devolved on her, which she managed with uncommon discretion, & Oeconomy— She was silently attentive to every want—& took the tenderest, & best Care of her aged Father— Her Brothers should arise, & praise her, for she has been a Mother to them. I am Glad her life was continued to smooth the Bed of Death, & close the Eyes of her venerable Parent— I trust she will soon join again his chearful Society, free from all the imperfections attendant upon humanity,—where Virtue has its full Reward— [3]

Sister Smith was here about three weeks ago, & carried away my Betsy Smith, my Child—my Friend—& Companion— But I feel willing to sacrifice my own wants—for the sake of her advantage,— Hers is a time of Life, when young Ladies, can with the greatest satisfaction, ease, & pleasure visit their Friends, & I would not deprive her of the Benefit which I hope she will reap from it—

Cousin Thomas I hear looks cleverly— I feel as if it would do me good to see him— This hot weather makes me feeble—as it always did—

I believe Sister Cranch has forgot that I am living, for I have not had a Line from her these three months, or she is wholly absorbed in your charming company—must I forgive her?—

I am my Sister every yours with affection   Elizabeth Shaw—

RC (Adams Papers); addressed: "Mrs Abigail Adams / Braintree"; docketed: "M$^{rs.}$ E Shaw" and "1791"; notation: "To be left at / Mr William Smith's."

[1] John Thaxter Jr. died in Haverhill on 6 July, ten days after his wife, Elizabeth Duncan Thaxter, gave birth to their daughter Anna Quincy Thaxter. JQA visited Haverhill from 7 to 9 July to attend Thaxter's funeral on the 8th (*Vital Records of Haverhill Massachusetts to the End of the Year 1849*, 2 vols., Topsfield, Mass., 1910–1911, 1:293, 2:480; Boston *Independent Chronicle*, 28 July; D/JQA/16, APM Reel 19).

[2] Rev. John Shaw of Bridgewater died on 29 April at the age of 83 (*Sibley's Harvard Graduates*, 8:627–629). Elizabeth Smith Shaw, in extolling her deceased father-in-law,

combines allusions to John Gay's fable "The Shepherd and the Philosopher," line 3; Job, 5:26; Psalms, 22:26 (as rendered in the *Book of Common Prayer*); and Matthew, 20:1–16.

³ Eunice Shaw (1743–1791), daughter of

Rev. John and Sarah Shaw of Bridgewater, died on 10 Aug. (*Vital Records of Bridgewater Massachusetts to the Year 1850*, 2 vols., Boston, 1916, 1:288, 2:553).

Abigail Adams to Martha Washington

my dear Madam   Braintree june 25 1791[1]

I was honourd with your much esteemed favour on the 15 of this month.[2] the state of my Health, Body and mind suffering most Severely with repeated attacks of an intermitting fever will plead my apoligy for omitting to thank you at an earlier date for your Friendly Letter. I have been so weakned & debilitated as to be unable to walk alone, and my Nerves so affected as to oblige me to seclude myself from all company except my most intimate connexions. I hastned Home with great ardour in hopes the Northern Air and the quiet country Breize might restore me, but my disorder was of too obstinate a Nature to quit me so easily. I hope I have now got the better of it, as it is more than a week since the Ague left me we have had more very Hot weather than is usual at this season. I fear you have sufferd by it in Philadelphia. I hope Heat there is not attended with a Sharp drought, as it is here. the Feilds which a few week ago wore a most pleasing aspect, are now Robd of their verdure and our vegatables droop & dye. I was most sincerly grieved at reading in a late Philadelphia paper an account of the death of Dr Jones. the more I had the pleasure of knowing him, the greater esteem I had for him, as an amiable Sensible and Benevolent Man. You Madam must more particularly feel his loss as he was your Family Physician.[3]

I am happy to learn by your Letter as well as by the publick accounts that the President has enjoyd his Health during his Arduous Southern Tour. I presume er'e this Time I may congratulate you upon his return to Philadelphia I must beg you Madam to present to him my most respectfull Regards and my congratulation upon his safe return. I hope you will have as agreable a journey to mount vernon as I should have had to massachussets but for that vile Ague which Tormented me. the whole Country through which we past was in full Bloom, and every spot wore the face of Peace & contentment. the people instead of murmers & complaints, expresst themselves happy and satisfied under the administration of their Government. there are however two inhabitants envy and Jealousy who are not perfectly content, but as they are characters for whom I have an utter aversion I can only pitty their folly and avoid them. Mr Adams desires me to present his best Respects to the President & to you Madam, and an affectionat remembrance to master Washington & miss Custos Compliments to mr and mrs Lear I hope the little Boy is finely recoverd from the small pox. shall I be an intruder if I ask again to hear from my dear mrs washington whose Health and happiness Shall ever be the Ardent & Sincere wish of her who has the Honour to subscribe herself her affectionat Friend and Humble servant   A Adams

To a Heart less benevolent I should apologize for relating my Grief, but I know that you Madam can sympathize with those who mourn as well as rejoice in their felicity

Dft (Adams Papers); docketed: "AA to M^rs. Washington / 1791."

[1] Although AA dated the Dft of her letter 25 June, she dated the RC 29 June (see Martha Washington to AA, 4 Sept., below). Internal evidence suggests that AA wrote most if not all of the letter at the latter time.

[2] Martha Washington to AA, 30 May, above.

[3] John Jones (1729–1791), a physician and surgeon born in Jamaica, N.Y., died in Phila-delphia on 23 June. His death was first reported the following day in the Philadelphia newspapers, the *Federal Gazette* and *The Mail*. Jones had attended Benjamin Franklin during his final illness in April 1790 and George Washington during his nearly fatal bout with influenza that May (Washington, *Papers, Presidential Series*, 5:395).

Thomas Boylston Adams to William Cranch

Dear William   Braintree August 4th: 1791

Either write upon larger paper, or give an outside cover to your letters, for in the act of opening yours which I have just rec^d: I took away with the wafer much of the connection of several sentences; and being interested in every word I felt rather out of humor; However I collected sufficient from the *whole* cloth to make quite a decent garment.[1] The only circumstance to be regretted is, that it was too long upon the road between here and the tailors, and thus disappointed the owner, by obliging him to appear in an old suit upon a publick occasion. Hieroglyphick's! I wish you much pleasure in decyphering them. Tomorrow morning our Family sett out for Haverhill. I have twice written a few lines to Uncle Shaw informing him of their intention, and the time appointed for going. The first time, they concluded to delay their journey for a few days, and yesterday I wrote again, but had no opportunity for sending the letter to Boston; therefore neither of the letters were sent. Prepared or not, you have them tom⁰: night bag & —age.[2] I take it you have allready ascended many steps toward attain'g the object of your wishes. Those of your hopes and expectation will probably be more difficult, as they are more important. Every thing as yet wears a cheerful countentance towards you. May those features never assume the gloom of despondency. Your account of Judge Sargeant, allows by this time very little hope of his life You I trust among his numerous mourners will not be the least. He has appeared to interest himself in your favor so far as he was capable, and from the benevolent disposition he has discovered, you have every reason to presume that you, with the rest of his friends will lose a kind benefactor;[3] the sympathetic feelings of your heart upon occasions of this kind do not require a prompter. As you have allready commented upon the kind of security you will give for a few symptoms, I shall make no additions to it; I only wish I were able to be your Banker at the lay you mention. I think a few Pounds, expended in purchasing some of the most valuable of Mr Thaxters professional Books, would not be badly applied. We go on after the goodly sort in Braintree, all except poor me, who I fear will have at the next general assembly of birds, the matter of 40 Indictments presented for murder, and many actions of tresspass vi et armis.[4] Poor Charles will be (*luged in for snacks*) as an accessory, for he was pretty generally as the great Sportsmen say. In at the death—of the birds which I killed. Your good family are all well, but you will be able to hear verbally by the folks. I should have been happy, had it been possible for me to have attended the rest in their tour; but I can be tollerable easy at Home. My love to *some*, only one or two out of your family, comps to all.

Yours &ca

Thomas B Adams

RC (OCHP:William Cranch Papers, Mss fC891c RM); addressed: "William Cranch Esqr: / Haverhill"; endorsed: "T.B.A. / Aug. 4. 1791."

[1] Not found.

[2] William Cranch had moved to Haverhill during the week of 17 July to take up the law practice and office of his recently deceased cousin John Thaxter Jr. Cranch boarded with the Shaws throughout his time in Haverhill ("Sketches of Alumni at the Different Colleges in New England," *NEHGR*, 1:78 [Jan. 1847]; D/JQA/16, 17 July, APM Reel 19; Christopher Pearse Cranch, "William

Cranch," in NEHGS, *Memorial Biographies*, 2:451).

[3] Nathaniel Peaslee Sargeant died in Haverhill on 12 October. He demonstrated his confidence in William Cranch by making the young lawyer sole executor of his will (*Sibley's Harvard Graduates*, 12:579; "Sketches of Alumni").

[4] With force and arms.

William Stephens Smith to John Adams

Dear Sir.   New York August 5th. 1791.

I should have long before this answered your affectionate Letter of Congratulation on my return to my family and friends but since my arrival, I have really been so perfectly and fully engaged, that I could scarcly call an hour my own— I had hurried myself for this week past in expectation of attending Mrs: Smith to Braintree, but the situation of my public and private business *tho' agreable* is such, that, I must deny myself that pleasure, my Brother and Sister however accompany her, and every other arrangement made in my power to render her voyage and Journey agreable— I will endeavour to be with you on the twenty first of September for the purpose of escorting her home— I wish'd much at this time to see you, not only to tell my long story about my European Visit, but to talk freely about domestick Politicks. The Letter I addressed to the President on my arrival, I got Charles to Copy, for you but I not only had not then time, to write you myself, but not even to read his Copy to see whether it was correct or not— Mr. Jay. Hamilton and King, were much pleased with the contents of it, But I beleive The President Mr. Jefferson & Mr. Maddison would have rather I had stayed at home— Inclosed I send you the Presidents answer to that Letter, and my reply to it, but being advised by Colo. Hamilton to take no notice of it, but leave it to its own operation on the minds of the Government, I reluctantly withheld it, and only replyed,— Thus "I have the honor to acknowledge the receipt of the Presidents Letter of the 13th. of July in answer to the Communications I thought it my duty to make on the 6th. of June after my return from Europe—["]¹ The[se letters] I have not time to Copy, and therefore must beg the favour of their being given to Mrs: Smith, who will safe keep them untill I see her— you will not I Know consider my forwarding a Copy of a letter sent to Mr. Robert Morris from one of those Gentlemen who waited on you soon after your arrival in London, as a member of a Committee of Merchants to converse on the Mercantile situation of affairs between England and America—as any mark of unjustifiable vanity—nor the Letter of the 10th. of May from London forwarded with a Copy of the Presidents Message as a superfluous accompanyment² for Minutiae I must refer you to Mrs: Smith, you may get a great deal from her by Question & Answer, but you know she is not so much exposed as her husband to fall into lengthy conversations except with Ladies in a half Whisper—

Or perhaps you will get more if you appoint under the small seal that able negotiator M^rs: A. she by gently speaking Sweetly smiling and calmly pursuing the subject, may find out what carried me to Europe—what I did while there—and what engages me here at present, more important than the office I hold—

With my most affectionate regards to M^rs: Adam, Mr John—Charles, Thomas & Eliza. I am Dr Sir. affectionately yours.

W. S. Smith

RC (Adams Papers); internal address: "To The Vice President / of The United States." Some loss of text due to wear at the fold.

[1] On 6 June, the day after his arrival at New York, WSS wrote a long letter to George Washington in which he reported on a private interview that he had had in London on 9 April with British home secretary Lord Grenville. Britain, Grenville had revealed, was ready to send a minister to the United States to negotiate a settlement of all differences between the two nations. Washington, in a 13 July answer, thanked WSS for the information and at the same time dismissed it, remarking "very soon after I came to the government I took measures for enquiring into the disposition of the british cabinet on the matters in question between us: and what you now communicate corresponds very exactly with the result of those enquiries." Neither the reply that WSS first drafted nor the acknowledgment that he instead sent has been found (Washington, *Papers, Presidential Series*, 8:241–255, 338–339). See also WSS to JA, 21 Oct., below.

[2] The letter to Robert Morris, which has not been found, was probably from Patrick Colquhoun (1745–1820), a Glasgow merchant and civic booster with whom Morris had both private business dealings and back-channel diplomatic communications. Sent to London in 1785 to confer with merchants there about a petition to Parliament for help in the recovery of American debts, Colquhoun and fellow Glasgow merchant Alexander Brown met with JA on 4 June, only nine days after JA had arrived to assume the post of U.S. minister to Britain (*DNB*; Hamilton, *Papers*, 20:141–142; Jefferson, *Papers*, 18:246, 275; JA to John Jay, 6 June 1785, PCC, No. 84, V, f. 491–496; JA, *D&A*, 3:180).

The 10 May 1791 letter from London, also not found, probably enclosed a copy of Washington's 14 Feb. message to the Senate and House of Representatives, which the president intended would spur Congress to enact legislation on trade and navigation that might goad Britain into negotiating a commercial treaty (Washington, *Papers, Presidential Series*, 7:346–347; Jefferson, *Papers*, 18:229–239).

John Quincy Adams to William Cranch

Boston August 17th: 1791.

I received almost a fortnight since your favour of July 23^d: [1] and should have answered it before now, if I was in the habit of doing as I ought I sued the note immediately, but have not heard from Johonnot since[2] The two actions to which you requested me to attend were both continued; I had not seen Nightengale, and thought it would be expedient to continue that:[3] the other was continued at a moment when I happened to be out of Court, and Robbins made so many fair promises that his client would do every thing to get the money by the next term, and such doleful lamentations of his poverty at present that I did not press the matter upon the Court much, and they were not very favorable to me.[4] I believe there will be no harm done in the end by it.

I hope you find such encouragement at Haverhill, as will give you full satisfaction upon the subject of your removal there, and I have no doubt you find it a more eligible situation for Business than Braintree: but you have a fund of happiness within yourself that is worth more, than all the law business in the Commonwealth.

Your Master Dawes went to Portsmouth last week; he intended to have paid you a visit on his return, but his brother Pierce who went with him, had an invalid's whim of returning through Newbury-Port, with which M^r. Dawes complied so that he did not see you.[5]

I saw him a few days before, and we had some conversation relative to you. His opinion does you justice, and I love him the better for his having appreciated your merit so truly. He too thinks that your removal was judicious, and has the same dependence upon your success with the rest of us: after making your panegyric, he added that if you should have Miss N. G. *as he supposed you would*, she would render you as happy, as you deserve to be; that she was calculated to cheer and enliven the most retired & humble station as well as to adorn the most dignified.[6] That you were both deserving of each other, and would enjoy together as much happiness as could result from good minds & congenial dispositions To this part of his story I did not so fully assent as to the other; and I thought I could perceive an obstacle to the completion of his prophecy, of which he was not aware. "Tis as one wedge drives out another" says Vellum in the drummer;[7] There will be somebody there who will cut the thread of your passion for Miss G.– that is my prophecy, and old Time will show before long which of us is right. It is your peculiar good fortune that in either case, your choice will justify the expectations of M^r. Dawes.

As for me, I could sit down and philippize upon my situation for an hour together, but I have got above it—res mihi subjicere conor.[8] indeed if I did not I should make but a pitiful whining fellow, I intend as soon as I am able to make myself a deep proficient in the stoic philosophy; it is the only consolation to a man upon whom the world frowns; and then if ever the cheating syren Fortune, should mistake herself so far as to smile upon me I will turn epicurean—that is my system. Epicure when a man is in luck, and Zeno, when the die is against him.[9]

I shall endeavour to be as little thoughtful or pensive, that is to think as little, as I possibly can; if I could but contrive not to think at all I should be the happier, but I cannot follow your advice of spending two or three months at Braintree. Think how my business would suffer by it: I defy you to calculate how many hundred pounds I should lose.— My health is indeed valuable; next to my conscience, and a very few friends, the most valuable object I have on Earth but it must take its chance. The *temptations* which you mention, I do not very well know; what should I be afraid of here— The only temptations that can be dangerous to me are such as would lead me away, but I am proof against every thing.

You will not fail to remember me to Mʳ· Shaw & the family, to our friend White, & generally to all the good folks whose remembrance is worth any thing, wherewith I remain as usual your friend

J. Q. Adams.

RC (DLC:William Cranch Papers); addressed: "William Cranch Esqʳ / Attorney at Law. / Haverhill."; endorsed: "J.Q.A. / Aug. 17. 1791."

[1] Not found. JQA remarked in his Diary that he received Cranch's letter on 4 Aug. (D/JQA/16, APM Reel 19).

[2] JQA's legal accounts record a bill of costs for the case of "Wingate vs Johonnot" under the date of 21 Feb. 1792 (M/JQA/18, APM Reel 215).

[3] On 19 Oct. 1791 JQA would argue and win the case of Whitemore (or Whittemore) *v.* Nightengale before the Suffolk County Court of Common Pleas (D/JQA/16, 19 Oct., APM Reel 19; D/JQA/18, 14 Feb. 1792, APM Reel 21).

[4] Edward Hutchinson Robbins (1758–1829), Harvard 1775, established his law practice in Milton in 1779. Elected to the Mass. house of representatives two years later, he remained a member until 1802, serving as speaker from 1793 (*Sibley's Harvard Graduates*, 19:forthcoming).

[5] Boston merchant Joseph Peirce (1745–1828) had been married to Ann Dawes, the sister of Thomas Dawes, since 1771 (Henry W. Holland, *William Dawes and His Ride with Paul Revere*, Boston, 1878, p. 67).

[6] Cranch would marry Anna (Nancy) Greenleaf (1772–1843) in 1795 (vol. 8:148; Greenleaf, *Greenleaf Family*, p. 222).

[7] Joseph Addison, *The Drummer*, 1715, Act V, scene i, line 188.

[8] A paraphrase of Horace, *Epistles*, Book I, epistle i, line 19: "et mihi res, non me rebus, subiungere conor," that is, to make the world serve me, not me the world.

[9] Epicurus was a classical Greek philosopher who defined happiness in terms of pleasure; Zeno, also a classical Greek philosopher, rooted happiness in virtue (*Oxford Classical Dicy.*).

Thomas Boylston Adams to William Cranch

My dear William   Braintree August 23ᵈ· 1791

I have somewhere heard an observation of this kind, "that a person should not be too anxious to return a kindness."[1] Had I strictly adhered to this injunction, an Answer to your last favor would not so soon have followed;[2] but as you expect shortly to be at Braintree in person, I must either remain in your Debt, or take this opportunity to discharge the obligation. I am happy to find that the novelty of your situation has not obliterated the remembrance of your now solitary companion, & when I tell you of the exertion which this poor scrap requires from me at present, you will think it of more consequence than otherwise it would deserve. Tomorrow will complete a fortnight since I was first seized with the Southern Plague, Viz. The Ague Fever;[3] and regularly every other Day since, I have had a severe fit, which has reduced me at least four degrees in point of flesh; as to Spirits, hardly any thing this side an inflamitory Rheumatism, will greatly diminish them. My mother when she returnd we found had been very ill most of the time in her absence, but happily, has had no fever fit since she got home. But you have enough of this. Charles left us on Sunday for New York, but Mrs Smith still continues with us, otherwise I should lose a little of my jolity; and should be quite impatient for your company. Truly if I may judge by your letter, I shall think you something more than a *sort of a Gallant*. I fear the good Judge had designs upon you, when he gave you the office of Executor. The facetious young Lady whom you sett at defiance may ensnare, in a course of time. How many a charm is born to be adored, yet ne'er to be enjoyed by those who worship the possessor's. This is all I have to say concerning one whom you have mentioned. Is it not possible for our heads together to invent a name for a cetain lady? I am not pleased with that she has at present. Your expedition to Exeter has at least made you acquainted with some impudent people. Above every thing I think the Judges of a Court of Justice should be treated with common respect, even if their *learning* will not entitle them to it. Much of the credit of a Layyer depends upon his manner of treating the Bench. Where the opinions of Judges are treated with contempt, the justice of a cause may as well be determined by the throw of a Dye, as the verdict of a Jury. A Gentleman Lawyer has many clients *in esse*.[4]

Betsey Smith is now at your father's; she with the rest of your family are very well and will be as happy to see you next week as

Thomas B. Adams.

RC (OCHP:William Cranch Papers, Mss fC891c RM); addressed: "William Cranch Esqr: / Haverhill"; internal address: "William Cranch Esqr:"; endorsed: "T.B. Adams / Aug. 23d. 1791. / Answd. Aug. 27.—"

[1] "He then that hasteth to restore and requite a kindness, hath not the mind of a grateful man, but of a debtor. And to conclude in few words, he that is desirous to pay over soon, doth owe unwillingly; he that unwillingly oweth, is ungrateful" (Seneca, *On Benefits*, transl. Thomas Lodge, London, 1899, Book IV, ch. xl, p. 178).

[2] Not found.

[3] From the seventeenth to the nineteenth century, ague—malaria—was seen in America as a southern disease because it appeared in northern latitudes only episodically but in southern ones continuously (Margaret Humphreys, *Malaria: Poverty, Race, and Public Health in the United States*, Baltimore, 2001, p. 23–29).

[4] In being, that is, actually existing. William Cranch apparently attended the Court of Common Pleas for Rockingham County, N.H., which convened in Exeter on 9 Aug. (*The Laws of the State of New-Hampshire*, Portsmouth, 1792, p. 70, Evans, No. 24585).

Thomas Boylston Adams to William Cranch

Braintree September 4th 1791.

Influenced by the same principle as when I last wrote, viz. That of discharging a debt before it has accumulated much on the score of interest, I have determined to come to a settlement to the date hereof.[1] You must not however expect the same degree of pure metal as that which produced the obligation; but make many grains of allowance for barrenness of Mint. Even should you be paid in *Script* subject to *speculation*, at least I shall not be subject to a Qui Tam prosecution. I am no less affected by the cause of your detainer, than the disappointment it occasioned; both cause and consequence however, I hope are temporary. The novelty of your scheme for getting yourself into business, is no less than its singularity. At any rate it discovers a fertility of invention, which in these *dull times*, is peculiarly serviceable to the possessor, more especially in our Profession. *Money* in puritanical times, was said to be "the root of all evil,"[2] A modern Churl, who sometimes indulges himself somewhat extensively in substitution or rather, prostitution of terms, has altered, by no means amended, the maxim, by which it reads thus "Women the reservoirs of all Scandal." Far be it from me to reveal the Author's name, for I have no inclination to immolate one of my fellow mortals on an Altar, the workmanship of his own temerity. I shall rather consider him as an object of commiseration, for having engaged in a most unequal contest. I am not the Jew for whose destruction the Gallows was erected.[3] Having thus expressed my opinion of the deplorable situation of a person engaged in this female war; it will be superfluous to add any thing by way of caution to you. The Ancient Ballad, afforded much entertainment to all true lovers of Atticism. Every one lamented the extinguishment of the Coal, and if any sudden blast from my bellows could have revived

226

the spark, the gentle fannings from every passing breeze, had soon restored it to its former glow. The subject original, was majestic, but the consequent effects are sufficiently ludicrous, and as such described, by the Balladist. "Hence in old dusky time a deluge came," &cª:⁴ The Ladies may make this passage of Thomson's applicable to their own case by erasing a single word. If you dare let them know that the history of their excursion has so soon passed the Merrimack, you may offer them my congratulations upon their arrival in safe moorings without being cast away.

When I mentioned my Sister to you in my last it was certainly an omission on my part not to mention her fine boys. If they could be under the government of your good mother for one week before you come, you would be pleased with their vivacity; but under present management I fear you will perceive very soon where the defect lies. I was yesterday threatned with a return of my Ague, but hope from the precautions I have taken, to escape its further attacks. It is almost a fortnight since I had a real fit. The Bark has been administered in copious effusions to your cousin   Thomas B Adams.

RC (OCHP:William Cranch Papers, Mss fC891c RM); addressed: "William Cranch Esqʳ / Haverhill"; endorsed: "T. B. A. Sep. 4. 1791."; notation: "post pd."

¹ Not found.
² 1 Timothy, 6:10.
³ In Esther, 5:9–14, the viceregent Haman, incensed by the failure of Mordecai the Jew

to show him due respect, has a gallows erected on which to hang the offender.
⁴ James Thomson, *The Seasons: Spring*, line 309.

Martha Washington to Abigail Adams

My Dear madam   Philadelphia September the 4ᵗʰ· 1791

Your frindly letter of the 29ᵗʰ of June¹—I should not have suffered to remain so long unacknowledge from any other cause than that of the severe illness of my dear Little Washington—who was confined to his bed with a cruel fevor for three weeks in the Months of July & August—² I beleive it is heardly necessary my dear madam for me to tell you that, during the time of his illness I was not in a situation to attend to any thing but him.— The fatague and anxiety which I underwent, were almost too much for me; but sine it has plased god to restore my dear child again to health, I find my self recovered, and begin to look round to see what I left undone—at that time, that I may attend to it now—

I had, with concern, heard of your illness before your Letter reched my hands; I assure you I was exceedingly rejoiced when that informed me that the ague had left you, and that you were getting much better.

If you have had reason to complain of the heat in New England— what must have been our situation in this city? whare a veriaty of circumstances combine with the climate to render the heat here at times almost insupporable: the heat of last week was more extreem than any we had experienced before—

The President returned from the southward in fine health—which was soon after interrupted for a little time—but I am now happy in saying that it is again restored;[3] and he unites with me in compliments and best wishes to your self—the Vice President—and your family—

I expect next week to set off with the President for Mount Vernon. I shall take my grand children with me in hopes that change of air will give them strength, as they are much relaxed with the heat of this city— I expect to be back by the latter end of october—when I hope I shall have the pleasure to see you perfectly well—

Nelly and Washington desire to be particularly remembered to your self and miss smith, to whome you will be so good as to give my kind regards.— M^r & Mrs Lear thank you for your remembrance of them and thair Little Boy, and request to be presented to you in very respectfull terms— a due and beleive me / Dear madam / your affectionate / friend & Hble / servant   M Washington

RC (Adams Papers).

[1] AA to Martha Washington, 25 June, and note 1 above.

[2] For George Washington Parke Custis' illness, see Washington, *Papers, Presidential Series*, 8:283, note 10.

[3] A tumor that George Washington had had removed from his leg in June 1789 returned sometime between 6 and 24 July 1791. Washington had it drained and was well again by 3 Aug. (same, 8:327, note 3).

Abigail Adams to John Quincy Adams

my dear son   Brookfield Sunday 9 oc^{br} 1791

I had not time to write to you before I left Braintree I was in so much trouble for your Aunt and Family, that I left home with a Heavy Heart indeed, nor can I look to Philadelphia with a much lighter one, for there mrs Brisler lies at the point of death with a fever, if living. I promised Lucy if any Letters should come from Gen^{ll} Knox or mr Brisler after I left home that you should open them and give them every information they might contain respecting her.[1] this I now request you to do.

I am extremely anxious to hear from your uncle cranch. I wish you could forward a Letter to me to be left a Smiths or the stage House at N Haven, should this reach you soon enough. I did not say enough to you a[bout] your Eye's. I would have you take a portion or two of Sal[ts] and then an oz of Bark, in 6 or 7 portions.[2] do not neglect it, if lost Health may be restored, lost Eyes cannot, and I am certain from my observation respecting your Health the summer past, that you stand in need of the Bark

your Father has stood his journey as well as could be expected. he is some what fatigued to day, but I hope his Heaviness arrises only from the exertions of the two last days, & from a South wind. if I had not past through the disorder myself and experienced the debility occasiond by it I should feel more anxious. convey the inclosed Letter as soon as you can to Braintree from your affectionate /
Mother   A Adams

p s I received your Letter and approve of what you have done[3]

RC (Adams Papers); addressed by TBA: "John Quincy Adams Esqr: / Boston"; endorsed: "My Mother. 9. Octr: 1791." and "My Mother. Octr: 9. 1791." Some loss of text where the seal was removed.

[1] JQA, when he wrote to AA on 5 Oct., forwarded a letter from Henry Knox, presumably that to JA of 28 Sept., in which Knox reported that John Briesler "has recovered and also his children, but his wife is dangerously ill" (both Adams Papers).

[2] JQA first noted "weak eyes" in his Diary on 3 August. He continued to complain of weak or sore eyes from time to time until 10 Oct. (D/JQA/16, APM Reel 19).

[3] In his letter of 5 Oct., JQA informed AA that he had purchased "a pair of hand-irons" less costly and more handsome than she had directed (Adams Papers).

Mary Smith Cranch to Abigail Adams

My dear Sister   Braintree [16] october [1791]

I wrote you last Sunday by Doctor Welsh & your son who were here & sent it to new-york where you now are I suppose.[1] I hope you found the Letter when you arriv'd as your Sympathytick heart would be in some measure reliev'd by the favourable account I gave you of mr Cranchs Leg— since that time it has continu'd to descharge well the mortified parts have been seperateing from the sound flesh & are now almost all come of but it has become such an offencive sore to dress as you scarcly can conceive of tis very painful too at times: I have dress'd it alone to day for the first time since it began to discharge in such a manner— tis still Bath'd once a day— Tis a slow & I fear will be a long peice of work before tis well we feed him yet with Bark & wine but not in such quantitys as at first— some parts of the Leg are heal'd but there is now a sore from the knee to the ancle. there are but two places which appear deep every part where the Blisters were not cut is sound— The swelling has in a manner left the Limb— he cannot walk a step nor bear his weight upon it yet his appetite is good

What charming Weather you have had for your journey I hope you all feel the better for your ride & that you will find all your Freinds in health & mrs Brisler recover'd—

Polly Tailor is with us waiting for Madam Jeffery to send for her.[2] She sent her wood She was ready to wait upon her & wonders that she is not sent for

cousin Betsy Smith is with mrs Norton who was well yesterday

Deacon Adams is dangerously sick with a slow Lung fever[3]

Mr Shaw is gone to Barnstable & to the ordination of mr Simkins[4] Sister Shaw was well but poor Billy grows worse I design to perswaid Mr Shaw to let mr Hughs see him— that man certainly has a faculty of seting Bones beyond many who are better theorests than himself[5]

William return'd last monday to haverhill & you must think my dear sister that I feel very lonely—but I hope the danger from mr Cranchs Leg is not so great as it was— tis a terrible sore now but it has been so much worse that I cannot help being incourag'd about it—but I hope I shall be resign'd be the event what it may— The support & kindness of my dear sister while she was here was a cordial to my spirits. & tho absent that she bears us upon her mind is a constant feast to my Soul— good grant that your health may be restor'd & that your Life so precious to us as well as to your own Family may be prolong'd many years yet to come & that we may have another happy meeting when the spring opens upon us—

Mr Cranch send his Love to mr Adams & you & begs me to renew his thanks for all your kindnesses & attentions

Lucy send her Duty & Love mr Adams I hope has not had a return of his dissorder I hop'd to have heard of you from some of your stages but I have not

Polly found half a dozen Tea spoons in the closet after you went away which she thought she had put up they are here with your other plate. She has put a hook upon the Kitchen chamber door or rather upon the door at the foot of the Stairs which effectually secures all the garrets— upon the wash house we shall put a Lock I have sent to mr Pratt for sea-weed to stop the cellar doors & bank the house. Polly has nail'd up all the Gates but the cow yard gate

I have your Pigs & hope to make fine ones of them— If there is any thing else I can do for you pray let me know it, nothing can give me more pleasure than to be able to discharge some of the obligations confer'd upon your / grateful & affectionate Sister

Mary Cranch

RC (Adams Papers); docketed: "Mrs M Cranch / to Mrs A Adams / October 1791." and "1791." Filmed at Oct. [*1791*].

[1] Mary Smith Cranch's letter of 9 Oct. has not been found.

[2] Mary Wilkes Storke Hayley Jeffery, for whom see vol. 7:273, note 4; 384, note 5. After a stay in Boston of over eight years, Mary Jeffery would return to Britain in Nov. 1792 alone; her husband, Patrick Jeffery, remained in Massachusetts (Boston *Independent Chronicle*, 10 Nov. 1792; Amanda Bowie Moniz, "A Radical Shrew in America: Mary Wilkes Hayley and Celebrity in the Early United States," *Common-Place*, vol. 8 [April 2008], www.common-place.org).

[3] JA's cousin Ebenezer Adams died on 22 Oct. 1791 (Mary Smith Cranch to AA, 23 Oct., Adams Papers). JQA traveled to Braintree for the funeral on the 25th (D/JQA/16,

APM Reel 19).

[4] John Simpkins (1768–1843), Harvard 1786, was ordained as minister of the Congregational Church in the north precinct of Harwich (now the town of Brewster) on 19 Oct. (Josiah Paine, *A History of Harwich, Barnstable County, Massachusetts, 1620–1800*, Rutland, Vt., 1937, p. 158–163).

[5] Probably either Robert Hewes (1751–1830) or his cousin Shubael Hewes (1732–1813), both of whom worked as bonesetters in Boston (Eben Putnam, *Lieutenant Joshua Hewes, A New England Pioneer, and Some of His Descendants*, N.Y., 1913, p. 323–326, 330–332; *Boston Directory*, 1803, Shaw-Shoemaker, No. 3862).

Abigail Adams to Mary Smith Cranch

my dear sister   N york Sunday october 17 [*1791*][1]

I arrived here last Night. my first inquiry was for a Letter from you, which I was happy enough to find, and great relief did it afford to my anxious mind.[2] I sent to the post office to see if I could get any further intelligence last evening but was dissapointed. I am ready however to attribute it more to your not getting an opportunity of conveyance than to any unfavourable circumstance, and I was much incouraged yesterday by seeing mrs judge cushing, who told me of a cure performed upon mrs Hyslops leg after a mortification had really taken place.[3] she made great use of Bark and wine. I am sure my dear sister neither mr Adams or I can ever think our wine used to a better purpose than in aiding the recovery [of so] dear & valuable a Friend, and we request you to get more from our cellar when that is expended. can there be a greater pleasure in Life than rendering kindness to those we love and esteem and who we know are every way worthy of our regard. how many of my anxious & painfull hours did you in the summer past alleviate by your sisterly kindness. how much too am I indebted to my dear Lucy for her goodness. I am anxious for her Health, and full of the mind that a free use of the Bark would relieve her Nervious Headacks Katy who is with me was relieved only in that way after a slow Nervious fever. I had a pleasant journey in point of weather. mr Adams found himself very weak and feeble when we came to travell. his Nerves were more affected than I was aware of before I left home. he has not had any return of his fever, but if I had not gone through all & more than he has sufferd I should be much more distrest. he gains strength by his journey, but what I fear is the buisness & company which he cannot avoid and which are very unfit for a person recovering from such a disorder. Thomas & Louissa are well— mrs smith & Family I found well—but I cannot learn a word from Philadelphia. Remember us all kindly to mr Cranch with our most sincere wishes for his perfect restoration to Health. I am my dear / Sister affectionatly yours

A Adams

RC (MWA:Abigail Adams Letters); addressed by TBA: "Mrs Mary Cranch / Braintree"; endorsed by Richard Cranch: "Letter from Mrs / A Adams (N York) / Octr 17. 1790"; docketed: "1790." Some loss of text due to placement of the seal.

[1] Sunday was the 16th.
[2] Not found.
[3] Either Mehetabel Stoddard Hyslop (1719–1792), wife of Boston wholesale merchant William Hyslop (1714–1796), or Betsey Williams Hyslop, wife of their son William Hyslop (1753–1792) (E. W. Stoddard, appendix to *Anthony Stoddard, of Boston, Mass., and His Descendants: 1639–1873*, N.Y., 1873, p. 124, 126).

William Stephens Smith to John Adams

Dear Sir.   New York October 21st. 1791.

The information I gave you relative to Mr. Hammonds official Character at the moment of your departure for Philadelphia, you will probably have confirmed previous to the receipt of this—[1]

The various important stations I have filled and the particular agency I had in producing this conciliatory advance of the British Court to the Government of The United States, Justifies to my mind the offer I propose making, of myself as a Candidate for the appointment at the Court of St. James's, in addition to this Mr. Hammonds Communications to me from Lord Grenville are so strongly marked with respect and Confidence, that I should not think, I did Justice to my Country, my family or myself should I omit presenting myself to The President at this period— particularly as the British Cabinet have pointedly instructed M^r· Hammond to pursue steadily the line, I marked out in my communications with Lord Grenville the last winter, as details in the Letter I addressed to the President on the 6$^{th.}$ of June last, viz. to enter into a full discussion & fulfillment of the unsettled points of the last Treaty, as a primary essential—to establish such Commercial regulations as the Interests of the two Country's require, and to leave all other points to their own operation, aided by the friendship & good understanding which the preceeding arrangements may produce,—

In addition to this mark of the esteem and Confidence of the Cabinet of England, M^r· Hammond is charged by his Court to take some proper opportunity and communicate to The President, not as if they were disposed to take the lead of his Judgement, in a Case like this, but that they conceived it a Compliment due from them to me, to assure the President, that on the appointment of a Gentleman to reside at the Court of London, no one would be more acceptable than myself or more likely to be agreable to the King and Cabinet of England— This Communication M^r· Hammond informed me he thought it his duty to make as early as possible

As I cannot reconcile it, to my feelings and the respect I entertain for you Sir, to attempt so important an object thro' any other medium, and relying on your friendship and disposition to promote my interest & the Honour of our connected families, I beg the favour of your presenting the enclosed letter to the President, and of supporting it by such observations as your better Judgement may dictate I am further induced to pursue the object thro' this Channel as the pursuit coincides with the letter, You once did me the Honor to address to The President on similar subjects, to aid you in this business, I will mention, that previous to the removal of Congress from New York, The President required of M^r· Jefferson a list of those Gentlemen whom he would recommend to his Consideration for foriegn Diplomatic appointment M^r· Jefferson told me in that case he had put my name amongst the first on the list— some time after M^r· Hamilton was called on to submit a few names to the President as persons proper to be employed to negociate the late loan— on that paper which contained 3 names, I was the second, but M^r· Jeffersons influence introduced M^r· Short tho' not mentioned by M^r· Hamilton & carried his point.[2]

However notwithstanding all this, should I not prove successful the knowledge of the failure, will be confined to my friends and for myself I shall not be at a loss to decide on the principles of it or find any difficulty in digesting the disappointment—

I am with great respect & regard / Your most Obed^t· / Humble Servt·

W: S: Smith

RC and enclosure (Adams Papers); internal address: "To / The Vice President / of The United States—"; docketed: "W^m S Smith / Oct 21st 1791"; notation on enclosure: "Copy of the Letter / addressed to The President." For the enclosure, see note 2, below.

[1] George Hammond (1763–1853) arrived in New York aboard the packet *Grantham* on 18 Oct. and apparently met with WSS before proceeding to Philadelphia, where he arrived two days later. Appointed British minister plenipotentiary to the United States, Hammond had been instructed not to assume that rank until the appointment of an American counterpart to Britain. In the meantime, he was authorized to act only as consul general. Hammond presented his credentials as minister on 11 Nov., just two days after George Washington finalized his choice for the London post, Thomas Pinckney. Hammond, whom JA had known as David Hartley's secretary during the 1783 peace negotiations, served as minister to the United States until 1795 (*New York Daily Gazette*, 18 Oct.; Washington, *Papers, Presidential Series*, 8:483; Jefferson, *Papers*, 18:280, 22:262).

[2] WSS enclosed not only the RC of his 21 Oct. 1791 letter to Washington, which JA forwarded along, but also a copy for JA, which is retained in the Adams Papers. Believing that his 9 April interview with British home secretary Lord Grenville had helped to secure the appointment of a British minister to the United States, WSS wrote to the president to claim credit and to offer himself as a candidate for U.S. minister to Britain. He did not receive the appointment. Chagrined at this second rebuff—Washington had dismissed his 6 June report on the interview—WSS on 7 Feb. 1792 resigned the office of supervisor of revenue for the district of New York in favor of "such private pursuits as may guard my own feelings from further unpleasant exercise" (Washington, *Papers, Presidential Series*, 9:104–105, 562–563).

John Quincy Adams to Thomas Boylston Adams

My dear Brother   Boston October 28th: 1791.

I received your favour of the 17th: inst^t: from New-York, and am happy to hear you had got well so far on your journey.[1] I hope you will be equally punctual on your arrival at Philadelphia.

I must request your attention to the memorandum, which I left with you last Spring; and that you would not forget to send my segars before the navigation closes for the Season. the numbers of the Gazette of the U.S. which I want are 99 and 101. of the 2^d: Vol: and 6 & 18 of the 3^d:

Nothing material has occurred since you left us. I was at Braintree a few days ago. M^r: Cranch is, we hope out of danger, but will have a very tedious time with his leg. I fear he will be confined through the whole winter.

Our Court of Common Pleas sat last week. I argued one cause to a jury; that of Nightengale, and obtained a verdict for him.[2] I found my confidence in myself growing much stronger, and acquitted myself more to my satisfaction than I had ever done before.— Since that time I have had another opportunity to take a practical lesson of public speaking. The Committee of the General Court, who are to report upon the petition of the North Parish in Braintree for incorporation, sat at Milton last Wednesday to hear the parties. I was employed with W. Cranch and B. Beale by the parish Committee to support the petition. We were all of a standing; but as I was the oldest in years, it fell to my lot to close the argument, and to answer, the objections from Dorchester and from the other parishes in Braintree. M[r]: Hichborn was a Committee man from Dorchester, and M[r]: Robbins was employed as Counsel for the other parishes.[3] The debate lasted about four hours. I was nearly one in my argument, and like Dogberry in the play "found it in my heart to bestow all my tediousness upon their honours."[4] You may well imagine I was not equal to the task, especially as I had not had even twenty four hours time for preparation, or for obtaining the necessary information relative to the facts. I was not at all satisfied with my performance, but believe I did not *lose* any ground, with the audience. These opportunities have both afforded me some consolation, as they have tended to convince me that I may, with the help of experience acquire at least a decent capacity for forensic contention. This has for these fifteen months past, been one of the greatest sources of my anxiety and apprehension. The present stagnation of professional business, must be temporary, but an utter disqualification for public speaking would have been perpetual, and would have cut the cable from the sheet anchor of my hopes.— You have often been witness to my fears on this head, and it is for that reason that I am thus minute in detailing the circumstances, which suspend at least their operation, and tend to give me some encouragement.— I expect to argue one cause more at the next session of our Court of Common Pleas in January, and if so, I shall again inform you, whether my diffidence continues to decline, and my hopes to assume consistency.

In the mean time business is as dull as ever. If I have very little to do, I find myself in very respectable company. Yet I cannot easily suppress the sigh when the reflection recurs that I still subsist upon paternal bounty.— If I cannot acquire my own subsistence, I will at least endeavour to deserve it, and in the long winter before us I intend to pursue, with as much ardour as if my prospect of reward was much greater than it is, the studies connected with my profession and with science in general.

Your friends in this town are well. Quincy told me he intended soon to write you.— Callender gallant as ever.— I saw Miss Breck last evening, at the assembly; she enquired particularly after Louisa.[5]

Write as often as you can. Love to all the family, and believe me to be ever affectionately, your brother.   J. Q. Adams.

October 29th

I have just received your's of the 23[d.] inst[t:] and am happy to hear you arrived agreeably at Philadelphia.[6] I shall take care of the enclosed Letters, and have nothing further to communicate.

RC (Adams Papers); addressed: "M[r:] Thomas B. Adams. / Philadelphia."; endorsed: "28th Oct: 1791."

[1] Not found.

[2] See JQA to William Cranch, 17 Aug., and note 3, above.

[3] In Jan. 1791, 129 men from Braintree's north precinct, or parish, along with 21 others from the middle precinct and adjoining parts of Dorchester and Milton, petitioned the Mass. General Court for incorporation as a new town. The senate took up the matter on the 28th, and an order was issued inviting the town of Braintree to comment at a hearing before the General Court scheduled for 16 February. Nine days before the hearing, the Braintree town meeting, dominated by men from the middle and south precincts who rejected any division of the town, voted to send six agents to oppose the petition and authorized them to hire an attorney at town expense to assist them. The town meeting at the same time directed Ebenezer Thayer Jr., Braintree's representative in the legislature, to use his influence there against the petition. What happened at the General Court hearing is not known, but the senate subsequently appointed a committee to consider the petition. In preparation for a hearing before that committee—the 26 Oct. hearing in Milton at which JQA spoke—the Braintree town meeting on 27 Sept. chose four agents to attend and oppose the petition. What occurred at the committee hearing is also not known, but the committee afterward returned a report in favor of the petition, which the senate accepted. On 21 Jan. 1792, the two houses of the legislature voted to allow the petitioners to bring in a bill to put their petition into effect. On 22 Feb., the bill passed, and a day later, Gov. John Hancock approved it, incorporating the town of Quincy (CFA, *History of Braintree, Massachusetts (1639–1708), the North Precinct of Braintree (1708–1792), and the Town of Quincy (1792–1889)*, Cambridge, 1891, p. 269–270; *Braintree Town Records*, p. 601, 611; Pattee, *Old Braintree*, p. 58–62; *Boston Argus*, 27 Jan. 1792; Mass., *Acts and Laws, 1790–1791*, p. 319–320).

[4] A paraphrase of Shakespeare, *Much Ado about Nothing*, Act III, scene v, lines 22–25, where Dogberry, having been accused by Leonato of being tedious, mistakes the gibe for a compliment and graciously replies, "but truly, for mine own part, if I were as tedious as a king, I could find in my heart to bestow it all of your worship."

[5] Josiah Quincy III and John Callender (1772–1833) were Harvard classmates of TBA studying law in Boston with William Tudor and Christopher Gore, respectively. Both young men would be admitted to practice before the Suffolk County Court of Common Pleas in 1793. Callender would go on to serve as clerk of the Supreme Judicial Court from 1815 until his death (*Harvard Quinquennial Cat.*, p. 203; William T. Davis, *Bench and Bar of the Commonwealth of Massachusetts*, 2 vols., Boston, 1895, 1:113, 265, 285; *Catalogue of Records and Files in the Office of the Clerk of the Supreme Judicial Court for the County of Suffolk*, Boston, 1897, p. 145; Amherst,

N.H., *Farmer's Cabinet*, 29 Nov. 1833).

Hannah Breck (1772–1846), daughter of Samuel and Hannah Andrews Breck, would marry JQA's Harvard classmate James Lloyd Jr. in 1809 (Samuel Breck, *Genealogy of the Breck Family Descended from Edward of Dorchester and His Brothers in America*, Omaha, 1889, p. 40–41, 208–209; *Harvard Quinquennial Cat.*, p. 201).

[6] Not found.

Abigail Adams to Mary Smith Cranch

my dear Sister   Philadelphia october 30th 1791

I wrote to you upon my journey whilst I was at Brookfield the sunday after I left you and was sorry to find by your Letter, that you had not received it.[1] I wrote to you from N york but have been so engaged in moveing, & so embarressd with company in the midst of it, tho only a complimentary call, that I have had scarcly a moment that I could call my own. it was kind in you [to l]et mr Cranch to superscribe your Letter. I thank you for [the] precaution, because I open every Letter from you with trembling and fear. I rejoice most Sincerely with you in your prospect of a recovering Limb. if the Life of our dear Friend is Spaired, we cannot be sufficiently thankfull to a kind Providence, even tho the recovery should be long and Tedious. my Heart bled to leave you in such distress

we Have nearly got through the Bustle of Removal, but my House is no way to my mind. the Rooms so small and not able to lay two together, renders it very troublesome to see so much company as we must be obliged to.[2] the weather is very pleasent and my Health better than for some months past Thomas is less threatned with Rhumaticks than he was on our journey. Louissa as well as usual. mr Adams is much recoverd to what he was, has been able to attend his duty in Senate, tho Sometimes a good deal exhausted.

you mention in your Letter getting the House blockd up. I forgot to inform you that there was cider and potatoes to be put into the cellar and that Brother had engaged to see the cellar Bank'd up, but if it should not be done I would wish to have it secured before the Frost. for the Reasons above mentiond I directed Polly to leave the keys of the House with them, the Keys of the cellar to bring to you. I wonder mrs Jeffry has not sent for Polly. she appeard so solicitious to get her. I hope no one has done her an injury. Polly had qualifications peculiarly fitted for my Family, and might still have been in it, but for a little unruly member. I like katy very well and beleive I could not have been better suited. mrs Brisler is with me, feeble & sick tho better than she was. I do not see but she must remain with me, unless Lucy returns to take care of her and her children.

my things have not yet arrived from Boston, I fear I shall lose my Pears.

I am anxious for Billy Shaw least he should be a criple all his day's

Let me hear from you often for I am still anxious. Remember me kindly to all inquiring Friends.

Yours affectionatly   A Adams.

RC (MWA:Abigail Adams Letters); addressed by TBA: "M^rs: Mary Cranch / Braintree"; endorsed by Richard Cranch: "Letter from M^rs / A Adams (Ph^a:) / Octr 30. 1791." Some loss of text due to placement of the seal.

[1] AA's 9 Oct. letter from Brookfield has not been found.

[2] Upon their arrival in Philadelphia the Adamses moved into a house at the corner of Fourth and Arch streets. Tench Coxe had found it for them on short notice after JA wrote him for assistance on 20 Aug., declaring, "I have determined in all Events to remove my family into Philadelphia from Bush hill, on account of the many Inconveniences We experienced last Year in passing and repassing." JA added, "As the time is short, I expect to be obliged to some disadvantage. But any house and any rent is better than what We Suffered last year" (JA to Tench Coxe, 20 Aug., PHi; Tench Coxe to JA, 3 Sept., Adams Papers).

John Quincy Adams to Thomas Boylston Adams

My dear Brother.   Boston December 3. 1791.

I received last week your favour of the 17th: of last month, and found in it none of that tediousness which you seem to apprehend:[1] indeed I suspect your fears were in some measure dictated by your indolence, and that you make them a pretext in your own mind, to relieve you from the tediousness of writing: but this pretence must not serve you: for I can assure you, that your Letters will always be tedious to me, only in proportion to their brevity, and that you are by far the most tedious when you do not write at all.

The arguments which you mention to have been held in the house of Representatives with respect to the ratio of Representation, were very amusing, and I have not seen those contained in your Letter, in any of the newspapers. The final decision of 1 to 30,000 has given as far as my conversation extends, very general satisfaction here, though I see most of our members voted against it.[2] The distinction which you say was held up, relative to the characteristic qualities of the Representative and Senatorial branches of the Legislature, was as far as I remember first suggested by Montesquieu, and afterwards adopted by Rousseau. Great as these names are and prevailing as the opinion is, I consider it as one of the idlest and most groundless distinctions that ever entered into the brain of a statesmen. It may be true that an individual or a body of men sometimes is deficient in wisdom, though very honest and well meaning; but wisdom, ought to be the characteristic mark of every branch of a legislature; and without integrity, there never can be any wisdom. To speak in the legal phraseology, wisdom is integrity, and more. For in every situation in life, whether in a public or in a private capacity, as an individual, or as a member of the legislative body, every man who departs from the line of honesty, departs just so far from the line of wisdom. If your house of representatives is only honest, without wisdom, they can be at best but useless to the community; and if your Senate is only cunning and are not thoroughly honest, they must be much worse than useless.—[3] But I have not time to expatiate any further upon this subject.

Mᵣ Woodward goes to Philadelphia next week, and will be the bearer of this Letter; and also of Miss Adams's book. Your father subscribed for three setts; and I have the other two in my possession. If he wishes to have them forwarded, you will let me know. I have one besides, as I was myself a subscriber.[4]

The numbers of the 2ᵈ Vol: of the U.S. Gazette which I want are 98 and 101. I believe I mistook one of them in my former Letter.— You may forward them by any convenient opportunity. I hope the segars will come soon, as I begin to be upon allowance, with the old stock.

Mᵣ Dana is appointed chief Justice of our Supreme Court, and Mᵣ Dawes is nominated to fill the vacant seat upon the bench.— If there was any business done this promotion might be serviceable to the younger Counsel at the bar, in this Town; but it is almost totally at a stand.— Never at a lower ebb: however, we live in patient expectation of better times.

Adieu; love and duty to all the family.   J. Q. Adams.

RC (Adams Papers); addressed: "Mᵣ Thomas B. Adams. / Philadelphia."; endorsed: "Decʳ 3ᵈ 1791"; notation: "Honᵈ by Mᵣ Woodward."

[1] Not found.

[2] Reapportionment in the wake of the 1790 census remained a matter of contention in Congress and later the executive branch for almost six months after the House of Representatives first took up the issue on 31 Oct. 1791. While debate revolved around certain technical details—the number of representatives, the ratio of representatives to constituents, and the division of representatives among the states—the substantive question at its core was the balance of power between large and small states, northern and southern interests, and Federalist and Republican sentiments.

On 15 Nov. the House of Representatives voted to set the ratio of representation at 1:30,000, and on the 23d it voted not to revise that figure to 1:34,000. Of the seven members from Massachusetts in attendance, six— Fisher Ames, Shearjashub Bourne, Benjamin Goodhue, Theodore Sedgwick, George

Thacher, and Artemas Ward—opposed the former measure and supported the latter; only one—Elbridge Gerry—took the reverse stance. By contrast all nine members from Virginia backed the first proposal and resisted the second. On 24 Nov. the House passed an apportionment bill with a ratio of representation of 1:30,000 and a House of 112 members and sent the legislation to the Senate.

After two weeks of consideration, the Senate voted to amend the House bill by changing the ratio to 1:33,000 and the size of the House to 105 members, effectively reducing the influence of the larger states. Because the initial tally produced a tie, JA cast the deciding vote. A week later, when the Senate voted not to withdraw the amendment even though the House refused to agree to it, another deadlock ensued and JA again determined the result. Together the refusal of the House to accept the Senate amendment and the refusal of the Senate to withdraw it left the two chambers at loggerheads.

On 23 March 1792 the House and the Senate narrowly passed a compromise bill establishing a House of 120 members divided among the states without reference to a ratio of representation, an approach that southerners, particularly Virginians, believed was intended to diminish their influence. Ten days later George Washington, in the first exercise of the presidential veto power, rejected the compromise bill as unconstitutional because, first, no single ratio of representation yielded a House of the character prescribed and, second, the ratio of repre-

sentation for several states exceeded 1:30,000. After failing on 9 April to override Washington's veto, Congress on the 10th passed yet another apportionment bill, which, like the original Senate version, set the ratio at 1:33,000 and the size of the House at 105 members. Washington signed the new bill into law on 14 April (Rosemarie Zagarri, *The Politics of Size: Representation in the United States, 1776–1850*, Ithaca, N.Y., 1987, p. 134–140; Michel L. Balinski and H. Peyton Young, *Fair Representation: Meeting the Ideal of One Man, One Vote*, New Haven, Conn., 1982, p. 10–22; U.S. House, *Jour.*, 2d Cong., 1st sess., p. 444, 454–455, 459–460; U.S. Senate, *Jour.*, 2d Cong., 1st sess., p. 351–354, 356, 422; *Biog. Dir. Cong.*).

[3] Both Montesquieu and Rousseau attributed to senates the quality of wisdom, despite having very different understandings of their composition and function (M. N. S. Sellers, *Republican Legal Theory: The History, Constitution and Purposes of Law in a Free State*, N.Y., 2003, p. 11–13).

[4] Hannah Adams, *A View of Religions, in Two Parts*, 2d edn., Boston, 1791, Evans, No. 23102. Author Hannah Adams (1755–1831), a distant cousin of JA, wrote to him on 21 Feb. 1791 (Adams Papers) to ask whether she could dedicate her forthcoming book to him. JA replied in the affirmative on 10 March, "only requesting that all Titles literary or political may be omitted and that the Address may be only to John Adams Vice-President of the United States of America" (MB:Paine Trust). He subscribed for three copies of the book at that time (*DAB*).

Abigail Adams Smith to Abigail Adams

my Dear Mamma   New York December 10th 1791—

I received last Evening your Letter of the 3d inst—[1] I began to think you had almost forgotten me. now and then I hear from you by persons who have seen you— they tell me that you appear to enjoy your health the weather grows so severe that I am almost discourage from thinking of quiting my own fire side. M̥ Smith does not find it convenient at present to Leave his official and private business— the latter however is much the most advantageous lands which he purchased of the State last summer for 3/3 pr acre he can now dispose of to people who wish to settle upon them for 10 shillings— Coll⁰ Smith wishes me to come without him but I dont like this plan much altho I have no small share of Curiossity to see the Wonderfull City of Philadelphia—

with respect to the appointment I have no desire that Mʳ S— should receive it and we have it from authority that he will not—and there is but one Person that I do not wish should have it— he has played such a double game that I hope he may be disappointed if he wishes it— I am sure that it will be much more for our interest to continue here as things are situated and I have no disposition to sacrifise *substance* to *shadow* but *we* hear that it has been decided at Court that no Person belonging to the senate or House of representative can be appointed for there is an express article in [the] Constitution against it—and I hope some body wi[ll] raise a dust if this is infringed upon

Browns Wife came to me day after day untill I was quite tired of hearing of her and at last I gave her twenty five shillings for which I inclose her receipt— I sent the Biscuit by Capt Bailie and I found the order and receipt of Browns Wife all which I enclose—²

Mʳ Rodgers takes the Charge of this Letter— he has called twice upon me— he looks very dejected—Poor Man,—³ Mʳˢ Clarkson has a Son a week old and is very well—⁴ the rest of the family are well—

by Charles Storer I heard from our friends at Boston and Braintree— my Unkle Cranch was recovering—but Mʳˢ Smith is very unwell I fear she is not long for this world pray write as frequently as you can find time— the Chrildren are very well present my Duty to my Father and Love to Louisa— is Thomas absorb[ed in] Business that we do not hear a word from him

adieu yours

A Smith—

RC (Adams Papers); addressed: "Mʳˢ· Abigail Adams / Philadelphia—"; docketed: "E Smith to / A Adams / 1791." Some loss of text where the seal was removed.

¹ Not found.

² Not found. The schooner *Dolphin*, Capt. Benjamin Bailey, sailed as a packet between New York and Philadelphia. The vessel cleared New York on 26 Nov. and arrived at Philadelphia on 2 Dec. (*New York Daily Gazette*, 21 Nov., 26 Nov.; Philadelphia *Federal Gazette*, 2 Dec.).

³ Abigail Bromfield Rogers, wife of Daniel Denison Rogers, died in Boston on 7 Oct. (*Boston Gazette*, 10 Oct.).

⁴ William Smith Clarkson, the first child of Matthew and Belinda Smith Clarkson, was born on 2 Dec. (Trinity Church [New York, N.Y.] Registers, www.trinitywallstreet.org/history/?registers).

Mary Smith Cranch to Abigail Adams

Braintree December 11th 1791

I again take my pen to write to my dear sister tis a long time I know you think since you have heard from me. I have the same complaints to make of you, but once since you arriv'd in Philadelphia have I receiv'd a line from you— I know your time must have been much taken up in arranging your House & receiving company. this I hope & not sickness has been the reason I have not hear'd from you oftener— as for me, how long an attendance upon a sick chamber is to be my portion I know not— When I wrote you last[1] I believe I told you that mr Cranchs Leg was almost heal'd but that he had taken a great cold by going down stairs at an improper time it was a very naughty trick he did we were lathing & plastering the Parlour. & he was affraid they would not do it right unless he could direct them— He thought he could cut Laths for mr Prat—& then he did not like mr Belchers manner of laying some Bricks which had fallen out of the room where it had been fill'd in so took the pail of Morter & did it himself—but being Weak it made him sweat & then the gown was pull'd of & the fire must be put out—& where was you I hear you say—reasoning intreating & at last almost scolding before I could get him back into his chamber. this was the begining of November He took such a cold as to make him very sick it fell upon his lungs & distress him much for a fortnight— he then seem'd to be almost well, rode out, went to Weymouth got to work in his Shop & except that his cough was not gone he was geting well fast—but unluckily he took another sudden cold last week which has again attack'd his Lungs & confin'd him to his chamber & he is now very ill. His stomack loaded with Phelm he begins to thro' it of & I hope will be better soon he is rather low than feverish his strength was much diminish by his confinement with his Leg but he was not sensible of it till he went to work. If he ever gets well again I hope he will be more attentive to himself. His Leg is perfectly well & seems to be as strong as the other— You know how he always groans when his lungs are distress this is the case now, all day & night asleep, or awake, I am almost sick for want of sleep myself— Lucy stands by me a good attentive child or I could hold out— She spent last week with her sister mrs Norton as is daily expectation of geting to Bed—[2] mrs Nortons Mother is with her & will stay till she gets up again I am very glad she can be with her as I cannot—[3] Richard grows a fine

Boy & can say any thing he is told to & speaks very plain— I have heard from Haverhill last week mr Cranch had a Letter from Willm he does not say but they are well at his uncles he gets some business but not enough to pay his expences

Miss Eunice is to be remov'd to Dorchester this week to board at a mr Mosleys⁴ she regrets leaving Braintree but to stay at the Doctors this winter she cannot mrs Phipps is very crazy & take no care scarcly of her Family—⁵ I feel sorry to have her go I shall miss her sadly her good sense I shall pine after. & I fear she will miss me more than I shall her upon some accounts— She is in good spirits & in pretty tolarable health for her She sends her Love to you— mrs Quincy spent a few days with us not long since desires to be remember'd to you

Polly Tailor has been here & spent four or five days likes her place very well & sends her Duty to you— mr Jeffery is gone to sea for his Health⁶ If I had not receiv'd your Letter the Day I did your cellar would have been stop'd I had spoken to mr Pratt & was to have had the sea-weed carried the next day & it would have been a sad thing to have look'd so meddlesome— your Hogs are all kill'd & salted one & an half from mr Pratts which were good The shoulders are so large that I shall Bacon them I thought it would not do to salt them your Pigs which I had are very fine they weigh'd eighteen score & seven pounds & I have more than two packs & an half of Hogs fat for you— shall you want much more Bacon than [life?] hogs will give you your Pork will be very fine I believe

[Floryr?] has retain'd Celias child She ask'd Phebe to let her keep thanksgiving with her & then refus'd to let her take her back again Said she had abus'd her but tis not true. She is there without any cloaths but what she had on Phebe would not let her have them

The widow Howard is or has been a widow bewitch'd Jo Bass the shoe maker is the person accus'd but he will not marry her—

pray let me hear from you soon I pine for a Letter Love as due from your Brother Neice & affectionate Sister   Mary Cranch

RC (Adams Papers). Filmed at 11 Dec. 1790. Some loss of text due to wear at the fold.

¹ Not found.

² William Smith Norton, second child of Jacob and Elizabeth Cranch Norton, was born in Weymouth on 29 Dec. (*History of Weymouth*, 4:444).

³ That is, Mary Porter Norton (1735–

1810), mother-in-law of Elizabeth Cranch Norton (*Vital Records of Abington, Massachusetts, to the Year 1850*, 2 vols., Boston, 1912, 1:173, 2:319; *History of Hingham*, 3:93).

⁴ Eunice Paine moved to Dorchester to board with Thomas Moseley (1728–1796) and

his family (Eunice Paine to Robert Treat Paine, 29 Dec., MHi:Robert Treat Paine Papers; Boston *Polar-Star*, 26 Dec. 1796).

⁵ Mary Brackett (1761–1831) of Braintree, daughter of James Brackett and his second wife, Mary Glidden Brackett, had married Dr. Thomas Phipps in 1780. The fourth of their seven children was born in April 1791 (Herbert I. Brackett, *Brackett Genealogy: Descendants of Anthony Brackett of Portsmouth and Captain Richard Brackett of Braintree*, Washington, D.C., 1907, p. 527, 537, 539; Amherst, N.H., *Farmer's Cabinet*, 22 Oct. 1831).

⁶ Patrick Jeffery (ca. 1748–1812), husband of Mary Wilkes Storke Hayley Jeffery and

partner with Joseph Russell Jr. in a Boston mercantile firm, sailed round-trip from Boston to the Madeiras aboard the brig *Mermaid*, Capt. Moses Grinnell, departing during the first week of December and returning during the last week of May 1792 (George Lyman Kittredge, *The Old Farmer and His Almanack*, Boston, 1904, p. 12–13; Boston *Columbian Centinel*, 1 Jan. 1791, 7 Dec.; Boston *Independent Chronicle*, 31 May 1792; Survey of Federal Archives, Division of Professional and Service Projects, Works Progress Administration, comps., *Ship Registers and Enrollments of Boston and Charlestown, 1789–1795*, Boston, 1942, p. 130–131).

Abigail Adams to Mary Smith Cranch

my dear sister   Philadelphia december 18 1791

I wrote to you on the 27 of Nov^br but company comeing in call'd me from my pen, and I have not since had leisure to reassume it. I have so little Time that I can call my own whilst here that I think when I return to Braintree I ought without suffering from any reflections to be able to live retired. on Monday Evenings our House is open to all who please to visit me. on twesdays my domestick affairs call for me to arrange them & to labour pretty well too, for the wednesdays dinners which we give every week to the amount of sixteen & 18 persons which are as many as we can accommodate at once in our Thousand dollors House on thursday the replacing & restoring to order occupies my attention the occasional intercourse of dinning abroad returning visits &c leaves me very few hours to myself. I feel that day a happy one, when I can say I have no engagement but to my Family I have a cleaver sober honest & Neat black woman as my daily cook. in this respect I am happier than formerly. I always hire for company. the greatest trouble I have, is that mrs Brisler is chiefly confind to her Bed wholy unable to do the least thing for herself or Family. she was better after I came here, but a return of the intermitting fever together with her old weakness & complaints not only deprives her of her usefulness, but is a great incumberance to me, and takes up much of the Time of my help. in short I know not how I get through, for I have no other help than those I brought with me except the cook. I have been very well myself till about a fortnight since. I have labourd under complaints [. . . .]¹ I am still afflicted. mr Adams is recoverd from his com-

244

plaints but labours under a great cold. Thomas has escaped better than I feard from the Rhumatism. it threatned him for several weeks Louissa is very well. cealia requests me to inquire after her child & prays you would write to me & inform her if it is well. mrs otis & cousin Betsy are well. we live Socible & Friendly together. in many respects I am much better off than when I lived out of Town. expence is not to be taken into consideration that is almost beyond calculation. What a dreadfull blow this defeat of Sinclair & his Army?[2] my Heart bleads for the Relatives of as worthy officers as ever fought or fell but, the justice the policy the wisdom of this cruel enterprize lies with higher powers to investigate than mine.

Your kind Letters of Novbr 6th & 11th came safe to Hand and made me truly happy[3] So little hopes had I of the recovery of our dear and valuable Friend that I feard to hear from you; I could never have imagind that a Leg such as his was, & which appeard to be so far gone in a mortification, could possibly have been restored & that so soon— thanks to that all gracious Providene whose kindness has been so frequently displayd towards us— I heard last week from mrs smith and her little ones.[4] they were all well. you begin I suppose to feel anxious for mrs Norten. I hope to hear in due time that she has a daughter. I feel anxious about our House at Braintree There was a place in the Roof that Leakd much. I sent for two Carpenters but they could not find out the place. I wish it might be lookd too. I spoke with Brother about it, but fear he has not thought about it. I see by the paper that mr Jeffrie is gone to the Madarics for his Health. I want to know how Polly does & how she is likd. I often think of your Neighbours saying she was as necessary to him as his daily Bread. I miss her very much in things which it will be hard for any other person ever to make up to me, in that ready offerd service which prevented my wishes, and which is always so pleasing. yet she balanced the account sometimes by the vexation which she occasiond me. I wish her well, and shall always value her good qualities, and freely credit her for them cealia is as good as I could expect, but would soon be led way if I did not strickly guard her. Katy has all the dispositions in the world [as] sterns says,[5] but wants experience, in a Service which is quite New to her. She is faithfull in her duty, but poor Girl has h[er] sister & two children to look after. in short I think sometimes it cost me as dearly for honesty & fidelity as it would for knavery and I seem to have got an entailment that follows me through the world, particularly a certain degree of sickness that I must take charge of— however it is I hope a part of the portion of good which I ought to do. if so I am in fault to complain— remember me kindly to all Friends mrs Payne I often think of. give my Love to her & tell her I hope to see her early in the spring with my other Friends pray if I did not mention the desk before give for it what you think it reasonably worth, and ask the dr for the money. let me hear from you as often as you can and be assured of the sincere affection / of your sister   A Adams

RC (MWA:Abigail Adams Letters); addressed by TBA: "M$^{rs:}$ Mary Cranch / Braintree"; endorsed by Richard Cranch: "Letter from M$^{rs.}$ / A Adams. Ph$^{a:}$ / Decr 18. 1791." Some loss of text where the seal was removed and due to a torn manuscript.

[1] One line at the top of the page has been cut off.

[2] On 4 Nov. an American army sent into the Ohio country under the command of Maj. Gen. Arthur St. Clair to subdue the Miami and Shawnee Indians was itself overwhelmed in a surprise attack. More than 900 of the approximately 1,400 Americans present—regulars, levies, and militia as well as women and children—were killed, wounded, or went missing, including 69 of the 124 officers (Wiley Sword, *President Washington's Indian War: The Struggle for the Old Northwest, 1790–1795*, Norman, Okla., 1985, p. 145–203).

[3] Neither letter has been found.

[4] AA2 to AA, 10 Dec., above.

[5] Laurence Sterne, *A Sentimental Journey through France and Italy*, ch. 20, "Montreuil."

Abigail Adams to Cotton Tufts

my dear sir   Philadelphia Dec^{br} 18th 1791

Tis more than two months since I left you yet I have neither written a word to you or heard from you. Since I left Home, I have been much occupied removeing, and living in the city subjects us to company at all times, so much so that I must either be denying myself through the whole day, or appoint one evening in the week as a publick Evening. this I have found to be the most agreeable to those strangers who are daily brought to this place either by buisness or curiosity, and to those who are more imediatly connected as members of the same body with us, & who wish to keep up an intercourse, but are become too numerous to do it in any other way. we have also found it expedient to see company to dinner one day in every week, so that a good House wife as I profess myself to be must be fully occupied. I have had more Health since my return here than for many Months before, and I hope to run away from the Ague in the spring, if congress will rise soon enough, but weighty concerns occupy them, and the important one of Representation has occasiond great discussions of the subject, but no intemperate heat. yet the great fish have a wonderfull appetite for the small fish, and the old dominion Strugles hard for an over balance in the scale. what is surprizing, is to see Some persons helping them, who mean well, but do not seem to apprehend the weight of the Negro Representitives as mr King calls them. the black cattle in the Northern states might as well claim to be represented. one of the southern rep's observed in debate that if virgina had been fully represented in senate the Question would not have gone as it has (mr Lee is absent).[1] the debates of congress are most misirably given to the publick, as the Members themselves declare. the sad and dreadfull Havock of our Army at the west ward cast a Gloom over us all. some of the best officers who remain to us after the Peace have fallen here. all our Boston youths who were officers are amongst the slain. a son of col Cobb I have heard much regreeted.[2] in short tis such a stroke as we Scarcly experienced through the whole of the War. not even Bradocks defeat is said to have caused such Slaughter. a poor Gouty infirm General, always unsuckselsfull, a misirable Bandity of undisiplind Troops—an excellent Choir of officers—who I am told went out like Lambs to the Slaughter, having no prospect of conquering— I apprehend much uneasiness will ensue—what is to be done is not yet determind? for Foreign affairs, mr *Madisson* is to go to *France*, and a mr pinckny who was an officer from S carolina and lost a Limb in the service, will be Nominated for England he sustains an amiable good character—[3] I presume congress will set Six months if not longer.[4]

with regard to our private affairs, sir mr Adams wishes you to engage mr Loud to make and have ready by spring two sashes for to make windows from my Chamber and two small ones for the chamber over that, and he thinks it would be best to paint the House again.[5] at what season can that be best accomplishd?

I should be obliged to you sir if you could engage a person to procure me two beds at vendue Bolsters & pillows I was obliged to Borrow all last summer. I would chuse they should be of the best kind, and you will think of me for Beaf in the season of it and a cask of Tongues, two of them I should like to lay in as I found them more usefull than large hams—and I should think it best to secure six Barrels more cider than we have. if we live we do not mean to remain here a week after congress rises even tho it should be in Feb[ry]

in Jan[ry] you will receive some interest for me. I wish you would send mrs Cranch 5 cords of wood on my account, but do not let even her know from what quarter it comes. mr Cranchs long sickness must have embarassed them. and there is a widow dawson very old and infirm, be so good as to direct mrs cranch to inquire into her necessities and to lay out two dollors for her in wood or other necessaries—[6] ‡ a mark of that kind in your Letter will inform me that what I request will be Complied with—

I hope you enjoy better Health this winter than in the summer past, and that you will take good care of yourself when the spring approaches. my best regards attend your worthy Family and all other Friends—

yours most / affectionatly   A Adams.

RC (Adams Papers); addressed by TBA: "Honble: Cotton Tufts Esqr: / Weymouth"; endorsed: "Mrs A. Adams / Dec. 18. 1791"; notation: "N°. 1."

[1] Senator Richard Henry Lee of Virginia did not take his seat in the 2d Congress until 21 Dec. (U.S. Senate, *Jour.*, 2d Cong., 1st sess., p. 358).

[2] William Gray Cobb (1773–1791), an ensign under St. Clair, was a son of Col. David and Eleanor Bradish Cobb of Taunton. At the time of his son's death, David Cobb (1748–1830), Harvard 1766, was chief justice of the Bristol County Court of Common Pleas, major general in the Massachusetts militia, and speaker of the state house of representatives (Bradford Adams Whittemore, *Memorials of the Massachusetts Society of the Cincinnati*, Boston, 1964, p. 106–108).

[3] On 21 Dec. George Washington nominated three men as U.S. ministers plenipotentiary: Thomas Pinckney to Britain, Gouverneur Morris to France, and William Short to the Netherlands. Rumors that James Madison would receive the appointment to

France had circulated for months. In a letter to Thomas Jefferson of 29 Sept., written from Paris, Short reported, "A letter from America informs me that the delay in the appointment of the minister here is supposed to proceed from your endeavouring to prevail on Madison to accept it and his hesitating and taking time to consider. As the person who writes me is a great friend of yours as well as mine I should have supposed what he said well founded if your letter did not prevent it" (Jefferson, *Papers*, 22:174, 262). See also WSS to JA, 21 Oct., above.

[4] Congress sat from 24 Oct. to 8 May 1792 (*Biog. Dir. Cong.*).

[5] Possibly Jacob Loud (1747–1820) of Weymouth (*History of Weymouth*, 3:376).

[6] Probably Mary Veasey Dawson, widow of George Dawson (Sprague, *Braintree Families*).

Thomas Boylston Adams to William Cranch

dear William   Philadelphia January 23^d: 1792.

The kind of silence which we have observed toward each other since I left Massachusetts, is not at all congenial with my feelings or disposition. You had just embarked in a cause in which I feel myself particularly interested; to know the success of the enterprize thus far would give me much satisfaction; the object of this letter is in some measure to draw from the source of information a detail of events, so far as they have contributed to success in the undertaking; The last time we heard of you, was in a letter from JQA, you had been engaged with him in supporting the petition of Braintree.[1] I have never heard the result of the affair, I have no doubt however, the parent received the ablest support from her Sons. The instance was somewhat singular, and I think the wisdom of Braintree was never better exercised than in employing her own Counsel upon the occasion. This Season of the year is generally remarkably gay in your part of the Country, and for the most part favorable to business of all kinds. I hear no complaints in this place of the scarcity of Clients or any thing else. People appear to be hastening to wealth rather too easily; all classes have been engaged in speculation, except those whose hands were tied; the inclination however has been wanting to very few; this has been attended with many bad consequences, it has opperated as a discouragement to industry, because the profits of the sober trader, were too slow for the *fashion*; the man who had been accustomed to calculate his wealth in proportion to his exertions, saw his neighbor who was lately his inferior both in fame and fortune, in a single day, without any apparent industry of his own, out strip him in both. Banks, Tontines, Canals, Lotteries, in short every thing which ingenuity can invent to gratify this spirit, are the rage of the present day. In New York, conversation is thought very uninteresting and insipid, if a man does not talk of Millions. They have within a week or two established another Bank which is called The Million Bank of N York.[2] A number of Gentlemen are about offering to lend Government two Millions of dollars at 5 p^r Cent, instead of the loan which is negociating in Holland. But I hope you won't think me infected with the Scripophobia. These things will find an end shortly. These unwieldy fortunes will change Masters; for the generality of the present owners, have not sense enough to keep them. Tis the opinion of sober Citizens that the monied interest as 'tis called, is the least informed of any set of people in the Country. That is, they think nothing of the great Bank—the Government, upon the sucess and preservation of which, all their wealth in the first instance depends.

We are happy to hear that your father has recovered from the alarming state in which we left him.

Cicero, has been greatly neglected by me this winter, I believe for want of an help mate. The sort of life, one is obliged to lead in this place, is not very favorable to literature of any kind. I have kept myself tolerably free from the vortex of disipation, but I am still subjected to more than is good.

You will please to present the love of our family to our friends.

249

Mine *particularly* to some, whom amidst all the gay circles I have not forgotten.

Affectionately yours   Thomas B Adams

RC (OCHP:William Cranch Papers, Mss fC891c RM); addressed: "William Cranch Esqr: / Haverhill"; endorsed: "T.B. Adams. / Jany. 23d. 1792. / Answd. feb. 18th."

[1] JQA to TBA, 28 Oct. 1791, above.

[2] Federalist taxation policies and the creation of the Bank of the United States combined to create a significant increase in paper wealth, which in turn led to considerable speculative business activity and a real estate boom throughout the United States, especially in major cities like Philadelphia and New York.

The Million Bank—one of three new banks attempting to establish themselves in New York around this time—reputedly sold thousands of shares within just a few hours, oversubscribing its million-dollar goal by a factor of ten. A few days later, the subscribers determined to merge the three new banks into a single "State Bank" designed to compete with potential branch banks of the Bank of the United States (Curtis P. Nettels, *The Emergence of a National Economy 1775–1815*, N.Y., 1962, p. 121–122; Young, *Democratic Republicans*, p. 220; New York *Gazette of the United States*, 18 Jan. 1792).

Thomas Boylston Adams to William Cranch

Dear William   Philadelphia Jan 28th 1792.

This day week I put a letter into the Post Office for you under cover to my Brother JQA. and this morning I have receiv'd your many dated letter, the last is the 16th:.[1] I complained in my other letter of our long silence, and am happy our thoughts should so well unite in breaking the charm. I should not have undertaken so suddenly to answer your letter, but for this circumstance. The last clause in your letter contains a few observations upon the Indian War, and a request for information concerning the original causes and the present continuation of Hostilities. This has been the enquiry, in this part of the Country; our newspapers are filled with invectives against *heads of departments*, which tho they come in an oblique direction yet they strike very forcibly upon The ——. It is a fundamental principle you know in the Constitution of England, as well as in most other Governments, that the King can do no wrong. This principle opperates as powerfully in this Country as in any other, only perhaps with this difference, that there is more *freedom* of expression and thought here, than in England. But the Minister of the War department has been and still is violently censured for continuing this War; but it is well known that he is but a Servant of Government; he however is the only mark too shoot at—and if this sort of warfare will kill him, I think he has but little chance for his life.[2] The people are not satisfyed that this is either a just or beneficial war, and they have repeatedly demanded information upon this head. Until this day they were as ignorant of the business as the people in your part of the Country. The enclosed, is the only official information that has appeared, and I am very happy that your request, and the means of gratisfying it, were put into my hands almost at the same instant.[3] Even this I fear will not entirely hush the clamors. The members of the house of Reps, are many of them dealing out to us, a kind of Newspaper Stuff as tis called, and they appear very unwilling to allow the demands upon the Treasury, to which this War gives rise. The first year, Congress were called upon for 100,000 dollars upon this score, the second year the sum was more than threble, and the last year the expense is calculated at a Million and a quarter.[4] The People have a right to be informed of the probable advantages of these expenditures, it ought also to be known whether they are absolutely necessary. Governor St Clair is in this City; he is not looked upon with much complacency, however whether his conduct has been culpable or not is still a question.—[5] He has certainly been unsucessfull, which in former ages was considered but one degree removed from a crime.

Sub— There is one part of your letter that has affected me in a very different manner from the rest. You will easily imagine what it was. I am almost afraid to write any thing upon the subject; but I will say this, that the destruction of our *whole frontire army*, did not affect me so *nearly*. In this I believe you will think me safe. How it happens that I should feel more interested in the health happiness and wellfare of that Y— L.— than in that of any other with whom I am equally acquainted, I am unable to conjecture; but such I acknowledge is the case. I shall not write enthousiastically upon this point, but will only say with My Uncle Toby and [. . .] She must not die, if she does, in my mind the brightest [star?] in H— will be extinguished. —Rosa.

My last letter was an attempt at describing [. . . .]ing features of the Times. The Rage for Scrip—is perhaps the m[ost] prominent; The Indian War is second at least. These things are exactly opposite in themselves—for the expenses of the War have counteracted all the benefit derived to the Govern^t from Speculation. I am glad to hear that business in your line has but one alternative, I presume you're in no need of a memento from me to perseverance. The Lawyers here as well as in Massachusetts can not boast of their business at first setting out. But there is this difference, that the old Lawyers here do have enough and to spare, so that age and experience are sure to be rewarded. But in the present state of business among you, there is no certainty upon this head. I see by the Newspapers they are making JQA a consequential committee man I hope he has something to excuse his negligence to his friends in this part of the world.[6] My best regards are at your disposal to Mr White's and other families, and my best wishes for you and your's.

Thomas B Adams

RC (OCHP:William Cranch Papers, Mss fC891c RM); addressed: "William Cranch Esqr: / Massachusetts / Haverhill"; endorsed: "T.B. Adams / Jany. 28th: 1792. / Answ^d. february 18th."; docketed: "Decr. 1. 1792." Some loss of text where the seal was removed.

[1] William Cranch's letter to TBA has not been found.

[2] An article signed "A" in the Philadelphia *American Daily Advertiser*, 6 Jan., opined, "That the military arrangements, and other governmental operations with respect to Indian affairs, have not been well ordered, is a truth as incontestable as the consequences have been deplorable. . . . Measures injurious to the reputation, the revenue, or the peace of the community demand immediate explanation, and if not promptly done, the minister should attone for the contempt by a loss of confidence, a loss of office, nay a *forfeiture*, of more consequence to him perhaps than both."

[3] The enclosure has not been found but was probably Henry Knox's "The Causes of the Existing Hostilities between the United States, and Certain Tribes of Indians North-West of the Ohio," Philadelphia, 1792, Evans, No. 24944. On 16 Jan., George Washington had written to Knox noting that "as the circumstances which have engaged the United States in the present Indian War may some of them be out of the public recollection, and others perhaps be unknown, it may ap-

pear advisable that you prepare and publish, from authentic documents, a statement of those circumstances, as well as of the measures which have been taken, from time to time, for the re-establishment of peace and friendship." Knox's response was published first as a broadside on 26 Jan. and then reprinted in the Philadelphia *Federal Gazette* and *The Mail* on 28 January.

[4] While Knox had originally suggested in 1789 that the cost to suppress the Northwest Indians would be around $200,000, by 1791, Congress had appropriated $313,000. After Maj. Gen. Arthur St. Clair's defeat in November at Fort Wayne, Knox requested that Congress authorize an additional $675,000 for a total to that point of slightly over $1 million (Francis Paul Prucha, *The Sword of the Republic: The United States Army on the Frontier 1783–1846*, N.Y., 1969, p. 19–20, 22; *Amer. State Papers: Indian Affairs*, 1:199).

[5] St. Clair arrived in Philadelphia on 21 Jan. 1792, presumably to defend himself against charges stemming from the Fort Wayne defeat (Philadelphia *Federal Gazette*, 23 Jan.).

[6] See JQA to TBA, 1 Feb., note 2, below.

John Quincy Adams to Thomas Boylston Adams

My dear Brother,—   Boston, February 1st, 1792.

I have been for more than three weeks indebted to you for two very agreeable Letters, which Mr. Otis brought from you.[1] They would not have remained so long unanswered but for a variety of circumstances which have concurred to engross all my time during that period. It is possible that you may have observed in the Centinel about a month since, that a Committee of 21 inhabitants at this Town was chosen in town-meeting, to report to the town what measures it might be proper to take in order to reform the present state of the police of the town; and you may have noticed that my name was among those of several of the most respectable characters in this Town upon that Committee; if you read the Centinels in course as they arrive, you must have seen that this Committee reported a certain plan, which after being debated in town meeting for three days was finally rejected by the votes of 700 men against more than 500 who were in favor of its adoption.[2] If you have noticed all these circumstances, it is probable you may feel some degree of curiosity to know something further upon the subject: You will perhaps wish to be informed what it is, that has thus agitated the whole town of Boston these five or six weeks, how it happened that I was placed upon this same Committee, and why the report was rejected—I will tell you, at the risque of fatiguing you with a tedious narration, which you may throw aside if it should become intolerable.

The Government of this town, in its corporate capacity, like that of all the other Towns in this Commonwealth, is a pure democracy; all the affairs of the town are transacted by the inhabitants in town meeting assembled, or by committees appointed by them; excepting certain powers which are vested in the Select-men, and which are very immaterial. The by-laws of the corporation are supposed to be enacted by the whole body of the people, and to be put in force by trials before Justices of the Peace.— In consequence of this system, the fact is, that no by-laws are enforced at all, and the inhabitants are subjected to various inconveniences, for the want of some internal regulation. Several attempts have been heretofore made to introduce a reformation, and to induce the inhabitants to request for a City charter. Those attempts have always been ineffectual, and the inconveniences have continued. About 6 weeks since, a town meeting was called, where after a debate upon the subject, in which the objects to be reformed were fully laid open and explained, the Committee, which I have already mentioned, were chosen.— It was a subject upon which I felt altogether uninterested, having been so short a time an inhabitant of the Town, and suffering personally very little from the inconveniences which had occasioned the complaints from whence that town-meeting resulted. I happened however quite accidentally to be present at the meeting and was nominated by Dr. Jarvis, to be a member of the Committee, and was accordingly chosen. He was indeed the last man in this town from whom I should have expected such a nomination, and I cannot very readily account for his motives.[3] Dr. Welsh asked him what his object was; and he answered, "that this Country were under great obligations to my father, and he thought it very proper that some notice should be taken of his Son; that he observed I generally attended the town-meetings, and appeared to interest myself in the affairs of the town; that I was a sensible young man" (excuse the vanity of the relation) "and he wished to hear my sentiments upon this subject."— I mention these circumstances because it will I believe, be somewhat surprising to your father, as it was to myself, that the first public notice ever shown me by the town of Boston should proceed from the nomination of Dr. Jarvis. I may now proceed to the transaction of the business itself.— The Committee met several times, and after discussing the subject amply and deliberating with great coolness and harmony agreed upon the plan which was proposed, and which you have perhaps read. The agreement was unanimous, with one exception, which was Mr. B. Austin, commonly called Honestus; he set his face against the reform from the beginning and did not agree to one article of the report. All the rest, though many of them differing widely as the poles, in most of their political sentiments, were fully agreed upon this point. When the report was debated in town-meeting Austin opposed it with the utmost degree of vehemence and absurdity. "It was to destroy the liberties of the people; it was a resignation of the *sovereignty* of the town; it was a link in the chain of Aristocratic influence; it was intended in its operation to throw the whole burden of taxation upon the poor." In short his speeches were such a farrago of nonsense and folly that it was hardly possible to imagine they could have any effect at all. On the other hand, Sullivan and Jarvis and Otis with several other Gentlemen argued the whole subject over and over with more popular eloquence than I ever saw exhibited upon any other occasion; yet upon the final Question, the result was as I have stated, seven hundred men, who looked as if they had been collected from all the Jails on the continent, with Ben. Austin like another Jack Cade, at their head outvoted by their numbers all the combined weight and influence of Wealth of Abilities and of Integrity, of the whole Town.— From the whole Event I have derived some instruction, and above all a confirmation of my abhorrence and contempt of simple democracy as a Government; but I took no part in the debate.— It was indeed a very good opportunity, that was offered me, of opening a political career, especially as I had been put upon the Committee; but for a variety of reasons I chose at least to postpone to some future period, my appearance as a speaker in town meeting; the principal of which was a want of confidence in myself, which operated most forcibly upon me. I hope, however, the time will come, when I shall not be so much oppressed by my diffidence.

But the sequel of the story is no less curious than the rest. The day after the question was decided, Russell the printer demanded of Austin, in the public street, satisfaction, for a personal insult he had received from him at the town-meeting; and upon Austin's refusing to give satisfaction, Russell treated him with every possible indignity, and gave him a severe corporeal bruising: upon which Austin spread abroad that Russell was the mere instrument of *aristocratic* revenge, and that he did not act from resentment for his own injury, but at the instigation of a few rich men, who were enraged at seeing the success with which he had advocated the cause of *the people*.— And such was the obsequious servility of his rabble, that in consequence of this suggestion, several hundreds of them assembled the same evening; threatened to pull down Russell's printing office, and the houses of the *aristocrats* who wished to enslave the people, and actually paraded the streets with clubs, and with violent menaces for two or three hours: however they did no real mischief, and the matter seems now to have blown over pretty generally; though the partizans on both sides are still warm and ready to quarrel.[4] I have from the beginning taken the part of a spectator rather than that of an actor in the scene, and I think the whole affair has given me some additional knowledge of human nature.

The present is quite a busy time in our political world; there are several other subjects upon which I could write you other letters as long and as tedious as this; but I must reserve some of my information for your father, to whom I am ashamed not to have written this long time. I intend soon to give him some account of another occurrence, which has made not a little political agitation in our atmosphere.

I have not much more to say to you respecting myself. Our Court of Common Pleas have sat again since I wrote you; I argued one more cause, and was successful. I gain my causes, but I get no business; that is at as low an ebb as ever, but I am tolerably habituated to the lot, and say, with Ancient Pistol, "si fortuna me tormenta, il sperare me contenta."[5]

The Petition from the North Parish in Braintree is hitherto successful. The Committee of the General Court before whom I mentioned to you our having argued the point, reported in favour of the petitioners: the bill for incorporating the town of *Quincy*, has past the Senate and is now before the House of Representatives. Hichborn has been indefatigable in his opposition to the business in every stage of it, but has not yet been able to defeat us.— The Question will not be finally decided till next week.

Mr. Cranch has been in town about a fortnight upon this affair, and attending the Court of Common Pleas. He has recovered to all appearance from his sickness, though he does not look so healthy, or in such spirits, as he was wont. Our other friends are all well.

Your brother,   J. Q. Adams.

MS not found. Printed from MHS, *Procs.*, 2d ser., 4:62–65 (1887–1889).

[1] Not found.

[2] The Boston *Columbian Centinel*, 31 Dec. 1791, noted the formation of a committee "to take into consideration the present state of the town, and adopt such measures, as may conduce to lessen, if not remove, the present embarrassment, either by an application to the Legislature to add new officers, with an increase of power, to the Corporation, or take such orders on the present police, as to give energy and respectability to the executive authority of all the Town Officers." The paper went on to reprint the committee's report and the debates around it on 14 and 21 Jan. 1792. On 28 Jan., it gave the final vote tally as 517 in favor of the committee's report and 701 against it at a meeting that JQA described in his Diary as "very disorderly. Hall overflowing" (D/JQA/18, 26 Jan., APM Reel 21). The plan would have divided Boston into wards and created a town council with increased authority to appoint officers and enforce the by-laws.

[3] For Dr. Charles Jarvis and his quarrel with JA, see vol. 8:413, note 2.

[4] Benjamin Russell (1761–1845) was the owner and editor of the Boston *Columbian Centinel*, a Federalist newspaper. At the town meeting, Russell was selected to count votes along with Benjamin Austin Jr. Austin initially accepted the task but then refused, saying he would not serve with "*such a fellow as Ben Russell*." Russell took offense and the next day, 27 Jan., called Austin out, threatening and spitting on him. That and subsequent evenings, a mob of mechanics—who supported Austin—gathered to tear down Russell's offices. They were stopped by the authorities.

Austin sued Russell for assault and battery, asking for £1,000 in damages. The Supreme Judicial Court found in Austin's favor in March 1793 but fined Russell only £1 (*DAB*; Philadelphia *Mail*, 25 Feb. 1792; Boston *Columbian Centinel*, 27 March 1793).

[5] Shakespeare, *Henry IV, Part 2*, Act V, scene v, line 102.

Richard Cranch to John Adams

Hon[d.] and dear Brother   Braintree Feb: 1[st.] 1792.

I have lately received a Letter from my worthy Friend and Nephew M[r.] William Bond of Portland, informing me that he wishes, thro' my intervention, to offer his Service to Congress as an assistant in the Mint of the United States which he supposes will be soon established. I have reason to think that very few Persons can be found at present in the United States who are so well acquainted with the Art of cutting and engraving the Dyes, or of working in Gold and Silver as he is. He was a chief Workman, while he resided in London, in making a most magnificent Service of Plate for the Empress of Russia, and has had all the advantages which that City affords for making himself a compleat Master in that Branch of Business. He particularly excells in the Art of Engraving. His moral Character is unimpeached, and his Circumstances in life are very respectable. I have enclosed a Copy of that part of his Letter to me which respects the subject of the Mint, together with some specimens of his Engraving of Dyes. If you should think him deserving the Notice of Congress in the Line in which he offers himself, you would oblige me much in using your Influence in making him known to that Department where the Business of establishing the Mint is to be conducted. A Line from you on the subject, after you have made such Enquiery as your Goodness will prompt you to make, will be very obliging to me.[1] The affair of incorporating the North Precinct of Braintree together with the Farms and Squantum, into a seperate Town, is now before the Gen[l] Court. I have been very closely engaged in the Matter for three Weeks past, as Agent for the Petitioners. We have had all the force of M[r.] Hitchborn against us, but he has not yet succeeded. The Report of the joint Committee who came to view the Premises, was in our favour, that we should be set off as a distinct Town together with the Farms and Squantum, but not to include Knights Neck. This Report was accepted in Senate, and leave given to bring in a Bill for that purpose, and was concurred by the House. A Bill was brought in accordingly (drawn by your Son) which passed the Senate, and was sent down to the House last Friday. I came home the next Day (being very unwell) and have not yet heard of its fate in the House, but I think it will pass. The Senate have named the Town *Quincy*.

Please to give my most affectionate Regards to Sister Adams, and let her know that my Gratitude to her is more than I can express, for her assistance to me in my late dangerous situation, when on the verge of Death; and for all the concern of a Sister and Friend that she has since had for my Recovery.– "Blessed are the Mercifull for they shall obtain Mercy".

Your aged and dear Mother, and your Brother and Family are well. Uncle Quincy is as well as usual. M[rs.] Norton is so well as to get down stairs again, and her little Boys are finely. The other Branches of our Friends are in usual Health as far as I have heard.

I hope this will meet you and your Family under agreeable Circumstances; and that every Blessing may attend you is the Wish of your obliged and affectionate Brother   Richard Cranch.

My dear M^rs. Cranch and Lucy send their Love to you all.

RC (Adams Papers); addressed: "To / the Vice President / of the / United States. / Philadelphia."; endorsed: "ans^d. 28. March 1792"; docketed: "A Letter from / Richard Cranch / Feb 1792."

[1] For William Bond of Falmouth (now Portland), Maine, Cranch's nephew by marriage, see vol. 7:176. He was probably one of the 400 craftsmen employed by silversmiths George Heming and William Chawner in 1775 to produce two complete dinner services and dessert sets for Catherine the Great—likely the largest single commission received in England from a foreign client in the eighteenth century (Hugh Honour, *Goldsmiths & Silversmiths*, N.Y., 1971, p. 206).

Bond's engravings are apparently no longer extant, but a copy of his letter of 3 Dec. 1791 to Richard Cranch in Cranch's hand is in the Adams Papers. In that letter, Bond notes that he has heard of the possible establishment of a U.S. mint and believes that his twenty years of metal-working experience, "some of the time in large Manufactorys in London," would be of use in the new office. "I have thoughts," he continues, "of offering my Services to the United States in the Line I have mentioned above, either to work at, or conduct the working part of the Gold and Silver; or to repair, or, if tho't able to do it sufficiently well, to cut such Dies as may be wanted, or as many of them as I can, or in any Line of the Department in which I could be usefull."

JA's reply to Cranch's request has not been found, but on 12 April 1792, Cranch again wrote to JA thanking him for a letter of 28 March and noting Bond's willingness to "accept of a subordinate Employment in the Mint Department, as his Business in Navigation is not so profitable now as it has been for some years past. . . . If when the Officers of the Mint are nominated you could introduce M^r. Bond as a Candidate, I think you would thereby promote the publick Good in that Department, and at the same time oblige a capeable, honest and worthy Man" (Adams Papers).

The establishment of a U.S. mint had been under discussion ever since the Constitution granted Congress exclusive authority to coin money. Congress formally established the mint in Philadelphia in April; David Rittenhouse was appointed its first director (Jesse P. Watson, *The Bureau of the Mint: Its History, Activities and Organization*, Baltimore, 1926, p. 3-7, 17).

Abigail Adams to John Quincy Adams

my dear son   Philadelphia Fe^bry 5 1792—

Tis a very long time since I wrote to you, or heard from you I have been more engaged in company than is my choice but living in Town has necessarily devolved more of it upon us than heretofore, and tho we have not seen more than in reality we ought to considering our publick Character, yet it is much of an Egyptian task, and fall some times much heavier upon me than my state of health will bear. we have regularly dined from 16 to 18 and sometimes 20 person every wednesday in the week Since I removed into Town, and on Mondays I see company. the rest of the week is or might be altogether taken up in Par[ties] abroad, many of which I have been obliged to decline on account of my Health. Your sister has been with me these 5 weeks and william, the col & Charles part of the time. they will leave me in a week or 10 days, and when we are to meet again, is in the Bosom of futurity The col & Family embark for England in the March Packet, not in a Publick capacity, but under such advantageous private contracts that tho it is with the utmost regreet I can consent to the seperation yet I think I ought not to say any thing to discourage them.¹ tis probable two years will be the least time they will be absent. the matter has been only a few days in agitation, and the determiniation of going in the March packet will hasten them from hence Sooner than I am willing to part with them. I am glad to see one of the Family in a prosperous situation, as from the col account I have reason to believe he is. I wish your Father would propose Thomass going with him. I think it would be advantageous to his Health and would give him a good opportunity of seeing Something more of the world he could be in the col's Family and of service to him in his transactions but I dare not venture upon the proposition, and as the cols going was communicated to him but yesterday I believe the thought has not yet occurd to him. Congress proceed so slowly in Buisness that I fear I shall be detaind here till May to my great regreet Post office Bill Representation & Indian War are great subjects of debate, the latter a melancholy one indeed— the secretary at War and of the Treasury are attackd and handled pretty Roughly in the News papers. your transactions for me in the Buisness way met my approbation. Cheeseman however did not act the Man of Honour and shall not be employd by me again. if I found Cealia, as I did, he was to have only 8 dollors which he was to call upon me for here. I never gave him any Authority to apply to you. When you receive the Rent of the House, Buy a Peice of Linnen and cambrick for them & get cousin Lucy Cranch to make your shirts and pay her for doing it out of the Rent. I know you must want a peice.

we are all in pretty good Health, the old intermitting still torments us at times tho it does not amount to the Ague yet—

inclosed is a Ticket:² see if it is worth any thing and let me know the cider you bought should be drawd of this month or the begining of March.

Let me hear from you soon and be assured that I am / Your affectionate Mother   A Adams we send you Espinasse printed here judge Lowel is so good as to take it[3]

RC (Adams Papers); addressed by TBA: "John Quincy Adams Esqr: / Boston"; endorsed: "My Mother. / Feb^y: 5 1792. Philadelphia" and "My Mother. 5. Feb^y: 1792." Some loss of text due to a torn manuscript.

[1] The exact nature of WSS's contracts is unknown, but they were probably an extension of the speculative ventures that he commenced during his 1790–1791 trip to England, for which see AA to Mary Smith Cranch, 12 Dec. 1790, note 2, above. WSS was apparently displeased with having to make this second voyage; he wrote bitterly to Henry Knox that the trip was "a money making pursuit, which was never suited to my genius nor my ambition, but you may tell the President that he & his minister of State have forced me to it." WSS blamed George Washington and especially Thomas Jefferson for their failure to provide him with what he considered an adequate governmental appointment. WSS, AA2, and their two children sailed for England on 29 March 1792 aboard the *Bristol*, Capt. Pierre de Pyster, arriving in England in early May (WSS to Knox, 27 March, MHi:Knox Papers; New York *Diary*, 30 March).

[2] Not found.

[3] Isaac Espinasse, *A Digest of the Law of Actions at Nisi Prius*, 2 vols., London, 1789, was reprinted and sold in Philadelphia by Joseph Crukshank and William Young (Philadelphia *Federal Gazette*, 18 Jan. 1792).

Abigail Adams to Mary Smith Cranch

my dear sister　　　　　　　　　　　　Philadelphia Fe^bry 5th 1792

I received your kind Letter of dec^br and sincerely congratulate you and my Neice upon the Birth of a son, tho I could have wishd it had been a daughter.[1] I have had the pleasure of having mrs smith and William on a visit to me for 5 weeks. the col has been part of the time here & Charles spent a fortnight with me. they expect to leave me in a week or ten days. this would be but a small matter to me as I should hope to see them again when I past through N york, but of that I have no prospect. the col has made a very advantageus contract with Some Gentlemen which will carry him abroad and keep him [there?] two years and accordingly he takes his Family with him and [plans?] to sail in the March Packet. this you may be sure is a heavy stroke to me, but I cannot wish them to decline it, as he goes upon a certain sure footing, and a probable great advantage mrs smiths is in circumstances which will make me more anxious for her, but my Family are destined to be scatterd I think.[2] I begin to long for the Time when I shall set out for Braintree. I fear it will not be earlier than the last year. my Health for six weeks has not been good. I still Labour under an Intermitting which I apprehend will increase with the warm weather. I am not confind, but am frequently obliged to decline going into company, of which this city is the General Resort during winter, and one continued Scene of Parties upon Parties, Balls & entertainments equal to any European city. the Publick amusements tis True are few, no Theatre here this winter an assembly once a fortnight, to which I have not been this season but the more general method for those who have Houses calculated for it, is to give Balls at their own Houses. The Indian War has been a distressing subject. who & who have been in fault is not for me to say. where a commander is to be found fit for the Buisness I believe will puzzel more wise Heads than one. the war is an upopular one. if it is a necessary War as I presume it is, it is to be hoped that measures will be persued to render it more Successfull than it has yet been, but I believe those whose judgments are good, have little expectations that it will be so.

what is become of Betty & her Husband? Cealia is very anxious about her child & very unhappy at the part her Mother has taken. I was glad to lea[rn] that Polly was well & pleasd with her place. we have had [. . .] weather here. the judge & mrs Lowell have been a month here and by them I shall forward this to you.[3] mrs Brisler is much better than she was, her disorder proved to be an intermitting fever

Let me hear from you and my Friends as often as you can it will give great pleasure to your / affectionate Sister   A Adams

RC (MWA:Abigail Adams Letters); addressed by TBA: "M^rs. Mary Cranch / Braintree"; endorsed by Richard Cranch: "Letter from M^rs. / Adams (Ph^a:) / Feb 5th. 1792." Some loss of text due to a torn manuscript.

[1] Not found.

[2] AA2 miscarried this pregnancy, apparently sometime en route to England; see AA2 to JA, 7 May; TBA to AA, 17 July; and Elizabeth Smith Shaw to AA, 26 Aug., all below.

[3] Rebecca Russell Tyng Lowell (1746– 1816), who had become Judge John Lowell's third wife in 1778 (*Vital Records of Charlestown Massachusetts to the Year 1850*, 3 vols., Boston, 1984, 1:379, 430; Ferris Greenslet, *The Lowells and Their Seven Worlds*, Boston, 1946, geneal. table).

John Adams to Charles Adams

Dear Charles   Philadelphia Feb. 13 1792

Your Letter of the 9th, gave me great Pleasure as it discovers a curiosity that is laudable and contains a very handsome Relation of political Events and Movements in New York of great Importance to that State and very interesting to the United States.[1]

The Writings which have excited your inquisitive disposition, were of Some importance in their day as they had Some Influence on the public Opinion; but are now forgotten and will probably never be again recollected except by you and your Brothers & sister. It is a great Consolation to me that no Party Virulence or personal Reflections ever escaped me, in all the sharp Contests in which I have been engaged.

My first Appearance as a Writer was in the Boston Gazette in 1763 or 1764 under the signature of U in opposition to a Writer in Fleets Paper whose Signature was, J.[2] My next Essays were the Essay on the Cannon and Feudal Law in 1765—[3] in the Same Year I wrote a few Pieces called Letters from the Earl of Clarendon to William Pym other Letters from Governor Winthrop to Governor Bradford.[4] in 1772 I wrote eight Letters to General Brattle on the subject of the Independence of the Judges. This is a Work of some Importance and deserves your Reading.[5] in 1774 and 1775 I wrote a long Series of Papers under the Signature of Novanglus, an extract of which was reprinted in England under the Title of History of the Rise and progress of the Dispute with the Colonies.[6] in 1776 I wrote at Philadelphia Thoughts on Government in a Letter from a Gentleman to his Friend.[7] in Holland in 1780 I wrote the Letters to Calkoen.[8] in England in 1777 I wrote the Defence of the Constitutions.[9] I had forgot, in Paris in 1780 I wrote a series of Letters which were printed in 1782 in England under the follish absurd Title given it by the Printer of Letters from a distinguished American.[10] in Holland in 1782 I wrote a Memorial to the Sovereigns of Europe on the Topick of American Independence[11] in 1790 & 1791 I wrote Discourses on Davila.[12] in Boston I always wrote in the Boston Gazette. that my Confession may be compleat I must tell you that I wrote a very foolish unmeaning thing in fleets Paper in 1762 or 1763 under the signature of Humphrey Ploughjogger. in this there was neither good nor Evil, yet it excited more merriment than all my other Writings together.[13]

Thus my son I have told you the whole Secret. You will find no offence against Religion Morals Decency or Delicacy and if your affection for your Father should ever induce you to look them up you will find in the most of them something to gratify your Curiosity tho there are not many of them of very great Importance. The Family are tolerably well. continue to write me the "Clashings of your Grandees."[14] I am with / much affection your Father

John Adams

RC (MHi:Seymour Coll.); internal address: "Mr Charles Adams."

[1] On 9 Feb., CA wrote to JA requesting "a list of the various publications of which you have been the author during your political life, The years in which they appeared, and

the papers in which they were printed. Such a present could you find leisure to make it would be greatly pleasing to me." The rest of the letter outlined some of the rivalries and in-fighting among New York State politicians (Adams Papers).

[2] JA's letters signed "U" were printed in the *Boston Gazette* on 18 July, 1, 29 Aug., and 5 Sept. 1763, in part as a response to Jonathan Sewall's letters signed "J" in the *Boston Evening Post*. For the text of the letters and analysis of JA's reasons for writing them, see JA, *Papers*, 1:59, 61, 66–81, 84–90.

[3] For JA's "Dissertation on the Canon and the Feudal Law," first published in the *Boston Gazette* on 12, 19 Aug., 30 Sept., and 21 Oct. 1765, see same, 1:103–128.

[4] The "Earl of Clarendon to William Pym" letters appeared on 13, 20, and 27 Jan. 1766 in the *Boston Gazette*; see same, 1:155–170. JA's "Governor Winthrop to Governor Bradford" pieces were printed in the *Boston Gazette* on 26 Jan. and 9, 16 Feb. 1767. For the purpose and history of the pieces—intended as a response to Jonathan Sewall's defense of Gov. Francis Bernard—as well as two unpublished works of the same title, see same, 1:174–176, 191–211.

[5] In Jan. and Feb. 1773, JA published under his own name seven letters to the *Boston Gazette* opposing the payment of judicial salaries by the Crown rather than the Mass. provincial government. He was countering the arguments of Maj. Gen. William Brattle, who, as moderator of the Cambridge town meeting, had opposed debating judicial salaries on both technical and theoretical grounds. For a thorough discussion of the controversy and the text of JA's essays as well as Brattle's response, see same, 1:252–309.

[6] For JA's Novanglus essays, which argued that the American colonies were not subject to parliamentary authority and appeared in the *Boston Gazette* between Jan. and April 1775, see same, 2:216–387. Portions of these essays were also published in England under the title "History of the Dispute with America; from Its Origins in 1754, to the Present Time" in John Almon's *Remembrancer, or Impartial Repository of Public Events*, 2d edn., London, 1775, p. 24–32, 45–54.

[7] JA wrote the pamphlet *Thoughts on Government, Applicable to the Present State of the American Colonies. In a Letter from a Gentleman to His Friend*, Philadelphia, 1776, Evans, No. 14639, while in Philadelphia at-tending the Continental Congress. For the text of this work, including its earlier incarnation as private letters, and analysis of its influence on American political institutions, see JA, *Papers*, 4:65–93.

[8] For JA's 26 letters to the Dutch lawyer Hendrik Calkoen, written in Amsterdam in Oct. 1780 in response to a series of questions from Calkoen, see same, 10:196–252.

[9] An inadvertence on JA's part. He published his *Defence of the Const.* in London in 1787 and 1788; see vol. 7:365–366, note 14.

[10] Responding to Joseph Galloway's *Cool Thoughts*, JA drafted his "Letters from a Distinguished American" in July 1780. JA sent them to his friend Edmund Jenings for publication, but Jenings failed to have them printed until the fall of 1782 when they appeared in the London *Parker's General Advertiser and Morning Intelligencer*. For a full discussion of the significance of the letters and for their texts in both draft and printed form, see JA, *Papers*, 9:531–588.

[11] JA's "Memorial to the Sovereigns of Europe," originally drafted in letter format but then converted to an essay for publication on the subject of a general peace for Europe and the United States, appeared in a variety of European newspapers in Aug. 1782 as well as in the *Boston Evening Post* in November; see same, 13:160–164.

[12] This is the first direct reference in the family correspondence to JA's *Discourses on Davila: A Series of Papers on Political History*. Beginning in fall 1789, JA began to study Enrico Caterino Davila's *Historia delle guerre civili di Francia*, Venice, 1630, using a French translation, *Histoire des guerres civiles de France*, Amsterdam [Paris], 1757. Davila (1576–1631), an Italian historian, spent over thirty years preparing the *Historia*, an account of the French civil war from 1560 to 1598. JA hoped that a close review of the earlier revolutions in France would shed light on the current one. His research once again affirmed for him—as had his previous studies of the Italian republics for the *Defence of the Const.*—the dangers of unicameral governments, especially as embodied in the French National Assembly. He was also offended by the French proposal to abolish all forms of rank and nobility, an attempt at leveling he found absurd. Typical for JA, the *Discourses* were a compilation of direct translations from the French of Davila's own work and summaries of the same inter-

mixed with JA's commentary. JA likewise borrowed heavily from the ideas of Adam Smith in *Theory of Moral Sentiments*, especially Smith's thoughts on distinction and rank.

Although published anonymously, JA was widely known as the author. These essays did little to ease growing tensions between Federalists and Republicans—who saw them as a defense of hereditary monarchy and in opposition to the popular French Revolution—or to improve JA's reputation outside of Federalist New England. Most notably, Thomas Jefferson took offense, indirectly attacking JA's "political heresies" in a letter of support contained in an American edition of Thomas Paine's *Rights of Man*. JA later claimed that he cut off the series abruptly because "the rage and fury of the Jacobinical journals . . . intimidated the printer, John Fenno, and convinced me that to proceed would do more hurt than good."

The *Discourses* were published as a series of unsigned essays in 32 numbers of the New York (later Philadelphia) *Gazette of the United States* between 28 April 1790 and 27 April 1791. All but the final number were subsequently reprinted, again anonymously, in a single volume in 1805 by Russell and Cutler of Boston. The 32d essay was not reprinted again until the twentieth century, when it appeared as an appendix in Alfred Iacuzzi, *John Adams: Scholar*, N.Y., 1952, p.

266–267. JA himself used the 1805 edition to revisit his work in 1813–1814, producing extensive marginalia in the copy in his library at MB. CFA reproduced some of that marginalia in his reprinting of the *Discourses* in *Works*, 6:221–403; even more extensive excerpts were published by Zoltán Haraszti in *John Adams & The Prophets of Progress*, Cambridge, 1952, p. 165–179. Finally, a manuscript draft of 17 of the numbers, as well as an unpublished 33d essay, exist in the Adams Papers, dated and filmed at [*April 1790*] (*Catalogue of JA's Library*; Haraszti, *Prophets*, p. 38–39, 165–179; Iacuzzi, *John Adams: Scholar*, p. 135–156).

[13] JA first published as Humphrey Ploughjogger—his favorite pseudonym—in Thomas and John Fleet's *Boston Evening Post*, 3 March 1763. Subsequent pieces appeared on 20 June and 5 Sept., as well as in the *Boston Gazette* in 1765 and 1767. For all of these items, see JA, *Papers*, 1:58–62, 63–66, 90–94, 146–148, 178–182.

For an earlier summary and evaluation by JA of his own writings in which he gives somewhat more detail, see JA to the Abbé de Mably, 17 Jan. 1783, same, 14:181–184.

[14] CA concluded his 9 Feb. 1792 letter to JA by noting that New York "has as many clashing Grandees as Florence or any of the Republics whose histories you have sketched" (Adams Papers).

John Adams to John Quincy Adams

My dear Son   Philadelphia Feb. 15. 1792

Your Letter of the 4th, has given me as much Pain by opening the Sceenes of Ambition in your neighbourhood as it has pleasure by the Elegance of its composition and the Intelligence with which it developes the Maneuvres of Parties and the Passions of Individuals.[1]

Another Drama at New York has been acted with equal Spirit and of more Importance.

At Philadelphia too We have had our Curiosities but I have not so much Courage as you, to undertake to explain them. When first Places are the Objects of pursuit to clashing Grandees, and the means of obtaining them are popular Arts, you know very well from History and even from your Short Experience, what is to be expected. For my own part I wish myself out of the Scuffle at almost any rate.

Your Mother is confined by rhumatick complaints complicated with others, but I hope will soon be better. The rest of the Family are well. Col Smith and your sister with their Children are to embark in the March Packet for England where they are to remain two Years upon his private affairs.

I hope to See you at Braintree before the first of May and there I shall live in tranquil retirement, Silently observing the Intrigues which may preceed and attend a great Election: and with more Indifference than you may imagine concerning their Effect.

Pray will not an Effort be made for Mr Jarvis, to take a Place in our Senate?[2] Write me as often as you can.

yours with great Affection   John Adams.

RC (Adams Papers); internal address: "Mʳ J. Q. Adams." Tr (Adams Papers).

[1] On 4 Feb., JQA wrote JA a lengthy letter on "the state of our parties in this State." He recounted the divisions caused by the appointment of Thomas Dawes to sit on the Supreme Judicial Court and the controversy surrounding the suggested reforms of Boston's town government, concluding that "the result of all the plots and counterplots will probably appear in the course of three or four weeks" (Adams Papers).

[2] Charles Jarvis was frequently mentioned in Boston newspapers as a possible candidate for the Mass. senate but was ultimately elected only to the lower house of the General Court (Mass., *Acts and Laws*, 1792–1793, p. 139–140); see, for instance, *The Argus*, 30 March; *Independent Chronicle*, 30 March; and *Columbian Centinel*, 31 March.

John Adams to Charles Adams

Dear Charles   Philadelphia Feb. 19. 1792

I wish you to take of Berry and Rogers as handsome a set of my Defence as you can find and packet them up handsomely and address them to The Reverend Joseph Priestley D. D. London, and send them by your Brother and Sister Smith. That Philosopher has made them so many Compliments in conversation as well as one in print; and as his sett was probably destroyed by the Rioters at Birmingham, I presume such a present will not be unacceptable to him.[1]

By a Letter from John,[2] I find that Ambition and Adventure, are as active at Boston as you represent them to be at New York. The Gales I hope will be gentle and only waft the Vessell forward on her Voyage. The Storms I hope I shall either not live to see, or be on shore under my own Peartree, when they come on to blow.

Your Sisters Voyage will oblige you to look out for Lodgings. Let Us know what are your Prospects.

I am my dear Charles your / affectionate   John Adams

RC (MHi:Seymour Coll.); internal address: "Charles Adams."

¹ On 14 July 1791, a mob attacked the Birmingham home of Rev. Joseph Priestley, destroying all of his books and papers. The rioters mistakenly believed that Priestley had helped to organize a pro-French dinner marking the anniversary of the fall of the Bastille. The attack on Priestley was widely covered in the U.S. press; see, for instance, Boston *Columbian Centinel*, 21, 24 September. JA sent him a set of the three-volume *Defence of the Const.*, which CA obtained from New York printers and booksellers Edward Berry and John Rogers. JA wrote to Priestley on 19 Feb. 1792, "I take an opportunity by part of my family bound to London, to remind you of a person who once had an opportunity of knowing you personally, and to express my sympathy with you under your sufferings in the cause of Liberty. Inquisitions and Despotisms are not alone in persecuting Philosophers. The people themselves we see, are capable of persecuting a Priestly, as an other people formerly persecuted a Socrates. . . . I am emboldened to hope that you will not be displeased to receive an other Coppy of my Defence, especially as that which was presented you formerly has probably had the honor to share the fate of your Library" (*DNB*; LbC, APM Reel 115).

² JQA to JA, 4 Feb., for which see JA to JQA, 15 Feb., note 1, above.

Abigail Adams Smith to John Quincy Adams

New York March 8ᵗʰ 1792

it has been oweing to the multiplicity of business that I have had upon my hands for a forghtnight past that I have omitted giving my Brother earlier information of *our* intended departure for Europe— we expect to sail in the course of this month— at first we intended going in the March Packett—but found it impossible to get ready we have therefore postponed our departure a few days untill the equinoxial storms have blown over— the World assign different motives for this rather sudden movement some say that a Foreign appointment has been given to Mʳ Smith—but it is not of much consequence what the world say— you my Brother are entitled to know from me, and tis confided to you only—that it is not a public appointment which carries us a cross the Atlantick—but an engagement which Mʳ S has made to transact some private Business in Europe which he supposes will engage him a year or two it is his wish and my desire to accompany him as it is for so long a period and I know so well the disadvantages and ill affects of seperating families that I had rather suffer almost any inconvenience in the voyage than submit to it— we take our Chrildren with us for I cannot consent to Leave them

it would afford me much pleasure if I could see you before I go but the time is now so short that I fear it is impracticable unless your Business could permit you to sett out immeadiately upon the receipt of this I do not urge it but it would afford me great sattisfaction upon many accounts

I have been upon a visit to our friends at Philadelphia this Winter which was lengthened out much beyond my intention by the severe indisposition of our excellent Mother a day or two before I had intended Leaving them she was seized with the inflamatory rhumatism which was followed by the intermitting fever and she has been very much reduced with it them I stayd with her as long as my time would possibly admit and untill I thought her better Thomas writes me that She began to take the Bark on Sunday and thought herself upon the recovery[1] Heaven Grant She may for her Life is very precious to us her Chrildren and to all who know her—

I frequently wished that you could have joined us there Charles was there a forghtnigt my Father received one or two Letters from you which pleased him much[2] he has recovered his health and appears very well except being subject at times to a depression of spirits Thomas is very thin but enjoys his health tolerably and is as steady in the pursuit of his studies as his friends can wish and I hope he will succeed

there were a few Dollars left in Dr Tuftss hands for the purchase of articles which we shall not want you may receive them if you please and if possible let them bring you to see us—or keep them untill I call for them[3]

remember me to all my friends tell them I shall think much of them all and beleive me yours affectionately   A Smith—

it is very Late—

RC (Adams Papers); endorsed: "My Sister—8. March 1792." and "M^rs: A. Smith. March 8. 1792."

¹ Not found.
² JQA to JA, 4 Feb., for which see JA to JQA, 15 Feb., note 1, above.
³ On 17 March, JQA replied to AA2 that "It would give me great satisfaction to pay you a visit before your departure, but the present state of my affairs is such as renders it impracticable. . . . I think I need not assure you that my most ardent wishes and prayers for your prosperity will attend you, in whatever climate of the earth your fortune may place you; and above all that you may, in due time, return to your family and friends; and with a full and satisfactory reward for all the troubles which a voyage of this kind may occasion to you." JQA also hoped that WSS would purchase law books for him in England and noted that Cotton Tufts would keep custody of the items he had purchased on AA2's behalf (AA2, *Jour. and Corr.*, 3:148–149).

John Adams to Abigail Adams Smith

My Dear Child: Philadelphia, March 10, 1792.

Your kind letter of the fourth of this month is before me.[1] I have frequently desired your mother to consent that I should send for other advice; but she has always forbid it, alleging that she was perfectly satisfied. The assiduity of her physician has, indeed, been very great; and his anxiety to do every thing in his power, most apparent. She is better to-day than she has ever been since her illness began, and I am much encouraged.

I rejoice that you are to wait till the equinox is over.

I do not read the New-York papers, having seldom an opportunity; but should be glad to have a hint of the various reasons which are conjectured for Mr. Jay's consenting to be a candidate.[2]

My love to Colonel Smith and my dear little boys.

I am, my dear daughter, with full intentions of corresponding with you frequently in your absence, and with sanguine expectations of pleasure in it, / Your affectionate father,   John Adams.

MS not found. Printed from AA2, *Jour. and Corr.*, 2:118.

[1] Not found.

[2] John Jay, although still chief justice of the U.S. Supreme Court, agreed to stand as a Federalist candidate for governor against Gov. George Clinton in 1792. Alexander Hamilton, who led the Federalists in New York State, recruited Jay as the only person who might have a chance to defeat Clinton. The contest generated considerable comment in the newspapers, including speculation on Jay's reasons for accepting the nomination. Jay's friends and foes alike believed personal interests guided his decision to run but put different interpretations on those interests. One supporter wrote, "Mr. Jay no doubt consults his ease and comfort in withdrawing himself from the fatigues to which his present appointment expose him, or is perhaps of opinion that he can serve this state and the United States more essentially as our first magistrate than as Chief Justice. In the first case gratitude for his long and important services in the most trying times impell us to support him, and in the latter the spirit of federalism will call forth our most earnest exertions." By contrast, an opponent sarcastically noted Jay's "noble instance of condescention and disinterested generosity;—he will give up £.1600 a year, and relinquish the pleasure of travelling nine months in the twelve—for the pitiful consideration of a continual residence in the most elegant mansion on the continent, and a salary, that by the next appropriation, will probably amount to £.2000." Jay was defeated after a highly partisan and sometimes controversial election (Monaghan, *John Jay*, p. 325–327, 333–337; New York *Daily Advertiser*, 20 Feb.; New York *Diary*, 22 Feb.). See also CA to JA, 20 Aug., below.

Abigail Adams Smith to Abigail Adams

New York March 11th 1791 [1792]

I received your Letter of March 7th my Dear Mamma and was very happy to find you so far recovered as to be able to use again your Pen[1]—altho I doubt not you find yourself very feeble and fear it may be long before you regain your strength; yet I hope by care and attention you will soon subdue this fever which afflicts you— I confess that I am but a novice in Phisick—yet I cannot reconcile it that so many weakening methods were necessary to subdue your dissorder— I hope you will be able to go to the Eastward as soon as the roads will admit I think—a change of Air may benefit you—but of this you are the best judge—

of the situation of my mind at leaving you in such an ill state of health—it is best for me to be silent— I can only say that anxiety must be my attendant— I think it is my Duty to go—but the contest is I confess almost too much to Bear— I feel myself obliged to Mrs Dalton and Mrs Otis for their attention to you— they are friendly good Women— I hope that *I* may be so fortunate as to meet with one or two such friendly spirits upon my Pilgrimage— it is but very Seldom that I allow myself to reflect upon this subject but when I do—it depresses my spirits not a little— I am fortunate as it respects a Lady who is going a Passenger in the same Ship with us. she is a Mrs Thomson who has lived as a companion and friend to Mrs Gates for three or four years—her Husband is a Clergiman a Scotchman [who] came over to this Country in the begining of the war and he purchased a little Farm at Johns Town above albany and was settled there—for two years but did not find success equal to his expectations— he returnd four years since to Dundee from whence he came but his People had settled some other Person in his Place during his absence— they have however settled an hund Guineas a year upon him during his Life—and he has sent for Mrs Thomson to come home—² Colln Duer has purchased her farm in this State—and she is going home in the Ship with us— She is a friendly cleaver Woman— her manners are mild and pleasing—and I think myself fortunate in her company—

with respect to the Chrildren—if you were settled in one place near a good school I should not object to Leaving Wm in your care— but you are travelling from Braintree to Philadelphia— at Braintree there is no school fit for him to go to; and if I Leave him here he will do just as he pleases with the whole family before one month is at an end: and Colln S. Mamma would think it hard that he should be from her all the time—so that I beleive it is best to avoid contests and evil consequences to take them both—with us— I suppose I shall be obliged to put Wm to a school from home—but I can see him every day—and I think he is too young not to require great attention from me—

I hope my Dear Mamma to hear that you are much better before I sail— I shall acquint you with the day before I go— in a Merchant Ship the period is never certain I wish it may be the last of the Month remember me to all the family with sincere affection / yours Daughter   A Smith—

RC (Adams Papers); addressed: "Mrs Abigail Adams / Philadelphia—"; docketed: "Mrs Smith to / her Mother / March 11th 1791." Filmed at 11 March 1791. Some loss of text where the seal was removed.

¹ Not found.
² Mary Vallance (ca. 1740–1810), a wealthy spinster, had become Horatio Gates' second wife in 1786 (Paul David Nelson, *General Horatio Gates: A Biography*, Baton Rouge, La., 1976, p. 284, 290). Rev. James Thompson briefly ministered to the Presbyterian congregation at Johnstown, N.Y., but his pastorate "was far from exemplary, and when he left, in 1787, quite a number of charges affecting his character were brought against him" (E. H. Gillett, *History of the Presbyterian Church in the United States of America*, rev. edn., 2 vols., Phila., 1873, 1:383–384).

Louisa Catharine Smith to Mary Smith Cranch

My Dear Aunt   Philadelphia March 18 1792

Excuse my intrudeing upon you a moment with a recital of a line from your Niece, Who is authorised from the feelings of her own heart And from a desire of her Aunts to gratify a request which she anxiously solicited me to comply with, I cannot object to the request altho it is a painful one, to informe you how extreemly sick my Aunt has been, I fear you have been anxiously distressed to hear particularly of her health If you should have heard of it transiently it will make you still more uneasy as I presume you have, news of this kind generaly drops from one person to another, Five weeks she has been confined to her Chamber with an inflammatory rheumatism and intermitting fever both combined together, one alone would have been quite enugh to contend with But where there is a complication of disorders, it makes them the more difficult to throw off, Wee are in great hopes that she is much better after haveing blisters applied and going through the various opperation's which a sick person has to undergoe, Wee think her greatly mended for the better, so much so that she begins to talk of giting in readiness to set out for Braintree the last of April,—

Wee have been whondering what is the reason their is not any letters from Braintree I heard my Aunt say it was a great while since she had heard from you, I hope Mrs Norton injoys her health very well, good health is an injoyment which we do not know how to prize untill we feel the want of it, give me leave to congratulate you upon the Birth of a nother grandson, little Richard I suppose begins to be very Talkative and amuseing to you, In a very short time wee are to loose Mrs Smith she with the family saile for England in a few days, and all of us very loth to part with her,

Please to present my Respects to my Uncle, and To rejoice in the recovery of his health Please to offer my Love to my Cousins,—

And believe me to be with the / most profound Respect and esteem / your affectionate Niece   Louisa Smith

RC (MWA:Adams Family Letters); addressed: "Mrs Mary Cranch / Braintree"; endorsed by Richard Cranch: "Letter from Miss / Louisa Smith, Ph^a: / Mar: 18. 1792."

Abigail Adams to Mary Smith Cranch

my dear sister   Philadelphia March 20 1792

I have obliged Louissa, much against her judgment, to give me a pen Ink and paper, that I might mak an effort however feeble to write a few lines to my dear sister Tis now the sixth week since I have been out of the door of this Chamber, or moved in a larger circle than from my Bed to the chair I was taken six weeks ago very ill with an Inflamitory Rhumatism and tho it did not totally deprive me of the use of my Limbs, it swelld and inflamed them to a high degree, and the distress I sufferd in my Head was almost intolerable. 3 Times was I let Blood, the state of which was like a person in a high Plurisy. I am now lame in my wrists from the 8th pr of Blisters which I have had. a week after the Rhumatism attackd me the intermitting fever set in, and under that I am still Laboring. it was necessary to quell the inflamitory disease first, & Bark could not be administerd for that. I am now reduced low enough to drive away the Rhumatism, but the old Enemy yet keeps possession. the dr promises me the Bark in a few days, but my dear sister you would scarcly know me reduced as I am. I have scarcly any flesh left in comparison of what I was, but blessed be God my Life is spaired and I am really mending, tho it must be slowly whilst this fever which daily visits me remains. in the midst of my Illness my dear mrs smith was obliged to leave me distress enough poor Girl, she then expected to have saild in 8 days but they have since determind to go in a merchant ship which is to sail this week. but tho absent from you my dear sister & deprived of the Tender care of my only daughter, I have not been without my comforts. Louissa has been a watchfull and attentive Nurse. Mrs Brisler has happily recoverd her Health and has been a comfort to me, but I have found in my old

Friend mrs dalton a Friend indeed, and in my good mrs otis & kind cousin Betsy all that I could wish or desire. one or other of them have been constantly with me, watching by Night & tending me by day as you my dear sister would have done. I have experiencd from all my acquaintance the kindest solisitude for me, & tho so long a sickness have always had more watchers to offer than I have had occasion to accept. I have had a most tedious cough through my disorder which has not yet left me. my weak state call upon me to quit the pen & lay me down. if well enough tomorrow I will take it up again

Wednesday 21.

I am much to day as yesterday, had a tolerable Night, find rather more agitation upon my Nerves. received a Letter from mrs smith who was to have saild this day, but is prevented by the cols being taken sick with his old Billious complaint so as to be obliged to be Bled and Blisterd; I am not a little anxious for him.[1] how soon may our fairest prospects be leveld with the dust and shew us that Man in his best estate is but vanity and dust?[2]

I am almost too weak to think of any arrangments for a journey, but as soon as I am able to travel I shall Set out for Braintree. if congress are not up, mr Adams will ask leave of absence. as I have not yet been out of my chamber, the middle of April is as soon as I can expect if I mend ever so fast, but that will soon be here. there is a little painting I wish I could get done to the House before I come, I mean the stairs and the Entry below & the china closset & the kitchen floor. I wish you would consult the dr & have it done if you can. mrs Black has her small Room painted as I should like the Entry and closset. I hope my wood is ready which I engaged to have got in the winter. if I had been well I should have written to the dr respecting Several things, but I am little capable of Buisness & mr Adamss whole time is taken up with the publick Buisness. I wish you to ask the dr if he does not think I had better have a Barrel of Brown sugar bought provided it can be had good. Sugars will rise. oats I suppose it will be time enough to think of, yet if they are reasonable I wish the dr to secure us a hundred Bushel. I thank you my dear sister for all the kind care you have taken for me. I still continue to be troublesome to you. my Love to my Neices & all other Friends. I find myself too feeble to continue writing. Cealia is well much concernd for her Child. adieu God Grant us a happy meeting prays your ever / affectionate sister   A Adams

RC (MWA:Abigail Adams Letters); endorsed by Richard Cranch: "Letter from Mʳˢ / A: Adams (Phᵃ⁾) / Mar 20. 1793."

[1] Not found.

[2] "For that which befalleth the sons of men befalleth beasts; even one thing befalleth them: as the one dieth, so dieth the other; yea, they have all one breath; so that a man hath no preeminence above a beast: for all is vanity. All go unto one place; all are of the dust, and all turn to dust again" (Ecclesiastes, 3:19–20).

Abigail Adams to Mary Smith Cranch

my dear sister   philadelphia March 25ᵗʰ 1792

I received your kind Letter of march eleventh yesterday.[1] I wrote to you last week which was the first time I had been permitted to use my pen, or indeed was able too, for six weeks. I have not yet been out of my chamber. the weather has been very unfavourable this Month. I was to have tried the carriage to day but the weather is against me. I am so feeble & faint, if I move that I do not think I could get down stairs without being carried. yet I grow impatient of confinement, and long to be well enough to set out on my journey. I fear I shall not have strength for it so soon as I wish, I would leave here the middle of April if I could.

you was so good as to make provision for me last year by procuring me those things which you thought necessary such as Loaf & Brown sugar Tea coffe meal &c as to Brown sugar I hope the dr will procure me a Barrel. I shall not have so many articles to provide as when I went last year in the furniture way, yet I did not arrive at a frying pan, or gridIron I think. I dont know whether I wrote the dr to procure me candles, if I did not you will speak to him

March 29ᵗʰ

Bad weather yet no riding out for which I am impatient. I yesterday received a Letter from mrs smith 24th she writes me that the col was better & that they expected to sail the first fair wind.[2] I have not learnt that they are yet gone indeed my dear sister it is very hard to part with my only daughter. it has depressd my spirits very much through my sickness, but we must all have our trials, some of one kind & some of an other as to Politicks, they begin to grow pretty warm. there are Honestus in congress as well as in Boston, there are Grumblers and antifeadelist, but very few from the North. the old dominion is in a Rage, because they could not carry the point of getting more than there share of Representation in the Government all the attacks upon the Secretary of the Treasury and upon the

Goverment come from that Quarter, but I think whilst the people prosper, and feel themselves happy they cannot be blown up. I most sincerely wish a stop could be put to the Rage of speculation, yet I think it is an Evil that will cure itself in Time. tis very curious, just before the News arrived of Sinclairs defeat, mr Gerry made a motion for an Equesterian Statue to be Erected to the President, agreeable to a former vote of congress— now the coin is not permitted to wear the stamp of the President because it would savor too much of Royalty.[3] so inconsistant are Men—and the same Men— but I feel that I must close. presenting my affectionate Regards to you & yours I am most Sincerely / Your affectionate / Sister

A Adams

RC (MWA:Abigail Adams Letters); endorsed by Richard Cranch: "Letter from M^rs / A Adams (Ph^a:) / Mar 25th. 1792."

[1] Not found.
[2] AA2 to AA, 27 March, below.
[3] On 6 Dec. 1791, Elbridge Gerry was named to a committee to consider the creation of an equestrian statue of George Washington, pursuant to an act of Congress of 7 Aug. 1783, but no further action was taken on it and the statue was not built at this time. The House of Representatives, in discussing the establishment of the mint, debated on 24 March 1792 striking out language from the Senate version of the bill that would have designed coins featuring an image of the president of the United States. Instead, the House voted to recommend an impression "Emblematic of Liberty" (*Annals of Congress*, 2d Cong., 1st sess., p. 228, 483–485).

Abigail Adams Smith to Abigail Adams

my Dear Mamma   New York March 27th 1792

I this day received your Letter of the 23^d inst and was rejoiced once more to see your own hand writing—[1] I have for some time feared that you were more indisposed than you would permit me to be informed of, I have suffered much anxiety on your account— inded my hands head and heart have been fully employed since I left you the former in preparing for my voyage and the latter by the indisposition of my best Friend— I have already written you an account of his health. we flatter ourselvs that he is recovering—but my fears at times overcomes my resolution— I am more and more convinced of the propriety of accompanying him he is I beleive more convinced than ever he was before of the necessity of attention to his diett— he has never since I knew him had so severe an attack— Mr Bailie says that the voyage will be of service to his health—and I hope it will—yet an anxious sollicitude for his wellfare must occupy my mind—and agitate my spirits—[2]

the Ship has been waiting for us a week and we have been detained by contrary winds since sunday which has been a most fortunate circumstance to us. the Blister which I mentioned to you has almost healed and my friend has recovered his strength— I have been on board this afternoon and have had our Beds arranged the accommodations are very tolerable much like those which you had in Callihams Ship—[3] the season is favourable and I will not anticipate evill consequences

I am happy to inform you that my friend has not been injured by this derangement of Mr Duers affairs—and it is almost a miracle that he was not— altho he had more confidence in Mr Duer than some other Persons yet he has been extremely cautious of committing his property to any one without receiving sufficient security— which has not consisted in any Mans name but the public paper and so long as that holds good he is secure— this I am sure will be a sattisfaction to you to be informed of but almost this whole City are some way or other connected in this Business— many Persons having endorsed his Notes from their relyance upon his stability who have received no equivalent have become responsible for many Thousands beyond their own ability— there must be knavery somewhare Charles has written to his Father his sentiments in full, how they will be received I dont know—[4] he is I must say very attentive to his office and Mr Troup has full employment for him—[5] I have done my duty and have made up my mind to say no more upon the Subject let what will happen— I have indeavourd to persuade Sally to go with us—and She had consented, but her Mamma would not give her consent because she would not go free and unbiassed in her mind— there is a strange jumble; in a variety of oppinions there is much perplexity— they are both equally obstinate, but *he* is to bear the blame;— but the radical fault is in treating him, or any other Gentleman with too much attention—without intending it should make an impression—and whare there does exist reasons to the contrary—[6]

I hope as the spring opens that you my Dear Mamma will recover your health— do not attempt to stay longer in Philadelphia than the roads will admit of your going Eastward— I shall be very anxious to hear of your health by every Packett— Mr Hammond will I dare say with pleasure inclose your letters— you know how painfull it is to be seperated from friends anxious to hear from them and disappointed in Letters.—

I scarce know how to close my Letter so many and various feelings operate upon my mind may you my Dear Mamma be restored to health is the sincere Prayer of / your Daughter   A Smith—

my respects to my Pappa and Love elsewhere—

RC (Adams Papers); docketed: "Mrs Smith to / her Mother / March 27ᵗʰ 1792."

¹ Not found.

² Possibly Dr. Richard Bayley (1745–1801), a prominent New York physician who was professor of anatomy and later surgery at Columbia College (*DAB*).

³ For AA's Diary account of her voyage on John Callahan's ship *Lucretia*, sailing home from England in 1788, see JA, *D&A*, 3:212–217.

⁴ CA's letter to JA has not been found. William Duer had been involved in land and bank stock speculation on a massive scale for several years, dating back to his time as secretary to the Board of Treasury in the mid-1780s. When the federal government finally brought suit against him for two unbalanced accounts, his financial empire collapsed and he was sent on 23 March 1792 to debtors' prison, where he remained, excepting a brief release, until his death in 1799. Duer's failure triggered a major financial panic in New York City as the speculative bubble burst and other financiers were driven into insolvency and bankruptcy. The collapse ultimately affected all levels of New York society (*DAB*; Young, *Democratic Republicans*, p. 298–299). For WSS's involvement in speculation, see AA to Mary Smith Cranch, 12 Dec. 1790, and note 2, above.

⁵ Robert Troup (1757–1832), King's College 1774, studied law with John Jay among others. He had previously served in the Continental Army and as secretary to the Board of War, and was a close political ally and friend of Alexander Hamilton (*DAB*).

⁶ This is apparently the first reference to a growing affection between CA and Sarah (Sally) Smith, AA2's sister-in-law (designated as SSA in *The Adams Papers*). The couple would eventually marry in 1795. For a 1785 description of her by JQA, see vol. 6:242.

Mary Smith Cranch to Abigail Adams

My dear Sister   Quincy April 8th 1792

I last Week receiv'd your Letter of the 20th & 21ᵈ of March with cousin Louisias giving me an account of your sickness If I had receiv'd hers first I should have been distress'd indeed. but I had not a hint of your Illness till I receiv'd those Letters When you wrote before you told me you felt an attack of your intermiting Fever I have been anxious ever since. I dare not indulge my fears I must always hope the best & endeavour to be prepair'd for the worst—& thank Heaven I am not yet call'd to this severe trial— I rejoice you have had such kind Friends about you—& that you have not wanted any alleviation that the comforts of Life could afford you— The world are much mistaken if they think you do not have your trials as well as others. but those in the lower walks of like are apt think the affluent must be happy

I hope before this your Fever has left you & that the next letter will bring me tydings of your restor'd health & that you are upon your journey to your quiet Habitation at Quincy

I went yesterday to Weymouth to consult the Doctor about what you wish to have done to your House & suppose it will be began next week to be painted— mr Prat will have the windows ready this week— mr Loud is remov'd to the eastward— I hope every thing will be done before you arrive— your wood is in the yard the Pine split up & put into the woodhouse— The Doctor Says he will look out for some sugar— If there is any thing you wish us to get into the House for you prey let us know it—

Lucy is return'd but mrs Norton is not well is troubled with a bad sore mouth & several other complaints—but her Baby grows finely & is as quiet as a Lamb—

I hear Coll: Smith has Sail'd so conclude his sickness was short but I pity Mrs Smith She must have an anxious Voyage

We have an amaizing forward spring—such an one was scarcly ever known here the verdure is delightful already—

Cousin Thomas is well I hope do not leave him to sicken in Philidelphia— William is well but poor Billy Shaw is not better—

I had a Letter from Sister Shaw the same eve I had yours—[1] She is full of trouble about her Son I really felt as if I had a cluster of woes presented me at once but when I consider'd I found they were greatly overballanc'd by mercies— may I never lose sight of them.

We are going wrong in our Politicks Doctor Tufts is like to be left out of the Senate there is a party who can never have their wishes granted while such men as he are in[2]

I am greatly oblig'd to my dear Louisia for her Letter but I have not time to answer it pray give my Love to her & my belov'd Thomas

May your health be restor'd & nothing happen to dissapoint the fondest hopes of your / affectionate Sister   Mary Cranch

RC (Adams Papers); addressed by Richard Cranch: "To / M^rs. Abigail Adams / at / Philadelphia."

[1] Not found.

[2] Cotton Tufts was not returned to the Mass. senate in the 1792 elections; he had served since 1781 (Mass., *Acts and Laws*, 1792–1793, p. 139; *Sibley's Harvard Graduates*, 12:497).

Abigail Adams to Mary Smith Cranch

My dear sister   Philadelphia April 20th 1792

I have just received your kind Letter as I was about to write to you to inform you that we proposed Sitting out on our journey on monday or twesday next. the weather has been so rainy that I have not been able to ride So often as I wishd in order to prepare myself for my journey, and how I shall stand it, I know not. this everlasting fever still hangs about me & prevents my intire recovery. a critical period of Life Augments my complaints I am far from Health, tho much better than when I wrote you last. I see not any company but those who visit me in my chamber nor have I once been out of my carriage, but to see my Friend mrs dalton who was sick before I got well, tho not till I was so much better as to do without her kind care. cousin Betsy smith has been with me for the greatest part of the Time the last Month, and a good child She is, tender and affectionate as her good Mother was. I thank you for your care about my things. we have sent last week to Boston by the Brigg Isabella a number of Boxes & Barrels. they are addrest to the care of J Q A. but I wish you to ask the dr to be so kind as to see that a carefull Team brings them to Braintree, & that Hay or straw is put into the cart, or the things will get Broken. the Bill of laiding was inclosed to mr Adams. I shall send by the Brig Maria my Trunk of cloaths &c she is now here.[1] I am glad to hear that Spring is forward as I hope to find the Roads good in concequence of it, but I always fear for the fruit. if the things you mention could be accomplishd before we arrive, it would be a great relief to me— I am grieved for my dear sister shaw, tho I have not been able to write and tell her so, for I was seazd with an inflamation in one of my Eyes when I was first taken sick which has not yet left me. I could not bear a light in the Room, nor even the fire to Blaize. it is much better—but writing reading or sewing are all painfull to me mr Adams has not had any return of his Ague but lives in continual apprehension. Thomas is thin & pale but does not complain. we must leave him on account of his studies yet it will be with apprehensions that I shall hear of his being sick— I do not particuliarly recollect any thing I want, you know as well I & better for you provided for me before. if you go to Boston I should like to have a pr of Brass Andirons at about 8 dollors price, Tongues & shovel proper for my best Room but you need take no extra trouble for them. you will be So good as to have the Beds aird &c if Bety is in Braintree She may be engaged for to stay if you think best till Cealia gets Home I shall send her by the vessel now here. I am not so perfectly easy on account of travelling Home as I should have been with Robert when he was sober, but he really got to such a pass that I have been obliged to part with him & have taken one who has not driven me more than once or twice, but I hope we shall reach Home safe— Terrible is the distress in Nyork, from the failure of many of the richest people there, and from the

Spirit of Speculation which has prevaild & brought to Ruin many industerous Families who lent their Money in hopes of gain— I was mortified to See our worthy Friend stand so low on the list of senators who I had been accustomed to see stand foremost, but such is the Instability of the people. popular Leaders catch their ear and they are credulous to their own injury— in the House of Representives of the U. states matters are not going better. the Southern Members are determined if possible to Ruin the Secretary of the Treasury, distroy all his well built systems, if possible and give a Fatal stab to the funding system. in senate they have harmonized well, no unbecomeing heats or animosity. the Members are however weary & long for a recess one after an other are droping off, which gives weight to the opposite side. Many of the southern Members have written long speaches & had them printed, which has had more influence than our Nothern Friends are aware of who depending upon the goodness of their cause, have been inattentive to such methods to influence the populace.[2] the V President, they have permitted to sleep in peace this winter, whilst the minister at war, & the Secretary of the Treasury have been their Game the Secretary of state & even the President has not escaped. I firmly believe if I live Ten years longer, I shall see a devision of the Southern & Northern states, unless more candour & less intrigue, of which I have no hopes, should prevail Should a War or any dire calamity assail us, then they would Hugg us, but politicks avaunt— my dear mrs smith has been a Month gone. it pains me to the Heart, but who of us can say, that we have not our troubles? our portion of happiness is no doubt equal to our deserts—

adieu my dear sister I hope to see you in a few weeks Remember me affectionatly to all our Friends / and believe me as ever yours

A Adams

RC (MWA:Abigail Adams Letters); addressed: "To / Mrs Mary Cranch / Braintree / or Quincy"; endorsed by Richard Cranch: "Letter from M[rs.] / A Adams (Ph[a:]) / Ap: 20[th.] 1792."

[1] The schooner *Isabella*, Capt. Abijah Luce, and the brig *Maria*, Capt. Isaac Pepper, had reached Boston and returned to Philadelphia by mid-May (Boston *Columbian Centinel*, 25 Feb., 17 March; Philadelphia *Federal Gazette*, 21, 31 May).

[2] During the House debate over the public debt and Alexander Hamilton's funding program on 30 March, several members gave lengthy speeches opposing the plan, including John Francis Mercer of Maryland, Abraham Baldwin of Georgia, Jeremiah Smith of New Hampshire, and William Findley of Pennsylvania. All were later reprinted in the newspapers (*Annals of Congress*, 2d Cong., 1st sess., p. 498–527; Philadelphia *American Daily Advertiser*, 31 March, 2, 5, 10 April).

Charles Adams to Abigail Adams

My dear Mamma   New York April 22—92

The pamphlet you have been so kind as to send me has met with much approbation here.[1] The boldness of the diction receives accumulated vigor from the too serious truths which it conveys. I think however something better might have been written upon those subjects. There is most certainly too much local partiality in the administration of our Government. People in this part of the world begin to see these things. They lament that Hamilton is so surrounded by enemies, and so greatly checked in a career which they conceive to be glorious to this Country. They view the Indian war as a measure ruinous to our Credit, as a squander of blood and treasure, which might be saved by a comparatively small tribute; Nor will they easily give way to the argument that it is degrading to give tribute to Savages. Are not say they some of the greatest Sovereigns in Europe tributary to a nest of pirates? Would it not be infinitely more to our advantage, and a saving of treasure to purchase peace? Most certainly it would. And they look forward to another defeat as a vital stab to the credit of their Country The foreign appointments, they detest, and begin to suspect that the Minister of State has rather too much influence with the executive.[2] These are things talked of with us. I hope I am not guilty of treason in mentioning them.

There is at this moment a seene of distress exhibited in this City which forms a horrid contrast to its former prosperity. This City which six weeks since was considered as the most florishing and the richest in America is now oppressed with misfortunes which create a general despondency The causes which have led to this you must have had detailed to you. The eagerness with which every individual who had property engaged in speculation The anxious desire of the widow and the Orphan to increa[se] their pittance by letting out their m[oney] at two three and four per Cent per m[onth?] The credit which Duer had acquired and the vast sums of money which he had drawn from the inhabitants His inability to fulfil his engagements and the consequent ruin of thousands begins this seene. An attempt to engross the 6 pr Cent debt of the United States by a company of Whom it is supposed McComb was the principal the great fall in the market the failure in their engagements their extensive connection with all the greatest speculators has created a universal bankruptcy There is not now a rich man in this City They were all engaged and they have all fallen The confidence between man and man is destroyed and every thing puts on the look of languor. We have for this week past been in great danger of a mob The people are exceedingly exasperated they wish to draw Duer and McComb from the goal to which they have fled for safety and to proceed with them to the last extremities They are now growing more cool and by proper management I think they will be pacified.[3] The Baron requested me to offer you his house when you came to town but I dare not do it[4] He is the best man in the world I sincerely beleive. I shall see Mrs Loring tomorrow and will write to you where I have procured lodgings[5] As I heard Congress would not adjourn till the middle of May I supposed I should [have] time. Be so kind as to present my resp[ects] to my father I fear this letter looks too m[uch] like treason to be shown to him. You may however use your discretion

Beleive me my dear Mamma your ever affectionate son

Charles Adams

RC (Adams Papers); addressed: "Mrs Abigail Adams. / Philadelphia"; docketed: "Charles Adams / to / his Mother / April 22nd 1792." Some loss of text where the seal was removed.

[1] Not found.

[2] In late Dec. 1791, George Washington had arranged for the appointment of Thomas Pinckney as minister to the Court of St. James, Gouverneur Morris as minister to France, and William Short as minister to the Netherlands. Contrary to CA's comments, Thomas Jefferson actually preferred Pinckney or Short for France because of Morris' opposition to the French Revolution, but he was overruled by Washington (Jefferson, *Papers*, 22:262). See also WSS to JA, 21 Oct., above.

[3] Alexander Macomb (1748-1831), a wealthy New York financier, was heavily involved in land speculation. He fronted a syndicate that had purchased from the New York State government—at greatly discounted rates, largely on credit—some 3.6 million acres of public land. Macomb was also a close associate of William Duer, with whom he engaged in bank stock speculation. When Duer's financial empire collapsed, Macomb's failed as well, and he too ended up in debt-

ors' prison, at which time his land dealings became public knowledge. On 10 April 1792, a mob of 400 or 500 people threw stones at the jail where Duer was held, breaking windows and lamps before dispersing. A week later, "a number of people collected before the gaol and seemed to be in great earnest about taking Mr. D——r, and using him in the genteelest manner circumstances would admit of. It occasioned a vast deal of clamor and commotion among the multitude, which after some time became very numerous." This group was dispersed without major incident (Young, *Democratic Republicans*, p. 237, 239-242, 298-299; New York *Diary*, 20 April).

[4] Baron von Steuben had a home at 32 Broadway in New York (*New-York Directory*, 1792, Evans, No. 24281).

[5] Probably Mary Loring (ca. 1735-1816), who ran a boardinghouse at the foot of Broadway (*New-York Directory*, 1795, Evans, No. 28598; New York *Commercial Advertiser*, 1 Feb. 1816).

Abigail Adams to Mary Smith Cranch

my dear sister   Sunday N york April 29 1792

I left Philadelphia on tweday Noon the 24 of April. my first stage was only twenty miles. I bore it better than I expected. the next day rode only 18. Rain came on & the Roads were Miry indeed. we did not get to this place till fryday Evening. here I find a vacancy which cannot be supplied, tho all my Friends are good & kind. the first being who welcomed me to the House, and met me at the door, was Billys little favorite dog who came skipping & hopping upon me. my feelings were awakned almost to Tears— Mrs smith I should have said moved into the Cols House when he went away N york is in great distress. many of my particulars acquaintanc whose affluence was great & well founded when I lived here, and even when I passt through last winter, are now in Ruinous circumstances, thousands worse than nothing. Such is the wheel of fortune—

we propose setting out tomorrow but shall not reach Braintree (Quincy I beg your pardon) till next week. I will endeavour to write you what day when we get into Massachuseets, not perhaps till wednesday week. my Health is better than when I set out, but the Weather is very Rainy, & I dare not travell in bad weather. my best Regards to you all

   adieu yours affectionatly   A Adams

RC (MWA:Abigail Adams Letters); addressed by CA: "Mrs Mary Cranch / Braintree"; endorsed by Richard Cranch: "Letter from Mrs / A: Adams (N:Y.) / Ap^l. 29. 1792."

Abigail Adams Smith to John Adams

My Dear Pappa—   Dover May 7th 1792

the Letter which I had the pleasure to receive from you before I left New York I had not time to answer,[1] I have now the pleasure to inform you of our safety after a Short but boisterous passage of 29 days and only 12 days from the Banks of Newfoundland to soundings in the English Channell, we were all very sick during the voyage but are now pretty well recovered and I hope to be able to proceed to London in a few days, I shall be very anxious untill I receive Letters from you and my good Mother I hope to hear that you are both recovering your health and that the ensueing season with air and exercise will establish to you both that invalueable Blessing—

you will I suppose ere this reaches you, have heard that the French have declared War against the Austrians that there has been an engagement at Tournay and that the French have been defeated with the loss of Six hundred Men—. the report is that the French army was at Breakfast in a Wood at Tournay and that the Austrians were concealed in this Wood fell upon the French and Cut them to peices. that General Dillon retreated with what Troops remained to Lyle where the People having an idea that he had intentionally sacrifised the Troops, hung him and quartered him— there are great Numbers of the French coming over daily, from Calais— many of them remain in this Country but more of them go from hence to Astend which being a free Port they perhaps feel themselvs secure—[2]

Mr Paine has been writing a second part of the rights of Man— and his Book has been stiled in the House of Commons an Infamous Libell upon the Constitution I will indeavour to send you the debates and the reviews of his Book the latter are rather civil to him—but perhaps the article was written by himself or his friends,[3] you will see by the papers that there is a party in the House aiming at a parliamentary reform which in the sequel will I fear produce confusion if not civil War— Mr Grey has made known to the House that early in the next seshions he shall bring forward a motion for a reform he is supported by Mr Fox Mr Smith and others in the House and by Mr Hollis Dr Kippis and a Number of others out of it—who have signed an association and hold meetings for the purpose—[4]

M^r G— Morris was here on his way to Paris the last week— he has been some time in London—and does not appear to be so much gratified with his appointment as his friends I beleive expected. I did not see him myself— he told Coll^n Smith that he was very glad they had not appointed him to this Court for he did not know a person they could have named who would have been so obnoxious as himself, he did not know how he should be received by the French Court for he had told them very candidly that they were going very fast to destruction—and now he should be obliged to hold his Tongue[5]

he says there is a party who are exerting themselvs to get rid of the Marquis La Fayette and he expects that they will succeed[6]

Coll^n Smiths business obliged him to go to London for a few days and as my situation would not permit me to take the journey so soon. he left me on Saturday I expect him in a few days when I hope to be able to proceed, my Chrildren desire to be pemembered to you with affection I hope to hear frequently from you it will ever confer pleasure upon your affectionate Child   A Smith—

RC (Adams Papers); addressed: "The Vice President / of the United States / Braintree / Massachusetts—"; endorsed: "M^rs. Smith. / Dover May. 7. 1792."

¹ JA to AA2, 10 March, above.

² France declared war on the Austrian empire, ruled by newly installed emperor Francis II, nephew to Marie Antoinette, on 20 April. The first major engagement of the war took place near Tournai, Belgium, and was a disastrous defeat for the French. A force of 5,000 men led by Gen. Théobald Dillon came under artillery fire before even reaching the town, leading to a panicked retreat. Dillon, sheltering himself in a peasant's home, was mistaken for a spy and taken to Lille, where a mob of soldiers and townspeople bayoneted him to death. The mob then hanged his corpse and paraded a severed leg around the town before finally burning the body (Schama, *Citizens*, p. 589–597, 599–600).

³ Thomas Paine's *Rights of Man, Part II*, received reviews in the March issues of both the London *Monthly Review*, p. 317–324, and *Critical Review*, p. 297–305. On 30 April in the House of Commons, William Pitt referred obliquely to "opinions published ... that were libels on the form of our government"; in reply, Charles James Fox disputed the characterization, mentioning Paine by name and arguing that Paine's works were not "any great danger" to the well-being of the British government (*Parliamentary Hist.*, 29:1312, 1314–1315). See also Descriptive List of Illustrations, No. 6, above.

⁴ Charles Grey, later 2d Earl Grey (1764–1845), member of Parliament for Northumberland, had announced on 30 April that he planned to introduce a petition to Parliament

from the "Society of the Friends of the People" advocating constitutional reform. He did so in 1793 but failed to move it into committee. Grey was a close lieutenant of Charles James Fox. Other supporters of Grey's work included Rev. Andrew Kippis and William Smith, M.P. for Camelford, both of whom the Adamses had known in England (*DNB*; *Cambridge Modern Hist.*, 6:476–477; vol. 7:27, 156).

⁵ George Washington named Gouverneur Morris as the American minister plenipotentiary to France in early 1792. Morris, who had lived as a private citizen in Paris since 1789, had previously spoken out in favor of a constitutional monarchy and in defense of Louis XVI, even helping to plot his escape attempt from Paris. In 1790–1791, he undertook an unsuccessful special mission to London to resolve lingering disputes over debts and commercial rights from the 1783 Treaty of Paris (*DAB*).

⁶ In Dec. 1791, Louis XVI, with the approval of the Legislative Assembly, had appointed the Marquis de Lafayette to command a portion of the French Army in the impending war against Austria. Lafayette, who continued to support a constitutional monarchy, became increasingly unpopular with more-radical groups in the Revolution, especially the Jacobins, who believed—without any evidence—that he was working with Louis XVI to subvert the Revolution by aiding the Austrians (Olivier Bernier, *Lafayette: Hero of Two Worlds*, N.Y., 1983, p. 235–237).

Thomas Boylston Adams to John Adams

Dear Sir   Philadelphia May 13th: 1792

Those Letters which I was directed to Copy and deliver to M^r. Cary for insertion in his "Museum", were prepared in season for last month; when I took them to Cary, he wished me to explain the occasion upon which they were written.¹ I told him that the Gentleman to whom one of the letters is addressed, (M^r. M. Weems), had

6. "TOM PAINE'S NIGHTLY PEST," BY JAMES GILLRAY, 1792
See page xiv

applied in England for Orders, as an Episcopalian Bishop, but that the law required every person before he could receive orders, to take the Oath of Allegiance to the British Crown,— That as M^r. Weems was an American, the design of his application would be frustrated, by a complyance with this law, so far as regarded taking the Oath,— And that because he had little hope of obtaining his object without a Compliance—he applied to you, by letter, in Holland, desiring your intercession on his behalf, with the Ministers from different Courts, where he might possibly succeed with less difficulty, than in England. That in consequence of this, you applied to Comte Reventlaw, (The Gentleman by whom the other letter was written); and that it was an answer to your's, addressed to Comte Reventlaw upon the subject of M^r. Weems's application. I am not certain that this explanation was right, or if it was, that it is sufficient However if it should be both right & sufficient, it was not satisfactory to Cary. He said it would be necessary to "Head" them with a short explanation, of their intent; as well as the occasion upon which they were written. I could tell him no more than I had done; therefore I must request you Sir, to explain the subject to me, that I may satisfy M^r. Cary, (if such a thing is possible). Monsieur Le Comte Reventlaw mentions a resolution of Congress transmitted by you to him; whether it related to this subject, I am ignorant. I can find nothing of the kind in the Journals of Congress, of the 21 March 1785 to which he refers.[2]

I hope to afford you an half hou[r's] amusement, in perusing the enclosed Pamphlett. It appeared a day or two since, and by those who have seen it, is thought to be well adapted to the purpose intended; which was to ridicule the too prevalent & fashionable doctrines of "Liberality." The 27 Article of the Confession of faith, is said to be the foundation of all the rest; these principles, if they may be called such, are openly avowed by those who profess to be deeply interested in the Politicks of France; and I believe it impossible to adopt the political, without avowing the religious opinions, of those Societies in France, which as M^r. Burke says, "are termed Philosophical." I have heard it suggested, that the Sec^y. of S— would subscribe cheerfully to all the Articles of the Creed; and that his name would not be an improper substitute, for "A liberal man."[3] It surely can't be treason in me, to relate what I have heard. The Letter is addressed to the young man, who advertized in the Newspapers a few weeks since, "that he proposed, preaching a number of discourses against, the divinity of Jesus Christ." His name is Palmer.[4]

I am Sir / your dutiful Son   Thomas B Adams.

RC (Adams Papers); addressed: "The Vice President of the United States / Braintree."; endorsed: "Th. B. Adams / May. 13. 1792." Some loss of text where the seal was removed.

[1] Mathew Carey (1760–1839), an Irish printer, had emigrated to Philadelphia from Dublin in 1784. He began publishing the *American Museum* in 1786 (*DAB*).

[2] Mason Weems (1759–1825) of Maryland traveled to England in the early 1780s to complete his divinity training. His ordination there was hindered, however, by the oath of allegiance to the British Crown required of all Anglican priests. In late Feb. 1784, Weems wrote to JA inquiring whether Weems might be ordained in another European country, specifically Sweden, Germany, or the Netherlands. JA consulted with the Danish minister to The Hague, Armand de Saint Saphorin (not the Comte de Reventlow, as TBA suggests), who supplied JA with a ruling that Americans could indeed be ordained in the Danish church, which JA in turn conveyed to Weems. In the end, Parliament lifted the requirement for the oath of allegiance in August, and Weems was ordained in the Anglican church the following month.

JA also submitted a copy of the Danish ruling to Congress. On 21 March 1785, Congress resolved to instruct JA to communicate to Saint Saphorin "the high sense the United States in Congress Assembled entertain of the liberal decision made by his Majesty on the question proposed to his Majesty's Minister at the Hague . . . respecting the Ordination of American Candidates for holy Orders in the episcopal Church." (TBA would not have found record of this resolution in the then-published Journals of Congress as it was entered into the Secret Journal, Foreign Affairs.) JA did so in a letter of 30 July to Frederick, Comte de Reventlow, Danish minister to Great Britain, as Saint Saphorin had since left his position at The Hague. Comte

de Reventlow's reply of 22 Aug. was presumably the second letter TBA sought to have published. Neither item appeared in the *American Museum* in 1792 (*DAB*; Weems to JA, [*ca.* 27 Feb. 1784], Adams Papers; JA to Weems, 22 April, LbC, APM Reel 107; JA, *Works*, 8:197–198; JCC, 28:187; JA to Reventlow, 30 July 1785, LbC, APM Reel 111; Reventlow to JA, 22 Aug., Adams Papers).

[3] Eliphaz Liberalissimus, *A Letter to the Preacher of Liberal Sentiments*, Phila., 1792, Evans, No. 24365. The pamphlet was written, possibly by Rev. Ashbel Green, in response to comments made by Elihu Palmer, for whom see note 4. Its "A Liberal Man's Confession of Faith" includes such statements as "I believe there is only one thing in religion essential; and that is to believe that nothing is essential" and "I believe every man should do just as he pleases."

[4] Elihu Palmer (1764–1806), Dartmouth 1787, initially served as a Presbyterian minister before becoming a Universalist and later a deist. He advertised in mid-March 1792 a "Discourse . . . against the divinity of Jesus Christ" to be given at the Long Room in Church Alley but was shortly thereafter barred from doing so. According to Palmer, "the Gentleman from whom he engaged the house, has taken an alarm at the novelty of the sentiment, and fearing a temporal injury, has forbid his entrance into the house." Palmer further observed that "the law of opinion, and the internal spirit of persecution, bear hard upon the rights of conscience." Palmer was eventually forced to leave Philadelphia but continued to preach and publish on deism (*DAB*; Philadelphia *National Gazette*, 15 March; Philadelphia *General Advertiser*, 17 March).

Thomas Boylston Adams to Abigail Adams

Dear Mama   Philadelphia May 14 1792

I received your kind letter of the 6th: this Evening, and feel happy that you advanced so far on your Journey, without receiving any injury.[1] I was somewhat anxious for your health, but the favorable account you give, has relieved me in a measure from the apprehen-

287

sion. I hope you may enjoy it much more this Summer than the last. The directions left with me respecting Mr. Harrison, are rendered of no consequence, by his declining in a very polite manner the kind offer you made him & lady.[2] He waited on me, and resquested that I would assure you how much he felt himself obliged; but that after reflecting upon the affair, he thought it most prudent to decline, as he expected very shortly to procure a "little Box" for him & Mrs. Harrison, and that the time he would be able to stay in the House, would hardly compensate for the trouble of removing. I confess to you, that I was not grieved at this answer—for tho I had rather have had them in the House than any body I know, yet I had found a Bachelors life so little irksome, that I had no inclination to change my situation. How long this will last I can't say; for my own sake, I hope during your whole absence. I find very little alteration with respect to the *sociability* of my meals; for you may recollect that we never were remarkably talkative An half dozen of insipid Newspapers, which the Printers still continue to send, generally fill up the intervals at Breakfast; and at dinner a Magazine, Museum, or Bolinbrook, make a substitute for companions.

I had thought of my duty to Madam Washington, and accordingly fulfill'd it on Friday Evening— She was very well, and enquired particularly if I had heared from you and how your health continued. Mrs. Dalton too, enquired—besides many others. You will pardon this small talk in me—I have nothing better at present. Miss B Smith had the civility to invite me to her *wedding*, through the medium of her Father; on thursday Evening; Her Bride maids were Miss A Hamilton, Miss Mead & Miss Keppele. The Bride Grooms attendants were Mr. Cutting, Mr. J Trumbull and Mr. Welsh; I don't know in what particular capacity I had the honor to Act, but as I was the only Gentleman, out of office, I thought myself highly honored.[3] The Ceremony was conducted with great decency & much propriety;— the Church service performed by Bishop White, was new to me; and except that part of it, in which the Lady says "I take thee Samuel" or whatever the name is, Miss S—— performed extreemely well.[4] She was dressed neat & simply—much frightened at first; but soon *composed*. Cutting made us very happy at a very handsome supper, and the Evening was spent in mirth and gayety. All formality and restraint seemed to be out of the question, especially as Mr. C. appeared perfectly in his element. On Saturday morning they sat out for NE—where you will probably see them in a short time.— M^rs: Dalton & M^rs. Otis direct me to remember them particularly to you; in doing which I subscribe your Son

Thomas B Adams

RC (Adams Papers); addressed: "M^rs: A Adams"; endorsed: "T. B. A. May 14. 1792 / Philadelphia."

¹ Not found.

² Probably George Harrison (1762–1845), son of former Philadelphia mayor Henry Harrison and a business associate of Robert Morris, who had recently married Sophia Francis (1769–1851), daughter of Anne Willing and Tench Francis (JA, *Papers*, 11:388; Charles P. Keith, *The Provincial Councillors of Pennsylvania*, Phila., 1883, p. 106).

³ Rebecca (Becky) Smith (1772–1837), daughter of the Episcopal priest Rev. William Smith, married Samuel Blodget Jr. (1755–1814) of Boston on 10 May. Another account of the wedding noted that the bride "was dressed in a sprig'd muslin *chemise*, and wore a bonnet with a curtain. The young ladies, her bridesmaids, had also on *che-*

mises, but their hats ornamented. . . . There was a monstrous company—forty-seven people—at supper. *That* was perfectly elegant in every respect, and not even a whisper or joke that could have raised a blush in a vestal" (Philadelphia *Federal Gazette*, 12 May; Horace Wemyss Smith, *Life and Correspondence of the Rev. William Smith, D.D.*, 2 vols., Phila., 1879–1880, 2:350, 514–519, 542; *DAB*, entry on William Smith).

⁴ Bishop William White (1748–1836) of Philadelphia served as the first Episcopal bishop for the diocese of Pennsylvania. He had dined with the Adamses in London in 1787 while there to be consecrated (*DAB*; vol. 7:443).

Thomas Boylston Adams to Abigail Adams

Dear M—— May 27th: [1792]

By one of the Newspapers I had the satisfaction to hear of your arrival at Boston, & have been anxiously enquiring for Letters at the post Office every evening.¹ I wish to hear how you stand the warm weather, and the effect of your Journey. The object of this letter is more immediately for the purpose of requesting a decisive answer to the proposal made by M^r. Bache of the House he has just left, for the accomodation of our family next winter. M^r. BF— Bache called on me this day in company with M^r: Randolph, and wished me, (if I had any authority or instruction upon this affair)² to give him an answer.—³ as, if my father had not thought of accepting the terms proposed, M^r. Randolph had expressed a wish of taking a lease of the House, if they could agree upon terms. I told him I had no instructions concerning the business, nor did I know whether my Father had made up his mind upon it; I agreed to write immediately and request an answer, which I would communicate as soon as received. His Father directed him to give you the first offer, and until he gets an answer, will not feel himself at liberty to look farther.

The terms, as mentioned by M^r. Bache are these. Rent £300,— Taxes—computed at ten or twelve pounds p^r Ann. Rent to Commence with the month of October next; possession sooner if you like. Will build Stables and require only the interest of the money expended in erecting them; & lastly shall be under no necessity to engage the House for more than six months certain—and as much longer as you please;— These are the whole—if you will enable me to give him a positive answer as soon as convenient—it will oblige him, and save me the trouble of further application

Have you seen Rights of Man, Second part? I presume however Boston is quite full of them as the first Copy was landed there.— I have hardly heard a single opinion expressed about it, since the publication of it here. This I presume is not because, opinions are not given, but because I have not been in the way of hearing them. Scarcely a line of censure or panegyrick has appeared in the papers.—[4] However I neither wish for printed or oral surmises concerning palpable absurdities, and if I must express my own reflections, they are shortly these: That Thomas Paine of 1792 is much fairer game for a Publicola than in 1791.[5] However, since he has undertaken to become his own Biographer—the attempt to perform this office by any other person, would be madness in the extreme. If, as he asserts, his political writings have hitherto met with a success, unexampled in those of any other, since the invention of printing to complete the climax I will add, his vanity has at least kept pace with his celebrity. His Sarcasms are addressed to the immagination of the vulgar, for whom he professedly writes; and if they should produce their intended effect; he, like his brother Apostle & Saint, Wat— Tyler—will deserve a monument in some field or Road, and the same inscription should answer for both. What that inscription will be, is yet unknown; The monuments however would answer this good and, like Buoys or Beacons they would warn us of our danger—and would say or seem to say—"Stranger pass not this way—lest thou catch the infection which is here entombed." I will close by subscribing,   Thomas B Adams.

RC (Adams Papers); internal address: "Mrs: A Adams."

[1] The Philadelphia *American Daily Advertiser*, 16 May, reprinted a 10 May piece from Worcester noting that AA and JA "passed through this town, on his way from Congress to his seat in Braintree" on 8 May.

[2] The closing parenthesis has been editorially supplied.

[3] Richard Bache (1737–1811), Benjamin Franklin's son-in-law and a former postmaster general, had inherited Franklin's properties at Franklin Court off of High Street in Philadelphia in 1790. Benjamin Franklin Bache, Richard's son, who had known the Adamses in France, was living in Franklin Court at the time while publishing his newspaper the *General Advertiser* (*DAB*; James Tagg, *Benjamin Franklin Bache and the Philadelphia* Aurora, Phila., 1991, p. 15, 60–61;

vol. 5:459). Mr. Randolph was probably Edmund Randolph (1753–1813), who was then serving as attorney general.

[4] American editions of the second part of Thomas Paine's *Rights of Man* had been published in Boston by T. and J. Fleet and in Philadelphia by Rice & Co. by 24 May 1792 (*Boston Gazette*, 21 May; Philadelphia *Federal Gazette*, 24 May). Except for a series of extracts in the *American Daily Advertiser* and the *General Advertiser*, no other pieces of commentary on the work had appeared in the Philadelphia newspapers by this time.

[5] Publicola was the pseudonym JQA used in a series of eleven newspaper pieces in the Boston *Columbian Centinel*, 8 June – 27 July 1791, critiquing Paine's *Rights of Man*. Mistakenly attributed to JA at the time, the Publicola articles attacked Paine's uncritical support of the French Revolution and the argument "that which a whole nation chuses to do, it has a right to do." Rather, Publicola contends, "The eternal and immutal laws of justice and of morality are paramount to all human legislation. The violation of those laws is certainly within the power, but it is not among the rights of nations" (JQA, *Writings*, 1:65–110).

Charles Adams to Abigail Adams

My dear Mamma   New York June 24th 1792

I have put off writing to you from post to post in hopes of hearing from some of the family that my father and yourself were well arrived and settled at Braintree, till at last I am quite tired of going to the Post office in fruitless search of letters. I have several times written to Pappa and in part informed him of the important struggle at present existing in this State.[1] I have intended to have been much more particular and to have requested his opinion of several questions which are now debating with much warmth amongst us. but I dare not give myself up too much to politicks. My examination will take place next month and I am anxious to appear to advantage at that period. I never felt so strongly the want of a conversation with him. Just about to set out in life and at a period when I find it will be impossible to remain neuter upon the various subjects which are agitating I wish him to fix principles or eradicate prejudices which I find I am imbibing My journey to Albany will lead me into some expence which cannot be avoided the fees of Court upon my admission, and a few books I could wish to purchase will call for a replenishment of my funds. I shall open an office in August as soon as I return from my examination I have not as yet fixed upon a Situation.[2] My dear Brother John owes me a letter or two I could wish him if he has not imbibed too many tontine notions, to make me prompt payment. I heard from Thomas last week he was very well and writes in good spirits.[3] We expect the May Packet daily, If we hear of Col Smiths arrival by her I shall immediately inform you. The Baron set out last week for Steuben quite dissappointed at the unexpected decision of the Canvassers[4] He says he will go up among his Yankees for there are no other honest people left in the world. Please to present my love and respects to all friends and beleive me my dear Mamma your dutiful son   Charles Adams

RC (Adams Papers); addressed: "Mrs Abigail Adams. / Braintree."

¹ On 7 June, CA wrote to JA about the continuing uncertainty as to the results of the gubernatorial election in New York. He also noted, "We enjoy a peace of Sentiment in general respecting national affairs excepting now and then a few chills from the Southern blasts which threaten to overturn our funding system. . . . Our hopes are in the firmness of the New England states We cannot but hope that they may see their danger before it is too late that they may rouse to repel this fatal stab to justice, but if our public faith is to be the Shuttle Cock for the Southern Nabobs to play with the sooner the matter is decided the better the sooner we are convinced who are to rule, the sooner we shall be settled in peace" (Adams Papers).

² Admission to the bar in New York required a college degree and the completion of a three-year apprenticeship under a licensed attorney (a seven-year apprenticeship without a college degree), followed by "a formal and superficial examination" (David McAdam et al., eds., *History of the Bench and Bar of New York*, N.Y., 1897, p. 178, 181).

³ There are no known extant letters between CA and TBA.

⁴ That is, of the canvassers appointed by the legislature to decide the gubernatorial election in New York. During the counting of votes, they noted irregularities in three counties and discounted those votes, leading to George Clinton's victory over John Jay (Young, *Democratic Republicans*, p. 301).

Abigail Adams Smith to John Quincy Adams

My Dear Brother   N 38 Argyll street London july 3^d 1792.

I had the pleasure to receive your kind Letter of the 18th of May by Barnard and was much releived by being informed that our Mother was recovering her health as rapidly as could be expected—¹ I feared from not having received a Single line from her; that she was not so well as my friends represented her to me we have had Letters from all my other friends except herself since our arrivall and I wonder not a little that she has been silent—and can impute it only to her indisposition—

the day after your Letter arrived Coll^n Smith went into the City to get the Books which you wrote for intending to send them by the first Ship which should sail for Boston but upon inquiring for the editions which you requested he found that they were the Dublin editions and that they were not permitted to sell them here the Bookseller told him if he searched all London he would not find an octavo edition of those works—and as they would be a third Cheaper he has concluded to write to Mr Wm Knox in Dublin and request him to send them out to you—which must delay some time before they can be sent—²

of Politicks I know so little that I cannot write you with any authentisity—of them— Tom pain as he is called continues to Busy himself very much and to Court persecution in every shape— he has undoubtedly a party here but the Sensible and judicious People do not join him and I beleive he is falling off fast in the minds of that class of Persons—

the late accounts from India are much talkd of and most People congratulate themselvs upon them it is said that Tipo has made terms of peace and gives up a Part of his Possessions and pays large sums to the British—[3]

the French are in greater distress than ever the Marquiss Fayettes Letter to the National Assembly it is supposed will put him into a very dangerous situation— he expresses himself very freely of the Jacobins—[4] the Kings palace has been surrounded and 4 thousand Peeople went through it—but no injury was done either to the King or Queen—so that it appears they had no system to do evill but were riotous they knew not why—[5]

Mr Short has been in London a few days on his way to the Hague— he is extreemly mortified & disappointed—at not having been appointed Minister in France he does not consider that he has been infinitly better treated than any person who has been employed in the Service of the U S. before he is to go to spain in the Course of the Summer that is if he has activity enough to get there—[6] you never saw any person less calculated to make exertions in the circle of your acquaintance I am sure— it is almost a miracle how he got from Paris to London he thinks he shall never survive a voyage across the Atlantick— he is the most enervated helpless Beeing that perhaps you ever beheld who we[ars] the Habit of a Man but this is entree Nous—

remember me to all my friends— I am Sorry to hear that my Father has left off his Wig—and hope it is only a temporary affair during the heat of the Summer—[7] I think he must look not so well— that his friend should not recognize him I do not wonder for I am sure it must make a great alteration in his appearance—and from that circumstance alone I should object to it pray write frequently to yours affectionate Sister   A Smith

you will oblige me if you could collect those peices written last summer under the title of Phi in answer to Payns first Book and Send them to me[8]

RC (Adams Papers); addressed: "Mr John Quincy Adams / Boston / Massachusetts"; endorsed: "My Sister—3. July 1792." and "My Sister. July 3. 1792"; notation: "p^r· Packett." Some loss of text where the seal was removed.

[1] Not found.

[2] Most Irish editions at this time were simply unauthorized reprints of earlier London editions sold at a lower price. London printers and booksellers strongly disapproved of this practice—which they considered piracy although it was not technically illegal—and discouraged the selling of such editions (Richard Cargill Cole, *Irish Booksellers and English Writers 1740–1800*, Atlantic Highlands, N.J., 1986, p. x).

[3] Reports of the surrender of Fath 'Ali Tipu Sultan, Nawab of Mysore (1753–1799), to the British Army, led by the Earl of Cornwallis, at Seringapatam on 23 Feb. reached London in June (London *Times*, 25 June; Franklin and Mary Wickwire, *Cornwallis: The Imperial Years*, Chapel Hill, N.C., 1980, p. 163–170).

[4] On 16 June, the Marquis de Lafayette sent a letter to the National Assembly accusing the Jacobins of undermining the French nation and arguing for the restoration of a true constitutional monarchy as mandated by the new French constitution. In response, leading Jacobins denounced Lafayette, and Maximilien Robespierre called for his death (Olivier Bernier, *Lafayette: Hero of Two Worlds*, N.Y., 1983, p. 237–238). The London *Times* printed an English translation of the letter in full on 29 June.

[5] On 20 June, some 10,000 French citizens gathered to petition the National Assembly to reinstate three radical leaders. A portion of the group broke off and went into the royal apartments in the Tuileries Palace, where they shouted protests for several hours at the king and queen but did them no physical harm (Bosher, *French Rev.*, p. 174; Schama, *Citizens*, p. 605–609).

[6] William Short was appointed minister to The Hague in early 1792; he had long been the American chargé d'affaires in France and had hoped to be made minister there instead. In Feb. 1793, he traveled to Madrid to negotiate, with William Carmichael, a commercial treaty with the Spanish (*DAB*).

[7] Wigs had begun to go out of fashion in the 1780s. Initially, men dressed their natural hair to match the look of a wig, but by the 1790s, short hair had become more fashionable (Richard Corson, *Fashions in Hair: The First Five Thousand Years*, N.Y., 1965, p. 296–298).

[8] Most likely a request for JQA's Publicola articles, for which see TBA to AA, 27 May [1792], note 5, above.

Thomas Boylston Adams to Abigail Adams

My dear Mother,   Philadelphia July 17–8th 92

I have just taken your letter from the Office and, as Briesler has not according to expectation sailed to day, I will add a few lines to what I have already given him. To hear from Col⁰ and Mʳˢ⸴ Smith was an agreeable circumstance, tho' much unhappiness is occasioned by it, under their peculiar situation. I had heard about a week since of their arrival at Dover, and of their illness—but had no conception of the dangerous situation of Mʳˢ⸴ Smith, till I read your letter.[1] I have written by most of the Vessels that have sailed from this Port, this Season, and am every day expecting letters myself.

As to Politics, I am very little acquainted with their present State— I have heard a suggestion of the same nature with that you mention— It will never succeed—but if I dared I would express a wish that it might. I wish this People to smart a little for their folly— I wish to have them taught by a little dear Bought Experience, to reward their best friends, and neglect those who despise them. They never will do this so long as they proceed upon the unwholsome absurd and dangerous principle, of changing a good man, for the chance of getting a worse. It may be mortifying to be neglected after having for a long course of years fulfilled every duty of every station with fidelity; but in my mind it would be much more so, to serve a people who could be capable of leaving so much virtue to languish in obscurity, (or if better) in retirement; when such an instance occurs He, against whom the slight is levelled—may say with the old Roman; "I banish my Country."[2] There may be secret machinations which are yet concealed under the garb of dissimulation, and which are waiting till time shall favor their appearance, but how extensive, or how deep they really are, I shall certainly not be the first to learn. It will turn out right if I have any luck at guessing: I go into no company where such subjects are talked off—therefore I guess upon my own bottom altogether. Everything which appears in public wears the face of peace & order as yet.

I have followed the advice of M^r. Coxe with respect to the House, and if I have any applications, I shall endeavor to take advantage of them; Briesler will give a particular account of all our movements hitherto, and I will transmit those which may follow— Money matters must be aranged suddenly—or I shall be dunned for Rent. M^rs. Keppele will in my [. . .] command a thousand Dollars, if she is determined upon it in the Fall—a[nd] Rents should come down else where— It is now comparatively a cheap house—and yet I can get no body who will even enter the House for nothing—for the time we have in it.[3]

I am &c   Thomas B Adams

PS. I have smoothed matters where they appeared to Rub a little—and I believe healed the breach effectually.

Tell John if you please to send me Blake's Oration, If worth it.[4]

Poor France, We had an attempt at Celebrating the Anniversary of their Revolution, but it was quite as lame & confused as the commemorated event— Even Odes composed upon the occasion, appear to be at war with Grammer, Meter, and even good sense—and I account for it in this way— These old standards, which have often witnessed many a hard battle, and always proved victorious, are now suspected of treachery, and being over powered by *numbers* have fallen a sacrifice to appease the rage of dullness and ignorance. In short—Good sense & Nonsense—ignorance & wisdom—are all Generals alike—like the French Army.[5]

Yours &c^a

RC (Adams Papers); addressed: "Mʳˢ: Abigail Adams / Quincy / near Boston." Some loss of text where the seal was removed.

¹ Not found.

² A paraphrase of Shakespeare, *Coriolanus*, Act III, scene iii. After Brutus says of Coriolanus, "There's no more to be said, but he is banish'd, / As enemy to the people and his country," Coriolanus replies, "You common cry of curs, whose breath I hate / As reek o' th' rotten fens, whose loves I prize / As the dead carcasses of unburied men / That do corrupt my air, I banish you!" (lines 117–118, 120–123).

³ Tench Coxe (1755–1824), a Philadelphia businessman, served as the commissioner of the revenue for the federal government. Coxe, who had previously helped the Adamses locate the home at the corner of Fourth and Arch streets in Philadelphia in the fall of 1791, recommended to JA that TBA attempt to find a new tenant for the house. The owner, Catharine Keppele (or Keppley), was unwilling to allow them to break their lease, and the rent amounted to $900 per year (*DAB*; Coxe to JA, 3 Sept. 1791, 20 Sept. 1791, and [*ante* 8 July 1792], all Adams Papers; *Philadelphia Directory*, 1793, Evans, No. 25585).

⁴ Joseph Blake Jr. (1766–1802), Harvard 1786, gave a "very pertinent and animated ORATION ... elegantly pronounced" at Boston's Independence Day celebration. Benjamin Russell subsequently printed it as a pamphlet (Boston *Independent Chronicle*, 5 July; Joseph Blake, *An Oration, Pronounced July 4th, 1792, at the Request of the Inhabitants of the Town of Boston*, Boston, 1792, Evans, No. 24123).

⁵ The Philadelphia newspapers reported "the Anniversary of the French Revolution, was noticed in this city, by demonstrations of joy." The celebrations included a French ship's firing its cannon in the harbor, "splendid" meals, and various toasts, after which "the evening was closed by a brilliant display of Rockets and other fire-works, which met with the greatest applause from a vast concourse of spectators." One ode published in the newspapers exhorted, "Sound, sound the minstrel, sound it high! / Till hardy Despots quake for fear, / And turn away their jaundic'd eye, / To let fair Liberty appear!" (*Federal Gazette*, 16 July; *American Daily Advertiser*, 17 July; *National Gazette*, 18 July; *General Advertiser*, 16 July).

Charles Adams to Abigail Adams

My dear Mamma   New York August 15ᵗʰ 1792

After a very fatiguing and a very anxious jaunt, I have returned from Albany with my Certificate of admittance to pratice the law I suffered much anxiety from the hesitation which the Court made at the certificate given me by Mʳ Lawrance who had not exactly pursued the form which is required in such cases. The great stumbling block was that he had expressed That "I entered his office" at a particular period mentioned and "studied law with him for two years" The Court said that in a certificate of that kind The words "Served a regular clerkship" were material. However trivial this objection appeared it required some efforts to remove it. Mʳ Lawrance was in Philadelphia and there was not time before the rising of the Court to obtain another certificate from him I suggested these things to the judges and offered to take an oath of the facts upon this and the certificates of several gentlemen who certified that they had often seen me at Lawrance's office employed at the business of a Clerk

&c[a] They after mature deliberation which kept me in hot water for two days gave up the point. A gentleman of the bar with whom I conversed upon the subject told me that he had privately expressed his surprise to the Judges that upon so trivial a point they should put me to so much trouble, that they had answered that they could none of them doubt but I had served regularly but that in my case it was necessary to be somewhat more severe than with any one else how far this excuse may be sufficient with men who ought to be independent I am not able to say. I was examined with seven more and have been flattered by being told I was not behind any of them in the propriety of my answers. I am now looking out for an office but the rents in the most public parts of the City are so extremely high that I cannot think it justifiable to take one in the center of business. I went today to look at a room in Hanover square not near so large as my brothers office, and I could not hire it under forty pounds. I received you kind letter of the 21st ult upon my return and also one from my brother John which I shall soon answer[1] He says We ought to submit to what has happened in this State he may be right but I doubt whether all his argumentative faculties could convince the people to acquiece. The flame instead of subsiding blazes more fiercely than ever, and the several Co[urts?] are preparing their remonstrances for the next session of our Legislature. Heaven grant a happy issue! There is too much warmth to expect a very quiet one. I am glad to hear of your resolution to remain at home this winter you will be much more at your ease than in Philadelphia Remember me with affection to my dear father to whom as soon as I can write in my own office I shall thank for his last letter.[2] My love to all friends and if they have any disputes to settle in New York I offer my services.

I am my dear Mother you affectionate and dutiful son

Charles Adams

RC (Adams Papers); addressed: "M[rs] Abigail Adams / Quincy." Some loss of text where the seal was removed.

[1] Not found.
[2] Not found.

Thomas Boylston Adams to John Adams

Dear Sir   Philadelphia Aug[st]: 16th: 1792

In my last Letter I promised to transmit the Result of the Town meetings which have been lately held in this City; the inclosed abstract will supersede the necessity of any additional remarks from me; It will be sufficient to say that the Party, which on the last meeting in which any business was transacted, had the majority, having gained all their measures prevented any further business on the last meeting by their obstinate Perseverance in opposing every Chairman who was nominated—The whole Afternoon was taken up in taking questions merely relative to the different Candidates proposed—and after many fruitless attempts a division was called for in favor of M^r. R Morris & Alderman Barcklay— the Parties were so nearly equal that no person could decide on which side of the *State House Yard* the majority lay. No business was done and the People dispersed not much satisfyed with the complexion of things.[1] It is said that we shall have an Antifederal Ticket—but I feel inclined to doubt the assertion. There is a Committee of Correspondence chosen to collect the *sense of the People* relative to this subject the Majority of whom are said to be of the old Republican Party in this State.[2] I find that when any important Question is agitated here— the distinctions of party are quite as familiar as they were formerly— every man knows his side of a Question by the *Countenances* he discovers when divisions are called for—not by it's conformity to, or connection with any particular system to which he is partial. When men are in this situation with respect to each other, we can hardly look for unanimity.

You have seen I presume the Pieces in Fenno's Gazette, signed an "American." I have not been able to learn upon whom the suspicion rests with respect to the Author. There has been for a long time a very free Animadversion upon the Speculations which have flowed through the National Gazette, as also upon the Editor. It has never arrived at the height to which an "American" has raised it, but I think the Sharpest key hast not been sounded yet.[3]

The Secretary of the Treasury has so arranged matters, that you will be at liberty to draw for a thou[san]d Dollars when you think fit— I presume the warrant may [. . .] by Attorney— The Secretary however will probably acquaint you with [th]e most practicable method.[4]

The House is yet upon my hands—we have as yet two months from this day—but I find no body disposed to take it even at fifty or forty dollars P^r month— M^rs. Keppele proposes going into it herself in October.

I find myself very happily situated in a very Respectable Private family, the Connections of which are somewhat numerous but all

Quakers— I consider myself peculiarly fortunate in being able to extend my acquaintance among this Society, with whom it is not an easy matter to be upon an intimate footing unless very strongly recommended,— Dr. Rush says I have made my fortune, but I can say that if I derive any benefit from the acquaintance it must in the first instance have proceeded from the D^{rs.} friendly assistance. He tells me to say for him that he would write you according to his promise, but that there is nothing worth communicating.

With presenting my best love to the family, I remain your Son

Thomas B Adams—

I have Received Mamma's letter of the 3^{d:} am glad to hear of the arrival of Briesler & family—[5]

RC (Adams Papers); addressed: "The Vice President of the United States / Quincy / near / Boston"; internal address: "The Vice President of the United States"; endorsed: "T. B. A. Aug 16. 1792 / Philadelphia." Some loss of text where the seal was removed.

[1] On 29 July, TBA had written to JA that he had "delayed writing several days hoping to be able to transmit the result of two meetings of the Citizens of Philadelphia for the purpose of forming a Ticket for Representatives, & Electors for President & Vice President; but nothing of importance has as yet been decided; and if I have had a true specimen of the general complexion of Philad^{a.} town meetings from those examples already afforded, I seriously believe no business of real utility will ever be transacted by them" (Adams Papers).

The abstract has not been found but was possibly a piece from the Philadelphia *Federal Gazette*, 1 Aug. (or a reprint thereof), which summarized the events of a town meeting held on the afternoon of 31 July. According to the report, "At half after three, an attempt was made to proceed to business, and Mr. McKean and Mr. Powel both named for chairman. After a noisy contest of *Yes* and *No*, those two gentlemen declined serving on the present occasion. Other names were brought forward, and among them, Messrs. Morris and Barclay. Mr. Wilson endeavoured to decide which name commanded a majority, a division for this purpose was three times effected; but the meeting was so numerous that it was found impossible to determine which was the largest mass, or to decide the question by enumeration. A last endeavour was made by the friends to con-

ferrees to place Mr. Morris in the chair, some confusion ensued, and the meeting was dissolved in a tumultous and unbecoming manner." John Barclay was a Philadelphia merchant and alderman (*Philadelphia Directory*, 1793, p. 7, 180, Evans, No. 25585).

[2] The Committee of Correspondence was appointed at the 30 July town meeting "to collect information of the sense of the People in different parts of the state, respecting the characters proper to be nominated as Members of Congress, and Electors of President and Vice-President." The committee consisted of Thomas McKean, James Hutchinson, Alexander Dallas, James Wilson, John Barclay, Hilary Baker, and Jared Ingersoll (Philadelphia *Federal Gazette*, 31 July).

[3] In the 4 Aug. issue of the *Gazette of the United States*, John Fenno published an article signed "An American" that attacked Philip Freneau's *National Gazette* as a means to denounce Thomas Jefferson. Freneau (1752–1832), a poet and journalist of French descent, had launched the paper in Oct. 1791 to counter Fenno's *Gazette*. The "American" accurately accuses Freneau of holding a public position—clerk of foreign languages for the State Department—and Jefferson of being the political force behind the paper. The piece goes on to question Jefferson's loyalty to the federal government, asking, "If he disapproves of the leading measures which have been adopted in the course of its

administration—can he reconcile it with the principles of delicacy and propriety, to hold a place in that administration, and at the same time to be instrumental in vilifying measures which have been adopted by majorities of both branches of the legislature *and sanctioned by the Chief Magistrate of the Union?"* (JA, *D&A*, 3:225; *DAB*; Jeffrey L. Pasley, *"The Tyranny of Printers": Newspaper Politics in the Early American Republic*, Charlottesville, Va., 2001, p. 63–66).

[4] On 16 Aug. 1792, Alexander Hamilton

wrote to JA that "a warrant for 1000 dollars in your favour has issued. If any authorisation from you had been sent to your son or any one else, your signature on the warrant would have been unnecessary. But as it is, it will be indispensable. Perhaps however the Treasurer may pay in expectation of it" (Hamilton, *Papers*, 12:208–209). See also JQA to TBA, 2 Sept., and JQA to AA, 19 Sept., and notes 1 and 2, both below.

[5] Not found.

Charles Adams to John Adams

My dear father   New York August 20 1792

I have this day opened an office in Hanover square.[1] The situation is as eligible as any in the City. There is but one objection, which is the high rents which are demanded for rooms in so public a situation. I have however been advised to take it, rather than go into a more retired seat. I wrote a few days since to my Mama, I then mentioned that forty pounds was the rent required for a small room; since when I have procured the one I now occupy, for twenty pounds until May. The difficulties I met with at Albany, were very fortunately removed, or I must have been obliged to have waited until October Term, as I did not receive the proper certificate from Mr Lawrance until after the Court had risen. Our politicians in this City, are more calm than those in the Country, All however seem to concur in the necessity of calling a Convention. "This Convention you say is a dangerous body." I doubt very much whether that observation has occured with proper force to our warm partizans. They look upon this body as an assembly who will meet, without dispute alter our election law, order a new election for Governor, and dissolve. They may find their mistake. I have not a doubt but a Convention chosen at the present moment from the people, would aim at establishing a Constitutional rot[ation?] in the first officers of the State; from this [they?] may go on from one thing, to another, and hatch at last, a very bad and defective Constitution.[2] I was astonished to find that one of the principal arguments used to the people, was the necessity of a change. I sometimes have conversed with Mr Troup upon that topic. I asked him if he could be serious when he advocated that doctrine; He answered It would take with the people! but are they to be deluded? are they to be persuaded to false tenets? Are the Community to be deprived of the first class of abilities, merely because the possessors have been a certain number of years in office? Is it just, or equitable, that a man who has served the public with virtue and integrity for a certain period, should constitutionally be deprived of his office, to make room for another, perhaps vicious and degenerate? Are you doing justice to yourselves, or benefit to the people whose interests you profess to espouse by disseminating such principles? But the influence which a man in office may acquire may be destructive of liberty! Have we not then the power of impeachment, and a still greater power that of changing our magistrates when they acquire corrupt or undue influence? I could wish Sir that politicians would content themselves with enforcing truths, without resorting to falsehood to obtain their purposes. but this is not the case, and yet there is something amiable in the principle, something in a strict adherence to truth, which is dignified and noble; it is a rock, over which the surges may lash, and billows beat in vain. Why then resort to falicy and chicanery? Because it is politic?

With every sentiment of respect and tenderness / I am dear Sir your affectionate son   Charles Adams

RC (Adams Papers); addressed: "The Vice President of the United States / Braintree / near / Boston.—"; endorsed: "New York. / Charles Adams / August 20. 1792 / ans^d 12. Oct^r." Some loss of text where the seal was removed.

[1] Hanover Square—still so named today, just off of Wall Street—was a center for business in New York City. It had been paved in 1789 (Thomas E. V. Smith, *The City of New York in the Year of Washington's Inauguration 1789*, N.Y., 1889, p. 34).

[2] In the wake of the contested 1792 New York gubernatorial election, Federalists called for a convention to revisit the decision of the vote canvassers and to review overall election procedures. The N.Y. State Assembly—with a Clintonian majority—ultimately undertook an inquiry, which found the canvassers free of "any mal or corrupt practise." No changes to the election laws were made (Young, *Democratic Republicans*, p. 310–313, 318–321).

Elizabeth Smith Shaw to Abigail Adams

My Dear Sister—   Haverhill August 26th 1792

I hope you will not think me criminally negligent in not particularly addressing myself to you before now— You may be assured I always think of you with the tenderest affection, & wish that I could have time, in a more correct manner to evidence the ebulitions of a Heart, filled with every sentiment of Esteem Love, & Gratitude— When I write to my Sister Cranch, I generally write in great haste, & think that if you wish to hear from me, you can easily satisfy yourself by enquiring of my Sister—

I thank you my dear Sister, for your kind attention to my Son— It was very pleasing to me that he was approved of by you— But you see in what a condition his poor Leg is— It has been a source of great Care, & anxiety to me ever since I saw you— Perhaps no one ever had a greater dread of seeing Persons useless than Myself. yet the whole of last winter, I feared that if my Sons life was spared, I should have the misfortune to see him a miserable Criple— And I know that our Circumstances were such as must add a double weight to the unhappy Lot— I had fondly hoped that he might one day, have been, not only a faithful Friend to his Sisters, but a kind Benefactor— But how often do find our best Prospects fail us, & Props raised up where we least expected them—

Joseph could not have given Bread to his Brethren & supported his aged Father if he had not have been cast into the Pit, & sold to the Ishmalites—nor perhaps would Mephibosheth been kindly allotted a Portion at the Kings Table, had he not been disordered in his feet—[1]

These Reflections (my Sister) are the bright gleams which sometimes serve to chase away those melancholly Ideas, which are too apt hover round me—

It is a dissagreeable Situation not to dare to trust ourselves with our own Thoughts— I know it is a vain thing for me to distress myself about future Contingences—& if in my Path of Life, I find many Thorns, & Briars dark & gloomy shades, yet I ought with a thankful heart to consider the many mercies that are strewed in the way, & with a meek, & humble temper view the soverign hand that guides the *Whole*, & with equal Justice, & tenderness sends his merciful, & afflictive Dispensations—

I was grieved to hear Mrs Smith was so sick, & suffered so much on her Passage to London— I think it was a dreadfull situation for a Lady to be in, on board Ship— She was so kind as to write to me just before her embarkation—[2]

I was dissapointed in not seeing Mr Adams & Louisa here— I expected them every day— Why should he not come— It is not Calypso's Island—there are no Syrens here—

I am sorry to hear your health is still so poor— Perhaps a Journey would do you good will not Mr Adams & you, favour us with a visit before his return to Congress— I long to see you— Cousin Betsy is not well yet, but a great deal better— I think she is recovering, though it seems to be a slow peice of work Sister Cranch wrote me word that Betsy Quincy was with you— She is full of life, & spirits—

there are many excrecences which must be discreety loped off, by the careful hand of Education– I think the Stock is good, & hope you will find it worth cultivating– You must let her work for you, & make her serviceable–she loves to serve–

When did you hear from Cousin Charles & Thomas– They must be very dull without there Sister, or you–

adieu my dear Sister– may your Health be restored & you continued a Blessing to all your Connections, as well as to / your affectionate   Elizabeth Shaw

RC (Adams Papers).

[1] Mephibosheth was the lame son of Jonathan, son of Saul, whom King David took into his home after Jonathan's death, saying, "Fear not: for I will surely shew thee kindness for Jonathan thy father's sake, and will restore thee all the land of Saul thy father; and thou shalt eat bread at my table continually" (2 Samuel, 9:1–13).

[2] Not found.

John Quincy Adams to Thomas Boylston Adams

My dear Brother.   Boston Sept[r]: 2. 1792.

I believe I am in arrears with you, for two or three Letters, which is owing in some measure to my indolence, but in a greater degree to the stagnation of events worthy of communication–[1] The purpose of my present Letter is to enquire of you respecting a warrant from the Treasury for some money, which it seems must be sent here to be signed by your father before it can be sent back for payment. It has been expected here this week, but as post after post arrives without bringing it, I write to you, to see that it be expedited: and indeed I believe it concerns you that the money should be speedily paid as much as any of us. If it should not be sent this way, before this Letter reaches you, I beg you would see it forwarded as soon as possible.

The National Gazette, seems to grow more and more virulent and abusive from day to day; but this is not surprizing, as Freneau must necessarily foam & fret, after his dastardly retreat from a charge, which he at first encountered, with a solemn affidavit.– One would think that circumstances so glaring would injure the credit with the public, both of the Great man & his parasite; but "It is no wonder" says David Hume, "that faction should be productive of such calamities; since no degree of innocence can protect a man from the calumnies of the other party, & no degree of guilt can injure him with his own."[2]

We are full of the small-pox in this Town; a general inoculation has taken place; and I suppose there are near ten thousand people now under its operation.[3]

All well at Quincy the last Time I heard from them which was about three days ago.

Your's affectionately   J.Q. Adams.

RC (Adams Papers); addressed: "Mr Thomas B. Adams. / Philadelphia."; endorsed: "2^d Sept; 1792."; notation: "4 Above Market 20."

[1] Not found.

[2] "It is no wonder, that faction is so productive of vices of all kinds: For, besides that it inflames all the passions, it tends much to remove those great restraints, honour and shame; when men find, that no iniquity can lose them the applause of their own party, and no innocence secure them against the calumnies of the opposite" (David Hume, *The History of England from the Invasion of Julius Cæsar to the Revolution in 1688*, rev. edn., 6 vols., London, 1762, 7:363).

[3] Because of the spread of small pox, on 29 Aug. the Boston town selectmen agreed to order a general inoculation in Boston. By 1 Sept., one newspaper had reported that more than 8,000 people were undergoing inoculation; another paper three days later put the number between 9,000 and 11,000 (Boston *Independent Chronicle*, 30 Aug.; Boston *Columbian Centinel*, 1 Sept.; *Salem Gazette*, 4 Sept.).

Abigail Adams Smith to Abigail Adams

My Dear Mamma: London, September 13, 1792.

It has been a subject of no small disappointment to me, not having received but one letter from you since you have been at Braintree, and only two since I left America.[1]   *   *   *   *   I have written you and my brother several times,[2] and have forwarded the newspapers, by which you will see the distressing situations in which the French are at present. The accounts from Paris are shocking to every humane mind, and too dreadful to relate; I shall send you the papers that you may learn from them their situation. Ship loads of poor, distressed, penniless priests and others, are daily landing upon this island; whether they will find hospitality and charity, I know not, but I fear they will not; for the lowest class of people here can never love the French, and the middling sort of persons do not relish so many Catholics and priests resident amongst them. There are persons who endeavour to find excuses for the cruelties which have been committed; they say that the friends of liberty have been deceived and betrayed in numberless instances; that supplies have been sent to their enemies; that their towns are given up without defence; that persons who have been employed in this country to purchase them arms and supplies, have sent them to the enemy; and that the aristocratic party were preparing to act the same scenes upon the jacobins, as have been practised upon themselves. They were not quite ripe for their operations when the others commenced. There are various opinions respecting the Duke of Brunswick's success; but at present he meets with very few obstacles to impede his course to Paris. Upon his nearer approach, I think the King and Queen will fall a sacrifice to the fury of the *mobites*, and is it not even better they should, than that the people should be annihilated by a general massacre?[3] One would suppose, that the English newspapers exaggerate in their accounts; but I fear they do not, for I saw, on Sunday last, a lady who was in Paris on the 10th of August, and she heard and saw scenes as shocking as are related by any of them; they seem to have refined upon the cruelties of the savages. These are confirmations strong, of the justice of my father's sentiments upon governments; yet the friends of liberty here, tell you the French are doing finely—surpassing us Americans; and I fear they will not be easy until they create disturbances in this country. One would suppose if any thing could check their discontents, it would be the picture they have before them. I wonder what Mr. Jefferson says to all these things?

* * * * * *

My friend has had an invitation from one of their Major-Generals and *Marechals de Camp*, to go over and fight for the French, but he declines—it is too uncertain a cause to volunteer in; but I have got so engaged in the cause of the French, that I have quite forgot myself. * *

It is supposed, if the democrats succeed in France, that the aristocrats will, many of them, go to America. The Vicomte de Noailles talks of it; the Marquis will, I dare say, when he gets released; Monsieur la Board thinks of it; they are only waiting to see how the event will terminate to make their decisions.[4]

Mr. St. John, brother to Mrs. Otto, dined with us last week. He left his father in Paris, and came over with a young Madame de Noailes, who was obliged to disguise herself in a sailor's habit, to get away from that land of iniquity.[5]

Sept. 29.

I expected to have sent my letter by a private hand, but I believe the gentleman does not go. I shall therefore request Capt. Bunyan's care of this packet.[6] It seems as if I were secluded from all my friends by an insurmountable barrier; not one single line from your pen since last May. Five months! It almost makes me homesick.

The latest accounts from France are that the National Assembly is dissolved, and a new Convention are convened who have chosen Petion their President, and have decreed that royalty is abolished in France.[7] Liberty and equality is the general cry. But the powers of Europe seem to have combined against them to bring them to subjection again. It is said that England dare not take a part; the Court party are very well disposed, but the people will not submit to it. The French are somewhat disposed to complain that their good friends, the Americans, do not step forward in their cause. Not one American officer has joined them, nor do they hear one word of comfort from them; and their minister is most obnoxious to the Republicans; and he refuses to pay them the debt due them, which they don't much relish. They will not permit him to quit Paris.[8] One of his friends said here, the other day, that he thought it not improbable that he would be taken off in some moment of confusion, but I do not believe this.

The Marquis is kept a close prisoner by the Austrians. It is said Madame La Fayette is in Holland. It has been said that Monsieur De Tournant is recalled from your Court.[9]

Write to me frequently, and believe me, / Your affectionate daughter,

A. Smith.

MS not found. Printed from AA2, *Jour. and Corr.*, 2:119–122.

[1] Not found.

[2] See AA2 to JQA, 3 July, above. Other letters have not been found.

[3] Karl Wilhelm Ferdinand, Duke of Brunswick (1735–1806), was leading the Austro-Prussian Army against the French and had successfully invaded France in mid-August. Shortly before this, on 10 Aug., a coalition of revolutionaries arrested King Louis XVI and Queen Marie Antoinette (Bosher, *French Rev.*, p. 168). See also Descriptive List of Illustrations, No. 7, above.

[4] Louis Marie, Vicomte de Noailles (1756–1804), had served in the American Revolution between 1780 and 1782. He emigrated to the United States in spring 1793 (JA, *D&A*, 4:85; Philadelphia *Federal Gazette*, 8 May 1793).

"Monsieur la Board" was probably François Louis Joseph, Marquis de Laborde-Méréville (1761–1802), who had also served in the United States during the Revolution. Supportive of the French Revolution in its early days, he was forced to leave the country after the fall of the monarchy (Hoefer, *Nouv. biog. générale*; François d'Ormesson and Jean-Pierre Thomas, *Jean-Joseph de Laborde: Banquier de Louis XV, mécène des Lumières*, [Paris], 2002, p. 250–251, 255–256).

[5] Either Guillaume Alexandre (b. 1772) or Philippe Louis (b. 1774), both sons of Michel Guillaume (Hector) St. John de Crève-coeur (1735–1813), the well-known author of *Letters from an American Farmer*. Crève-coeur's daughter, America Francès (b. 1770), had married Louis Guillaume Otto, the private secretary to French minister to the United States Anne César, Marquis de La Luzerne, in April 1790 (Thomas Philbrick, *St. John de Crèvecoeur*, N.Y., 1970, p. 11–13; vol. 6:249–250).

Anne Paule Dominique de Noailles (1766–1839) was the sister of Marie Adrienne Françoise de Noailles, Marquise de Lafayette. Pauline, as she was called, and her husband, Joachim de Montagu-Beaune, Marquis de Bouzols, emigrated from France to England in late 1791 (Georges Martin, *Histoire et Généalogie de la Maison de Noailles*, La Ricamarie, France, 1993, p. 86, 88–89).

7. "JOURNÉE DU 10 AOÛST 1792 AU CHÂTEAU DES THUILLERIE," BY MADAME JOURDAN, CA. 1792

See page xv

[6] James Bunyan captained the ship *Montgomery*, which ended up taking 74 days to reach New York from London, not arriving until early Jan. 1793 (*New York Daily Gazette*, 5 July 1792; Philadelphia *General Advertiser*, 9 Jan. 1793).

[7] Following the arrest of the king and queen, the revolutionaries created a National Convention, which met for the first time on 20 Sept. 1792. It quickly abolished the monarchy and established a republic. Jérôme Pétion de Villeneuve (1756–1794), a lawyer, was the mayor of Paris until he resigned in October to sit in the Convention (Bosher, *French Rev.*, p. xix, liii, 177–178).

[8] In the wake of the fall of the monarchy, the first meeting of the National Convention, and the beginning of the Terror, many foreign diplomats fled Paris. Gouverneur Morris—whose support of the monarchy and nobility made him extremely unpopular in revolutionary France—chose to remain; while not technically under house arrest, he nonetheless faced mobs invading his home and would likely have had difficulties if he had tried to leave the city (William Howard Adams, *Gouverneur Morris: An Independent Life*, New Haven, Conn., 2003, p. 228–229, 239–242). See also WSS to JA, 5 Oct., below.

[9] After the collapse of the constitutional monarchy, the Marquis de Lafayette fled from France to Belgium, ostensibly neutral territory, where he was promptly arrested by the Austrian Army for attempting to overthrow the king of France. He was eventually handed over to the Prussians, who imprisoned him in a fortress north of Berlin. At the same time, Adrienne Lafayette was briefly arrested at their estate at Chavaniac on 10 Sept. by the Committee of Public Safety. She was allowed to return to the chateau after Jacques Pierre Brissot de Warville intervened on her behalf (Olivier Bernier, *Lafayette: Hero of Two Worlds*, N.Y., 1983, p. 242–248).

Jean, Chevalier de Ternant, had served as an officer with the French Army during the American Revolution. He was appointed France's minister to the United States in 1791 and remained in the position until 1793 (Jefferson, *Papers*, 6:161–162; *Repertorium*, 3:144).

Abigail Adams to John Quincy Adams

Dear child   Quincy Sep^br 14 1792

As we have some skitish persons in the Family who are apprehensive of the small pox, and of every Body from your infected city, we shall not have the pleasure of your company, nor the office a visit from you this week. your cousin Lucy informd me to day that you had a letter from your sister.[1] pray send it me or such extracts from it as will inform me how she does and the col and Boys. I am very anxious for Thomas and fear he is Sick as I have not any Letters from him for a fortnight mr Black will be in Town & you may send any Letters by him to night. the Boston Newspapers we want to see, do not forget to send them. you will probably receive a Letter from salem or marblehead respecting a young woman who is comeing to live with me.[2] Should she fix any day for comeing to Boston, I must get you to engage the Salem stage man to take her to Boston & let me know on what day, when I will send Brisler to Town for her. She has had the small pox— I wish you would ask mrs Welch to let her come to her House, and I will not trouble her for more than one Night, perhaps not that

We have not yet got the necessary article from philadelphia nor can we devine why it comes not.

adieu your affectionatly   A Adams

RC (Adams Papers).

[1] Probably AA2 to JQA, 3 July, above.

[2] Not found.

John Quincy Adams to Abigail Adams

Dear Madam.   Boston Sept[r:] 19. 1792.

I wrote to my brother Thomas more than a fortnight ago, respecting the warrant, & requesting him to see it forwarded— But whether from an apprehension on his part of an additional delay, or from what other cause I know not, he has not done it, and last Evening in answer to my Letter I received from him one urging very strongly the necessity of his having an order to receive the money.—[1] Two lines from my father six weeks ago, might have prevented all the perplexity.— I enclose a Letter from Thomas to him, wherein I suppose he states his necessities himself—[2] In that to me dated the 10[th:] he says "I cannot wait more than a fortnight longer." Will you please to request my father to write an order of only two lines, addressed to the officer at the treasury who pays the money; if I knew who it was I would send you one ready written. it will be I presume sufficient to say. Sir— Please to pay M[r:] T. B. A. the sum of —— dollars on my account & his receipt, shall be your discharge.— And pray send it to town to-morrow by all means, that it may go by the next post.

I enclose also, a Letter to you from my Sister; the seal of which I took the Liberty to break.— I find with pleasure they were all well; which did not clearly appear, by her letter to me, which I sent you yesterday.[3]

It will be best I believe to empower Thomas to receive all the money due at the treasury, and to direct him to send forward bills to you, after deducting the sum which he must have. Or perhaps it will be better to direct him to take an order upon General Lincoln from the treasury, for so much, as is to come to you, and to receive the rest himself.— It is a science to obtain money from thence, through all the offices and formalities that are made essential; and as I am wholly ignorant, of the usual proceeding I have not been able to do the business for you.— But pray, let not the order be delayed an hour longer.

Thomas wishes also for directions, with respect to engaging lodgings for my father this winter: and he wishes they may be very precise and minute— You will be so kind as to give him all proper information upon that head.

I sent your Letter to Salem,[4] last week; but have not yet received an answer.

Your's affectionately.   J. Q. Adams.

RC (Adams Papers); addressed: "M^rs: A. Adams. / Quincy."

[1] TBA's letter to JQA, apparently dated 10 Sept., has not been found.

[2] On 10 Sept., TBA wrote to JA reminding him that he would need to expressly authorize the Treasury Department to pay TBA the money the department owed to JA in order for TBA to collect it. TBA was anxious for this authorization as "I have been for some time past upon pretty short allowance—but hope I shall not lose my credit before I hear from you." JQA followed up on this matter in a letter to TBA of 20 September. JQA noted that the Adamses had already sent TBA the necessary warrant two weeks earlier (both Adams Papers).

[3] Probably AA2 to AA, 13 Sept., and AA2 to JQA, 3 July, both above.

[4] Not found.

William Stephens Smith to John Adams

Dear Sir—   London Oct^tr. 5th. 1792.

M^r. Bond delivered your Letter of the 20th. of april[1] I should have answered it sooner, but I really have been so much occupied in my private affairs, that I have scarcely had time to attend to any of my Correspondents out of the line of real business—but I now have a pretty clear prospect of getting well thro' the great points I embraced— I shall however, I find, make more reputation than money, but upon the whole I have done vastly well, the wide spead ruin of speculation has not in the least effected any of my negotiations, nor the property of my friends committed to my direction, they are of course very much satisfied, and make very grateful returns, both in the line of civility & further unbounded confidence— in short sir, I feel agreably the effects of my prompt decissions on the score of public employment, the last winter, I feel myself in a great measure independent of the smiles or frowns of Courtiers, which I am grevied to find our Capital abounds, with— should any change take place in the administration of the affairs of our country, so as to introduce men who do not require too great a suppleness of Character to fill the offices of Government, but will be content, with the strict integrity & unblemished honour of Candidates, not absolutely deficient in abilities— perhaps my ambition may induce me to join them, but never while I possess abilities sufficient to bouy me above the lash of poverty or independence of soul enough–to dispise the low intregues of designing ministers, will I join the career of those who in the infancy of Government lay it down as a principle that great suppleness of Character is a primary essential & that those who do not possess it, are not fit, for public employments–

I send you the papers to the present date–& should be glad to know what our able minister of foreign affairs thinks of his french alliance now, I think if he has any modesty left or my friends have any Justice, they will acknowledge the propriety of my opinions & the Justness of my conduct on that subject–& as the affairs are connected with the appointment of a Minister to the Court of france,– you will find that M^r. Morris is more detested in Paris, than he was hated here, a Gentleman from france lately here in public employment–asked me a few day's past a plump Question–thus– my God sir, how came your Country to send such a man as m^r. Morris as its minister he surely cannot be the representative of America either in opinions or manners– The people of france are so much disgusted with him & enraged at him–that if he did not bear the name of an American & a Commission from Washington, his head would have been paraded upon a pike before this day– this I put by slightly, by saying I was in pursuit of my private affairs & did not know a sufficiency of the interior of the politicks of our great men to say from what scource he sprang into that political situation, excepting that it was by the apparent independant nomination of the President– he said, that Washington friends in france were much electrified, to find such a man with such Morals & Character, possessing his Confidence &c. &c. I suppose you will hear more of this from other quarters, & on this ground, I shall also be found to have been right, which will encrease the hatred of my enemies, & give me more cause to laugh at, if not despise them– We are all well here & are about making an excursion into Devonshire & to take bath in our return to London, for tho' we are but private people we cannot help being a little fashionable– M^rs: Smith has written to M^rs: Adams & I suppose given a greater detail of politicks than I have time to enter into She loves it; you may guess where she got it from, & her Judgement on those points are astonishingly good, we chat a little now & then on these subjects, but keep ourselves out of the Circles of the Court, & shall continue to do so– she Joins me in affectionate Love to you, Madam Loisa & *T. B. Adams* Esqr.–& wish you would present our most particular respects to M^rs: Washington–

I am D^r. Sir. / Your most Obe^dt. / Humble ser^vt.   W: S: Smith

RC (Adams Papers); addressed: "The Vice President of The United States / at / Philadelphia"; internal address: "The Vice President"; endorsed: "Col. Smith."

[1] Letter not found. Mr. Bond was probably Phineas Bond (1749–1816), an American loyalist who served as the British consul in Philadelphia. He had sailed to England in June (Joanne Loewe Neel, *Phineas Bond: A Study in Anglo-American Relations, 1786–1812*, Phila., 1968, p. 5, 9, 14–15, 91–94, 174–176).

Charles Adams to Abigail Adams

My dear Mamma   New York Oct[r] 8th 92

It is a long time since I have heard from you although I have not omitted writing. I hope it is not illness which hinders you from sometimes informing me how things are going in Massachusetts. The Baron returned from Steuben last week and I had intended to procure lodgings at some private boarding house, but when I mentioned to him my intention, he took me kindly by the hand "My dear Adams said he When your sister went from New York I invited you to come to my house, at least till you could find more convenient and pleasant Lodgings; I then had not the pleasure of a long acquaintance with you, but I was pleased that in our little society we could be of mutual advantage to each other, and that our improvements in the French language and in other branches of literature would render my table the seat of improvement and pleasure. I have since you have been here formed a very great and sincere friendship for you. You must now allow me the right of friendship; Indeed you must not leave me. What is it? Is there any thing you do not like? Is any thing inconvenient? I wish I could give you a better apartment, but the house will not aford it. I told him there was not a desire I could form but what was accomplished in his house; but that I did not think it proper that I should any longer take advantage of a kindness I had not a right to expect. And will you not then allow me to be any longer your friend and patron? You must not make such objections. It is not from any favor I can ever expect from your father. I am not rich, nor am I poor: and thank God I have enough to live well and comfortably upon; your being here does not make any difference in my expences. I love you, and will never consent that our little society should be broken, untill you give me more sufficient reasons for it.["] To this affectionate and fatherly address, I could only reply that I would do any thing he wished and would not leave him if he was opposed to my doing so. My dear Mamma there is something in this man that is more than mortal. We have late accounts from Europe, Our friends are well. I can not here enlarge upon french affairs but my father is a prophet and ought as the Baron says to be ranked next after Isaih. I have a necessity for about fifty guineas Will you tell me how I shall procure them. I do not know unless I borrow them and I do not like that very well. But should necessity prompt me I must do it. When does Pappa mean to pass through New York, I fear he will be most terribly perplexed the next session, There is a party formed to abolish this government. It consists of Officers of the late army. Antifederalists, and Southern men who from many reasons are endeavoring to subvert the funding system and of course every obligation which a nation can be under. Our Eastern delegates are complained of It is said their eyes are not open that they rest in security while America is in the greatest danger That they sleep while every body opposed to them is on the watch. God Grant that we may not be ruined, That we may not discard our name as a nation. You may depend upon it there is great danger of it. And my dear father what will be his sensations when all his toils are forgotten and his labors sunk in oblivion. what will be the path for his Children to persue when they see such an event will any encouragement remain to follow the road of public virtue Will any wish remain to be ranked among the list of patriots: Colonel Burr is appointed a judge of our Supreme Court and will without doubt accept the office. He aims at the Gubernatorial chair of this State and it is thought he will be able to obtain more influence as a Judge than he can by his present station.[1] Mr Jay has been at death's door but is now somewhat recovered.[2]

I should be glad to hear oftener from Braintree where is my Brother John I hear no more of him than if he was in Asia.

Adieu my dear Mamma beleive me your affectionate son

Charles Adams.

PS I requested that some shoes might be sent to me, but I suppose you did not recollect it. I can not get them here they are very bad and at a very high price. If three or four pair can be sent it will much oblige me.

RC (Adams Papers); endorsed by JA: "C. A. Oct. 8. 1792. / New York."

[1] On 2 Oct., George Clinton and the N.Y. Council of Appointment nominated Aaron Burr, then a New York senator, to become associate justice of the N.Y. Supreme Court. He declined the position (Milton Lomask, *Aaron Burr: The Years from Princeton to Vice President 1756–1805*, N.Y., 1979, p. 176).

[2] John Jay became dangerously ill with an eye inflammation and rheumatic fever in late September; he finally recovered in November

(*Selected Letters of John Jay and Sarah Livingston Jay: Correspondence by or to the First Chief Justice of the United States and His* Wife, ed. Landa M. Freeman and others, Jefferson, N.C., 2005, p. 213–214).

John Adams to Charles Adams

My dear Charles   Quincy October 12. 1792

I congratulate you on your Admission to the Bar and your taking Possession of an Office in So good a Part of the Town, and I would not advise you to exhange it for any other, without an absolute necessity. There is a great Advantage to a Lawyer in being always to be found in the Same place. I wish you as much Success as you can desire and all the Pleasure and Profit from your Practice in a Country like ours and in times like these. Honour and Integrity in all your concerns, a constant Attendance at your Office, and an ardent Application to your Studies will soon acquire you a reputation in the World and a Crowd of Clients about you

I am much pleased with your Observations on political subjects and approve entirely that Rectitude of heart which must have dictated your Attachment to Truth in all political Transactions. Falshood is never Politick. So far am I from admiring the old Monkish Maxim Populus vult decipi: decipiatur.[1] for although I must confess from Experience, that the People sometimes choose to be deceived, yet I cannot agree to the other Part of the Proverb, so far as to take any part in the deception.

The Time has been when I had less unfavourable Notions of Rotations than I have at present. That Time however has been long Since past. Reading Reflection and Observation have wholly weaned me from that delusion and I believe that nothing has contributed more to my conversion than the Observation that in all History and Experience Rotations have been the favourites only of the Aristocracy. The People in contradistinction to the Aristocracy Seldom approve of Rotations and are never fond of them, except when at times they have been deceived by the Aristocrats.

It will be found at this instant that they are the Aristocrats in France and some of the worst of them too, who, by exciting Mobs and Tumults among People who may be hired to any Thing by a few Liards[2] apiece, are playing Mischief with their Constitution and the Rights of Man.

You must write me as often as you can and not wait always for regular Answers from me, as my Engagements sometimes and my health at others will not allow me to write.

My Regards to the Family We are connected with and particular Compliments to the worthy Baron.

I am my dear Charles your affectionate / Father

John Adams

RC (MHi:Seymour Coll.); addressed: "Charles Adams Esqr / Councillor at Law / New York"; internal address: "Mr Charles Adams"; notation: "Free / John Adams."

[1] The people wish to be deceived, let them have their wish (attributed to Cardinal Caraffa, legate of Pope Paul IV).

[2] A small French coin of little value (*OED*).

Thomas Boylston Adams to Abigail Adams

My dear Mother,   Philada: Octr: 17th. 92

I have not received any letters from you, for a considerable time, and I experience the same kind of apprehensions for the cause which you have often expressed concerning me. I fear least the cold weather which is fast approaching should affect your health, by bringing a return of your Rheumatism. I have repeatedly written concerning engaging lodgings for my Father before all the places are engaged, but I have yet recd: no instructions, and if they should even come now I fear no very eligible accomodations can be easily obtained. Mrs. House has the most commodious Rooms of any I know, but 'tis probable they may all be engaged by this time, as many of the former lodgers will return there;[1] I know of no other place where there is even a tolerable prospect of obtaining suitable lodgings; however it cannot be my fault if they are not now attainable. Every body of your acquaintance seem to regret your determination to remain behind; but I differ from them in opinion, tho' I may be presumed more interested in your return than any of them. I do not despair however of again seeing you in Philada: provided you think proper to return next Fall—[2] The Reelection is I believe very safe—there can be no hindrance on that score then; but your health is the principal objection, but this I hope will be removed by that time. The Election for Representatives in Congress has been held in this State, and from the returns allready recd: it is said to be Federal; there was a very formidable interest however in opposition; they were indefatigable in their endeavors to carry their Ticket, but are obliged to knock under at last.[3] The Electors for P & VP are to be chosen in a few days; we hear very little said of them; indeed there was scarcely ever know an Election however trifling, that was conducted with so much peace & order in this place.[4] But the City has disgraced itself by the countenance given to Rank Anti's while the Counties have deservedly gained a great share of applause by an opposite conduct. Mess.rs: Hutchinson, Dallas Fox & Co: feel themselves heartily mortifyed by their ill success, in those places where their presence could not overawe or influence the people.⁵ We never shall get a splendid Representation for this State while there are so many distinct interests or rather prejudices to encounter; but we may get an *harmless* one.

I got a Letter from M.rs: Smith dated 5 Aug.st: she was just going to the Review at Bagshott—⁶ What dismal accounts we have from France if true— A Letter has been received by a Merch.t: in this City from a Correspondent in Charleston SC, informing him of the Slaughter of 5000 Parisians—and the Assassination of the Queen— The King & M. La Fayette were missing—& the Duke of Brunswick within 30 leagues of Paris. This intelligence is from Paris by the Georgia Packet wh[ich] sailed on the first of Sept.r:— Doubts are suggested of its authenticity but tis said to be direct[. For] my part, if the last circumstance concerning the [Duke] of Brunsw[ic]k be true I can easily credit all the rest. Otherwise it seems improbable.⁷

I sent the Carriage by Capt.n. Carver; but the price Binghurst charges for Casing, is extravagant especially in the manner it is done—⁸ If the Carriage gets injured I won't pay him a Farthing—he asks six Doll.s. which I would have given if it had been well done; I'll thank you to let me hear how it arrives. I have payed M.rs. Keppele her third quarter, and resigned the Key of the House, she has allready removed her Family & taken possession. I have also paid my Board. The Store Rent, and my Taylor's Bill—for my Winter & Summer cloath's. I want some shoes from Hardwick if you will please to send them. My best love to all Friends   Tho.s: B Adams

RC (Adams Papers); addressed: "M.rs: A Adams / Quincy / near Boston—"; internal address: "M.rs A Adams"; endorsed by JA: "T.B.A. Oct.r 17 1792." Some loss of text where the seal was removed and due to a torn manuscript.

¹ Mary House ran a boardinghouse at the corner of High (now Market) and Fifth streets (Washington, *Diaries*, 5:155–156).

² In fact, AA would not return to Philadelphia until May 1797, after JA had become president.

³ TBA's assessment of the 9 Oct. 1792 election was premature. The returns as counted and reported in the newspapers by 17 Oct. indicated that eight Federalists and five Democratic-Republicans would be sent to Congress from Pennsylvania. The final results put the tally at five Federalists and eight Democratic-Republicans (Philadelphia *Gazette of the United States*, 17 Oct.; Philadelphia *American Daily Advertiser*, 31 Oct.; *Biog. Dir. Cong.*).

⁴ The election of electors for president and vice president took place on 6 November.

⁵ Dr. James Hutchinson (1752–1793) studied medicine in Philadelphia and London prior to the Revolution, during which he served as the surgeon general of Pennsyl-

vania from 1778 to 1784. He was active in Philadelphia politics. Alexander James Dallas (1759–1817), of Scottish descent, was born in Jamaica. In 1783, he moved to Philadelphia where he practiced law and became a naturalized citizen. From 1791 to 1801, he served as secretary of the Commonwealth. Both men played active roles in promoting Democratic-Republicans in the 1792 election. Fox may have been Edward Fox (1752–1822), an Irishman who held various positions in the Pennsylvania government and also served as secretary and treasurer of the University of Pennsylvania from 1791 until his death (*DAB*; Harry Marlin Tinkcom, *The Republicans and Federalists in Pennsylvania 1790–1801*, Harrisburg, Penn., 1950, p. 51–54; Edward Fox, Penn Biographies, University of Penn. Archives, www.archives.upenn.edu).

⁶ Not found. On 7 Aug. 1792, King George III conducted a review of the British Army at their encampment at Bagshot roughly thirty miles southwest of London. According to newspaper reports, some 200,000 people attended the event, which featured a military parade, demonstrations of precision marching, and target firing (London *Times*, 9 Aug.).

⁷ The Philadelphia *Federal Gazette*, 15 Oct., printed the item that TBA paraphrases here under the headline "Melancholy Intelligence, If True." This was just one of many reports appearing in newspapers throughout the United States on the situation in France, often offering contradictory information. The report was a mixture of fact and exaggeration; see AA2 to AA, 13 Sept., and notes, above.

⁸ John Bringhurst (1726–1795) was a noted Germantown carriage maker. Capt. Reuben Carver sailed the schooner *Friendship* between Boston and Philadelphia (Laurens, *Papers*, 7:574; Boston *Columbian Centinel*, 15 Aug.).

John Adams to Abigail Adams Smith

My Dear Daughter: Quincy, October 29, 1792.

I received with great pleasure your kind letter from Dover,¹ and rejoiced in your safe arrival in England; but I have not been able to write you until now. When I was at the bar, I had commonly clerks who took off from me much of the manual labour of writing. While I was abroad I had commonly Secretaries to assist me. But now, when my hand shakes and my eyes fail, I have no one even to copy a letter, so that I am obliged to lay aside all pretensions of answering letters. My inclination has been strong to write to you and Col. Smith long ago, but ability has been wanting.

You are in Europe at a critical moment, more proper perhaps to make useful observations and reflections than any other which has occurred for centuries; but the scenes about you—at a distance, are terrible; and those which are near you, must be infested with a party spirit very anxious and very unsociable. You will soon wish yourself at home. We, indeed, have our parties and our sophistry, and our rivalries, but they proceed not to violence. The elections are going on in New-England with a spirit of sobriety and moderation, which will do us honour; and, I have not heard of any thing more intemperate than might be expected, in the southward or middle states.

For myself, I have made up my mind, and am more anxious to get out of public life than to continue in. I can say, with infinitely more sincerity than Cæsar, that I have lived enough to glory, however feeble the glimmer may be. I am not disposed to say with him, that I have lived enough to life, for I should like to live to see the end of the revolutions in Europe, and that will not be these hundred years.[2] My kind regards to Col. Smith and my dear boys, and to all friends.

Your mamma, I suppose, has told you all the news among our acquaintance, and it will be no pleasure to you to hear me repeat it. One thing she has forgotten: Capt. Beale of Squantam has set up, between me and my brother, a new house, the largest and handsomest ever built in their neighbourhood.[3]

What says my friend Brand Hollis to the French democrats now? Does his admiration of Mr. Paine continue or diminish? If my friend really loves king-killing, he is like to be satiated. I own I do not. My faith is immovable, that after ever so many trials, the nations of Europe will find, that equal laws, and natural rights and essential liberties can never be preserved among them without such an unity of the executive power.

I am, my dear child, / With much affection, / Yours,

John Adams.

MS not found. Printed from AA2, *Jour. and Corr.*, 2:123–125.

[1] AA2 to JA, 7 May, above.
[2] "I have lived long enough to satisfy either nature or glory" (attributed to Julius Caesar).
[3] The Beale House is now part of the Adams National Historical Park.

Thomas Boylston Adams to John Adams

My dear sir,   Philadelphia Oct^r: 30th: 1792,

Your kind favor of the 11th: reached me some time since.[1] The reasons you assign for delaying your journey to Philad^a: would be sufficient to satisfy me, but I have been particularly requested by several of your warmest Friends, to mention that your determination may be viewed in a different point of light by those who seek occasions & opportunities to injure you or your cause. It has become a matter of pretty general enquiry why the VP—is not to be here at the first of the Session, and it is feared that your final resolution concerning your journey hither, is only to be decided by the event of the Election. There has been such a spirit discovered in this, & the Southern States within a few months past, that the Friends & advocates of the present state of things, feel themselves extreemly alarmed; and one of their principal reasons for wishing your presence as soon as possible at the head of the Senate, is the weight which your influence may have, to counteract the progress of dangerous measures. A single vote taken from any of the Eastern States, at this particular juncture, is thought to be of great consequence in the Political Ballance; especially as at this Session, a Reinforcement is expected from Kentucky.[2]

The dreadful scenes now acting in France, and the universal anarchy which appears to prevail, has excited terrors even in the breasts of the warmest enthousiasts for Revolution; and the justice of your principles with respect to Government begin to be openly acknowledged, tho' they have long been *silently* seen.

'Tis said to be your *happy fate* to be the most obnoxious character in the United States, to a certain party, (whose hatred & opposition is the glory of every honest man) who for a long time have considered you as the first barrier to be removed in order to the success of their designs. If this be true, the necessity of your presence at this time will appear more striking than ever, as 'tis thought every exertion will be made on their part the coming Session to embarrass the most important measures, and even to subvert some that have allready received sanction. You will recollect that all the momentous questions which were agitated in Senate last session, were finally decided by the casting vote, and altho' upon some accounts it may not be a very pleasing reflection, that the President of the Senate must necessarily encounter the Odium of half the Assembly in the honest discharge of his duty, yet there is some consolation to be derived from the involuntary veneration which that firmness of conduct must inspire, even in the breasts of those he may disappoint.[3]

The open opposition to the excise Law in the back parts of this State, has occasioned much anxiety to the President of the U, S,. His Proclamation has been treated with contempt, and some publications in the Pittsburgh Gazett have gone so far as to defy any attempts to enforce the law.[4]

Your goodness will I hope excuse [the] liberty I have taken in suggesting these inducements [in] hastening your Journey. If they appear to you of the same consequence as to those at whose request I have communicated them, I shall feel happy in having complyed with their desires; if not, I hope you will attribute it to the interest I feel in every thing that appears particularly to relate to you or your Office.

I have not yet been able to procure accomodations for your Reception; but hope to do it in a few days. M^r. & M^rs. Otis have made a very obliging offer of a Room in their House, but no exertion on my part shall be wanting to procure the appartments mentioned in your letter.

Presenting my best love to the Family at Quincy and all other friends

I subscribe myself your dutiful / Son   Thos B Adams

RC (Adams Papers); addressed: "The Vice President of the U,S, / Quincy / near / Boston"; internal address: "The Vice President of the U,S,"; endorsed: "T. B. Adams / Octr. 30. 1792 / ans^d Nov. 14. / rec^d 13." Some loss of text where the seal was removed.

[1] Not found.

[2] Kentucky, which became a state on 1 June, sent two senators for the second session of the 2d Congress: John Edwards and John Brown, both of whom attended the Senate for the first time on 5 November. Edwards (1748–1837) had served in the Va. House of Delegates and helped to frame Kentucky's state constitution. Brown (1757–1837), a lawyer, had represented Kentucky in the Va. senate and had also previously served as a congressional representative from Virginia from 1789 to 1792 (*Biog. Dir. Cong.*).

[3] While most of the Senate's deliberations were secret, the *Annals of Congress* indicate that JA cast deciding votes on several procedural motions related to the bills for apportioning representatives and for conveying land to the Ohio Company (2d Cong., 1st sess., p. 47, 49–50, 51, 123–124).

[4] Although Congress had passed into law a tax bill that included an excise on distilled liquor in March 1791, no one attempted to enforce it in western Pennsylvania until Aug. 1792. People in that region, as well as in many other areas of the country, had been and remained strongly opposed to the law. They argued that the excise disproportion-

ately affected those who lived in the western parts of the United States and laborers and the poor, primary consumers of domestic spirits. Opposition to the excise took a variety of forms, including petitions, assemblies, and occasionally violence, and would grow into what became known as the Whiskey Rebellion by 1794.

By fall of 1792, Alexander Hamilton's concern at the continuing opposition to the excise—especially resolutions by a Pittsburgh assembly calling for "every other legal measure that may obstruct the operation of the law, until we are able to obtain its total repeal"—led him to push for the use of the military to enforce it. While he could not convince the rest of George Washington's administration to support military action at that time, he did convince Washington to issue a proclamation, dated 15 Sept., decrying the "violent and unwarrantable proceedings" and directing "all courts, magistrates and officers" to take appropriate action to enforce the law (Thomas P. Slaughter, *The Whiskey Rebellion: Frontier Epilogue to the American Revolution*, N.Y., 1986, p. 105, 109–124; Philadelphia *Federal Gazette*, 25 Sept.).

Thomas Boylston Adams to Abigail Adams

My dear Mother,   Philadelphia Nov; 2^d. 1792

I have received your favor of the 21st. [1] and as I want a little private conversation with you, must oblige you to pay the Postage of my answer. At the request of several of our Friends I addressed a Letter to my Father a day or two since—stating certain reasons for hastening his Journey to Philad[a:] and most of those were of a public nature; but I omitted to mention any inducements of a personal nature to him, because I chose rather to communicate them to you. It is feared lest his absence from the Seat of Gov[t:] at this critical period, will give a handle to his Enemies, who will use every effort to divert the votes of the Electors in some of the States from him, and thereby prevent his having a Majority. I know there is not a man connected with the Gov[t:] who is less disposed to trouble his friends upon an occasion of this kind, or who has less dread of the arts of his opponents, yet the question is whether his absence at this time may not be construed by them as an unfavorable symptom in public affairs. The spirit of opposition increases to the southward, and every opportunity which can be seized, will be eagerly employed to embarrass the public Counsels. The reasons assigned by my Father in his letter to me, for delaying his Journey, were perfectly satisfactory, because I considered the delacacy of his situation with respect to the coming Election, and am acquainted with his wish to have it pretty clearly decided before he undertakes the Journey. The anxiety which is expressed by his friends arises from the apprehension lest he should be absent the whole session, which they are now willing to acknowledge might have considerable influence upon public measures. It seldom happens that any business of great importance is transacted in the first weeks of a Session, so that he would not be so much missed as at a later period, but if the complexion of the Election should be unfavorable, he may determine not to come at all, which, every one knows would injure the Federal interest materially. I hope therefore both Public & private considerations will induce him to come on. I hear no doubts or surmises expressed with regard to the Election; nor do I hear of a single Candidate whose Rivalship may be dreaded. If any thing like a serious or formidable contest were meditated, I should certainly hear of it from my young Companions at least, who have never discovered a disposition to conceal any thing of this kind from me. Burr is mentioned—but so faintly that I doubt whether he secures three votes, notwithstanding he has the support of P—— Edwards[2] or A J Dallas. Maryland is said to be favorable to the present State of affairs, altho', Mercer has been reelected.[3] But enough of this— Now with regard to Lodgings, I know not where to apply further than I have allready. It seems as if the whole City was full even to an overflow— I shall be constantly upon the look out, but all the Lodging Houses are full, as I find most of the members of Congress bespoke their old places before they left this place last year; we must wait therefore till some favorable opening occurs.

There are no complete setts of the National Gazett to be procured from its Commencement, and my Patiotism is too strong to give so small an encouragement as the price of a single Paper, to such an engine of party opposition; I shall wait therefore till you tell me what effect this reason has with you, before I send orders to the Editor— Fenno will have nothing to do with him. The negociation therefore must be carried on in my name, to which I oppose the above objection.

I have taken a huge fancy to some of your Cheese, and as I still retain a share of affection for my native soil, a little of its produce would be particularly acceptable, at this time; My Quaker Friends, are the most hospitable people in the Circle of my acquaintance, and my good Lady, by her friendly offices, renders your absence infinitely less irksome than I could expect; I wish therefore to make her a small present of this kind, provided you can spare half a Dozen or so, from your stock; you may think it a singular request, but I hope not unreasonable. They may be put in a small Cask & sent by water, if convenient.

My health has mended much since the Cold weather set in; I prevent any *kinks* in my bones by regular exercise, and as to the Ague, the Bark proved too strong for it this season, tho I come within an ace of it several times; The Wine which was left me, was of great service, I say *was* because I finished the last of it yesterday— I can wait conveniently till my Father comes to have it replenished, if you think it a reasonable expence. My paper says, good by to you,—my best love to Unkles Aunts, Brothers Cousins &c

T B A.

RC (Adams Papers).

[1] Not found.

[2] Pierpont Edwards (1750–1826), Princeton 1768, was an influential Connecticut lawyer who had previously been a delegate to the Continental Congress in 1787–1788. Edwards was also Aaron Burr's uncle (*DAB*).

[3] John Francis Mercer (1759–1821), William and Mary 1775, had served as a delegate to the Continental Congress from Virginia in 1783–1784 but now represented Maryland (*Biog. Dir. Cong.*).

Abigail Adams to Abigail Adams Smith

My dear Mrs Smith   Quincy Nov'br 3.d 1792

Mrs Jeffry sails in Captain Scott and is so good as to say that she will take Letters to you. I have written to you by Captain Barnard who generally has quick passages—and by his return I hope to hear from you. I had Letters last week from Charles. he writes that our Friends in N york were all well, excepting chief Justice Jay who had been dangerously Sick, but was then on the recovery. The complextion of politicks in that state was rather against the National Goverment. the Governours Party having carried all their Projects, and Burr was rewarded for his opinion upon the Legality of the Election with a judgeship of the supreem Court. From Philadelphia Thomas writes me that the returns for Representatives were generally Federal[1] in Conneticut the old Members are all rechosen with the addition of two new Members.[2] Hampshire the old set, in senate Wingate is out, and judge Livermore in his Room.[3] the Choise in this state will be on fryday next when from the complextion of affairs I presume we shall get a good set.[4] Mr Gerry has declined serving again. I wish you to write me when you think it likely you shall return. I hope you will not go to sea again in the circumstances you went in before. you was certainly in the greatest Danger of losing your Life. I was much surprizd at the circumstance of mrs Copleys never having received her Money for the silk she purchased. I wrote to mrs Welch directly and as it hapned the dr had a Receit for the money deliverd to a mr Hubard 30 dollors which according to the Bill which accompanied the silk would have been sufficient, had it been left. mr Hubard was out of Town but has been written to about it and mrs Gray assures me that as soon as she can learn how the affair hap'ned she will inform me and that the money which she supposed she had advancd at the Time the silk was procured, shall be sent by captain Barnard.[5] I certainly should never have askd such a favour for myself, much less should I have done it for an other person, and I am extreemly sorry that mrs Copleys delicacy has prevented her from informing me before I beg you to make every apology for me who was only a mere agent in the Buisness—but would sooner pay the money myself than mrs Copley should lay any longer out of it.

if you will with the china Send me a Bill of it, I will either remitt you the Money or pay it to whom ever you direct. I find that Barnard will not sail so soon as scott. I put one Letter into the Bagg the other I shall give to mrs Jeffry. The Print you mention of the death of Chatham is come to Philadelphia, but we have not yet got it, or learnt where it is lodg'd, the Captain dye'd a few Days after his arrival.[6] when your Father goes to Philadelphia Brisler will take measures to find it. my Love to the dear Boys.

present me kindly to Mr Vassel and Family to mr & mrs smith, and to all other Friends[7] Let me hear often from you, and where you have been whom you have seen of our old acquaintance, my old servants I should be glad to hear of.

Your Aunt Cranch desires me to remember you to her I ought first to have mentiond your aged Grandmother who always kindly inquires after you. Send her a fan or any triffel by Barnard. the Idea that you remember her at such a distance gratifies her tenfold more than the value of the present. I mention a fan because a dog tore hers to peices which she had long had, and highly valued. The old Lady is as well this summer as the last, and is now in her 84th year. my Love to the Col Tell him to take care of his Health. I am my dear Daughter your ever affectionate / Mother   A Adams

RC (Adams Papers); addressed: "To / Mrs Smith / Argile Street No 38 / London."

[1] TBA to AA, 17 Oct., above.

[2] AA was slightly mistaken. One Connecticut representative, Jonathan Sturges, was not reelected. The three new members of Congress—all Federalists—were Joshua Coit, Zephaniah Swift, and Uriah Tracy (*Biog. Dir. Cong.*).

[3] Samuel Livermore and Paine Wingate switched roles: Livermore moved from the House of Representatives to the Senate, while Wingate stepped down from the Senate to the House. Livermore (1732–1803), Princeton 1752, originally studied law in Waltham, Mass., but moved to New Hampshire in 1758. He served in the Continental Congress and as chief justice of New Hampshire's state supreme court, 1782–1789. Wingate (1739–1838), Harvard 1759, was a Congregational minister who later turned to farming and politics, serving in a variety of state and federal positions between 1781 and 1809 (same).

[4] Massachusetts reelected Caleb Strong and George Cabot as its senators. For the House of Representatives, the state elected Fisher Ames, Shearjashub Bourne, David Cobb, Peleg Coffin Jr., Henry Dearborn,

Samuel Dexter, Dwight Foster, Benjamin Goodhue, Samuel Holten, William Lyman, Theodore Sedgwick, George Thacher, Peleg Wadsworth, and Artemas Ward. Ames, Bourne, Goodhue, Sedgwick, Thacher, and Ward had all previously served in the 2d Congress, and all were Federalists except Dearborn, Holten, and Lyman (same).

[5] On 6 Oct. 1789, Susanna Clarke Copley wrote to AA that she had sent twenty yards of silk "according to your direction" (vol. 8:419). See also AA to Thomas Welsh, 15 Nov. 1792, and AA to Susanna Clarke Copley, [*post 15 Nov.*], both below.

[6] On 20 April, John Singleton Copley wrote to JA (Adams Papers), indicating he was sending two copies of the recently completed engraving of Copley's 1781 painting *The Death of the Earl of Chatham*, one for the Adamses and one for George Washington. Because the Adamses were in Quincy at the time the engravings arrived in Philadelphia, they were unable to receive them directly. By 27 Jan. 1793, however, JA was able to write to Copley to thank him for the engraving and to assure him that JA had delivered one to Washington personally (MB).

The copy belonging to the Adamses remained in the family and hangs in the dining room at MQA.

⁷ William and Margaret Hubbard Vassall and William and Frances Coape Smith had been social acquaintances of the Adamses during their time in London (vol. 6:305, 311, 381, 388).

Mary Smith Gray Otis to Abigail Adams

Dear Mʳˢ Adams   Philadelphia Novʳ: 3ᵈ· —92

It was my intention to have written to you earlier after my return than this, but have found my time very much taken up, with puting my house in order.— You will not however think me less sincere for being late in my enquieres after your health, which I am sorry to hear is not yet confirmed. Your friends here regret very much, being deprived of your society this winter and are only reconciled to it, by the consideration of its being benificial to you.— The Vice President has been anxiously expected here, at this time by his friends, & his delay is considered as an unfortunate curcumstance, as it respects himself & his country, the former consideration I know, he is too much above, the latter I trust has still some influence upon his mind.— Haveing said thus much, give me leave to adde, that I think, there is no lodging house sutable for the Vice President to be at, to be with other boarders, will not assuredly do; & there is no place that he can come to, with so much propriety as to our house, we have rooms enough and will accomodate him the best in our power.— Mʳ Bryslar knows all his wants, and with his assistance, I think he will be as well of as at a Boarding House.— This is not ment as a complement, but as what would give Mʳ Otis & myself great pleasure.—

The ladies of Congress are all here there is no addition to the number, but only Mʳˢ Ames,[1] the city begins to be gay, but they have not yet enter'd into the spirit of Card Partys

Remember me to Mʳˢ Cranch & family love to Louisa.— And whenever you can find time to write me, you will give pleasure to /
Your Affecᵗ Cous[in]   M Otis

[*ca. 7 November*]

Mʳ Otis encloses a copy of the speech & informs that Mʳ Lees having declined public business &, the Vice President not arrived Mʳ Langdon is Pres: pro tem:— Mʳ O encloses the Speech[2] & will send the minutes the next post.[3]

RC (Adams Papers); addressed: "Mʳˢ: Adams / Quincy." Some loss of text where the seal was removed.

¹ Fisher Ames had married Frances Worthington (b. 1764) of Springfield, Mass., in July after a lengthy courtship (Winfred E. A. Bernhard, *Fisher Ames: Federalist and Statesman 1758–1808*, Chapel Hill, N.C., 1965, p. 200–203).

² Otis emphasized this word by circling it in curlicues.

³ Richard Henry Lee, the Senate's president pro tempore, had resigned on 8 Oct.;

John Langdon was elected on 5 Nov. in his place (*Biog. Dir. Cong.*). The speech enclosed (not found) was likely George Washington's address to Congress of 6 Nov., which first appeared in print in the Philadelphia *Gazette of the United States*, 7 November. On 12 Nov., Samuel Alleyne Otis wrote to JA enclosing the minutes of the proceedings of the Senate, including its response to Washington's address (Adams Papers).

Abigail Adams to Thomas Welsh

Dear sir   Quincy 15 Nov^br 1792

I inclose to you a memorandum which I received from Mrs Smith,¹ the Receit given you for the Money I have received and will forward in a Letter to mrs Copley but at the same time I wish to know how she is to come at the money lodged in the Bank. perhaps mrs Gray has taken measures for that, but as I feel myself in some degree responsible to mrs Copley I wish when I write to her & state the facts, that she may at the same time receive her money.

My son takes Fennos paper in which is a peice dated Annopolis & signed a consistant Republican I think, for I have not now the paper by me. I would suggest to you sir whether it might not be proper for Russel to republish it.² the people of this state appear to feel themselves safe and I believe are happy under the National Goverment, but if they mean to continue so they must be more vigilint, for never since the commencment of the Goverment has there been so formi[dable] a combination to overthrow it. there are no falsehoods too barefaced for the Antis to circulate. the zeal with which a certain Gentleman in Boston is brought forward for a Representitive shews plainly that like Moles, much work has been done in this state underground.³ mr Ames I find in one place has been Represented as having made an immence fortune by speculation, in an other place the people have been told that he was an Enemy to the Rights of the People and in an other, where such a report was known to be unpopular, that he was in favour of the Petition of the officers of the late Army, but they may be assured that Massachusetts has not a Member who has more uniformly supported the National Goverment since its commencment and with abilities which his Enemies dread.⁴ let our Country men look at France and ask themselves do the Rights of Men consist in the destruction & devastation of Private property do the Rights of Man consist in Murder &

8. "HIGH STREET, FROM NINTH STREET. PHILADELPHIA,"
BY WILLIAM RUSSELL BIRCH AND THOMAS BIRCH, 1799

See page xvi

Massacre without distinction of Age or youth of sex or condition, Scenes which Humanity Sickens at, the very recital of which at this [distan]ce from the scene of carnage, the Youthfull Blood is frozen, and each particular Hair as shakspear expresses it, stands an End, like quills upon the fretted Porcupine.[5]

Mr Adams sets of on monday next could you ride up and dine with us on sunday we shall be very happy to see you. my kind Regards to mrs welch and family—

yours affectionatly   A A

RC (Adams Papers); addressed: "Dr Thomas Welch / Boston"; docketed: "M^rs· A Adams '92." Some loss of text due to a torn manuscript.

[1] Not found.

[2] "To the People of Maryland," which was signed "A Consistent Federalist" and dated Annapolis, 19 Oct., appeared in the Philadelphia *Gazette of the United States*, 31 Oct., reprinted from the *Maryland Journal and Baltimore Advertiser*, 23 October. Benjamin Russell reprinted the article in the Boston *Columbian Centinel*, 17 Nov., under the signature "A Constant Federalist." The article, responding to a suggestion that Charles Carroll of Carrollton replace JA as vice president, argues that Antifederalists had long opposed JA "because his abilities and principles were formidable to their views and ambition; and because to prevent his re-election would be a point gained over the constitution itself." It goes on to summarize much of JA's diplomatic career in glowing terms and to suggest that "the knowledge he acquired, in these several missions, of the *interests and views of the courts of Europe*, fit him in a peculiar manner to fill, to the greatest advantage, the station he now occupies."

[3] Benjamin Austin Jr., who was defeated by Fisher Ames for Suffolk County representative (Boston *Columbian Centinel*, 3 Nov.).

[4] During the weeks before the election, various newspaper items appeared questioning Ames' disinterestedness and suggesting his collusion with speculators; see, for example, Boston *Independent Chronicle*, 25 Oct., and *Boston Gazette*, 29 October. After the election, the *Boston Gazette*, 5 Nov., printed a satirical piece breaking down who voted for Ames into categories such as "Branch Bank Officers, Directors and Runners"; "Persons interested deeply in the Funds, alias Paper-Men"; and, finally, "A noted, idle stroller, who *has been too fat* to engage in any Business but Speculation!" Two years earlier, Ames had been accused of withholding from Congress a petition signed by thousands of soldiers in opposition to the funding bill (Stewart, *Opposition Press*, p. 42).

[5] Shakespeare, *Hamlet*, Act I, scene v, line 20.

Abigail Adams to Susanna Clarke Copley

my dear Madam   [*post 15 November 1792*][1]

I was not a little Surprizd at receiving intelligence through mrs smith soon after her arrival that you had never received the Money for the Silk you was so good as to purchase at my request three years ago— I am extreemly sorry that your delicacy prevented you from giving me this information at an earlier period. most assuredly Madam I would not have askd such a favour for myself nor could I have ventured it for any other person. upon my Receiving mrs smiths Letter I immediatly informd mrs Gray of it who was not less surprizd than I was—for 30 dollors was sent with the Letter and Mrs Gray supposd that it was paid for at the Time the silk was sent tho she now recollects that the Bill which she received was not receited. a Mr Russel Hubbard was the person who received the money and not finding mrs Copley at Home when he left the Letter he lodgd the money in the Bank of England where it now is. he thought no more of it, and mrs Adams did not see mrs Gray till two years after when she thanked her me[2] for having procured her silk through mrs Copley

I inclose you the Recit which will enable you to receive at the Bank the 30 dollar with one pr cent interest from the time it was lodg'd there, as I am informd. I am unacquainted with the mercantile method of doing Buisness but suppose it is Regular. if there should still be any diffiulty remaining I hope you will be kind enough to inform me

our late dear suffering Friend mrs Rogers I shall always remember with a sisterly affection She was happily for her releazd and I believe I may add made perfect as humane Nature was capable of, through Sufferings if ever there was a sincere mourner mr Rogers may be rankd in that Class—

My dear Mrs Smith expresses herself happy in the Renewal of her acquaintane with you—and in the continuence of your Friendship. I hope she will not be in a situation to call upon you for such assistance as you have formerly renderd her, but if she should, I shall more than ever solicit your kind attention to her. I hope she will never venture to sea in circumstances similar to those in which she made her last voyage which nearly cost her her Life.

My own Health has sufferd so much by my Residence at Philadelphia that I do not propose going there this winter.

I hope mr Copley & the Ladies your daughters enjoy their Health. miss Copleys Rose Tree I still preserve & tho it has out lived several seasons & many of the productions of Nature Time has Rob'd it in some measure of its Bloom.[3]

I am dear Madam with my best wishes for your Health & happiness / Your Friend & Humble servant   A. A

Dft (Adams Papers). Filmed at [1792].

[1] The dating of this letter is based on AA's letters of 3 Nov. to AA2 and of 15 Nov. to Thomas Welsh, both above.

[2] AA initially wrote "her" then added "me" directly above it.

[3] AA brought two rose bushes back from England in 1788, a red Lancaster and a white York, which she planted at the Old House. The Lancaster survived into the nineteenth century; the York is still flourishing at the Adams National Historical Park.

John Adams to Abigail Adams

My dearest Friend   Hartford Nov. 24. 1792

The Weather has been so disagreable and the Roads so bad, that I have not been able to advance farther on my Journey than to Bulls Tavern in this Town where I arrived last night after an unpleasant ride in the snow from Springfield.[1] It Snowed all last night and has blocked up the roads so that I cannot move onwards till monday.

I have fallen into Several curious Conversations, on the road, which however would be too trifling to commit to Paper. a Gentleman of very respectable Appearance told me last Evening without knowing or Suspecting me, all the Politicks of New York and Philadelphia for and against the V. President. "The V. P. had been as all Acknowledged a great Friend to this Country, but had given offence to his Fellow Citizens in Massachusetts, by writing something in favour of hereditary descent. That he had been long in Europe and got tainted." I told him laughing that it was hard if a Man could not go to Europe without being tainted. that if Mr Adams had been Sent to Europe upon their Business by the People, and had done it, and in doing it had necessarily got tainted I thought the People ought to pay him for the Damage the Taint had done him, or find some Means to wash it out and cleanse him.

Govr H. has been here and made a Dinner for the Gentleman of this Town.[2] one asked after the V. P. "The Governor had not Spoken to the V. P. this year; He was not one of the Well born." A Gentleman remarked upon it afterwards what would Mr H. have been if he had not been well born the Nephew of the rich Uncle Thomas.? in short his Silly Envy of the V. P. is perceived & ridiculed by all the World out of Massachusetts. He is considerd as a mere rich Man prodigal of his Wealth to obtain an empty Bubble of Popularity.

I am told that an unanimous Vote will be for me in Vermont New Hampshire, Connecticut and Rhode Island. This is generally expected, but I know full well the Uncertainty of Such Things, and am prepared to meet an Unanimous Vote against me. Mr P. E. came off miserably. He gave such offence by mentioning his Nephew, that they would not appoint one Man who had any connection with him.[3]

I would not entertain you with this political Title tattle, if I had any thing of more importance to say. one Thing of more importance

to me, but no News to you is that I am / yours with unabated Esteem & / affection forever   J. A.

RC (Adams Papers); internal address: "Portia."; endorsed: "Novbr / 24 1792."

[1] Capt. Frederick Bull (d. 1797) ran a tavern in Hartford (Hartford *Connecticut Courant*, 21 Oct. 1793; Middletown, Conn., *Middlesex Gazette*, 24 Feb. 1797).

[2] John Hancock traveled to Connecticut
in October, primarily to visit family and

friends in Fairfield (Herbert S. Allan, *John
Hancock: Patriot in Purple*, N.Y., 1953, p. 352;
New York *Diary*, 16 Oct.).

[3] That is, Pierpont Edwards and his
nephew Aaron Burr.

Abigail Adams to John Adams

my Dearest Friend   Sunday Quincy Nov[br] 26 1792

Such has been the weather Since you left me, that I cannot form
any accurate judgment where you now are. I sometimes conjecture
that you are not farther than Brookfield. at any rate you must have
had an unpleasent week, tho perhaps not so severe a snow storm as
we have had here. Monday afternoon & all twesday it raind then
cleard up very cold and blustering. on fryday came on a snow storm
wind very voilent at North East. it continued so through fryday
Night and saturday even untill sunday morning, when the snow was
over the tops of the Stone walls and so Bank'd that no wheel carriage can stir. we had not any meeting to day, and some person had
their sheep to digg out from under the snow Banks. ours very fortunately experienced the comfort of their new habitation. the Hay was
housed on fryday, & bedding provided for the Horses, but the Boat
is not carried to the Island. after the storm of twesday shaw[1] and
Tirril went to see if she could be got of, but the very high Tide had
thrown her up so high that they pronounced it impossible untill the
Tides rose again, and that it would be more adviseable to turn her
over where she now is, & secure her there for the winter, this Snow
storm confirms them in the opinion I never remember so severe a
snow storm in November. I hope to hear from you this week. I have
felt much anxiety for you, more perhaps than if I had been a fellow
traveller with you with Books about me I have felt dismal & Lonely.
you left the only ones you intended to take; and an Inn seldom furnishes any entertainment of a literary kind. I hope Brisler minds to
have a fire in your Bed Room and that your sheets are well aird and
your Bed well cloathd. remind him of this injunction yet I know not
whether this will reach you soon enough to put it in practise. Porter
who was to cut our wood and Timber is confind to his Bed with the

Rhumatism.[2] most families I find are caught without wood, so that it is to be hoped they will turn out & make roads. I think you will find it necessary to take a sleigh and if so you will travel with more ease to yourself than with wheels

I cannot tell you any news not having seen to my great mortification any News paper since you went away nor have I been out of the House since I returnd after leaving you. I did not think I should have felt so lonely. it seems so still all day long as if half the Family were gone.

Let me hear from you as soon as you get to Philadelphia, and sooner if this should reach you at Nyork as I design it shall—

I am most affectionatly / yours   A Adams

I hope poor Cheeseman is not cast away with your Trunk of cloaths, but if he was within reach of the storm I know not how he could stand it. I presume we shall hear many a melancholy ship wreck[3]

RC (Adams Papers); addressed by JQA: "The Vice-President of the United States / Philadelphia."; endorsed: "Portia / Nov. 26. 1792."

[1] Ezra Shaw Jr. (b. 1771) of Abington (*Vital Records of Abington, Massachusetts, to the Year 1850*, 2 vols., Boston, 1912, 1:204).

[2] David Porter (1753–1827) of Abington (Joseph W. Porter, *A Genealogy of the Descendants of Richard Porter*, Bangor, Maine, 1878, p. 55–56).

[3] Capt. Samuel Chesman's ship, the *Trion*, arrived safely in Philadelphia by early December (Philadelphia *Gazette of the United States*, 8 Dec.).

John Adams to Abigail Adams

My dearest Friend   New York Dec[r.] 2. 1792

At Hartford, finding the Roads obstructed with Such Banks of Snow, as were impassable with Wheels I left my Chaise with M[r] Frederick Bull of that town to be sent to Boston, and my Horses to be sent after me, and took to the Mail Stage. We happened to have agreable Passengers, and arrived here on Wednesday night. as I had little sleep for several nights, I found myself fatigued, a little fevourish with a bad Sore throat, and have been nursing here till sunday. tomorrow morning I go off for Philadelphia. Charles and our Friends are well— Some Persons have rec[d] letters from our Children in London who expect to come home in the Spring.

Governor Clinton is to be V. P. of U. S. and Gov[r] of N. Y. too, at least this is the Sanguine Stile both of his Friends and Enemies.

Some of both I mean. The C. J. has been very Sick but is recovered. He looks very thin and pale however.

Charles has had some Business, and has argued and gained his first Cause. It is no small Thing to make the Beginning at the Bar. He wants Books and I must help him to purchase a few of the most necessary.

I wrote you from Hartford and shall write again from Philadelphia. I hear many Stories of Marches and Countermarches Intrigues and Manœuvres of Burke[1] Dallas, Edwards Clinton &c &c to form Combinations v$^{s.}$ the V. P. but I know not how much of it to Credit. at all Events I hope I shall not be obliged to lie alone next Winter, and with this Wish I close my Letter—

yours forever & forever   J. A.

RC (Adams Papers); addressed: "Mrs Adams / Quincy / near / Boston"; internal address: "Portia"; endorsed: "Dec^{br} 2. 1792"; notation: "Free / John Adams."

[1] Aedanus Burke (1743–1802), an Irishman who settled in Charleston, S.C., had been an Antifederalist during the ratification debate. He served a single term in Congress before returning to South Carolina where he was appointed chancellor of the equity courts (*Biog. Dir. Cong.*).

Abigail Adams to John Adams

my dearest Friend   Quincy Dec^{br} 4th 1792

I was very happy to receive on thanksgiving day the 29 of Nov$^{br.}$ your Letter dated Hartford. I feard that you had not reachd so far the weather was so dissagreable, but if the Roads have mended as much with you as they have this way, you have reachd Philadelphia by this time. I shall with impatience wait to hear of your arrival there. the snow remaind with us but one week Since which we have had pleasent weather. there has not anything occurd material that I know of since you left us— if you get Russels paper you will see a little deserved Burlisque upon the Govenours speach respecting the expressions made us of by Congress which gave him such umbrage.[1] Tomorrow is a very important day to the united states, much more important to them, than it can possibly be to you or to me for think of it as they please tomorrow will determine whether their Government shall stand four years longer or Not. mr Clinton Seems to be the only competitor held up. I fancy he will receive no aid from N England. I hope you will order Fenno to continue his paper to me. We have had a Gang of Thieves infesting this Town since you left it.

333

the thursday after you went away Shaw & James went into the woods & in the day time the best saddle was stolen out of the Barn closset. the same Night mr Cary had his best Horse stolen[2] and mr smith who lives on mrs Rows place had his taken the same night[3] and last Sunday morning James came Running in to inform me that his Stables had been attempted, & his Lock broken, but being doubly secured the villan could not effect his purpose. he tried the Coach house door & split of a peice of the door, but could not get the Bar out. he went on to mr Adams's at Milton & stole his Horse[4] a Traveller lodged at Marshes Tavern on saturday night, who got up in the Night Rob'd the House of various articles of wearing Apparal and made of. we Suppose that he was the person who attempted our stables and that he belongs to a Gang. they are in persuit of him[5]

your Mother was well this day she spent it with me. She and your Brother & family all dinned with me on thanksgiving day as well as our Son. tis the first thanksgiving day that I have been at Home to commemerate for Nine years. Scatterd and dispersed as our Family is, God only knows whether we shall ever all meet together again much of the pleasure and happiness resulting from these N England Annual feltivals is the family circles & connections which are brought together at these times, but whether seperate or together I am sensible that every year has been productive of many Blessings, and that I have great cause of thankfulness for preserving mercies both to myself & Family.

I inclose a Letter for Brisler[6] I wish him to inquire the price of Rye that I may know whether it would quit cost to send me a dozen Bushel tis five & six pence pr Bushel here. Superfine flower I want to know the price of, it has taken a rise here[7]

my Love to Thomas tell him to write me often I hope the House of Reps will be in a little better humour after all Elections are over. I ~~hope~~ trust they will not follow the French example & Lop of Heads, even of departments. they appear to have a great terror of them I see a Lucius & a Marcus, I should like to know who they are.[8] [. . . .]hee many compliments & respects to all my good Friends in Philadelphia. I flatter myself I have some there, and be assured of the affectionate Regard / of your   A Adams

RC (Adams Papers); addressed by JQA: "The Vice-President of the United States. / Philadelphia."; endorsed: "Portia. Decr 4. / ans^d. 19. 1792." Some loss of text where the seal was removed.

¹ On 12 Nov., John Hancock addressed the Mass. General Court. In his speech, he took exception to a directive from Congress that "the Supreme Executive of each State SHALL cause three lists of the names of the Electors of such State to be made and certified." Hancock believed that the use of the word "shall" was inappropriate; he argued, "that Government applies itself to the People of the United States in their natural, individual capacity, and cannot exert any force upon, or by any means controul the officers of the State Governments as such: Therefore, when an Act of Congress uses compulsory words with regard to any Act to be done by the Supreme Executive of this Commonwealth, I shall not feel myself obliged to obey them" (Boston *Columbian Centinel,* 14 Nov.).

² Alpheus Cary (1761–1816) of North Bridgewater later served as a selectman in Quincy (Sprague, *Braintree Families*).

³ Probably Hannah Rowe of Milton (Pattee, *Old Braintree,* p. 60).

⁴ Lemuel Adams (1748–1833) of Milton (Sprague, *Braintree Families*).

⁵ The tavern proprietor may have been Jonathan Marsh (1753–1822), who lived on Hancock Street and held various town offices (same; Pattee, *Old Braintree,* p. 171).

⁶ Not found.

⁷ In Dec. 1792, rye was priced at three to three and a half shillings per bushel in Philadelphia; superfine flour cost forty shillings per barrel (Philadelphia *Federal Gazette,* 1 Dec.).

⁸ Lucius, probably Melancton Smith, argues in two articles in the Philadelphia *American Daily Advertiser,* 14 and 24 Nov. 1792, that JA's writings in *Defence of the Const.* and *Discourses on Davila* demonstrated his attachment "to a goverment of king, lords, and commons," making him unsuitable to be reelected vice president. Comparing JA and George Clinton, Lucius writes, "The characteristic difference, then, in their political principles simply amounts to this, that those of Mr. Adams vary radically from the constitution, in the main features of the republican system; whereas those of his competitor harmonize with it in that essential point." Marcus' essay, which initially appeared in the Philadelphia *Gazette of the United States,* 21 Nov., replies to Lucius in defense of JA, arguing that the *Defence of the Const.* "is the best defence of a free republican government in the English language" (Young, *Democratic Republicans,* p. 331).

John Adams to Abigail Adams

My dearest Friend   Philadelphia Decr 5. 1792

last night I arrived at Philadelphia in tolerable Health and found our Friends all well. I have concluded to accept of the kind offer of Mr and Mrs Otis and taken a bed in their House. Thomas is charmingly accommodated and is very well. This Day decides whether I shall be a Farmer or a Statesman after next March. They have been flickering in the Newspapers and caballing in Parties: but how the result will be I neither know nor care. I have met a very cordial and friendly reception from the Senate. All lament that Mrs Adams is not here: but none of them so much / as her Friend forever

John Adams

RC (Adams Papers); internal address: "Portia."

John Adams to John Quincy Adams

My dear son   Philadelphia Dec[r] 5. 1792

at 9 last night I arriv'd and this Morning have taken my Seat from whence I write this. I have just rec[d] yours of 22. Nov. with its Inclosure.[1] I am told most confidently that all the Votes in N. Y. will be for Clinton and all the Votes in Pensilvania for me. I believe neither.

If the People of the Union are capable of being influenced by Such Characters as Dallas and Edwards, I should be ashamed of them and their Service. but I know better Things. The Writings are weaker than the Agents.

If any Thing disagreable happens it will be a dissipation of the Votes upon various Characters, merely to throw them away. and these follies will be occasioned by Causes much more ancient than the federal Govt or my Writings. I mean Jealousies of South vs North and dubitations about federal Towns and foreign Debts.

Charles is very earnest for you to write to him. He is turning Politician & Writer. He has made his Essays at the Bar and begins to have Business.

Thomas is studious and is happily lodged. M[rs] smith is expected in the Spring.

I shall lodge at M[r] Otis's where I shall feel myself at home. Write me as often as you can.

God bless you   J. A.

RC (Adams Papers); internal address: "M[r] Adams." Tr (Adams Papers).

[1] Not found.

Charles Adams to Abigail Adams

My dear Mama   New York [*post* 5] December 1792[1]

Some years since you was so kind as to purchase for your children a certain tract of Land in Vermont. What number of acres the Lots contained I know not. I beleive that little or no pains has been taken to secure the title to them they were indeed thought but of Little value. The price of new Land has of late risen so much and the demand becoming greater every day It would I think be a prudent undertaking to make a few enquiries respecting the family property which lies in that State. There is a M[r] Morris who lives in Vermont upon whom I can depend for information respecting this business, but my total want of knowledge upon the subject renders it impossible for me to make the necessary enquiries.[2] My Brother will I have no doubt assist you in making out a statement of the business. The questions I wish to propose are these Of whom the Land was bought? In what year? In what part of the State it lies? What title was given? What consideration paid? How many acres were contained in the lots. Which is my particular part? and if possible how bounded separately: if not; how the whole tract is bounded? I hope to be able to gain such information as will redound to the benefit of us all.[3] We have no forcing news. Our Clintonians have made a great noise about their Hero's election to the office of Vice President and their dissappointment must be extremely keen as from the returns I have been able to see that the present Statement of the votes is that the present incumbent has 71 votes and M[r] Clinton 15 which leaves a majority of 7 votes provided all the other States vote unanimously for Clinton South Carolina North Carolina Virginia Kentuckey and Georgia are not included in this calculation We have had no accounts from those States. I received by my father your kind present the Stockings were very acceptable I rejoice to hear of your mending health. if my finances will allow I intend to pass a few days with my dear Mother at Braintree during the winter but this is altoge[ther] an uncertainty. Thomas spent a few days with [me in] September he appears to be well and grows fat [his] lodgings at Philadelphia are very pleasant. He is a good Brother. Let me not be forgotten by any of my friends. I shall answer my brothers letter very soon he has been so good a correspondent of late that it is a pitty to loose him.[4] Besides he is very good Counsel upon all occasions!

Beleive me your affectionate son forever   Charles Adams.

RC (Adams Papers). Filmed at Dec. 1792. Some loss of text where the seal was removed.

[1] This letter was written sometime after 5 Dec., the day on which the New York State presidential electors cast their votes for George Clinton for vice president.

[2] Probably Lewis R. Morris (1760–1825) of Springfield, Vt., who had served as secretary to Robert R. Livingston in the early 1780s. Morris moved from New York to Vermont in 1785 and in 1791 acquired 2,650 acres of Vermont land from his father, Richard, who remained in New York (Hugh H. Henry, "General Lewis R. Morris/Barry/Mollica House," Connecticut River Historic Sites Database, Connecticut River Joint Commissions, www.crjc.org/heritage/V07-14.htm).

[3] For the Vermont land AA purchased in 1782, see vol. 4:315, 316–317, 345; 7:457, 459; 8:34.

[4] Not found.

John Adams to Abigail Adams

My dearest Friend   Philadelphia Dec[r.] 7. 1792

I am lodged at M[r] Otis's and am personally well accommodated: but I am So little pleased with living alone at any Lodgings, that this shall be the last time. You must come to me another Year or I will come to you. I am convinced if you were now here you would again be sick for the damp and chill is very penetrating. Next fall, I hope your health will be better.

How the Election is gone I know not. It cannot go amiss for me, because I am prepared for every Event. Indeed I am of the Cat kind and fall upon my feet, throw me as they will. I hear some very good stories to this purpose sometimes.

Benson propagates a beautiful Anecdote of this kind.[1] A large Company mixed of Federalists and Antis, Whigs and Tories, Clintonians & Jaysites were together at New York in Conversation about French Affairs. All Parties it seems condemned and execrated the Plans and Conduct of the Jacobins. Unluckily at length a Jaysite and Federalist observed that We had Jacobins in this Country who were pursuing objects as pernicious by means as unwarrantable as those of France. This roused the Resentment of a Clintonian Anti whose name is Gilbert Livingston, who took the Reflection to himself and his Party and grew warm.[2] "Nothing says he mortifies me so much in the Misconduct in France and America too, as to see that the Fools are all playing the Game into the hands of that M[r] John Adams."

Why Said Benson to Livingston who it seems is a serious Man. M[r] Adams reads the Scriptures and there he finds that Man is as stupid as the Wild Asses Colt.[3] He believes what he reads and infers his necessary Consequences from it, that is all. M[r] Adams is not to blame. He did not write the Scriptures. He only reads and believes.

Benson got the laugh upon Livingston but I love Livingston the better for the story. It shews Integrity and Candor at Bottom, 'tho Prejudice and Party Spirit were att top.

The President & Lady and all others Enquire anxiously and affectionately for You. I have given Charles my Coach Horses to buy him Law Books. For the future your Pair of Horses will be all I shall keep. My Love to all   J. A.

RC (Adams Papers); internal address: "Portia"; endorsed: "Dec[br] 7 1792."

[1] Egbert Benson (1746–1833), King's College 1765, was a New York lawyer. He represented New York in the Continental Congress from 1781 to 1784 and in the U.S. Congress from 1789 to 1793 (*DAB*).

[2] Gilbert Livingston (1742–1806), a distant cousin of the more prominent Livingstons, was an Antifederalist lawyer from Poughkeepsie, N.Y. (Staughton Lynd, *Anti-Federalism in Dutchess County, New York*, Chicago, 1962, p. 25–27).

[3] "For vain man would be wise, though man be born like a wild ass's colt" (Job, 11:12).

Charles Adams to John Adams

Dear Sir   New York Decr 8th [1792]

I had yesterday the honor of receiving your kind letter of the fifth.[1] Our electors have returned from Poughkeepsie but are determined by the information I have procured to keep the State of their votes a secret. There is it is true a report that they were unanimous, but I beleive it arises from no good authority A certain nephew of our Governor has held out hopes of twelve votes from the eastern States but such ideas can intimidate none but very feeble minds[2] New Jersey are unanimously federal if the information we receive by the papers be just. I this day received a Letter from my Brother John.[3] He gives me very favorable accounts of my dear Mothers health He seems to be fixed in the system of Optimism and looks or affects to look with vast sang froid upon the various hurly burlies that are happening in the world. The horses are not yet arrived I have written to Mr Bull to send them on immediately I have received no answer I shall write again tomorrow. We have had no arrivals from Europe since you left us and have nothing new stirring The account of the Capture of Dumorier's army is not beleived[4]

Our Legislature are still upon the examination respecting the rejection of the votes at the last election for Governor how long it will last and whither it will tend I know not. It serves at least to keep animosity alive.

I am Dear Sir your Dutiful son   Charles Adams

RC (Adams Papers).

[1] Not found.

[2] DeWitt Clinton (1769–1828), Columbia 1786, was the son of George Clinton's brother James. DeWitt had studied law and was admitted to the bar before becoming his uncle's private secretary (*DAB*).

[3] Not found.

[4] Charles François du Périer Dumouriez (1739–1823) briefly served as minister of foreign affairs and minister of war in the French revolutionary government. He led the French Army from 1792 to 1793. Rumors of his capture were in fact false and would shortly be contradicted in the New York newspapers. Dumouriez continued to lead the army successfully until March 1793 when, after a major defeat, he defected to the Austrians (Bosher, *French Rev.*, p. xxxvi, 166, 183; New York *Weekly Museum*, 1, 8 Dec.).

John Adams to Abigail Adams

My dearest Friend   Philadelphia Dec[r] 8. 1792

D[r] Blair has resigned and D[r] Green is our Chaplain, but Miss Blair is married to M[r] Roberdeau the Bearer of this Letter, son of my old Friend the General.[1]

There is an universal and respectful Inquiry after you and your health, and as general a respect and Attention shewn to me. The Savages who shoot from the Swamps and thickets, from the Brakes and Briars from the Mud and Dirt, are all hidden Skulkers, and dare not shew their heads or make known their Names. You will know more of the Election before this reaches you than I do. It does not appear that I am born to so good Fortune as to be a mere Farmer in my Old Age, notwithstanding the kind Intentions and benevolent Endeavours of some People to excuse me from future Journeys.

Your son and your Friends are all well.

I dont know whether I have told you that I came from Hartford in the Stage, that I have given my Horses to Charles to buy Law Books.

With Affections and tenderness inexpressible at this distance I am

J. A.

RC (Adams Papers); internal address: "Portia."

[1] Rev. Ashbel Green (1762–1848), Princeton 1783, was appointed chaplain to the U.S. Congress on 5 Nov., a position he held until 1800. Green replaced Rev. Samuel Blair (1741–1818), Princeton 1760, who declined to be renominated. Both were Presbyterians (Sprague, *Annals Amer. Pulpit,* 3:268–269, 479–486; Philadelphia *General Advertiser,* 6 Nov.).

Isaac Roberdeau (1763–1829), a civil and military engineer helping to lay out the new city of Washington, D.C., had married Susan Shippen Blair, Rev. Blair's daughter, on 7 Nov. 1792 (*DAB*; Philadelphia *Federal Gazette,* 12 Nov.). For Roberdeau's father, Gen. Daniel Roberdeau, see vol. 2:350.

John Quincy Adams to John Adams

Dear Sir.   Boston December 8. 1792.

Our Electors met in this town on Wednesday last, and their Votes for President and Vice-President were unanimous this was generally expected here, and the event is supposed to have been nearly if not wholly the same in all the New-England States— New-York it is imagined was unanimous for M[r:] Clinton as V.P. their Electors are chosen by their legislature, where their Governor has a bare majority, determined to support upon all occasions his party and his politics. From the other States you will probably hear before us.— And upon the whole, I presume the election will be favourable.[1]

The Governor has at length prevailed in routing the players. On Wednesday, the Attorney General received orders from him and the Council, to prosecute the violators of the Law, immediately. He applied for a warrant, to a Justice of the Peace returnable before two Justices of the Quorum. The Sheriff arrested one of the actors behind the Scenes in the course of the play on Wednesday Evening, and informed the company that unless they dispersed immediately he should arrest all the other performers for the Evening. The Company immediately assumed the form of a deliberative assembly, and debated the Question, whether they should retire, or direct the players to proceed and bid defiance to the Sheriff. They concluded that obedience to the Law, was the safest party and withdrew, not without many imprecations against the Governor, and the Law, upon which they were interrupted.— The next morning the examination upon the warrant was to take place and the Justices met at Faneuil Hall, their own offices being too small, and the Court-House occupied, by the district Court.— The Hall was about half-full of Spectators, who took every opportunity, to express their disapprobation of the proceedings.— An objection was taken by M^r: Otis, counsel for the defendant, to the warrant, as not being founded upon *oath* but only upon an official complaint of the Attorney-General. Whether Sullivan committed the blunder from ignorance, or from inattention, or from design, is doubtful; but the by-standers enjoy'd a hearty laugh at his expence.— He has affected a kind of neutrality upon this occasion, and has avoided giving offence to either party by being active on either side. It was supposed by many persons, that he proceeded thus irregularly on purpose to give the players an opportunity to escape, and he himself wishes to have it understood that he acts only in consequence of express directions from the Governor and Council.— The objection however prevailed and the player who had been arrested was discharged amid the loud and very improper plaudits of the audience. Justice Barrett, with proper Spirit reproved their conduct in the Hall, upon which they were quiet; but as soon as they got out of the Hall, they closed the business with three huzza's. The players in the mean time, had taken the alarm, and most of them are gone; so that I hope we shall have no more altercations upon this Subject.[2]

We have no other news at present peculiarly worthy of communication, and I therefore close my Letter with the assurance that I am with all due respect and affection, your Son.   J. Q. Adams.

RC (Adams Papers); addressed: "The Vice-President of the United States. / Philadelphia."; endorsed: "J.Q. Adams. Dec. 8 / ans^d. 19. 1792." Tr (Adams Papers).

[1] When the final votes were tallied on 13 Feb. 1793, George Washington received 132, JA received 77, George Clinton received 50, Thomas Jefferson received 4, and Aaron Burr received 1. New Hampshire, Massachusetts, Rhode Island, Connecticut, Vermont, New Jersey, Delaware, and Maryland all supported JA unanimously. New York, Virginia, North Carolina, and Georgia supported Clinton unanimously, while Kentucky gave its vice presidential votes to Jefferson. Pennsylvania and South Carolina each split its votes: Pennsylvania gave 14 to JA and 1 to Clinton, while South Carolina gave 7 to JA and 1 to Aaron Burr (U.S. Senate, *Jour.*, 2d Cong., 2d sess., p. 485).

[2] Opposition to theater in Boston was a longstanding tradition dating to the seventeenth century, and by 1750 the General Court had passed "An Act to Prevent Stage-Plays, and Other Theatrical Entertainments," which levied substantial fines against anyone running, acting in, or attending a theatrical production. In 1792, the Boston Tontine Association, after failing to secure the repeal of this law, decided to challenge it by building the Board Alley Theatre and hiring a company of players, led by Joseph Harper, to perform there. In order to circumvent the law, they described their space as an "exhibition room" and called the plays "moral lectures." JQA attended a number of these performances during the fall but found the acting quite poor: "very ill performed: the best bad: the worst inexpressible."

On 5 Dec., Boston sheriff Jeremiah Allen, at the direction of Attorney General James Sullivan, exercised a warrant against Harper provided by justices Benjamin Greenleaf and Samuel Barrett. The audience reacted unhappily to the interruption of the performance, tearing down the state coat of arms and trampling a portrait of John Hancock. At the hearing the next day, Harper, defended by Harrison Gray Otis and William Tudor, was released when the justices declared the warrant illegal (William W. Clapp Jr., *A Record of the Boston Stage*, Boston, 1853, p. 2–3, 5–13; Heather S. Nathans, *Early American Theatre from the Revolution to Thomas Jefferson: Into the Hands of the People*, N.Y., 2003, p. 65–67; D/JQA/18, 8 Oct., APM Reel 21).

Samuel Barrett (1739–1798), Harvard 1757, of Boston became a lawyer after failing as a merchant. He was made a justice of the Court of Common Pleas in 1789 (*Sibley's Harvard Graduates*, 14:135–137, 140, 142).

John Adams to John Quincy Adams

My dear Son   Philadelphia Decr 9. 1792

This Letter will be delivered you, by Mr Roberdeau a Son of General Roberdeau my ancient Friend, lately married to Miss Blair a Daughter of Doctor Blair, whom your Mamma knows. I pray you to Shew all the Civility to Mr Roberdeau in your Power. invite him to Quincy with you to keep sunday with your Mamma and shew him Boston and Cambridge, Colledge Library Apparatus &c and give him all the Advice and Aid you can in his pursuits. I have been under Obligations to his Father.

It is Said that the Electors in Jersey have been unanimous and those of Pensilvania had but one dissentient.[1] I have rec^d Returns from both but have not opened either. It is Said too from good Authority that Maryland is unanimous.

There is a general Interest taken in my Reelection in such a number of States as affects me. The Utmost Efforts of my Ennemies have undoubtedly been exerted, and what success they may have had in Virginia and the States to the southward of it, is uncertain. New York it is expected will show their vain Spite against New England. It is not Antifederalism against Federalism, nor Democracy against Aristocracy. This is all Pretext. It is N York vs N. England.

I am affectionately your Father   John Adams

RC (Adams Papers); internal address: "John Quincy Adams Esq."

[1] The dissenter was Robert Johnston (d. 1808), University of Pennsylvania 1763, a physician from Franklin County, Penn. (*Colonial Collegians*; Boston *Columbian Centinel*, 5 Dec.).

John Adams to Abigail Adams

My dearest Friend   Philadelphia Dec[r] 10. 1792

Your Account of our little domestic affairs and the Arrangements of the Farm, was very entertaining to me, and I hope you will continue to inform me of every occurrence of any consequence.[1] I should be glad to know who is engaged to take the Care of the Place this Winter: What prospect you have of hiring a Man in the Spring by the Year: and your opinion whether I had not better engage a complete farmer in the County of Worcester or Hampshire. none however are Superiour to some in Bridgwater. I am very comfortable at M[r] Otis's. Thomas is very well and very good.

My Friends have been more anxious than I have been about a certain Reelection. There has been an Ardour upon this occasion among all the Friends of the Constitution, order and good Government, which I did not expect. The Votes of New Jersey have been unanimous both for President and V. P. Those of Pensilvania were unanimous for P. and 14 out of 15 for V. P.— it is reported, but not certain that Delaware and Maryland were unanimous. It is almost an universal opinion that N. Y. will be unanimous for Clinton, merely to give him an Ecclat and to shew their disapprobation of the V. P. without even a hope or a wish, to have C. elected. I am not however clear that they will be unanimous. The Virginians and N. Carolinians are Said to be zealous against the V. P. not, as some of them say, that they wish to get him out, but to shew a marked disapprobation of his Politicks. But enough of this Electioneering Stuff. My Duty to my Mother and Love to Louisa and all friends.

Tell my Brother that I hope he will Use his best Endeavours that

Mr Strong may be reelected.[2] He is an excellent head and heart. They cannot do better.

yours   J. A

RC (Adams Papers); addressed: "Mrs Adams / Quincy / near / Boston"; internal address: "Portia"; endorsed: "Dec^{br} 10 1792"; notation: "Free / John Adams."

[1] AA to JA, 26 Nov., above.
[2] Caleb Strong was reelected to the Senate in 1793 (*Biog. Dir. Cong.*).

Thomas Boylston Adams to Abigail Adams

My dear Mother,   Philadelphia Dec^r: 11th: [*1792*]

It is just a week since I had the pleasure of receiving a visit from my Father at 8 oClock in the Evening of a very stormy day, after he had become almost exhausted by the fatigue of his ride from Elizabeth Town. He stoped at my lodgings, & as he was much fatigued he declined going any further that night. The next day I went to the place where I had after much trouble procured lodgings and while I was settling all affairs for his reception he saw M^r & M^{rs}: Otis who persuaded him to stay with them, which proposal he immediately closed with & I was left the disagreeable business of undoing my engagements, & paying thirty Dollars for the three weeks the Rooms were reserved; besides being *abused* & *berated* by the tongue of the ostensible character who managed the affairs of the family being the Daughter of the Old Lady who keeps the house. In short I was obliged to take these or none, which is the only reason I have; & I consider it a real happiness after what I know & have hear'd that my Father is so happily rid of them, tho' he had no reasons of this kind for changing his resolution, being totally unacquainted with Every thing relating to the family. To be sure it was not so pleasant for me to transact the last part of the business, but at all events I rejoice in the change— He knows nothing of the altercation which pass'ed between me & those people, & I wish he may not. It is our usual luck you know to sink money for nothing; some compensation was reasonable however as the people say they were prevented taking any one else. My Father is very happily situated now, where you will be much better pleased to hear of him. I think myself under many obligations to M^r & M^{rs}: Otis for their kindness, & hope they will not have much trouble for their politeness. The season hitherto has been remarkably fine here; we have none of your mountain snow banks to wade thro', tho' it begins to be very cold. All the Gay Circles have commenced, tho' I am very happily less troubled with invitations to partake in them than when you were here. I attend the Assemblies pretty regularly & sometimes go to the Drawing Room, which makes the greatest part of my dissipation. There is one source of pleasure & amusement which I enjoy more than formerly; that of visiting without reserve the families connected with the one I live in. They are numerous, and all of them perfectly friendly; what is more, there are a considerable number of young people of both sexes, the females of whom especially, are the finest women I have met with in Philadelphia. Sensible, accomplished, well educated, amiable; in short their persons are adorned with beautiful simplicity, but their minds are richly improved & cultivated. You won't think by these encomiums which I think due to their merrit, that I am upon the point of "joining their meeting," or of persuading any of them to a "runaway match." I hope however when you return to this place, you will have an opportunity of acknowledging the justice of my remarks.

Politicks hitherto go tolerably smooth, & while this is the case nothing can be very interesting in the relation. I have seen the Return of votes for Pres[ident] & Vice Pr^{et:} from the four middle States. N-Jersey—Pennsylvania Delaware & Maryland; The number of Electors was 34. for these four States, of which 33 are *Federal*. One Elector in this State voted for Clinton, not it is said from party views, but from motives of personal acquaintance & friendship for him. This has not much the appearance of being afraid of Kings, Lords & Commons.

I am your dutiful Son   Thomas B Adams.

PS. I thank you much for the Cheese, which is praised considerably, I have also rec^{d:} my Shoes. I will with pleasure attend to the request of Cousin Lucy, to whom present my love, as well as the rest of our friends—

My Fathers Trunk had a pas[sage of] 19 days, but arrived safe at last.

Dec 12th.

Accounts from N York [say the?] Electors were unanimous for the two Georges—[1]

RC (Adams Papers); addressed: "M^{rs:} Abigail Adams / Quincy / near / Boston." Some loss of text where the seal was removed.

[1] The last two sentences were written sideways in the margin.

Thomas Boylston Adams to William Cranch

My dear William   Philadelphia [*post 15*] Dec^r: [*1792*][1]

I have for some time past had it in contemplation to take my pen & devote its impressions to your service, but that noted thief, Procrastination must answer for my negligence, & supply an excuse where I have not the hardiness to offer one. It often happens that the best friendships have the fewest documents to prove their existence; as a well-kindled fire, such an one as now warms your addresser, needs least fuel to keep it alive. But after all, there may be at least some shew of reason, in a friendly enquiry now & then; this shall excuse me for withdrawing your attention from more important pursuits for the simple purpose of acquainting your friend T, B, A—with the minute History of your fire-side in those Nothern Regions upon the Banks of Merrimack. Ay, but you must tell me more too; and yet I think you need not, for I do'nt confine you to one, two, or three particular circles, but let your statement be co-extensive with your acquaintance; particularise only, where particulars may be worth relating. Here sure is latitude enough; to make you still more free, write me what you please, and it will follow, as my heart unto my hand, you cant displease me.

Shall we together range the Trackless Wilderness where war & havock rage, to find some dire calamity, or among the cultured fields of civilized man seek for some object, whereon we may descant? Or shall the agonizing groans of fast expiring Despotism in convulsed Europe call forth our hearty congratulations? It seems as if the anxious struggles of our Tranatlantic bretheren must terminate in good— The means we must deplore—the ends, tho' yet unknown, ca'nt fail of being glorious. We have various accounts indirectly from several ports in Europe of the flight of Brunswick with his whole Army, that is, so much of it as has escaped famine, disease & Captivity; the story has been repeatedly circulated, but as yet does not meet general credit, The wishes however of most people among us seem to favor its truth; should it prove a fact, we must then begin a new score of wishing, which perhaps will be more liable to defeat, at least for a long time, viz That the French Nation may speedily come to its senses, and by quelling the frantic enthousiasm which has hither to frustrated all attempts toward a settled order of things, reassume a character which has so long been sacrificed at the shrine of Anarchy. Years however may elapse before this desirable end shall be attained, for when the blood of a whole nation is once thoroughly heated to a degree of fermentation, many powerfull purgatives must be administered to reduce it to its natural temperature. Liberty is to the mind, what Light is to the Eye— when too suddenly received, it destroys for a short time the very sense it was intended to restore. As the free exercise of Natural rights shall become more familiar to Frenchmen, they will be less bewildered by their novelty, & consequently more prepared for a Government of salutary laws.

Our National legislature has been more than a month convened— they have as yet entered upon no business of great moment—of course they are tolerably good humored as yet.[2] A uniform system of Bankruptcy will probably be created this session, which seems to be the most important subject that will claim their attention; all the objects which hitherto excited anxiety have allready been embraced; it now remains to preserve pure & uncontaminated that system which has procured us National respectability.[3] It appears from returns already received that the present VP— has nearly two thirds of all the votes; NYork & Virginia are in much disgrace. I am happy to see so good a Representation from Massachusetts; you will undoubtedly stand very high [in po]int of Respectability & talents. Your County might better itself perhaps—tho Goodhue is a good Merchant—he does not shine as a statesman.

Present my love, &c[a] to all friends, and take a great share for yourself from   Thomas B Adams

RC (OCHP:William Cranch Papers, Mss fC891c RM); addressed: "William Cranch Esq[r:] / Attorney at Law / Haverhill / near Boston."; endorsed: "T.B. A. / Dec[r.] 1792." and "Rec[d.] 19. ans[d.] 22[d.] Jan. 1793." Some loss of text due to a torn manuscript.

[1] The dating of this letter is based on reports of the Duke of Brunswick's "flight," which first appeared in the Philadelphia newspapers on 14 and 15 December.

[2] Congress began sitting again on 5 Nov.; it would adjourn on 2 March 1793 (*Biog. Dir. Cong.*).

[3] Although a "bill to establish an uniform system of bankruptcy throughout the United States" was introduced into the House of Representatives on 10 Dec. 1792, Congress failed to pursue it further. Various versions of the bill would be considered in multiple sessions of Congress until one was finally enacted on 4 April 1800 (*Annals of Congress*, 2d Cong., 2d sess., p. 741; *An Act to Establish an Uniform System of Bankruptcy*, Phila., 1800, Evans, No. 38697; Peter J. Coleman, *Debtors and Creditors in America: Insolvency, Imprisonment for Debt, and Bankruptcy, 1607–1900*, Madison, Wis., 1974, p. 18).

John Quincy Adams to John Adams

My dear Sir.   Boston Dec:^{r:} 16. 1792.

I received last evening your favour of the 5^{th:} instant— The votes of the Electors in Connecticut and Rhode-Island, were unanimous it seems, as well as in this State; I have not heard any further, but we presume there was the same unanimity in New-Hampshire, which if it be the case, will I think do credit to New-England. We expect nothing but the voice of Faction from New-York; and we know not enough what the disposition of the Southern States was.—

I gave you in my last some account of the Governor's having at length succeeded in overthrowing the players, but some other circumstances have taken place, which at that time, I had not heard.— Two days after the arrest of the player which I mentioned in my last, those who still remained had announced another play, but upon being advised by their own friends to desist, they postponed the performance.[1] At night however a mob of about two hundred people, collected together and went up to the Governor's house, to ask his leave to pull down the play-house. Upon their approach towards his house, the family were thrown into great consternation, upon the idea that they were of the other party, and were coming to insult him. He received however a deputation from them, and as it is said authorised them to proceed upon their riotous design. They accordingly went, and began to destroy the fences round the house, but were soon dispersed by a Justice of the Peace, of the other party, who went among them, with the riot act in his pocket, ready to read it to them if there had been occasion.[2] There has been since then no further attempt to act more plays, and all the actors are now gone.

But the Governor and his instruments were not content with this victory: they must appeal to the public, for approbation of all his conduct on the occasion and for censure upon that of the opposers to the Law; and Sullivan, with the intrepidity of face peculiar to himself came forward in last Thursday's paper, under the signature of a friend to Peace, with the professed design to criminate the breakers of the Statute, and to justify the executive authority.[3] You will probably see in the two next Centinels, a couple of pieces signed *Menander*, in answer to him.— I presume he will reply, but I think the discussion must terminate unfavourably to him. The subject cannot be very interesting to you, but perhaps an interest in the success of the writer may induce you to peruse the discussion. I will send you the publication of the friend to Peace by the next Post, and as you will receive the Centinel regularly, you will there find the answers of *Menander*.[4]

The unanimity of the Electors in this State, was by all accounts a sore mortification to his State Majesty. It anger'd him to the heart, and he vented his peevishness upon the first objects that presented themselves to him. It was on the same day with the Election, that he made his attack upon the players. He made several difficulties about signing the warrant upon the treasury for the pay of the Electors, and delayed untill a third message, from them was accompanied with an intimation to him that unless he signed the warrant immediately, they should go to their homes without receiving their pay at all. This implied menace had its effect; and he signed the warrant.— But he has affected to be much alarmed for his own safety; and to be in terrors lest a mob should attack his person or his house. There have been in the public prints several foolish inflammatory squibs threatening him with tar & feathers, or with breaking his windows. but they have been treated with general contempt, and there has not been the slightest symptom of any popular excesses against him, though he has endeavoured to excite them in support of his whimsical passion against the theatre.[5]

A french and English news-paper has been commenced in this Town, which is to contain among other things a summary account of the french Revolution.[6] This account is very handsomely written, by one of the Aristocratic party now here, having been driven from the Island of S^t: Domingo, by the triumphant faction there.[7] He has aimed at impartiality as much as he could, but if you read the narrative you will find he is very bitter against the Duke of Orleans to whom he attributes all the Calamities of his Country. The first number only has been published, and the Editor has forwarded one of them to you which he will continue to do. The translation of that part of the paper will be done by me, and I imagine the paper itself will not be continued long after that publication is finished. The proposals are only for six months.

I hope you will not consider me as trifling with my time, for spending it in translating french politics and discussing theatrical questions— My pen has lain dormant for near a year and an half, and perhaps its revival may with some propriety be, by essays upon subjects not of the first magnitude. There has been upon my mind a strong sentiment of delicacy, which has kept me silent in the midst of all the scurrility of which you have been the object. The charges which private malice and public faction have employed as instruments against you have been so despicable in themselves that common sense and Common Honesty, must have felt some degradation in descending to the refutation of them. I have thought that where they could have any possible effect, sober reason and plain truth could not counteract it, because the minds affected must be too blind or too wicked, to feel the operation of just Sentiments. The Event of the election as far as we know it has corroborated my opinion. As to the general measures of the federal government, when I have seen them attacked artfully and insidiously, as has frequently been the case, I have often thought of defending them; but as often have concluded that my assistance, could not be necessary, and could be but feeble. The Government I supposed needed it not, and as to my own advancement, I could really see nothing in public life, but what it was my object to avoid. I have been really apprehensive of becoming politically known, before I could establish a *professional* reputation. I knew that my independence and consequently my happiness in life depended upon this, and I have sincerely wished rather to remain in the shade than to appear as a politician without any character as a Lawyer.— These Sentiments have still great weight in my mind, and if therefore you should think me squandering my attention upon subjects of too trivial import, I hope you will do me the Justice to believe that it is not for want of judgment in my comparative estimation of things.

I have run into great prolixity already, and will therefore only add that I am as ever, your affectionate Son.   J. Q. Adams.

RC (Adams Papers); endorsed: "J. Q. Adams / Decr 16. ans^d 26 / 1792." Tr (Adams Papers).

[1] A final advertisement for a "Comic Lecture," a performance of David Garrick's *The Lying Valet*, and a "Musical Lecture," *The Padlock* by Isaac Bickerstaffe, appeared in the Boston *American Apollo*, 7 December. The following day, Joseph Harper placed an advertisement in the Boston *Columbian Centinel* expressing his gratitude to the people of Boston "for their many favours: And while he laments the necessity he is under, thus early to leave this hospitable *capital*, he shall ever bear in remembrance the obligations he is under for their liberality, benevolence, and candour."

[2] Apparently AA reported the same events in a letter to JA (not found); he responded on 29 Dec., "Who is that Justice Cooper who read the Riot Act? The Town Clerk or his son? If the Mob Swore they had the Governors orders to pull down the Theater, I shall beleive that the Mob swore to a lie: for it is impossible the Governor should have given Such orders or such Leave" (Adams Papers). Boston town clerk William Cooper (1721–1796), a longtime justice of the peace and register of probate for Suffolk County, read the Massachusetts Riot Act of 1786, which gave officials the power to order crowds dispersed and said that anyone who did not depart within one hour of the reading of the

act faced criminal penalties (*NEHGR*, 44:56 [Jan. 1890]; Mass., *Acts and Laws*, 1786–1787, p. 87–90).

³James Sullivan's piece, signed "A Friend to Peace," appeared in the Boston *Independent Chronicle*, 13 Dec. 1792. Sullivan argued that "if the law is unconstitutional, there is ample provision made for a remedy"; consequently, "if there is a constitutional remedy, the violent measures which have been resorted to, and the open defiance to a law established by the Legislature, and recognized several times, as proper and expedient, cannot be justifiable."

⁴JQA published his three Menander pieces in the Boston *Columbian Centinel*, 19, 22, and 26 Dec., responding to "A Friend to Peace." He writes in support of those attending the theater, "In a free government the minority never can be under an obligation to sacrifice *their rights* to the will of the majority, however expressed. The constitution of this State is expressly paramount to the laws of the legislators, and every individual in the community has the same right with the legislature to put his own *honest* construction upon every clause contained in the constitution."

⁵A "correspondent" in the *American Apollo*, 7 Dec., decried the government's illegal warrant against the theater players as "so flagrant a violation of the constitution" and noted that "if such illegal measures are still pursued, and our sacred rights thus daringly violated, let the infringers remember, that 'the tar and the feathers are with us, apples and eggs, yea, rotten ones in abundance.'"

⁶The *Courier Politique de l'Univers*, edited by Rev. Louis de Rousselet, a Catholic priest, and printed by Joseph Bumstead, published its first number in Boston on 10 December. Originally designed to appear only in French and to offer an extended summary of the events of the French Revolution from 1788 on, the editor instead decided to publish in both French and English. He engaged JQA to provide at least some of the English translations, which JQA worked on throughout December. The newspaper published at most six numbers, closing sometime in mid-Jan. 1793, but no issues are extant (Col. Soc. Mass., *Pubns.*, 24:296–299 [April 1921]; D/JQA/18, 3, 17 Dec., APM Reel 21).

⁷The writer of the account was likely a M. d'Hauteval, with whom JQA had dinner on 16 Dec. 1792. JQA described him to JA in a letter of 5 Jan. 1793 as "a french Gentleman from the Island of Sᵗ⁺ Domingo, where he had lately the misfortune to lose a plantation of great value, by the devastation of the insurgent negroes" (Adams Papers; D/JQA/18, APM Reel 21).

The revolution in St. Domingue (now Haiti), inspired by the French Revolution, began with demands for rights first by white colonial leaders, then in 1790 by the free black community—a movement that colonial forces quickly suppressed. In 1791, however, the situation escalated with a massive slave revolt that displaced many plantation owners, forcing them to migrate to the United States and elsewhere. The insurgent slaves, with the assistance of French republicans, succeeded in abolishing slavery by 1794, then began a move for national autonomy led by Toussaint Louverture. Although he was captured and killed in 1803, Haiti achieved its independence from France in 1804 (Laurent Dubois, *Avengers of the New World: The Story of the Haitian Revolution*, Cambridge, 2004, p. 1–4, 8, 87–88).

John Adams to Abigail Adams

My dearest Friend   Philadelphia Decʳ 19. 1792

Your favour of the 4ᵗʰ· arrived by Yesterdays post. The Votes on the important day you mention, are now known to have been unanimous as far as Cheasapeak Bay, excepting one in Pensilvania and all in New York. The whole Flock in Virginia as well as in N.Y. run for Mʳ Clinton.

They tell me it is a compleat Tryumph of Fœderalism over Antifœderalism: but I own I can See no Tryumph in obtaining more

Votes than Mr Clinton: if the Services of J.A. can be compared to those of G. C. if the Sacrifices, if the Sufferings, if the Talents if the Experience, if the Knowledge of one can be brought down to a Comparison with the other, it is high time to quit Such a service. There is not the Smallest degree of Vanity in this. In one Point only will I allow that his Merit is superiour to mine: he has had more Sense than I have in feathering his nest, and making Provision for his Children.

Lucius and Marcus, after whom you enquire I have never read and know not their Writers. I give myself no trouble about Such Writings as are personal against one.

The Plan has been concerted, the Agents and Instruments mustered from Georgia to N. H. The Misrepresentations to the southward have been as gross as they have been numerous: in short they have plainly discoverd an opinion that all their hopes were suspended on the Removal of one Man from office. Mr Parker of Virginia,[1] I am told boasts that the Plan was his own and Mr Burke of S. C. Mr Dallas of this Town, Mr P. Edwards of New Haven, are reported to have been his principal Coadjutors.

The Prices of Rye and Flour are as high in Proportion here as at Boston: but Brisler will enquire particularly and write the Result.

You have many Friends who enquire affectionately after your health and all regret, that you cannot be here. Thomas is very hearty: and well Spoken of.

It would not be prudent to enter very minutely into the Anecdotes which the late Electioneering has produced; but Some of them are very curious.— Judge Cushing and Judge Griffin[2] were divided in opinion on the Cause of so much Expectation in Virginia, which will continue sometime longer the Effervescence in that State, and produce Admirers of Clinton from an hatred to or rather from a desire to hate if they could Jay, and me. I am / tendrement yours

J. A.

RC (Adams Papers); addressed: "Mrs Adams / Quincy / near / Boston"; internal address: "Portia"; endorsed: "Dec^br 19. 1792"; notation: "Free / John Adams."

[1] Col. Josiah Parker (1751–1810) represented Virginia in Congress from 1789 to 1801, initially as an Antifederalist but later as a Federalist (*Biog. Dir. Cong.*).
[2] Cyrus Griffin was appointed federal judge for the District of Virginia in 1789 (*DAB*).

John Adams to Charles Adams

Philadelphia Dec[r] 19. 1792

I have rec[d] from you one Letter and no more Since I left N. York.[1] Your Electors appear like a large black Spot in a bright Circle of Unanimity which extends from N. H. to Maryland inclusively. Then the Region of Darkness begins again and extends I know not how far.

A decided Reprehension from N. York and Virginia would very Sensibly affect me, if there were not most unequivocal Marks of a Party Spirit, unworthy of Freemen in both. The Cry of Monarchy and Aristocracy is so manifestly false, and is so clearly but a Pretext to cover mean Prejudices and little Passions that I feel no mortification for myself but much for my fellow Citizens, in this pitiful Manœuvre.

The Spirit of falshood which has appeared both in Newspapers and in private Letters upon this Occasion is allarming to every fair mind, and augurs very ill for the Tranquility of this People if not for the duration of their Gov[t.]

You are very indolent, Charles,. You [should write] oftener to me than you do. Let me [know] [. . .] turns up.— The Gentlemen with whom I conversed in N. Y. were right in their Opinions of M[r] Osgood.[2] I own I found great difficulty in believing that Man capable of Sacrificing his sentiments to a Party So grossly. But America will See enough of that kind of Conduct.

The Ambition and Turbulence of Virginia is becoming intollerable: with a President, a Secretary of State an Attorney General, an Ambassador and what not, in the general Gov[t.] she discovers a disposition to insult all the rest of the Union: but she may depend upon it her Pride will have a fall.

I am tenderly yours   J. A.

RC (MHi:Seymour Coll.); internal address: "M[r] Charles Adams." Some loss of text due to a torn manuscript.

[1] CA to JA, 8 Dec., above.

[2] Samuel Osgood, who had previously represented Massachusetts in the Continental Congress, moved to New York to take up the position of postmaster general in 1789. He chose to resign and remain in the city when the federal government relocated to Philadelphia. As a presidential elector in 1792, he voted for George Clinton, to whom he was distantly related by marriage. JA commented to JQA in another letter of 19 Dec. that "The Vote of Osgood is a Strong Instance that Friendship, Services, Gratitude are Chaff, before the Wind of Party Passions" (Adams Papers; *DAB*; New York *Daily Advertiser*, 21 Nov.).

Abigail Adams to John Adams

my dearest Friend   Quincy dec^{br} 23. 1792

I congratulate my Country upon the uninimnity exhibited in the Nine states whose votes are made known, and I congratulate my Friend upon the same occasion as it is much more pleasing to serve a people whose willing and general suffrage accompanies their Choice, than when spairingly given. I think it a proof not only of the wisdom and integrity of the people but of their Satisfaction & content with the administration of the Government and their Resolution to support it. the Newspaper warfare seems only to have Strengthend the Friends of Government, and enlightned its opposers. I cannot however flatter myself that the 5 remaining states will be so well agreed in their vote, yet I think we may presume upon half their Number.

I was happy to learn by your last of your safe arrival at Philadelphia and upon several accounts that you was at mr otis's you will feel yourself more at Home, and find some domestick Society in mrs otis & the pratling Harriot. I have not yet had resolution sufficient to leave my Home. I wishd the Bustle of Election over before I went to Boston, and the weather has been so winter like that I have been fearfull of quitting my own fireside your Mother was well this day she has been out with me to meeting all day, and bears the cold well. no one appears more anxious or interested in the choice of V P than she does— she sends for the Newspapers and reads them very Regularly. I see by yesterdays paper that our Son is one of a committe to present an address to the Govenour for to request his aid in procuring a repeal of the AntiTheatrical Law which a large Majority of the inhabitants have voted at their late meeting to Petition the Legislature to repeal, and to co operate with the Representitives in such measures as may be judged expedient to give effect to the Petition.[1] a writer in the Centinal handles his Excellency without fear. he tells him in plain words that it was both unnecessary and irregular in the chief Magistrate to complain to the Legislature that the Law was voilated. they had nothing to do with it, their functions consisting in enacting not in executing Laws. Charge him with acting from Passion & encourageing a Mob to commit outrages— the poor Man has certainly burnt his fingers and will have the Gout most bitterly as soon as the General Court convene, he has other subjects of mortification at this time I trust.

I should be glad to hear from you once a week at least. do you sleep warm?

Thomas does not write to me. he contents himself with hearing from me by you— you will let Brisler know his Family are well. Faxon wants money to Buy stock, he wants three Cows and 4 young cattle he says—[2]

He and the two Nightingales have valued savils meddow, at 12 pounds pr Acre. I askd Faxon what rule he went by, mentiond this meddow of Bass's that you gave seven pounds for, but he is wild; that would fetch 20 he says, and this of savils, is as well worth 12 as Frenchss was six.[3] I have askd your Brother he thinks it too high, but I suppose your son will write you about it. I have advised him to allow 9 pounds ten shillings as you Love Land better than money, or to take the meddow for the debt.

Grain rises daily so does every article of produce Mutton excepted. are things as much higher at Philadelphia as they are here? I mean have they risen in the same proportion? I hope they will stop or the Banks fail. one thing I am pretty certain of, *that Farmers* should have produce to sell instead of purchaseing every article Regards to all inquireing Friends from your ever affectionate

A Adams

RC (Adams Papers); addressed by JQA: "The Vice-President of the United States. / Philadelphia."; endorsed: "Portia. Dec.r 23d / 1792."

[1] The Boston *Columbian Centinel*, 22 Dec., printed a series of resolutions thanking those who had previously worked to repeal the anti-theater legislation, encouraging them to continue their efforts, and naming a number of people, including JQA, to "a Committee to co-operate with them in such measures, as may be thought expedient, to give effect to the petition and remonstrance, which the town will present to the Legislature on this subject."

[2] James Faxon (1744–1829), a boot maker who was married to Mary Field, Esther Field Briesler's sister, was an Adams tenant farmer from 1792 to 1794 (Sprague, *Braintree Families*; Laurel A. Racine, *Historic Furnishings Report: The Birthplaces of Presidents John Adams and John Quincy Adams*, Quincy, Mass., 2001, p. 39).

[3] "Savils meddow" may have been land belonging to Benjamin Savil (1711–1794), which JA purchased from Savil's heirs on 5 Oct. 1795. JQA indicated that he had arranged for brothers John (1757–1804) and Ebenezer (1759–1823) Nightingale to appraise the land in his letter to JA of 22 Dec. 1792 (Adams Papers; JQA, *Writings*, 1:130–133 [in part]). JA had purchased on 17 Nov. four acres of salt marsh from Moses French (1731–1807), moderator of the Quincy town meeting, for the price of six pounds per acre (Sprague, *Braintree Families*; Adams Papers, Wills and Deeds).

Abigail Adams to John Quincy Adams

my dear   Quincy 25 dec^{br} 1792

Prince will bring this to you; the inclosed Letters I wish you to direct, the thin Paper, to your Father The other to Thomas;[1] Prince is to return on thursday mor͠g by him send the papers and any Letters which you may have; if the weather should prove pleasent, I shall send a Horse for you on saturday. I have seen the dr since I wrote to you, and talkd with him about the meddow. he thinks that if they will give a deed of the meddow for the debt, that as your Father Loves Land better than Money, and considering he once told them, that he would take it for the debt; (tho two years interest have since arrisen), that he will be better satisfied than to let the land be Sold to any one else, but if you have Enterd the action there will be time enough to take his orders upon it before Execution. I congratulate my Country upon the uninimmity exhibited in the votes of the Electors. tis much more there concern than mine, & next to my Country, myself and Family have a Right to be gratified as it is much pleasenter to spend & be spent for those who are sensible of ones merrits abilities and services, than to serve them against the will of half of them. whether N York are ashamed of their vote or not I think it strange that we should hear sooner from maryland than from them—

Yours affectionatly   A Adams

RC (Adams Papers).

[1] AA to JA, 23 Dec., above; the letter to TBA has not been found.

Charles Adams to John Adams

My dear Sir   New York Decr 26 1792

I am very sorry that Mr Bull has been so very dilatory that I received the horses but a day or two since He I find can make good promises. I am now looking out for a purchaser and hope to find one soon The horses do not look so well as I expected they would. We have accounts from Europe of the retreat of the combined armies from France. In this event I am only able to see a state of Anarchy continue for a longer space of time for They disposition of The French people is now much less inclined to a state of Tranquillity than ever. This unhappy Country will I fear be ruined de fond encomble[1] The Federal party in this State bite their chains while Clinton and his party Lord it over them with uncontroled sway. In his appointments he thrusts all kind of real merit asside and opens the door to none but his devotees. He has made Morgan Lewis a brother in law of Chancellor Livingston a judge of the Supreme Court, a man who is as unfit for a judge as any lawyer at our bar in preference to Mr Benson or Mr Jones[2] He has made Nathaniel Lawrence attorney General a man who never opens his lips at the Bar but has this merit that he is his.[3] And even poor me he has chosen to vent his spite upon by preferring one of his young adorers to hold a Notarial Seal.[4] He makes thorough work I assure you. I will venture to ask you one question Whether it is not propable if he goes on in this way for three years longer he may not fix himself very firmly in the saddle? There are two more measures which we expect A vote of thanks to the majority of the Canvassers a William Livingston as member from this City to Congress.[5] If These two things happen I suppose they will have finished this winters Campaign They are more mortified than they are willing to allow at the unsuccesful attempt of their head for the office of Vice President. The Baron desires his respects he intends to visit Philadelphia in a few days We have had a sorrowful house for sometime my poor friend Mulligan lost two of his sisters in one day by an epidemical fever which is raging with great violence in this City.[6] Do not think me indolent I am not and will write constantly to you.

Adieu my dear father beleive / me your dutiful and affectionate son   Charles Adams

RC (Adams Papers).

[1] The French Army defeated the Austro-Prussian Army at Valmy on 20 Sept. and Jemappes on 6 November. This success allowed the French revolutionary government to begin a push for imperial expansion and formally annex territory, starting with Savoy in late November (Bosher, *French Rev.*, p. 182).

[2] Morgan Lewis (1754–1844), Princeton 1773, was a lawyer, member of the N.Y. State Assembly, and attorney general. He had married Gertrude Livingston, sister of Chancellor Robert R. Livingston, in 1779. He would serve as a justice of the N.Y. Supreme Court until 1801. Samuel Jones (1734–1819) was a noted lawyer who had helped to compile the authoritative edition of New York legal statutes in the wake of the Revolution.

He served in the N.Y. state senate from 1791 to 1797 (*DAB*).

[3] Nathaniel Lawrence, who replaced Morgan Lewis as attorney general, represented Queens County in the N.Y. State Assembly. He had previously served in the N.Y. state ratifying convention (Hamilton, *Papers*, 9:247).

[4] Probably Francis Bloodgood (1769–1840) of Albany, a lawyer, who on 15 Sept. 1792 married Eliza Cobham, a ward of Clinton (*New-York Directory*, 1793, p. 227, Evans, No. 25422; Dexter, *Yale Graduates*, 4:532; New York *Diary*, 24 Sept. 1792).

[5] Col. William S. Livingston had been elected to the N.Y. State Assembly as a Federalist in 1791 but sided with Clinton in the gubernatorial election controversy the fol-

lowing year. The Republicans nonetheless declined to endorse Livingston in the subsequent congressional race, and he lost to John Watts, a Federalist (Young, *Democratic Republicans*, p. 334–335).

⁶ John W. Mulligan (1774–1862), Columbia 1791, studied law with Alexander Hamil-

ton. Like CA, he was a close friend of Baron Steuben. Two of Mulligan's sisters, Frances (b. 1782) and Mary (b. 1787), died on 24 and 25 Dec. 1792, respectively (Michael J. O'Brien, *Hercules Mulligan: Confidential Correspondent of General Washington*, N.Y., 1937, p. 153–156).

John Adams to John Quincy Adams

My dear Son   Philadelphia Decr 26. 1792

I rec^d by the last post your favour of the 16. The Votes from New Hampshire to Maryland inclusively have been unanimous excepting the factious Voice of New York, and one Dr Johnson of Conecocheague formerly a New Yorker a Particular Friend of Mr Clinton and by his own confession under particular Obligations to him. Southward of Chesapeak all are for Clinton except S. C.

I thank you for your History of Tragedy Comedy and Farce: but I cannot believe that Mr H. gave any encouragement to the Men of hand, to meddle with the Play house or the Board fences.

I have read the "Friend to Peace" and have no Small Penchant to see Menander. The Translation of the French account of the Revolution is well done and deserves to be continued. I Scarcely know of a greater Service that could be now rendered to the People of this Country, than a faithful and impartial Account of French affairs would be. I wish the Leyden Gazette could be regularly translated as well as reprinted in the Courier. I mean that part of it which relates to French affairs.

Your Observations on the Scurrility disgorged at me, as well as on the insidious Attacks on the general Government, are just to a certain degree. but not wholly so. The Newspapers guide and lead and form the public opinion. Gutta cavat lapidem, non vi sed sæpe cadendo. a continual dropping will wear a stone. We shall never have a fair Chance for a good Government untill it is made a rule to let nothing pass unanswered. Reasoning must be answered by reasoning: Wit by Wit, Humour by Humour: Satyr by Satyr: Burlesque by Burlesque and even Buffoonery by Buffoonery. The stupidity of Multitudes of good Friends of their Country and its Government is astonishing. They are carried away with every Wind of Doctrine and every political Lye: but the Docility with which they receive an answer when it is put into their Mouths is the only resource We have left.— hundreds even of the Officers of Government, Stand aghast like Children not knowing what to think nor what to Say, untill another Gazette furnishes them with Matter.

Franklin was pursued by an Opposition all his Lifetime. He was sometimes rejected at Elections by the Citizens of Philadelphia. He generally answered and sometimes very bitterly the Pieces against him. But He and his F[riends] made it a rule all his Life to let no Paragraph [go] unanswered.[1]

The Mortification of our well born State Monarch at the Unanimity of the five New England States, is in Character. He did me a Service by his late Journey to Connecticut. He put all the Stern farmers upon their Guard, and made them avoid all his Admirers even his Cousin, Thaddy Burr.[2]

I am grieved at the Weakness in the Conduct of this Gent[n] and his venerable Lieutenant towards me, but they can do me no harm: and I Say very little about them. Write me as often as you can.

We are all well— Love to your Mamma &c   J. A.

RC (Adams Papers); addressed: "John Quincy Adams / Councillor at Law / Boston"; internal address: "M[r] J. Q. Adams"; endorsed: "My Father Dec[r]. 26. 1792"; notation: "Free / John Adams." Some loss of text where the seal was removed. Tr (Adams Papers).

[1] This paragraph was written at the end of the letter but before the complimentary close and marked for insertion here.
[2] For Thaddeus Burr of Fairfield, Conn., see JQA, *Diary*, 1:306.

John Adams to Abigail Adams

My dearest Friend   Philadelphia Dec[r.] 28. 1792

Your Friends who are numerous enquire continually after your health and my answer is that you have not informed me that it is worse, from which my conclusion is that I hope it is better.

The Noise of Election is over, and I have the Consolation to find that all the States which are fœderal have been unanimous for me, and all those in which the Antifœderalists were the predominant Party, unanimous against me: from whence my Vanity concludes that both Parties think me decidedly fœderal and of Some consequence. Four years more will be as long as I shall have a Taste for public Life or Journeys to Philadelphia. I am determined in the mean time to be no longer the Dupe, and run into Debt to Support a vain Post which has answered no other End than to make me unpopular.

The Southern States I find as bitter against M[r] Jay as they are against me and I suppose for the same Reason. I am Surprized to find how little Popularity Mr Hancock has in any of the states out of Mass.

Mr Pierpoint Edwards has been here: although he did not vouch-Safe me the honour of a Visit or a Card, he was Seen in close Consultation at his Lodgings with Mr Jefferson and Mr Baldwin. I am really astonished at the blind Spirit of Party which has Seized on the whole soul of this Jefferson: There is not a Jacobin in France more devoted to Faction. He is however Selling off his Furniture and his Horses: He has been I believe agreater fool than I have, and run farther into Debt by his French Dinners and Splendid Living.[1] Farewell for me all that Folly forever. Jefferson may for what I know pursuing my Example and finding the Blanket too short taking up his feet. I am sure, all the officers of Government must hall in their horns as I have done.

Mr Ingersoll has wrote me for his Fee with Thomas and I must pay it, if the House make any Appropriation.[2] My Love to all— My Duty to my Mother. I am as impatient to see you as I used to be twenty year ago.

J. A.

RC (Adams Papers); internal address: "Portia"; endorsed: "Decbr. 28 1792."

[1] Thomas Jefferson faced lingering debts not just from his years of extravagant living in France and the cost of relocating back to the United States but also from the time of his inheritance of his father-in-law's estate in 1774. By 1794, he owed approximately £6,500, largely to two British firms (Malone, *Jefferson*, 3:167, 176–179).

[2] Letter not found.

Abigail Adams to John Adams

my dearest Friend   Quincy decbr 29th 1792

I received your two kind favours of 7th & 12 of this Month.[1] I have written to you regularly every week since you left me. we have not had any deep snow since the first in which you was caught upon the road. the greater part of that soon left us, & has been succeeded by two slight snows of a few inches depth. the weather has however been steadily cold & generally with a clear Sun shine. I find the cold creates as great an irritation upon my Nerves producing a Tremor, as the heat does by relaxation. I suffer more on that account than any other. I have not past a whole winter here for Nine years before. I think I mentiond to you that I had setled with shaw for the 5 Months he had lived with us, and agreed with him at the price we talkd of, for four Months more. He is very Steady, carefull & constant to buisness, tho not so string and active as some others. I have not yet any prospect of getting such an additional Hand as you want. I have desired mr Cary to inquire for me but they do not incline to let themselves till Spring. they do not know what price to ask. these Pernicious Banks will undoe us. yesterday mr Cranch gave a dollor pr Bushel for Rye. Bills which you know were three & four pr cent above Par when you went away are now as much below par. large Quantities have been sent here from the [sou]thard to be sold. tis said here that the demand for grain abroad, is the occasion of it, but I suspect some political manœuvre tho I know not what, and upon this occasion I am like some other person's perhaps jealous without a cause. I see the Banks multiplying in every state, and I consider them as so many Batteries raisd against the General Government. I think this one instance amongst many others in which the state sovereigntys will prove pernicious we daily feel the banefull Effects of such an overplus of paper

after what took place in Nyork with respect to the Election of mr Jay—I had no expectation but that the Same Party would oppose your Election to the v P. but I did not think that they would have led virgina by the Nose so compleatly the vote of those two states have declared to the world the Hostile Sentiments they possess towards the Government, for at that, much more than at you personally, is it aimed. as to disliking your politicks, I do not believe that they know what your politicks are. I am sure they do not if they rely upon the Representations which have been made to them by those whose sole intention was to deceive them— I own I cannot feel that cordiality towards those States which I do for those who have been unanimous towards you. I respect individuals of each, and I pitty those who are blinded by Party. if I know myself I do not think it is because I have such a fondness for the station, but because I think much of the tranquility & happiness of the Government depends upon having in that station, an establishd Character for firmness integrity and independence, and such must be the Character who can divest himself of all personal feelings, and do equal justice to those who are declareedly in opposition to his Principals, as to those who unite in sentiment with him. thus much for politicks. the best written peice I have read, and one which shews the Author to have had an acquaintance with all the transactions which have taken place for a number of years past, was that which was addrest to the Free and independent Electors of President & V. P. in Fennos paper of the 1 of dec^br— I have a curiosity to know the writer.[2]

Tomorrow I have a Number of hands going to cut the Timber for the Corn House that it may be ready for the first snow. your mother and Friends are all well. I received a Letter from Thomas, shall write to him soon affectionate Regards to mr & mrs otis and to all other Friends I have the advantage of you, I have Louissa for a bed fellow but she is a cold comfort for the one I have lost. pray continue to write weekly to your ever affectionate   A Adams

RC (Adams Papers); addressed by JQA: "The Vice President of the United States. / Philadelphia."; endorsed: "Portia. Dec.r 29. / 1792." Some loss of text due to the placement of the seal.

¹ JA to AA, 7 Dec. and 10 Dec., both above.

² An article by Philanthropos entitled "To the Free and Independent Electors of President and Vice-President of the United States" appeared in the 1 Dec. issue of the Philadelphia *Gazette of the United States*. An advocate for JA, Philanthropos argues that "In important national questions, misrepresentations often bias the public mind, and party interests create divisions, calculated only to subserve the designs of demagogues and temporizing politicians, who, strive to seduce the affections of the people from their real and substantial friends, and to erect their own fame upon the fall of those whom they have conspired to ruin. Superior merit is peculiarly the object of envy—Contracted minds delight in collecting the failings of others, that they may make a sacrifice to their own pride; and as the best of men are subject to imperfections, no one is secure from the attacks of malevolence." Philanthropos suggests the need to counter such misrepresentations and proceeds to provide a lengthy outline of JA's merits to demonstrate his worthiness to continue as vice president, describing JA as "a man of genius and extensive erudition; an eminent lawyer, politician and civilian; a warm friend to civil and religious liberty; an early and decided patriot; a strenuous advocate for the rights of his country."

Elizabeth Smith Shaw to Abigail Adams

My Dear Sister—   Haverhill Dec. 31. 1792

I wish I could be satisfied, & *know* what is my duty towards my William, & Abigail, I could then feel easy, & cheerful— To day is the last day for our inoculation for the small-Pox— There is an hospital about half a mile above our house The people are passing, & repassing every hour of the Day, & I cannot think William secure & yet I am fearful of his going in the winter— I thought we were determined to let them both go, but there is so many things in the way that I believe it will be omitted— I have been hoping the town would permit the hospital to be continued till in the spring—but they have had a meeting & will not allow it— they say it has been 500 Dollors mischeif to us alreaddy— Winter here, is our harvest in Trade—

You cannot conceive how much I have suffered, I am perplexed— & distressed I fear they will never have so good a chance again— The two Doctors take turns in tarrying with them the whole time—

46 come out to Day & tomorrow & Mr Shaw think there was never a Class that did better, though he is very averse to his own Children going in—[1] The Class has suffered terribly with the cold—but their symtoms have none of them been dangerous in the least—

enough of the small pox—I am almost crazed with it— But out of the abundance of the heart, I find the hand will write—

However my Mind has been absorbed it has not been so much so, as not to be anxious for you, & my Countries welfare

I looked with eargerness into every newspaper & am happy to find that my fellow ctitizens were wise—that they understood the things that belong to their *peace*, though many falsehoods, & misrepresentations have been invented to blind, & hide them from thier Eyes—

I know the unaimity which appeared in the votes, must give my Brother & you more pleasure on the account of the approbation, gratitude—& respect they discovered, than on any private Emolument arising from the Station—

Notwithstanding what you have said, I cannot but hope to see you here— We shall all think it a pleasure to make you warm, & comfortable— Our high ground & clear northwest winds will brace your nerves, & restore your health—

Whenever you may chance to see the sensible Menander, please to tell him that since he is so great an advocate for the Theatre, there are many friends in Haverhill, who would wish to see him act his part here— If in the Character of a conscious Lover, I will not be angry— any Character which *he* may think *proper* to assume will please—for some can please in all but in none can he please your *Sister* more than in that, of an *affectionate Nephew*—

May the close of this, & every succeding year find you surrouned with every circumstance of Felicity, is the wish of your ever / grateful Sister

Elizabeth Shaw

PS I have not time to write to Sister Cranch now— please to give my Love to all—

RC (Adams Papers).

[1] Shaw reported to her sister Mary Smith Cranch on 11 Feb. 1793, "I shall have the pleasing intelligence conveyed to you, that my Children have had the small-pox—very favourably—indeed Just as I could have wished— William was in fine Spirits all the time— Had just soreness enough in his arm to know that the small pox had taken—was suddenly seized, & was unwell about ten hours, & had no more trouble, he had about an 100 pox, which filled, & were as good humourd as himself— Little Abigail suffered more with her arm, & had the symtoms a great while—had the rash very full— She was quite sick for 6 or 7 days—but after she broke out, the soreness of her flesh went of, & she felt relieved though she had three or four hundred—& considerable number filled

nicely– The language of my heart is, what shall I render to their great preserver, for this renewed instance of his kindness–" (DLC: Shaw Family Papers).

John Adams to Charles Adams

My dear Charles   Philadelphia January 1. 1793

on the Commencement of the new Year I wish you health, honour, Profit and Pleasure through the Course of it, and as many repetitions of these anniversaries as shall be for your own happiness and the benefit of your Friends and Connections in the World. Application and that alone will Secure you, under the Smiles of divine Providence the Blessings of Life.

Make for me the Compliments of the Season to all our Freinds in New York. The disagreable Symptoms of Disaffection to the Union which have appeared in your State, have given me much Anxiety, but have not diminished my regard to their Welfare, nor my Wishes for their Prosperity. They must reflect, if they are not past reflection and they must feel if they are not past feeling on the Unanimity of all their Neighbours against them.

Governor Clinton and his Adherents have discovered an Ambition which will not soon be forgotten in America. and it is not probablle that the People of America will suffer their Union to be dissolved, or the Administraters of their Government to be embarrassed to gratify the Jealousy Envy Ambition or Revenge, or any other Passions litle or great of Mr Clinton or his Mirmidons: though another mortified faction at the southward may be found to magnify the miserable Baggatelle of his services to the Size the first Characters in the Community. The fraud is too gross to deceive the most undiscerning among impartial Men. Let him go on with his arbitrary Exclusions of the best Characters in his State merely because they will not be his Spaniels, and see the Consequence. I rely upon your discretion however. dont neglect to write to   J. A.

RC (MHi:Seymour Coll.); addressed: "Charles Adams Esqr / Councillor at Law / Hanover Square / New York"; internal address: "Charles"; notation: "Free / John Adams."

Abigail Adams to John Adams

my dearest Friend   Quincy Jan^ry 2. 1793

our son brought me your favour of the 19 december on sunday last, by which I find that the same Ideas have past through both our minds on a late Election amidst all that has been written upon the occasion, no one has ventured to state the comparative merrits, and services of the Candidates, but have contented themselves with saying that they would not bear a comparison, that clintons were lighter than a feather when weighd against yours. the Peice I mentiond to you in my last Letter, did you more justice than any which I have before read. the Characters who have been most active against you, are many of them such as a Man would rather chuse to be in opposition to than upon terms of civilitity with. the misfortune is that they have their weight and influence in society. possessing some talants and no principals they are fit agents for mischiefs of the blackest kind. by the candidate they have opposed to you, they have come forward and openly declared themselves opposed to the Government. mark their measures, watch their movements and we shall see them strugling whenever they dare shew themselves, for the assendency. the late success of the Arms of France against their Enemies, seems to give much satisfaction to the half thinking politicians, as tho the Retreat of the King of prussia was to give Peace to France and heal all her internal wounds, establish a quiet Government and build up a Republick in a Nation shaken to its center, and Rent to Peices by Faction. when I read citizen President, & citizens Equality, I cannot help feeling a mixture of Pitty and contempt for the Hypocrisy I know they are practising and for the Tyranny they are Executing. I was visiting at mr Apthorp the other day. he mentiond to me the surprize he was in when he read Pains Letter and the account he gave of the treatment he received from the custom house officers who Searchd his papers, to find that the P——t had any correspondence with a man whom he considerd as an incenderary and a Character unfit for to be trusted. he could not but consider it as degrading his Character and doubted the Authenticity of the Letter. tho it struck me in the same manner when I read the account, I was determind not to say so to him. I only observd to him that the passage publishd could not do any injury to any Character, tho no doubt mr Pain took pains to have it known Publickly that he had the honour of a Letter from the President in order to give himself weight & importance—[1]

Inclosed are a few lines which pleasd me from a symplicity of stile as well as for the truth they contain. the Author I know not they are taken from the Centinal.[2]

You inquired of me in a late Letter[3] whether I had any prospect of hireing a Man by the year. a Young Man of a good countanance has offerd himself this week. he lived the last year with a mr Williams at Roxburry. he is from the state of N Hampshire and has lived four years at Roxburry in different places a year at a time. he talkd of 30 pounds by the year. I told him that would not do, I did not hear that more than 24 was given by any body the last year, and that it must be a very extrodinary hand to earn such wages— I told him we did not want a hand till the first of march he said he wishd to let him self immediatly—but we fi[nally] came to these terms if upon inquiry his character would answer and you approved I would hire him from the 1 of Feb'ry & he came down to 26 pounds, which you will think too high perhaps—but I am not bound to take him if you do not chuse— I mentiond the first of Feb'ry that I might have time to write to you, and in the mean time I shall inquire his Character.

present my Love to mrs otis, and Regards to all inquiring Friends from your ever / affectionate   A Adams

P S the Timbers for the corn House is all cut & drawn to gether in the woods waiting for snow to get it home we have very cold weather but little snow about 2 inches depth

RC (Adams Papers); addressed by JQA: "The Vice-President of the United States. / Philadelphia."; endorsed: "Portia Jan. 2 / ans^d 14. 1793." Some loss of text where the seal was removed.

[1] George Washington's letter of 6 May 1792 to Thomas Paine was one of a number of papers a customs official attempted to seize when Paine passed through Dover en route to Paris to take a seat in the French National Convention. In Paine's 15 Sept. report of this incident, he included a short excerpt from Washington's letter, which was written to thank Paine for sending Washington several copies of Paine's *Rights of Man* (Boston *Columbian Centinel*, 12 Dec.; Washington, *Papers, Presidential Series*, 10:357).

[2] The enclosure has not been found but was possibly a piece entitled "Dr. Parr's Opinion of Mr. Paine," which dismissed Paine's understanding of government as "too partial for theory, and too novel for practice, and under a fair semblance of simplicity, conceal a mass of most dangerous errours" (Boston *Columbian Centinel*, 2 Jan. 1793).

[3] JA to AA, 10 Dec. 1792, above.

John Adams to Abigail Adams

My dearest Friend   Philadelphia January 2. 1793

Our Antifœderal Scribblers are so fond of Rotations that they Seem disposed to remove their Abuses from me to the President. Baches Paper which is nearly as bad as Freneaux's begins to join in concert with it, to maul the President for his Drawing Rooms, Levees, declining to accept of Invitations to Dinners and Tea Parties, his Birth day Odes, Visits, Compliments &c—[1] I may be expected to be an Advocate for a Rotation of Objects of Abuse, and for Equality in this particular. I have held the office, of Libellee General long enough: The Burthen of it ought to be participated and Equallized, according to modern republican Principles.

The News from France, so glorious for the French Army, is celebrated in loud Peals of Festivity and elevates the Spirits of the Ennemies of Government among Us more than it ought: for it will not answer their Ends. We shall now see the Form of the French Republick. Their Conventions will have many Tryals to make before they will come at any thing permanent. The Calamities of France are not over.

I shall claim the Merit of Some little Accuracy of foresight when I see General Lincoln, who you remember was inclined to think the Duke of Brunswicks march to Paris certain, while I was very apprehensive that the numerous fortified Towns in his Way would waste his army and consume the Campain.

We Shall Soon See the Operation in France of Elections to first Magistracies.[2] My Attention is fixed to this Object. I have no doubt of its Effects: but it is a curious Question how long they can last. We have lately Seen how they have Suceeded in New York and what Effect that Election has had upon the Votes for President. Cabal, Intrigue, Manœuvre, as bad as any Species of Corruption We have already seen in our Elections. and when and where will they Stop?

tenderly.   J. A.

RC (Adams Papers). Filmed at 2 Jan. [1794].

[1] Benjamin Franklin Bache's *General Advertiser*, 2 Jan. 1793, included a piece, "To the Noblesse and Courtiers of the United States," ostensibly advertising for a poet laureate for the United States and explaining the duties of the position and the nature of the poetry to be written: "To give a more perfect accommodation to this *almost new* appointment, certain *monarchical prettinesses* must be highly extolled, such as LEVIES, DRAWING ROOMS, STATELY NODS INSTEAD OF SHAKING HANDS, TITLES OF OFFICE, SECLUSION FROM THE PEOPLE, &C. &C. It may be needless to mention certain other trifling collateral duties, but that the poet may be acquainted with the whole circle of requisites, it may not be amiss to hint, that occa-sional strokes of ridicule at *equality*; the absurdity that the *vulgar*, namely the people, should presume to think and judge for themselves; the great benefit of *rank and distinction*; the abomination of supposing that the officers of government ought to *level* themselves with the people by visiting them, inviting them to their tables, &c. may be introduced by way of episode to the Poem."

[2] The National Convention required new elections to all local and municipal administrative bodies after the establishment of the republic. Most of these took place in late 1792 and early 1793 (Malcolm Crook, *Elections in the French Revolution: An Apprenticeship in Democracy, 1789–1799*, N.Y., 1996, p. 98–101).

John Adams to John Quincy Adams

My dear son   Philadelphia January 2. 1793

I am again entertained by your kind Letter of the 22. Ult.[1] The Intrigues of Mr Clinton Mr Burke Mr Dallas Mr Pierpoint Edwards, &c with Several Members of Congress from Virginia N. C. Georgia and Kentucky aided by Governor Hancock, have given a very odd cast to the Election: but they have Seperated the sheep from the Goats— There must be however more Employment for the Press in favour of Gov^t. than there has been, or the Sour, angry, peevish, fretful, lying Paragraphs which assail it on every Side will make an Impression on many weak and ignorant People.

It is better that the People of Boston should be employed in disputing about a Theatre, than in reading the gloomy falshoods which have disgraced their public Prints for some time in disparagement of the general Government.

In Answer to General Lincoln's Inquiry, I can only Say at present that when an Appropriation Law shall have past, I will draw the Money and pay it where he points out.[2] but if no Appropriation should be made I will borrow the Money of a Friend and repay him in Boston—but I shall know more in a few days.

I am astonished both at the Judgments and Consciences of those who appraised the Marsh at twelve Pounds an acre.— Go on with the Action and levy the Execution—at whatever Price, Appraisers under Oath shall affix, I must take the Land finally and shall acquiesce but I will not be so imposed on, as to take it voluntarily at such an exorbitant Valuation. Mr Savil may sell the Meadow and pay me if he will— if he getts 12^£ or 20^£ I shall be easy, for I am by no means attached to the Land. His whole Conduct shows that he means to injure me as much as he can. and I am now determined to be injured by him as little as I can. I bought 4 Acres of Marsh as good as that for 24^£ a few days before I came away.

The French Arms have been Successful beyond their own Expectations and if their national Convention Should be as wise as their Army has been brave their affairs may be happily settled. A Republick must have Laws and those Laws must be executed. Mankind Seems to be bent upon trying over again, the Experiments with which all Governments began of elective first Magistrates. Elective Legislatures or at least an Elective Branch of a Legislature may do very well in France: but I have long thought and still think that

Elective Executives will do only in America. We shall Soon see how they operate in Europe. An hereditary Executive cannot be admitted in a free Government without an hereditary senate to contrast it. on the other hand an hereditary senate without an hereditary Executive would be equally dangerous & destructive. My Opinion has always been that in France a free Government can never be introduced and endure without both an hereditary Executive and Senate. But the Voice of all the World seems to be against me. A few Years will shew whether the French Republic will last longer than the English one did in the last Century.

I think however there will be a general Revolution in Religion and Government all over Europe. how many Centuries will be employed in civil distractions and what new form of Things will rise up I pretend not to foresee or conjecture. If the Influence of their Confusions does not produce Anarchy among Us, We may be happy

yours   J. A.

RC (Adams Papers); endorsed: "My Father. Jan^y: 2. 1793." Tr (Adams Papers).

[1] JQA wrote on 22 Dec. 1792 congratulating JA on his reelection and offering additional details of the ongoing debate regarding theater in Boston. JQA also indicated that Benjamin Lincoln was hoping to collect $600 owed by JA (Adams Papers; JQA, *Writings*, 1:130–133).

[2] Congress confirmed the continuation of the vice president's salary at $5,000 per annum on 18 Feb. 1793 (*U.S. Statutes at Large*, 2d Cong., 2d sess., p. 318).

Charles Adams to John Adams

My dear Sir   New York Jany 5th 1793

I yesterday received your affectionate letter of the first instant. In return for your kind wishes, I present my respects, with an ardent hope, that you may yet many years be spared to your children, your friends and your Country; and that each returning season may still, as they ever have, find you happy, in that greatest of blessings to the just, an applauding conscience. Many are the mortifications which the Federal party experience in This State. The tyranny of a majority is exerted without controul. The Constitution of This State provides for the enumeration of the inhabitants but once in seven years: since the last census the Northern and western parts of This State have increased quadruply in numbers so that the representation from Those Counties is very inadequate.[1] These Counties are mostly peopled by The New England States and are universally Federal— Mr Clinton it is true appoints his Sattelites to offices among

369

them but they are too discerning to be wheedled from their sentiments If our Electors had been chosen by the people as they ought
to have been we should not have laboured under our present disgrace. There are two anecdotes circulating in this City for the truth
of which I must rely upon you One is That a certain man in high
office in the United States his name I did not hear wrote to Govr
Hancock That as the Constitution of the United States was manda-
tory in that part which directs That The Electors "shall" return their
votes sealed to the Seat of Government It was an insult upon the
dignity of the People of the particular States who chose the Electors
That Govr Hancock caught at this and communicated to The Legislature his ideas upon the Subject That they laughed and ordered the
votes to be returned. There is something too ridiculous in this to be
beleived.— The other that a committee of the officers of The Massachusetts Line had waited upon you and offered their Suport if you
would use your influence in support of their petition That you answered "You had always served your Country, and always would"[2] I
receive many congratulations upon your reelection The various
machinations which have been put in play against you have I think
served to rivet the affections of the people more strongly. They begin to perceive that nothing has been spared to injure you. That
every species of falshood has been used to alienate their veneration
and respect. They see through the deceit, and turn with horror
upon your accusers. The success of The French against the combined armies has excited a blind joy in this City. But anything will
go down with the cry of liberty Our Tammany Society have given
another specimen of their folly and rashness in the toasts which
they drank upon the celebration You may have seen the list[3] I think
the name of Petion too destestable to receive the Euge[4] of true
Americans. But "They know not what They Do" The Contest of The
French is not yet ended with foreign powers, but if it were They
have a hydra to contend with at home which will not so easily be
subdued. We are much surprised at the idea of reducing the military
establishment of the United States at This moment Are we likely to
succeed in our treaties with The Indian tribes?[5] Or are our militia
the only proper troops to contend with them? I cannot beleive it
consistent with policy or oeconony. I should be very glad to get
Fenno's paper Our Printers give us but partial accounts of the debates in the house of Representatives If you could send it to me
without inconvenience to yourself it would be a feast. I am sorry

that I did anything wrong with Seymour Bull has behaved like a villain but it is now useless to complain. If I had had money enough to pay Seymour I should not have sent an order to Philadelphia but by his return I had picked up sufficient to discharge it which I did. Mr Bull must answer to you for his ill conduct. It is very difficult to sell horses at this time I have held them up at a hundred pounds but shall sell them at any rate next week The horses look very ill I beleive their keeper has not only used them but made them eat but little I will do the best I can with them.

In your letters you ask me respecting Mr Wilcox The piece you allude to under his signature was respecting the election of Vice President. He is one of the bar, but has never been celebrated; a modesty and diffidence which at his first appearance as a lawyer, was rendered unsurmountable by being too severely brow beaten, by an Elder brother in the profession. An honest, candid, firm man in his principles and politickes He made his first appearance upon the Contest in our election of Governor. His intentions were good; He meant to speak independently; He would examine principles; He had no partialities, except such as were founded in honesty and honor; He should say nothing he was ashamed to avow; He should asperse no man in the dark; There was no necessity for concealment; He should therefore use no fictitious signature. He has uniformly adhered to his system. He has written more upon that subject than any other writer; and more to the purpose than all put together The sneaking subterfuge of rotation he despised He called the Child by its right name whilst those who had more influence than he had were afraid to call it Federal. He does not write one of the most brilliant styles but he has gained much consideration by his manly and nervous sentiments. Such Sir is the man you have enquired after and such the sentiments he supports and I sincerely hope his writings may raise him from obscurity.[6] I made application to Berry and Rogers to make out their account for you They told me they must procure from Mr Dilly the true statement as they had most of the first volumes from them.[7] That Mr Berry was going to England by the next packet and would return in the Spring when every thing should be adjusted. I have not seen Menander but have this moment a promise from a gentleman for a constant perusal of The Centinel Please to give my love to my Brother and beleive me your dutiful and affectionate son   Charles Adams

RC (Adams Papers).

[1] CA exaggerates somewhat but is correct in noting an increase in population in the northern and western portions of the state. Between 1790 and 1795, the population of eligible voters in those counties (usually described as the eastern and western districts) increased from 18,000 to 35,000, while the southern areas (the southern and middle districts) grew only from 20,000 to 29,000 voters (Young, *Democratic Republicans*, p. 585, 588).

[2] Since the Revolution Massachusetts officers had petitioned Congress for additional pay for their military service. Most recently, they had appealed for compensation for officers who had sold to speculators depreciated government bonds that Congress had since agreed to honor under the Funding Act. The latest petition was read and tabled by the House on 31 Dec. 1792 and resulted in no additional compensation (Sidney Kaplan, "Pay, Pension, and Power: Economic Grievances of the Massachusetts Officers of the Revolution," *Boston Public Library Quarterly*, 3:17, 21 [Jan. 1951]; U.S. House, *Jour.*, 2d Cong., 2d sess., p. 657).

[3] Reacting to reports that the French had defeated the Prussian Army, the Tammany Society of New York met on 27 Dec. to celebrate with songs and toasts. Besides drinking to the French Republic and various leaders, including Pétion and Dumouriez, the participants also toasted Thomas Paine, the Marquis de Lafayette, "Destruction to all Kingcraft and to all Priestcraft, the poisons of public happiness," and "Contention and confusion in the councils of all despots" (New York *Daily Advertiser*, 29 Dec.).

[4] "Approval, commendation" (*OED*).

[5] On 20 Dec., John Steele of North Carolina proposed a resolution in the House of Representatives to "reduce the military establishment of the United States" in order to provide better frontier protection and to lower spending. Actual debate on the motion began on 28 Dec. and continued at length until the bill was ultimately defeated on 8 Jan. 1793 (*Annals of Congress*, 2d Cong., 2d sess., p. 750, 762–768, 773–790, 791–802).

[6] William Willcocks (1750–1826), Princeton 1769, a New York lawyer and justice of the peace, had staunchly supported John Jay in the 1792 New York gubernatorial election, going so far as to challenge Marinus Willett to a duel over the matter (*Colonial Collegians*). Willcocks' article, which appeared in the New York *Daily Advertiser*, 15 Dec., argued that Clinton's antifederalism made him ill suited to serve as vice president under the Constitution. Willcocks also defended JA against charges that his writings were an endorsement of the British government: "That part which he took in the political drama with Great Britain, at the earliest hour, and uniformly maintained throughout those times which tried men's souls, to the present day, is alone sufficient to acquit him of any unfavourable presumption."

[7] For the London bookseller Charles Dilly, see vol. 1:73–74.

Abigail Adams to John Adams

my dearest Friend   Quincy Jan^ry 7th 1793–

I received your Letter by mr Roberdeau who with our son and young mr Quincy came out and dinned with me to day.[1] I was pleased to see a son of your old Friend and acquaintance for whom you have so often expresd a Regard; as well as the agreeable Husband of miss Blair that was; we had much conversation about my acquaintances in Philadelphia, many of whom he could give me a particular account of. we past a very pleasent day. I once or twice last summer exprest an anxiety at not hearing from Thomas so often as I wishd: I recollect you askd me, if I was equally anxious about you when absent my days of anxiety have indeed been many & painfull in years past; when I had many terrors that encompassed me around I have happily Surmounted them, but I do not find that I am less solicitious to hear constantly from you than in times of more danger, and I look for every saturday as a day on which I am to receive a Boon. I have received a Letter every week since you left me, and by this days post two—one of the 28 & one of the 29th dec^br—for which receive my thanks, particularly that part in which you say you are not less anxious to see me than when seperated 20 years ago—[2] Years subdue the ardour of passion but in lieu thereof a Friendship and affection deep Rooted subsists which defies the Ravages of Time, and will survive whilst the vital Flame exists. our attachment to Character Reputation & Fame increase I believe with our Years. I received the papers National Gazzet and all I see the dissapointed Electors wish to excuse their vote by Representations respecting you, that prove them to have been duped and deceived, while the Antis fly of assureing the publick that the Monarchy Men, & the Aristocracy have become quite harmless.[3] if so it is to be hoped that their hue & cry will subside— present me kindly to all the good Ladies who favour me by their inquiries after my Health. it is better than the last winter tho very few days pass in which I can say that I feel really well.

I have not heard any thing of the Chaise since you wrote me that it was left at Harford I believe it will not reach Home till spring. the Narrow Ro[ad] to the water have been so blockd up with snow that shaw has not been able to get up any sea weed lately: he attempted it but could not succeed, & the ground has been bare in the Road The Timber for the corn House is all cut & part of it got home, one day more will compleat it. Faxon was going this last week to the Ceadar Swamp it being now a fine time but very unfortunatly a Man on the Road near it, broke out with the small Pox & refused to be moved so that he cannot go. we have not had any sleding in the Road this winter yet the Ground has been pretty much coverd with a thin snow & Ice, the weather in General very cold. Hay is fallen I am told to 4 & 6 pence pr hundred. Grain still holds its price, superfine flower 7 dollors pr Barrel oats 3 shillings pr Bushel. I have not had occasion yet to purchase. my Horses are so little used that they are high Spirited enough with 8 quarts a day. James takes very good care of them. I do not regreet your parting with the others. one pr are sufficient here, and a good able Farm Horse will do us more service & be much more prudent for us. I hope you live prudent enough now for the most Rebublican spirit of them all. from the debates there appears a jealous carping ill naturd spirit subsisting and a great desire to crush the Secretary of the Treasury & the minister of War

you was right, the chief Majestrate denies his having given permission to the Mobility to pull down the Theater. His Prime minister under the signature of a Friend to Peace, has undertaken to defend his whole conduct, whilst a writer under the signature of Menander defends his fellow citizens, to say no more like an able counsel these Peices you will find in the Centinal of december 19 22 & 26th those of the 19 & 22th are written in a masterly stile.

Your Friends here are all well excepting Brother Cranch who has had a very ill Turn. I fear he will not tarry long with us.

I am my dear Husband with the tenderest Regard and attachment your affectionate   A Adams

RC (Adams Papers); addressed by JQA: "The Vice-President."; endorsed: "Portia Jan 7 / 1793." Some loss of text where the seal was removed.

[1] JA to AA, 8 Dec. 1792, above. JQA, who dates this dinner to 9 Jan. 1793 in his Diary, identifies Mr. Quincy as "J. Quincy," presumably Josiah Quincy III (D/JQA/19, APM Reel 22).

[2] The letter of 28 Dec. 1792 is printed above. On 29 Dec., JA wrote to AA again, weighing in on the theater controversy in Boston and the presidential election (Adams Papers).

[3] Various pieces linking JA with a pro-monarchy philosophy appeared in the Philadelphia *National Gazette*. On 2 Jan. 1793, one article suggested that the threat of "all efforts toward monarchy and aristocracy," however, had been overcome: "The current of popular opinion is become so strong against every idea, intimation, and attempt of that nature, that the advocates and planners of such schemes no longer dare venture abroad with their propositions for giving the government a twist towards royalty, the eager though somewhat concealed object of a well known faction for at least four years bypast."

Thomas Boylston Adams to Abigail Adams

My dear Mother   Philadelphia 8th: Jany: 1793

I am somewhat surprized by the information given in your letter of the 23d: Decr: viz. that you have not received a single line from me since my Father left you.[1] Certainly there must have been some fault in the Post Office, or some person who has taken the letters therefrom has neglected to deliver them. I wrote the first week after my Fathers arrival, informing you of several circumstances relative to his determination of residing at Mr. Otis's— I wrote an other letter upon a different subject a few days after, and there has been ample time for their reaching you before the date of your letter. I hope you have before this received them—[2] I rejoice with you at the unanimity that has appeared in the late Election— It seems something extraordinary that the two Candidates should be supported in different

States with so much apparent spirit. Nine States nearly unanimous for one and five for the other. You are misinformed as it respects Pennsylvania—there was but *one* vote for Clinton all the rest being unanimous; this vote was given him from motives of personal Friendship as well as private interest; the point of Federal, or Anti— seems not to have been considered, for the man who gave it is warmly Fed[l.]— South-Carrolina cast a reflection which will be sensibly felt by Burr in giving him one vote, which was known to be confered for no other reason than that it might be lost. The Election is great, we have now only to wish that the *People* may be *generous* or rather *just*. Our Finances are at present much deranged— however you feel it more than I do— The final decission of the Treasury cut off more than 700 Dollars—

Tomorrow is the day fixed by M[r:] Blanchard for his 45[th:] Flight in the Balloon from the Jail yard— He intends if wind and weather permit to dine in N-York. It excites you may suppose the curiosity & astonishment of all *us* novices in such spectacles—mine however is reduced to a Philosophical indifference almost bordering on Stoicism; I shall never the less, gaze like other simple ones at the painted baubles, without deriving either amusement or instruction from the experiment.[3] As to Congress—I give every one that ask the same answer, that I scarcely think them worth my notice, I certainly have not thought them worth my personal attention as yet—they have become much less consequential as a public body since they have made every body rich & happy, except the V— P—, and unless they create business for themselves—their sessions will or ought to be very short in future. However they have not yet done all, and instead of a disposition to do more the spirit of undoing seems to be gaining ground— You will have from Massachusetts a good Representation for the next Congress—but ours has little to boast in point of splendor, or genius.

I shall attend to your request concerning the Museum as soon as I have cash enough to pay for the binding &c[a:] There is no Register published that I hear of— I have not been able to procure the Books for which Cousin L— Cranch wrote me.[4] I ought to address her in person, but I hope she will remember I never was *vastly polite*. My regard for her & all the family however shall not diminish by separation. As to visiting Massachusetts next Summer, nothing but necessity such as an Ague would impose, will suffer me to hope it. My time will be too precious I fear at that time to devote to amusement. Your absence this Winter from the gay circles is much comented in words—doubtless by many in reality. I am very little troubled with those insipid invitations which used to waste more time & health than they ever aforded amusement, but still a sufficiency of those which I deem more flattering as I have the vanity to think my company is desired.

My best love to all friends, both in-doors and out, and belive me truly affectionate   Thomas B Adams—

RC (Adams Papers); internal address: "M^rs: A Adams"; endorsed by JA: "T. B. Adams / 8. Jan. 1793."

¹ Not found.
² The first letter is at 11 Dec. [1792], above; the second letter has not been found.
³ The Adamses as a family had long been interested in ballooning, and TBA's parents, JQA, and AA2 had attended balloon flights in Paris, though none by Jean Pierre Blanchard. Blanchard (1753–1809), a French balloonist, was attempting his 45th flight but his 1st in

the United States. On the morning of 9 Jan. 1793, he successfully crossed from the prison court in Philadelphia to Deptford, N.J., in a fifteen-mile flight lasting slightly less than an hour (vol. 6:x–xi; Jean Pierre Blanchard, *Journal of My Forty-Fifth Ascension*, Phila., 1793, p. 10, 14, 26, Evans, No. 25207). See also JQA, *Diary*, 1:216–217, 222.
⁴ Letter not found.

John Adams to Abigail Adams

My dearest Friend   Philadelphia January 9. 1793

In your Letter of Decr 23^d you Say "Faxon wants Money to buy, three Cows and four young Cattle."— I know not the Price of Stock: but if you can purchase him what he wants at a reasonable rate and can finds means to pay for them I shall be content. but I would employ Some one to purchase them in Bridgwater or Abington. Faxon himself is not So judicious as he ought to be, in Some Things.

I have the same aversion to the multiplication of Banks and the Same Apprehension of their pernicious tendency as you express: but so many People live upon them, that they will have their Course. We shall soon be perplexed and distressed, in consequence of them. I consider myself already as taxed one half of my Salary and one half of all the Interest of my Money to support Bankers and Bankrupts. In Short Debtors and Men of no Property will find means, in our State of society, to compel others who have something not only to pay their debts for them but to support them. It falls hardest on Widows orphans, Salary Men, and those who have Money at Interest, we except such of those last as are at Liberty to Speculate. They are able to make what Money they please.

I received yesterday the Votes from Kentucky. They are said to be all for Mr Jefferson. Let Us, my Dear prepare our minds and as well as We can our Circumstances to get out of this miserable Scramble.

It gives me pleasure to read that you are making Preparations of Timber for a Corn house, and I hope shaw will be as attentive as he can through the whole Winter to all my Manufactures of manure, that We may make a good Corn field in the Summer.

I had Yesterday a charming Letter from Charles; according to him, had the Electors of that State been chosen by the People, their Votes would have been very different. The Representation of the People in their present Legislature is very unequal and partial in favour of the Anti's, and Clinton; as he has explained very intelligibly and intelligently.

M[r] Taylor the new Senator from Virginia,[1] has made a Motion for opening our Doors and building a Gallery: but he will not be assisted in his Argument by the late Example of Virginia, where the Electors at Richmond opened their Doors, and held debates and made Phillippicks before "The Marseillois," by which means Six Votes are said to have been converted, either by reasoning or by fear.[2] This Example will not convince the Majority of the Senators of the Necessity, Expediency or propriety of opening their Doors.

I have a warm Chamber with a Southern Exposure and have a fire in it day and night. I am warm enough a nights but cannot Sleep as I ought. I have Scarcely had a compleat nights Sleep since I left you, which keeps me apprehensive of the Fever and Ague in the Spring. I hope however to escape it. I shall not be able to leave this Place till the fifth or sixth of March.[3] The Roads will be bad and the Journey by the Stage fatiguing, but I who was born to be a slave must fullfill the End of my Creation.

Tenderly   J. A.

Blanchard to day is to sett all the World upon the broad Stare at his Balloon. I wish H. could make it an Interlude and send him back to Europe.

RC (Adams Papers); internal address: "Portia"; endorsed: "Jan[ry] 9th / 1793."

[1] John Taylor (1753–1824), William and Mary 1770, a lawyer and farmer from Caroline County, Va., replaced Sen. Richard Henry Lee in late 1792 (*Biog. Dir. Cong.*).

[2] "La Marseillaise," composed in the spring of 1792 in Strasbourg by Rouget de Lisle, who gave the song the title "Chant de Guerre de l'Armée du Rhin" (Song of the Rhine Army), had been conceived as a military theme but quickly became popular as a revolutionary anthem (Schama, *Citizens*, p. 597–599).

[3] The congressional session concluded on 2 March 1793 (*Biog. Dir. Cong.*).

John Adams to Abigail Adams

My dearest Friend   Philadelphia January 14. 1793

This day I rec^d yours of the 2^d.— I have rec^d all the Votes from all the States. it is known that Georgia voted with N.C. V. and N.Y. and Kentucky voted for Jefferson.

There is no other Newspaper circulated in the back Country of the Southern States than Freneau's National Gazette, which is employed with great Industry to poison the Minds of the People. The Fœderal Court has again had a Sitting in Virginia and by reason of Mr Jays Sickness the great Cause is again continued, which serves to keep up the Rage in that State, and N. C. which is its Eccho.[1]

If you hire the Man you mention, you should know beforehand what kind of skill and Experience he has in farming as well as his Integrity and good disposition. I shall leave it however to you.— Twenty Six Pounds are too high. 24 are enough: but if you cannot get one for less We must give 26.

I expect e'er long to hear that Pain is Split and pliced for an Aristocrat: perhaps roasted or broild or fryed. He is too lean to make a good Pye, but he is now in company with a Number, who are admirably qualified and disposed to feed upon each other.

The foolish Vote of the constituting Assembly in favour of a Rotation and excluding themselves from being re-elected has cost every Man of Weight and Talents among them his Life or his Country and his fortune. all are murdered banished and confiscated. Danton Robertspiere, Marat &c are Furies.[2] Dragons Teeth have been sown in France and come up Monsters.

The Army has behaved better and the People seem to be zealous: but if they have not some system by which they can be united, what is to be expected?

We have our Robertspierres and Marats whose wills are good to do mischief but the Flesh is weak. They cannot yet persuade the People to follow them.

If the national Assembly can Subdue the mutinous Rabble at Paris as well as Dumourier has driven the Prussians, they may be free and do something, but what I know not.

tenderly yours   J A

RC (Adams Papers); internal address: "Portia."; endorsed: "Jan^ry 14 1793."

[1] The Circuit Court for the District of Virginia sat between 23 Nov. and 6 Dec. 1792, but the only justice to attend was William Cushing. The court met again in Virginia be-

tween 22 May and 8 June 1793, with John Jay and James Iredell in attendance, at which time they considered "the great Cause," the case of Ware *v.* Hylton. One of more than 200 suits filed by British creditors seeking to recover debts from Virginia citizens, Ware *v.* Hylton raised questions about the strength of the contract clause of the Constitution (Art. 1, sec. 10) and the supremacy clause (Art. 6). It was ultimately decided in favor of the British creditors in 1796 (*Doc. Hist. Supreme Court*, 2:338–339, 380, 539).

[2] When the French Constituent Assembly was replaced by the Legislative Assembly on 30 Sept. 1791, the dissolving assembly—at the suggestion of Robespierre—voted that its members would be prohibited from serving in the new congress. This made it impossible for prominent conservatives to continue to serve and cleared the way for radicals to dominate the government. After the National Convention in turn replaced the Legislative Assembly in Sept. 1792, Robespierre and fellow radicals Danton and Marat were active members (François Furet and Mona Ozouf, *A Critical Dictionary of the French Revolution*, transl. Arthur Goldhammer, Cambridge, 1989, p. 530; Stanley Loomis, *Paris in the Terror, June 1793 – July 1794*, Phila., 1964, p. 49, 73, 93).

Abigail Adams to John Adams

my dearest Friend   Boston Jan[ry] 22 1792 [1793]

I received your kind favours of Ja'n[ry] 8 & 9th and on saturday a Letter from our daughter[1] I have been in Town for a few days—for the first time I chose not to come till all the Bustle of Election was past Election for a Representitive has taken place since I came here. Honestus's Friends and emisaries have been indefatigable in procuring votes for him, and their success has been Such that he stands highest upon the list, and tho it is presumed that their will not be a Choice, he & dr Holten will be the Candidates.[2] dr Jarvis is sitting up for Federal senator in the Room of mr strong.[3] Speculation is the popular Topick when a man is to be crushd, and that is the crime of which mr strong is said to be guilty, and tho I presume it is quite groundless, yet it will answer a Party purpose an other Idle story is that mr Pitt has resignd,[4] and that the President of the u s is going to resign in March, as tho there could be any connextion between the resignation of the first minister of state in England and the chief majestrate here, nor can I devine the policy of the Report unless it is meant for a stock jobbing purpose, yet there are persons here stupid enough to swallow such reports. you will see by the papers the whole Town of B— laid under a tax of 3 dollors pr head which they dare not refuse, even those who in their hearts dislike the Festival and will join in it no further than to pay the money: the Civick Feast of the Cits, pushd down their Throats for fear of being stiled Aristocrats.[5] Such is the infectious spirit, of the Times—

Mr B— is here.[6] I saw him at the assembly, where he was very social. there were some compliments paid to him, which tho in the Character of this Town, belongd not to a private citizen—such as waiting the dances for him for more than an hour and finally being obliged to begin without him, as he did not make his appearence till near Nine oclock dinning at five oclock to conform to his hour, &c one compliment however he has received not so much to his taste, a W—— for Arerages of old martinec affairs—

do you suppose that Congress will meet after their dissolution on the 3^d of March? I fear you will have as dissagreeable a time Home as you had when you went. Love to mrs otis her Friends here are all well— my Health is better than it has been. I have not had any return of a Fever for two Months. I cannot say as much for two years before

my Love to Thomas I will write to him next week when I return to Quincy

Yours most affectionatly   A Adams

RC (Adams Papers); endorsed: "Portia / Jan. 22. 1793."

[1] On 8 Jan., JA wrote to AA with yet more commentary on the recent elections. In particular, he related various anecdotes being relayed in the South about his relationship with George Washington, commenting, "There is no End of the Fictions and Falshoods which were propagated and not contradicted in those remote States." JA also told two stories of individuals' criticizing his *Defence of the Const.* without actually having read it. He cynically noted that "These Anecdotes show the real Genius of this enlightened Age. Such is a great part of the Light, which We boast of So much" (Adams Papers).

The letter from AA2 may have been of 13 Sept. 1792, above.

[2] Dr. Samuel Holten (or Holton) was elected to Congress; Benjamin Austin Jr. was not (*Biog. Dir. Cong.*).

[3] Charles Jarvis failed in his election attempt; Caleb Strong and George Cabot remained senators from Massachusetts for the 3d Congress (same).

[4] The rumor was false; William Pitt remained prime minister until Feb. 1801.

[5] For the civic feast, see AA to JA, 1 Feb. 1793, and note 1, below. Tickets to the event cost three dollars each and were advertised several times in Boston newspapers (William Parker Cutler and Julia Perkins Cutler, *Life, Journals and Correspondence of Rev. Manasseh Cutler, LL.D.*, 2 vols., Cincinnati, 1888, 1:489; *Columbian Centinel*, 19 Jan.; *Boston Gazette*, 21 Jan.).

[6] Possibly Samuel Breck Sr.

John Adams to Abigail Adams

My dearest Friend   Philadelphia Jan. 24. 1793

Our good Friend General Lincoln gave me this morning your favour of the 7th which compensated in Part of my Disappointment by Mondays Post. I sett my heart on one Letter a Week and as many more as you please.

I cannot say that my desire of Fame increases. It has been Strong in some Parts of my Life but never so strong as my Love of honesty. I never in my Life that I know of sacrificed my Principles or Duty to

Popularity, or Reputation. I hope I am now too old ever to do it. But one knows not how tryals may be borne, till they are made.

The Hellhounds are now in full cry in the Newspapers against the President, whom they treat as ill—as ever they did me.

The Same insolent and impudent Irishman who is said to have written so much against me, is now suspected to be writing against him.

Both Houses of Congress are making strict Inquisition into the Treasury: with upright and patriotic Views no doubt. Hamilton will find no more mercy than is due from a generous nation to a faithful servant. But I presume his Character will Shine the brighter. However it is still but an Experiment, whether the Ministers of state under an elective Executive will not be overborne, by an elective Legislature. I believe it to be certain that two elective houses of Legislature, or even one, have it in their Power whenever they shall have it in their Will to render any Minister of state or even any elective Executive unpopular, though he may be possessed of the best Talents and most perfect Integrity. I presume that neither of our Houses will be disposed to such Injustice. but the time may come.

I am so well satisfied with my present simplicity, that I am determined never to depart from it again so far as I have. My Expences in future forever shall at all Events be within my Income nay within my Salary. I will no longer be the miserable Dupe of Vanity. My Style of Life is quite popular. What say you to living with me in Lodgings next Winter? This shall be my Plan if I cannot hire a house for Six months only. Your Friends who are very numerous enquire tenderly after your health. Benson says he is for making Mrs Adams Autocratrix of the United States. This however must be Secret because it is a sort of Treason.

tenderly yours   J. A.

RC (Adams Papers); endorsed: "Jan^ry 24 1793."

John Adams to Abigail Adams

My dearest Friend   Philadelphia January 27. 1793

I was not a little Surprized, a few days ago at receiving a Letter from Dr Hutchinson as Secretary to the Philosophical society in this City certifying my Election as a Member of that Body. This Gentleman you know has been celebrated for his opposition to my Election as V.P. one of the Society since told me, that when I was nominated they all rose up and cryed out that I had been a Member these twenty Years.

The Truth it seems is that I was elected as long ago as 1779 but the Records for some years preceeding and following that time are not now to be found.[1] The Secretary of that day has run Mellancholly and Fanatic, and knows nothing of the Records if he kept any.

The Sickness of my worthy Brother Cranch, which you mention in your last has given me many a melancholly hour Since I rec^d it.— Although the immense Load of Care that has oppressed me for so many Years has rendered me incapable of enjoying his Conversation, as I used to in my Youth, I have ever loved him, and shall never cease to love him. I hope he will recover his health and be preserved to his Friends for many years. My Love to sister. Duty to my Mother, Love to my Brother and all Friends. Louisa I hope has conquered all her disposition to the Ague and all its crawls & Chills. My Love to her.

I am very well accommodated here for my self: but not for Company.

I Shall not get away from hence before the fifth of March, and then there will be a long unpleasant Journey before me.

But I will make up for all by Enjoyment on the Farm, during the summer. provided always that I dont get the Ague. That is not quite annihilated in its seeds. I am bilious and otherwise reminded to beware of the first hot day.

I am, with all the Ardour of / Youth yours   J. A

RC (Adams Papers); internal address: "Portia"; endorsed: "Jan^{ry} 27 1793."

[1] Dr. James Hutchinson served as secretary of the American Philosophical Society. His letter to JA has not been found, but on 24 Jan. JA wrote to Hutchinson and Jonathan Williams thanking them "for the honor" of election to the Society (PPAmP). For discussion of JA's possible earlier election, see vol. 3:297, 299–300.

John Adams to John Quincy Adams

My dear John   Philadelphia January 27 1793

Although your modesty would not inform Us, of your commencement as a Faneuil Hall Orator, it is impossible to conceal from the Public so important an Event, when there are 500 talkative noisy Witnesses of it, and accordingly it has come to me from an Eye and Ear Witness, as I suppose, your young Friend Breck.[1]

I rejoice that you have taken the Unpopular Side of the Questions concerning Incorporation of the Town, and Dramatic Entertainments; not because I love Unpopularity or wish you to be unpopular; but because I believe the unpopular Side in these Instances to be right; and because it will Serve to keep you back in the political Career for some time and give you Leisure for study and Practice, in your Profession.

Menander I think was free enough for a Statesman, but Eccho has been full free for a Witt and a Droll.

> Ere o'er the World had flown my mob-rais'd Fame
> And George and Britain trembled at my name;
> This State, then Province, pass't with wise intent
> An Act Stage Plays and such Things to prevent:
> You'll find it, Sirs, among the Laws Sky-blue
> Made near that time, on brooms when Witches flew
> That blessed Time, when Law kept wide awake
> Proscrib'd the faithless, and made Quakers quake.
>   &c
>
> Yet in an Act, have Congress Said of late
> That the Supreme Executive of State
> *Shall*—What a Word to Governors to Use
> By Men unworthy to unloose their shoes
> *Shall*! I repeat the abusive term once more
> That dreadful offspring of Usurping Power. &c[2]

When Where, Ah! Where my son will these Things end? If ever Mortal had provocation to become a Party Man, and revenge his Wrongs upon his Ennemies, in their own Way, it is I.— but for the World, I would not.— You will never see me involving Massachusetts in the Perplexities that New York is in.— The Persecution against me, set on foot in Boston by the little Passions of little Minds, is the most unprovoked, the most destitute not only of Grounds but of even Pretexts that ever happened in this World. Yet Jealousy Envy and Terror haunt their frivolous souls like Spectres. so be it— This is Punishment enough to gratify all my Resentments— I would not feel the smart of the Sting of Envy as they do for all their Popularity and for as absolute a despotism over those with whom they are popular as they possess.

Boston Seems however to be breaking out with a Distemper worse than the small Pox. Anarchical Dinners and Anarchical Elections, will be worse than the Plague.

There are some alarming symptoms even in Congress: but I hope the French when they begin to build will assist us. hitherto they have only pulled down.

yous affectionately   J. A.

RC (Adams Papers); internal address: "J. Q. A."; endorsed: "My Father Jany. 27. 1793." Tr (Adams Papers).

¹ Samuel Breck Jr. (1771–1862), son of Samuel and Hannah Breck, had recently moved to Philadelphia from Boston to join his parents. The younger Breck had been educated in France and was pursuing a career as a merchant. JQA had attended the Boston town meeting on 21 Dec. 1792 at Faneuil Hall "to remonstrate against the anti-theatrical Statute" (J. Francis Fisher, *Memoir of Samuel Breck*, Phila., 1863, p. 8–

10, 12–13, 17; D/JQA/18, APM Reel 21).
² These lines are excerpts from Connecticut Wit Richard Alsop's satirical poem *The Echo*, No. IX. The piece, which first appeared in the Hartford *American Mercury*, 14 Jan. 1793, parodies John Hancock's opposition to theater in Massachusetts (Carl Holliday, *The Wit and Humor of Colonial Days (1607–1800)*, Phila., 1912, p. 262, 264–265).

Charles Adams to John Adams

My dear Sir   New York Jany 31st 1793

I received your favor of the 29th yesterday¹ I had sold the horses the day before for £70:.

The Baron returned on teusday his visit has been of service to him He said to me upon sitting down to supper that evening "I thank God my dear Charles that I am not a Great man and that I am once more permitted to set down at my little round table with Mulligan and yourself enjoy more real satisfaction than the pomp of this world can afford." He thinks that parties are too high to remain long in a quiet situation. That Antifederal [spiri]t which wishes to imitate the geniuses of France is boiling with much force among the members of Congress. I hear that They charge the Secretary of the Treasury with having embezzled two millions of the public money.² Surely if accusations like this without foundation are suffered to pass by without censure we have arrived at a republican liberty of Speech. Is it ignorance or malice which forges these charges? The Baron told me You were well, prudent and respected, but that The other great officers of the Goverment were very uneasy How often when reflecting upon the trials you have undergone and the rewards you have generally met with have I repeated to myself those beautiful lines of Horace

"Justum et tenacem viri propositum
Non Civium ardor non prava jubentium
Non vultus Instantis Tyrranni
Mente quatit Solida.["][3]

The President too has at last become the subject of open invective? I beleive him very illy calculated to bear it. He is in a measure unaccustomed to being abused by libels and whether he will have fortitude enough to despise them I am very doubtful

We received letters from our friends in England on Sunday last[4] They write pleasingly of their health and prosperity We hear also that Prusia has acknowledge the Republic of France and that an alliance between them is shortly to take place The French army under Dumourier have captured Mons Bruxells and Gent and made 15000 prisoners[5] Where will all this end? We are quite peaceable in this City for the present The assembly are about to impeach Judge Cooper for malpractice during the last election for Gover[nor. He] will be taking up the hatchet upon the oth[er side?] probably they will still tyrannize as they have before Their majority is so decided in both houses that Cooper will stand but a poor chance however innocent he may be.[6] That we may be speedily releived from oppression is the sincere prayer of your / affectionate son

Charles Adams

RC (Adams Papers). Some loss of text where the seal was removed.

[1] JA wrote to CA on 29 Dec. 1792, commenting on the vice presidential election and encouraging CA not to become embroiled in any political battles. "My Advice to you," JA instructed, "is to preserve the Independence of your own Mind and bow the Knee to no Man for the sake of a National Seal. Behave like a Gentleman towards Mr Clinton and his Friends but preserve your Veneration for Mr Jay who deserves it" (MHi:Seymour Coll.).

[2] Democratic-Republican leaders in Congress, suspicious of Alexander Hamilton's handling of the proceeds of two loans authorized in 1790, approved on 23 Jan. 1793 a series of resolutions—known as the Giles Resolutions, for William Branch Giles of Virginia, who proposed them—demanding a full accounting. Hamilton complied, sending reports to both houses in February. Although the reports failed to satisfy the Republicans, they were unable to muster sufficient support for another round of resolutions condemning Hamilton's actions. For a full discussion of the situation, including the text of the resolutions and Hamilton's reports, see Hamilton, *Papers*, 13:532–579; 14:2–6, 17–67, 68–79, 93–133.

[3] "The man tenacious of his purpose in a righteous cause is not shaken from his firm resolve by the frenzy of his fellow citizens bidding what is wrong, not by the face of threatening tyrant" (Horace, *Odes*, Book III, ode iii, lines 1–4).

[4] Not found.

[5] Dumouriez's army captured Mons on 7 Nov. 1792, Brussels on 14 Nov., and Ghent shortly thereafter. By 28 Nov. what remained of the Austrian Army had evacuated from the Netherlands (*Cambridge Modern Hist.*, 8:416–417).

[6] William Cooper (1754–1809), a major New York landowner, proprietor of Cooperstown, and staunch Federalist, served as

judge of Otsego County. Clinton supporters accused him in a petition to the state legislature of trying to influence the vote in Otsego during the 1792 gubernatorial election, but the charges were dismissed (*DAB*).

John Adams to Abigail Adams

My dearest Friend   Philadelphia January 31. 1793

I have, this minute rec[d] your favour of the 22[d.] The Report of the Presidents Resignation is probably designed to prevent the Rise of the Stocks: but the Insolence which appears every day in Baches and Freneaus Papers, proceeding from the Same Persons who are tired of abusing me, may be carried to a point that he will not bear. He has not been used to such threshing and his skin is thinner than mine.

Cit. H. and Cit. A. I presume will grace the Civic Feast. Cit and Citess is to come instead of Gaffer and Gammer Goody and Gooden, M[r] and M[rs], I suppose.

Congress I presume will not sitt after the Second of March. I shall not be able to sett off till the 5[th.] but I will not wait if I travel but ten miles a day.

We Shall See, in a few months, the new French Constitution, which may last Twelve months, but probably not more than Six. Robertspierre and Marat with their Jacobin Supporters I suspect will overthrow the Fabric which Condercet Paine and Brissot will erect. Then We shall see what they in their turn will produce.[1]

M[rs] Washington requests me to present you her very particular regards. Many other Ladies do the same.

Citizen Brisler and Citizen V. P, are very happy together— Since they are equal and on a Level it is proper that sometimes one should be named first and sometimes the other.

Our Countrymen are about to abandon the good old grave solid manners of Englishmen their Ancestors and adopt all the Apery Levity and frivolity of the French.

Ca ira. / tenderly yours   J. A.

RC (Adams Papers); internal address: "Portia"; endorsed: "Jan[ry] 31 / 1793."

[1] Both Marie Jean Antoine Nicolas Caritat, Marquis de Condorcet (1743–1794), and Jacques Pierre Brissot de Warville (1754–1793) were members of the so-called Girondin faction in the French National Convention. They, along with Thomas Paine and others, helped to write a liberal constitution, which was completed by 15 Feb. but had little effect because of the ongoing Terror. After the arrest of the Girondins later in 1793, Condorcet died in prison and Brissot was guillotined (Bosher, *French Rev.*, p. xxvii, xxxii, 178).

Abigail Adams to John Adams

my dearest Friend   Quincy Feb^{ry.} 1. 1793.

your last date, as yet received, was the 14 of Jan'^{ry}, I may have Letters in Town; but as the week has been stormy I have not got them: I wrote you last from Boston the day before the Civic Feast, as it was Stiled. the day past in much better order than was apprehended; for to men of reflection the Cry of *Equality* was not so pleasing, and to men of Property very alarming it was agreed amongst them to indulge a spirit they could not supress, & unite with the Mobility in their Feast, to keep a strickt watch and gaurd over them: and to appoint steady persons upon [who]m they could depend to conduct the sacrifice, for such indeed was [the] *citizen ox–* the whole was managed without any Riot except the distribution of the ox; a Table being placed at the upper End of State street, the ox was paraded there, together with a load of Bread & 2 Barrels of Punch but no sooner was the ox cut in peices than they were seazd by some sailors & *citizen Mobility*, and thrown in every direction amongst the spectators. the Tables split to peices the plates &c made one Crash, the Punch & Bread were instantly driven of, the one to the Mall, where the Mobility followd and enjoyd it, the Bread to the Alms House; the day closed with much quietness & all was still by 12 oclock at Night. you will have read the Toasts which shew the spirit that gave rise to the Feast, & the prodigious pains which they took to avoid drinking the Healths of anyone but washington whom they avoided stiling citizen–[1] tis said Citizen samuel did not so well relish the Term, least the Ears of his followers should be too much accustomed to it, and join with those who wish to have the Town incorporated.[2] the two Candidates of Representives are no doubt Holten, & Austin; mr B——n has descended to such Popular arts as have disgusted his Friends, it is said, but falshood is so current a coin on such occasions that I am slow of belief: I was very splendidly entertaind at his House whilst I was at Boston; having heard Some things, I was more attentive to what past.[3] I found by his conversation that he was one of those, who thought that the President might unbend, and visit, & mix with Tom dick and Harry. he askd me if I had heard that the secretary of War was going to resign. I replied that I had not. he said he had been informd so from a Gentleman, who heard it from Knox's mouth [last ni]ght the President had been very unfortunate in that appointment. this brought to my mind mr danes conjecture of the Author of the Strictures.[4] I askd after ward if any known cause existed for a personal animosity? but could not learn any thing further than their owning eastern Lands together perhaps some altercation might have arrisen. I was at the Assembly, and received many polite attentions. mr S——n & his Lady were civil beyond my conception. Such kind inquiries after the health of the V. P. and such solicitude to accommodate me. the high sheriff too was vastly politee. mrs S——n & her daughter visited me a day or two after which was what I did not expect.[5] I calld upon mrs Gill. she afterwards sent for me to take Tea with her, which I did mr Gill was at Prince Town. She proposed to me a Family match which was to send my Son J Q A to England for her Neice miss Hollowell and to give her in marriage to him.[6] She wishes to have her Neice return to her, for mrs Adams says she I am all alone in this Country, I have no connextion to call my own— thus with an immence property She looks round her without a being for whom she feels any natural attachment to bestow it upon. there must be a some thing to Mar all our enjoyments in a state of Probation like this Life, "a Cruel something unpossessd"[7]

we have had a very open winter the day before yesterday we had a pretty fall of snow—which I hope will enable us to get Home the remaining Timber, and my Wood; shaw laments that he has not a stronger Team. Faxon makes up two and is in constant employ for some one or other. he has not however assisted me but one day which was in getting Timber. we have sent into the ceadar swamp and got out Some Rails. Faxon whose Eyes always see double, says that 2000 may be cut upon one acre and a Quarter. I am glad however from Belchers & shaws account to find that it is like to turn out well worth the money. I am anxious to get all the Buisness done which you left me in Charge but the season has not been so favourable as we wisht—

our Friends are all well Remember me kindly to mrs otis. her sister is with me. she was so good as to spend a few days with me on my return from Boston

yours most affectionaty   A Adams

RC (Adams Papers); addressed by JQA: "The Vice-President of the United-States / Philadelphia."; endorsed: "Portia / Feb. 1. ans^d· 12 / 1793." Some loss of text where the seal was removed.

[1] A committee of Boston citizens organized a civic feast for Thursday, 24 Jan., to celebrate "the SUCCESSES of their French brethren, in their glorious enterprize for the establishment of EQUAL LIBERTY." The food for the feast was carried through the

city on carts, after which, "From the immense number of citizens assembled in *State-street*, the refreshment provided, could not be so *equally* distributed, as was wished; but notwithstanding this circumstance, the highest degree of cheerfulness and good-will prevailed; and the sacrifice being speedily demolished, the citizens retired in good order." Leftover bread was donated to the jail and almshouse. Following a second procession, the organizers gathered and several toasts were offered, including "The Rights of Man" and "The fraternity of Freemen." The toast to George Washington, given by "Citizen" Charles Jarvis, was, "We propose but one individual, and your hearts will tell you that this is WASHINGTON" (Boston *Columbian Centinel*, 26 Jan.).

[2] Various groups of people had tried to incorporate the town of Boston into a city, beginning as early as 1708. The most recent attempt had been in 1791, when the lack of an efficient police system led to calls for a town reorganization; see JQA to TBA, 1 Feb. 1792, and note 2, above. Later attempts gained greater popular support but were thwarted by the lack of a provision in the 1780 Massachusetts constitution allowing the state to create cities. The 1820 constitutional convention amended the state constitution to address this issue, and Boston was subsequently incorporated in 1822 (Winsor, *Memorial History of Boston*, 3:219–222).

[3] For James Bowdoin Jr., son of the late governor, see vol. 1:327. At this time, he was being promoted—unsuccessfully—to represent Suffolk County in Congress; see, for example, Boston *Columbian Centinel*, 19, 29 Dec. 1792.

[4] Probably a reference to an article signed "A Uniform Federalist," which initially appeared in the Philadelphia *American Daily Advertiser*, 29 Nov., but was reprinted with the title "Strictures on Mr. Adam's Political Character" in the Philadelphia *National Gazette*, 1, 5 December. The piece challenged an earlier one by "A Consistent Federalist," for which see AA to Thomas Welsh, 15 Nov., note 2, above. Attacking JA as a monarchist and suggesting that his time in Great Britain had corrupted him, "A Uniform Federalist" proclaimed, "if you wish to persevere in the happy and honorable experiment of governing yourselves; if you wish not a king; if you be not prepared to *open your purses* to pay his ordinary and extraordinary revenues, his *church*, his *armies*, his placemen, his pensioners &c. &c. and in short, to *defray the expences* of your own *slavery*; then, abandon Mr. Adams; annihilate his political existence; . . . stigmatize him as an *apostate* from his own political creed; and, what is worse as an apostate from your political creed and the political creed of your constitution."

[5] For Martha Langdon Sullivan, see vol. 7:384. Mehitable Sullivan, Martha's step-daughter, would marry James Cutler on 5 Feb. 1793 (Thomas Coffin Amory, *Materials for a History of the Family of John Sullivan of Berwick, New England*, Cambridge, 1893, p. 152).

[6] Mary Hallowell, whom the Adamses had met in London, eventually married John Elmsley, who became the chief justice of Canada (vol. 7:17, 26; Robert Hallowell Gardiner, *Early Recollections*, Hallowell, Maine, 1936, p. 4).

[7] "Against our peace we arm our will: / Amidst our plenty, something still / For horses, houses, pictures, planting, / To thee, to me, to him is wanting. / That cruel something unpossessed / Corrodes and leavens all the rest" (Matthew Prior, "The Ladle," line 165).

John Adams to Abigail Adams

My dearest Friend   Philadelphia Feb. 3. 1793

General Lincoln setts out Tomorrow, and I should not dare to let him go without a Love Letter to you.

After a November December and January the fairest softest and finest that ever were known in this Place, The Month of February has been ushered in by a considerable Snow: but the Weather is again so fine that the sun will soon restore Us the naked ground: I should like it better in its White Robe of Innocence till the 20th of March.

I dined Yesterday at Mr Daltons. Mrs Dalton enquires affectionately and sends her regards &c

Fryday night I Spent with the Philosophical society. The Meeting was thin: but I was not able to perceive any great superiority to our Accademy, except in the President.[1] There are able Men however, and I was agreably entertained. Mr Jefferson was polite enough to accompany me: so you see We are still upon Terms. I wish somebody would pay his Debt of seven Thousand Pounds to Britain and the Debts of all his Country men and then I believe his Passions would subside his Reason return, and the whole Man and his whole State become good Friends of the Union and its Govt. Silence however on this head, or at least great Caution.

I hope the Boston Rejoicings were at the success of the Arms of France, and not intended as Approbation of all the Jacobinical Councils. I am enough in the Spirit of the Times to be glad the Prussians and Austrians have not Succeeded, but not to exult in the Prison or Tryal of that King to whom though I am personally under no Obligation, my Country is under the greatest.[2] It is Providentially ordered that I who am the only ~~man~~ American who was ever Accredited, to him and retired from his Court without his Picture, and under his displeasure Should be the only one to bewail his Misfortune. The accursed Politicks of his knavish Favourite have cost him his Crown if not his head. The Duke de la Rochefaucault too, is cutt to Pieces for his Idolatry.[3] If I had not washed my own hands of all this Blood, by warning them against it, I should feel some of it upon my soul.

Macchiavels Advice to cutt off a numerous Nobility had more weight than mine to preserve them and Franklins Plagiary Project from Marchement Nedham had more Weight with Fools than all my Proofs strong as holy Writ.[4] The Vengeance of Heaven for their Folly, has been revealed in more shivering Terms than in any of my numerous Examples

yours kindly   J. A.

RC (Adams Papers); endorsed: "Febry 3. 1793."

[1] JA is making fun of himself; he was elected president of the American Academy of Arts and Sciences in Boston on 24 May 1791 after the death of the organization's first president, James Bowdoin. He would remain in that position—albeit largely in an honorary capacity—until his resignation on 4 June 1813. David Rittenhouse was president of the American Philosophical Society (Frank E. Manuel and Fritzie P. Manuel, *James Bowdoin and the Patriot Philosophers*, Phila., 2004, p. 250–253; Amer. Philos. Soc., *Trans.*,

3:xxviii [1793], Evans, No. 25103).

[2] Louis XVI, who had been arrested in Aug. 1792, was tried by the National Convention and executed on 21 Jan. 1793. Marie Antoinette was guillotined on 16 Oct. (Bosher, *French Rev.*, p. xiv, xx, 180). See also Descriptive List of Illustrations, Nos. 9 and 10, above.

[3] Louis Alexandre, Duc de La Rochefoucauld d'Anville (1743–1792), a *philosophe* and friend of the United States who had corresponded with JA, was stoned to death by a French mob in Sept. 1792 (JA, *D&A*, 4:42; Hoefer, *Nouv. biog. générale*).

[4] In *The Prince*, ch. 9, "Of the Civil Princedom," Niccolò Machiavelli warns of the difficulty of a prince coming to power through the support of the nobility because he "finds many about him who think themselves as good as he, and whom, on that account, he cannot guide or govern as he would." Machiavelli further notes that the prince "need not always live with the same nobles, being able to make and unmake these from day to day, and give and take away their authority at his pleasure" (Machiavelli, *The Prince*, transl. N. H. Thomson, N.Y., 1910, p. 35).

Marchamont Needham (or Nedham) (1620–1678), a provocative British journalist, was best known for his satirical writings and frequently shifting allegiances during the English Civil War. Needham wrote several tracts in defense of Oliver Cromwell's Commonwealth and the overthrow of the monarchy, including *The Case of the Commonwealth of England Stated*, London, 1649; *The Excellencie of a Free-State; or, The Right Constitution of a Common-wealth*, London, 1656; and *Interest Will Not Lie; or, A View of England's True Interest*, London, 1659 (*DNB*). JA believed that Franklin had been unduly influenced by Needham's antimonarchical writings and that the French, in turn, were unduly influenced by Franklin. See, for example, JA to TBA, 26 April 1795 (PWacD) and 7 April 1796 (DLC).

Abigail Adams to John Adams

my dearest Friend   Quincy Febry 9th 1792 [1793]

I received your kind favour of the 24th of Jan'[ry] together with the News papers. the writings of the American Mirabeau, if he is an American & those under the Signature of Cincinnatus are insolent indeed, and are in unison with a Number of papers Published in the Boston Chronical calld the crisis, Supposed to be written in Philadelphia and sent here for publication as I was told in Boston that there was a Club, who were in constant correspondence with the s——y of state those papers are leveld at the Government & particularly against Hamilton, who will however I hope stand his ground.[1] a very viruelent peice has appeard in the same paper signd stephen Colona Threatning the Government with the vengence of a hundred thousand Men, if certain Characters formerly stiled Antifeaderal were not more notised & appointed to office this writer says that the constitution was addopted by means of Artifice cagoiling deception & he believes corruption I read the peice at the time it was publishd, but had no Idea that the Author could be our former P——h Friend.[2] a very good answer followd it written; by mr davis, signd Publius with a Quotation as the introduction from the Play calld the Ladies of castile—[3]

9. LOUIS XVI, BY JOSEPH DUCREUX, 1793
See page xvi

10. "LA REINE MARIE-ANTOINETTE EN HABIT DE VEUVE À LA PRISON
DE LA CONCIERGERIE," BY ALEXANDRE KUCHARSKI, 1793
See page xvi

I received a Letter to day from our daughter dated Nov^br the col children &c were all well.[4] she writes that our minister complains loudly of expences that he had no Idea of them. mrs P—— complains of the impudence of trades people in that Country. they must be strangly alterd—for I never saw more civility in any country. Nay I have often been surprized at their confidence in strangers, but perhaps these people have been accustomed to slaves, and expect the same servility. mr M—— renders himself very obnoxtiuous in France by an active and officious Zeal in favour of the Aristocracy he has lately been obliged to keep close—for the Jacobines declare that if he was not an American with a commiss[ion] from Washington they would have had his Head upon a Pike long ago. they are astonishd that such a character should be sent them. short tis said is very voilent in Holland. Humphries is really going to marry a Lady of Ample fortune.[5] his countrymen who have been in Lisbon speak highly of his polite attention to them, but complain that they are not noticed *by others* mrs smith had visited mrs Beach who was well and vastly pleasd with England—[6] if there is any vessel going from Philadelphia pray write to mrs smith for she complains very much that she does not hear from her Friends. tis uncertain whether she returns in the Spring

I had a Letter to day from Charles he writes me that he had been sick with a fever which prevaild very much in NYork, but was quite recoverd.[7] we have had a fortnight of Sad weather here one day very cold the next a warm rain and thaw. this has convinced me that I am still to suffer from my former complaint. I have been attackd with the old intermitting and am still struling with it.

we have accomplishd drawing home the remainder of the Timber, & shaw has been employd with Faxon & two other hands whom I have hired in getting stuff from the ceadar swamp, in which they have found four or five pine Trees—old & fit for Boards these I have had cut & drawn to the saw mill we hope to get 2 thousand of Boards from them. we still have to cut and draw from the woods Trees for Jistes, but our snow comes & lies only a day or two, by which means we do not accomplish all we wish.

My affectionate Regards to all inquiring Friends tell Benson I do not know what he means by abusing me so, I was always for Equality as my Husband can witness. Love to Thomas, from your affectionate

Abigail Adams

RC (Adams Papers); addressed: "Vice President of the / United States / Philadelphia"; endorsed: "Portia / Febr^y 9th 1792." Some loss of text where the seal was removed.

¹ In the Philadelphia *Federal Gazette*, 7 Jan., "Mirabeau" addresses a letter to "Fellow Citizen" Thomas Jefferson, begging him to forgo retirement to continue his work as "the colossus of opposition to *monarchial deportment, monarchial arrogance, and monarchial splendor.*"

Addressed to members of Congress, the president, and the "Victorious & Patriotic Officers of the French Army," Cincinnatus' letters were published in the Philadelphia *General Advertiser*, 8, 11, 14, 21 January. Cincinnatus takes both George Washington and Congress to task for their failure to compensate fairly former members of the Continental Army, arguing that "the present government has been liberal to the late army in nothing but neglect and contempt" (11 Jan.).

Beginning the previous September, the Boston *Independent Chronicle* had been publishing a lengthy series of articles entitled "The Crisis," signed "A Republican," which would eventually total fourteen installments, concluding in Aug. 1793. The wide-ranging pieces cover various topics, including trade and commerce, taxation, public credit, the Indian War, economic relations with Europe, and the establishment of a national bank. The author attacks Alexander Hamilton as a "superficial financier" (15 Nov. 1792) and disputes the efficacy of many of his policies, especially his support of national and branch banks over state banks (*Independent Chronicle*, 6, 27 Sept.; 11, 25 Oct.; 1, 15, 30 Nov.; 10, 24 Jan. 1793; 7 Feb.; 26 April; 18, 25 July; and 8 Aug.).

² The article by Stephen Colonna appeared in the Boston *Independent Chronicle*, 20 Dec. 1792. It complains of the poor treatment of Antifederalists, "excluded from any places of honour or emolument," concluding, "And be assured, the awakened wrongs, and the active resentment of a hundred thousand men are not easily done away, or alleviated." The Adamses' "former" friend from Plymouth was James Warren.

³ Publius' article, which was printed in the Boston *Independent Chronicle*, 10 Jan. 1793, decried Stephen Colonna's piece as "indecent and intemperate invective . . . a libel on the government and people of the United States." Mercy Otis Warren's play *The Ladies of Castile*, written in 1784, was published in *Poems, Dramatic and Miscellaneous*, Boston, 1790, Evans, No. 23035. Publius quotes from Act II, scene v, lines 42–45: " 'Tis all a puff—a visionary dream– / That kindles up this patriotic flame; / 'Tis rank self love, conceal'd beneath a mask / Of public good." Mr. Davis was probably Caleb Davis (1738–1797), a Boston merchant and Federalist who had been a delegate to the Massachusetts state ratifying convention (*Doc. Hist. Ratif. Const.*, 4:xxxv; 5:909).

⁴ Not found.

⁵ David Humphreys eventually married Ann Frances Bulkeley, the daughter of a wealthy English merchant, in Lisbon in 1797 (*Colonial Collegians*).

⁶ Sarah Franklin Bache (1743–1808), Benjamin Franklin's daughter, had served as his hostess until his death in 1790. She and her husband, Richard Bache, visited England in 1792 (*Notable Amer. Women*).

⁷ Not found, but on 20 Jan. 1793, CA wrote to JA, "I have but just now recovered from an attack of the epidemical fever which has for some time past raged in this City. It confined me somewhat more than a week to my chamber" (Adams Papers).

Abigail Adams Smith to Abigail Adams

New-York, Feb. 9th, 1792. [1793]

It is with very great pleasure that I address you, my dear mamma, from this place again. You will be as agreeably surprised as our friends here were, the evening before the last, to see us, and find us safe at New-York; for our arrival was wholly unexpected to them. We avoided informing our friends of our intentions, knowing that their anxious solicitude for our safety would render them unhappy. We left England the 23d of December, in the Portland packet, at a season when our friends there thought we were almost out of our senses.[1] But we have been highly favoured, having had a very pleasant passage—not knowing what cold weather was until a day or two before we landed; we neither saw nor experienced the want of a fire during our passage; and for three weeks had such warm weather that we were obliged to sleep with our windows open in the cabin. Our course was to the southward as far as the latitude of 30 degrees, and we were greatly favoured in coming upon our own coast. I can scarcely realize that it was mid-winter. We have all been very well upon our passage; the children look finely, and Col. Smith is very well; for myself, I was never so well at sea before. We had an excellent ship and a good captain; our accommodations were convenient; we had four poor expatriated French priests, on their route to Canada, as fellow-passengers, but they did not incommode us, we having two cabins. We had a passage of 45 days, and feel ourselves quite at home again. You would have been amused to have seen the meeting in Dey-street; surprise and joy were the most prominent sensations.   *   *   *   *   *   *   *   *

They could scarce believe their eyes; it was between eight and nine o'clock when we landed. But it is time to tell you the cause of our leaving England, which was the prospect of a war on the ocean in the spring, and we did not like the idea of crossing it with bullets whizzing round our heads. Some business, also was an inducement.

England informs France that if they attempt to open the navigation of the Scheldt, that they shall join the Dutch; this is the ostensible cause for arming, which they are doing with great vigour.[2] But they dread internal commotions, and are fortifying the Tower, directing the guns upon the city, preparing to build barracks in the Royal Exchange—placed a double guard at the Bank; breaking up all societies for reforms of Parliament, and forbidding, by proclamations, the meeting of all societies who call themselves republicans; burning Tom Paine in almost every capital town in England in effigy, with the rights of man in one hand, and a pair of old stays in the other. In short, doing just what he wishes, I presume, making him of more consequence than his own writings could possibly effect. He is falling off pretty much in France.

Col. Smith sets off on Tuesday for Philadelphia. I shall remain here. I shall have a strong inclination to make you a visit, for I must be a visiter until May, as we have no house. We think to take one in the country for the summer. If you were in Philadelphia, I should soon be with you. I hear my father has quite renewed his youth, and that he is growing very popular; that the abuse is directed to another quarter.

Remember me to my brother, and all other friends, and believe me, / Your affectionate daughter,   A. Smith.

MS not found. Printed from AA2, *Jour. and Corr.*, 2:115–117.

[1] The packet *Portland*, Capt. James, arrived in New York on 8 Feb. after a 45-day voyage from Falmouth, England (*New York Journal*, 9 Feb.).

[2] In the wake of victories by the French Army, France declared war on both Great Britain and the Netherlands on 1 February. The British had rejected France's request for neutrality the previous fall, feeling threatened by France's re-opening of the Scheldt River after the French seizure of Antwerp—in violation of an agreement among the Dutch, British, and Prussians giving the Dutch exclusive rights to it—and by the execution of Louis XVI. Before AA2 and WSS left England, George III "had thought it prudent to order an addition to his naval armament, and a speedy equipment, and a general inspection and embodiment of the army and militia, to enable him to support, on all emergencies, a respectable defensive, or in case of treaty obligation, to be able to fulfill them &c. &c." (Bosher, *French Rev.*, p. 182–183; *Cambridge Modern Hist.*, 8:418; *New York Journal*, 9 Feb.).

Abigail Adams to Abigail Adams Smith

My dear Child   Quincy Febry 10 1793[1]

I received yesterday by way of Nyork your kind Letter of two dates october 28 & Nov[br] 8th a fortnight before I received a Letter sent by captain Bunyan I wrote you by mrs Jeffry & once since by way of Liverpool[2] I designd to have written by the last vessel which saild in dec[br] but I waited to see how the Election would turn for v. P & the vessel saild without my getting a Letter on Board. no old Country has perhaps exhibited more intrigue & falshood than the Clintonian Party have done to influence this Election the Antifeaderal Party throughout N York Virginna North Carolina & Gorgia were indefatagable not to have any Scattering votes but to unite in one Man that he might be the more formidable competitor.[3] in order to accomplish this they Represented the v. P. as a Man who by his conduct and his writings was endeavouring to introduce a Government of Kings Lords & commons, as a high Aristocrat, & Clinton as a man opposed to this system, the best Friend to the Libeties of the Country quite a democrat.[4] the Party tried their Arts in N England but they were rejected with disdain and ten States tho not the most

Numerous gave an almost unanimous vote, only 2 dissenters. their were a Number of very well written Peices upon the subject publishd in Fennos Gazett but mr Freaneu was all the time publishing the grosest falshood & abuse & that paper alone was circulated through the southern states with as much assiduity as ever Pains Rights of Man were by the Revolution society. the Jacobines as they have been justly termd considerd one Man in their way—could he be removed and in his stead the Personal Enemy of Hamilton Elected, then could they overthrow him & with him all his systems & Plans together with the constitution Such is the spirit of a Party who are mad with the cry of Liberty and eaquality, yet have they no Clergy to level no Nobilitity to anihilate all are intitled to the same natural Liberty have equally the protection of the Laws & Property is in the hands of so numerous a Body of the people that they cannot strike at that without striking at a majority of the people. they have no real cause of complaint,[5] yet are they continually abusing the Government the officers of Government & Since the new Election they attack the President in an open & insolent Manner—abuse him for his Leves[6] his Birth days & because he does not mix in society, abuse him because he does not advocate a further compensation to the officcers of the Army & even tell him that a greater misfortune cannot befall a country than the unanimous suffrace of his Countrymen as it tends to render him self important & supercilious and creates a Belief that the safety of the Government rests upon one Man—alass poor humane nature.[7] yet how angry are they with the only Man who has had the courage to point out to them the Nature and disposition of the humane Heart, to tell them the concequence resulting from a Government not properly balanced & proving this doctrine by a Labourous reserch into Government both ancient & Modern the most virulent party Man of them all has not however dared to impeach eitheir the Honour the Honesty or the integrity of the v. P nor have they once charged him with seeking popularity. they are not all so honest as a Robert Levingstone of N york who said nothing vexd him so much in all the French Revolution & in the advocates for it here, as to see the fools by their conduct playing the Game into the Hands of that there mr Adams and proving the truth of his Books.[8] Why said Benson to whom the observation was made, mr Adams reads the scriptures and he reads there that Man is as stupid as the wild Asses colt, mr Adams does not write the scriptures he only reads and believes. but enough of this. your Father Lodges at mr otis's where he is as happy as he can be Seperated from his Family. the time is drawing nigh when he will return home for the summer. Thomas got through the summer better than I expected. he is very agreably Lodgd with a Quaker Lady whose good will he has secured as well as a Numerous Family connextion of Friends, from whom he says he receives every mark of kindness and attention. dr Rush tells him he has made his fortune by attaching the Quakers to him. he says he has found a most agreeable acquaintance with the young people of Both sexes and that the most accomplishd Women he has met with are in that society. forbiden the Amusements of the Gay world they turn their attention to the cultivation of their mind, & he hopes to convince me of the truth & justness of his observations by introducing a Number of them to my acquaintance When ever I reside again in that city.

I spent a fortnight in Boston, in Jan'ry you will be surprizd when I tell you it was my first visit there since my return from Philadelphia, but my Health sufferd such a shock last winter and spring, that I dared not go at all into company. I even found whilst I was there that the small deviations from the Regularity which I had been for several months habituated to affected me more than I could have supposed, and within this week past I have had a more regular & severe attack of the intermitting than for Many Months past. our society at Quincy is small but we enjoy it, and I have our good cousin Betsy smith who Nursd me so kindly last winter with me Louissa is my companion Polly Tailor my chamber maid a hired man & woman who Love each other cordially & mean matrimony soon; James is my Postilion & Prince my footman I ought not to have forgotten Becky Tirril whom I have taken to bring up in the List of my domesticks, all of whom are Good in their Particular Provinces[9] these constitute my domesticks and I have not lived so quiet a Life so perfectly to my mind Since you made one of a small Family at the foot of Pens Hill in former days— your Brother visits me some times and keeps sunday with me. your venerable Grandmamma who is now sitting by me desires me to present her kind Love to you and tell you she longs to see you & the dear Boys. she has her Health better than for several years past which I in some measure attribute to the attention I have been able to pay to her this winter. your Friend mrs Guile is disconsolate. she has retired with her daughter to malbourough taken a chamber in a House next to her sister Packard, where she refuses to be comforted, will not see her acquaintance or mix at all in society.[10] her two sons She has placed with mrs Cranch who has a young Clergyman as a preceptor to them and Cornelias. I wish my two Grandsons were with them. they are two very likly children Ben both reads & writes well he is very like his Father. Josiah is all the mothers mildness animated with her vivacity. Richard sometimes joins the Party and a droll peice of solidity he is. Mrs Norten spent a day or two with me the last week she desires me to remember her kindly to you, says her conscience accuses her for not writing to you. Lucy has been here there & every where—but at Quincy. I believe she has not been at home more than three weeks for many Months— William is getting fast into Buisness at Haverhill. mrs Guile has laid upon him the Guardianship of her sons. your Aunt Shaw was well when I last heard from her. When I was in Town all your acquaintance inquired kindly after you. Mrs storer always expresses a sincere attachment to you mrs smith is the kind amiable Benevolent woman her last son she named for our dear uncle. she has four children.[11] I visited mrs Gill & she sent for me to take Tea we talkd much of her sister and Neice.[12] she told me that she felt alone in the world and longd to have her Neice come to this Country. she wisht I would consent to send my son for her and then we would make a match, laughingly said she would propose it to him. she sent her maid up stairs for Marys minature that I might tell her if I thought it a likness I pro-nouncd it a very good one. she treated me with great Hospitality & politeness & urgd my going to Prince Town next summer— mr Gill was then there. she expresst great anxiety for her Sister and affec-tion for her Neice.—

I hope you will return in the spring. we are a scatterd Family. Charles I had a Letter from last week[13] he is still with the Baron whom he speaks of with the sincerest affection and esteem. Re-member me affectionaly to the col. tell william I have not any to-ken of remembrance to send him, but he must not forget me I loved his little dog for his sake and John that he shall have the best Lamb in my flock if he will come home & live with me. Josiah Guile says he knows why I love him, because William is near his age & big-ness. tell him that Josiah can read in his Testament like a Man

Remember me to all our Friends both in London & Clapham I fear mr Hollis will Root me out of the Hyde if I do not write to him & substitute some French Plant in my Room, but tell him I claim a place there as one of the Rights which belong to me for I have not ceased to respect & Love him tho I have been too neglegent in personal assurances of it and tho we do not agree in politicks, we unite in wishing happiness to all Mankind. you will see by our Newspapers how citizen Mad our people are, and what a jubelee they have exhibited for the success of the French Arms over the Prussians & Austerians. when they establish a good Government upon a solid Basis then will I join them in rejoicing, tho the 17 Centry is staind with their crimes & cruelties[14]

I am my dear daughter most tenderly your / affectionate Mother

A Adams

Dft (Adams Papers). Printed in AA, *Letters*, ed. CFA, 1848, p. 359–362.

[1] The printed version dates the letter to 11 February.

[2] Letters not found.

[3] The printed version adds, "and in every State where this party prevailed, they have been unanimous for Clinton. Several of the States were, however, duped by the artifice and lies of the Jacobins, particularly North Carolina. The cry of rights of man, liberty and equality were popular themes."

[4] The printed version reads: "For this purpose they made unfair extracts from his writings, upon which they put their own comments. In one company in Virginia they roundly asserted that he had recommended to Congress to make a son of George the Third, King of America. In another, that he was opposed to the President, and that all the difficulty which he had met with from the Senate originated with him. This story the President himself contradicted. Another was, that the keeping the door of the Senate shut was wholly owing to his influence. In short, there was no end of the arts that were used."

[5] The printed version reads: "yet do we daily see in embryo all the seeds of discord springing up from an elective executive, which, in the course of a few years, will throw this nation into a civil war, and write in letters of blood those very truths which one of their best friends has forewarned them of, and that at the expense of his present popularity. I hope, however, that the period may be so distant that neither he nor his children may behold the dreadful scene."

[6] The printed version also adds, "Mrs. Washington abused for her drawing-rooms."

[7] The printed version reads: "They compare him to a hyena and a crocodile; charge him with duplicity and deception. The President has not been accustomed to such language, and his feelings will be wounded, I presume."

[8] That is, Gilbert Livingston. See JA to AA, 7 Dec. 1792, and note 2, above.

[9] Probably Rebeckah Tirrell (b. 1780), daughter of Nathan Tirrell (Sprague, *Braintree Families*).

[10] Elizabeth Quincy Guild's only daughter was Eliza Ann Guild (b. 1789). Elizabeth's husband, Benjamin Guild Sr., had died in the fall of 1792 (Charles Burleigh, *The Genealogy and History of the Guild, Guile, and Gile Family*, Portland, Maine, 1887, p. 85).

[11] William and Hannah Carter Smith had by this time four children: William (b. 1788), Elizabeth Storer (b. 1789), Mary Carter (b. 1791), and Isaac (b. 1792), named for his grandfather Isaac Smith (1719–1787).

[12] For Mary Hallowell, see AA to JA, 1 Feb. 1793, and note 6, above.

[13] Not found.

[14] The printed version concludes: "Time enough for these exultations when they can soberly unite in a form of government which will not leave one man to prey upon and murder his fellow-creature with impunity. When I see them united for their common benefit, and returning to a sense of justice, wisdom, and virtue, then will I rejoice in their prosperity. Until then I mourn over them as a devoted people."

John Quincy Adams to John Adams

My dear Sir.   Boston Feb$^{y:}$ 10. 1793.

As I was going to meeting this afternoon a Gentleman met me in the street, and desired me to fill him a writ immediately which he intends to have served as early as possible in the morning. I accordingly did it, and as it is now too late to attend the afternoon service, I think I cannot employ the leisure time thus thrown on my hands better than in giving you an account of the commercial catastrophe now taking place in this Town, which occasioned the singular application to me, that I have just mentioned.— The bubble of banking is breaking, and I am very apprehensive, that it will prove as distressing to this Town, as that of stock-jobbing was about twelve months since, at New-York. Seven or eight failures of considerable consequence have happened within these three days, and many more are inevitable I think, in the course of the ensuing week.[1] The pernicious practice of mutual indorsements upon each others notes has been carried as now appears to an extravagant length, and is now found to have involved, not only the principals who have been converting their loans from the bank into a regular trading stock, but many others who have undertaken to be their security. The stagnation of trade produced in the fall of the year by the small-pox; and very much increased by a remarkably open winter, which has not admitted of the usual facility of communication with the Country, upon the Snow, have undoubtedly accelerated this Calamity, which however would have been the more oppressive, the longer it would have been deferred.

These misfortunes, will undoubtedly, give a degree of activity to my particular profession, which has not for several years been allotted to it. But I shall personally derive but very little immediate benefit from it: I see no prospect of its adding much to my business at present; and if it should, there is no satisfaction in thriving by the misery of others

I received last Evening your favour, with a quotation from the Echo, which has been read here as well as the Hartford news-carrier's wit, with pleasure by those who are fond of laughing at the follies of our great man.—[2] The Situation of our affairs is such, and the passions and rivalry's of our most conspicuous characters assume an aspect so alarming, that we have indeed much to apprehend for the fate of the Country. It is a subject upon which my mind does not dwell with pleasure; and I am the more desirous to keep myself altogether unconnected with political topics, because my sentiments in general I find are as unpopular, as my conduct, relative to the Town-police, or to the theatrical questions. I have no predilection for unpopularity, as such, but I hold it much preferable to the popularity of a day, which perishes with the transient topic upon which it is grounded, and therefore I persisted in refusing to appear at the anarchical dinner which was denominated a civic feast, though I was urged strongly by several of my friends to be-come a subscriber, upon principles of expediency Those friends dis-liked the whole affair quite as much as I did, but thought it neces-sary to comply with the folly of the day.— Upon the whole however, it appears to me that the celebration of that day, has had rather an advantageous than an injurious effect. The specimens of Equality exhibited in the course of it, did not suit the palates of many, who had joined in the huzzaes. The Governor thought proper to be sick, and not attend; and I believe has ventured to express his disappro-bation of the proceedings in several particulars.— We have Jacobins enough; but in this instance they overshot themselves, and shewed their teeth and claws so injudiciously, as to guard even the weaker members of the community against them.

My mother spent a fortnight in this Town, in the course of the last month; and I am very happy to find that her health continues so much improved. We hope to have the pleasure of seeing you again in the course of five or six weeks.

I have received, and have now in my hands the whole money, that was due upon Savil's bond, which is cancelled. It will be necessary for you to discharge the mortgage on your return as I have not a power sufficiently ample to authorise me to do it.

I am, my dear Sir, yours with the sincerest / affection.

J. Q. Adams.

RC (Adams Papers); endorsed: "J.Q. Adams / Feb. 10. ans^d. 19 / 1793."

[1] JQA further noted in his Diary, "Several failures. Unknown to me but by report" (8 Feb., D/JQA/19, APM Reel 22). The Boston *Columbian Centinel*, 13 Feb., also com-mented that one of the failures totaled £14,000 and that "Prudential motives, and the security of equal justice to all *bona-fide* creditors, were the cause of several recent failures."

[2] "Addressed by the Boy Who Carries the *American Mercury*, to the Subscribers," Hartford, 1793, Evans, No. 46684, is usually attributed to Richard Alsop, also the author of *The Echo*. He makes fun of the French, Antifederalists, and especially John Han-cock's opposition to theater in Boston: "Here *Plays* their *heathen names* forsake, / And those of *Moral-Lectures* take; / While, thus baptiz'd, they hope to win / Indulgence for all future sin. / Now HANCOCK, fired with

patriot rage, / Proscribes the Morals of the Stage; / Claps HARPUR under civil durance, / For having dared, with vile assurance, / By

Interludes, and *Plays* profane, / Pollute the glories of his reign."

Abigail Adams to John Adams

my Dearest Friend   Quincy Febry 16 1793

I received your kind Letters of Jan^ry 28 & 30th 1 I well recollect receiving a Letter from mr Gerry soon after you went first to France informing me of your being Elected a member of the Phylisophic society in Philadelphia and when you received the vol^m in England of their transactions, I never could account for not finding your Name with the Members.[2] the loss of the Records at that time accounts for it. you will hear before this reaches you of the Transactions in England which I consider the begining [of] Trouble. God only know where it will end, and whether we in this Country shall not be involved in the same whirlpool

Febry 18

Thus far I wrote and was prevented from proceeding last night our son came up from Town with the joyfull tyding of the arrival of the col mrs smith & Family. I received a Letter from her at the same time dated Nyork the col you will have seen before this reaches you, and from him you will learn more particulars Relative to the threadned overturn of England, but I will say no more upon politicks at this Time, as I am not able to write much, and a few domestick concerns occur that I wish to mention. dr Tufts desires me to mention to you Clover seed. he wishes Brisler to inquire the price & if it can be purchased as low as 10 pence or a shilling pr pound to procure a Barrel of it & ship it round tis 18 pence here and he says we shall want some & he will take the rest. an other article I would mention is some Porter & some segars for your comfort and the last is whether it would not be adviseable to purchase a strong Farm Horse in conneticut & let Brisler take home the chaise. our great oxen have performd pretty well while they could be used in the Cart, but in the snow without any leader before them they cured & Hawl, is the carters term in such a manner that they cork themselves and have been useless unless when I could prevail with Faxon to let me have a yoke from the Farm to go with th[em] which he has done when we have sent to the Ceadar swamp [. . .] that broke his two Teams which he keeps constantly employd. Shaw was much mortified & begd me to buy him a yoke as he had Hay enough to keep them & could not possibly accomplish the work unless I did. I sent him out to see several yoke, but they were too low in flesh & 55 dollors a pr. he solisited me to let him go to Abington & try I consented and he last night brought home a yoke comeing seven years for which he gave 58 dollors— he says they are *right Handsome cattle* used to make stone wall kind & smart in very good flesh &c. I hope what I have done will meet your approbation—which will always recompence me for what ever exertions I may make.

I was taken sick on that day twelve month that I was the last year. I have been confined to my Chamber for a week, but have not the Rhumatick complaints which I had last year. the fever rather tends to an intermitting I have been Bled which has lessned the inflamitory symtoms and I hope it will terminate without any long confinement. I have very good Nursing, and tho a deaf I believe a safe Physician[3]

Mrs smith is desirious of comeing on to pass a Month with me before she goes to Housekeeping perhaps she may so contrive it as to come with you. you will see her soon and settle the accommodation. mr Cranch is well again as usual & sends his Love with many thanks for your kind expressions towards him. I caught the opportunity of writi[ng] whilst sister was gone down to dinner but she schools me for it.

adieu in hopes to see you soon / most affectionatly yours

A Adams

Love to Thomas I hope he does not feel any Ague complaints

RC (Adams Papers); addressed by JQA: "The Vice-President of the United States / Philadelphia."; endorsed: "Portia / 1793." Some loss of text where the seal was removed.

[1] JA to AA, 27 and 31 Jan., both above.
[2] AA received two letters from Elbridge Gerry on the subject of JA's election to the American Philosophical Society, one of 17 April 1780 and the other of 16 May, both in response to her letter of 13 March (vol. 3:297–299, 323–325, 350). On 26 June 1786,

David Rittenhouse sent to JA two copies of the second volume of the transactions of the Society, one for JA and one to be forwarded to Thomas Jefferson (Adams Papers).
[3] Dr. Thomas Phipps, for whom see Mary Smith Cranch to AA, 4 July [1790], note 1, above.

John Adams to Abigail Adams

My dearest Friend   Philadelphia Feb. 17. 1793

We have had Such falls of Snow and rain that I Suppose the Mail has been retarded and I have no Letters; and you may be in the same Case. I have written however as regularly as usual. I have no Letters nor Message from our dear Family at N. York Since their arrival excepting a Line from Charles the next morning announcing it.[1] another fort night and I shall sett out on my return home I shall make a short stay at N. Y. for fear of worse roads as well as from a zeal to get home. Indeed I have so little affection for that *southern State* as it has lately become, that the sooner I get thro it the better.

I have a great Mind to send home our furniture. My Salary has become ridiculous, sunk more than half in its Value and about to be reduced still lower by another Million of Paper to be emitted by a new Bank of Pensilvania.[2] Before I was aware I got abominably involved in debt and I shall not easily get out.— by I will be no longer a Dupe. The hospitality of Philadelphia would have kept me, the whole Winter at Dinner with one Family and at Tea and Cards with another: but I have made it a rule to decline all Invitations excepting Such as came from Families where I had never dind before, and excepting once with the senators who have families here, once with our Ministers of State and once with foreign Ministers. It has been Employment enough to write apologies in Answer to Invitations. I should have been down with the Ague long before now if I had accepted Invitations to Evening Parties. I never dine out without loosing the next nights Sleep, which shews that there is still a disposition to a fever.

I live in terror least the State of Europe should force the President to Call Congress together in summer. I am not without hopes however that the national Convention of France will give England Satisfaction about Holland, the Austrian Netherlands and the Scheld, that We may still be blessed with Peace: but if there should be war We shall be intrigued into it, if possible.

The Personal hatreds and Party Animosities which prevail here, have left me more in tranquility than any other Person. The Altercations between the humble Friends of the two or three Ministers have done no service to the Reputation of either. The S. of the Treasury has suffered as much as the Secretary of State. Ambition is imputed to both, and the Moral Character of both has Suffered in the Scrutiny. They have been sifted by Satan like Wheat and all the Spots that have been discoverd have been circulated far and wide. I am afraid that Hamiltons Schemes will become unpopular, because the State Legislatures are undermining them and Congress will be obliged either to let them fall in the Publick opinion, or to support them by measures which will be unpopular. Hamilton has been intemperately puffed and this has excited green Eyed Jealousy and haggard Envy. Jays Friends have let Escape feelings of Jealousy as well as Jeffersons. And it is very natural. Poor me who have no Friends to be jealous, I am left out of the Question and pray I ever may.

Yours tenderly   J. A.

RC (Adams Papers); endorsed: "Febry—17 1793."

[1] Not found.
[2] On 5 Feb., the Penn. house of representatives began consideration of a bill to create a new Bank of Pennsylvania. The bank, as signed into law on 30 March, initially offered $3 million in capital stock (Philadelphia *Federal Gazette*, 9 Feb., 3 April).

John Adams to Charles Adams

Dear Charles   Philadelphia Feb. 17. 1793

I have not answered your favour of 31. of Jan. nor that which announced the Arrival of your Brother and Sister.

> Justum et tenacem Propositi Virum
> Non Civium Ardor prava jubentium
> Non Vultus instantis Tyranni
> Mente quatit Solida,

was repeated by Cornelius De Wit on The Rack and in torture; as you may See in Cerisiers Tableau.[1] I know not whether the Rack is to be borne or not; but I know, the most disgusting, Sickening, disheartening grieving, provoking, irritating Feeling of the soul, is excited, by the Meanness, the Baseness of political Lies and popular Injustice. There is no Country upon Earth where the People will hear and read this contemptible Ribaldry with so little Resentment, or so much malignant Pleasure against their best Men. The hornets, the Wasps the Fleas, the Lice and the Ticks are now Stinging the President and if the People bear it, they deserve to be eaten by Fleas, as you was in Spain.

We Shall See next fall, how Parties will Stand; if Congress Should not be called together Sooner. The War in Europe may compel an earlier Session.

> Weigh well your part, and do your best
> Leave to your maker all the rest,

I read last night in the Almanack and cannot give you a better precept.— Another very good rule from the Same respectable Authorty is

> He who contracts his swelling Sail
> Eludes the Fury of the Gale.

another still is worth transcribing

> Regard the World with cautious Eye
> Nor raise your Expectation high.
> Life is a Sea, where Storms must rise
> 'Tis folly talks of cloudless Skies.[2]

I had, from your Letter, entertained hopes of seeing Mr Smith here before now: but the Roads must be so bad that I now despair of it. My Love to him, your sister, and my dear little Boys. I must make but a Short Stay at New York, on my return. My affairs at Quincy require my Attention, and Presence.

I envy no Man but the Baron and General Gates. If I had a Steuben, I would remove with all my Family and live upon it.—[3] I could yet cutt down Trees and clear Land, which I am convinced is the happiest Employment of human Life. If you ever was present at Stubbing Bushes and burning them you must have felt it. hunting deers is not so transporting to a Savage, as clearing Land to a Farmer. Feeding Cattle, which is very pleasant is not equal, to the Work of Creation in the Woods which converts a Forrest into a fruitful field. War, Negotiation, Legislation, Administration hide your diminished heads, in Comparison with Husbandry for a happy Life. a Proportion of Solitude is essential to happiness. Man was not made nor borne to be alone it is true: nor was he born to be always in Company. Alternate Retirement and Society is the only System of Wisdom. so thinks and so will Act your affectionate Father

John Adams.

RC (MHi:Seymour Coll.); internal address: "Charles Adams."; docketed: "Vice President."

[1] For Antoine Marie Cerisier's *Tableau de l'histoire générale,* see vol. 4:81. Cornelius de Witt, a seventeenth-century Dutch official and brother of grand pensionary Johan de Witt, was falsely accused of planning an assassination attempt against William III, Prince of Orange. Refusing to admit guilt even under torture, de Witt was found not guilty but was nonetheless deprived of his offices and sentenced to exile. Before that could take place, he and his brother were murdered by members of the civic guard loyal to the prince (Rowen, *Princes of Orange,* p. 120, 127-129). See also JA, *Papers,* 10:354, 355, 438; 13:416, 424.

[2] All of the quotations, in somewhat different order, come from Nathaniel Cotton, "Content. Vision IV," *Visions in Verse,* London, 1751, lines 153-154, 147-148, 138-139, 145-146.

[3] Like Baron von Steuben, Gen. Horatio Gates had retired to a large estate just north of New York City in 1790. Rose Hill Farm included a "large & handsome" house and a "garden which was filled with every variety of the best & choicest fruit" (Paul David Nelson, *General Horatio Gates: A Biography,* Baton Rouge, La., 1976, p. 287-288).

Charles Adams to John Adams

My dear Sir   New York Feby 19th 1793

I have this moment received your kind favor of the 17th. I am not ignorant that dayly abuse is poured upon not only the officers of Government, but even upon the President himself who heretofore has been exempted from public attacks of this nature. I console myself by reflecting that the authors of these libels are a few hirelings of Antifederalism in the City of Philadelphia. The Philadelphia Gazetts it is true circulate through the Union, but our Printers in this City have sense enough not to reprint their scandal and I should never have heard of it but from you and several friends who have remarked it at the Seat of Government This City has shown itself in the late election for Representative to be disgusted at the men and measures of the Antifederal party The majority of votes for Mr Watts are beyond the calculation of any one a majority of eleven hundred cannot fail to do honor to the politicks of this City.¹ Peculiarly unfortunate is this City in being destitute of men who are able and willing to serve them in public Mr Watts is not the man who should represent us in Congress and this is the opinion of a great many of the people He is a well meaning man but not a shining character. what can be said! We had the choice between a vilain and an honest man.

The principal subject of conversation is respecting the minister who is on his voyage from the French Republic to the United States.² Various opinions are advanced with regard to his reception. Some say that we cannot but receive him out of a principle of gratitude to France who was so early in acknowledging our Independence! but should we carry this so far as to draw all the Nations of Europe into a war with us? Can we receive a minister who comes from we know not who? England and Holland must join against the French in the Spring if they insist upon opening the Scheld And can they resist so many formidable [. . .]? Where are the treasures which can keep up [. . .] when according to statement the last event [. . .] and the troops who were but three months in the field cost France nineteen million Sterling it is impossible! the mines of Peru would not suffice. Is there no delay which can be employed to put this reception off? I know very well that Our Government will be urged I hope not forced to commit themselves by such a measure.

Feby 20

By the Bristol which arrived last evening we have accounts from Europe to the 25th of Decr It appears that great exertions are making by the Emperor Russia and the rest of the combined powers The Emperor alone sends three hundred and fifty thousand men into the field.[3] That Genl Miranda was at Antwerp and the French flag was flying in that port That the Dutch were in consternation fearing an invasion every moment.[4] We have also received a number of resolutions of the National convention which are somewhat extraordinary. They swear never to lay down their arms till all the Nations of Europe shall have tasted the sweets of liberty. This is one among a number equally extraordinary They have decreed that the whole family of the Bourbons shall be exiled except those who are in confinement in the Temple, and even the monkey trick of Monsr Egalité has been of no service to him he is indicded with the rest.[5] The National Convention by their proceedings appear little less unreasonable than the Assembly. This I think is very certain that while their present ideas remain they can never hope for tranquillity though they should be the Conquerors of Europe.

Will the new Congress be called together on the fifth of March? I think we should look round us While so universal a war pervades Europe we ought not to be asleep?

I am my dear father with every sentiment / of respect your affectionate son   Charles Adams

RC (Adams Papers); addressed: "The Vice President of the United States— / Philadelphia"; endorsed: "C. Adams / ans^{d.} 27. Feb. 1793." Some loss of text where the seal was removed.

[1] John Watts (1749–1836), speaker of the N.Y. State Assembly, defeated William S. Livingston by a vote of 1,872 to 707 (*Biog. Dir. Cong.*; *New York Daily Gazette*, 21 Feb.). See also CA to JA, 26 Dec. 1792, and note 5, above.

[2] For Edmond Charles Genet, the recently appointed French minister to the United States, see JA, *D&A*, 2:355.

[3] Emperor Francis II (1768–1835) succeeded his father, Leopold II, as leader of the German empire on 1 March 1792 (*Cambridge Modern Hist.*, 8:398; 13:table 33). Reports brought in from the ship *Bristol*, dated Vienna, 24 Nov., indicated that by the end of that month, the Austrian Army intended to have 360,000 soldiers participating in the campaign against France (Philadelphia *American Daily Advertiser*, 23 Feb. 1793).

[4] Gen. Francisco de Miranda (1750–1816) was born in Venezuela. He had served with the French in the American Revolution and now led a portion of their army alongside Dumouriez. The French had occupied Antwerp in December (Hoefer, *Nouv. biog. générale*; *Cambridge Modern Hist.*, 8:417).

[5] At a meeting of the National Convention on 15 Dec., the assembly determined that "The Generals in all those countries, which are, or may be occupied by our armies, shall immediately proclaim in the name of the

republic, the abolition of the ancient contributions, nobility, taxes, feudal rights, real and personal servitude, the exclusive right of hunting and fishing, and all privileges. They shall declare to the people, that they bring them peace, liberty and fraternity." It also established new administrative bodies and representative assemblies and declared, "The French nation swears never to down its arms until the countries into which they have entered shall be free and their liberty secured."

The next day, the Convention adopted another decree that "All the members of the family of the Bourbons, Capets, except these who are detained at the Temple, shall quit the Department of Paris in 24 hours, and in three days the territories of the Republic and the countries in which the French armies presently are."

For Louis Philippe Joseph, Duc d'Orléans, who now called himself Philippe Égalité, see vol. 7:156. At this time, after considerable debate, he was exempted from the decree requiring all members of the royal family to leave France but was executed later in 1793 (Philadelphia *American Daily Advertiser*, 23 Feb.).

John Adams to John Quincy Adams

My son   Philadelphia Feb. 19. 1793

I have great Satisfaction in your Letter of the 10th. The Breaking of the Bubble of Banks would be a Blessing if it could teach our People to beware of all other Bubbles. But I fear We shall have a Succession of them. I hope however at least they will teach you caution.

"The Rivalries of our most conspicuous Characters" are such as human Nature produces under the Cultivation of such a Constitution as ours, and they never will be less. If they should have the Effect to convince this nation of one of the most obvious, Simple, certain and important Truths vizt ["]The Necessity of Subordination—in Society" it will be well. if otherwise We must have Anarchy.

Your Sentiments will not always be unpopular; if they are you will have nothing to loose, if you have nothing to gain, for no Man will be able to call his Life Liberty Reputation or Property his own. I Should not advise you to indulge any uncommon Ardour or distinguished Zeal about the Town Police or Theatrical Questions. in you it must be hypocricy to pretend to any other sentiments than those you have manfully expressed.

Your refusal to appear at the delirious Dinner, I cannot but approve. It will do you no harm in the End.

I am afraid your Mother caught her Ague at Boston: but so it must be.

I shall see you in 3 or 4 Weeks at farthest I hope.

Col Smith is here but not in good health: your sister and Nephews are well. so is your Brother Thomas and / your affectionate father   J A.

RC (Adams Papers); internal address: "Mr Adams."

Abigail Adams to John Adams

my dearest Friend   Quincy Feb'ry 22 1793—

my Last Letter was written to you in Bed I write this from my chair, my fever is leaving me and I am mending So that I can set up the chief of the day. the dr says it was the unexpected News of mrs smiths return that had so happy an effect upon me as to Break my fever. I am languid & weak but hope to be well by the Time you return. I shall forward my next Letter to you, to be left at N york as it might not reach you in Philadelphia if you set out as soon in March as you propose. I would mention to you your Coupons for the year least it should slip your mind.[1] I believe I mentiond in my last all that I could think of respecting domestick concerns. our Weather is so changeable that it retards the kind of Buisness which I should be glad to have compleated. this week we have had floods of rain, which has carried of the chief of the heavy snow which fell the week before. o I forgot to mention to mr Brisler to cut me some of the weeping willows, & put on Board any of the vessels comeing this way, some of mr Morriss peach tree Grafts. we have some young plumb trees which will answer for stocks.[2] your Brother told me on monday Evening that the senate had made choice of mr Strong; I presume the House will concur tis an ill wind which blows no good to any one. the late failures in Boston have thrown Some buisness into the hands of our son he is well and grows very fat.

present me affectionatly to all my Friends particularly to mrs Washington whom I both Love and respect. Remember me to mrs otis and tell her that her sister Betsy complains that she does not write to her. a kiss to miss Harriot, tell her she must find out how I sent it. your Mother desires to be rememberd to you. one day last week whilst I was the most sick, the severest N East snow storm came that we have had through the winter. we could not pass with a carriage, and I desired my People not to let her know how ill I was as she could not get to See me, but no sooner was there a foot tract than she put on stockings over her shoes, and I was astonishd to hear her voice below stairs. she has had better health than for some years past

Adieu all Friends send their Regards / ever yours   A Adams

RC (Adams Papers); addressed: "The Vice President of the / United States. / Philadelphia."; docketed: "AA 1793."

[1] On 1 March, JA, as a subscriber to the sixth Dutch-American loan of 2 March 1791, sent to Wilhem and Jan Willink coupons that entitled him to interest on his investment. JA

asked that the money be shipped to Cotton Tufts in the form of gold or Spanish dollars (JA to Wilhem and Jan Willink, 1 March 1793; Willinks to JA, 22 April, both Adams Papers; Winter, *Amer. Finance and Dutch Investment*, 2:1086–1091).

² Probably Robert Morris, who has been

credited with the development of two varieties of peaches: "Morris's White Freestone" and "Morris's Red Free Stone" (George Lindley and Michael Floy, *A Guide to the Orchard and Fruit Garden*, N.Y., 1852, p. 189).

John Adams to Abigail Adams

My dearest Friend   Feb. 27. 1793 Philadelphia

I am so anxious for your health, Since you inform'd me of the return of your Intermittent, that I shall take the Stage on Monday for N. York, but whether I shall go by the Packet to Providence, or continue in the Stage to Boston, I know not. This will depend upon the Wind and other Circumstances to be learn'd at N. York.

C. Smith is here in good health. He is returned from France and England, almost a Revolutionist, if not quite. The Fermentation in Europe distresses me, least it should take a turn which may involve Us in many difficulties. Our Neutrality will be a very delicate Thing to maintain: and I am not without Apprehensions that Congress or at least the Senate may be called together in the summer if not earlier. however We must be prepared as well as We can for Events.

The Attorney General, in opening the Information to the Jury, at the Tryal of M[r] Paine, was pleased to quote large Passages from Publicola, with Some handsome Compliments: so that Publicola is become a Law Authority. M[r] Erskine in his Answer cryed, Well, let others do like Publicola answer the Book not prosecute the author.[1]

I am weary of reading Newspapers. The Times are so full of Events, the whole Drama of the World is such a Tragedy that I am weary of the Spectacle. Oh my Sweet little farm, what would I not give to enjoy thee without Interruption? But I see no end to my Servitude, however the nations of Europe and even of Africa may recover their Liberty.

Hamilton has been Sufficiently fatigued with demands for Statements and Information. I hope his health will hold out, and his Character be Supported: but We have broad hints of what may be expected by, Executive Officers, who depend upon an Elective head, from Elective Legislatures. Ambitious Members of a Legislature will too easily run down the Popularity of Ministers of State, or I am egregiously mistaken. But Ca ira.

France will Soon Shew Us Examples enough of Ministers falling before ambitious Legislatures, if she has not exhibited enough already. Calonne Neckar, Montmorin and 20 others, where are they?[2]

I am, my dear, most tenderly your   John Adams

RC (Adams Papers); internal address: "Portia"; endorsed: "Febry 27th 1793."

[1] Thomas Paine's first part of the *Rights of Man*, published in London in March 1791 and reprinted in the United States in May, elicited JQA's response as Publicola the following month. Paine's publication in 1792 of the second part of *Rights of Man*, which was more widely distributed than the first part and considered a threat to the British monarchy, resulted in Paine's being charged with seditious libel. He appeared in court in June, but the trial was postponed until December. Attorney general Archibald Macdonald led the successful prosecution. Thomas Erskine (1750–1823), an opposition leader and attorney general to the Prince of Wales, represented Paine, who did not attend (*DNB*).

TBA reported similar news to JQA in a letter of 26 Feb. 1793, in which TBA noted that he had obtained information about the trial from a pamphlet entitled *The Whole Proceedings on the Trial of an Information Exhibited Ex Officio by the King's Attorney-General against Thomas Paine*, London, 1793, which he quoted at length to JQA (Adams Papers). See also TBA to AA, 27 May [1792], note 5, above.

[2] Charles Alexandre de Calonne, the former French controller general of finances, had successfully emigrated to England, and Jacques Necker, the former director general of finances, had retired to his home on Lake Geneva. Armand Marc, Comte de Montmorin de Saint-Herem, one of King Louis XVI's advisors and a former ambassador to Spain, had been arrested and killed by a mob in Aug. 1792 (Bosher, *French Rev.*, p. xxviii, l, li).

Abigail Adams to Abigail Adams Smith

My dear Mrs Smith.   Quincy February 28. 1793.

I wrote to you by your brother making a proposal to you which you might not consider me in earnest about—[1] Since then I have two additional motives to request the Col^s consideration and your's of the subject. If setting aside family connexions it is with respect to business a matter of indifference which city you reside in I certainly could wish it might be Philadelphia for four years to come. The late vote respecting salary will certainly prevent our becoming House-keepers there in public life. We have suffered too much already by being involved in debt at the close of the four years and obliged to give up our house, dispose of one pair of horses and in other respects retrench our expenses. The five thousand dollars at this period is not in the purchase of any article of life more than half equal to what it was at the time it was first granted— Knowing as I do what the expense of living there as well as here is I cannot think of seeing your father again subjected to the like inconvenience—yet to live half the year separated of the few years which I have reason to think are remaining to me is a sacrifice that I do not consider at this day my duty— I shall not make any observation upon past services or my own estimation of things— I will conform to what is and should be glad to enjoy the Society of my family as much as I can. My furniture is stored in Philadelphia. If the Colonel and you think it inconsistent with your arrangements and prejudicial to his affairs to reside in Philadelphia I shall think it best after consulting your Father to order the furniture home, though I know not what to do with the greater part of it. I should be tempted to sell what I have not room for if I did not know that it must be at a great loss. If you think proper to go there I will endeavor to have it stored till such time as you might incline to take a house there— If we take lodgings with you, 'tis probable that our family will not exceed five persons, and we could I presume make such arrangements as would render each of us happy— I will not again take charge of a family and sacrifice my health in that city as I have done— Though a small family we are and always have been a scattered flock, my infirm state of health leads me to wish for those pleasures which domestic life affords. I love society, but 'tis the rational not the dissipated which can give true delight.

I fear the roads will be so bad as to prevent your coming to see me so soon as I wish but in April the passage by way of Rhode Island will be both pleasant and safe and as you are an old and experienced sailor you will find that way much pleasanter than by land and much less fatiguing.

Let me, my dear daughter, hear from you as often as possible remember me affectionately to all friends

Your's most tenderly   A. Adams.

Tr in CFA's hand (Adams Papers).

[1] Not found.

John Adams to Abigail Adams

My dear   Philadelphia March 2. 1793

Your Letter from your Sick Chamber if not from your Sick bed, has made me so uneasy that I must get away as soon as possible.—[1] Monday Morning at Six, I am to Sett off in the Stage, but how many days it will take to get home will depend on the Roads, *and* or the Winds. I dont believe Nabby will go with me. Her Adventurer of an Husband is so proud of his Wealth that he would not let her go I suppose without a Coach and four, and such Monarchical Trumpery I will in future have nothing to do with. I will never travel but by the

Stage nor live at the seat of Government but at Lodgings, while they give me so despicable an Allowance.— shiver my Jibb and start my Planks if I do.

I will Stay but one night at New York. Smith says that my Books are upon the Table of every Member of the Committee for framing a Constitution of Government for France except Tom Paine, and he is so conceited as to disdain to have any Thing to do with Books.

Although I abused Smith, a little above he is very clever and agreable: but I have been obliged to caution him against his disposition to boasting. Tell not of your Prosperity because it will make two Men mad to one glad; nor of your Adversity for it will make two Men glad to one Sad.— He boasts too much of having made his fortune, and placed himself at his ease; above all favours of Government.[2] This is a weakness, and betrays too little knowledge of the World: too little Penetration; too little discretion. I wish however that my Boys had a little more of his Activity— I must soon treat them as The Pidgeons treat their Squabs—push them off the Limb and make them put out their Wings or fall. Young Pidgeons will never fly till this is done.

Smith has acquired the Confidence of the French Ministry and the better sort of the Members of the national Convention: but the Executive is too changeable in that Country to be depended on, without the Utmost caution.

Adieu, Adieu, tendrement   J. A.

RC (Adams Papers); internal address: "Portia"; endorsed: "March 2ᵈ 1793."

[1] AA to JA, 16 Feb., above.

[2] WSS's ongoing land speculation had provided the Smith family with considerable wealth at this time. Also, WSS had visited Paris in late 1792 and agreed to serve as the French government's agent in the United States, tasked with negotiating full and immediate payment of America's outstanding debt to France (*Colonial Collegians*; Jefferson, *Papers*, 25:243–245).

Thomas Boylston Adams to Abigail Adams

My dear Mother   Philadelphia 2ᵈ· March 1793

I am grieved to hear of the fresh return of your old persecuter the Ague; I had flattered myself that the Air & Climate of New England would chase away all Billious complaints. I am suspicious that the Bark of which so free use is made in this disorder will not effectually remove it, at least I have found it the case with myself. There is a weed known here by the name of Cardis, which is much used in this disorder, and I think it has proved servicable to me; I can't recollect ever to have heared of it in Massachusetts, but wish you could get some of it for trial.[1] My own health has been better this, than the last winter, but I have periodical returns of what I think the seeds of an Ague. However I don't live in continual dread of it— if it comes I must stand the charge, & endeavor to conquer it.

The arrival of Col: & M^rs: Smith was unexpected, but not the less agreeable. The Col, has been, & still is, in this City; I rejoice to hear of his success, which (he says and I have no reason to suspect the truth of it) has placed him & his Family in eligible circumstances. You will have the satisfaction to see them & learn more fully the circumstances—

I wrote you some time since concerning our furniture, & wish you to think what arrangements will be most proper, so that I may know in season what measures to take— Nothing is determined concerning them, and (as usual) you must be applied to in the last resort.

The old business of hunting down the sec^y of the Treasury has employed a considerable share of the present session, of which this is the last day— He has risen superior to all the unmanly insinuations that have been promulged against him; and it must be the ardent prayer of every honest patriot that he may still maintain his superiority. My Father will inform you the tenor of Giles's Resolutions which have been canvassed the three last days; It will suffice for me to say that so far as I hear they are universally condemned; and the large majority against them, speaks the truth of my information.

Your good friend M^rs: Powell, directs me to give her love: to you, and to say, that *I am a very sad young man*, for not visiting her Family; this is what *M^r· Hill* calls a *homely compliment* to me; and I might say with great truth, (as I did last night to him in his *own house*) had it come from him, that with him it was certainly *homely*.[2] I must relate this little anecdote for your amusement, otherwise you won't understand what I meant above. A party, of whom I had the honor to make one, were invited to sup with M^r: Hill on the 1st: of March. It consisted of Col & M^rs: Hamilton; Genl & M^rs: Knox, M^r & M^rs: Wolcott, M^r: Breck & Family, M^r· & M^rs: Peters M^r: Dalton and Family & Col. Smith; the younger class, were M^r: & M^rs· G Harrison, Miss Knox Miss *Patty Meredith* Miss Peggy Clymer, and one or two others, beside four or six young Gentlemen;[3] after dancing a little and making merry we were called to a splendid supper which was not a little enlivened by the presence of Judge

Peters who sung one or two fine songs—the greater part of the company retired at half past eleven, and at twelve all were gone except Miss Meredith & Miss Clymer, whose carriage had not arrived; I perceived these young Ladies had come without a gallant and therefore requested permission to see them safe home. The ladies grew impatient; we were some what fatigued by dancing, and I belive, (at[4] least I speak for myself) had rather more inclination for the pillow of repose, than for the company of *the Graces*, (including M[r.] Hill) during this suspence, endeavoring to keep each other awake, we indulged in what M[r.] Hill termed homely compliments, and when he made the remark he happened to address Miss Meredith. Without adverting to the particular *appropocity* of the *pun*, of which M[r] Hill is remarkably fond, I observed that those compliments coming from him were most assuredly *homely*, meaning only, that as he was in his *own house*, they implied hospitality, of which nature they were, for I think he offered the ladies his embroydered bed—however as ill luck would have it, a young gentleman present took the pun in a different and less favorable sense, and sett up a titter which communicated like wild fire till it was universally understood I preserved my muscles as smooth as the nature of the case would admit, and by a few subsequent observations, strongly emphacised, turned it off tollerably well; & without giving offence. Soon after the carriage for the ladies came, and I had the pleasure to land them safely home at a little past one o Clock.

Thus I have given you a history of one Party of this season, the only one I have attended that afforded even one incident worth relating; in fact I apologise for this, which, if other matter had been so readily at hand, should have supplied its place.

I am your dutifull son   Thomas B Adams

PS I must request you not to mention this Annecdote of M[r] H— to any one coming to Philad[a] for I should forfeit all his good offices were he to know how I understood the above—

RC (Adams Papers); endorsed: "T B Adams March / 2[d] 1793–"

[1] Probably *carduus*, Latin for thistle, which was used for treating pleurisy, inducing vomiting, and other medicinal purposes (OED; E. Smith, *The Compleat Housewife; or, Accomplish'd Gentlewoman's Companion*, Williamsburg, Va., 1742, p. 195–196, 198, 219, Evans, No. 5061).

[2] Henry Hill (1732–1798) was a Philadel-phia wine merchant (Washington, *Papers, Presidential Series*, 8:148).

[3] Elizabeth Schuyler Hamilton (1757–1854) of Albany, N.Y., had married Alexander Hamilton in 1780 (*Notable Amer. Women*).

Oliver Wolcott (1760–1833), Yale 1778, served as comptroller of the U.S. treasury and succeeded Alexander Hamilton as secretary of the treasury in 1795. He had married Elizabeth Stoughton (1767–1805) in 1785 (Dexter, *Yale Graduates*, 4:82–85).

Lucy Knox (1776–1854), eldest child of Henry and Lucy Flucker Knox, married Ebenezer Thatcher in 1804 (Thomas Morgan Griffiths, *Major General Henry Knox and the Last Heirs to Montpelier*, Lewiston, Maine, 1965, p. 48, 73).

Martha Meredith (d. 1817), daughter of Samuel and Margaret Cadwallader Meredith, married John Read, a lawyer, in 1796

(Philadelphia *Gazette of the United States*, 28 June 1796; *Boston Daily Advertiser*, 3 April 1817).

Margaret Clymer (1772–1799), daughter of George and Elizabeth Meredith Clymer, married George McCall in May 1794 (Gregory B. Keen, "The Descendants of Jöran Kyn, the Founder of Upland," *PMHB*, 6:213–214 [1882]).

[4] Opening parenthesis editorially supplied.

John Adams to Charles Adams

My son   Quincy March 18. 1793

I had the Pleasure of receiving your favour of the 1st. on Saturday night:[1] by your Brother, who has been admitted this Term at the Supreme Court and is rising in Practice as well as in litterary fame.

We cannot be too cautious in forming our Opinions of french affairs, and We ought to be still more Slow in discoursing on them. Our amiable and excellent Friend, the Baron is like many others, too Sanguine in his Expectations of irresistable Combinations against the French Republic, and in his Predictions of Partitions Famine, Civil War &c on the other hand our fellow Citizens in general, have too much Enthusiasm in their Applauses of the present Leaders and too sanguine hopes and assurances of Glory and Tryumph to the Jacobins. at least this is my impulse, who have however small Pretentions to better lights than others.

To me, it has ever been astonishing that The King La Fayette, Rochefaucault &c Should have had So little Penetration as to believe that the late Constitution could endure.

The Report of the late Case in the Supream national Court will soon be made public and the Arguments of the Judges weighed. If it Should be necessary for Congress to interfere by Submitting that part of the Constitution to the Revision of the State Legislatures, they have Authority to do it.[2]

I congratulate you on the national Complextion of the N. York Representatives, which justifies a hope that So material a part of the northern branch of the Union is not likely to become compleatly a Southern State. I regret with You that Mr Kent is not elected.[3] My faith is very faint in the Story of 30 Spanish ships with English Jacks.[4]

Although I have no personal Obligations to the King of France, being the only American, accredited to his Court, whom he formally affronted, I do not less acknowledge his Friendship to my Country, nor less regret his unhappy fate. If it were in my Power I would restore him to his Crown and Dignity, well and faithfully limited by a senate and an adequate Representation of the People: for to such a form of Government the Nation must aspire or they will never establish their Liberty. In this opinion I am as Sanguine, as the Baron is in his Predictions, or a Boston Populace, in their civic Rejoicings. possibly as erroneous. The French national Convention, in their Letter to the President have reflected, an honour on me, and a disgrace on the Memory of Franklin, which I believe they never intended. "The United States of America will hardly credit it; the Support which the ancient French Court had afforded them to recover their Independence, was only the fruit of base Speculation; their Glory offended its ambitious Views, and the Ambassadors bore the criminal orders of Stopping the Career of their Prosperity." Mr Madison and Franklins friends will understand and feel this: but they will prevent the American People from understanding it, if they can. It is a confirmation of my Representations and a Justification of my Conduct: but it is a Refutation of all Franklins corrupt Sychophancy and a severe Condemnation of his Conduct. The N. York News Writers will Suppress this Letter if they can, because it reflects an immortal Glory on Mr Jay.[5]

Your Mother is better but has had a severe Confinement of five Weeks.

I am &c   John Adams

RC (MHi:Seymour Coll.); internal address: "Mr Charles Adams."; endorsed: "March 18 1793–"

[1] CA wrote briefly to JA on 1 March touching on a variety of topics, including Thomas Paine's trial, the Publicola writings, New York's election of congressional representatives, and a possible Anglo-Spanish alliance against the French (Adams Papers).

[2] See TBA to AA, 10 Aug., note 3, below.

[3] James Kent (1763–1847), Yale 1781, a Federalist lawyer, had assisted John Jay in the contested gubernatorial election. He was defeated by his brother-in-law Theodorus Bailey in the race to represent Dutchess County, N.Y., in Congress (*DAB*; New York *Daily Advertiser*, 28 Feb.).

[4] In his 1 March letter to JA, CA noted that "A vessel arrived yesterday from Cadiz which fell in with a fleet of thirty ships of the Line Spaniards. They carried the English Jack with the Flagg of Spain so that this has the appearance of an alliance" (Adams Papers). The *Baring*, Capt. Cooper, arrived in Philadelphia on 24 Feb., having left Cadiz on 5 January. It reported that at Cadiz "there were several Spanish ships of war sitting out there, and they had an English Jack flying at the top mast head." Spain, however, did not join the growing European alliance against France until 7 March (New York *Daily Advertiser*, 28 Feb.; Bosher, *French Rev.*, p. 183).

[5] For the letter of the French National

Convention to George Washington, dated 22 Dec. 1792, see Washington, *Papers, Presidential Series*, 11:538–540. A translation was printed in the New York *Diary*, 21 Feb. 1793.

Thomas Boylston Adams to John Adams

My dear sir.   Philadelphia 7[th:] April 1793—

I am requested by M[r:] Dobson to enquire of you what disposition you desire to be made of your Book's of which he has a considerable supply of Coppies.[1] Whether some of them should not be sent to Boston & New York, or whether you would wish them to remain where they are. He thinks you gave him no possitive directions about them before you left the City.

Various events have taken place in France since you left us; and tho' not unexpected are not the less important. Since the Execution of the King & Queen nothing can be thought too mad or extravagant for the National Convention to commit, and the conjecture is not unfair that the Royal Family is e're this extinct. Every arrival since the death of the King has brought some rumor of war—but no authentic information has come to hand till by the arrival of the Packet at New York, Official Dispatches were received by M[r] Hammond of a declaration of war on the part of France against England & Holland. There have been some speculations in our Newspapers relative to the Reception & acknowledgment of the expected Minister from the new Republic: If indeed that can be called a Republic, where no laws exist, or if they do, where there is no power Supreme to enforce obedience to them. The term as applied to France, must signify the actual state of the Country, not the form of its Government—Res-Publica, or the Public Afairs, in confusion. Under any other construction, nothing would be easier than to create a Republic in any Country, for they have only to destroy the existing Government—and they are at once resolved into a Frenchifyed system, which if they chose they may call a Republic.

The propriety of receiving the expected Minister in a public capacity has been doubted; indeed Bache's paper some time ago asserted that the President of the U,S, had resolved not to acknowledge him; but little credit I believe is to be given to this report, considering the quarter from whence it came.[2] If there would be no impropriety in commiting your opinion upon this subject to a private letter, I will make a request that it may be directed to me.

I presume the Spring begins to show itself with you by this time, for the Fruit Trees have been in full bloom for some days in this

City— I hope the warm weather will restore health to my Mother, to whom I present my best love and affection, and remain / your dutiful Son

Thomas B Adams

RC (Adams Papers); internal address: "The Vice President of the U,S."

[1] Thomas Dobson (d. 1823), a Philadelphia printer and bookseller, was selling copies of JA's *Defence of the Const.* (Philadelphia *American Daily Advertiser*, 30 Dec. 1791; *Baltimore Patriot*, 11 March 1823).

[2] Benjamin Franklin Bache's Philadelphia *General Advertiser*, 27 March 1793, announced, "A report has been prevalent for some days past, that our executive had come to a determination of not acknowledging the minister who is daily expected from France. This report from its nature is not entitled to much credit; we state it, however, as we heard it, leaving it to our readers to stamp its true character." On the same day, the Philadelphia *Federal Gazette* chastised Bache for

"the attempt . . . to injure the supreme executive. . . . The well-known prudence so characteristic of the president of the United States, would, with a candid mind, have been sufficient to deter the publication of the nature alluded to."

George Washington and his advisors debated the appropriate reception for Edmond Genet: first, whether or not to receive him at all, and second, if he were received, with what qualifications. They eventually decided unanimously at a 19 April cabinet meeting to indeed receive him but left open the question of qualifications (Washington, *Papers, Presidential Series*, 12:392–393, 459).

Elizabeth Smith Shaw to Mary Smith Cranch

My Dear Sister—   Haverhill April 21st 1793

I have been exceedingly grieved at hearing of our dear Sister Adams's Illness— She was so well in the winter, that I hoped she would have escaped any inconvenience from the return of the fever & ague— When it gets such fast hold of a Constitution, it appears to be a very formidable Disorder, & is attended with very disagreeable Consequences— I have heard she was growing better, & hope by this time, she is enjoying a confirmed state of health— It must give her great Satisfaction to find that her Daughter, & Family have once more escaped the dangers of the Sea, & have arrived safe at New-york— The early return of the Vice President to his Family, must be to her, an additional Source of pleasure— But the Commotions which are taking place in almost every part of the world, will (I fear) make it necessary for the Congress to meet again very soon— Perhaps it will not be possible for the active Genius of America to sit still, & be a silent spectator of those great Events; filling their Coffers, & making their own advantage of the Follies, & Vices of Mankind— But whether we are involved in the War, or not, I know we must suffer, at lest Individuals must— The price of Articles have risen a quarter higher in the course of the last week— Indeed the price of the necessarys of Life, have been very high through the whole of the last year, & those whose maintanence is fixed to a stated Sum, must severely feel it—

Have you my Sisters put on any *external* marks of mourning for the unfortunate Lewis to whom America is so much indebted—[1] I am sure you could not read the fate of his unhappy Family without tender regret— It was his misfortune, & seems to be his only crime that he was born, & a King at this particular period of time— Had he have lived in some former age, he might have been idolized, & buried with his ancestors— His virtue, his benevolence, his condescendsion & Lenity was the Cause which effected his Death— The french Nation verified the old Proverb, "Give an Inch, & they will take an Ell—["] They felt the advantages arising from a greater degree of *Knowledge*, & *Liberty* than their Fathers had possessed, but had not virtue enough to sustain, & make a wise use of it— They thought they could not obtain *too* much of so great a *Good*— They precipitately made vast strides, & the pendilum of Power has vibrated with such voilence, as has thrown them into such Scenes of horror, & confusion as we now see them— Lewis the 16th. like Charles the 1st. has suffered for wishing to preserve inviolate, those Laws, which there own Subjects had made— unhappily for them, the *Temper* & *spirit* of the People was changed, but the *Laws* were the same— Thus may the greatest Monarchs fall, & their dust mingle with the lowest of their Vassals—

> "*This is the state of Man*: to day he puts forth
> The tender leaves of Hope; tomorrow blossoms,
> And bears his blushing honours thick upon him;
> The third day comes a frost, a *killing frost*,
> And when he thinks, good easy man, full surely
> His Greatness aripening, *nips his root*."[2]

Every day we are taught by some Occurrence, or other on what an uncertain tenor, we hold every earthly Enjoyment, & the vanity of building, on less than an immortal basis—

My dear Brother Cranch (I presume) views these political Commotions, with the Eye of a Christian Phylosopher,—as a prelude, & introductory of much greater Events in the moral word— I often wish to hear him converse—

I never wished to read History more in my Life, than now— It was always a Source of Entertainment & Instruction to me— But my dear Sister you must pity me, for my Eyes are so weak, that I fear sometimes I shall be blind— I can read but a few moments before my sight is gone, & it makes me sick, & dizzey—[3] Thanks to my good Angel, that induced me to lay up a Stock in early life, which (though small indeed) I would not exchange for Gold— I think I should be miserable without it—

Your Son (my Sister) is indeed very dear to me— He is just such a Friend as every one wants near them— I think he is exceedingly like his Father— *He made every body love, & respect him—*

This letter layed last week because I did not love to send it by the Post— I intended to have added more, but Col Hurd is waiting, so I must bid my dear Sister adieu— E Shaw—

RC (Adams Papers); addressed: "Mrs Mary Cranch / Quincy—"

[1] Enthusiasm in the United States for the French Revolution diminished in the wake of Louis XVI's execution. In Boston, the head and horns of the ox used for the civic feast in January was ceremonially buried in commemoration of the "melancholy fate of the first Princely Hand which was stretched forth to relieve America, in the hour of her distress." But not everyone was as sympathetic to the king's fate. The Philadelphia *National Gazette* noted sarcastically, "It is said that the *American Royalists* have been much embarrassed, as to the manner of evincing the sincerity of their grief for the 'murder' of his *most Christian Majesty—* Whether by muffling the bells in all the large towns and cities, for the space of *twelve months at least*; or by cloathing themselves in the sable garb of mourners on the occasion. The last mode has met the approbation of a majority; but *a respect for men in power*, which is characteristic of these mourning gentry, has deterred them from hastily putting their scheme in execution, until *the court* shall have time to lead the way" (Charles Downer Hazen, *Contemporary American Opinion of the French Revolution*, Baltimore, 1897, p. 253–259; *Massachusetts Spy*, 4 April; *National Gazette*, 23 March).

[2] Shakespeare, *King Henry the Eighth*, Act III, scene ii, lines 352–357.

[3] Shaw had suffered previously from inflammations of her eyes (vol. 6:500, 506; 8:276).

Thomas Boylston Adams to Abigail Adams

My dear Mother, Philadelphia 5th: May 1793—

Your last letter to me is dated the 18th: of March, since which time I have not heared a single word of the family, either verbally, or in writing.[1] We have news from France as late as the 15 of March, and one would think a letter from Quincy might have traveled the distance of 350 miles in the course of seven weeks. 'Tis my happiness, (some may think it a misfortune) not to distress my mind with unpleasant surmises upon such occasions; but I had rather be accused of a little Stoical apathy, than upon every intermission of more than usual duration in the correspondence of my friends, to attribute it to unfavorable causes. Mrs. Smith & her family have all been sick since their return, but I heared nothing of it till they had recovered their health— This may be the case with the Family at

Quincy, but I hope they have not yet to wait to inform me of their reestablishment— On Friday last the French Frigate which brought the French Minister from Paris came up the Delaware—she had been expected for some days, and when she got up, she saluted the City with fifteen Guns—which were answered from the Shore— There was a vast collection of people on the Wharves who saluted the Vessel with repeated huzza's, which were warmly returned by the Crew— Great numbers went off to the Ship as she lay in the River, and met a most cordial reception from the French Officers— the next day I went on board, but without making my self known I wished merely to gratify my curiosity, and I could do it as well In-cog—as if I had been introduced— the officers were civil, and shewed all that was to be seen—which cheifly consisted in 300 dirty Sailors in a dirty vessel, all á la mode de Francàise the Sailors Sing Ci, Ira—and dance the Marselais call each other Citoyen and in short exhibit the true spirit of the Revolution— There are the Crews of seven prizes which she has made since she left France on board, the Captains & mates of which are permited to walk the Deck— So much for L'Ambuscade The Minister has not yet arrived—he comes by land from Carolina—[2]

Your Friends here desire to be particularly remembered to you, I shall do it however only in this general way, which for civilities like these, is quite sufficient— Indeed I am at a loss to think what the generality of these mighty civil folks would find to say to me, were it not for my absent relations, whose health & wellfare seems to be a never failing source of enquiry & congratulation. I have a method of discovering whether the compliment in such cases is intended for me, or the person enquired for— "Your Father and Mother were well I hope when you heared from them last?" "Sir—or Madam (as the case may be) you do me honor by your friendly enquiries." If any thing further seems to be expected—I descend into particulars—but for the most part, the conversation seldom goes beyond a proposi-tion & reply—very rarely to a rejoinder— You see I must be in the fashion—I cant avoid a little *Scandal*

With presenting my best love to all Friends / I subscribe

Thos B Adams

PS, Mrs. Lynch has heared of the arrival of the Vessel in which her husband went last to Sea, at Boston, and has desired me to make enquiry of Mr Briesler, whether Lynch has returned and whether he intends coming to Philad^a:— The poor woman thinks herself deserted, and I believe nothing gives her more comfort than the prospect of Col & M^rs. Smith's residing here.

Monday 6th:

After I had sealed this Letter I received my Fathers of the 27th: of April—which I will answer in a short time—[3]

RC (Adams Papers); addressed: "M^rs: A Adams / Quincy / near Boston."

[1] Not found.

[2] Edmond Genet arrived in Charleston, S.C., on the frigate *Embuscade* on 8 April. Although the ship continued on to Philadelphia, Genet decided to remain in the South and travel overland by carriage, finally reaching the capital on 16 May. During the course of its trip up the eastern coast of the United States, the *Embuscade* took seven prizes, two of which—the brig *Little Sarah* and the ship *Grange*—the crew brought with them to Philadelphia when they arrived on 2 May (Harry Ammon, *The Genet Mission*, N.Y., 1973, p. 44, 55; Philadelphia *American Daily Advertiser*, 27 April; Philadelphia *Independent Gazetteer*, 4 May).

[3] Not found.

Charles Adams to John Adams

My dear Sir   New York May 10th 1793

It is sometime since I have written to you but still longer since I have had a line from my dear father. I do not repine for while you are happy in your feilds I will willingly give up that share of pleasure and instruction which I constantly received from your kind communications. It appears as if this City was fated to be the scene of constant disquietude and jarring cabal no sooner have the inhabitants cooled a little upon one subject than another source of contention arises and they begin with redoubled animosity. This cannot excite our astonishment if we consider the motley complection of the Citizens. A collection from all parts of the Globe The English Irish Scotch Dutch and Germans compose a very numerous body whose peculiar pride consists in fostering their national prejudices. The English Irish and Scotch swarmed to this City where they found a protection which in some States was denied them.[1] By their close connection and mutual assistance many of them are among the richest people. But far from a grateful sense of what they owe and without considering that were they again in their own Countries they would fall from their self opinianative importance they constantly strive to depreciate the American character. Most Americans are friends to the Revolution of France however they may view with horror the enormities which have been committed during the unfortunate course of five years they still separate the people desirous of liberty from the cabal of a National Assembly or the murderous demagogues of a National Convention. They hoped and still hope that under a good form of Goverment The French Nation may be restored to order, but when they hear themselves damned for their impudent ideas by a small cluster of Englishmen who lurk within the bosom of their Country when they hear repeated threats that the thunder of the British nation may be hurled upon them they are fired with indignation at the insult. Conduct like this from a club of Englishmen in this city has roused the spirits of the people and unless they learn more prudence fatal consequences may ensue. The low state of our funds is in some measure owing to an apprehension that America may be drawn into The war. For myself I see not much danger conscious that every endeavor will be used to maintain a neutrality and that measures the most strenuous will be put in operation to preserve this Country in a state of peace. These apprehensions however ill founded fail not to make some considerable impression upon the public mind. Another cause is the caution with which The Banks discount and the difficulty of procuring large quantities of specie. This it has been found is necessary as the multiplicity of banks has created distrust. That they cannot long hold out I think is certain they have had a pernicious influe[nce] upon the price of every article of consumption and I know of nothing except Salaries and la[wyers] fees that has not doubled within these two years. The Baron setts out tomorrow for Steuben I am sorry to loose his company for so long a period but he is almost as fond of his farm as you are and delights in the society of his Yankee's as he calls them. My Sister talks of beginning her journey sometime next week, she wished me to accompany her but I must deny myself that pleasure

Adieu my dear Sir Beleive me your / affectionate son

Charles Adams.

RC (Adams Papers); addressed: "The Vice President of the United States / Quincy / near / Boston—"; endorsed: "C. Adams / May 10. 1793." Some loss of text where the seal was removed.

[1] The 1790 census for New York State found an ethnic breakdown of approximately 52 percent English, 17.5 percent Dutch, 8 percent German, 8 percent Irish, and 7 percent Scottish. In New York City in the following decade, new immigrants continued to arrive from Great Britain, Ireland, and France, and a political split emerged as English immigrants tended toward the Federalist Party while the Scottish, Irish, and French favored the Democratic Republicans (Young, *Democratic Republicans*, p. 98, 401–402, 569).

Thomas Boylston Adams to Abigail Adams

My dear Mother   Philadelphia 21 May. 1793.

Your kind letter of the 12 has reached me, in complyance with Mr Brieslers request I enclose the Receipt of Mrs Lynch.[1] She was in much need of the little assistance, and expressed gratitude for the receipt of it. The Porter also shall be attended to; I have been so fortunate as yet to have received no warning from the owner of our Store— The furniture still rests there and I have some hope will not yet be disturbed. The most disagreeable trouble on my hands at present is to find a suitable place for my own head. My good Quaker lady intends giving up house-keeping about the middle of next month, and of course we are all under the necessity of changing our lodgings. The reasons of her taking this step are such as might naturally be expected from one who was brought up in a very different course of life. She finds that house Rent is increasing, that every article of life is nearly double in price, and that her expences in living far exceed the trifling assistance she derives from her lodgers. Unless she took a large house and admited every comer & goer, her present course of life cannot be profitable, & for this she is by no means calculated; so that she has by the advice of her Family & Friends come to a resolution to quit house keeping & return to her Father's. I shall regret the change of lodgings because I am persuaded it cannot be for the better— However I have not much longer to reside here, and I shall do as well as I can. I have no particular place in view as yet— The terms of board will be higher I know than at present but I won't go If I can avoid it to a common lodging house—

Col Smith has been some time in town, and finds little prospect of accomodating himself with an house at present. All the best houses in the City are taken up, and I know he wont live in an ordinary one. There may be opportunities between this & next fall to suit himself, at present Rent is monstrous, & houses very scarce— I have not met with the Publications you mention; no judicious peices will be republished here you may rest assured. People will not think for themselves—nor in all cases will they be guided by the judgment of others—so that we must be content with the dictates of the ignorant Multitude. I will say nothing of French Affairs. Calculation & conjecture have so often been lost upon them that the event ought rather to be acquiesced in when it shall arrive, than deplored by anticipation. I am out of all patience with the eternal folly of palliating every calamity & seting it down to the score of necessity— I think the excentricities of a Commet might as well be calculated, as the probable effects of such & Such particular events. Whilst France was successful in beating her first enemies, & conquering foreign states—I wished her spirit might be humbled— A Country really desirous of establishing a peaceful Government, has no business with foreign Territories— War is by no means its proper Element. Since the universal combination of powers against her, whether she has provoked it or not, I feel a powerful principle of humanity taking Root in my mind, as an advocate for the weaker party; 'tis a rule, & a very good one for individuals no less than Sovereign powers, to examine the justice of the cause about which Nations are quarreling. Considering France in her present situation, without examining the means by which it was acquired, the justice of the dispute seems to lay on their side. They have abolished an odious & oppressive Government too effectually ever to be reared again from its ruins—we will not say a word whether this was done by the general sense of the Nation— It suffices that having reduced themselves to Anarchy—the nation now see the necessity of a Government in some shape—still there is no Cry for a King, a Nobility, an established Clergy, &c^{a.} The very sound is odious; nothing that has the smallest tendency to superiority or eminence of rank will be received as yet. Here then is the great danger, the Shivre de Freze— that may cause Shipwreck—[2] The first axiom of civil Government, is authority & Subordination; But all confidence is destroyed between man & man; who then shall dare to take the helm. No man has a right to challenge the obedience of another, unless his authority is confered & derived from the original source— here is no original source, because the people are divided in their sentiments too far to unite upon any common measure of utility. What then must be the first step towards Government in France in such circumstances? It will be trod by a military force—whether they maintain their own ground against the combination, & establish their independance, or whether they become their slaves & vassals. This Combination of powers are practising injustice so far as they distract the attention of the French from Pacifick institutions, & prevent their worshiping Liberty & Equality in peace at home. I have become a wellwisher to the French so far as they are to be considered struggling with adversity, even tho' 'tis merited. I justify no single event that has taken place—since they are so, make the best of them, they cannot be recalled. They anticipated declarations of war, so far they act on the defensive. I can only further add, that seeing things are so, the event must sanctify the means— Conscientious people will exclaim, but necessity is not under the influence of dominion. These are my sentiments of French politics, so far as they go— I began by declining them altogether, & fully intended to stop at the first sentence— but you see the difference—

With all due affection / I remain your son

Thomas B Adams

RC (Adams Papers); notation: "May 23ᵈ."

¹ Not found.
² Possibly cheval de frise, literally "horse of Friesland," a defensive mechanism for halting cavalry charges or other military advances (*OED*).

Charles Adams to John Adams

My dear Sir   New York May 29ᵗʰ 1793

It is with great pleasure I hear that my brother is appointed to speak the town Oration, on the fourth of July next. It would give me infinite satisfaction to hear him, but as I cannot, I request a few copies if they can be procured, as soon as they appear in print.[1] Confined as he must be, by the shackles which are, I think erroniously, imposed upon those who have this duty to perform; I have no doubt but he will greatly add to his already far extended reputation. Publicola, has been reprinted in Edinburg and in London; and in an European Magazine, there is a contradiction of your being the Author of those publications, as was indicated by the edition printed in Scotland.[2] The reports of Dumourier's defection, come from so many different quarters, that we begin to give credit to them; nor do I think it so very extraordinary, no man in his right senses could submit to be the instrument of so mad a faction, as now seem to govern in France. We have in our papers this day, a dialogue said to have passed between the General and the Commissioners sent to carry him to Paris: In which Dumourier says "your Convention consists of three hundred fools, governed by four hundred rascals. They have formed a Government infinitely more imbecile, dangerous and destructive, than the former. They will annihilate the nation."[3] I am very much pleased with a writer with the signature of Marcellus; I have seen but one Number reprinted in Fenno's Gazette, but his sentiments are perfectly coincident with those, which I think every well wisher to his Country, every real American ought to adopt: but alas! what will not this people swallow, if gilded over with the foil of liberty and equality. Where is the Lover of this Country who will not join in the wish? "that laurelled victory may sit upon the sword of *Justice* and that success may always be strewed before the feet of *virtuous Freedom*" but we should learn to discriminate; We should learn to distinguish virtuous freedom, from unprincipled licentiousness; then, and then only, can we be a happy or a dignified people.[4] While we are continually hunting in the catalogue of improbabilities, for excuses, to palliate the enormities of an enraged clan of Jacobins, we are injuring our morals and destroying our reputations.— Dumourier seems to have expressed great surprize that Condorcet, should not have pointed out a constitution, more worthy of his abilities: but what could he do? Might he not have fallen a victim to just ideas? and I think it is quite time that martyrdom should be discarded at least from France; there is but little encouragement. Mon^rs Genet is received with open arms in Philadelphia, I know of no objection which can with propriety be offered to this; provided it did not convey the idea of an acquiescence in the transactions in France. I know very well that such ideas as these, are termed Aristocratic. I disclaim the faith. My sentiments are dictated by the purest philanthropy. Can those who with the stern eye of apathy behold murder carnage and every affliction which can desolate a Country, following as a consequence of the unbridled machinations of a few: men Can they love mankind? No person can be more an advocate for civil liberty and civil equality than myself, but name not the French as models; name not that barbarous, that cruel people, as examples worthy to be followed by Americans, who are happy in equal laws and a just Government. Happy! thrice happy people! if they would reflect upon their own prosperity. I have found it adviseable of late, again to peruse with attention the writers upon Natural law. Grotius, puffendorph, Vattel, Burlemaque. many questions interesting to the community, and to individuals, dayly arise. These studies, blended with that of the law, have lately occupied my attention. I think I have pitched upon a method of reading, by far the most preferable: instead of reading the Reporters in course, I take up Espinasse's Law of actions, a book of great authority and credit, and constantly refer to the cases in the Reporters: a method which fixes much more firmly in my memory the principles of every case: in this manner I intend to go through him, and have no doubt of reaping ample reward for my pains. It has been my endeavor to select in the first instance The Reporters during the time of Lord Mansfield. I have purchased

Burroughs	Durnford and East }	Richardson's pra K B
Cowper Reports	Bacon's abridgment	Crompton's practice
Douglass	Espinasse Nisi Prius	Powell on Mortgages
		Do on Contracts
W Blackston	Lilly's Entries	Highmore on bail
	Lovelace laws disposal	Kyd on bill of exchange

Laws of the State of New York.—[5]

Our parties in this City begin to cool down of late; it was quite time, for very warm blood was raised, and it was very much feared that serious consequences might have ensued.

Perhaps you may recollect, that when I was last at Quincy you offered me a work entitled Cours D'Etudes:[6] I had then no method of conveying it to New York: should you now remain of the same mind, Brizler will pack them up, and send them to me by Barnard. I had occasion while I was there to peruse several parts of that work, and was highly delighted with it, as containing a very useful and instructive epitome of the Sciences. Judge Duane in his kindness has been pleased to appoint me one of the Commissioners to examine the claims of invalid pensioners. He may think it an honor conferred, but there is no emolument to be derived, and except its being a charitable duty, would be rather tedious. I accepted it on that account; but the late law of Congress has so restricted applicants, that I doubt much whether any one will be able to take advantage of it.[7] Our latest arrivals from Europe bring intelligence to the fifth of April only; it appears that communications from France have been of late so impeded that we are led to suspect much of our information has been coined in England. I fear I have long since tired your patience And I will bid you adieu

Beleive me my dear Sir your ever affectionate and dutiful son

Charles Adams.

RC (Adams Papers); addressed: "The Vice President of the United States / Quincy"; endorsed: "Charles Adams / May 29. / ansd June 5. 1793."

[1] On 4 July, JQA delivered an address at Boston's Old South Meeting House, which Benjamin Edes & Sons published some days later. "Seventeen times has the sun, in the progress of his annual revolutions, diffused his prolific radiance over the plains of Independent America," JQA said. "Millions of hearts which then palpitated with the rapturous glow of patriotism, have already been translated to brighter worlds; to the abodes of more than mortal freedom." The press reported an enthusiastic reaction to the address: "The elegance and spirit of the composition, and the forceful elocution of the

Speaker, excited such a *burst* of *admiration*, as would have flattered a CATO" (JQA, *An Oration Pronounced July 4th, 1793*, Boston, 1793, p. 12, Evans, No. 25076; *Massachusetts Mercury*, 5 July). An incomplete Dft and Tr of the oration are in the Adams Papers, filmed at 4 July.

² JQA's Publicola articles were first published in Edinburgh in 1791 as *Observations on Paine's "Rights of Man"* without any identifying author, though they were commonly attributed to JA. John Stockdale—a friend of JA—subsequently published them in London in 1793 under the title *An Answer to Pain's Rights of Man. By John Adams, Esq.* but stopped the printing when he learned that JQA, not JA, was the author. The *European Magazine*, Feb. 1793, p. 85, included a note avowing that JA had not written the pieces (JQA, *Writings*, 1:66; John Stockdale to JA, 16 March, Adams Papers). See also TBA to AA, 27 May [1792], and note 5, above.

³ Reports of the French National Convention for 1 April 1793 included an extended dialogue between General Dumouriez and the commissioners from the Convention. This dialogue suggested that it was Dumouriez's "fixed intention" to go to Paris to protect the queen and her children, and he further threatened that "the convention will not exist three weeks longer" and expressed his determination to restore the monarchy (*New York Journal*, 29 May).

⁴ Marcellus appeared in the Boston *Columbian Centinel*, 24 April, and 4, 11 May. The third installment was also reprinted in the Philadelphia *Gazette of the United States*, 25 May, and CA quotes from the final lines of that piece. Marcellus examines the role the United States and its citizens should play in the war among the European powers, arguing that "a rigid adherence to the system of Neutrality between the European nations now at war, is equally the dictate of justice and of policy, to the individual citizens of the United States, while the Nation remains neutral." Furthermore, he suggests that "the natural state of all nations, with respect to one another, is a state of peace."

⁵ Henry Cowper, *Reports of Cases Adjudged in the Court of King's Bench: from . . . 1774, to . . . 1778*, London, 1783; William

Douglass, *A Summary, Historical and Political, of the First Planting, Progressive Improvements, and Present State of the British Settlements in North-America*, 2 vols., Boston, 1747–1752, Evans, No. 5936; Charles Durnford and Sir Edward Hyde East, *Reports of Cases Argued and Determined in the Court of King's Bench*, London, 1787; Matthew Bacon and others, *A New Abridgement of the Law*, 5 vols., London, 1736–1766; John Lilly, *Modern Entries, Being a Collection of Select Pleadings in the Courts of King's Bench*, London, 1723; Peter Lovelass, *The Law's Disposal of a Person's Estate Who Dies without Will or Testament*, 4th edn., London, 1787; Robert Richardson, *The Attorney's Practice in the Court of King's Bench*, London, 1739; George Crompton, *Practice Common-placed; or, The Rules and Cases of Practice in the Courts of King's Bench and Common Pleas, Methodically Arranged*, 2 vols., London, 1780; John Joseph Powell, *A Treatise upon the Law of Mortgages*, London, 1785; Powell, *Essay upon the Law of Contracts and Agreements*, London, 1790; Anthony Highmore, *A Digest on the Doctrine of Bail in Civil and Criminal Cases*, London, 1783; Stewart Kyd, *A Treatise on the Law of Bills of Exchange and Promissory Notes*, London, 1790; *Laws of the State of New York*, Albany, N.Y., 1777– .

⁶ Étienne Bonnot de Condillac, Abbé de Mureaux, *Cours d'étude pour l'instruction du prince de Parme*, 16 vols., Parma, Italy, 1775. Copies of all but vol. 13 are in JA's library at MB (*Catalogue of JA's Library*).

⁷ On 28 Feb., George Washington signed into law "An Act to Regulate the Claims to Invalid Pensions," which modified the earlier "Act to Provide for the Settlement of the Claims of Widows and Orphans . . . and to Regulate the Claims to Invalid Pensions," enacted the previous year. The new law created higher bars to establish legal claims of disability from military service during the Revolutionary War, including oaths from two doctors and multiple witnesses testifying to the injury and strict deadlines for applications. The act also required that all evidence be submitted either to a district court judge or to a three-person commission appointed by the judge (*Annals of Congress*, 2d Cong., 2d sess., p. 1346–1348, 1436–1437).

John Adams to Charles Adams

Dear Charles   Quincy June 5 1793

I thank you for your, agreable Letter of the 29. Ult. Your Brother is destined to be celebrated and consequently envyed and abused. He has great Talents, and equal Industry. Publicola has passed through Several Editions in Ireland and Scotland as well as England, and I am well informed that the Speaker of the House of Commons, Mr Pitt and Several other Characters high in office besides the Attorney General have pronounced it one of the ablest Things of the kind they ever read. Marcellus deserves as high an Encomium. I am of Dumouriers opinion that the last Fugitive Piece, which the French call a Constitution is worse than the first, and, as La Croix Said of the latter that it would last as long as it should please God the former will have the same fate.[1]

If Dumourier had known Condorcet as well as I do, he would not have been surprized at his Constitution. He has been ignorant and indiscreet enough to commit himself in Print, Several years ago, in favour of a crude and shallow Idea of his three Idols Turgot Franklin and the Duke de la Rochefaucault, and now he will never get rid of it, till he is murdered like the last of them.[2]

You are very right. The Spirit of Liberty is a Sober and a temperate Spirit. Rage, Violence & fury are inconsistent with it.

I am pleased to perceive that your Taste for Books is a growing Appetite and your Love of study an increasing Passion. Go on my son. You will find your Account in the study of Ethicks, and the Law of Nations. Such Writers not only enlighten the Understanding but they rectify and purify the heart. The Love of Justice, of Humanity and of Wisdom, are the never failing Effects of frequent and constant Contemplation of the Principles Maxims and Reasonings of those Writers.

Your Plan of Studying Espinasse, is judicious and I hope you will pursue it to the End.— The Catalogue of Books you have purchased is no Doubt valuable, and you do well to admire Lord Mansfield, yet you must be upon your guard and not always adopt his Ideas, nor should you forget, Hale Coke or Holt[3]

Brisler shall Send you, The Abbe Condelae's Course of Study as you desire.

Judge Duane has made you a very handsome Compliment, which

demands and I presume will have your gratitude. Tho there may be no Profit there is honour, and a fair Opportunity to do good and to approve your humanity, Justice, publick Spirit Patience Politeness and Address before many People, which to a good young Man is a prescious Advantage. I hope therefore you will attend this Duty as punctually as if it was lucrative. *A Sincere desire to do good is the best Trait in a young Man's Character.* A Selfish Indifference to the good of others, is one of the worst.

My regards to our Connections. I am &c   John Adams

RC (MHi:Seymour Coll.); internal address: "Charles Adams"; endorsed: "June 5. 1793."

[1] Jean François de Lacroix (1754–1794), a lawyer, was a member of the National Convention and an ally of Danton (Hoefer, *Nouv. biog. générale*).

[2] Condorcet had argued for "the unprofitableness of the division of legislative powers into several bodies," first in a *Supplément* to his *Influence de la révolution d'Amérique sur les opinions et la législation de l'Europe*, n.p., 1786, and later in his *Lettres d'un bourgeois de New-Heaven* (published in Philip Mazzei's *Recherches historiques et politiques sur les*

États-Unis de l'Amérique septentrionale, 4 vols., Paris, 1788), written in response to JA's *Defence of the Const.* He believed that a single unicameral legislature better served a democracy, a notion to which JA took considerable exception (Haraszti, *Prophets*, p. 235–236).

[3] Sir John Holt, Thomas Farresley, and Giles Jacob, *A Report of All Cases Determined by Sir John Holt, Knt., from 1688 to 1710*, London, 1738.

Thomas Boylston Adams to John Adams

Dear sir,   Philadelphia 9th: June 1793—

I have procured the Warrant from the Treasury for the payment of D 1250. and taken two Orders on the Branch Bank at Boston in the name of my Brother. One for Dls800. & the other for Dls1,190, which will be paid him on demand, on your behalf. The surplus I have reserved for the following purposes. Viz For five months Board Dls66. 50Cts; One hundred Dls sent to my Brother Charles; For two Quarters Store Rent Dls 36. For nine Doz of Porter Dls 16. For myself Dls 41— 50Cts— Or, to state it in a more Mercantile way—

	Dlls	Cts
To Charles at NYork.	100	
For five months Board for myself.	66	50
For two quarters Store Rent for the furniture	36	
For Nine Doz of Porter.	16	
For myself.	41	50
	Dls 260 "	0

I have inclosed the Orders to my Brother John;[1] he will be upon the Spot, and can transmit the money to you at Quincy without delay; As they are drawn in favor of my Brother, no Indorsment will be necessary on your part. My good Quaker Landlady is upon the point of giving up house keeping, which has obliged me to seek another residence— I have found one at another Quaker house, but at a higher price than before— They demand at the rate of seventy five pounds Pr Ann. and I was under the necessity of closing with the terms, as I could hear of no place equally reasonable— The situation is much preferable to that which I left, & my accomodations are better; but I did not make the exchange from choice. The name of the Family is (Staal) they bear a very respectable character, and are to appearance civil folks—[2]

I must apologize for troubling you with my personal concerns— I hope my next letter may contain more interesting matter.

Presenting my best love to all friends / I subscribe / your affectionate son   Thomas B Adams

RC (Adams Papers); internal address: "The Vice President of the U,S."

[1] Not found.

[2] China merchant John Stall Sr. and his wife, Frances, operated a boardinghouse at 72 North Third Street in Philadelphia (Rush, *Letters*, 2:688–689, 747; *Philadelphia Directory*, 1793, Evans, No. 25585; U.S. Census, 1790, Penn., p. 222).

Elizabeth Smith Shaw to Abigail Adams

My Dear Sister—   Haverhill June 11th 1793

I am extremely sorry to hear, that you have had another attack of your ague, since Cousin Betsy left you— I hope you are in the use of every probable means for your releif, & restoration to Health— That glow in your features, which I have contemplated with so much satisfaction, I should be grieved to see injured by Sickness, or any disaster— But you my dear Sister have a double Security—Nature & Grace have both conspired in your favour—For *that Beauty* which depends principally upon the Mind,—upon the Divinity that stirs within cannot easily be defaced by Time, Sickness, or any accidenttal Circumstance—

I am very glad you was so kind as to let Cousin Betsy have your Horse & Chaise to make a visit to her Mother— you was mistaken if you thought I was unwilling, to have her go,— To *tarry* with her, was what I thought would be prejudicial to her health— But I have wanted all this Spring to have gone, & to have taken Betsy with me, to see my unhappy sick Sister—who has no relation, or connection but ourselves, to visit, or befriend her—

I am very sorry Cousin Polly has not receivd a Letter I sent to her by my Cousins—[1] It was designed to encourage in her filial piety, approving, of her readiness to quit her business, though in a very fine way—& shewing the benifit which I supposed would be derived from her attending upon her Mother, rather than any one else— I know it is a hard, & tedious Task, for so young a Daughter— Yet I seldom knew an absolute necessity for firmness, strength of mind, & the exercise of great Virtues but that they *came* obedient to the call—were ready attendants upon the Summons—

Happy for us that it is so— The belief of it, has kept many a one, from sinking under the weight of Affliction—

The weekly Papers are filled with accounts of the Commotions which have taken place in almost every part of Europe France exhibits to our view a Scene too Shocking, & too full of horror for the tender Mind to dwell upon— Is anything more to be deprecated than a civil War? What bloody Scenes—what murders, & massacres—What want of publick Confidence?— The smiling Sycophant to Day,—Tomorrow the cruel Assasin—Nothing to designate the Friend, from the bitter Enemy— Can anything be more dreadful than such intestene Convulsions—such publick Factions, & all the Evils of Pandora's Box, & ten thousand more if possible, are in thy horrid Train— Let me turn from it—& with Gratitude reflect upon the Goodness of that Being, who when we had every thing to Fear, has caused us so soon to sit down in peace, enjoying the rich Blessings of a wise & good Government—& may he who holds the hearts of all in his hands, long continue Men of Wisdom, & Virtue to guide & direct the publick Weal—

I have not yet heard of Mrs Smiths being at Quincy— I hope you will all favour me with a visit—

If you please you may tell Celia that I had rather not take a Child so far off— It must be attended with inconveniences— I am obliged to hire a Spinner half the year—& we cannot afford to multiply our Family without profit— If Mr Shaw could take Scholars, the profits of which would furnish us with cloathing, I would never turn the Wheel again for I perfectly hate the work, in a place where we are obligd to see so much company, & then I would take a little Girl immediately—& keep Betsy Quincy wholly to sewing.— She might do as much again, if I had any new work for her to do— Cousin Lucy is

a lovely woman, & makes us too—too short a visit to your affectionate Sister   E Shaw—

RC (Adams Papers).

¹ Probably Mary Smith, daughter of Catharine Salmon and William Smith Jr.

John Quincy Adams to Thomas Boylston Adams

My dear Brother.   Boston June 23. 1793.

I have received your Letter containing the orders upon the
branch bank, and also that with the bill of lading of 3 barrels;¹ I
ought to have written you this information a post or two ago, but
some business, more indolence, and most of all forgetfulness was
the occasion of my omission.

I suppose you will soon commence Attorney, and I understand
you have some thoughts of retiring into one of the back Counties of
Pensylvania, to commence practice. let me know what your intentions are, and when you expect to commence your career— I am not
quite in statu quo I have a sort of Pisgah-sight² of future milk and
honey—but not yet much enjoyment of it in person.

I have an Oration to deliver on the 4th: of next month, as you
know I have written and committed it to memory, and am thoroughly disgusted with it.— While I was writing I thought myself
quite brilliant as I advanced; and was pleasing myself with future
applauses at almost every sentence that issued from my pen— Now,
it appears to me a mass of dull common-place, composed of stale
facts, hacknied sentiments, veteran similies, and trite allusions, with
scarce a single gleam of originality shooting through the solid darkness of the composition.— The humble merits of the average of similar performances, are now my greatest consolation— However indifferent my execution, I shall not easily place myself in a style of
inferiority upon comparison.

The most extraordinary intelligence, which I have to convey, is
that the wise and learned Judge & Professor Wilson, has fallen most
lamentably in love with a young Lady in this town, under twenty; by
the name of Gray. He came, he saw, and was overcome. The gentle
Celadon, was smitten at meeting with a first sight love—unable to
contain his amorous pain, he breathed his sighs about the Streets;
and even when seated on the bench of Justice, he seemed as if
teeming with some woful ballad to his mistress eye-brow.— He obtained an introduction to the Lady, and at the second interview pro-

posed his lowly person and his agreeable family to her acceptance; a circumstance very favourable to the success of his pretensions, is that he came in a very handsome chariot and four. In short his attractions were so powerful, that the Lady actually has the subject under consideration, and unless the Judge should prove as fickle as he is amorous and repent his precipitate impetuosity so far as to withdraw his proposal, You will no doubt soon behold in the persons of these well assorted lovers a new edition of January and May.—Methinks I see you stare at the perusal of this intelligence, and conclude that I am attempting to amuse you, with a *bore*; no such thing. it is the plain and simple truth, that I tell—and if you are in the habit of seeing the Miss Breck's as frequently, as your wishes must direct you to see them, you may inform them, that their friend and mine, *Miss Hannah Gray,* has made so profound an impression upon the Heart of judge Wilson, and received in return an impression so profound upon her own, that in all probability they will soon see her at Philadelphia, the happy consort of the happy judge.[3]

Cupid himself must laugh at his own absurdity, in producing such an Union; but he must sigh to reflect that without the soft persuasion of a deity who has supplanted him in the breast of modern beauty, he could not have succeeded to render the man ridiculous & the woman contemptible upon the subject of politics I wish not to enter; they would lead me too far; and they are at this time unpleasant beyond the common proportion.— I enclose a few lines written upon some of the insolence proceeding from your shoe-black of the Muses, who thinks himself a poet because he knows himself a lyar.—[4] They are only for your perusal, and have never been seen by any other person [. . . .] Write me what you think of the point in the four concluding [verses The] sarcasm appeared severe to the parental partiality of the author; but who can be admitted as the judge of his own composition.

I remain your cordial friend & affectionate brother.

J. Q. A.

RC (Adams Papers); addressed: "M^r: Thomas B. Adams / Philadelphia."; endorsed: "J Q A / June 23– 93–"; notation: "Due Cook 16 cents / gon out of town." Some loss of text due to a torn manuscript.

[1] Not found.

[2] "A faint view or glimpse of something unobtainable or distant" (*OED*).

[3] Judge James Wilson, age fifty, married nineteen-year-old Hannah Gray of Boston on 19 Sept. (*DAB*). Celadon, from James Thomson's *The Seasons*, refers to any "lady-love" (Brewer, *Reader's Handbook*).

[4] Not found.

Thomas Boylston Adams to William Cranch

My dear William   Boston July 20th: 1793

I have only two or three minutes at present to devote to the purpose of answering a long & agreeable letter I received from you
before my departure from Philadelphia—[1] I had anticipated with
pleasure an expected interview at Cambridge, & feel no small mortification in the disappointment. After passing a very happy week in
the company of my friends & former associates I am upon the point
of returning to Quincy—where I shall remain a few days, & then
hasten to return from a place, which litterally speaking, I had no
buisiness to leave at this season. I make but one observation more
which is, that if we should unfortunately miss each other this time,
we must supply by this *pen*, that antidote to separation the absence
of the person. As to my visiting Haverhill, it's out of the question—
my stay won't admit. Inclination attracts, but necessity repels. Give
my best Compliments &ca &ca: to inquiring Friends in general you
may employ farther particulars at discretion.

Believe me   Thomas B Adams

RC (OCHP:William Cranch Papers, Mss fC891c RM); addressed: "William
Cranch Esqr: / Atty at Law / Haverhill"; internal address: "William Cranch Esqr:";
endorsed: "T.B.A. July 20 '93."

[1] Not found.

Charles Adams to John Quincy Adams

My dear Brother   July 29th [1793]

I received the copies of your Oration by Mr Atkinson for which I
give you my own and the thanks of my friends Unwilling to trust my
own partial judgment upon the performance I have endeavored to
collect the opinions of those of my friends here who are most remarkable for their taste and my own ideas have been justified by the
universal applause which has been bestowed upon your Oration. I
cannot but admire the prudence which you have observed in steer-
ing so cautiously between the Scylla and Carybdis of public opinion
and surely it was your duty to offend no one in a performance of
this kind. In a late letter you observe that some of my friends think
me too strenuous upon the wrong side.[1] I must be thought so if I
deny a single democratic principle. Every man who now ventures to
disapprove of a single measure of the French is according to mod-

ern language an Aristocrat and I had rather submit to the imputation than indiscriminately to approve of every transaction of that nation God forbid that I should ever become the advocate of tyrany whether exercised by a single or a many headed monster. How stenuous are the party in Philadelphia to engage us in a war What abuse and reviling constantly fill that mint of defamation the National Gazette How determined should be the conduct of The Executive. Surely the conduct of a foreign Minister is reprehensible who talks of appealing to the people from the decision of the first Magistrate.[2] If ever there was a time when firmness was required it is now. What do you think of the decision of Judge Peters in your part of the world? I would ask one question Suppose a French Ship should come up to the wharves of New York and carry away to Philadelphia twenty or thirty British merchantmen Could our Court of admiralty have jurisdiction of it? We have had a case similar to that of the ship William before our District Court it was argued on the part of the Libellants last week and more ingenious and learned argument I never heard in a Court Messrs Troup and Harison shew themselves to the greatest advantage to be sure the concluding quotation of M^r H applied to judge Duane could not but raise a smile in the countenance of those who know his character. He is suspected of leaning towards the opinion of Judge Peters for whom he has a great veneration but I am inclined to beleive that after the argument and the application of the Verse from Horace "Justum et tenacem" & he will not have obstinacy enough to decide similarly.[3] We dayly expect a French fleet in this port I dread the moment— We have many turbulent people in this City who would wish to take advantage of such an event. We have already been witnesses to the commencement of very tumultuous proceedings. A writer in the philadelphia papers Pacificus has claimed the attention of the public I am happy to find most men of character accord with the sentiments of this writer who he is I know not The Secretary of the treasury, amongst us, has the credit of being the author the peices would not disgrace his pen.[4] Entre nous it seems to me rather surprising that The VP has not been called to Philadelphia surely his Counsel is necessary in the present circumstances of this Country pray explain to me you may have a better opportunity of knowing the reasons than myself or the multitudes who ask me the question. My Respects and Love to all friends

    Yours affectionately   Charles Adams

PS The Boston Frigate Commanded by Captain Courtnay is now off the Hook as he has thirty two guns and has sent a challenge to The Ambuscade who is now under sail to meet her hundreds of people have gone down to be witnesses to the expected encounter which will no doubt be very desperate.[5]

RC (Adams Papers); addressed: "John Quincy Adams Esqr / Boston—"; endorsed: "C: Adams. July 29. 1793."

[1] Not found.

[2] On 22 April, George Washington issued his Neutrality Proclamation, which states that, as regards the war between France and the rest of Europe, "duty and interest of the United States require, that they should with sincerity and good faith adopt and pursue a conduct friendly and impartial toward the belligerent powers." In practice, this policy meant that French privateers could not be outfitted in American ports nor could France enlist American citizens to serve in the French Army or Navy. Edmond Genet, frustrated by this situation, threatened to ignore Washington's ruling and appeal directly to the people through their congressional representatives (Washington, *Papers, Presidential Series*, 12:472–474; Jefferson, *Papers*, 26:687–688). See also CA to JA, 25 Aug., and note 3, below.

[3] On 21 June, Judge Richard Peters ruled in the case of the capture of the British merchant ship *William* by the French *Citizen Genet*. The libellants argued that the *William* had been captured illegally in American territorial waters, while the defendants insisted that the United States did not have standing to adjudicate a case between two nations at war with one another. Peters agreed with the latter, stating that the U.S. district court had no jurisdiction "in a matter growing out of the contests between belligerent powers." In a similar case, Richard Harison, the U.S. district attorney in New York, and Robert Troup were involved in legal proceedings regarding the capture of the British brig *Catharine* by the French frigate *Embuscade*. Harison and Troup argued that the ship had been "taken within the territory, and under the protection of the United States." In Jan. 1794, Judge James Duane of the district court ruled that his court did not hold jurisdiction over such matters; any restitution would have to come from the executive branch. Shortly thereafter, in another case, the U.S. Supreme Court ruled that district courts did have jurisdiction, and in August, the *Catharine* was restored to its owners, who also received an award for costs and damages (Jefferson, *Papers*, 26:200–201, 254; Richard Peters, *Admiralty Decisions in the District Court of the United States*, 2 vols., Phila., 1807, 1:12–30).

For the quote from Horace, see CA to JA, 31 Jan. 1793, and note 3, above.

[4] Pacificus—a lengthy defense of Washington's Proclamation of Neutrality—appeared in seven essays, five published by the Philadelphia *Gazette of the United States*, 29 June, 3, 6, 10, 13, 17 July, and two by the *Federal Gazette*, 24, 25 July. Alexander Hamilton was indeed the author; see Hamilton, *Papers*, 15:33–43, 55–63, 65–69, 82–86, 90–95, 100–106, 130–135.

[5] Capt. George William Augustus Courtenay brought the British frigate *Boston* from Nova Scotia to stop harassment of British shipping by Citizen Jean Baptiste François Bompard of the French frigate *Embuscade*. At sea off New York, Courtenay sent a challenge to Bompard in the city, who responded that he would meet the British off Sandy Hook. In a two-hour battle before hundreds of spectators on 1 Aug., Courtenay was killed and the *Boston* fled to sea. A heavily damaged *Embuscade* returned to New York to the cheers of French partisans (William R. Casto, "French Cruisers, British Prizes, and American Sailors: Coordinating American Foreign Policy in the Age of Fighting Sails," in Kenneth R. Bowling and Donald R. Kennon, eds., *Neither Separate Nor Equal: Congress in the 1790s*, Athens, Ohio, 2000, p. 212–217).

Thomas Boylston Adams to Abigail Adams

My dear Mother   Philadelphia Aug[st]: 10th: 1793.

I ought to have written you from New-York, of my safe arrival there in little more than three days, after a pleasant Journey, with only one constant companion from Boston, who was a French Gentleman now a Merchant in that place— We found the roads remarkably fine, and the Country at 20 Miles distanc from Boston presenting a more favorable appearance. Our journies were between 70 & 80 miles distance each day, & you will readily suppose I wanted no further rocking to lull me to sleep. I found our friends in N.Y— all well–& as Col Smith was upon a small Jouney in the Country, I was persuaded to wait his return, as he was anxious to hear what account I could give of his wife, with whom he accuses me of having run away

The people of N York many of them are raving mad with French Politicks, & the sober part are asleep—or if awake dare only yawn & gape. The Sea Duel between Bompard & Courtney engrossed all conversation, and the partizans of each are equally imprudent in their behavior— The Coffee-House, proper only for the resort of Merchants, is converted into a *den of thieves* & Jacobins,[1] and the Citizen Mechanicks have deserted their Shops & occupations for the less arduous task of settling the affairs of the Nation. In Philadelphia things have been carried to greater lengths in some respects. The Household of the Citizen Minister have been convicted of conduct, which in any other Country would deserve no other name than Treason, & would probably meet a punishment adequate to that crime. Handbills have been distributed representing the President and Judge Willson with their heads under the Guillotine, and proclaiming their death to the Citizens of Philadelphia on account of the acquittal of Henfield lately tried for entering into the service of France.[2] If such things do not destroy our Government it will be because we have none to fall a sacrifice. Like the City of Paris however in the heighth of their Massacres, we are said to be in perfect tranquility; and because the consequences are not immediate, nobody appears alarmed.

The Sup Court of the U, S. having no business ready for trial sat but two days—the State of Massachusetts did not appear & the same process will be observed against her as against the State of Georgia—[3]

Our friends in Philad^a are well, those who remain in the City, which is but a small proportion. The sudden death of Mrs Lear will no doubt distress you—she fell a victim to neglect of her person when in a bad habit, not as at first represented from eating too freely of unripe fruit.[4] Mr Lear is inconsolable under his loss, & has suffered himself to be seen by none but the Family since the funeral.

Presenting love &c^a / I remain / your son   Thos B Adams.

RC (Adams Papers); internal address: "M^{rs:} A Adams."

[1] The Tontine Coffeehouse was a center of pro-French sentiment in New York. It hosted banquets for visiting Frenchmen and auctions of prizes taken by French privateers (Edwin G. Burrows, *Gotham: A History of New York City to 1898*, N.Y., 1999, p. 318–320; New York *Daily Advertiser*, 13 Aug.).

[2] Gideon Henfield, a Salem, Mass., sailor, was prosecuted by the Washington administration for enlisting in the French Navy, which the president considered a violation of American neutrality. Supreme Court justice James Wilson presided over a special session of the U.S. Circuit Court of Pennsylvania to try the case. The government made the argument that although Congress had not passed a law specifically forbidding such enlistments, Henfield's actions nonetheless violated U.S. treaties with Britain, the Netherlands, and Prussia. The jury acquitted Henfield on 29 July of all charges (Jefferson, *Papers*, 26:130–131).

[3] During an abbreviated session in Philadelphia on 5 and 6 Aug., the U.S. Supreme Court considered the cases of Chisholm v. Georgia and Vassall v. Massachusetts. In the Chisholm case the state of Georgia had refused to send a representative to the February session of the court because it denied the legitimacy of a suit brought against it by a citizen of another state. At that time the justices ordered Georgia officials to appear in August or face a default ruling. A representative did attend the August session and the case was continued. The Vassall case was similar but involved an Englishman suing the state. Massachusetts also claimed sovereign immunity by denying the legitimacy of a suit brought by a citizen of another country. Massachusetts officials had been subpoenaed to appear at the August session, but they did not do so and Vassall was continued as well. Both cases remained unresolved until they were nullified by the ratification of the Eleventh Amendment, which prohibits such suits (*Doc. Hist. Supreme Court*, 1:217–219; 5:134–137, 364–369).

[4] Mary Long Lear died of yellow fever in Philadelphia on 28 July (Ray Brighton, *The Checkered Career of Tobias Lear*, Portsmouth, N.H., 1985, p. 114–115). See also TBA to JA, 9 Oct., and note 2, below.

Charles Adams to John Adams

My Dear Sir   New York Augt 25th 1793

By Colonel Smith who setts out for Boston tomorrow I have the pleasure of addressing a few lines to you. If you procure the Newspapers from New York you will observe by them that events of some importance have passed lately in this City with an almost incredible rapidity. Though much has been feared, from the turbulence of some and much apprehended from the inactivity of others yet happily for us nothing very serious or alarming has as yet happened. We have had some small riots at Our Coffee house and one or two of the Citizens have received the bastinado but the steady and nervous arm of the law has cooled the tempers of those who were disposed to riot, and at length the respectable inhabitants have come forward to discountenance such unwarrantable proceedings.[1] The Great Mʳ William Livingston has been the ostensible head of a party composed of Drunken Porters idle Carmen and three or four men who though once they had some claim to respectability at the present moment could not fail of approaching nearer the zenith by a turn of the political ball.[2] The whole consisting of perhaps three or four hundred people. yet small and despicable as they really were they tyrannized with uncontroled sway and it was sufficient for them to denounce a man for him to meet with the most ignominious treatment. These people Addressed the French Minister. This step called forth the resolutions approving The Presidents proclamation which have awed them into a Deathlike Silence.[3] Mʳ Genet has written to The President requiring that he would exculpate him from the various charges which have been brought against him of want of respect for him and of imprudent conduct &c Mʳ Jefferson returns for answer That it is not proper for Diplomatic characters to communicate with the President but through his ministers.[4] He is continually falling in the estimation of the people. I hope for peace and tranquility. All our friends are well The Baron does not return until the latter end of October I expect he will pass a few days with you before the Session as he tells me I must be ready [to] accompany him.

Adieu my Dear Sir Your dutiful / son   Charles Adams

RC (Adams Papers); addressed: "The Vice President of the United States / Quincy"; endorsed: "Mʳ Charles / August 25. 1793." Some loss of text where the seal was removed.

[1] On 18 Aug., French and British sailors clashed in the streets of New York. "It is said to have arisen from several insults given by a number of British to some French sailors who were quietly enjoying themselves in this land of freedom," the *New York Journal*, 21 Aug., reported. "Not willing to brook the gross treatment of having their cockades trampled under the feet of Britains, struck with axes, tongs, &c. three to one, the Frenchmen collected some of their comrades and pursued their antagonists—but they averted their vengeance by secreting themselves. Some of them, however, in the evening, were imprisoned."

[2] William S. Livingston championed the cause of the New York Society of Cartmen, which was organized in March 1792 to resist the policies of Federalist New York mayor Richard Varick. In a move the Republican opposition characterized as a "Reign of Terror," Varick denied cartmen freemanship and announced in 1791 that any who did not support the Federalist Party would be denied city licenses (Graham Russell Hodges, *Slavery, Freedom & Culture among Early American Workers*, Armonk, N.Y., 1998, p. 13–15).

[3] Throughout Aug. 1793, various towns, cities, and organizations met to pass resolutions supporting George Washington's Neutrality Proclamation. The citizens of New York City, on 8 Aug., stated that Washington's pronouncement was "a wise and well-timed measure of his administration, and

merits our warmest approbation." Likewise, on 6 Aug., the New York Chamber of Commerce resolved, "That the Proclamation of the President of the United States, declaring their neutrality towards the powers at war, was in our opinion a measure wisely calculated to promote the interests and preserve the tranquility of our country; and that we conside[r] the same as a new proof of that watchful regard for the honour and prosperity of the nation, which has uniformly distinguished the administration of our first magistrate" (New York *Diary*, 8 Aug.; New York *Daily Advertiser*, 7 Aug.).

⁴ Edmond Genet's letter to Washington of 13 Aug. and Thomas Jefferson's reply of 16 Aug. both appeared in the New York *Diary*, 21 August. Genet was attempting to defend himself against attacks by Rufus King and John Jay claiming that he planned to cir-

cumvent the decisions of the president and "appeal to the people," a statement he had allegedly made in a conversation with Alexander James Dallas. Genet demanded "an explicit declaration" from Washington that "I have never intimated to you an intention of appealing to the people; that it is not true that a difference in political sentiments has ever betrayed me to forget what was due to your character or to the exalted reputation you had acquired by humbling a tyrant against whom you fought in the cause of liberty." Washington forwarded the letter to Jefferson, who replied to Genet that "it is not the established course for the diplomatic characters residing here to have any direct correspondence" with the president. Jefferson also noted that Washington "declines interfering in the case" (Jefferson, *Papers*, 26:676–678, 684).

Thomas Boylston Adams to John Adams

My dear Sir   Woodbury Oct^r: 9th: 1793—

After repeated, tho' unsuccessful attempts to procure the letters, which I was informed by my Mothers letter, must be in the Post Office at Philad^a: this night's Post has brought me *six*: four from Boston and Quincy, & two from my other friends;[1] I feel no little gratitude to my friends in General, & my Parents in particular for the anxious solicitude they have expressed for my wellfare, upon the alarming occasion which now exists in Philadelphia.[2] I have shuddered at the thought, when I reflect on the danger to which I now perceive I was for many days exposed before I left the City; while there, I was insensible to the innumerable instances of mortality, which daily occurred; but since my residence in this place, I have become more acquainted with the calamities of the City, & more regardful of my own safety. Had I received your's & my Mothers letters sooner; or before I left the City, I should probably have made some town in the interior Counties of Pennsylvania the place of my residence; it might have been useful to me in my future pursuits, by giving me an oportunity to form a further acquaintance with the manners of the people, & also of determining upon the place of my future residence. The short notice I had for departure, (being only one day) precluded my making those arrangements which would have been necessary for a journey of any length or distance; & even at the short distance I now am from Philadelphia, I find myself destitute of winter cloaths, pretty short of *cash*, having left the greater part I possessed in the City, and wanting many conveniences, which would make my exile more comfortable. However I, in com[pany] with many of my acquaintance am amply provided with necessaries, & I can submit to any thing when I perceive others more un-provided, & willingly contibute my proportion to render their situation more tolerable. This place tho' a small distance from the City, is by far the least crouded with inhabitants of any in the neighborhood, & from the little communication that exists with the City, I feel myself tolerably secure. My Friend Mr Freeman & myself were the two first strangers that came to this town; while every small village on the other side of the River was filled with deserters; for this reason I thought it more safe to retire to this place.[3] Many have followed us, but they bear no proportion to the towns of Pennsylvania. I could write in this strain till morning, but it would afford you no satisfaction— I will therefore reserve further communications for the next Post,—

Subscribing myself / your Son   Thomas B Adams

PS, I have just heared of the death of your old friend J D Sergeant; he has fallen sacrifice to his public spirit & humane exertions— he was appointed a manager of the Hospital at Bush Hill, & undertook the trust—[4] While we lament the cause, we cannot but admire the principles with which he was actuated.

Oct^r: 15. 93—

The accounts from the City are much the same;

RC (Adams Papers); addressed: "The Vice President of the United States / Quincy / near Boston."; internal address: "The Vice President / of the U. S."; endorsed: "T. Adams / oct. 9. 1793." Some loss of text where the seal was removed.

[1] None of these letters has been found.

[2] Yellow fever appeared in Philadelphia in August and soon spread to become a devastating epidemic that killed an estimated 5,000 in the city before dissipating with the first frost of December. The pestilence was at its height in October and on the date of this letter the daily death toll passed 100 for the first time (J. H. Powell, *Bring Out Your Dead: The Great Plague of Yellow Fever in Philadelphia in 1793*, Phila., 1949, p. 233–234, 281–282).

[3] During the yellow fever epidemic TBA fled across the Delaware River to Woodbury, N.J., ten miles south of Philadelphia. His companion was perhaps Ezekiel Freeman, a clerk in the Philadelphia Auditor's Office (*Philadelphia Directory*, 1793, p. 167, Evans, No. 25585).

[4] Jonathan Dickinson Sergeant (1746–1793), Princeton 1762, a lawyer, met JA while attending the Continental Congress as a New Jersey representative. He moved to Philadelphia in 1776 and served as Pennsylvania's attorney general. He died of yellow fever on 7 Oct. 1793 (*DAB*; Philadelphia *National Gazette*, 9 Oct.). For the use of Bush Hill as a hospital during the epidemic, see Descriptive List of Illustrations, No. 4, above.

Abigail Adams Smith to Hannah Carter Smith

my Dear Madam   New York October 12ᵗʰ 1793

I have executed your commission but not exactly conformable to your request— the muslin like the pattern was all gone there was a peice which I thought would do to match it very well which I purchased and have sent by Mʳ Charles Storer I hope you will not disapprove of my taking it I thought you would not be likely to get any thing so near it in Boston & I wish it may meet your approbation the muslin is rather finer I think

you will I flatter myself feel sollicitous to know our situation respecting the fever now rageing in Philadelphia I am Sorry to inform you that it does not in the least abate in that Place but is said to be more fatall in its consequences— we found our friends here greatly alarmed—and we this day hear that a Number of Persons have by some means got into this City the last night from Philadelphia notwithstanding a guard is kept constantly upon the Shoars by the inhabbitants of the City—and one Person has been this day carried upon Governors Island—ill with the fever—¹ the Philadelphians are much displeased att the arrangements which are made to prevent Persons from thence comeing into this City: and other intermediate Towns— I hope our friends will not think of going on to Philadelphia be so good as to present my Compliments to Mʳ Smith and Cousin Betsy and / beleive me very sincerely your / friend   A Smith—

RC (MHi:Smith-Carter Family Papers); addressed: "Mʳˢ William Smith / Boston"; endorsed: "A. Smith / N Y'k 1793"; notation: "favour'd by / Mʳ Storer."

¹ On 13 Sept., New York appointed a committee to institute measures to keep yellow fever from spreading to the city from Philadelphia. Inspectors and night patrols guarded all landing places and ordered any vessels from Philadelphia into two-week quarantine. Any people showing symptoms were sent to a temporary hospital on Governor's Island. Sporadic attempts at evasion were reported, including one by a ship ordered to quarantine on 17 Sept. that landed Philadelphia travelers in the city at two o'clock the following morning. Newspapers published regular updates on yellow fever cases at the hospital, including a 19 Oct. report that a man recently sent from a quarantined ship was now ill with fever (New York *Daily Advertiser*, 2, 19 Oct.; New York *Diary*, 17 Sept.).

Thomas Boylston Adams to Abigail Adams

My dear Mother   Woodbury 20ᵗʰ Octʳ⁺ 1793—

I am happy in having it in my power to give you more favorable accounts respecting the Fever in Philadᵃ⁺ than I have yet been able—

Not more than three or four persons have died p$^{r:}$ Day for 4 or 5 days past, at the Hospital and there is a prospect of safety in returning to the City in the course of a Fortnight. Indeed many Families have allready returned, but those who could stay away with any convenience have declined. The disorder is found to submit to the cold weather; & the Phisicians entertain great hopes that the next month will dispel all infection. The City has suffered an immense loss of property, independent of many valuable lives, & 'tis apprehended that there will be many failures among the Merchants, who appear to have suffered most in point of interest of any Class of People. In addition to the general calamity which affects us more nearly, there has been a report that the City of Charleston SC, has partly been destroyed by an Earthquake; but we are not as yet certain as to the truth of it. I have enjoyed my own health tolerably, during the Fall, tho' in a Country much subjected to Agues & Intermittants a circumstance I did not know when I first came here. As the Season is past for those disorders, I am not afraid of alarming you by mentioning it. I am at a loss to know where Congress will assemble this Winter; even should the Fever subside in a short time, the Country has been so generally alarmed that many will be fearful of going to Philad$^{a:}$ & I am uncertain whether the President has the power of assembling Congress in any other place.

I have scarcely read a Newspaper since I left the City, & am therefore ignorant as to the State of Public affairs at present ether in Europe or America; I don't know that I ever experienced the value of public prints, by the want of them before now. Hereafter I shall always be opposed to the tax upon Newspapers, because it may have a tendency to prevent their general circulation. The minds of the People have been so much agitated by the disease in Philad$^{a:}$ that no one gives the least attention to politic's or government. There has lately been an Election in Pennsylvania for Governor, & it was thought Mifflin would be out-run by Muhlenberg; but I am told he has three votes in his favor to one against him in all parts of the State.[1] At last I find that your Governor is not Immortal; what a pity! That Self-opininated Omnipotence, should finally expire like common Mortals. The last Office your people can pay to his Memory, is that of ranking him among the Cannonized Saints of Antiquity; and I expect the Almanacks of the next year will run under the date of Anno Domini 1794 & "Mortis Sancti Johannes Hancock—Primus," For the year of our Lord one Thousand seven hundred & ninety Four, & of the death of the Sanctifyed John Hancock, the

First. I suppose however he is to be succeeded by somebody, & I wish to hear who is talked of.[2]

Present my best love to my Father & the Family / and believe me, / your Son   Thomas B Adams

RC (Adams Papers); addressed: "M^rs: Abigail Adams / Quincy / near / Boston"; internal address: "M^rs: A Adams / Quincy."

[1] In the final tally, Thomas Mifflin defeated Frederick Augustus Muhlenberg for governor by a vote of 19,590 to 10,700 (Philadelphia *American Daily Advertiser*, 12 Dec.).

[2] John Hancock died at the age of 57 on 8 October. On 14 Oct., the city of Boston marked his passing: "At sunrise the bells in all the publick edifices in his town, opened the scene, by tolling, without cessation, an hour; and the flags in town, at the Castle, and on the masts of the shipping in the harbour, were half hoisted. At one o'clock, all the stores and shops were shut, and numer-ous citizens, in their individual capacities, paid various marks of unfeigned respect to the deceased." JA rode in the procession, along with acting governor Samuel Adams and other political, judicial, military, and religious leaders; one observer estimated that 20,000 people participated all together. Samuel Adams was subsequently elected governor in his own right in 1794 (Herbert S. Allan, *John Hancock: Patriot in Purple*, N.Y., 1953, p. 358–360; Boston *Independent Chronicle*, 17 Oct.; *DAB*).

Thomas Boylston Adams to Abigail Adams

My dear Mother   Woodbury 3^d: Nov^r: 1793—

Since my Brother informed me of the miscarriage of some of my letters, I am determined to suffer no Post to pass without writing to some of the Family. The Fever in Philadelphia is a never failing source of subject-matter, when every other is exhausted, but it gives me real joy that I have it in my power to assure you from the best Authority, that no danger is to be apprehended from returning to the City in its present state; the only circumstance to be feared is, that people will croud in too fast, without taking those necessary precautions which are recommended after they return; airing the Houses thoroughly & white washing the Walls &c^a:— In order to cause you no uneasiness on my account, I have resolved not to go into the City for 10 days to come, & even when that time is elapsed, my return will depend altogether on the fullest conviction that the disease is entirely subdued.

It will hardly be prudent for Congress to meet in Philad^a: this Season, tho' I confess I know not where, or in whom the power resides of convening them in any other place. They cannot be accomodated in any of the neighboring towns, and I see no more safe method than that the President should prorogue their meeting to a later period. It may be necessary however that Congress should meet at this Period more particularly to correct the Insolence of that French Jacobin of a Minister, who if suffered to proceed will soon dictate law to the United States. I have not seen a Newspaper for a Month past, till yesterday, when I had the perusal of one belonging to a traveler, which contained Genet's letter to M^r. Jefferson; of all barefaced insults from a public Minister, I think this newfangled Republican's the most brazen, how it will be received I know not, but how the Author of it ought to be treated is more easy to conceive.[1] I am sorry our Juries are so much warped to the side of French madness, but I am well convinced they will not suffer an insult to be given to their chief Magistrate, however their conduct may have given birth to it.

I hope the next letters from me will be dated at Philad^a:, you will know however in season from / your affectionate & dutiful / Son

Thomas B Adams

RC (Adams Papers); internal address: "M^rs: A Adams."

[1] On 27 Oct., Edmond Genet wrote to Thomas Jefferson complaining strenuously about the dismissal of Antoine Charbonnet Duplaine (d. 1800) as French vice consul at Boston. A few weeks earlier, on 3 Oct., Jefferson had written to Duplaine revoking his exequatur in response to Duplaine's decision to seize forcibly a prize originally captured by the French privateer *Roland* but in possession of Massachusetts' deputy federal marshal. Genet's letter, which appeared in the New York *Columbian Gazetteer*, 31 Oct., among other newspapers, charged that "the constitution of the United States has not given the President the right which he now appears desirous to exercise. . . . I demand of you, sir, to ask the President of the United States to procure an examination, by the legislature representing the sovereign people of Massachusetts, of the conduct of Citizen Duplaine." Samuel Adams, acting governor of Massachusetts, declined to take any action on the matter (Jefferson, *Papers*, 26:797; 27:184–185, 272–274).

Thomas Boylston Adams to Abigail Adams

My dear Mother   Woodbury Nov: 17th: 93

Your favor of the 28th: Oct^r: has been received, & as I omited writing by the last Post, I will defer it no longer, lest, your fears should again be excited on my account.[1] If I felt the same degree of alarm that appears to have taken hold of the People at a distance from Philadelphia, the proposal you were kind enough to make me of passing the Winter with you would probably be accepted, but from a full conviction that I can reside in Pennsylvania with perfect security, I think it most prudent to decline the invitation. If it should be unsafe to remain in Philadelphia, I can take up my residence in some of the interior Towns, where I shall have an opportunity of attending the County Courts, & forming an acquaintance which may be useful to me hereafter. But the City itself is at present perfectly free from the contagion, & I see no reason to apprehend a fresh eruption of the disease—besides the old saying of "Nothing venture, nothing have" is so deeply impressed upon my mind at present, that I would not hesitate to run some risque if there were a prospect of introducing myself into professional business by it. So far as my observations of life extend, I am convinced that there never was a Man of Eminence in the world, that was not indebted in some degree, for his fame to what is commonly termed fortune or accident. This is perhaps more frequently the case with Military than litterary characters, in one respect, viz. their continual exposure to danger & death. Their reputation is well earned no doubt, & is rather extorted from mankind as a just debt, than confered gratuitously. But I will not at this time descant upon a subject which can bear very little analogy to that which introduced it. All I wish to enforce by it is, that I could justify to my own mind, a remote hazard of my life, provided the occasion was sufficiently important to myself or others, to warrant the trial. I have been nearly Ten Weeks out of the City, and have met with some interruption in my studdies, but I shall make application for admission to the Bar soon after my return to the City. Mr Ingersoll returned last week, and expects me to attend the Office to assist him 'till my admission, & as Dr Rush assured me I might return with perfect security, I shall not disappoint my Master. There is a certainty that much law business must be done this Winter and I dont see why I should be excluded from a share of the Loaves & Fishes, tho' it may be a very small proportion.

Business of every kind is lively in Philadelphia, & most of the Citizens have returned. The Air which when I left it was extremely offensive in every part of the City, is now perfectly pure. We have lately had several heavy rains & some snow, & there is no doubt but we shall have a severe winter. The price of wood is high at present, but this is owing to the want of intercourse not to the scarcity, for there are thousand of Cords now lying on the Banks of the Creeks in this County, ready for transportation.

I have heared but once from my Sister since [her] return to New York—[2] She wrote me by a Lady [who] lives in this town & was on a visit to NewYork but unfortunately the Trunk which contain[ed] my letter's was left on the Road & has not yet been forwarded.

Presenting my best love to all the Family / I remain / your Son

Thomas B Adams

PS, Please to send my Boots round by Water, as I am in great want of them. The Schooner Neptune, Captn: Cheesman, is in the employ of JD Blanchard at Philad^a and will sa[il from] Boston in a week or two. M^r [Bris]ler may hear of her by applying at No 10. L Wharf & may send my Boots round by her[3] your next letters may be directed to me at Philad^a:

RC (Adams Papers); addressed: "M^rs: Abigail Adams / Quincy / near Boston"; internal address: "M^rs: Abigail Adams"; endorsed: "Thomas Letter / Nov^br 10. / 1793." Some loss of text where the seal was removed.

[1] Not found.
[2] Not found.
[3] The middle two sentences of the postscript were written sideways along the margin of the page and marked for insertion at this point.

John Quincy Adams to Thomas Boylston Adams

My dear Brother   Boston Nov^r: 20. 1793.

Your father will be the bearer of this Letter, and probably will find you at Philadelphia, which our late accounts represent as being totally free from the pestilence, which raged with so much violence for two or three months.— Remember however and be cautious— In the midst of the general calamity, for which your friends participate in the general affliction, they recollect with pleasure, proportioned to the extreme anxiety they felt for you, that you were spared, and they are therefore earnest in their recommendations, that you would not expose yourself by any particular omission of precautions, when the danger is principally past.

I apprehend from the tenor of your last Letter to me, that one Letter which I wrote you, had not yet reached you. It was dated if I mistake not the 15th: of September;[1] and some part of the contents, were such as I should be very sorry to have fall into any other hands. If you have the Letter now, or should receive it hereafter, I wish you to give me notice of it, for my own satisfaction: but if you have it not yet, do not perplex yourself with conjectures upon the subject, as possibly you might without this caution, from the manner in which I now speak: if this appears mysterious to you, upon explanation, you would discover that like most other mysteries, it would turn out to be something very simple.

The approaching Session of Congress is like to be somewhat tempestuous; though I really think, the extravagance of the french fire-brand's absurdities, will operate as an antidote against them.[2]

His measures appear to be as weak, as his designs are destructive: but the example which he sets to future European agents, is so pernicious, it may be so easily imitated by the representatives of any foreign power; that I am alarmed at the tameness with which it is received by this people.— In this part of the Country indeed there is scarcely any body so thoroughly depraved in his politics as not to disapprove of his madness, but if the President had treated him as he did Duplaine, he would scarcely then have been punished in a degree equal to his deserts.

I hope you will not be much longer delayed in the attainment of your legal degrees, and I dare say the time you have past in your sequestration has not been lost. I most earnestly wish that your success, in your profession may be greater, and especially more rapid than mine has hitherto been. You have not quite so many disadvantages to encounter as have fallen to my lot— Three long long years of painful suspense and tedious expectation and at the close of them suspense and expectation still, is not an encouraging prospect.— Yet it has been and still is mine. I have however long since got above or below repining at it, and in spite of all my evils can fatten upon it, like one of the genuine pigs from the sty of Epicurus.[3]

Whereupon I conclude myself your brother   J. Q. Adams.

RC (Adams Papers); addressed: "Mr Thomas B. Adams. / Philadelphia."; endorsed: "J Q Adams. / Novr. 20th: 93—"

[1] Neither of these letters has been found.

[2] The third Congress began its first session on 2 Dec. and concluded on 9 June 1794 (*Biog. Dir. Cong.*).

[3] "Amid hopes and cares, amid fears and passions, believe that every day that has dawned is your last. Welcome will come to you another hour unhoped for. As for me, when you want a laugh, you will find me in fine fettle, fat and sleek, a hog from Epicurus's herd" (Horace, *Epistles*, Book I, epistle iv, lines 12–16).

John Adams to Abigail Adams

My dearest Friend   Hartford Nov. 24. 1793

We have had an agreable Journey to this Town, have been to Meeting all Day and heard two excellent Discourses from Mr Strong:[1] We are to drink Tea at Col Wadsworths. Trumbul and his Lady are at New Haven.[2] At four or five O Clock in the Morning We proceed. The Weather to day is Soft and fine, tho We had last night a violent Wind & Rain. Accounts from Philadelphia are unanimous in favour of the Healthiness of the City: Yet I think with Col Wadsworth that a Pause at Trenton to consider and inquire will not be much amiss.

The Virginia Assembly have taken up the Presidents Proclamation and Seventy Odd against forty Odd, voted it right.[3] But When the Minority found themselves cast they prevailed with the Majority to vote that they had nothing to do with it. Enough however was done to convince Us that We shall not be, wholly under the Directions of a foreign Minister.

Thatcher has taken for his Vade mecum Fontenelles History of oracles. I mentioned to him Farmer upon Devils: a Title that charmed him so much that he is determined to send for Farmers Works.[4]

M^r storer requests that you would let his Family know We are thus far safe. Brisler does the same. I am, my dearest / yours forever

J. A

RC (Adams Papers); addressed: "Mrs Adams / Quincy / near Boston"; internal address: "Mrs A."; endorsed: "nov^br 24. / 1793."; notation: "Free" and "Free / John Adams."

[1] Rev. Nathan Strong (1748–1816), Yale 1769, had served as minister of the First Church of Hartford, Conn., since 1774 (*Colonial Collegians*).

[2] Poet and attorney John Trumbull and his wife, Sarah Hubbard Trumbull, who had lived in Hartford since 1781. Trumbull had attended Yale and practiced law in New Haven early in his career (*DAB*).

[3] By a vote of 77 to 43, the Va. House of Delegates passed a resolution on 1 Nov. 1793 declaring George Washington's Neutrality Proclamation "a politic and constitutional measure, wisely adopted at a critical junc-

ture, and happily calculated to preserve to this country the inestimable blessings of peace" (Philadelphia *Federal Gazette*, 12 Nov.).

[4] Peter Thacher's "vade mecum," or guidebook, was Bernard Le Bovier Fontenelle's *History of Oracles, and the Cheats of the Pagan Priests*, transl. Aphra Behn, London, 1688. Hugh Farmer (1714–1787), a noted dissenting minister and theologian, had published a number of tracts, including *An Essay on the Demoniacs of the New Testament*, London, 1775 (*DNB*).

Thomas Boylston Adams to Abigail Adams

My dear Mother   Philadelphia 24 Nov^r: 1793—

I have now been in the City since the 19th: and am happily able to give you the fullest assurance of our freedom from danger, on account of the malignant Fever. The Citizens have most of them returned, & universally in good health, business has revived, & is fast returning into its former train; from all present appearances, nobody would think that any Calamity had befallen us. It is surprising how soon a person wears off those impressions of terror, which tho' all alive when he first enters the City, are forgotten in the course of a few hours. The idea of danger is dissipated in a moment when we perceive thousands walking in perfect security about their customary business, & no ill consequences ensuing from it. Many of the

Inhabitants are in mourning, which still reminds us of the occasion, but a short time will render it familiar. No person that has not been exiled from their usual residence upon such an occasion can realize the joy that is universally felt at meeting a former friend or acquaintance— The congratulations for each others wellfare are as mutual as they appear to be sincere. I find a small number of my former acquaintance who have participated in the Calamity, & a few who were victims to the disease, but by far the greater proportion have escaped. My present Landlord lost a Son, who was a pupil of Dr Rush, & the most promising young Physician of any that have died.[1] He was seized with a delirium in the first Stage of his disorder and refused all medicine that was offered him. Indeed this was the case with many, & it allways proved fatal in such instances. Among those who have been swept away, I believe Mr Powell & Mr Sergeant are the only two with whom you were acquainted.[2] The disease proved most fatal to tradesmen & Mechanics, whose circumstances would not admit of their leaving town;[3] but no class of Citizens have been totally exempted. The Disease however is now dissipated, & I apprehend no danger can exist during this Season. I doubted before I came to town whether Congress would be safe in assembling here this Winter, & I still believe it will be a difficult matter to persuade them that no danger remains, but if they will come & judge for themselves only by two days residence they must be convinced that their fears are groundless.

My Examination for the Bar comes on next week; it is time I was, if I am not prepared to receive it. It is just three years since I entered Mr Ingersoll's Office, & tho' I expect no business unless by accident, yet I choose to take my station at the Bar as an Att^y. provided my Examinors will give me a passport. If you wish any thing sent round from here, there will be an opportunity before the Winter sets in. I am in great want of my Boots, & I hope you will not forget the Books also that I packed up to be sent me.

Remember me Affectionatly & believe me your son

Thos: B Adams

RC (Adams Papers).

[1] John Stall Jr., a medical student of Benjamin Rush, died on 23 September. Five months later Rush sent Stall's mother a silver cup in his memory (Rush, *Letters*, 2:674–677, 688–689, 747).

[2] Samuel Powel (or Powell) (1739–1793) had been the mayor of Philadephia and served as speaker of the Pennsylvania senate from 1792 to 1793. He died on 29 Sept. (Washington, *Papers, Presidential Series*, 1:125, 10:444; Philadelphia *National Gazette*, 9 Oct.).

[3] Although ten doctors and ten ministers were included on a list of yellow fever vic-

tims compiled by Philadelphia bookseller Mathew Carey, the majority of the dead were tradesmen, laborers, and servants. "It has been dreadfully destructive among the poor," Carey wrote. "It is very probable, that at least seven eighths of the number of the dead, were of that class" (Mathew Carey, *A Short Account of the Malignant Fever Lately Prevalent in Philadelphia*, 4th rev. edn., Phila., 1794, p. 60–61, Evans, No. 26736).

Hannah Quincy Lincoln Storer to Abigail Adams

Boston Nov[r] 27 —93

Had you My respected friend join'd the Small, tho' social Circle the last Thursday, it would have been an addition to our pleasure, but by your first friend I was Soon prevented Saying Much upon the Subject—["]as none he Said ought to be present at the parting of *Hector* and *Andromache* but the Nurse and Child"—[1]

I have his permission to ask your Company for a day but a Night he would not consent to, as being so long in Boston at a time always made you Sick: I added if you'd Come and Stay with Me you Should *eat, drink, and Sleep,* as you pleased— the weather is Now very fine, I should be exceeding glad to See you with Miss Smith any day this week that would Sute you—in that Sociable way that I flatter Myself would be grateful to you / and pleaseing to / Your / Affactionate friend

H Storer

P S My Sister Guild and My Daughter calls upon you in their way to M[rs.] Cranches M[r] Storer desires his Compliments—and joins Me in the above request

RC (Adams Papers).

[1] Homer, *The Iliad*, Book VI, lines 456–647.

Abigail Adams to John Adams

my dearest Friend   Quincy Nov[br] 28 1793

My early rising still continues, and I am writing by candle light. it is a week this day since you left me. I have rejoiced in the fine weather for your Sake. it has sometimes been cold and Blustering, but the Air has been pure and bracing. on saturday Night we had a plentifull Rain Succeeded by a fine day. I presume you reachd N York yesterday. I hope you found all our Friends well tho I have not heard from mrs Smith for a long time. I could wish if you must go to Philadelphia that you could have gone immediatly to your old Lodgings Brisler could make Breakfast & coffe in the afternoon even if you was provided with dinner in some other place. all accounts however agree that the City is clear from infection. I Sincerely hope it is, but I do not know what cause need be given to so many, as must suffer through anxiety and apprehension for their Friends, when Sitting a few weeks out of the city might remove it.

Cousin Lucy cranch came from Town last Evening and brought your Letter dated Hartford I also received one from Thomas of the 17ᵗʰ· I suppose you will find him in the city upon your arrival there. he writes that dr Rush assures him that he may come with safety.

our people here at home have been engaged some days in getting wood—one at the high ways one in getting sea weed. by the way savil continues every day in bringing two & sometimes 3 Load I do not know how much you agreed with him for, so I have not Stopd him, as I knew you was desirious of getting a quantity I expect he will cart till he has a pretty high Bill

last Night accounts were received of a Bloody Battle between General Wayne and the Indians tis said Wayne kept the Feild tho with the loss of 500 m[en] and that the Indians left as many dead upon the Fie[ld] tis a great point gaind to keep the Feild against them I hope they will now be convinced that we have men enough to fight them—[1]

Mrs Brisler was well yesterday she has been here two days, and went home last evening

Let me hear from you every week it will be the only thing to keep me in spirits.

I am glad the virginians had some sense & some cunning as both united produced a proper measure. the Tone in Boston is much changd of mr Consul. he begins to make his Feasts and to coax & whine like a Hyena, as if having made use of big threatning language he had terrified the puny Americans and now was willing to kiss & make Friends—

present me to all those Friends who have Survived the general calimity, and as ever I am / most affectionatly yours   A Adams

RC (Adams Papers); addressed by JQA: "The Vice-President of the United States. / Philadelphia."; endorsed: "Portia / Nov. 28. 1793." Some loss of text where the seal was removed.

[1] On 27 Nov., the Boston *Columbian Centinel* reported 500 U.S. and 600 Miami casualties in a battle in the Northwest Territory. The article attributed Gen. Anthony Wayne's victory to the assistance of Kentucky volunteers under Gen. Charles Scott who arrived in the midst of the fighting. The report was apparently a much-exaggerated account of a 17 Oct. attack by the Miami on a supply train near Fort St. Clair in which fifteen soldiers were killed and seventy horses lost. Scott and his men arrived immediately after the skirmish and were assigned to guard future convoys. In his official dispatch, Wayne

voiced concern that news of the conflict would "probably be exaggerated into something serious by the tongue of fame, before this reaches you" (*Amer. State Papers: Indian Affairs*, 1:361).

John Adams to Abigail Adams

Col Smiths Cottage,[1] near New York

My Dearest Friend   Nov. 28 1793

I arrived here Yesterday, and had the Pleasure to dine with our Children and The Baron: All are very well and send their Duty. Charles is well, fat and handsome, and persists in the Line of Conduct which We so much approved. His Business increases & he will do well.

Accounts from Philadelphia continue to be favourable. M[r] Otis has written for his Family to come on, as M[rs] Smith informs me. if so I shall be at no loss.

M[r] Genet has made a curious Attack upon M[r] Jay and M[r] King which you will see in the Papers.[2] My Duty to Mother, Love to Brothers Sisters Cousins, particularly Louisa. I go on towards Philadelphia to day. yours   J. A.

RC (Adams Papers); internal address: "M[rs] A."

[1] WSS and AA2 resided at 18 Cortlandt Street in New York (*New-York Directory*, 1794, Evans, No. 26919).

[2] On 14 Nov., Edmond Genet wrote to both Thomas Jefferson and Attorney General Edmund Randolph claiming that John Jay and Rufus King had "published in the newspapers a libel against me" in August when they reported that Genet intended to "appeal to the People" over the decisions of the president. See CA to JA, 25 Aug., note 4, above. Genet's letters were published in various newspapers, including the New York *Diary*, 22 November. They first appeared in Boston in the *Independent Chronicle*, 2 Dec. (Jefferson, *Papers*, 27:367–368).

John Adams to Abigail Adams

My dearest Friend   Philadelphia Dec[r.] 1. 1793

We may ever remember[1] The Thirtieth of November because it was the Day on which We were absolved from Infamy; in 1782 and because it was the Day on which I entered this City in 1793.[2] Finding by all accounts that the Pestilence was no more to be heard of, and that M[r] Otis had returned to his House, I drove directly to Market Street and took Poss[n.] of my old Chamber and bed. The principal Families have returned, the President is here, Several Members of Congress are arrived and Business is going on with some Spirit. The greatest Mortality appears to have been in bad Houses and among loose Women and their gallants among the Sailors and low foreigners. Some Persons of Note have fallen. Dr Hutchinson is thought to have been the Victim of his own french Zeal, by admitting infected Persons and goods from French Vessells from the French West India Islands.[3] if, however the Contagion was imported the State of the air and of the Blood, which was prepared to catch like tinder was not imported.

Mr Otis has written for his Family. Our son Thomas has been once in Town but has returned to Woodbury.

Mr Anthony came in last Evening and gave me an account of his Enquiries, the Result of all is that the Destroying Angel has put up his sword, and Said it is enough.—[4] It will be enough I hope to convince Philadelphia that all has not been well. Moral and religious Reflections I shall leave to their own Thoughts: but The Cleanness of the Streets I shall preach in Season & out of Season.

My Duty and Love where due / yours forever   J. A.

RC (Adams Papers); addressed: "Mrs Adams / Quincy / near / Boston"; endorsed: "Dec^br 1 1793"; notation: "Free / John Adams."

[1] JA interlined the previous four words above the following line.

[2] The Preliminary Peace Treaty between Britain and the United States was signed on 30 Nov. 1782; see JA, *Papers*, 14:103–108.

[3] James Hutchinson died on 5 Sept. 1793

from yellow fever, which he contracted while nursing others during the outbreak (*DAB*).

[4] Probably Joseph Anthony (d. 1798), a prominent Philadelphia merchant (*Philadelphia Gazette*, 29 Sept. 1798).

John Adams to Abigail Adams

My dearest Friend   Philadelphia Decr 5. 1793

I wrote you from Hartford, New York and once from Philadelphia: but have not yet had the Pleasure of a Letter from you Since I left home.

The Night before last We had a deep Snow, which will probably extinguish all remaining apprehensions of Infection. We hear of no Sickness and all Seem at their Ease and without fear.

The Presidents Speach will Shew you an Abundance of Serious Business which We have before Us: Mr Jefferson called on me last night and informed me, that to day We should have the whole Budget of Foreign Affairs British as well as French. He Seems as little Satisfied with the Conduct of the French Minister as any one.[1]

Thomas Spent the last Evening with me. He has had an opportunity of Seeing the Courts, Judges Lawyers &c of New Jersey, in the Course of the last fall, and has I hope employed his time to Advantage. This Day he is to be examined and this Week Sworn in. May a

Blessing Attend him. Although I have attended and shall attend my Duty punctually in Senate, I shall not run about upon Visits without caution: yet I believe there is little or no danger.

The Viscount Noailles called on me, and I enquired after all his Connections in a Family which I knew to be once in great Power Wealth and Splendor.[2] He Seems to despair of Liberty in France and has lost apparently all hopes of ever living in France. He was very critical in his Inquiries concerning the Letters which were printed as mine in England. I told him candidly that I did not write them and as frankly in confidence who did. He says they made a great Impression upon the People of England. That he heard M[r] Windham & M[r] Fox Speak of them as the best Thing that had been written, and as one of the best Pieces both of Reasoning and Style they had ever read.[3] The Marquis he says is living, but injured in his health. Your old Friend the Marchioness still lives in France in obscurity in the Country. He thinks that a Constitution like that of England would not last three days in France, and that Monarchy will not be restored in a dozen Years if ever.—

The Partitioning and arbitrary Spirit of the combined Powers will contribute more than any Thing towards Uniting the French under their old Government. Frenchmen cannot bear the Partition of their Country: and rather than see it divided among their neighbours they will unite in something or other.

It will require all the address, all the Temper, and all the Firmness of Congress and the States, to keep this People out of the War: or rather to avoid a Declaration of War against Us, from some mischievous Power or other. It is but little that I can do, either by the Functions which the Constitution has entrusted to me, or by my personal Influence. But that little shall be industriously employed untill it is put beyond a doubt that it will be fruitless, and then I shall be as ready to meet unavoidable Calamities as any other Citizen.

Adieu

RC (Adams Papers); addressed: "M[rs] Adams / Quincy / near / Boston"; endorsed: "Dec[br] 5 1793."; notation: "Free / John Adams."

[1] In his annual address to Congress, delivered on 3 Dec., George Washington called for legislative action to preserve peace with the warring nations of Europe, to secure peace with the hostile Indians of the Ohio Country, and to solidify peace with the disaffected Creeks and Cherokees. Describing American relations with Europe as "extremely interesting," Washington promised to report on them in detail "in a subsequent communication." Within two weeks, he sent to Congress three separate messages on foreign affairs—one dedicated to France and Britain, another to Spain, and a third to Mo-

rocco and Algiers—each conveying extensive documentation of the administration's diplomatic negotiations.

The first of these messages, delivered on 5 Dec. and dealing with France and Britain, announced that Edmond Genet's actions "have breathed nothing of the friendly spirit of the nation which sent him" and that Washington had requested Genet's recall. At the same time, Washington submitted to Congress the correspondence that led up to this decision, including Thomas Jefferson's letter to Gouverneur Morris, [23] Aug., asking Morris to make the formal request to the French government. By October, the French government—now dominated by the Jacobins—had responded, agreeing to the recall, although news of that did not reach Phila-

delphia until early 1794 (*Annals of Congress*, 3d Cong., 1st sess., p. 10–13, 14–16; *Amer. State Papers: Foreign Relations*, 1:141–300; Jefferson, *Papers*, 26:685–692).

[2] Several members of the Vicomte de Noailles' extended family would be executed by guillotine in June and July, including his father, Philippe de Noailles; his wife, Anne de Noailles; and his mother-in-law, Henriette Anne Louise de Noailles (JA, *D&A*, 4:84–85).

[3] William Windham (1750–1810), member of Parliament for Norwich, was a political ally of Edmund Burke and a strong opponent of the French Revolution (*DNB*). For JQA's Publicola writings, see CA to JA, 29 May 1793, note 2, above.

Charles Adams to John Adams

My dear Father New York Dec[r] 6 1793.

The very interesting situation of our Country at present cannot fail to call forth the serious reflections of those who are anxious for its wellfare What we are destined to can only with certainty be divulged by the operation of time. Individuals reason from the experience of past ages and often draw different conclusions from the same premises. We are as yet but a young Country. Yet we have gone through some ordeals to gain experience, but we must go through many more before a Government can be established in this Country sufficiently energetic to act with a proper dignity both towards foreigners and our own citizens. We boast of freedom of security to our persons property and reputation and yet we do not find that the laws are always executed in such a manner as to secure what we boast of or to punish invaders upon those rights Through the negligence timidity or design of men who ought to exert themselves to give just and good laws their proper operation we are daily exposed to gross invasions. Through the unwillingness of men of reputation to come forward to State truths to the people we are often exposed to the rash proceedings of an ignorant Mob. Many instances of these serious facts may be exhibited. This City has from time to time subjected to the lawless depredations of the mob, and The instigators have as often been overlooked and have passed without the punishments due to their crimes. The reasons assigned for this lenity are that it is better to let such conduct pass unnoticed than to irritate the minds of people by severe punishment But surely exam-

ples ought to be made or the evil will increase with double rapidity.
We have of late had an alarming instance fury of a mob in this City
A young man was indicted at the last Court of Oyer and Terminer
for a rape Upon the trial no evidence was given to convict him of
the crime and the jury gave a verdict Not guilty. During the course
of this trial The people in the Galleries to applaud or hiss as it
suited their fancy The Counsel for the Prisoner were insulted in the
most gross manner in open Court Yet the judges either did not dare
or neglected to punish this contempt. In the evening a mob collected and very composedly pulled down a half dozen houses The
Mayor to whom much praise is due as an active and determined
Magistrate did what was in his power to quell the riot but he was
hindered in the execution of his office and obtained nothing but
bruises and kicks The next day threats were heard in the City
against the Counsel for the prisoner They were told their houses
would be pulled about their ears One man said he would show them
how those things were done in France The Governor promised that
the Militia should be called out to protect them. Evening came on
and no signs of Militia were seen and they were obliged to quit their
houses for safety. It is said the Governor never ordered them out If
he did they disobeyed his orders This is not probable as by late appointments he has the Militia officers at his beck all the principal
officers being chosen from his *band*. The mob contented themselves
with tearing down six or seven more houses that evening and then
disbanded in a very orderly manner.[1] Luckily the freak of pulling
down half the City did not take them or I see no impediment to the
execution. Notwithstanding all this no prosecutions no indictments
no commitments have been heard of. It is said These were houses
of ill fame, but they were no less private property and as such
should be protected. If once the principle is admitted that the mob
according to their whims have a right to destroy and execute their
vengeance; whose person or property is safe? But no pains are taken
to oppose such conduct and when the Citizens see or hear of such
fracâ's they stare and wonder what has got into the people. Where
are we to look for remedies for these outrages if men who have it in
their power to prevent them sit still and wink at them? We are in
danger of having many evil examples set us by the number of unprincipled foreigners who are daily pouring in upon us and they will
no doubt be made tools to serve party purposes If then such violence is not nipped in the bud we have but a melancholy prospect
before us—

By The last Federal Militia Law—the appointment of Officers is left to the different States.[2] I have doubts respecting the policy of this measure. If it is true as has been suggested That the office of Governor of a State from its nature leads the persons holding such office to an opposition of the Federal Government is it not placing a very dangerous weapon in the hands of those who unless they are more disinterested than mankind in general will not act with energy in support of the Federal cause? I do not know whether these ideas are perfectly just, they are such as have occured to me and if I am wrong I wish to be corrected.

Adieu my dear Sir / Beleive me your affectionate son

Charles Adams

RC (Adams Papers); endorsed: "C. Adams. Dec. 6 / ans[d] 8. 1793."

[1] On 8 Oct., Henry Bedlow, a notorious gallant, was tried for the rape of Lanah Sawyer, a seventeen-year-old seamstress, before the Court of Oyer and Terminer and Gaol Delivery of the City and County of New York. New York attorney general Nathaniel Lawrence presented the case for the prosecution but left the argument of it to his more junior colleagues Josiah Ogden Hoffman and James Kent. Counsel for the defense included William A. Thompson, James M. Hughes, Brockholst Livingston, Robert Troup, John Cozine, and Richard Harison.

To save their client from conviction and execution—rape then was a capital crime in New York—Bedlow's attorneys worked hard to discredit his accuser. They savaged Sawyer's character, conduct, and motives, denigrating her testimony as self-serving invention. At the same time, they struggled to establish the credibility of the witnesses who appeared on their client's behalf, in particular Mary Cary, the brothel keeper in whose house the encounter between Bedlow and Sawyer had occurred. Whitewashing Cary's obvious moral shortcomings, the lawyers for the defense painted her testimony as disinterested truth. In the end, their strategy proved successful. After a trial lasting fifteen hours, the jury deliberated for just fifteen minutes before returning a verdict of not guilty.

Six days later, however, popular anger over the trial incited a mob to demolish Cary's house and destroy all of its furnishings. Several other brothels suffered the same treatment that night and the next. By the third night Mayor Richard Varick and the city magistrates had restored order, apparently without assistance from Gov. George Clinton (William Wyche, *Report of the Trial of Henry Bedlow*, N.Y., 1793, Evans, No. 26513; Franklin B. Hough, *The New-York Civil List*, Albany, 1858, p. 30, 36, 428; *New-York Directory*, 1792, Evans, No. 24281; New York *Diary*, 7 Nov. 1793; Paul A. Gilje, *The Road to Mobocracy: Popular Disorder in New York City, 1763–1834*, Chapel Hill, N.C., 1987, p. 87–88).

[2] Congress intended the Uniform Militia Act, passed on 8 May 1792, to strengthen national defense through the establishment of a militia system consistent throughout the states. The act's failure to promote uniformity or improve preparedness led George Washington to call for new legislation in the annual address that he delivered to Congress on 3 Dec. 1793 (*U.S. Statutes at Large*, 2d Cong., 1st sess., p. 271–274; C. Edward Skeen, *Citizen Soldiers in the War of 1812*, Lexington, Ky., 1999, p. 6–8).

Thomas Boylston Adams to Abigail Adams

My dear Mother   Philadelphia 9th: Dec[r:] 1793—

I believe you are indebted to me for a letter or two, but as your late loss has been my gain, it is more incumbent on me to attempt to compensate in some measure by my communications the absence of my Father.

You have doubtless provided yourself with a comfortable supply of Winters Stores for a severe campaign, as there is reason to anticipate a long one— The Winter has but just commenced with us, but we hope its continuance will not be short, for much of our security against a return of the late disorder is thought to depend on this Season. Congress have commenced their Career with the interesting transactions of the Executive department during their recess— The budget was opened last week and has already occupied three or four days in the mere reading. They are to be published shortly, when you will have an opportunity to gratify your curiosity, which I can easily immagine is excited on the occasion.[1] Altho' the making public the heretofore private negociations of the Executive may wear the appearance of novelty, & excite alarm in those who are acquainted with former usage, as establishing a dangerous precedent, yet I trust the fairness, candor and liberality of our Government will be no more liable to imputations unfavorable for its reputation, than its character for firmness and decission can be impeached by Foreigners.

There seems to be a wish in the Executive that the letters which have passed between him & Foreign Ministers should meet the public eye at this time, and I believe it a very happy circumstance that the conduct of the Minister of France has called them forth. There are many people who think we shall be under the necessity of arming our Merchantmen, so as to protect our trade & make reprisal whenever it appears that our Vessels have been unjustly captured or detained. The Merchants complain of the defenceless state of our Commerce, of the imposibility of trading to advantage, or with so much Safety as if we were actually engaged in War. Congress will probably take these things into consideration in the course of the present Session, & I hope place us in a mo[re] respectable situation as to the means of defence in case of an actual rupture, than at present we are—

My Examination for the Bar is passed, and the Oath of Office administered to me—[2] I am at liberty therefore to undertake the cause of the oppressed, & attempt to render justice to him that is wronged— I anticipate very little of this kind of business this winter—if it comes it will be more acceptable.

My Father was well when I saw him last; he had rec[d:] no letter from you since his arrival & would have been anxious if my Brother

JQA had not quieted his apprehensions by a few lines—[3] Believe me your son

Thomas B Adams

RC (Adams Papers). Some loss of text where the seal was removed.

[1] *A Message of the President of the United States to Congress Relative to France and Great-Britain. Delivered December 5, 1793,* Phila., 1793, Evans, No. 26334. Published by order of the House of Representatives, this pamphlet was initially released in two parts. The first part, which contained George Washington's message along with the papers that he had forwarded regarding relations with France, appeared by 5 Jan. 1794; the second part, which contained the papers relative to Britain as well as the original French versions of papers presented earlier in translation, appeared on 22 Jan. (JA to CA, 5 Jan., Adams Papers; Philadelphia *American Daily Advertiser,* 23 Jan.).

[2] TBA was admitted to the Philadelphia bar on 7 Dec. 1793 (John Hill Martin, *Martin's Bench and Bar of Philadelphia,* Phila., 1883, p. 243).

[3] JQA's letter to JA has not been found, but on 10 Dec., JA acknowledged a letter from JQA of 28 Nov., commenting that "considering your Mothers usual Goodness in writing to me in my too frequent Absences, I have been under some Anxiety for her health, because I have not received any News from her since I left her" (Adams Papers).

John Adams to Abigail Adams

My dearest Friend   Philadelphia Dec[r] 12. 1793

This Day having been devoted to Thanksgiving by the Governor of Pensilvania, Congress have adjourned to Fryday.[1] We have had a great Snow and afterwards a great Rain but not enough to carry off all the Snow. The Weather therefore is still cool, tho fair and pleasant. All Apprehension of the Fever Seems entirely departed, a Circumstance the more comfortable to me, as, having been among a few of the Earliest who came into Town, if any Thing unfortunate had followed I might have been reproached for Setting a precipitate Example.

our Son Thomas was examined approved and Sworn the last Week; so that We have three Lawyers upon the Theatre of Action. May they be ornaments to their Country and Blessings to the World.

Congress has a great Task and a very unpleasant one before them. With Indians and Algerines for open Ennemies and so many other Nations for suspicious Friends, besides so many appearances of ill Will among our own Citizens, who ever Envies a seat in that Body I believe the Members have no great reason to be delighted with theirs.[2] My own is a situation, of Such compleat Insignificance, that I have Scarcely the Power to do good or Evil: yet it is the Station the most proper for me, as my Eyes and hands and Nerves are almost worn out.

The two Houses have been tolerably unanimous in giving to the Presidents system a kind of rapid approbation: but what will be the Result of the Negotiations with France and England I know not.[3] M[r] Jefferson has regained his Reputation by the Part he has taken, and his Compositions are much applauded by his old Friends and assented to by others. The fresh depredations of the Algerines are so well calculated to prevent Emigration to this Country from England scotland and Ireland, that People are ready enough to impute their Truce with Portugal and Holland to British Interference. our Trade is like to suffer by the Arbitrary Decrees of England Spain and France as well as by the ferocious Pyracy of Affrica.[4]

This Winter will Shew Us the Temper of England as well as France. Americans cannot see with Pleasure the French Islands fall into English hands, nor will even French Emigrants be gratified with the Partition of their Country.[5] But Foresight is impossible in such a Chaos. I am with great Anxiety for / your health, your

J. A

RC (Adams Papers).

[1] On 14 Nov., Pennsylvania governor Thomas Mifflin declared 12 Dec. a day of thanksgiving to mark the end of the Philadelphia yellow fever epidemic. Four days later nineteen city clergymen signed an address encouraging participation in the observance (Philadelphia *Federal Gazette*, 11 Dec.).

[2] The ongoing problem of U.S. relations with Algiers came to the fore again in late 1793 when Portugal—which had customarily protected U.S. ships from Barbary pirates around the Strait of Gibraltar to ensure continuing imports of American corn and flour—signed a peace treaty with Algiers. This new situation left U.S. ships vulnerable to piracy, and the Algerines immediately took advantage, capturing eleven vessels by December and enslaving their crews. Some in the United States also blamed the British for the situation, arguing that the British were allied with the Algerines, had encouraged the peace treaty with Portugal, and had possibly incited the Algerines to make their captures. These events pushed Congress to act on the crisis in early 1794, authorizing a million dollars to purchase peace and ransom captive sailors and additional money to establish a U.S. Navy (Frank Lambert, *The Barbary Wars: American Independence in the Atlantic World*, N.Y., 2005, p. 73–77).

[3] George Washington's Neutrality Proc-

lamation received the endorsement of the House of Representatives on 6 Dec. 1793 and of the Senate on the 9th in their respective replies to his annual address, even though neither body had completed its review of his intervening message respecting relations with France and Britain (*Annals of Congress*, 3d Cong., 1st sess., p. 17–18, 138–139).

[4] After the outbreak of war in Europe in the spring of 1793, Britain and France each maneuvered to starve the other of provisions from the United States by unilaterally decreeing neutral trade with the enemy illegal and then seizing American merchant vessels caught in violation (*Cambridge Modern Hist.*, 7:318–319).

[5] In the spring and summer of 1793, Britain expanded the war with France to the Caribbean. After capturing Tobago in April, British forces invaded St. Domingue, and the colony was divided between the warring armies. The French government of St. Domingue responded by freeing the colony's slaves and inviting them to join the army, a move that eventually turned the conflict in France's favor (Michael Duffy, "The French Revolution and British Attitudes to the West Indian Colonies," in David Barry Gaspar and David Patrick Geggus, eds., *A Turbulent Time: The French Revolution and the Greater Caribbean*, Bloomington, Ind., 1997, p. 83–85).

Abigail Adams to John Adams

my dearest Friend   Quincy dec^br 14. 1793

I hope this days post will bring me a Letter from you at Philadelphia, and that I shall hear you are well and at mr otis's tho obliged as they say to keep Batchelors Hall for a short period. mrs otis I trust will be with you before this Letter. I wrote by her tho I had little to inform you of. your Farm will occupy your mind I know Sometimes and you will wish to know if the ground is broke up which you left unfinish'd. the stones have been removed and one days work after a Rain has been performd. the people were anxious to compleat it the next day tho the ground was stiff, but [in] the attempt they Broke the beam of the plough & were obliged to quit. we have sent it to be repaird & the first opportunity it will be compleated. the weather has been pleasent & the Sea weed is attended to every day when, wood is not. Arnold is very anxious to tarry with me and has offerd to stay at six dollors the winter Months. at present I thought I could do without him but gave him encouragement that I would hire him if snow came so as to get the stones across the pond.[1] what can be done with the set of wretches who have begun their winter depredations upon the cedar pasture, Cut down trees lately as Arnold informs me, Some of those which the fire past over have been seen at wilsons door. Humphries informs me that the lot call'd Ruggles's a bound tree containing 5 foot has been recently cut down & others near it & carried of, by nobody knows whom.[2] Boilstone Adams has had his shop broke open this week 2 sides of soul Leather Boot legs & several calfs skins carried away. they broke the Glass & then unfastned the window in shrt we seem to live amongst a people who have no sense of Right & wrong— Remember me kindly to all inquiring Friends. read columbus—and let me know the opinions of those who do.[3]

Yours most affectionaly   A Adams

mrs Brisler & family are all well

RC (Adams Papers); addressed by JQA: "The Vice-President of the United States / Philadelphia."; endorsed: "Mrs Adams / Decr. 14. ans^d 23^d." Some loss of text where the seal was removed.

[1] Possibly Joseph Neale Arnold (1764–1816), a Quincy neighbor whose wife, Mehitable Adams Arnold, was a daughter of JA's first cousin Ebenezer Adams (Sprague, *Braintree Families*; vol. 6:238).

[2] Probably Levi Humphrey (b. 1767), "a transient man" of Braintree. "Ruggles's" lot was likely the woodlot AA purchased in 1783

that was formerly owned by Samuel Ruggles (b. 1700) of Braintree and Boston (Sprague, *Braintree Families*; vol. 5:285, 288).

³ JQA published in the Boston *Columbian Centinel*, 30 Nov., and 4, 7, 11, 14, 18 Dec. 1793, four essays (over several issues) under the name Columbus in response to the activities, writings, and controversy surrounding Edmond Genet's mission. Columbus describes Genet in the first essay as "the most implacable and dangerous enemy to the peace and happiness of my country," then uses the subsequent three to outline his reasons for this opinion, attacking Genet's attempts to circumvent George Washington's neutrality policy and to draw the United States into the European war.

John Adams to John Quincy Adams

Dear Sir   Philadelphia December 14. 1793

Congress have rec^d from the President all the Negotiations with France and England as well as those with the Indians. On Monday We expect those with Spain and all the Intelligence rec^d respecting the Algerines. The whole forming a System of Information which Shews our dear Country to be in a critical Situation. So critical that the most sanguine are constrained to pauze and consider.

The Truce between the Regency of Algiers and the Court of Portugal will be imputed by a Party to the Influence of England, and No Other Party that I know of can contradict them. The Event has been daily expected, for Years, as it has been known that Portugal has been all along Suing for Peace, without offering Money enough to Satiate the Avidity of the hungry Barbarians. The Disposition to emigration in England Scotland and Ireland will be checked, and our growing Navigation will be impeded so much by these Corsairs, that the British Government will be Suspected to be highly delighted with it.

Congress must take a cool Survey of our Situation and do nothing from Passion.

I have read two Numbers of Columbus. The Compass of Observation, maturity of Reflection and Elegance of Style Suggested to me Conjectures that the Statute of Limitations might not be the only Apology for my short Letter. It is a Mortification to reflect, that a few Ironies, a merry Satirical Story, or a little humour will make more Impression than all these grave Reasonings, polished Eloquence and refined oratory. The President however, with the Unanimous concurrence of The Four Officers of State, has formed the Same Judgment with Columbus, and I hear no Members of Congress who profess to differ from them.

How does your Democratical Society proceed in Boston? There ought to be another Society instituted according to my Principles, under the Title of the Aristocratical Society: and a third under that of The Monarchical Society and no Resolution ought to have Validity, untill it has been considered & approved by all three.

These Democratical Proceedings have brought upon Us, the Jealousy of the Combined Powers, and of all the French who do not concur with the Jacobin Clubbs, and these will soon be, if they are not at present the Majority of the Nation. Our People would do well to consider, to what Precipice they are running. When Junius Said The opinions of the People were always right and their Sentiments never wrong, I wonder what World he lived in.[1] Is not a Mahometan Religion, the opinion of a People as well as the Christian and have not the Sentiments of the People of England for Example been furious against Monarchy in one year and for it in another. Such Popular Adulation is to me most contemptible, Although it is so pernicious that it ought to excite more Indignation than Contempt.

For myself, my Race is almost run. You have a long Career before you, and I am happy to observe that you have not accommodated your opinions nor Sentiments to the momentary Fashions of the present times, but have Searched for Principles which will be more durable. I am affectionately   J. A.

RC (Adams Papers); internal address: "Mr Adams"; endorsed: "My Father 14. Dec^r: 1793." and "My Father Dec^r: 14. 1793." Tr (Adams Papers).

[1] Junius, "To the Printer of the Public Advertiser," 13 Oct. 1769, *The Letters of Junius*, London, 1770, Letter XXVII. JA is also quoting JQA's own work back to him; JQA had just used the same quotation in the second article in his Columbus series.

John Adams to Abigail Adams Smith

My Dear Daughter: Philadelphia, December 14, 1793.

I thank you for your kind letter of the tenth of this month.[1]

Mr. G. may well be shocked at the Message. It is a thunderbolt. I cannot but feel something like an apology for him, as he was led into some of his enterprises by the imprudence of our fellow-citizens. The extravagant court paid to him by a party, was enough to turn a weak head. The enthusiasm and delirium of that party has involved us, and will involve us, in more serious difficulties than a quarrel with a Minister. There is too much reason to fear that the intemperance of that party has brought upon us an Algerine war, and may compromise us with all the maritime powers of Europe.

It is a very difficult thing for a man to go into a foreign country, and among a strange people, and there act a prompt and sudden part upon a public political theatre, as I have severely felt in France, Holland, and England; and if he does not keep his considering cap always on his head, some party or some individual will be very likely to seduce him into snares and difficulties. This has been remarkably Mr. G.'s unhappy case. Opposition to the laws, and endeavours to set the people against the government, are too gross faults to be attempted with impunity in any country.

The scandalous libel on the President, in a New-York paper, is a proof to me, that foreign politics have had too much secret influence in America; indeed, I have known enough of it for fifteen years to dread it; but this desperate effort of corrupt factions, is more than I expected to see so soon.[2]

Present my love to my two dear boys. You have a great charge upon you, my dear child, in the education of these promising children. As they have not had the regular advantages of public schools, your task in teaching them literature must be the more severe. A thirst for knowledge early excited, will be one of the best preservatives against that dissipation and those irregularities which produce the ruin of so many young men; at the same time that it will prompt them to acquire those accomplishments which are the only solid and useful ones, whether they are destined to any of the liberal professions, to the gallant career of soldiers, or to the useful employments of merchandise and agriculture.

Your mamma complains that she has not received a letter from you in a long time. Remember me to Colonel Smith.

Your affectionate, J. Adams.

MS not found. Printed from AA2, *Jour. and Corr.*, 2:125–127.

[1] Not found.

[2] Thomas Greenleaf's *New York Journal* printed "a letter from a gentleman in Virginia" in the 7 Dec. issue that attacked George Washington without ever mentioning him by name. The piece suggested that Washington "looked up to the Mogul of England for high preferment" at the close of the Revolutionary War and accused him of being "most infamously niggardly" and "a most horrid swearer and blasphemer." On 11 Dec., at the Tontine Coffeehouse, "a numerous and respectable meeting of Citizens" issued a series of resolves condemning the piece and Greenleaf for having published it. That same day, Greenleaf apologized in his newspaper for the publication, claiming, "The person at whom it is said to be aimed, is as highly respected and revered by me, as by any citizen of the United States, and I do most sincerely regret, that it ever was published" (New York *Daily Advertiser*, 11 Dec.).

John Adams to Abigail Adams

My dearest Friend   Philadelphia Dec[r] 15. 1793

Having taken a cold which makes it inconvenient to go out this morning I cannot employ myself more agreably than by writing to you. The President and M[rs] Washington enquire after you very respectfully every time I see them. M[rs] Washington enquires after all of Us and particularly Miss Louisa— She wishes, with an Emphasis and I dare Say very sincerely, that I had brought you along with me.— M[r] Dandridge acts at present as The Presidents Secretary and I dont find that he has any other Secretary or Aid de Camp at all.[1] Miss Nelly went over into Maryland in the Course of the Summer and there got the Ague and Fever. The poor Girl looks pale and thin, in Consequence of it: but will soon got the better of it.

Brisler has engaged some Rye Flour for you, but when you will receive it, I know not. Cheesman is not yet Arrived. Yesterday was brought me an Account of which I had not the least Suspicion for above an hundred dollars, from Bringhurst. Will it not be adviseable to sell the Cochee? and the Chariot,? and buy a new Chariot? Perhaps Some Coachmaker in Boston would exchange. We Shall have little Use for the Cochee, and have no Room at present to dispose of the Coach. I only mention this for Consideration. Furniture and Carriages have made Mischief enough for Us.— Rocks are much better, at least they do less harm.

I went to See M[rs] Wilson, but she was gone out. The Judge was at home, and is very young notwithstanding his Spectacles and White Hair.— M[rs] Hammon looks portly enough for a Lady who has been the Wife of an Ambassador half a Year and more.[2]

I told you in a former Letter that Thomas was examined approved and sworn.

For Want of a virtuous Magistracy or *a virtuous Attorney General Pro Tempere,* to prosecute convict and punish disorderly Houses at New York, the Sovereign Mobility took the Guardianship of the public morals into their own Hands and pulled down Seven or Eight houses, turning with exemplary Inhumanity many Ladies into the cold Air and open Street. The public was irritated by two or three Charges of Rapes, and the Lawyers treated the Subject with too much Levity, treated virtuous creditable Women with too much indifference and Mother Cary the old Beldam with to much respect. This is what I hear. I am sorry that Mobs should have a plausible

Excuse for Setting up for reformers. But I never could feel an intollerable Indignation against the Riots called Skimmington Ridings[3]
when they really were excited by gross offences against Morals.

Yours as ever   J. A.

RC (Adams Papers); endorsed: "Dec^br 15 1793."

[1] Bartholomew Dandridge Jr. (ca. 1772–
1802), Martha Washington's nephew, had
replaced Tobias Lear as George Washington's
secretary earlier in 1793 (Washington, *Papers, Presidential Series*, 8:234–235).

[2] Margaret Allen, daughter of Andrew
Allen of Philadelphia, had married British
minister plenipotentiary George Hammond

on 20 May (*DNB*; Philadelphia *Federal Gazette*, 21 May).

[3] "A ludicrous procession . . . usually intended to bring ridicule or odium upon a
woman or her husband in cases where the
one was unfaithful to, or ill-treated, the
other" (*OED*).

John Adams to Charles Adams

Dear Charles   Philadelphia Decr 16. 1793

The Revolution in France is commonly Said to be without Example in the History of Mankind: But although there may be circumstances attending it, peculiar to itself, I cannot think it altogether
unlike any Thing that has happened. The Revolution in England in
the time of Charles the first has so many features in common with
it, that I think the History of England from the Year 1625 to the Year
1660 deserves to be more attended to than it is in these days. It
would well become all young Gentlemen to read it, not for the Sake
of imbibing the Spirit of Party from it, but to observe the Course
and Progress of human Passions in Such Circumstances. In this
View let me recommend to you to inquire where you can borrow
Lord Clarendons History of The Rebellion and Civil Wars in England and to read it through in Course. To me who read it, within the
first Year after I was admitted to the Bar, in the Winter of 1758 and
1759, it has been as Useful as any Work I remember to have read. It
has put me on my guard against many dangers, on on hand and on
the other to which in the Course of my Life I have been exposed.[1]
Whitelock is another Writer on the Same Times who is well worth
your reading.[2] You may indeed read the Account given by Rapin,
Maccauley Hume, smollet or any of the Historians, but none of
them in my opinion will render the reading of Clarendon Useless or
unnecessary.[3] There is the Life of Oliver Cromwell written by Harris, and if my Memory Serves me, some other Lives by the Same
Author, which, although they are Apologies for Oliver and his
friends, will through much Light upon the Transactions of that Pe-

473

riod.[4] Rushworths Collections you may perhaps find in some of your Public Libraries and Rimers Fadera may contain Usefull Papers.[5]

The Monarchy was voted down the King was beheaded, the House of Lords were decreed Useless and Prelacy or the Hierarchy were demolished as compleatly as they have been lately in France. Yet in 1660 Monarchy Aristocracy and Hierarchy were restored and became more popular than ever. The Interregnum continued twelve years from 1648 to 1660: Oliver Cromwell however and his Army held the Place of Government. How long the Commonwealth could have lasted without his Aid is uncertain. Whether the Commonwealth of France will last as long, time will determine. The national Convention Seem to be determined that none of their Generals, shall live long enough to acquire Power either to Support or counteract them. This System will probably shorten the duration of their own Influence. In reading the Events of this Period of Republicanism in England, you will naturally increase your Esteem of real Liberty and your Affection for it, while you Satisfy your Understanding that it cannot exist without Government wisely tempered & well organized. You will find much Entertainment as well as Instruction. That you may receive both from these and all other Studies is the sincere Wish of your Father   J. A

RC (MHi:Seymour Coll.); internal address: "M[r] Charles Adams"; endorsed: "Dec[r] 16 1793."

[1] Edward Hyde, 1st Earl of Clarendon, *The History of the Rebellion and Civil Wars in England Begun in the Year 1641*, 3 vols., Oxford, 1702–1704. Portions of two volumes of a 1720 edition are in JA's library at MB (*Catalogue of JA's Library*).

[2] Bulstrode Whitlocke, *Memorials of the English Affairs; or, An Historical Account of What Passed from the Beginning of the Reign of Charles the First, to King Charles the Second His Happy Restauration*, London, 1732.

[3] Paul de Rapin-Thoyras and N. Tindal, *The History of England*, 25 vols., London, 1725; Catherine Macaulay, *The History of England from the Accession of James I. to [the Revolution]*, 8 vols., London, 1763; David Hume, *The History of England*, 6 vols., London, 1754–1762; Tobias George Smollett, *A Complete History of England*, 4 vols., London, 1757–1758.

[4] William Harris, *An Historical and Critical Account of the Life of Oliver Cromwell*, London, 1762. Other titles by Harris include *An Historical Account of Hugh Peters*, London, 1751; *An Historical and Critical Account of the Life and Writings of Charles I, King of Great Britain*, London, 1758; *An Historical and Critical Account of the Life of Charles the Second, King of Great Britain*, 2 vols., London, 1746; and *An Historical and Critical Account of the Life and Writings of James the First*, London, 1753.

[5] John Rushworth, *Historical Collection of Private Passages of State, Weighty Matters in Law, Remarkable Proceedings in Five Parliaments*, 8 vols., London, 1721–1722; Thomas Rymer, *Foedera conventiones, liter, et cujuscunque generis acta publica*, 20 vols., London, 1704–1735.

Charles Adams to John Adams

My dear father   New York Dec[r] 19th 1793

I received your favour of the 16th yesterday. I am sorry that from
what I said in my last to you it should be inferred that I wished to
advocate the cause of infamy or that I had partially related circumstances. All I meant by there being no evidence was that was not
such evidence as would warrant a jury to find the prisoner guilty of
the charge laid against him. I most earnestly request that you would
not too easily take up ideas prejudicial to me Your letter if it was
intended to give pain had the desired effect but I have to observe
that many things have been told respecting me which are false
many things reported which I attest Heaven are not true. Lord
Hale's history of the Pleas of the Crown I have read and some of the
other authors you have recommended.[1] My attention shall be
turned to the others. I do not look upon the French Revolution as a
new thing many circumstances have perhaps contributed to make it
more replete with crimes than any other. The great ignorance of the
mass of the people made them easy tools for the factious and unprincipled demagogues to work with Many men at such periods will
arise who are continually endeavoring to promote the reign of anarchy well knowing that their only chance of keeping upon the top of
the wheel is in a continued scene of tumult. In France there does
not appear to be one two or three or four parties but five or six hundred and most indubitably it is better to have one Cromwell than
five hundred. I have lately read a pamplet Entitled Plaidoyer pour
Louis seize par Mon[r] Lally Tollendal. It is a morsel of eloquence
which I am anxious you should see Much information is to be gathered from it. The history of the author is remarkable. During the
reign of Louis 15th his father was executed in a most ignominious
manner for surrendering Pondicherry to the English His son found
protectors and applied himself to the study of the laws with the intention to vindicate the memory of his father. At the age of 22 he
proffered a Memorial to Louis the 16th requesting a revision of the
decree against his father. It was granted and he appeared himself as
the Solicitor before the parlement of Paris and the memory of his
father was relieved from disgrace his property and title restored.[2]
Such is the man who was anxious to defend his King but was denied
the privilege of doing it before the National Convention A man as I
am informed [of si]ngular eloquence and most persuasive Oratory.

I have received your kind assistance of an hundred dollars for which accept my sincere thanks.

The people I think show an unusual degree of dejection at the prospect of affairs. Nor are those who have been most instrumental in exasperating the powers of Europe against this Country among the least cast down. Civic feasts. Kicking British Officers out of Coffee houses King killing toasts &c[a] &c[a] are things which some begin to think were imprudent. and perhaps not altogether justifiable I see nothing but sad experience that can bring all right.

I am my Dear Sir your dutiful son   Charles Adams

RC (Adams Papers); addressed: "The Vice President of the United States / Philadelphia"; endorsed: "C. Adams. Dec[r.] 19. / 1793." Some loss of text where the seal was removed.

[1] Sir Matthew Hale and Emlyn Sollom, *Historia placitorum coronne* (*The History of the Pleas of the Crown*), 2 vols., London, 1736.

[2] Trophime Gérard, Marquis de Lally-Tolendal, *Plaidoier du Comte de Lally-Tolendal pour Louis XVI*, London, 1792. Lally-Tolendal (1751–1830), an orator and scholar, had initially supported the French Revolution but grew disenchanted with its increasing violence and eventually fled to England. His father had been the commander-in-chief of the French Army in India, but in 1766 he ran afoul of court politics and was summarily tried and executed by beheading. His son eventually persuaded Louis XVI to reverse the judgment in 1783 and his estates were restored (*Ann. Register*, 1830, p. 255–256).

John Adams to Abigail Adams

My dearest Friend   Philadelphia Dec[r] 19. 1793

M[rs] Otis arrived with her little Rosignal, in good health and Spirits the night before last, and brought me your favour of Dec[r] 7.—[1] Why am not I so fortunate as to be able to receive my best Friend, and to Spend my Days with her whose Society is the principal delight of my Life. If I could make Twelve Thousand dollars at a Bargain and Several of Such Bargains in a Year: but Silence.— So it is ordained and We must not complain.

If a Suitable Season should occur for ploughing, our Men may plough, if not they may leave it till Spring.

I like your Plan very well to Stock one Place with young Cattle, and to apply to shaw if Humphreys and Porter decline, to take care of the Dairy in the other.

I am pleased with D[r] Tufts's Plan.

Citizen Genet made me a Visit yesterday while I was in Senate and left his Card: I shall leave mine at his Hotel Tomorrow: as Several of the Senators have already hastened to return their Visits: but We shall be in an Awkward Situation with this Minister.— I write you little concerning public affairs, because you will have every Thing in Print. How a Government can go on, publishing all their Negotiations with foreign Nations I know not. To me it appears as dangerous and pernicious as it is novel: but upon this occasion it could not perhaps have been avoided. You know where I think was the Error in the first Concoction. But Such Errors are unavoidable where the People in Crowds out of Doors undertake to receive Ambassadors, and to dictate to their Supream Executive.

I know not how it is: but in proportion as dangers threaten the Public, I grow calm. I am very apprehensive that a desperate Antifœderal Party, will provoke all Europe by their Insolence. But my Country has in its Wisdom contrived for me, the most insignificant Office that ever the Invention of Man contrived or his Imagination conceived: and as I can do neither good nor Evil, I must be born away by Others and meet the common Fate.

The President has considered the Conduct of Genet, very nearly in the Same light with Columbus and has given him a Bolt of Thunder. We Shall See how this is supported by the two Houses. There are, who gnash their Teeth with Rage which they dare not own as yet. We Shall Soon See, whether We have any Government or not in this Country. If the President has made any Mistake at all, it is by too much Partiality for the French Republicans and in not preserving a Neutrality between the Parties in France as well as among the Belligerent Powers: But although he Stands at present as high in the Admiration and Confidence of the people as ever he did, I expect he will find many bitter and desperate Ennemies arise in Consequence of his just Judgment against Genet. Besides that a Party Spirit will convert White into black and Right into Wrong, We have I fear very corrupt Individuals in this Country, independent of the common Spirit of Party. The common Movements of Ambition every day disclose to me Views and Hopes and Designs that are very diverting. But these I will not commit to Paper. They make sometimes a very pretty Farce, for Amusement, after the great Tragegy or Comedy is over. What I write to you must be in Sacred Confidence and Strict discretion.

Mrs Washington prays me, every time I see her to remember her to you very affectionately. I am as ever / your   J. A.

RC (Adams Papers); endorsed: "Dec^br 19. 1793."

[1] AA's letter to JA of 7 Dec. discussed difficulties she was having coming to terms with her farmhands and reported on Cotton Tufts' plan to pay off a portion of one of the Adamses' notes (Adams Papers).

Abigail Adams to John Adams

my Dearest Friend   Quincy december 20th 1793.

I have to acknowledge your two kind Letters one of the first the other of the 5th of december from philadelphia my anxiety has in some measure abated since I found you went immediatly to your old Lodgings, as no person was sick in that house if the air of it had been properly Changed by opening & airing I should hope theire might be no danger, this winter. the spring will be the most danger-ous Season. I would fain hope that when publick danger threatens, all personal views & interests will vanish or be swallowd up in the more liberal and enlarged Policy of Love of Country & of Mankind. the speach of the President is that of the wise Man who foreseeth the danger & Gaurdeth against it. I never liked the translation, hid-eth himself, that looks too cowardly for a wise and brave Man.[1] I would hope that congress may be so united in their measures as to dispatch important matters in a short period. the message relative to foreign affairs was more full and decisive than I expected. every one may see that the President is much in earnest and that tho cool, he has felt properly warm'd Genet has renderd him self contemptable indeed. Columbus has not done with him, by what I can learn he has carried conviction to those who before doubted for want of proper information. I have not seen any attempt to answer him. I should like to know what the opinion of the peices is with your members. Some persons have said they were written by Ames others ascribe them to mr Gore to mr otis & some to an other hand. Russel has been Questiond, he say they are not in his hand writing, "but sir I know the writer there is but one man capable of writing them!"

I rejoice that Thomas has got through his studies and examina-tion. I hope he will get into buisness I know he will be attentive in-dusterous and obliging. I sincerely pray that he may be prosperous— the season is fine with us. I have written to you every week Since your absence & was surprizd to find by your Letter of the 9th to our son that you had not heard from me.[2] mrs otis is with you before this time, and will add to the comfort and happiness of the Family. when I found that no danger was apprehended I wrote to urge her to go on. I hope your Health is better for your journey. I have not been sick, but have [had] a Remembrancer of my old Ague tho I have not been in Boston Louissa at the same time had a much Se-verer attack so as to Shake an hour. I hope we have queld it for the present. our Friends are all well. I propose visiting a New Nephew to day, mrs Norten has an other son.[3] Girls seem to be denied our Families I hope we shall not have occasion for so many soldiers— remember me to all my old acquaintance whether in or out of Congress.— is mrs washington with the President. my particular regards attend her from your / ever affectionate   A Adams

I have seen the dr to day he tells me that he took up the Note and payd three hundred pounds, gave his own for the other three hundred which he proposes to pay of the next month, as he does not like the trouble of a monthly renewal, besides that it amounts to seven pr ct as the interest must be pay'd Monthly. I believe I mentiond to you before that he designd the interest due in Jan'ry as part of the Sum. if you can other ways provide for me I would not break in upon his plan. I have purchased 30 Bushels of oats the price 2s·10d pence pr Bushel I must soon procure an other load of hay. savil has carted 30 load of sea weed. he has not yet call'd for his pay. our people have carted 13 load and very different ones from savils. his object was to get up three loads pr day, and load all himself, it could not be large I have as you directed, askd mr Pratt for his account. he will bring it in a few days— I have payd Arnold and he is gone for the present. thus much for Buisness—

I received Thomas Letter of december 9th and will write him soon. it already Seems a long time since you left me. I fear I shall not be able to look forward to your return at so early a period as the last year.

RC (Adams Papers); addressed by JQA: "The Vice-President of the United States / Philadelphia."; endorsed: "Portia Decr. 20 / ansd 30. 1793." Some loss of text where the seal was removed.

¹ "A prudent man foreseeth the evil, and hideth himself; but the simple pass on, and are punished" (Proverbs, 27:12).
² For JA's 10 Dec. letter to JQA, see TBA to AA, 9 Dec., note 3, above.
³ Elizabeth Cranch Norton gave birth to a third son, Jacob Porter Norton, on 16 December.

John Adams to Abigail Adams

My dearest Friend   Philadelphia Decr. 20. 1793

This Morning I returned Mr Genets' Visit. The Conversation was confined to Some Inquiries I made concerning his Mother, and Sisters with whom I was acquainted at Versailles in 1778. 1779. and 1780,[1] and some little discussion about the form of the new Constitution: but not one Word or hint or Allusion concerning himself his Conduct, or the Conduct of our Government or People towards him. I perceive Some Traits of his Countenance which I knew in 1779.

He appears a Youth totally destitute of all Experience in popular Governments popular Assemblies or Conventions of any kind: very little accustomed to reflect on his own or his fellow Creatures hearts; wholly ignorant of the Law of Nature & Nations, the civil Law, and even of the Dispatches of ancient Ambassadors with which his own Nation and Language abound. A declamatory Style a flitting fluttering Imagination, an Ardour in his Temper, and a civil Deportment are all the Accomplishments or Qualifications I can find in him, for his Place.

The Printer in Boston cannot afford Room for Columbus, though' he has Space enough for the most miserable Trash. The Writer had better print Such Things in a Pamphlet—in that Way a Printer might make Money. He cannot be too cautious to avoid all Expressions, which may be thought inconsistent with the Character of a Gentleman.

I thank him for his masterly defence of the Writers on the Law of Nations and for laying before the Public Such Passages as are extreamly to the Purpose.

Your Children must conduct the affairs of this Country, or they will be miserably managed, for I declare I know of nobody but them or some of them rising up who are qualified for it. If they Suffer as much in the service, and get as little either of honour Profit or Pleasure by it as their Father has done, they will deserve to be pitied rather than envied.

The President and M[r] Jefferson have handled Genet, as freely as Columbus. How Jefferson can feel I know not. There are Passages in Genets Letters which imply that Jefferson himself contributed very much to lead him into the snare.

yours as ever

RC (Adams Papers); endorsed: "Dec[br] 20th / 1793."

[1] Marie Anne Louise Cardon had married Edmé Jacques Genet, a chief clerk in the French foreign ministry, in 1752. Together they had nine children, including four daughters who lived beyond infancy: Jeanne Louise Henriette, Julie Françoise, Adelaïde Henriette, and Anne Glaphire Sophie (Meade Minnigerode, *Jefferson, Friend of France, 1793: The Career of Edmond Charles Genet*, N.Y., 1928, p. 5–7). For JA's acquaintance with the Genet family in 1778–1780, see JA, *D&A*, 2:354–355, and JA, *Papers*, vols. 6–10 *passim*.

John Adams to Abigail Adams

My dearest Friend   Philadelphia Decr 22. 1793

I went this morning to Dr Greens and this afternoon to St. Pauls where I heard Dr Magaw: but I am not Sure it is prudent to go to Church or to Meeting for if there is danger and can be infection any where it is as likely to be in these Assembleis as in any Place. All the World however says and believes there is no danger.

Our son Thomas opened at the Bar, on Fryday and acquitted himself to his own Satisfaction at least, and that is a great Point. His Cause was a Prosecution of a disorderly house and consequently his Audience was crouded. Two of your sons are thus engaged in the great Work of Reformation and I wish them success. Mr Ingersol thinks, that as Charles is not necessitated to push into the Country for an immediate subsistance, he had better remain in the City where there is the greatest Quantity and Variety of profitable Business. But advises me to let him ride the Circuits in the Summer, to see the Country and the People as well as practice. This Plan upon the whole I approve, among many others for this decisive one, that he will avoid the danger if there should be any in the Summer Months.

I cannot write you upon public affairs. I should write in Shackles. There will be many weak Propositions no doubt. it is even possible there may be some wicked ones: none I hope Stark mad.

The Antifœderal Party by their ox feasts and their civic feasts, their king killing Toasts, their perpetual Insolence and Billingsgate against all the Nations and Governments of Europe their everlasting brutal Cry of Tyrants, Despots, Combinations against Liberty &c &c &c have probably irritated, offended and provoked all the Crowned Heads of Europe at least: and a little more of this Indelicacy and Indecency may involve Us in a War with all the World. on the other hand It is possible the French Republicans may be angry with Us for preventing their Minister, from involving Us in War & Anarchy. The State is in critical Circumstances, and have been brought into them by the Heat and Impatience of the People. If nothing will bring them to consideration, I fear they will suffer Severely for their Rashness. The Friends of the Government have been as blind as its Ennemies in giving Way to the Torrent. Their great Error was in suffering Publicola to be overborn and Paines Yellow Fever to be

Spread and propagated and applauded, as if, instead of a Distemper, a putrid, malignant mortal fatal Epidemic, it had been a Salubrious shower of Blessings from on high. It is reported this Luminary is coming to America.[1] I had rather, two more Genets should arrive.

M[rs] Dalton and too many others to be named, desire their respects to you.

My office renders me so compleatly insignificant that all Parties can afford to treat me with a decent respect, which accordingly they do, as far as I observe or hear or suspect. They all know that I can do them neither much good nor much harm.

My Health has been pretty well, excepting a Cold, which I regularly have upon entering this City two or three Weeks, every Year.

I am afraid We shall have a long session. But I hope We shall rise in April. My Duty to my Mother & Love where due.

yours unceasingly　　　　　　　　　　　　　　　　　J. A

RC (Adams Papers); endorsed: "Dec[br] 22 1793."

[1] Thomas Paine did not return to America until 1802; in late Dec. 1793, he was imprisoned by the French as a British national after he broke with the increasingly radical National Convention (*DAB*).

John Adams to Charles Adams

Dear Charles　　　　　　　　　　　　　　Philadelphia Dec[r] 23. 1793

The Papers, furnish Us this Evening with more flowers of Jacobinical Rhetorick from New York. Crushing Monarchy Confusion to Aristocracy and Monarchy: a Brutus to Tyrants &c are Still not only panting in the Bosoms of the Guests at the new Civic Feast, but they must publish their Breathings to the World.[1]

It is so customary for the Members of the Corps Diplomatick, to make Ex officio representations of Such Ebullitions in Newspapers to the Administration of the Government to which they are Accredited; that it must be acknowledged to be much to the honour of the Gentlemen who are here from Spain Holland and England, that they have not hitherto persecuted the President & secretary of State with Remonstrances against our Newspapers. Their Silence is a Proof of their Moderation, their Patience and their Tenderness for the Freedom of the Press. I Suppose too that they make allowances for our Youth and Inexperience of the World. For Our Ignorance of what in Europe is known and acknowledged to be the Delicacy and Decency, due to all foreign nations and their Governments. We claim a Right, very justly to the form of Government We like best. Every Nation in

Europe has the Same Right and if they judge Monarchy to be necessary for their Happiness, What Right have We to reproach, much less to insult them? Supposing ourselves to be Judges of what kind of Government is best for them, a Supposition however which We cannot modestly make and which is certainly ill founded, We should have no right to impose upon them our Ideas of Government, any more than our principles of Religion or systems of Faith. There is an Ungenerosity in this disposition So often displayed by so many of our Countrymen, nearly bordering on meanness of Spirit, and an illiberality, Strongly marked with littleness of Soul.

Should a foreign Minister complain to the President against the grossest of these Libels, and demand that the Printers, Writers &c should be punished, what could he answer? He must answer that he would give orders to the Attorney General to prosecute them: should the Attorney General Prosecute and the Grand Jury not find a Bill or the petit Jury not convict what would be the Consequence? Resentment, Vengeance and War as likely as not. At the present Moment the Combination of Powers is so strong, that We may expect they will be irritable in Proportion to their feeling of their own Superiority of Power. And I am really apprehensive that if our People cannot be persuaded to be more decent, they will draw down Calamities upon our Country, that will weaken Us to such a degree that We shall not recover our Prosperity for half a Century.

What assistance can France give Us, or We afford her in the present Posture of affairs? We should only increase each others Miseries, if We were involved in War, with all her Ennemies.

our People Seem to think they could now go to War with England and be at Peace with all the rest of Europe: a delusion so gross that I am amazed it should have deceived the Sagacity of the meanest of our Citizens: so sure as We go to War at present with any one European Power We must go to War with all, excepting Denmark and Sweeden, and the Consequences of such a War have not I fear been maturely weighed by my dear Countrymen. I am my dear Charles your / affectionate Father   J. A.

RC (MHi:Seymour Coll.); endorsed: "Decr 23 1793."

[1] The Philadelphia *American Daily Advertiser*, 23 Dec., reprinted a letter from New York regarding a farewell dinner for Edmond Genet, which he was ultimately unable to attend. Nonetheless, the guests gathered and made various toasts in support of the French Revolution, including "Success to the French cause—May every Frenchman be a Hercules to crush despotism and monarchy" and "The Rights of Man universally acknowledged."

John Adams to Abigail Adams

My dearest Friend   Philadelphia Decr. 26. 1793

I have enough to do to write Apologies in Answer to Invitations to dinner and to Tea Parties: but I have long Since taken the Resolution that I will not again loose myself and all my time in a wild vagary of Dissipation. As it is not in my Power to live on equal terms with the Families and Personages who exhibit so much real Hospitality in this City, I would not lay myself under Obligations to them which I could not repay. But besides this I have other Motives. I have Occasion for some time to write Letters to my friends, and for more, that I may read something, and not be wholly ignorant of what is passing in the litterary World. There is more pleasure and Advantage to me, in this than is to be found in Parties at dinner or at Tea.

Columbus is republishing in New York, in a public Paper, of whose Title I am ignorant, whose Editor is Mr Noah Webster who is lately removed from Hartford to that City, and is Said to conduct his Gazette with Judgment and Spirit upon good Principles.[1] He has given a conspicuous Place and a large handsome Type, as I am told to the Speculations of the Bostonian. Here they are unknown, except to two or three, but I have heard they are to appear a Printer having heard Mr Ames Say they were *a very compleat Thing* and that there was but one Man in Boston that he knew of who could write them

our Friend Mr Cabot has bought a Farm in Brokelyne, adjoining to that of my Grandfathers, where he is to build an House next Summer. He delights in nothing more than in talking of it. The Searchers of Secret motives in the heart have their Conjectures that this Country Seat in the Vicinity of Boston was purchased with the Same Views which some Ascribed to Mr Gerry in purchasing his Pallace at Cambridge and to Gen. Warren in his allighting on Milton Hill.[2] Whether these Shrewd Conjectures are right or not, I own I wish the State may never have worse Governors, than Gerry or Cabot, and I once thought the Same of the other.

I am told Mr Jefferson is to resign tomorrow. I have so long been in an habit of thinking well of his Abilities and general good dispositions, that I cannot but feel some regret at this Event: but his Want of Candour, his obstinate Prejudices both of Aversion and Attachment: his real Partiality in Spite of all his Pretensions and his low notions about many Things have so nearly reconciled me to it, that I will not weep. Whether he will be chosen Governor of Virginia, or whether he is to go to France, in Place of Mr Morris I know not. But this I know that if he is neglected at Montecello he will soon see a Spectre like the disgraced Statesman in Gill Blass, and not long afterwards will die, for instead of being the ardent pursuer of science that some think him, I know he is indolent, and his soul is poisoned with Ambition.[3] Perhaps the Plan is to retire, till his Reputation magnifies enough to force him into the Chair in Case. So be it, if it is thus ordained. I like the Precedent very well because I expect I shall have occasion to follow it.— I have been thirty years planning and preparing an Assylum for my self and a most admirable one it is, for it is so entirely out of order, that I might busy myself, to the End of my Life, in making Improvements. So that God willing I hope to conquer the fowl Fiend whenever I shall be obliged or inclined to retire. But of this prattle, (entre nous) enough.

Yours as ever

RC (Adams Papers); endorsed: "Dec^{br} 26 1793."

[1] Noah Webster's recently established New York newspaper, *American Minerva*, reprinted the second and third Columbus essays on 16, 17, 19, 21, 23, 24 December.

[2] George Cabot (1752–1823), Harvard 1770, had been a Beverly, Mass., sea captain and merchant. He served as one of Massachusetts' senators from 1791 to 1796. In 1793, he purchased a large farm and house in Brookline, Mass. If he had political designs on the Mass. governorship, they never materialized, though he was considered for a diplomatic mission to France (*Sibley's Harvard Graduates*, 17:344–367). JA's grandfather Peter Boylston had been a Brookline shopkeeper.

[3] In Alain René Le Sage's *The Adventures of Gil Blas of Santillane*, transl. Tobias Smollet, Book XII, ch. xi, the Count d'Olivares, upon losing his public position, retires to his garden where he is haunted by a ghost: "I am the prey of a morbid melancholy," he reports to Gil Blas, "which eats inwardly into my vitals: a spectre haunts me every moment, arrayed in the most terrific form of preternatural horror. In vain have I argued with myself that it is a vision of the brain, an unreal mockery: its continual presentments blast my sight, and unseat my reason. Though my understanding teaches me, that in looking on this spectre I stare at vacancy, my spirits are too weak to derive comfort from the conviction." He dies shortly thereafter. Gaspar de Guzmán, Count d'Olivares (1587–1645), served as minister under King Philip IV of Spain from Philip's ascension to the throne until 1643 when he was forced to retire (*Cambridge Modern Hist.*, 4:635–637, 654).

Thomas Jefferson formally retired on 31 Dec. 1793. He would spend the next three years primarily at Monticello, where he improved his farms, built a grist mill and nail factory, and generally focused on agricultural and building concerns. He remained out of public office until his election to the vice presidency in 1796 (*DAB*).

Abigail Adams to John Adams

my dearest Friend   Quincy dec[br] 28 1793.

The weather is so extreemly cold that my Ink almost freezes whilst I write, yet I would not let a week pass without writing to you, tho I have few occurrences to entertain you with; I received last saturday your two Letters one of the 12 and one of the 13th, december;[1] I have not yet had a Philadelphia paper. when the pamphlets are out containing the correspondence between the ministers I hope you will send me one. in Edds paper of the last week appeard a low abusive peice against the British minister for the conduct of his court towards America but it was really too low for notice.[2] the Chronical exults, without reason however at Dallas'es Reportt, it has become as much of a party paper as Freaneus.[3] there is a great & general Allarm arising from the depredations which it is reported & feard the Algerians have made upon American vessels. All imported articles particuliarly west India produce has risen in concequence of it; congress will indeed have their Hands full of Buisness—and will have no time I hope, and very little disposition to quarrel. I am solisitious to know what Genets conduct will be at Philadelphia. I presume he does not shew his Head at the Levee, nor will he venture a visit to you in his publick Character; I think he is much like Cain after he had murderd Abel. Columbus closed last Saturday. I hope you have seen all the Numbers we have had in the course of the last week a very suden Death dr Rhoads was taken sick with a nervious fever and dyed the 3 day leaving a most distrest family 5 children 2 of them quite Babies, and mrs Rhoads hourly expecting to get to Bed, and in want of every necessary of Life. I never was witness to a more distresst Scene. I attended the funeral, and found her in fits, the children and people in the Room all terifye'd not knowing what to do with, or for her. dr Phips had run home for some medicine; and every person seem'd to be thrown into the utmost distress. the dr was a kind Husband and an innofensive man, dejected & disspirited tis Said by his prospect, her situation is pityable indeed. she has since got to bed and happily I may say lost her Baby which no doubt sufferd from her distress of Body and mind[4]

our Friends here are all well. I do not learn that any persons have been endangerd by going into the city of Philadelphia, so that my fears and apprehensions are much quieted. this very cold weather if it reaches you will tend to preserve the Health of the inhabitants, but I fear it will pinch you severely. it gives me the Rhumatism

I am with every sentiment of affection and Regard most tenderly your   A Adams

RC (Adams Papers); addressed by JQA: "The Vice-President of the United States / Philadelphia."; endorsed: "Mrs Adams 28. Dec^r / 1793 / ans$^{d.}$ 6 Jan. 1794."

[1] JA wrote a brief letter to AA on 13 Dec., acknowledging hers of 28 Nov., above. He mentioned attending church services on the day of thanksgiving and also noted Edmond Genet's arrival in Philadelphia (Adams Papers).

[2] The *Boston Gazette*, 23 Dec., contained a piece signed "A Merchant" attacking George Hammond, "one of the diplomatic Agents of our late detestable Tyrant," for declaring the British intent to seize U.S. provisions being shipped to France. "The Ignorance of this person becomes as conspicuous as his Impudence is insupportable," the article continues. "The Principles of the War against the *French* are well known to be precisely the same with those which instigated the late cruel and unprovoked attack upon the Liberty and Independence of this Country." The piece also excoriates the British government for its part in the Indian wars and "their late manœuvres in ALGIERS."

[3] Alexander James Dallas published a report in the Philadelphia *American Daily Advertiser*, 9 Dec., outlining his version of events related to Genet's ongoing battle with John Jay and Rufus King over the French minister's alleged "appeal to the people." Dallas' report, while describing Genet as "intemperate" and accusing him of issuing "angry epithets," nevertheless stated unequivocally that the expression that Genet would "appeal from the President to the People" was in Dallas' words, not Genet's. The Boston *Independent Chronicle*, 19 Dec., reprinted Dallas' statement. In the same issue, the newspaper also published an editorial celebrating Dallas' "*strict probity*" and decrying, "it is evident that every unfair measure has been taken to injure Mr. *Genet*, in the opinion of the people—to destroy his reputation, and to throw him into a 'dilemma' in the execution of his office."

[4] Dr. Joseph Wanton Rhodes (or Rhoades) (b. ca. 1752) died on 19 December. He had been married to Catherine Greenleaf (b. 1760) since 1780 (Boston *Independent Chronicle*, 30 Dec. 1793; Boston, *30th Report*, p. 447; Greenleaf, *Greenleaf Family*, p. 196).

Elizabeth Smith Shaw to Abigail Adams

My Dear Sister—   Haverhill Dec. 29th 1793

It is a long time since I have written to you, or received a Line from either of my much loved Sisters— I have done like many others, in the more important Concerns of Life, who, though convinced of their Duty, put off the performance of it, to a more convenient Season—not considering, that the present moment, is the only one we may be favoured with—

I know that my Sister looks back upon the last year, & now sees the close of it, with peculiar gratitude—that Heaven has been pleased to preserve the lives of all her Family—& to spare *her Son* when surrounded on every side, with that most awful pestilential Dissease which has torn so many Mothers from the arms of their clinging Infants, & with a cruel despotic sway, in quick succession made, "wild Inroads on a Parents Heart—"[1] But *he* who is the repairer of breaches—who hears the young Ravens when they cry, will not be deaf to the cries of those helpless Infants, but will raise up Friends to those distressed Orphans, who will be the guide of their tender Years—

When the Congress first met, I felt very anxious, & I know your mind must have been much agitated—least the City should not have been properly cleansed—& the air prove prejudicial to your best Friend— I never think of him, but with a petition to heaven, that his most useful Life might be spared, that he might see the blessings of that Government, of which he has been so instrumental,—preserved, inviolate to his Childrens, Children—

A nervous putrid fever has prevaield in the Towns round us, & carried of a number of Persons— Mr Welch, a Class-mate of your Son's, is among the number—

"Lamented Youth! in life's first bloom he fell"[2]

He was a young minister beloved by every one—happy in the affections of the People of his Charge—Zealous in promoting the intereste of Religion, without too great a degree of Enthusiasm—meek—& serious—with out affectation—cheerful, without Levity—complacent & affable without familiarity gentle in his manners—excellent in his Morals he enforced, & gave a double weight to his Precepts, by the purity of his Life—which was uncommonly useful, improving in knowledge & virtue— What! though short his *date*—if it has answered Life's great end—it is enough— Scarce one year has elapsed since he was united to an accomplished Lady—in the silken bands of Hymen—whom in the pangs of Death, he pressed to his fond faithful Heart—& beged of her Mother, to again receive, & protect both her, & *hers*, if heaven should be pleased to bless his widowed, pensive, solotary mate, with the tender appellation of *Parent*—which alas! he must never know—[3] It was a Scene almost too tender, for Description— I will say no more than that

"In Sorrow, may I never want a Friend
Nor, when others mourn, a Tear to lend—"[4]

Mr Cranch went away suddenly, & I had not time to finish this— May it find you in health—& the new born year be replete with Blessings—

I wish you would be so kind as to lend me the Rights of Women— the first opportunity—[5] when you write to your Children, please to give my Love to them all— / & accept of the unfeigned Love, & Grati- / tude of your affectionate Sister   E. Shaw—

Please to excuse the writing, as Abby is round all the time chattering like a Mag-pye—

RC (Adams Papers).

[1] Isaac Watts, "To Mitio, My Friend," line 99.

[2] Homer, *The Iliad*, Book XVII, line 348.

[3] Francis Welch (1766–1793), a classmate of JQA at Harvard, served as the minister at West Amesbury, Mass., until his death on 15 December. He had married Priscilla Adams (1772–1817) in Dec. 1792; their only child, Priscilla Perkins Welch, was born in Feb. 1794 (William Prescott, "Philip Welch of Ipswich, Ms., and His Descendants," *NEHGR*, 23:421 [Oct. 1869]). For JQA's sketch of Welch, see *Diary*, 2:236.

[4] Anne Steele, "The Friend," in *Poems on Subjects Chiefly Devotional*, 3 vols., Bristol, Eng., 1780, 1:237–239, lines 41–42.

[5] Mary Wollstonecraft, *A Vindication of the Rights of Woman*, London, 1792.

Abigail Adams to John Quincy Adams

my dear   Quincy dec[br] 30 1793—

I inclose to you your Brothers Letter I should have Sent for you last saturday but I expected a snow storm. I suppose your Father has written to you. he is vex'd with the Printer for Publishing in three Numbers what ought all to have been in one. he says the writer of Columbus had better publish in a pamphlet by which a printer may get money, and as pamphlets are much in vogue at present. suppose you should hint it to him your Father sends his thanks to the writer, for his masterly defence of the writers upon the Law of Nature and Nations and for laying before the publick such passages as are extreemly to the purpose Genet made him a visit as he did to other Senators who all *hastned* to return it. he was at home when your Father returnd his. there conversation was confind to inquiries after his mother & sisters, &c and to some discussion about the form of their New constitution. Take Genets Character from one who has long been accustomed "to look quite through the deeds of Men"[1] ["]He appears a youth totally destitute of all experience in popular Governments popular assemblies or conventions of any kind: very little accustomed to reflect on his own or his fellow creatures Hearts; wholy ignorant of the Law of Nature & Nations, the civil Law and even of the dispatches of Ancient Ambassadors with which his own Nation and Language abounds A declamatory stile a flitting fluttering Imagination an Ardour in his Temper, and a civil deportment are all the accomplishments or qualifications to be found in him for his place" and this Character I would send to the Printer if I dared.[2] you may if you will venture. it is the most favourable one that is due to him. mr Jefferson treats him I think quite as freely as Columbus Have the Libel which was printed upon the President by Greenleaf & the Resolves which past at the Coffe house in concequence of it, reachd Boston. your Father mentions it in one of his Letters.[3] the P— finds that there is more than one Church left in America. I dont know where he could find ports enough to make them all into Consuls— I own that is a little spightfull, yet I do Revere respect honour and Love the President.—

I shall send next saturday for you. if you have an opportunity to send to Charles the remaining Numbers do. the Tigers paw will delight him. I felt the down of it when I read it.[4] I do not mean however to single out this beautifull metaphor as the only object worth consideration I have read all the Numbers with attention and consider them a valuable present to the publick tending, to place in a true and just point of view the conduct of a Man who has disgraced his office, and made himself so obnoxious as scarcly to be entitled to common decency. partizans may Rail, but sound reason will enlighten and prevail. I see a scene opening before me which will call for as great exertions from the rising generation as their Fathers have already pasd through. may all those to whom talants and abilities are entrusted qualify themselves for the Guidence and protection of the common Weal. Parties are arising and forming themselves upon Principals altogether Repugnant to the good order and happiness of society. No fire, says an Author I have lately been reading assails a civil edifice so voilently as the Flame of National Passion, for it consumes the very stones of the Fabrick levels merit to the Ground and makes reason tremble excites tumults and insults and makes way for the triumphant entry of Ambition those Hearts which ought to be cordially united by the Bonds of Brotherly Love Breathe nothing but vengance & Rancour[5]

adieu yours affectionatly

A Adams

RC (Adams Papers). Tr (Adams Papers).

[1] From Julius Caesar's description of Cassius: "He reads much, / He is a great observer, and he looks / Quite through the deeds of men" (Shakespeare, *Julius Caesar*, Act I, scene ii, lines 202–204).

[2] AA is quoting from JA's letter of 20 Dec., above.

[3] On 13 Dec., JA wrote to AA, "A great Indignation has been excited at New York by a Libel on the President, which I have not Seen as it is Suppressed at present as much as possible. Greanleaf has published an Apology, at least as Sawcy as it is modest" (Adams Papers). See JA to AA2, 14 Dec., note 2, above.

[4] In the fourth part of the Columbus essays, JQA writes that the French ministers "have not been able to disguise their real contempt for the Americans. They have interspersed numerous menacing insinuations

amid their warmest pretences of friendship; and the murderous fangs of the tyger, peep through the downy velvet of her paws, at the moment when she fawns the most" (Boston *Columbian Centinel*, 18 Dec.).

[5] AA is quoting from Benito Jerónimo Fiejóo y Montenegro, "On the Love of Our Country, and National Prejudice or Prepossession," in *Essays, or Discourses, Selected from the Works of Feyjoo*, transl. John Brett, 4 vols., London, 1780, 2:99–100.

Charles Adams to John Adams

My Dear Father   New York Decr 30th 1793—

The effusions of our Jacobin spirit had been smothered if some evil minded person in Philadelphia had not published an extract of a letter from one of the party relating the circumstances The whole conduct of the feast had been carefully concealed nor was it possible to procure any information respecting it until the extract appeared.[1] The partisans of M[r] Genet fall off daily. some still remain and it is said that most of them will find their purses somewhat lightened by their connection. As to our other Citizens they are very much troubled least the Gentleman should cover himself with the black mantle. Your last letter I have a desire to give it to one of our Printers, but I would not do it without your consent It abounds with such truths as I think must forcibly strike the public mind which now appears open to conviction. It is not difficult to fix upon the author of the peices signed Columbus. They are very highly esteemed and have been reprinted in all our papers except Greenleaf's in which I should be sorry to see them. He is the veriest imp of sedition that was ever suffered in a City. but he has lately received a lesson which he will not soon forget He published an infamous peice against the President which has cost him dear and excited a general detestation against him. Heavens! what a change! but four year ago and we thought the voice of calumny dared not attack this man. I recollect a conversation I had with you Sir upon this subject before they had commenced their attacks in that quarter. I remember well the apprehension you expressed least they should strike even there. We now see that those apprehensions were not groundless. The consequences are to be feared. How poor a reward for virtuous exertions in the service of our Country.

The high winds for these few days past have prevented the Mails from Philadelphia passing the river. Will it be possible to persuade the State Government to cooperate in the defense of the Country? What alterations are proposed in the Militia law? Fenno does not send me his papers so that I do not obtain regular information from the Seat of Government. At This crisis so interesting and important the papers would be peculiarly acceptable.

My Love to my brother I am glad he has began his carrere with so much propriety.

Adieu my dear Sir beleive me your / affectionate son

Charles Adams

RC (Adams Papers).

[1] See JA to CA, 23 Dec., note 1, above.

John Adams to Abigail Adams

My dearest Friend   Philadelphia Decr 30. 1793

This morning I received your favour of the 20$^{th.}$ The House I am in was aired and Smoked with Tar & Powder and the Vaults Slaked with Lime &c before I came in.

I hope with you that Congress will not remain here late in the Spring: but the Extent of Business before Us Seems to be immense. Perhaps the less We do the better. Something however must be done.

When Russell Said "there is but one Man capable of Writing Columbus" he Said what I have thought all along.— The Persons I converse with are too wise to give any Opinions or Say any Thing about Such Writings. most are too wise to read them. I wish Columbus may not be inflated with Vanity, and too much emboldened. *festinelente*.[1] He will have more Influence in his Closet, than upon the Stage.

I Sympathise with you and Louisa. My own health has been better for my Journey: but I have a great Cold every Year, before I have been a fortnight in the City and you know it lasts Six Weeks. I never find any Benefit from any thing I do for it, so I leave it to take its Course

But as Mr Izard and his Wife say "We are grown too old to live Seperate"— Mr Izard is here keeping Batchelors Hall—she at New York with Mrs Marrigold. It is very hard upon me in my old age to be obliged to live from my Family, after having been a slave for thirty Years— Oh Columbus, Columbus you know not what you are about.—

Mrs Washington is here and never fails to make the kindest Inquries and to send the most cordial Regards.

I this day received a Visit from Mr Joseph Priestley the oldest son of Dr Priestley, with a Letter from his Father. The Letter with a Card was left when I was in the Senate: as soon as I came home and found the Letter, I returned the Visit—and found Mr Joseph Priestly with his Wife and his youngest Brother, with another Enlishman whose Name is Colman I believe. I revere the D^r and his sons are likely Men: but they will do no good in America, untill they are undeceived. They are blinded by Ignorance or Error: blinded beyond the most stupid and besotted of our American Jacobins.[2] entre nous. They are young however and will be corrected by Experience.

I like the Drs Plan very well— I can send you, what you may want I hope— There cannot be too much Seaweed, provided the Loads are heavy enough. I hope The Bedding of the Animals is changed often.

We have pleasant Weather here.— We hear nothing of Cheesman— Mrs Dalton Mrs Otis hear nothing of their Adventures which were on board Phillips. There has been terrible Gales at sea and many Small Craft lost. I do not yet despair of Cheesman, but We are in Trouble on his account.[3]

We Shall sooon See The Lt. Governors Speech to the General Court.[4] Some curious metaphisical if not Jesuitical Subtilties I warrant you: The Dotage of a Man who was never equal to the Station he now holds may demand some Excuse. But no Man in that Chair will be independent. Independence is not compatible with popular Elections I fear. These are Truths that even, I, am not independent enough to say to every Body. But although The Popular Voice will overawe every Man in some degree, I hope We shall be able to Steer the Vessell clear of the Rocks and Sands. God knows!

yours   J. A

RC (Adams Papers); endorsed: "Dec^br 30 1793."

[1] That is, "Festina lente" (Hasten slowly).

[2] Dr. Joseph Priestley's letter of 20 Aug. (Adams Papers) was carried to JA by Priestley's eldest and youngest sons, Joseph (1768–1833) and Henry (d. 1795). Joseph Jr. had married Elizabeth Ryland (d. 1816) in 1792. Both sons had immigrated to the United States in Aug. 1793 with the goal of locating land on which the whole family could settle. Accompanying them was Priestley's friend Dr. Thomas Cooper (1759–1839), a British doctor and lawyer who was also interested in settling in the United States. JA disapproved of the Priestleys' pro-French stance. Joseph

Priestley Sr. had been made a citizen of France in 1792 and elected to the National Convention, though he never sat in that body. The family eventually settled in Northumberland, Penn. (*DNB*; *DAB*).

[3] On 27 Nov. 1793, the schooner *General Heath*, Capt. Samuel Chesman, left Boston for Philadelphia carrying a trunk from AA to JA. After a week at sea the vessel encountered a severe gale off the Delaware Capes. Chesman, the first mate, and a boy named Joseph Willcut were swept overboard, and although the two men made it back aboard the boy was lost. The damaged vessel arrived

in Charleston, S.C., on 11 Jan. 1794 and in Philadelphia by 1 April when JA received his trunk (AA to JA, 8 Feb.; JA to AA, 1 April, both Adams Papers; Boston *Columbian Centinel*, 16 Nov. 1793, 8 Feb. 1794).

⁴ On 17 Jan., Lt. Gov. Samuel Adams, as acting governor, gave a speech to the Mass.

General Court commenting on the nature of the U.S. Constitution and the need for balance between federal and states' rights, supporting the creation of a similar constitution in France, and advocating education for all young people (Mass., *Acts and Laws*, 1792–1793, p. 706–711).

Abigail Adams to John Adams

my dearest Friend   Quincy Dec'br 31 1793

Your two kind Letters of the 19 & 20th reachd me on the 28th they are my saturday evenings repast. you know my mind is much occupied with the affairs of our Country. if as a Female I may be calld an Idle, I never can be an uninterested Spectator of what is transacting upon the great Theater, when the welfare and happiness of my Children & the rising generation is involved in the present counsels and conduct of the principal Actors who are now exhibiting upon the stage. That the Halcion days of America are past I fully believe, but I cannot agree with you in sentiment respecting the office you hold; altho it is so limited as to prevent your being so actively usefull as you have been accustomed to, yet those former exertions and Services give a weight of Character which like the Heavenly orbs silently diffuse a benign influence. Suppose for Instance as things are often exemplified by their contraries, a Man, in that office, of unbridled Ambition, Subtile intriguing, warpd and biased by interested views, joining at this critical crisis, his secret influence against the Measures of the President, how very soon would this country be involved in all the Horrours of a civil War. I am happy to learn that the only fault in your political Character, and one which has always given me uneasiness, is wearing away, I mean a certain irritability which has some times thrown you of your Gaurd and shewn as is reported of Louis 14'th that a Man is not always a Hero— Partizans are so high, respecting English and French politicks, and argue so falsly and Reason so stupidly that one would suppose they could do no injury, but there are so many who read and hear without reflecting and judging for themselves and there is such a propensity in humane Nature to believe the worst, especially when their interest is like to be affected, that if we are preserved from the Calamities of War it will be more oweing to the superintending Providence of God than the virtue and wisdom of Man. How we are to avoid it with France supposing Genet should not be recall'd I know not. must we

494

Submit to such insults? judging from the manner in which France has carried on the present War, I should not wonder if they feard a Partition of their Kingdom. A Frenchman reminding an English man of the Time when in the Reign of Henry the sixth, the English were almost absolute Masters of France Said sneerlingly to him "When do you think you will again become Lords of our Kingdom?" to which the Englishman replied, ["]When your iniquities shall be greater than ours."[1] how can any Nation expect to prosper who War against Heaven?

By this time you will have seen all the Numbers of Columbus. I should like to know the Presidents opinion of them, as well as some other Gentlemen who are judges. they assuredly are ably written, and do honour both to the Head and Heart of the writer, who deserves well of his fellow citizens for the information he has thrown upon a subject of so much importance at so critical a period—but their is a "barberous Noise of asses Apes and dogs" raisd by it in the Chronical.[2] nevertheless sound reason and cool Argument will prevail in the end.

Having spun my thread out with respect to politicks I will think a little of our own private affairs. dr Tufts has paid two hundred pounds and become responsible himself for the remainder. I wrote to you his further intention,[3] the 17 of Janry he proposes to discharge two hundreds pounds more. I have closed my account this day I have kept an exact account of my expenditures & payments since you left me, which I inclose to you.[4] mr Cary offerd to bring me an other load of Hay at the same price. what he brought is agreed to be of the first quality, and it was all weighd, but I did not feel myself in a capacity to engage it absolutely. we have heitherto had so little snow that Buisness is dull mr Belcher has cleard of all the sea weed untill some high Tide brings more. he is now getting home the pine wood.

our Friends desire to be rememberd to you. mrs Brisler and family are well. you will present me affectionatly to mrs washington who I respect and Love

My Love to Thomas. I hear he is for fighting the Algerines, but I am not sure that would be the best oconomy, tho it might give us a good pretence [for] Building a Navy that we need not be twichd by the Nose by every sausy Jack a Nips— he had better find Law for his countrymen and prevail upon them to take it.

I am as ever most affectionatly / yours   · A Adams

RC (Adams Papers); addressed by JQA: "The Vice-President of the United States / Philadelphia."; endorsed: "Mrs A. Decr 31. 1793 / ans. Jan. 9. 1794." Some loss of text where the seal was removed.

[1] From "A Frenchman" on, AA is quoting from Benito Jerónimo Fiejóo y Montenegro, "The Most Refined Policy" in *Essays, or Discourses, Selected from the Works of Feyjoo*, transl. John Brett, 4 vols., London, 1780, 1:145.

[2] "When straight a barbarous noise environs me / Of owls and cuckoos, asses, apes and dogs" (Milton, Sonnet XII, lines 3–4). On 26 Dec., Americanus attacked Columbus' analysis of the Consular Convention and interpretation of the Constitution in the Boston *Independent Chronicle*, disputing that Columbus' arguments were "founded on the law of reason, and on the Constitution."

[3] AA to JA, 20 Dec., above.

[4] Not found.

Appendix

Appendix

LIST OF OMITTED DOCUMENTS

The following list includes 71 documents that have been omitted from volume 9 of *Adams Family Correspondence* and 10 documents that have come to the editors' attention since the publication of the volumes in which they would have appeared. Each entry consists of the date, correspondents, form in which the letter exists (Dft, LbC, RC, etc.), location, and publication, if known. All copies that exist in some form in the Adams Papers are noted.

1775

[*ca. 19–29 Nov.*]   Mercy Otis Warren to Abigail Adams, RC (Adams Papers); filmed at n.d.

1776

9 June   John Adams to [*Abigail Adams?*], LbC (Adams Papers), APM Reel 90.

1777

20 July   John Adams to Cotton Tufts, RC offered for sale, University Archives, Westport, Conn., June 2004, item 34042-001.

1779

27 Aug.   James Lovell to Abigail Adams, RC (Adams Papers); filmed at 27 Aug. [*1777–1781*]; PRINTED: Smith, *Letters of Delegates*, 13:421–422.

1780

24 Jan.   Elizabeth Smith Shaw to Abigail Adams and Mary Smith Cranch, RC (DLC:Shaw Family Papers).

1781

16 June   John Adams to Richard Cranch, RC offered for sale
           and PRINTED (in part): *The Collector*, Dec. 1951,
           item W1946.

1783

[*ca. 1 April?*]   Benjamin Waterhouse to Abigail Adams, RC offered
           for sale and PRINTED (in part): *The Collector*, Feb.
           1895, p. 58.

1784

6 Sept.   John Quincy Adams to Richard Cranch, RC
           (MeHi:Fogg Autograph Coll.).

1785

18 April   Elizabeth Smith Shaw to [*Abigail Adams?*], Dft
           (DLC:Shaw Family Papers).

1789

27 Sept.   Charity Smith to Abigail Adams, RC (Adams Pa-
           pers); filmed at 27 Sept. 1790.

1790

9 Jan.   Hannah Hunt Jeffries to Abigail Adams, RC (MHi:
           Adams-Hull Coll.).

23 Jan.   Cotton Tufts to Abigail Adams, RC (Adams Pa-
           pers).

5 Feb.   Abigail Adams to Unknown, Dft (Adams Papers).
[*ca. March*]   Hannah Hunt Jeffries to Abigail Adams, RC (MHi:
           Adams-Hull Coll.).

28 April   John Quincy Adams to Cotton Tufts, RC (MH-H:
           Schaffner Coll.).

14 June   George and Martha Washington to John and Abi-
           gail Adams, RC (Adams Papers).

27 June   Abigail Adams to Mary Smith Cranch, RC (MWA:
           Abigail Adams Letters).

29 June   Rebecca Leppington Hurd to Abigail Adams, RC
           (Adams Papers).

15 July   John Adams to John Quincy Adams, RC (Adams
           Papers).

15 July	John Adams to Cotton Tufts, LbC (Adams Papers), APM Reel 114.
9 Aug.	John Quincy Adams to John Adams, RC (Adams Papers).
27 Aug.	Mary Smith Cranch to Abigail Adams, RC (Adams Papers).
5 Sept.	Abigail Adams to John Quincy Adams, RC (Adams Papers).
21 Sept.	Thomas Welsh to John Adams, RC (Adams Papers).
3 Oct.	Abigail Adams to Cotton Tufts, RC (NHi:Misc. Mss. Adams, Abigail).
4 Oct.	Mary Smith Cranch to Abigail Adams, RC (Adams Papers).
10 Oct.	John Adams to Cotton Tufts, LbC (Adams Papers), APM Reel 115.
11 Oct.	John Adams to John Quincy Adams, RC (Adams Papers); Tr (Adams Papers).
13 Oct.	John Quincy Adams to John Adams, RC (Adams Papers).
2 Nov.	Lucy Ludwell Paradise to Abigail Adams, RC (Adams Papers).
7 Nov.	Abigail Adams to Mary Smith Cranch, RC (MWA: Abigail Adams Letters).
7 Nov.	Hannah Storer Green to Abigail Adams, RC (Adams Papers).
20 Nov.	Thomas Welsh to John Adams, RC (Adams Papers).
8 Dec.	John Adams to John Quincy Adams, RC (Adams Papers); Tr (Adams Papers); PRINTED (in part): JQA, *Writings*, 1:64, note 1.
11 Dec.	William Cranch to Abigail Adams, RC (Adams Papers).
17 Dec.	John Adams to John Quincy Adams, RC (Adams Papers); Tr (Adams Papers).
17 Dec.	John Adams to Thomas Welsh, RC (MHi:Adams-Welsh Corr.); PRINTED: *M.H.S. Miscellany*, no. 12:2–3 (Dec. 1970).

1791

30 Jan.	Thomas Lee Shippen to Abigail Adams, RC (Adams Papers).
20 Feb.	Mary Smith Cranch to Abigail Adams, RC (Adams Papers).
6 May	Abigail Adams to Mary Smith Cranch, RC (MWA: Abigail Adams Letters).
5 Oct.	John Quincy Adams to Abigail Adams, RC (Adams Papers).
23 Oct.	Mary Smith Cranch to Abigail Adams, RC (Adams Papers).
5 Nov.	John Quincy Adams to Abigail Adams, RC (Adams Papers).

1792

9 Feb.	Charles Adams to John Adams, RC (Adams Papers).
17 March	John Quincy Adams to Abigail Adams Smith; PRINTED: AA2, *Jour. and Corr.*, 3:148–149.
17 March	John Quincy Adams to William Stephens Smith, RC offered for sale, Robert H. Dodd, Catalog No. 20, April 1916, p. 25.
28 March	Abigail Adams to Cotton Tufts, RC (Adams Papers).
28 March	John Adams to Cotton Tufts, RC (Adams Papers).
12 April	Richard Cranch to John Adams, RC (Adams Papers).
7 June	Charles Adams to John Adams, RC (Adams Papers).
28 July	Josiah Quincy III to Thomas Boylston Adams; PRINTED (in part): *Boston Weekly Advertiser*, 17 Nov. 1864.
29 July	Thomas Boylston Adams to John Adams, RC (Adams Papers).
29 Aug.	John Quincy Adams to Abigail Adams, RC offered for sale, Swann Galleries, 3 May 1990, item 178.
30 Aug.	Abigail Adams to John Quincy Adams, RC (Adams Papers).
10 Sept.	Thomas Boylston Adams to John Adams, RC (Adams Papers).

20 Sept.	John Quincy Adams to Thomas Boylston Adams, RC (Ia-HA).
29 Oct.	Elizabeth Palmer Cranch to Abigail Adams, RC (Adams Papers).
[*ca. 10 Nov.*]	Abigail Adams to John Quincy Adams, RC (NHi: Misc. Mss. Adams, Abigail).
19 Dec.	John Adams to John Quincy Adams, RC (Adams Papers).
22 Dec.	Abigail Adams to John Quincy Adams, RC (Adams Papers).
22 Dec.	John Quincy Adams to John Adams, RC (Adams Papers); PRINTED (in part): JQA, *Writings*, 1:130–133.
29 Dec.	John Adams to Abigail Adams, RC (Adams Papers).
29 Dec.	John Adams to Charles Adams, RC (MHi:Seymour Coll.).

1793

7 Jan.	John Quincy Adams to Abigail Adams, RC (Adams Papers).
8 Jan.	John Adams to Abigail Adams, RC (Adams Papers).
20 Jan.	Charles Adams to John Adams, RC (Adams Papers).
12 Feb.	John Adams to Abigail Adams, RC (Adams Papers); PRINTED: JA, *Letters*, ed. CFA, 2:124–125.
26 Feb.	Thomas Boylston Adams to John Quincy Adams, RC (Adams Papers).
1 March	Charles Adams to John Adams, RC (Adams Papers).
2 March	John Adams to John Quincy Adams, RC (Adams Papers).
16 March	Abigail Adams to John Quincy Adams, RC offered for sale and PRINTED (in part): Thomas Madigan, *The Autograph Bulletin*, March 1923, p. 64, item 678.
20 March	John Adams to Thomas Boylston Adams, Dft (Adams Papers).
9 June	Thomas Boylston Adams to John Adams, 2d letter, RC (Adams Papers).
[*ca. 16 July*]	John and Abigail Adams to Sarah Cobb and Robert Treat Paine, RC (MHi:Robert Treat Paine Papers).

2 Aug.	Abigail Adams to William Cranch, RC (PHC: Charles Roberts Autograph Coll.).
14 Nov.	John Adams to John Quincy Adams, RC (Adams Papers).
7 Dec.	Abigail Adams to John Adams, RC (Adams Papers).
10 Dec.	John Adams to John Quincy Adams, RC (Adams Papers).
13 Dec.	John Adams to Abigail Adams, RC (Adams Papers).
23 Dec.	John Adams to Abigail Adams, RC (Adams Papers).
28 Dec.	John Adams to Charles Adams, RC (MHi:Seymour Coll.).

Chronology

Chronology

THE ADAMS FAMILY, 1790–1793

1790

4 Jan.: The 2d session of the 1st Congress convenes in New York.

2 March: Abigail Adams Shaw, daughter of John and Elizabeth Smith Shaw, is born in Haverhill.

12 March: Richard Cranch Norton, son of Rev. Jacob and Elizabeth Cranch Norton, is born in Weymouth.

17 April: Benjamin Franklin dies in Philadelphia at the age of 84.

28 April 1790 – 27 April 1791: JA's *Discourses on Davila*, a series of unsigned essays, is published in 32 installments in the New York (later Philadelphia) *Gazette of the United States.*

29 May: Rhode Island ratifies the Constitution, the last of the original thirteen colonies to do so.

15 July: JQA is admitted to the Massachusetts bar.

16 July: George Washington signs an act to move the temporary seat of government from New York to Philadelphia and establish a permanent seat on the Potomac River in ten years' time.

21 July: TBA graduates from Harvard; JQA and William Cranch receive their master's degrees.

July: William Cranch is admitted to the Massachusetts bar and opens a law office attached to his father's shop in Braintree.

7 Aug.: AA2 gives birth to her third son, Thomas Hollis Smith, in New York.

9 Aug.: JQA opens a law office at the Adamses' Court Street property in Boston.

12 Aug.: The 2d session of the 1st Congress adjourns in New York.

10 Sept.: TBA joins the Adamses in New York.

Oct.: TBA leaves New York for Philadelphia to begin a legal apprenticeship in the office of Jared Ingersoll.

12 Nov.: The Adamses take up residence at Bush Hill, an estate outside of Philadelphia, after a five-day journey from New York.

Nov.–Dec.: TBA suffers an acute rheumatic attack, lying "18 days totally deprived of the use of his Limbs"; he is attended by Dr. Benjamin Rush.

6 Dec.: The 3d session of the 1st Congress convenes in Philadelphia.

Dec.: WSS leaves for England to pursue business opportunities.

1791

20 Jan. – 3 March: JQA visits Philadelphia from Boston.

3 March: The 3d session of the 1st Congress adjourns in Philadelphia.

4 March: Vermont is admitted to the Union.

4 March: While still in Europe, WSS is appointed supervisor of revenue for the district of New York, having served as marshal since 25 Sept. 1789.

21 March – 6 July: George Washington makes a tour of the southern states, visiting Richmond, Charleston, and Savannah; he is greeted with great fanfare.

April: AA2 and her family relocate within New York City, from 13 Nassau Street to Dye (now Dey) Street.

2 May: JA, AA, and TBA leave Philadelphia for an extended visit to Braintree, stopping in New York and Fairfield, Conn., due to AA's illness.

May: Thomas Paine's *Rights of Man* is published in the United States; Thomas Jefferson pens the new introduction, indirectly attacking JA's "political heresies" in *Discourses on Davila*.

5 June: WSS returns to the United States from England on the British packet.

8 June – 27 July: JQA, under the pseudonym Publicola, publishes eleven letters in response to Paine's *Rights of Man* in the Boston *Columbian Centinel*; JA is widely believed to be the author.

20–25 June: Louis XVI, Marie Antoinette, and their children are stopped at Varennes while attempting to flee the capital and brought back to Paris.

6 July: John Thaxter Jr., AA's cousin and former secretary to JA, dies in Haverhill.

8 July: Thomas Hollis Smith, AA2's third son, dies.

July: William Cranch moves to Haverhill to take up the law practice of John Thaxter Jr.

Aug.: AA2 and the children, accompanied by WSS's brother and sister, visit JA and AA in Braintree; CA also visits for a time before leaving for New York on 21 August.

24 Oct.: The 1st session of the 2d Congress convenes in Philadelphia.

31 Oct.: Philip Freneau launches the Philadelphia *National Gazette* to counter John Fenno's *Gazette of the United States*.

Oct.: AA and JA depart Braintree for Philadelphia, visiting the Smiths in New York on their way.

Oct.: Richard Cranch suffers from a severe gangrenous leg injury and is weakened by sickness through the winter.

late Oct.: JA and AA take up residence in a home in Philadelphia at the corner of Fourth and Arch streets.

1 Nov.: WSS is appointed supervisor and inspector of the district of New York.

29 Dec.: William Smith Norton, son of Rev. Jacob and Elizabeth Cranch Norton, is born in Weymouth.

1792

Winter: AA suffers from an "Intermitting" fever, preventing her from attending most social events in Philadelphia.

Jan. – mid-Feb.: AA2, WSS, and William Steuben Smith make an extended visit with the Adamses in Philadelphia; CA also visits for a fortnight.

23 Feb.: Quincy is set off from Braintree and incorporated as a town.

29 March: AA2, WSS, and their two children sail for England aboard the *Bristol*, arriving in England in early May.

24 April: The Adamses leave Philadelphia for Quincy.

8 May: The 1st session of the 2d Congress adjourns in Philadelphia.

1 June: Kentucky is admitted to the Union.

July: CA is admitted to the New York bar.

10 Aug.: The French Revolution intensifies with the invasion of the Tuileries Palace and the arrest of the royal family. Ten days later the Marquis de Lafayette emigrates from France to Austria.

20 Aug.: CA opens a law office in Hanover Square, just off of Wall Street.

late Oct. – 9 Nov.: WSS visits Paris, where he agrees to act as an agent for the French government in collecting debts owed to France by the United States.

5 Nov.: The 2d session of the 2d Congress convenes in Philadelphia.

19 Nov.: JA departs for Philadelphia, arriving on 4 Dec., and takes a room with Samuel and Mary Otis; AA remains in Quincy for the winter owing to her ill health.

19–26 Dec.: JQA publishes three letters in the Boston *Columbian Centinel* under the pseudonym Menander protesting the anti-theatrical actions taken by Massachusetts attorney general James Sullivan.

1793

21 Jan.: Louis XVI, having been tried by the National Convention and found guilty of conspiring against the nation, is executed by guillotine in Paris.

9 Feb.: The Smith family returns from England on the *Portland* packet.

13 Feb.: The Electoral College votes are counted and read by JA in Congress: George Washington is unanimously reelected president and JA wins a plurality for vice president.

2 March: The 2d session of the 2d Congress adjourns in Philadelphia.

4 March: Washington takes the oath of office at a special session of Congress and delivers a brief inaugural address; JA attends along with foreign ministers, representatives, and many spectators.

mid-March: JA departs Philadelphia to join AA in Quincy.

8 April: The French ambassador to the United States, Citizen Edmond Genet, arrives in Charleston, S.C., and makes an overland journey to Philadelphia arriving on 16 May.

July–Aug.: TBA visits the Adamses in Quincy and the Smiths in New York.

July–Nov.: A yellow fever epidemic breaks out in Philadelphia, eventually taking 4,000 lives; thousands, including TBA, flee to the surrounding countryside.

5 Sept.: The Reign of Terror begins in France; over 17,000 executions occur before Robespierre is overthrown and put to death himself the following summer.

16 Oct.: Marie Antoinette is executed by guillotine.

30 Nov.: JA arrives in Philadelphia after a brief stopover in New York; AA again remains in Quincy for the winter.

30 Nov. – 14 Dec.: JQA, under the pseudonym Columbus, publishes three letters in the Boston *Columbian Centinel* challenging the current fervor for Citizen Genet and the French Revolution.

2 Dec.: The 1st session of the 3d Congress convenes in Philadelphia.

7 Dec.: TBA is admitted to the Pennsylvania bar.

16 Dec.: Jacob Porter Norton, son of Rev. Jacob and Elizabeth Cranch Norton, is born in Weymouth.

31 Dec.: Thomas Jefferson resigns as secretary of state.

Index

NOTE ON THE INDEX

The index for volume 9 of the *Adams Family Correspondence* is designed to supplement the annotation, when possible, by furnishing the correct spellings of names, supplying forenames when they are lacking in the text, and indicating dates, occupations, and places of residence when they will aid in identification. Markedly variant spellings of proper names have been cross-referenced to what are believed to be their most nearly standard forms, and the variant forms found in the manuscripts are parenthetically recorded following the standard spellings. Cross-references under maiden names are used for women who were single when first mentioned in the text and were married subsequently but before December 1793.

Branches, departments, and positions within the U.S. federal government are indexed individually under the name of the entity, with subdivisions as appropriate. For example, the Supreme Court is found as a subentry under "Judiciary, U.S." while "Presidency, U.S." stands as a main entry.

Subentries appear in alphabetical order by the primary word of the subentry. Abbreviations are alphabetized as if they were spelled out, thus "JQA" is alphabetized under "Adams, John Quincy."

The Chronology, "The Adams Family, 1790–1793," has not been included in the index.

The index was compiled in the Adams Papers office.

Index

OPINIONS AND BELIEFS

Index

ADAMS, THOMAS BOYLSTON
(*continued*)
Individuals: William Cranch's relationship with Nancy Greenleaf, 225, 226–27; Edmond Genet, 443, 450–51; Benjamin Goodhue, 347; John Hancock, 449–50; WSS, 428

PUBLIC LIFE
bar examination, xxviii, 456, 460, 465, 466, 472, 478; career plans of, xxviii, 83, 107–108, 109; legal career, xix, 438, 440, 452, 456, 460–61, 465, 478, 481, 492; visits New Jersey courts, 460

RELATIONSHIP WITH PARENTS
AA's health and, 416–17; JA advises, 152; JA's books and, 421; advises JA, 318–19, 320–21; arranges lodgings for JA in Philadelphia, 315, 319–20, 321–22, 344, 374; correspondence with AA, xxx, 17, 18, 19, 20, 34, 54, 85, 103, 107, 299, 308, 323, 334, 355, 356, 362, 372, 380, 446, 453, 458, 479; correspondence with JA, xv, xvi–xvii, 107, 299, 309, 310, 320–21, 426; as parents' agent, xxviii, 82, 284, 286, 287, 288, 289–90, 295, 296, 298, 309, 310, 316, 417, 428, 435–36, 438; parents' financial support for, xxvi, 105–106, 112, 115, 143, 309; requests and receives goods from AA, 322, 345, 453, 456; as secretary for AA, 181, 186, 211, 214, 229, 232, 238, 246, 248, 260, 261; as secretary for JA, 216; sends pamphlet to JA, 286; separation from, 83

RELATIONSHIP WITH SIBLINGS
with CA, 144, 337; JQA's romantic relationships and, 110; assists JQA, 52–53, 208, 212, 234, 239, 303; with brothers, xxix; correspondence with AA2, 241, 267, 316, 452; correspondence with CA, 291, 292; correspondence with JQA, 209, 210, 213, 236, 239, 248–49, 250, 252, 309, 310, 414

SOCIAL LIFE
attends balloon flight, 375, 376; goes fowling, 220; in Philadelphia, xxix, 288, 344–45, 376, 417–18, 425; visits New York, 11, 12–13; visits to Braintree, 209, 210, 225, 375; visits to Haverhill, 24, 53, 85

TRAVELS
to Massachusetts, 15, 211, 440; moves to New York after graduation, xxviii, 85, 87–88, 92, 95, 103, 106, 107, 108, 109, 119, 124; moves to Philadelphia, 124, 127, 144; to Philadel-phia, 234, 236, 237, 248, 443, 449; possible visit to England, 259

Adams Family Correspondence: editorial method, xxxv; letters omitted from, 499–504
Adams National Historical Park. *See* Old House
Adams Papers: digital publication of, xxxvi
Addison, Joseph: *The Drummer*, 223, 224
Aesop: *Fables*, 51, 52, 187
Africa, 413, 467
African Americans: employment of, 136; re-apportionment debate and, 247; revolution in St. Domingue and, 351; as servants, 51, 244; as possible servants for Adamses, 199, 201, 211; as possible tenants for Adamses, 183. *See also* Slavery
Agriculture: AA hires farmhand, 365–66; construction of corn house, 362, 366, 373, 377; dairying, 37, 476; effect of drought on, 218; effect of duties on, 138; failure of at Birthplace, 112; farming implements, 125, 468; fruit trees, 412, 421–22; government promotion of, 4; hay, 495; hemp production, 135; manure, 44, 377; in Massachusetts, 134–35; at Monticello, 485; preparing land for, 408, 468, 476; purchase of cattle, 355, 376; seaweed as fertilizer, 373, 458, 468, 479, 493, 495; team for plowing, 404–405; tending livestock, 149, 231, 331, 373, 493; theft of horses and equipment, 334
AHA. *See* Harrod, Ann (1774–1845)
Ainsworth, Robert: *Dictionary, English and Latin,* 129
Akenside, Mark: "Love, an Elegy," 41, 42, 44
Albany, N.Y., 269, 291, 296, 300, 357, 418
Algiers. *See* Barbary States
Allen, Andrew (of Phila.), 473
Allen, Anne Penn (daughter of James), 167, 182; identified, 168
Allen, Elizabeth Lawrence. *See* Laurance, Elizabeth Lawrence Allen
Allen, James (of Phila.), 168, 182
Allen, Jeremiah (Boston sheriff), 341, 342, 388
Allen, Margaret. *See* Hammond, Margaret Allen
Allen, Margaret Elizabeth (daughter of James), 167, 182; identified, 168
Allen, Mary Masters (daughter of James), 167, 182; identified, 168
Alleyne, Abel (son of Thomas), 88, 120
Alleyne, Thomas (of Braintree), 21, 22

331; cost of, 155; Marsh's Tavern (Quincy), 334, 335; Mason's Arms (Haverhill), 25

House, Mary (of Phila.), 315; identified, 316

House of Representatives, U.S. *See* Congress, U.S.

Houses: Adamses' in Philadelphia, 242, 244, 246, 295, 296, 298, 310; Beale House, 318; building and renovation of, xii–xiii, 242, 484; mob attacks, 463, 464; purchase of, 288; rents on, 94–95, 289–90, 344; size of, 170; for Smiths, 428; U.S. mansions, 151. *See also names of individual estates*

Hovey, Joseph (Boston factory owner), 136

Howard, Elizabeth Clarke Mayhew (1st wife of Simeon), 191–92

Howard, Jerusha Gay (2d wife of Simeon), 157, 191–92; identified, 159

Howard, John Clarke (son of Simeon), 107, 108

Howard, Jonathan Mayhew (son of Simeon), 192

Howard, Mary (of Braintree), 243

Howard, Rev. Simeon (of Boston), 107, 108, 157, 159, 191–92

Hubbard, Nicholas (Amsterdam banker), 133

Hubbard, Russel, 323, 329

Hudson River, 74, 99, 149, 171, 491

Hughes, James M. (N.Y. lawyer), 463, 464

Hume, David: *Essays and Treatises on Several Subjects*, 41, 43, 66; *History of England*, 303, 304, 473, 474

Humphrey, Levi (of Braintree), 476; identified, 468

Humphrey Ploughjogger (pseudonym). *See* JA–Writings

Humphreys, Col. David (U.S. diplomat): appointments of, 133, 175–76, 193, 194; rumored death of, 165; marriage of, 394, 395; reputation of, 394

Hunt, Cornelius (of the West Indies), 20, 22, 120, 400

Hunt, Hannah (of Braintree), 6

Hunting, 100, 220

Hurd, Elizabeth (daughter of John): identified, 34

Hurd, Elizabeth Foster (1st wife of John): identified, 34

Hurd, John (Boston insurance broker), 33, 424; identified, 34

Hurd, John Russell (son of John): identified, 34

Hurd, Katharine (daughter of John): identified, 34

Hurd, Mary Russell Foster (2d wife of John): identified, 34

Hurd, Rebecca Leppington (3d wife of John), 33, 34; letter to AA listed (1790), 500
  Letter: To AA (1790), 34

Hutchinson, Dr. James (of Phila.): identified, 196, 316–17; American Philosophical Society and, 381–82; appointed to committee of correspondence, 299; correspondence with JA, 381–82; death of, 460; influence of, 316
  Letter: To AA (1791), 196

Hyde, The (Brit. estate): Adamses visit, 99, 163, 165; gardens of, 101, 400–401; Thomas Brand Hollis on, 164

Hyslop, Betsey Williams (wife of William, Jr.): identified, 232

Hyslop, Betsey Williams or Mehetabel Stoddard, 231

Hyslop, Mehetabel Stoddard (wife of William, Sr.): identified, 232

Hyslop, William, Sr. (1714–1796, Boston merchant), 232

Hyslop, William, Jr. (1753–1792, son of William, Sr.), 232

Iacuzzi, Alfred: *John Adams: Scholar*, 264

Immigration: AA on, 180; from France, 283, 304, 305, 306, 414, 427, 476; mob violence and, 463; naturalization laws, 4; to U.S., xvi, 269, 351, 426, 427, 467, 469, 493

Independent Chronicle (Boston): Adamses on, xxii–xxiii, 5, 173; "The Crisis" published in, 391, 395; critiques of, 127; "A Friend to Peace" published in, 351; Genet and, 459, 486, 487; Harvard commencement reported in, 83; lotteries advertised in, 46; political alignment of, 6; political attacks in, 83, 127, 328, 495, 496; political reports in, 24, 108–109; Publius published in, 395; Stephen Colonna published in, 395; mentioned, 119

India, 293, 294, 476

Ingersoll, Jared (Phila. lawyer): TBA studies with, xxviii, 166, 208, 360, 452, 456, 481; appointed to committee of correspondence, 299; education of, 152; mentioned, 153

Ingraham, Joseph (of the *Columbia*), 92

Investments: CA on, 169; JQA on, 162; of Adamses, xiii–xiv, xxvi, 6, 7, 64, 84, 125, 126, 131, 172, 176, 184–85, 186; Appleton's loan certificates, 197 (illus.); in Bank of Pennsylvania, 406, 407; in Bank of United States, 195; commissioners to oversee public, 108; in continental securities, 125; depreciation of war bonds, 372; Funding Act and, xii, 95, 144, 184–85, 186;

wife of Asa): AA2 on, 188; AA on, 9, 93; leaves Braintree, 120, 190; Lucy Cranch visits, 158; marriage of, 8, 9, 12, 13, 85, 88, 90; possible marriage to JQA, 91; mentioned, 10, 399

Packard, Rev. Asa (of Marlborough), 8, 9, 12, 13, 90, 158

Page, John (Va. representative), 99

Page, Margaret Lowther (wife of John), 98; identified, 99

Paine, Eunice (sister of Robert): AA's charity toward, 141; TBA and, 174; boards with Cranches, 75–76; in Dorchester, 243–44; health of, 58–59, 75–76, 88; mentioned, 89, 246

Paine, Robert Treat (Mass. politician), 29, 32, 77, 88; letter from JA and AA listed (1793), 503

Paine, Sarah Cobb (Sally, wife of Robert), 76, 88; identified, 77; letter from JA and AA listed (1793), 503

Paine, Thomas: AA2 on, 292–93; AA on, 365; JA on, 318, 378, 416; burned in effigy, 396; cartoon of, xiv, 285 (illus.); correspondence with Washington, 365, 366; French Revolution and, 291, 386, 481–82; newspaper articles on, 366; *Rights of Man*, xiv, xxvii, 205, 264, 293, 366, 396, 398, 414, 483; *Rights of Man, Part II*, xiv, 283, 284, 290, 291, 414; toast to, 372; trial of, xiv, 413, 414, 420; possible visit to U.S., 482

Paintings: of AA, 158, 184; of American Revolution, 101, 103; by Thomas Birch, xvi, 327 (illus.); by William Russell Birch, xvi, 327 (illus.); of Bush Hill, xii–xiii, 111 (illus.); cartoons, xi–xii, xiv, 79 (illus.), 285 (illus.); of George Clinton, 101, 103; conference on, 83; engravings of John Singleton Copley's, 324–25; by William Cranch, 158, 159, 179, 184; by Joseph Ducreux, xvi–xvii, 392 (illus.); of French Revolution, xv–xvi, 307 (illus.); of Mary Hallowell, 400; by Alexandre Kucharski, xvi–xvii, 393 (illus.); of Louis XVI, xvi–xvii, 392 (illus.); by James Peller Malcom, xii–xiii, 111 (illus.); of Marie Antoinette, xvi–xvii, 393 (illus.); of nuns and monks, 164, 165; of Philadelphia, xvi, 327 (illus.); by Edward Savage, xi, 56 (illus.), 57 (illus.); of scientists, 152; by John Trumbull, 101, 103; of George Washington, xi, 56 (illus.), 101, 103; of Martha Washington, xi, 57 (illus.)

Palmer, Elihu (Deist minister), 286; identified, 287

Palmer, Elizabeth. *See* Cranch, Elizabeth Palmer

Palmer, Gen. Joseph (of Germantown, Mass.), 18, 37, 120

Palmer, Mary (Polly, daughter of Joseph): AA on, 17; boards with Cranches, 59, 76; correspondence with AA, 29; correspondence with JA, 28, 29; death of mother and, 21, 28; financial difficulties of, 19; health of, 141; stays in Old House, xxvii, 18, 26, 27, 37, 49, 62; travels of, 141, 188
    Letter: To AA (1790), 27

Palmer, Mary Cranch (wife of Joseph): AA's charity toward, xxvii, 6; burial of, 22; death of, 15, 17, 19, 21, 28; Mary Palmer on, 28; stays in Old House, 18, 37

Paradise, John (of Va. and London), 102, 181, 182

Paradise, Lucy Ludwell (wife of John), 102–103, 181, 182; letter to AA listed (1790), 501
    Letter: From AA (1790), 101

Paris, France: balloon flights in, 376; Bastille, xxxiii, 266; education at, 152, 153; possible invasion of, 305; mayor of, 308; Prison de la Conciergerie, xvii, 393 (illus.); Temple Prison, xvii, 410, 411; Tuileries, xv–xvi, xxxiii–xxxiv, 293, 294, 307 (illus.); violence in, xv–xvi, xxxiii, 103, 304, 316, 443; mentioned, 35, 36, 133, 262, 283, 284, 293, 306, 311, 366, 367, 378, 416, 425, 433, 475

Park, James Allan: *Law of Marine Insurances*, 66, 68

Parker, Josiah (Va. representative), 137; identified, 138, 352

Parker's General Advertiser and Morning Intelligencer (London), 263

Parsons, Theophilus (Newburyport lawyer): JQA's legal training with, xxvii, 14, 36, 37, 64, 73, 78, 105; law practice of, 30, 41; travels of, 41; mentioned, 71

Partridge, George (Mass. representative), 105, 159

Passaic Falls, N.J., 72

Patronage: CA's bar examination and, 296; federal, 104, 105, 195; for WSS, 92–93, 109–10, 147–48, 149, 156, 165, 170, 175–76, 199, 200, 203–204, 215, 216, 221, 222, 232–34, 241, 260, 266, 310–11; sought from JA, 104, 105, 108, 109, 114–16, 153–54, 256–57, 258; sought from JA through AA, 21–22, 26, 33, 34, 39, 48–49, 153–54, 195; sought from JA through JQA, 143–44, 145; Steuben denies seeking, 312; for veterans, 153–54, 191

Paul IV, Pope, 315

Peacefield. *See* Old House

Peirce, Ann Dawes (wife of Joseph), 224

569

❡The *Adams Family Correspondence* was composed in the Adams Papers office using Microsoft Office Professional with style sheets and programs created by Technologies 'N Typography of Merrimac, Massachusetts. The text is set in eleven on twelve and one half point using the Linotype-Hell Postscript revival of *Fairfield Medium*, a design by Rudolph Ruzicka that includes swash characters especially designed for *The Adams Papers*. The printing and binding are by Edwards Brothers of Ann Arbor, Michigan. The paper, made by Finch, Pruyn & Company and distributed by Lindenmeyr Munroe, is a grade named *Finch Fine Vanilla*. The books were originally designed by P. J. Conkwright and Burton L. Stratton.